WASHINGTON DC ACCESS ®

Charles A Grace February 1990

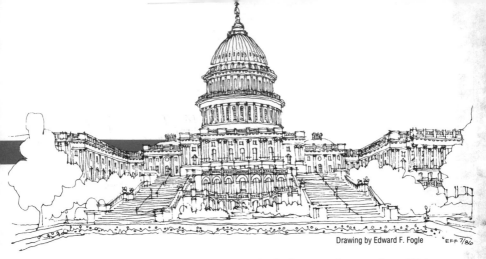

Drawing by Edward F. Fogle EFF 7/86

Washington DC's abundant space and greenery stand as a welcome contrast to the nation's other major cities. However, the visitor who presumes it's possible to cover DC in a few days just because it seems uncongested is making a big mistake—it's easy to spend a week navigating the halls of the Smithsonian Institution's museums.

The city itself offers an exhilarating, puzzling, and sometimes frustrating blend of official pomp and hometown intimacy, wealth and poverty, and power and impotence. Even first-time visitors should make a point of getting off the Mall to experience the charming little tidewater city beyond its perimeter—to sit in the sun next to Dupont Circle's splashing fountain, explore the ethnic restaurants of Adams-Morgan, admire the brick sidewalks and pampered elegance of Georgetown and the Victorian townhouses of Capitol Hill, or watch the old men trying to snare catfish at the foot of the Kennedy Center.

Airports

National: Washington's oldest and smallest airport, located on the Potomac River in Arlington VA, is just $3^1/2$ miles from the US Capitol; thus it remains a perennial favorite of congresspeople and other local Pooh Bahs, as well as plain old residents. Because of its short runways, it carries only domestic flights of moderate distance; a major overhaul of its antiquated terminals and parking will continue through the 1990s (page 180).

Washington-Dulles: Located 26 miles west of Downtown in Northern Virginia, Dulles is the end of the line for nonstop transcontinental flights and many international flights. Note: the tremendous increase in traffic through Dulles can make for crowds at Customs and the baggage claim (page 191).

Baltimore-Washington International: BWI, formerly *Friendship International*, lies 32 miles north of Washington in Suburban Maryland and serves as both a local airport for Baltimore and as an international airport for the Washington region. Combined with Dulles, it gives Washington-bound travelers the choice of 2 modern, relatively accessible international airports (page 149).

BWI ✈

Dulles ✈ - - - - - - - - -
    National ✈

Getting into town: Buses run from all 3 airports to major DC hotels. The **Airport Connection**, 301/441.2345 or 301/261.1091, serves BWI; the **Washington Flyer**, 685.1400, serves National and Dulles. (BWI is also served by some **Amtrak** trains, 484.7540.) **Metrorail** serves National Airport (Metro stop: National Airport) with a free shuttle bus to the terminals. Taxi and limousine service is available as well.

MARC Commuter train service connects Union Station, Harper's Ferry, Martinsburg, Brunswick, and Baltimore. ♦ 800/325.RAIL

Getting Around Town: If you find Washington a bewildering place to navigate, you are not alone: this is a city that is all show and no tell. Tourists and new arrivals far outnumber longtime residents, but they are left to find their own paths through the jungle. Signs are few, confusing, and obscurely sited—notably in the megamillion-dollar subway. The National Park Service has designed theirs for horse-and-buggy traffic, not for the harried motorist trying to find the right lane on the Mall or Rock Creek Parkway. Most bus stops carry but one piece of information: a phone number that rings busy—in the unlikely event that you can find a pay phone. And you must penetrate to the bowels of Metro Center to buy the official bus map. It is hard to decide whether this lack of guidance is the result of bureaucratic incompetence, a desire to keep the marble and greenery unblemished, or a strategy to lead strangers off course—much as the British removed road signs in anticipation of a German invasion 50 years ago.

Take these inconveniences as a challenge and enjoy Washington's many assets. The street plan may be tough on motorists, but it's a cinch to figure out on the map (see **Street Plan**, page 6). The natives (if you can find one who has been here for more than a few months) are friendly. A car is the most convenient way to get around, except in the tourist and business districts, where parking is expensive and/or scarce. Walking can be rewarding for the first few miles; however, all but the very fit soon get footsore: Washington was designed for horses and carriages, not pedestrians, and is deceptively large in scale. Tourists are best advised to use the **Tourmobile** (page 5), a shuttle that links most of the major sites. Other options include **Metrorail**, **Metrobus**, and taxis

Metrorail A steadily expanding system, part subway, part surface transit, comprising 5 color-coded lines that snake from the suburbs through Downtown and back. Designer **Harry Weese** has been acclaimed for his coffered concrete vaults, which give commuters a Roman sense of grandeur. The coffers hold sound-absorbing material and air-quality control systems that make the interior airy and quiet. The stations and the air-conditioned stainless-steel cars are immaculate, due to an antigraffiti architectural design and an army of custodians that scrubs away when the system closes down at night.

Over 300,000 passengers use this system on a daily basis. Federally funded construction began in 1969 and will continue well into the 1990s. Sixty-four stations and 70 miles of track are currently in service. (When the system is eventually completed, it will encompass 87 stations and 103 miles of track.) Metrorail's 5 lines currently serve Downtown and outlying suburban areas and link up with Union Station and Washington National Airport. (Although the entire system could run by computer, an operator rides each train, and each car has an intercom that allows passengers to talk to the operator in case of trouble. Stops are announced over the PA system.)

Each station entrance is marked by a tall brown pylon. A large letter **M**, the system logo, is displayed on all 4 sides. Beneath the logo, brightly colored stripes indicate which lines serve that particular station, e.g., blue line/yellow line. (Although all trains have official names based on their starting and destination points, most locals refer to them by color.) It is essential to know the end destination of the line on which you wish to travel; knowing the color of the line is not enough. The front of each train is clearly marked.

To get to the trains, passengers sometimes descend long, dramatic escalators. (At 228 feet 6 inches, the escalator at the soon-to-be-completed **Wheaton Station** will be the world's longest.) Passengers arrive at the mezzanine or ticketing part of the station, which has ticketing machines and a booth with an attendant as well as large colored maps of the system. In general, maps of the rail system are not easy to obtain; your best bet is to write ahead or ask at the Metro service windows at Metro Center.

Disadvantages include a fare system so confusing that it must have been designed by moonlighters from the IRS, suburban parking lots that fill to overflowing, station lighting too dim to read a newspaper by, and design flaws that cause the system to freeze up during snowstorms. After the disastrous blizzards of 1987, Metro scrambled to redesign the aboveground tracks, but the system has not been seriously tested since then. Although Metrorail is handicap-accessible, the elevators are sometimes hard to find.

The fare you pay depends on where you get on and off and what time of day you travel. To deal with the cumbersome price hierarchy, Metro created the *Farecard*. These paper cards with an encoded magnetic stripe are read by turnstiles that subtract the proper fare. The fare structure and maps are posted at station entrances, along with the Farecard purchase machines.

Before entering the platform, insert your card into the entrance turnstile. The time and place are recorded and your Farecard returned. When you get off the train and prepare to leave the station you will pass through an exit turnstile. Insert your Farecard. The correct value of the trip will be subtracted. If value remains on your card, it will be returned. If there isn't enough value on the card, you will be directed to an *Addfare* machine, which will tell you how much money is needed to make up the differ-

ence. Put in the money, retrieve the card, and pass through the turnstile. Do not throw away your card on the train! Not only is this littering, it can be expensive. (In theory, the machines accept coins and bills, sell you a Farecard containing up to $20 worth of travel, and make change. In practice, the balky machines often spit back bills not to their liking—try pleating and unfolding a bill lengthwise before giving up and seeking help from the attendant in the entrance kiosk.) Free Metrorail-to-bus transfers are available from machines inside your station of origin; no bus-to-Metrorail transfers.

One-day family/tourist passes are available by mail or at selected hotels. Special discount fares for students, senior citizens, and the handicapped are available. Up to 2 children age 4 or younger travel free with a paying customer. Metro also sells fortnightly *Flashpasses* for a variety of Metrorail/Metrobus ride combinations. Bicycles are allowed on Metrorail during off-peak hours. Bicyclists must take an orientation class and carry a permit. Although parking is available at suburban stations, the lots fill up as early as 7:30AM in many areas. Take the bus, Metro officials say. Rush-hour fares are in effect weekdays (excluding federal holidays) from 5:30 to 9:30AM and 3 to 6:30PM.

Metrobus More than 1500 buses thread their way along 700-plus routes at speeds seldom exceeding 35 mph. Many are designed as feeder routes to the rail system. For some areas, however, the bus remains the sole source of public transportation.

Georgetown, for instance, vetoed a Metrorail stop—no hoi polloi, thank you. As a result, traffic congestion is a perennial Georgetown problem. The even-numbered **30** buses (30, 32, 34, 36) connect Georgetown to Downtown and Upper Northwest. In fact, a ride on a 30 bus provides a soup-to-nuts tour of Washington, traversing the city from the upper-crust enclaves of Upper Northwest and the National Cathedral, through Georgetown, past the White House along Pennsylvania Ave, down the Mall, past the

Orientation

House office buildings on Capitol Hill, and into the poorer black neighborhoods of far Southeast.

No change is given. Bus-to-bus transfers are free within DC, with some surcharges on routes to the suburbs. ♦ Metrorail: M-F 5:30AM-midnight; Sa 8AM-midnight; Su 10AM-midnight. Route, fare, and parking information 637.7000; schedules by mail 637.7000; handicapped, student, and senior citizen fares 637.7000; bike-on-rail permits 962.1116; handicapped on-call service 962.1825; TDD for hearing-impaired 638.3780; lost and found 962.1195; transit police 962.2121 &

Local Bus Services:

Montgomery County: Ride-On, 217.RIDE

Prince George's County: Call-a-Bus, 372.1255

Alexandria: Dash, 370.DASH

Fairfax City: CUE, 385.7859

Fairfax County: Fairfax Connector, 339.7200

Greyhound/Trailways The old Art Deco Greyhound station Downtown is scheduled to be restored and turned into an office building. The new terminal, at 1st and L Sts NE, behind Union Station, serves both Greyhound and Trailways. ♦ 565.2662

Taxis DC's taxi system is a national embarrassment. Cabs are often dilapidated, and many of the drivers are rude, unscrupulous, and ignorant of the city's geography. If your driver speaks English, consider yourself lucky. The blame should be laid partly to Congress, which has resisted efforts to install meters, and partly to the district, whose regulation of the taxi system is a scandal in itself. The only good thing to come of this mess is that DC cabs are cheap compared to other cities. There are over 9000 cabs; hailing one is usually not too difficult.

Fares are based on a zone system, with an additional charge for each zone traversed. A surcharge is added onto the fare for additional passengers and during evening rush hour. Fare information, along with zone maps, is supposed to be displayed in each cab (be sure to specify *which* quadrant of the city you want). Unfortunately, this system, in combination with the low fares, encourages drivers to overcharge, particularly if their passengers don't appear local. Caveat emptor. Drivers are allowed to pick up multiple fares, which is great if you're the second or third fare on a rainy day, not so great if you're in a hurry. You *can* refuse to share your cab, but unless you have a steel hide, this course is not recommended. Fares from DC to the airports are based on mileage.

The 3 largest DC cab companies are **Yellow** (544.1212), **Diamond** (387.6200), and **Capitol** (546.2400): they all radio-dispatch cabs.

Maryland and Virginia cabs use meters; they can take you into DC and out to the suburbs or to an airport, but not within DC itself.

Automobiles The metropolitan area functions on automobile transportation, despite Metro's popularity. The **Beltway** (I-95, I-395, I-495) bypasses Downtown and connects the suburban areas; it is also known for epic backups due to the region's tremendous suburban growth. Geography also plays a part: there are few bridges over the Potomac, and those few (the American Legion Bridge and the Woodrow Wilson Bridge on the Beltway, the Roosevelt Bridge on I-66, and Key and Memorial bridges) quickly become rush-hour bottlenecks. Radio traffic reports are useful.

Washington rush hours offer other quirks. Rock Creek Parkway becomes one-way during rush hours, and some major thoroughfares, such as Connecticut Ave, switch several lanes to match the traffic flow. Interstate 66 is restricted to carpools with 3 or more people inbound during morning rush hour and outbound in the evening. Interstate 395 has restricted carpool lanes during rush hours. Ever-ingenious Washington commuters have been known to put inflatable dummies on board to beat these rules. Others pick up carless commuters at suburban parking lots. This ad hoc hitchhiking system has become so institutionalized that attempts to shut down the evening pickup point Downtown were halted by protests from suburbanites.

Downtown parking garages are plentiful but expensive. Metered street parking generally runs for a 2-hour maximum: carry lots of quarters. Be forewarned that the DC government is anomalously efficient in its parking enforcement. Expired meters are worth a hefty ticket, and cars left in rush-hour zones are swiftly towed, at a painful price. Do not consider becoming a scofflaw if you plan to remain in the area for any amount of time. The district keeps scrupulous track of repeat offenders and will sock you with the hated *boot*, a metal contraption that fits over a tire and immobilizes your car until you pay the back tickets plus a hefty boot-removal fee. In recent years the DC police have also instituted strict weekend parking regulations in Georgetown in an effort to reduce congestion. Obey the special signs explicitly or risk emerging from a bar at 1AM and discovering that your car has been impounded. Parking on the Mall is free but scarce and allowed for only 3 hours at a time. All handicapped spaces are monitored; if your car doesn't have a handicapped license plate, don't tempt fate.

One last quirk of DC driving: diplomats. Washingtonians have long cringed at the vehicular mayhem caused by some members of the diplomatic corps. Diplomatic immunity protects them from criminal prosecution and civil suits resulting from an accident, although concern over the situation in the 1980s resulted in the passage of a law granting victims of diplomatic drivers some financial compensation in lieu of insurance payments. The State Department issues red-white-and-blue license plates to the diplomatic corps. Give them a wide berth.

FYI

Staying Safe: Much has been made of DC's tragically high murder rate, fueled by a booming drug trade. The drug markets, and the crime that accompanies them, are by and large far away from most neighborhoods frequented by travelers. However, Washington remains a big city, with the usual big city crime problems. So stay alert: Washington neighborhoods change quickly, with only a few blocks separating safe from fairly dangerous. Stick to well-lit, well-traveled areas at night, don't carry large amounts of cash or flaunt expensive jewelry, and go out of your way to avoid people who look like trouble.

Newspapers and periodicals: *The Washington Post* is the region's major daily, with *The Washington Times* offering a more conservative slant. The free weekly *City Paper* is particularly good for news on the local entertainment scene, as is the *Post's* "Weekend" section, published every Friday. *Regardie's* gives the inside scoop on business real-estate and corporate takeovers, while the *Washingtonian* covers the lifestyles and comings and goings of DC's movers and shakers. *Capital Spotlight* offers a black perspective on local and national events; *Northwest Current* deals with music, lectures, and shops in Georgetown and the Upper Northwest; and *Museums and Arts Washington* lists current museum, gallery, and historic-home exhibitions.

Telephones: As of this writing, pay phone calls within Washington cost 20 cents. Although the outlying areas have their own area codes, 301 for Maryland and 703 for Virginia (804 for Charlottesville VA), you don't usually need to dial the area code when calling from DC (area code 202).

Money: Deak International exchanges foreign currency, as does the National Bank of Washington and several other major banks. Travelers checks are available at all local banks.

Tipping: A 15-percent tip is standard in restaurants; DC tax is 6 percent, so double the tax and you're almost there. Taxi drivers are tipped 15 percent of the fare. Hotel bellmen and station porters expect $1 per bag. A tip is a reward for service; if you don't get it, don't pay for it.

Smoking: It is illegal to smoke on public transportation, in theaters, in designated areas of restaurants, and in most shops.

Drinking: The drinking age in DC, Maryland, and Virginia is 21. Bars in the district can serve liquor until 2AM Monday through Thursday and on Sunday and until 3AM Friday and Saturday. Retail liquor store prices are generally cheapest within DC.

Touring DC

Tourmobile is the tourist's friend. These boxy, articulated buses ply their way around the Mall hitting all the major sights: the Smithsonian museums, the Capitol, and the Lincoln and Jefferson memorials, as well as out-of-the-way spots such as Arlington National Cemetery. An all-day ticket allows you to get on and off as often as you like; guides point out the sights along the 90-minute Mall loop. ♦ Fee. Tour

schedules vary, and reservations are sometimes required; call for information. 554.7950, group tours 554.7020

Old Town Trolley Tours of Washington Small green-and-orange buses offer 2-hour guided tours from major hotels to the National Cathedral, the Capitol, and the Mall and memorials. For a single fee you can get on and off as often as you like. ♦ Fee. Daily 9AM-4PM, Jan-Memorial Day, Labor Day-Dec; daily 9AM-7PM, Memorial Day-Labor Day. 269.3020/1

Gold Line/Gray Line Large air-conditioned buses offer 8 tours, from all-day overviews to half-day tours of Mount Vernon and Alexandria to a 3-hour *Washington by Night* tour. ♦ Fee. 386.8300

The Street Plan

Although newcomers to Washington on their twelfth circumnavigation of a traffic circle may feel like socks caught in the spin cycle, there really *is* an elegant logic to the city's layout. Once you have it down, you'll be able to get around easily.

Pierre L'Enfant designed the city as a grid overlaid with diagonal spokes radiating from the major traffic

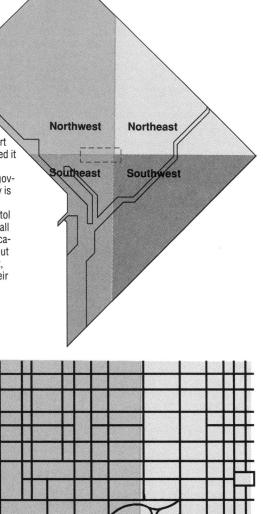

Northwest   **Northeast**

Southeast   **Southwest**

Orientation

circles. It's the diagonal streets, named after the states of the union, that usually confuse visitors. So ignore those for now and start at the beginning: **the central grid**. L'Enfant focused it on the **Capitol**, not on the White House—an apt metaphor for a country based on representative government. With the Capitol as *ground zero*, the city is divided into 4 quadrants—Northeast, Northwest, Southeast, and Southwest. North and South Capitol streets serve as the east/west division, and the Mall and East Capitol Street as the north/south demarcation. Once you accept the fact that L'Enfant's layout allows for the existence of 4 different, and distant, buildings, all properly claiming 500 10th St as their address, you're well on the way to mastering the system. (See **L'Enfant's Plan**, page 208.)

The Grid

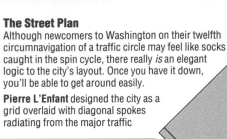

Each quadrant is divided into a **regular grid of lettered and numbered streets**, with the quadrants set up as mirror images of each other. The numbered streets run north-south, starting from North and South Capitol streets. Thus, First Street NW and First Street NE are only 2 blocks apart, but 10th Street NW and 10th Street NE are 22 blocks apart. When the numbered streets cross the north/south divider of the Mall and East Capitol Street, they automatically take on the suffix for the new quadrant: say, 10th Street SW and 10th Street SE.

The lettered streets complete the grid. Starting at the Mall/East Capitol Street meridian, they run east-west. A and B streets are preempted by the Mall and

Constitution and Independence avenues, which flank the Mall to the north and south. So the letter streets start with C and proceed apace. Even this system has its quirks, though: J Street is nonexistent, with legend holding that the exclusion was a slap at unpopular **Chief Justice John Jay**, and I Street is often spelled *Eye* so that it's not confused with the numeral 1. Q Street sometimes appears as Que. After the 26 letters of the alphabet are exhausted, the east-west streets continue on with 2-syllable streets in alphabetical order: Adams, Bryant, Channing. When the 2-syllable alphabet runs out, 3-syllable names take over: Albemarle, Brandywine, Chesapeake, and so on.

The Diagonals

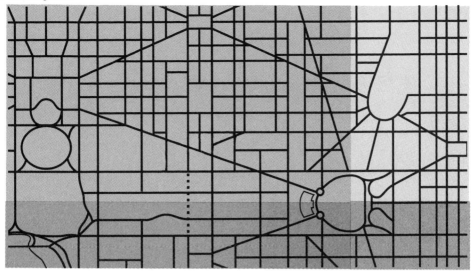

The wild cards in the system are the **broad diagonal avenues**—Pennsylvania Avenue, which runs from M Street at the foot of Georgetown past the White House, breaks temporarily at the Capitol grounds, and then continues southeast across the Anacostia River into far Southeast, is the best-known. The state streets intersect at traffic circles. Thus, Dupont Circle is transected by Connecticut, New Hampshire, and Rhode Island avenues, with P Street NW and 19th Street NW thrown in for good measure. These multiple entrances and exits to circles make for traffic-flow nightmares, a problem that the city's planners have attempted to alleviate, without much success, by channeling some circles, such as Dupont, into express and local lanes.

Forbearance is the only surefire way to negotiate circles unscathed. But the avenues, besides being broad beautiful boulevards act as handy shortcuts across the grid pattern, as well as functioning as some of the city's major thoroughfares. Wisconsin and Connecticut avenues ferry residents to the Maryland suburbs, while New York Avenue connects to Route 50 (to Annapolis) and the Baltimore-Washington Parkway, and Pennsylvania maintains its own special status as the nation's *Main Street* and path of the inaugural parades.

Put it all together, and you've got a foursquare grid overlaid with idiosyncratic diagonals and circles, combined to make a city that, while businesslike at heart, is sometimes overtaken by fits of whimsy that can be either inspired flights of genius or hopeless detours. L'Enfant, it seems, knew the character of the United States all too well, and fashioned its capital accordingly.

DC Reading

A Kid's Guide to Washington, D.C. by **Diane C. Clark** (1989, Gulliver Books of Harcourt Brace Jovanovich, Inc.)

American Express Pocket Guide to Washington, DC by **Christopher McIntosh** (1989, Prentice Hall Press)

Away for the Weekend: Washington, D.C. by **Eleanor Berman** (1989, Clarkson N. Potter, Inc.)

Best Restaurants & Others: Washington D.C. & Environs by **Phyllis C. Richman** (1989, 101 Productions)

Frommer's 1989–1990 Guide to Washington, DC (1989, Simon & Schuster)

100 of the Best Real Estate Agents: Washington, D.C., and Suburban Maryland (1989, C&M Publishing, Inc.)

The Smithsonian Guide to Historic America: Virginia and the Capital Region by **Henry Wiencek** (1989, Stewart, Tabori & Chang)

Successful Gardening in the Greater Washington Area by the **Men's Garden Club of Montgomery County** (1989, in bookstores or by mail from P.O. Box 34863, Bethesda, MD 20817)

Zagat Washington, D.C./Baltimore Restaurant Survey (1989, Zagat Survey)

Washington in Focus: The Photo History of the Nation's Capital by **Philip Bigler** (1988, Vandamere Press)

Ghosts: Washington's Most Famous Ghosts by **John Alexander** (1987, The Washington Book Trading Co.)

Rainy Days, Sunny Days, Saturday's Child: Family Activities in Metropolitan Washington by **Deborah Churchman** and **Anne H. Oman** (1987, Washington Book Trading Co.)

Washington, D.C., Guidebook for Kids by **Carol Bluestone** and **Susan Irwin** (1987, Noodle Press)

Washington, Past and Present: A Guide to the Nation's Capital (1987, The U.S. Capital Historical Society)

Washington's Embassies of the World: Five Walking Tours and Directory by **Donald C. Dilworth** (1986, Communications Press, Inc.)

Beauty and Bounty: One-Day Nature Trips In and Around Washington D.C. by **Jane Ockerhausen Smith** (1983, EPM Publications)

One-Day Trips Through History: 200 Excursions Within 150 Miles of Washington, D.C. by **Jane Ockerhausen Smith** (1982, EPM Publications)

The Washington One-Day Trip Book: 101 Offbeat Excursions In and Around the Nation's Capital by **Jane Ockerhausen Smith** (1981, EPM Publications)

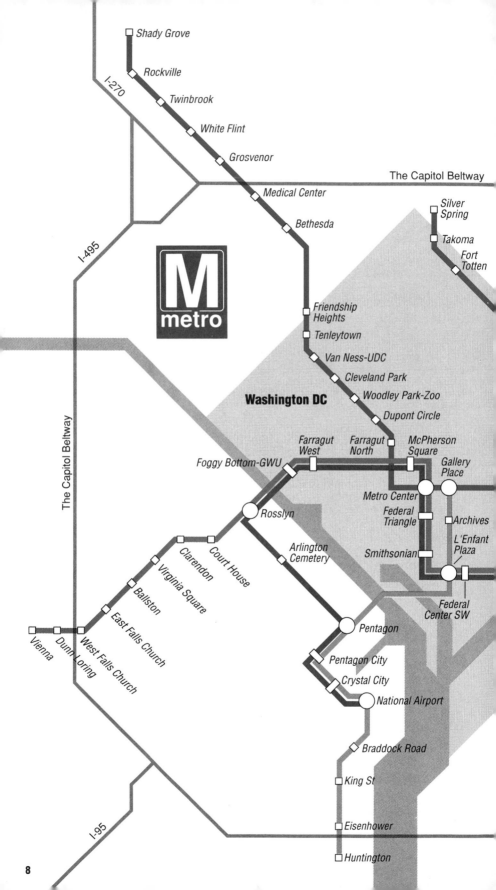

Orientation

Phone Numbers

Emergencies
Fire/Police/Ambulance	911
Fire/Police/Ambulance (nonemergency)	832.4537
TTY/TDD Deaf Emergency	727.9334
Poison Control Center	625.3333
Ask-A-Nurse	760.8787
Rape Crisis Center	333.7273
Suicide Prevention Hotline	546.6232
AAA Emergency Road Service	222.5000

Visitor Information
Washington Area Convention and Visitors Association	789.7000
International Visitor Information Service	783.6540
Handicapped Visitor Information (voice)	472.6770
(TTY)	472.5764
Tourmobile Sightseeing	554.7950
Smithsonian Institution	357.1300
Travelers Aid	347.0101
Washington Metropolitan Area Transit Authority, Metrorail and Metrobus route and schedule information	637.7000
Handicap Services	962.1245

Recorded Messages
Event Information	737.8866
Dial-a-Museum (Smithsonian)	357.2020
Dial-a-Park (National Park Service)	426.6975
Dial-a-Phenomenon (Smithsonian)	737.8855
Sports Update (Washington Post)	223.8060
Time	844.2525
Weather	936.1212
White House	456.7041

Important Numbers
Amtrak Railroad Service	800/872.7245
Greyhound/Trailways Bus Lines	565.2662
Better Business Bureau of Metropolitan Washington	393.8000
Dental referral service	686.0803
Doctor referral service	466.2870
U.S. Capitol	
Senate	224.3121
House of Representatives	225.3121
U.S. Customs	566.8195
U.S. Passport Office	783.8200
Visa Information (Department of State)	663.1972
Youth Hostel	737.2333

Capitol Hill NE/SE

Downtown

17

16

M

L

15

K

I

14 H

G

13 G

M 12 F Union Station

M Judiciary Square

F

E

D 9

11 10 8

C

7 Consitution Ave

3 2 6 E. Capitol

4 1 28

5 Independence Ave

32

30 31 33 34

M Federal Center SW

29 D 36 37 38 39

M Capitol South E F

Virginia Ave G 41 M

Southeast Fwy 43 44

The Mall I 42

K

L

M

46 N

45

O P

Anacostia River

Frederick Douglass Memorial Bridge

11th St Bridge

Anacostia Fwy

Q R

Ridge Pl

S T

Good Hope Rd

U

V W

Martin L King Jr Ave 13th 14th 15th 16th 47

New Jersey Ave
No. Capitol
So. Capitol
1st 2nd 4th 5th 6th 7th 8th 9th 10th 11th 12th 13th 14th 15th 16th 17th
Florida Ave
West Virginia Ave
Morse Ave
Neal Ave
Montello Ave
Queen
Trinidad Ave
Bladensburg Rd
Mount Olivet Rd
Maryland Ave
Massachusetts Ave
Tennessee Ave
North Carolina Ave
South Carolina Ave
Kentucky Ave
Pennsylvania Ave
Potomac Ave
Eastern Market
Potomac Ave H
Potomac Ave

When that irascible Frenchman **Pierre L'Enfant** looked up at grassy **Jenkins Hill** in 1790, he saw "a pedestal waiting for a monument."

What he put atop it was the **Capitol** of the new republic. It is from here, the heart of the city he planned, that one can still best see the outlines of this last of the Baroque cities.

Not all the subsequent builders and planners of the national capital have seen the city through L'Enfant's eyes. Indeed, virtually the whole of Washington, but especially the area around the Capitol, has been a touchstone of city planning as that concept has

Capitol Hill/Northeast/Southeast

changed through the years. Whether planners have been called upon by the nation to build—or rebuild—the capital, or whether they have assigned themselves the task, no other American city so reflects the nation's changing sense of itself. A walk from the would-be Napoleonic grandeur of the **Library of Congress** to the starkness of the **Hart Office Building** is a brief tour through the national character.

The Hill, as Washingtonians know it, is full of stops. Along with the Capitol, which includes both the **Senate** and the **House of Representatives**, there are also the **Supreme Court Building** and the office buildings of **Congress**. The **Folger Shakespeare Library** was placed on *The Hill* by its founder, Standard Oil executive **H.C.Folger**. A revitalized **Union Station** once again lives up to the vow of its original designer, **Daniel Burnham**, to "make no little plans, they have no magic," soaring splendidly above the inevitable flotilla of shops, restaurants, and theaters. The **Capital Children's Museum** is just east, as are a thriving restaurant district along Massachusetts Avenue NE and many stately Victorian townhouses.

One of **Northeast Washington**'s best known institutions is **Gallaudet University**, which has been pioneering in education and autonomy for the deaf since 1857. It sits on **Kendall Green**, land deeded to it by a member of Andrew Jackson's famous *kitchen cabinet*. The **Catholic University of America**, with its prominent undergraduate and graduate schools, and the **National Shrine of the Immaculate Conception** are major forces on the Northeast skyline and in the nation. The **National Arboretum** offers an unexpectedly pastoral refuge to the north along New York Avenue at the city's hectic gateway to the north, as do the **Kenilworth Aquatic Gardens**.

Southeast Washington, comprised largely of residential neighborhoods for middle- and lower-class families, is most famous for **RFK Stadium**, home of the **Washington Redskins**, who have not played before an unsold seat in more than 2 decades. The football team, perhaps more than anything, binds Washington's unusually disparate population together. Close to the stadium is the all-but-forgotten **Congressional Cemetery**, established in the days when it seemed not just a quick hop from the Capitol but a long, lugubrious carriage-ride away.

Southeast shows signs of an otherwise long-vanished Washington. The city, for example, once featured 3 major markets. Central Market, the largest, is long gone, as is Western Market. But **Eastern Market**, famous for its fresh produce and crabcake sandwiches, continues to serve this part of the city. Many

well-known persons used this market over the years, including **John Philip Sousa**, one of Southeast's native sons (he even wrote a novel about the area). And many of its customers were—and doubtless are—employees of the **Marine Barracks and Navy Yard**, now primarily a museum.

The neighborhood of **Anacostia**, across the muddy **Anacostia River**, is in some respects an independent community—self-contained and proud. In **Good Hope Road** and **Martin Luther King, Jr., Avenue** it has its own Main Streets. In **Fort Stanton Park** and the banks of the Anacostia, it has its own serene relief from Washington's heat. In the **Anacostia Museum**, located in **Uniontown**, a community settled in the wake of the Civil War by freedmen, it has its own museum. Today, the neighborhood includes some of the city's most economically depressed areas, in addition to handsome and secluded residential streets whose houses command a sweeping view of the city from Anacostia's heights.

Fiery abolitionist leader **Frederick Douglass**, a former slave who came to be known as the Sage of Anacostia, remains the area's most honored hero. His then-suburban home across the Anacostia River, **Cedar Hill**, has been restored by the National Park Service and is now a **National Historic Site** and museum.

Courtesy Bureau of Engraving and Printing

1 The Capitol (1793, Dr. William Thornton) **George Washington** officiated at the cornerstone-laying ceremony (the sandstone for the building came from his Aquia Creek quarries), but it was not until 22 November 1800, at **President John Adams'** insistence, that the House and the Senate moved into the Capitol and officially called the first joint session of Congress to order. The building at this time was a 2-story square structure. By 1807, a second similar edifice had been built for the House of Representatives. A wooden walkway linked the 2 buildings.

In 1814, British troops invaded Washington and convened in a little session of their own in the Senate building. The decision that day was to burn the Capitol along with the city's other federal buildings. Only a sudden summer rainstorm spared the building from total destruction. Five years later, the structure was repaired. Congress returned home, and what you see today is an outgrowth of the 1819 Capitol. Most visitors enter the building via the **East Front**, where every 4 years on 20 January the presidential inauguration ceremonies take place. (In 1981, **Ronald Reagan**'s inauguration took place on the **West Front**; the location of each ceremony is determined by a joint congressional committee.) As you walk up the steps toward the magnificent bronze

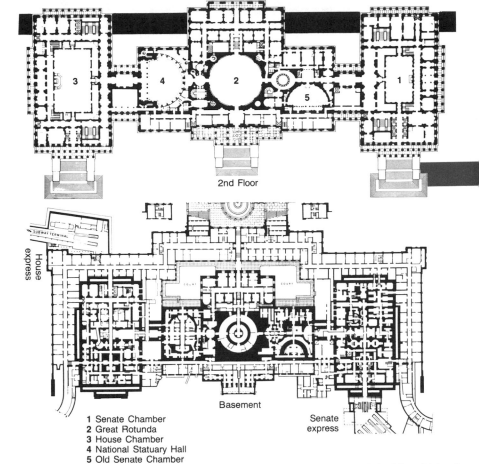

2nd Floor

Basement

House express

SUBWAY TERMINAL

Senate express

1 Senate Chamber
2 Great Rotunda
3 House Chamber
4 National Statuary Hall
5 Old Senate Chamber

Columbus Doors, keep in mind that it was here that **William Henry Harrison** delivered the longest inaugural speech on record ($1^{1}/_{2}$ hours) in a drizzly downpour, only to die of pneumonia 3 weeks later. Here, too, **Franklin Delano Roosevelt** reassured a nation beset by the Depression, declaring that "the only thing we have to fear is fear itself." On the East Portico steps in 1961, **John F. Kennedy** set the tone for his presidency with the words, "Ask not what your country can do for you, but what you can do for your country."

There had once been a small wooden dome sheathed in copper atop the Capitol, but in the 1850s Congress decided it was unsafe and badly proportioned. It commissioned a much bigger one, designed by **Thomas U. Walter** and raised with the engineering expertise of **General Montgomery Meigs**. Erratic financing and then the Civil War impeded the progress of construction, and when the Secretary of War wanted to divert the iron and manpower to the war effort, it seemed likely that the project would be scrapped entirely.

At the time, Washington was a shambles and morale was very low. The Capitol itself had been forced into double duty as a field hospital. **President Lincoln** appraised the situation and decided that construction must go on "as a symbol that our nation will go on."

And so, while doctors and chaplains ministered to the wounded, workmen hammered overhead. Late in 1863, amid tremendous fanfare, the $19^{1}/_{2}$-foot *Statue of Freedom* was raised to the top of the 9-million-pound iron dome. From a distance, the figure looks like an American Indian: she wears a helmet rimmed by stars and finished with an eagle's head, actually symbols from ancient mythology. But when first designed by **Thomas Crawford** in the late 1850s, she wore a *liberty cap*, the hat worn by freed Roman slaves. **Jefferson Davis**, then Secretary of War and in charge of construction, objected to the antislavery implication and had the design changed. Ironically, Davis left Washington in 1861 to become president of the Confederacy, and the *Statue of Freedom*, sculpted in Italy, was shipped to America and cast in bronze by slave labor.

Much of the artwork in the Rotunda and throughout the Capitol is a testament to one man: **Constantino Brumidi**. A political refugee, Brumidi spent 25 years (1852–77) painting the Capitol's interior as a way of thanking his adopted homeland. The fresco in the dome's eye, with its 15-foot-high colonial statesmen mingling with classical deities (they look life-size from the Rotunda floor), is Brumidi's work, as is the frieze, which from the floor looks 3-dimensional.

13

Four of the 8 large historical paintings lining the Rotunda walls were done by **John Trumball**, an aide to (then) General George Washington. Trumball did not paint from second-hand reports. He has been an actual witness to each of the scenes he depicted.

To the south of the Rotunda is **Statuary Hall**. In 1864 each state was asked to contribute statues of its 2 most celebrated citizens. Ninety-two of these statues, representing such people as **Will Rogers** (Oklahoma), **Robert E. Lee** (Virginia), and **Brigham Young** (Utah), are displayed in this room. The House of Representa-

Capitol Hill/Northeast/Southeast

tives met here until 1857. **John Quincy Adams**, serving in the House in his postpresidential years, discovered an acoustical phenomenon: at certain spots you can clearly hear conversations from across the room, although anyone standing in between hears nothing. In 1848, Adams suffered a stroke in this chamber; a small gold star on the floor designates where the sixth President died.

North of the Rotunda, the public areas include the **Old Senate Chamber**, the **President's Room**, and the **Old Supreme Court Chamber**. If you wish to sit in the **Visitors Galleries** in either the **Senate Chamber** or the **House Chamber** and you're not on the official tour, you'll need to stop by the office of your senator or representative (depending on which chamber you wish to observe) and pick up a gallery pass. If you don't know your representative's name or office location, call the Capitol's House switchboard at 225.3121, or its Senate switchboard at 224.3121. (For easy access from the Rotunda to the representative's office, use the subway—a must for children!—which links the Capitol with the surrounding office buildings.) Foreign visitors can enter the galleries by showing their passports. Space is reserved in each gallery for handicapped visitors.

Be sure to check beforehand to verify that Congress is in session and, if so, what's on the day's schedule. You can do this by calling 224.3121 or by checking the *Washington Post's* daily *Activities in Congress* column. If an American flag is flying over the chamber you wish to visit (south: House, north: Senate), that legislative body is in session, and if a lantern glows from the Capitol dome, at least one of the chambers is at work.

The action on Capitol Hill builds in intensity in December as the elected officials attempt to tie up loose ends and still make it home for the holidays. If your visit to Washington is primarily to see Congress in action, this is the time to come. Throughout the year, if you're looking for drama and pacing, a visit to the chamber galleries is pro forma, but the real place to be is at the committee meetings. Schedules are also listed in the *Washington Post*. Just make sure it's an open meeting and show up on time.

To write your senator or representative:

Senator (name)   Representative (name)
Senate Office Building   House Office Building
Washington DC 20510   Washington DC 20515

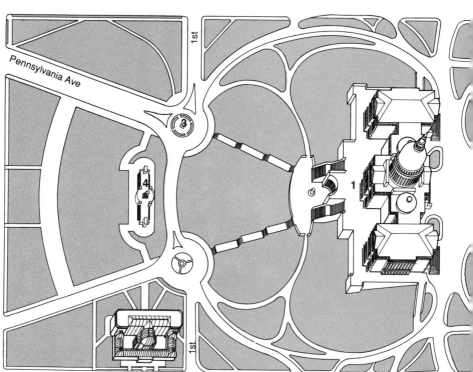

Pennsylvania Ave

Independence Ave

During the summer, the Capitol's **West Terrace** hosts free evening concerts, beginning at 8PM:

M   US Navy Concert Band
Tu US Air Force Band
W   US Marine Band
F   US Army Band

Special concerts are offered on Memorial Day, the Fourth of July, and Labor Day. The West Terrace also affords an outstanding view of the city and a closeup of the original sandstone West Front, which has been handsomely restored. It narrowly escaped a proposal to extend and rebuild it in as harshly unsympathetic fashion as the East Front.
♦ Daily 9AM-8PM, Memorial Day-Labor Day; daily 9AM-4:30PM, Jan-Memorial Day, Labor Day-Dec. Tours daily 9AM-4:45PM. Capitol Rotunda and Statuary Hall open in the summer until 8PM. When the House or Senate is in night session, that wing remains open. Daily tours lasting 30-45 minutes leave from the Rotunda every 5-10 minutes. Free. Write your senator or representative well in advance to arrange a VIP tour of the Capitol. East Front entrance at E. Capitol St on Capitol Hill. Metro stops: Capitol South, Union Station. 225.6827

2 Spring Grotto (1875, Frederick Law Olmsted) A cool and quiet hideaway best visited on a hot summer day, designed by the creator of New York's Central Park. ♦ Constitution Ave NW (1st St-New Jersey Ave) Metro stops: Union Station, Capitol South

3 The Peace Monument (1877, Franklin Simmons) A marble memorial to sailors slain in the Civil War. The figure of America weeps on the shoulder of History. Inscribed in America's book: "They died that their country might live." ♦ Pennsylvania Ave at 1st St NW

4 General Ulysses S. Grant Memorial
(1927, Henry Schrady) Scores of statues in Washington commemorate wars, great leaders, and fallen warriors, yet few are as striking in their realism or as strong a condemnation of war as this monument in Union Square.

Capitol Hill/Northeast/Southeast

In the center of the installation is the 17-foot bronze of Grant. To the north is the *Cavalry Group*. Seven mounted men prepare to charge. Their officer holds up his sword, his mouth wide open as he shouts the advance. To his side, a horse has stumbled, pitching its rider headlong onto the mud. The soldier behind pulls desperately on his mount's reins, trying to avoid the fallen man. The group seems alive with tension and movement.

To the south is the *Artillery Group*. Three horses, one with a rider, pull a cart holding a cannon and 3 soldiers. The horses are rearing back in response to a sudden order to turn. Each soldier shows a different face of battle. One is ready, another frightened, another weary to the bone.

Henry Schrady was only 31 years old and largely unknown when he was chosen by a jury of the most respected sculptors of his day, **Augustus Saint-Gaudens** and **Daniel Chester French** among them. Despite the consternation of the artistic establishment and his own poor health, Shrady plunged into his work, dedicating the remaining 20 years of his life to this single project. The completed memorial was finally dedicated in 1927, 2 weeks after his death. ♦ Union Square (Pennsylvania-Maryland Aves NW)

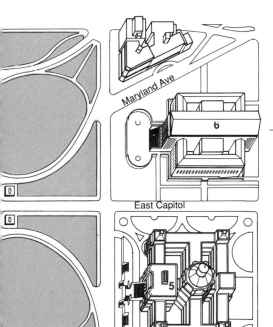

For people with an interest in comparative statistics, here is a set compiled by *Congressional Quarterly Inc.* It records the output of Congress as of 31 March 1989 in years following the election of a new president.

	1977	1981	1989
Senate			
Days in session	47	39	27
Bills reported out of committee	71	62	46
House			
Days in session	46	43	30
Bills reported out of committee	133	13	15
Both			
Bills clearing both houses	17*	6*	12

*1977 and 1981 include only those that eventually became law.
Courtesy of Congressional Quarterly Inc.

Places a bill may die

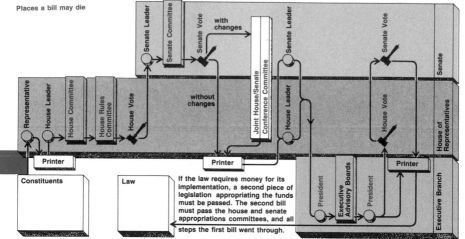

Together, the **Senate** and the **House of Representatives** form the 2 chambers of **Congress** called for in the Constitution. Congress makes federal laws, sponsors studies and investigations, assesses taxes, and appropriates funds for government projects. Although every new law must pass through both chambers before going to the president, each of the 2 chambers does have some powers exclusive of the other.

In general, the Senate plays a stronger role in foreign policy. It ratifies treaties and approves presidential appointments. It also sits as a court of impeachment on federal officials.

All legislation having to do with taxation or appropriations must be initiated in the House of Representatives. In addition, the House alone has the authority to bring charges of impeachment.

Big numbers have a way of blunting their own significance, but in the interest of demonstrating the monumental task of governing America, here are a few to ponder. In 1988, 4013 measures were proposed in the Senate, and 7269 in the House of Representatives, for a total of 11,282. Fourteen hundred thirty were passed by the Senate and 1502 by the House. Of these, only 761 became public law (a passing rate of 6.7%); the rest ended up somewhere in the **National Archives**.

When one considers the many paths a piece of legislation may take, it's amazing that even that many made it. What follows is a simplified explanation of how a bill originating in the House might become law:

The initial impetus for a bill may come from a wide array of sources: the president and his advisory commissions, congressional committees, lobbyists, private citizens, your congressperson. No matter what its origin, in order for a bill to be considered, it must be sponsored by at least one senator or representative.

The first step is the drafting of a bill. This may be done by an individual citizen, but more frequently it's done by executive commissions, congressional committees, the **Legislative Reference Service** of the **Library of Congress**, or an individual congressperson's staff.

The bill is then dropped into a box (hopper) on the desk of the **Clerk of the House**. It's assigned a number, read into the *Congressional Record*, and sent to the **Government Printing Office**, which makes and distributes copies. The **Speaker of the House** then assigns the bill for study to a specific committee or subcommittee, depending on what the bill concerns—agriculture, defense, judicial matters, etc.

A committee hearing is really the first trial by fire for any new bill. The committee can table the bill, effectively killing it before it comes to a general vote. The committee may also revise the bill and/or report it out. In that case the committee's report of recommendations is printed up and distributed, and the bill is eligible to be voted on by the full House.

Before the vote, the bill must make its way through the Rules Committee. This group decides only on matters of procedure, but its decisions can be a matter of life or death for proposed legislation. The committee determines what type of amendments, if any, will be allowed and what type of debate procedure will be followed. It also assigns the bill a place on the calendar. A lot of important lobbying goes on between sponsoring representatives and members of the Rules Committee, for they can bury a bill so deep that it will never see the light of day while Congress is in session. If that happens, the whole process must begin again—starting at the hopper.

The bill eventually comes up for a **Second Reading** in front of the House. Any debate or amending takes place at this time. Majority and minority opponents and proponents of the bill are busy marshaling forces, persuading, and determining who will speak for their side on the floor of the House.

Finally, the bill gets a **Third Reading**, although, in fact, all that is read is its legislative number. A vote is then taken. In most cases only a simple majority is needed to pass a bill.

It's possible that while a bill has been moving through the House, a similar **companion bill** has been going through pretty much the same procedure in the Senate. In the event that both bills are passed, any differences between them are hammered out in a **Joint House/Senate Conference Committee**.

If there is no companion bill, a bill passed by the House moves across the Capitol building to the Senate, where it starts a new round of committee hearings and votes. Any changes are put before a Joint Committee, and in most cases, a compromise version is arrived at. The revised text is printed and then goes before both chambers of Congress for another vote.

If the bill is passed in both houses, it is **enrolled**. This means a special copy is typeset on parchment. It goes to the Speaker of the House and the **President of the Senate** for signing, before it is sent to the president.

The president has 10 days in which to act on the bill. If he signs the bill it becomes law; if he allows 10 days to pass without taking any action it automatically becomes law. In the event that he vetoes the bill, $2/3$ majorities in both the House and the Senate are needed to **override** his decision. A rarely used third option is the **Pocket Veto**. If the bill comes to the president when there are fewer than 10 days left to the session of Congress and the president declines to sign it, it dies.

The Roving Capital

The **Continental Congress** first convened in 1774. From then until 1800, when it moved into official headquarters in the District of Columbia, the Congress resembled nothing so much as a roving band of Bedouins in knee breeches. During that time the members met in 8 different cities, each having the right to call itself the capital—at least for a moment. Congress was so transitory that when a statue in honor of **George Washington** was proposed in 1783, **Francis Hopkinson**, a representative from Pennsylvania, suggested that it be mounted on wheels—the better to follow Congress in its wanderings.

Philadelphia was the capital more frequently than any other city, but in 1777, with the British closing in, Congress hightailed it to the town of **Lancaster** PA, which became capital-for-a-day. From Lancaster, Congress moved across the Susquehanna River to **York**, where it remained until June of 1778. The Articles of Confederation (the first constitution of the 13 American states) was passed there, and **Benjamin Franklin** had his press moved up so he could print $1 million worth of much-needed Continental money. Congress moved back to Philadelphia, but was again threatened by the British and moved to **Baltimore** MD in 1779.

In 1783, the Revolutionary War was over, but the nation was broke and the union tenuous. Congress was once again meeting in Philadelphia and might have continued to do so had a group of soldiers not invaded the city and rioted for back pay. Congress fled to **Princeton** NJ, where it met in **Nassau Hall**, still part of the Princeton University campus and then the largest building in the country. However, there wasn't enough room in town for the growing bureaucracy, which soon moved on to **Annapolis** MD, where there was presumably more hotel space. In Annapolis, Congress decided that the new government needed its own city, but no one could agree on the site.

Every town in the country immediately began lobbying to be named capital, including **Trenton** NJ. (Congress met there briefly in 1774 before rejecting the proposal.) **New York City** became the capital in 1774, and in 1789, George Washington was inaugurated there. Later that year, Congress moved back to Philadelphia and remained there until 1800.

Debate on where to put the capital was fierce. Northerners wanted it near a financial center, while agrarian Southerners feared the power of northern financiers and special interests. It took a political compromise between **Alexander Hamilton** and **Thomas Jefferson** to decide the issue in 1790. During the Revolutionary War, the South had managed to pay her soldiers, but the North had not. Led by Hamilton, the northern states wanted Congress to absorb their debt. The South, led by Jefferson, was opposed. Finally the 2 men worked out a deal whereby the North was relieved of its debt and the South gained the prestige of a national capital.

Congress specified the size of the site and that it be somewhere on the Potomac, but the choice was left to Washington, who had once been a surveyor. Although he was hounded by land speculators, he made an independent choice, picking a diamond-shaped area where the Potomac and Anacostia rivers merged. He hoped the Anacostia would provide a deep-water naval port, while the Potomac would be a link to western provinces by way of the proposed **Potowmack Canal**. Perhaps it was no accident either that the capital would be an easy day's ride from Washington's home at **Mt. Vernon**.

Yearly, $116,000 is allocated to a quarterly cleaning of the capital's 56 principal statues and monuments, including the **Lincoln** and **Jefferson** memorials, the **Juarez** statues, and the **DC War Memorial**. The process consists of a 5-person crew operating a steam-pressure-system hose. This is attached to a mobile tank truck filled with 1500 gallons of pure water. A complete 4000-gallon washdown of the Lincoln Memorial takes 6 working days and nights.

While a congressman, **John Lindsay** said: "New York has total depth in every area. Washington has only politics; after that the second biggest thing is marble."

5 Library of Congress (Thomas Jefferson (Main) Building, 1897, Smithmeyer and Pelz; John Adams Building, 1939, Pierson and Wilson; James Madison Memorial Building, 1980, DeWitt, Poor, and Shelton) Here are some figures, although they're impossible to grasp: nearly 90 million items, 400 more added every hour; nearly 6000 books printed before the year 1500; 5 **Stradivarius** violins; 1500 flutes; the world's largest collection of comic books; 3.5 million pieces of sheet music; recordings of traditional songs of the Sioux; one of only 3 remaining perfect **Gutenberg** bibles, circa 1455. There is no doubt that this is the world's largest library and collection.

Funded in 1800 with $5000, the library began as a 1-room reference collection for Congress. When it was burned in 1814 by the British (we had just burned theirs in Canada), **Thomas Jefferson**, retired and in need of money, offered his fine private library as a replacement.

The Jefferson Building is an ornate Italian Renaissance/Beaux-Arts confection. Most striking is the **Main Reading Room**, a soaring, domed octagon built in 3 colors of veined marble—the copper roof of the dome was once gilded. Twice in the last 40 years the library has been forced to expand: first into the white Georgia-marble John Adams Building at 2nd St and Independence Ave SE; then into the 6-story, 46-acre James Madison Memorial Building, 101 Independence Ave SE, where you can see a part of the library's collection of over 12 million photos and prints. Most of these were obtained as copyright submissions and span the history of photography. **Mathew Brady**'s work is well represented, and the entire photo collection of *Look* magazine is here. The Madison Building also contains the nation's largest film archive, and its jewellike Mary Pickford Theater (on the 3rd floor) screens classics at no charge (707.5677).

Special collections include the **Manuscript Division**, which comprises volumes from many of the presidents' private libraries; the **Local History and Genealogy Division**, where family records may be researched; extensive **Asian** and **European collections**; and the **National Library Service for the Blind and Physically Handicapped**.

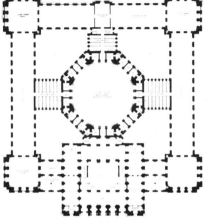

Concerts are offered year-round, and include those by the **Juilliard String Quartet**, which plays the library's collection of Stradivariuses and other fine stringed instruments. Literary events run October through May, and feature poets and authors of note.

This is the nation's library, and as such is open for use by researchers over 18 years of age. (Visitors of all ages are welcome in the exhibition halls.) An 18-minute slide/sound presentation, *America's Library*, runs hourly weekdays from 8:45AM to 8:45PM, Saturdays from 8:45AM to 5:45PM, and Sundays from 1:45 to 4:45PM. Follow this with a tour that will take you into the stacks; these leave from the **Visitor Services Center** weekdays from 10AM to 3PM. There is a gift shop in the James Madison Memorial Building that sells books, cards, and crafts.

Renovations on the Jefferson (Main) Building began in 1988 and will continue at least through 1989, with the Main Reading Room closed and many exhibitions and collections moved. Check with the Visitor Services Center, or call 707.5000 to see which areas are open.
♦ Free. M-F 8:30AM-9:30PM; Sa 8:30AM-6PM; Su 1-5PM. Visitor Services Center: M-F 9AM-4PM. Jefferson (Main) Building, 1st St SE (E. Capitol St-Independence Ave) Metro stops: Capitol South, Union Station. 707.5000, reference 707.6500, tours 707.5458, reading room schedules 707.6400 &

Within the Library of Congress:

Madison Building Cafeteria ★$ On the 6th floor of the Madison Building is one of official Washington's best restaurant bargains, with high-quality soups, salads, sandwiches, and entrees served in an attractive dining room with a panoramic view of the city. ♦ American ♦ M-F 9-10:30AM, 12:30-3PM. No credit cards. 707.8300

6 Supreme Court (1935, Cass Gilbert) Armed only with the US *Constitution* and a carefully fashioned authority, the Supreme Court determines the complexion of American society more than almost any other single power. For this reason a session at the Supreme Court is one of the most rewarding experiences for those who come to Washington DC as a pilgrimage to honor and explore the federal government.

The court's 9 justices are called into session the first Monday in October. They hear cases for 2 weeks, then retire to formulate their decisions for another 2 weeks, continuing to work through the end of April. During the in-session weeks, the court is open to the public during hearings (Monday and Tuesday). No passes are needed to attend, but there are only 100 to 150 seats available to the public, so you must come no later than 9:30AM to get a seat. The *Washington Post* will report the cases due for review on in-session days, and you will be able to anticipate the crowd. Following argument, the court takes the bench every Monday, usually until 4 July, to hand down orders and opinions, so if possible make that the day of your visit and feel the true drama of the nation's highest court.

When the Supreme Court is in session, in-courtroom lectures are given weekdays 3:30 to 4PM. When the court is out, lectures are given 9:30AM to 3:30PM every hour on the half-hour. In addition, there is a half-hour film featuring the **chief justice** and others on the bench explaining the history and day-to-day workings of the court.

The Supreme Court began hearing cases in 1790, but so little was thought of its prestige that the first chief justice, **John Jay**, resigned to become governor of New York. It took almost 150 years before it was deemed worthy of its own home, a dazzling white Neoclassical edifice. Although the building is restrained and commanding, there is evidence that Gilbert perhaps didn't take the commission as seriously as he could have: he and some of his nonjudicial contemporaries are among the robed figures in the main pediment.

The massive building has one of the best government cafeterias, but plan your visit carefully—it closes to the public 4 times daily. ♦ Court: free. M-F 9AM-4:30PM. Cafeteria M-F 7:30-10:30AM, 11:30AM-noon, 12:15-1PM, 1:15-2PM. 1st St NE (Maryland Ave-E. Capitol St) Metro stops: Capitol South, Union Station. 479.3211, cafeteria 479.3246 ♿

7 Sewall-Belmont House The **National Women's Party** has turned this house into a museum of American women's political achievements. The original structure dates from the late 1600s or early 1700s. Sewall

Capitol Hill/Northeast/Southeast

added to the house in 1800, and parts were burned by the British in 1813. Numerous remodelings have made it a crazy quilt of architectural styles: Queen Anne, Georgian, classical, and French influences are evident. **Albert Gallatin**, Jefferson's and Madison's Secretary of the Treasury, is purported to have worked out the *Louisiana Purchase* deal here.

In 1929, the NWP bought the house. Today it serves as the party's headquarters. Displays commemorate **Alice Paul**, author of the original *Equal Rights Amendments*, and trace the history of the women's movement from suffrage to the present. ♦ Free. Tu-F 10AM-3PM; Sa-Su noon-4PM. 144 Constitution Ave NE (1st-2nd Sts) Metro stops: Capitol South, Union Station. 546.3989

8 Cafe Berlin ★★$$ Dine inside or out on stick-to-your-ribs dishes like sauerbraten, potato dumplings, and red cabbage; or beef goulash with spaetzle in a rich gravy. The dessert menu is huge. Best choices: apple strudel, Black Forest cake, and Linzer torte. ♦ German ♦ M-Th, Su 11AM-10PM; F 11AM-11PM; Sa 4-11PM. 322 Massachusetts Ave NE (3rd-4th Sts) Reservations recommended. Metro stop: Union Station. 543.7656

To see how **Statuary Hall** in the Capitol looked when it was used by the House of Representatives, visit the **Corcoran Gallery of Art**. An enormous group portrait there shows the 17th Congress preparing for an evening session. Eighty-six figures are identifiable, including 67 congressmen, 6 Supreme Court justices, members of the press and the House staff, and even a visiting Pawnee chief. The artist of this gigantic undertaking? **Samuel F.B. Morse**, who was a highly regarded painter before he invented the telegraph.

"It could probably be shown by facts and figures that there is no distinctly native American criminal class except Congress." **Mark Twain**

The **Capitol Dome** is cast iron painted to look like marble. It must be repainted every 6 or 7 years, a job requiring 600 gallons of paint.

Restaurants: Red **Hotels**: Blue
Shops/Parks: Green **Sights/Culture**: Black

8 Two Quail ★$$ Creative (and sometimes uneven) new American cuisine emphasizing grilled tuna, swordfish, Key lime cheesecake, and other homemade desserts in 3 intimate rooms quirkily furnished with mismatched chairs and silverware. ♦ American ♦ M-F 11:30AM-2:30PM, 5:30-10:30PM; Sa 5:30-10:30PM; Su 10:30AM-3:30PM, 5:30-10:30PM. 320 Massachusetts Ave NE (3rd-4th Sts) Reservations recommended. Metro stop: Union Station. 543.8030

9 Bob's Famous Homemade Ice Cream Capitol Hill outpost of the local lawyer-turned-

churnmeister, and the original home of **Oreo ice cream**. ♦ Daily noon-midnight. 236 Massachusetts Ave NE (2nd-3rd Sts) Metro stop: Union Station. 546.3860. Also at: 3510 Connecticut Ave NW. 245.4465; 4706 Bethesda Ave, Bethesda MD. 986.5911

10 La Brasserie ★★$$ A charming townhouse serves as home base for good nouvelle and classic country fare, from quiche to rabbit to a killer crème brûlée with fresh raspberries. When it's warm, the outdoor terrace is open for dining. ♦ French ♦ Daily 11:30AM-11:30PM. 239 Massachusetts Ave NE (2nd-3rd Sts) Reservations recommended. Metro stop: Union Station. 546.6066

11 The Monocle ★★$$$ Traditionally an after-work watering hole for Senate-side powerbrokers, the Monocle also serves good pastas, steaks, and seafood; particularly pleasant when Congress is out. ♦ American ♦ M-F 11:30AM-midnight. 107 D St NE (1st-2nd Sts) Reservations recommended. Metro stop: Union Station. 546.4488

William Howard Taft was the first US president to use the **Presidential Suite**, now the **Adirondacks** restaurant, in **Union Station**. Other luminaries have included **Queen Elizabeth II**, **King George VI**, **King Albert of the Belgians**, **King Prajadhipok of Siam**, **Queen Marie of Rumania**, and **King Hassan II of Morocco**.

The 24-hour **Servicemen's Canteen** opened in December 1941 in **Union Station**. Throughout its 5-year operation, a 5-cent ceiling was imposed on every food item.

The cornerstone that **George Washington** laid in the **Capitol Building** in 1793 is apparently lost forever. (A thorough search was conducted in the 1950s when the East Front of the Capitol was rebuilt.) The stone, which was set into a silver plate, marked the 13th year of American independence.

12 Union Station (1908, Daniel Burnham; restoration, 1988, Harry Weese; urban and retail design, 1988, Benjamin Thompson & Associates, LaSalle Partners, and Williams, Jackson, Ewing) This magnificent monument to the Beaux-Arts optimism of the early 1900s has had a bumpy ride in the latter part of the century but appears to be back on track. The original granite building, based on the *Arch of Constantine* (outside) and the *Baths of Diocletian* (inside), had its own bowling alley, mortuary, icehouse, liquor store, swimming pool, nursery, and silver-monogramming shop. In 1937, in its heyday, as many as 42,000 travelers passed through the concourse on a daily basis (250 redcaps stood waiting to serve them), and a round-the-clock medical staff awaited any emergency.

With the decline of rail travel, the station was allowed to run down: a leaking roof caused huge chunks of plaster to fall from the ceiling, water pipes burst constantly, and toadstools sprang from the muddy floor. In 1976, railroad operations were moved to a squalid temporary terminal behind the station, and the original vaulted waiting room was transformed into a Bicentennial visitors center, with a giant pit dug into the floor. After further decay, the building was rescued by a $160-million public/private partnership. In 1988, Union Station reopened in the reincarnation closest yet to Burnham's grand intention. Original walls, columns, and windows have been restored, while much of the building has been transformed into office and retail space. Master craftsman **John Barianos** is responsible for much of the painting, stenciling, and restoration of the moldings and scagliola (imitation marble); his handiwork can also be seen at the Willard Hotel and at the Capitol.

The Main Hall, with its magnificent 96-foot-high barrel-vaulted ceiling, now contains a kiosk with a newsstand, a concierge station, and several cafés and restaurants, including **Sfuzzi** (an offshoot of the popular New York restaurant).

The **Station Concourse** behind the Main Hall has 3 levels, with perhaps 110 shops: **Cignal**, **Benetton**, **The Limited**, **Nature Company**, **Brookstone**, **Putumayo**, **Tannery West**, and **Victoria's Secret** among them.

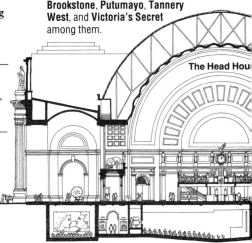

The Head Hou

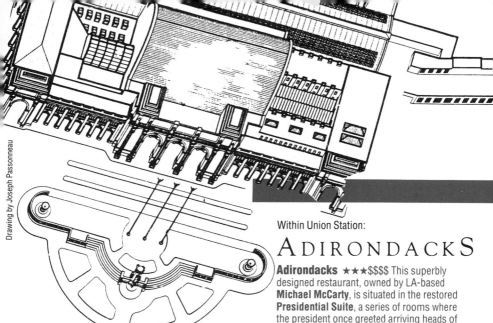

The **Train Concourse** just north of the Station Concourse includes Amtrak train access and connects the station to the adjacent 1381-space parking garage behind.

Internal access to **Metrorail** is provided on the **Metro Concourse**, where approximately 25 international fast-food shops and a 9-screen movie theater complex are dramatically positioned among Roman-bath-inspired 25-foot-deep piers and arches that have been left intact and unadorned.

All of this commerce is pumping new economic life into the area, but most importantly, Union Station has been restored to its former vital self—a living, breathing train station.
♦ Station 24 hours. Stores: M-Sa 10AM-9PM; Su noon-6PM. Restaurant hours vary. Massachusetts Ave NE (1st-2nd Sts) Metro stop: Union Station. 371.0441, Amtrak information 800/872-7245

Notice the strategically placed shields on the 36 Roman legionnaire statues in the **Main Hall** of **Union Station**. They were originally cast as nudes. To avoid public outcry, railroad officials demanded that the shields be added before the statues were installed.

Within Union Station:

ADIRONDACKS

Adirondacks ★★★$$$$ This superbly designed restaurant, owned by LA-based **Michael McCarty**, is situated in the restored **Presidential Suite**, a series of rooms where the president once greeted arriving heads of state (**Eisenhower** was the last president to use these rooms). Hand-painted canvas panels adorn the main dining room, while **David Hockney**'s 20-painting suite *Blue Guitars* hangs in 2 of the smaller dining rooms (once the changing rooms for the president and first lady). Indiana duck with Grand Marnier and California blood oranges, Norwegian salmon with beurre blanc, and a chocolate caramel torte (layers of vanilla mousse and caramel custard covered with white and/or dark chocolate, surrounded by a ribbon of dark chocolate) are among McCarty's inventive dishes.
♦ American ♦ Daily noon-2PM, 6-10PM. Street level. Reservations recommended. 682.1840

Great Train Store A continuously chugging model train beckons windowshoppers, who, once inside, will discover railroad caps, railroad books, shot glasses decorated with railroad logos, even videotapes celebrating the train. An assembled wooden **Brio** train set keeps the kids busy while their parents shop.
♦ M-Sa 10AM-9PM; Su noon-6PM. Station Concourse. 371.2881

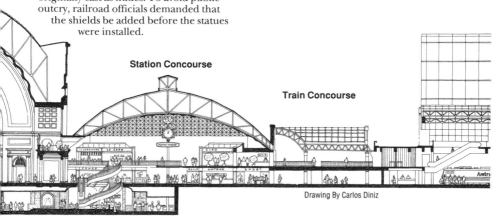

Station Concourse

Train Concourse

Drawing By Carlos Diniz

Contrast One-of-a-kind gifts: stenciled pillows made of Mongolian lamb or Brazilian cowhide, picture frames (marble or stained glass), bookends, stationery. Everything here is black-and-white and abstract or geometric in design. ♦ M-Sa 10AM-9PM; Su noon-6PM. Street level. 371.0566

13 National Capital Station, US Postal Service (1914, Graham & Burnham) Designed to complement nearby Union Station (also by Burnham), this smaller and less opulent Beaux-Arts building is rendered in white Italian marble and trimmed with an Ionic

colonnade. ♦ M-F 7AM-midnight; Sa-Su 7AM-8PM. Massachusetts Ave NE (N. Capitol-1st Sts) Metro stop: Union Station. 523.2337

14 Capital Children's Museum (National Learning Center) Learning and playing finally meet in fine hands-on children's museums such as these, where it's equally amusing to see the grownups getting involved with the touchy-feely gismos, play clothes, and climb-ons. Here, children explore other cultures by trying on the clothes and sampling the foods of foreign lands, and learn how to use the city by play-riding in a bus or taxi. They learn by doing, whether it's computing, building, or painting. The **Penny Exchange** gift shop sells all kinds of toys, most as educational as they are fun. ♦ Admission. Daily 10AM-5PM. 800 3rd St NE (H-Eye Sts) Metro stop: Union Station. 543.8600, recorded information 638.5437 ₠

15 Greyhound-Trailways Bus Center This modern bus station, tucked 3 blocks behind Union Station in a dusty industrial area, serves as the terminal for most interstate bus lines. ♦ 24 hours. 1005 1st St NE (K-L Sts) Metro stop: Union Station. 289.5155, bus schedules 565.2662

"Sir...no man in the nation wants peace more than I; but I prefer the troubled ocean of war...with all its calamities...to the tranquil and putrescent pool of ignominious peace!" **Henry Clay**
Speaker of the House
1811–1825

As early as 1894, members of the **Bisons**, the football team of **Gallaudet University**, used a circular formation to shield their sign language from the opposition. The *huddle* proved an effective way to conceal play signals, and the rest is history.

"Liberty, when it begins to take root, is a plant of rapid growth."
George Washington
Maxims of Washington

16 Gallaudet University (1867, Calvert Vaux and Frederick Law Olmsted) **Edward Miner Gallaudet**, youngest son of deaf school patriarch **Thomas Hopkins Gallaudet**, helped create the beautiful Gothic-style college to serve as a higher-learning institution for the deaf. Today, it is the world's only accredited liberal arts college for the hearing-impaired, providing education for 2200 students. The formal stone buildings epitomize the Victorian Gothic style; the campus grounds reflect Olmsted's master touch. Tours of the campus are arranged through the **Visitors Center**. ♦ 800 Florida Ave NE (Brentwood Parkway-W. Virginia Ave) Metro stops: Union Station, Rhode Island Ave. Visitors Center 651.5000, TDD 651.5104 ₠

17 Union Market, also known as the *Florida Avenue Farmers Market*, is open year-round and includes several warehouselike wholesale centers that carry freshly cut meats, fish, and fresh produce, fruit, and eggs. Emphasis is on ethnic foods, such as the Italian products at **A. Litteri Inc.**, where pastas, cheeses, and sausages are sold by the pound. ♦ Tu-Su 8AM-4PM. Florida Ave NE (4th-5th Sts) Metro stops: Union Station, Rhode Island Ave.

18 Trinity College Founded in 1897 by the **Sisters of Notre Dame de Namur**, this women's liberal arts college, with nearly 1000 students, includes a strong continuing-education program for working women. The granite **Main Hall** (1899) features marble parquet and stained glass in a 4-story atrium and is a landmark in Northeast DC. ♦ 125 Michigan Ave NE (Franklin-4th Sts) Metro stop: Brookland-CUA. 939.5000
Within Trinity College:

Chapel of Notre Dame (1924) Byzantine chapel with 67-foot dome contains **Bancel La Farge**'s mosaic of a scene from **Dante**'s *Divine Comedy*—the Coronation of the Virgin.

19 Dance Place The area's largest producer of contemporary and avant-garde dance, with 42 weeks of weekend performances by national and international troupes like **Eiko & Koma**, **BeBe Miller**, and **Liz Lerman**. Ongoing modern dance classes, and an **African Dance Festival** in June. ♦ Seats 200. Shows: Sa 8:30PM, Su 4PM, Jan-Mar, Nov-Dec; Sa 8:30PM, Su 7:30PM, Apr-Oct. Box office: M-F noon-6PM; Sa 9:30AM-2PM, 5-8:30PM; Su 3-4PM, Jan-Mar, Nov-Dec; M-F noon-6PM; Sa 9:30AM-2PM, 5-8:30PM; Su 4:30-7:30PM, Apr-Oct. 3225 8th St NE (Kearney-Lawrence Sts) Metro stop: Brookland-CUA. 269.1600

20 Colonel Brooks Tavern ★$ It's not easy to find a restaurant in the Brookland area, so this casual, reliable place is something of an oasis in the desert. Good burgers, potatoes, egg dishes, and desserts. Jazz Tuesday nights, with local Dixieland bands. ♦ American ♦ Daily 11AM-2AM. 901 Monroe St NE (9th-10th Sts) Metro stop: Brookland-CUA. 529.4002

Restaurants: Red	Hotels: Blue
Shops/Parks: Green	Sights/Culture: Black

cals. Thespian alumni include **Susan Sarandon**, **Jon Voight**, and playwright **Jason Miller**. Founded in 1887 by **Cardinal James Gibbons**, this is the only university that is run by the US hierarchy of the Roman Catholic Church. It is notable for its schools of canon law, sacred theology, and diaconal services. ♦ Guided tours by appointment 3 weeks in advance. Hartke Theatre: seats 500. Box office M-F 10AM-6PM when school is in session. 620 Michigan Ave NE (Harewood-McCormack Rds) Metro stop: Brookland-CUA. 635.5000 box office 635.5367, tours 635.5305

Capitol Hill/Northeast/Southeast

21 National Shrine of the Immaculate Conception (1914–1939) The key word here is *huge*: 459 feet long, 157 feet wide, and 329 feet high, with a capacity to hold over 6000 people. This Catholic church stands as a magnificent testimony to the faith of Marianism and its object, the Virgin Mary. Construction started in 1914, when the rector of Washington's Catholic University obtained papal sanction for a new monument dedicated to the *Heavenly Patroness of the US* (as determined by **Pope Pius IX** in 1847). The final 1959 completion of the world's seventh-largest church—and the largest Catholic church in the Western Hemisphere—showed a contemporary massive cruciform structure incorporating both Byzantine and Romanesque elements. Thirty-two chapels in the upper church contain bright mosaic altars devoted to Marian interpretations from all over the world. Light streams through 200 windows of stained glass, hitting an immense mosaic shrine whose construction demanded the depletion of an entire Italian quarry. Although the crypt gallery holds a contemporary relic, **Pope Paul VI**'s crowning tiara, the ultimate masterpiece must be **Millard Sheet**'s colossal mosaic *Triumph of the Lamb*, affixed to the sanctuary dome.

Since every parish in the US contributed to the building fund, the shrine now belongs to every American Catholic. With this in mind, the church administration actively encourages sacred pilgrimages, and sacraments are celebrated daily for pilgrims who come to the shrine. There is a gift shop downstairs. Mass hours vary: call for information. ♦ Daily 7AM-6PM. Tours every half hour M-Sa 9-11AM, 1-4PM; Su 1:30-4PM. Michigan Ave NE (4th-N. Capitol Sts) Metro stop: Brookland-CUA. 526.8300 &

22 The Catholic University of America The nearly 100-year-old coeducational institution manifests a paradoxical union of past and future. While some students are studying the university's highly respected traditional ecclesiastical curriculum, others are studying the science of storm control in the high-tech **Atmosphere** and **Aerospace** laboratories. Catholic University is also renowned for the **Hartke Theatre**, justly famous for the quality of its plays, which range from Greek and Shakespearean dramas to opera and American musi-

23 Franciscan Monastery Officially the *Commissariat of the Holy Land for the United States*, this monastery provides a fascinating insight into life behind holy walls. Its main function, to preserve and maintain shrines in the Holy Land through fund-raising, has been possible due to the enterprising minds of the **Order of the Friars Minor**, the resident acolytes and keepers of the beautiful grounds. A 30-minute tour of the rose garden and the monastery's central part, an early Italian Renaissance church completed in 1899, includes faithful replicas of several Holy Land shrines. Even a small authentic reproduction of a Roman catacomb has been dug underneath the church to demonstrate the plight of early Christian worshipers. ♦ Tours: M-Sa 9, 10, 11AM, 1, 2, 3, 4PM. 1400 Quincy St NE (14th-17th Sts) 526.6800

24 Moore's Love and Peace A basic local bar featuring not-so-basic local jazz acts. ♦ M-Th, Su 5PM-2AM; F-Sa 5PM-3AM. Live music Tu, Th 9PM-1AM; F-Sa 10:30PM-2AM; Su 8-11PM. 1509 Rhode Island Ave NE (15th-16th Sts) Metro stops: Rhode Island Ave, Brookland-CUA. 635.2471

Who makes more money than the president? After all, isn't his office the most important in the land? Surprise! The president's salary falls far behind those of certain Washington-born or -based athletes, writers, actors, TV correspondents, doctors, business execs, and lawyers. It seems, in fact, that almost any profession other than politics has top-dollar potential. In 1987, for example, cardiac surgeon **Dr. Jorge García** earned $1,000,000; **Larry King**, professional provocateur, brought home $1,515,000; for his lectures and no-holds-barred anchoring style on ABC, **Ted Koppel** earned $1,700,000; the salary, bonus, stock options, and fringe benefits of Giant Food chairman, president, and CEO **Israel Cohen came** to $3,448,186; insurance agent-turned-author **Tom Clancy** earned a staggering $5 million; and **Sugar Ray Leonard** pocketed a cool $10.8 million, most of it earned in a 36-minute bout with **Marvelous Marvin Hagler**. What did **Ronald Reagan** earn? A paltry $200,000.

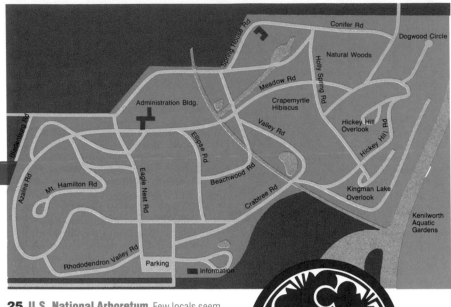

25 U.S. National Arboretum

Few locals seem to know about this 440-acre stretch of garden and woodland overlooking the Anacostia River, because it's practically deserted except for the few weeks in spring when the azaleas and the tourists run riot. All the better for cognoscenti, as the arboretum is one of the capital's loveliest secrets.

Established by Congress in 1927 as a research institution, the arboretum harbors such rare plants as the *Siberian larch* and *Manchurian lilac*, as well as green things that even non-herbophiles can enjoy, like the 70,000 azaleas, masses of rhododendrons, ornamental crabs, cherries, and dogwoods. During Washington's languorous spring, each week brings a new cascade of color and fragrance. Amid all the live things rises an incongruous stand of Neoclassical columns salvaged from a renovation of the US Capitol and erected here in 1988.

Perhaps its most prestigious collection, valued at $4.5 million, is the **National Bonsai Collection**, given to the US as a 1976 Bicentennial gift from the people of Japan. Housed in a specially constructed garden pavilion adjacent to the **Administration Building**, the 53 trees of 34 species range from 30 to 350 years of age. The once-normal plants, artfully trained to stunted growth in shallow pots, stand no more than 1 or 2 feet in height. An elaborate alarm system now protects the collection—after a local student once pilfered a tree to decorate his apartment. The plant was immediately returned when the thief found the bonsai's value to be $75,000! Another structure boon to the vast grounds is the **Herbarium**, filled with over 500,000 dried plants to maintain a technical reference system.

Early summertime is the peak season for the arboretum, when daily crowds of 20,000 visitors view the blooming azaleas and flowering dogwood and crab apples. During winter, the 1500 dwarf and slow-growing conifers assembled on a 5-acre hill dominate the scene; early spring is the time for jasmine and camelia blossoms. The arboretum regularly presents special demonstrations, films, and flower shows. Group tours for 10 or more are arranged by calling 3 weeks in advance. ◆ Free. M-F 8AM-5PM; Sa-Su 10AM-5PM. Bonsai collection daily 10AM-2:30PM. 3 entrances: 3501 New York Ave NE; 24th and K Sts NE; Maryland Ave and M St NE. 475.4815

26 Anacostia Park

Extending 8 miles along the Anacostia River, the 1355-acre area qualifies more as a natural reserve than as a conventional park, with mostly fertile marshland and small, sunny glades hidden in the forests. The northeastern part holds **Kenilworth Aquatic Gardens**; another area is designed as a bird sanctuary, where songbirds and wading birds like green herons and great blue herons inhabit the woods. During migrating season, a large number of ducks and geese also congregate in the park. You can walk almost anywhere, except to the upper reaches of the river, which are inaccessible due to their natural wild state.

There is a multipurpose pavilion located at the lower end of the park that offers environmental educational programs, community exhibitions, and roller-skating. Dinghy boat rentals and larger outboards are available from the yacht clubs along the river. ◆ Open all year during daylight hours. E. Capitol St SE (Pennsylvania Ave-Anacostia Naval Annex) 433.1190

27 Kenilworth Aquatic Gardens Fourteen acres of hydrophilic flora and fauna are contained within this hidden, seldom-visited **Anacostia Park** marshland. Founded in 1882, war veteran **W.B. Shaw** began the collection with a few water lilies from Maine. The native trees— willow oaks, red maples, and magnolias— provided natural shelter for the ponds, which attracted a variety of water dwellers. Muskrats, raccoons, and opossums now coexist happily with species of frogs, toads, and turtles. Plan for an early- morning visit, since many of the night-blooming lotuses close during harsh daylight. Group tours on advance notice. ♦ Daily 7AM-4:15PM. 900 Anacostia Dr SE (Kenilworth Ave) 426.6905

Constantino Brumidi's *The Apotheosis of George Washington* is painted on the ceiling of the **Capitol**'s Rotunda. The painting's seated central figure is surrounded by 13 maidens who symbolize the original 13 states. Apparently, a number of these women resemble certain *ladies of the evening* for whom the artist had a particular liking. It seems Brumidi was not inspired solely by the Confederation.

The **Metrobus** covers nearly 50 million miles annually. This impressive figure is equivalent to 101 round trips to the moon.

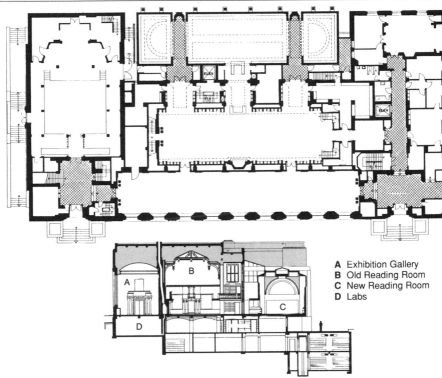

A Exhibition Gallery
B Old Reading Room
C New Reading Room
D Labs

28 Folger Shakespeare Library (1932, Cret & Trowbridge; remodeling, 1979, Hartman-Cox) Founded in 1930 by **Henry Clay Folger**, a Standard Oil executive and Shakespeare maven, the library now contains the world's largest collection of plays and poetry by *the Bard*, including several copies of the 1623 **first folio**, the first printed collection of Shakespeare's plays, and the only surviving quarto of *Titus Andronicus*, found in a cottage in Sweden. Selected works from the collection are on display in the gallery. The building, one of **Paul Philippe Cret**'s finest designs, reconciles a Greek-influenced Art Deco exterior (which features 9 bas reliefs with Shakespearean scenes) with an Elizabethan interior; the late-1970s additions are sensitive and well-done. The museum shop sells all kinds of things with Shakespeare's face or words printed on them. Shakespeare's birthday open house takes place in April. ♦ Free. M-Sa 10AM-4PM. Walk-in

tours M-Sa 11AM-1PM. Group tours by appointment. 201 E Capitol St SE (2nd-3rd Sts) Metro stop: Union Station, Capitol South. 544.4600

Within the Folger Shakespeare Library:

The Shakespeare Theater at the Folger, incorporated as a separate entity in 1986 under artistic director **Michael Kahn**, presents a 4-play classical season October through June in a replica of a 16th-century theater. The resident **Folger Consort** also performs here, and acting classes for both professionals and nonprofessionals are offered. ♦ Seats 250. Shows: Tu-Sa 8PM; Su 2, 8PM. Box office: M 10AM-6PM, Tu-Su noon-8PM in performance weeks; daily 10AM-6PM in nonperformance weeks. 546.4000

Renovation of the US Capitol's west facade (completed 1987) cost $29 million, $20 million less than the allotted $49 million.

29 Anton's Loyal Opposition ★$$$ The brass-and-glass decor provides an elegant setting for cocktails and piano music. The overpriced menu of steaks, seafood, pasta, and veal doesn't live up to the music. ♦ American ♦ Daily 7AM-11:45PM. Music nightly 7:30-11:45PM. 400 1st St SE (D St-N. Carolina Ave) Reservations recommended. Metro stop: Capitol South. 546.4545

29 Bullfeathers ★$$ House-staffers throng like crazed bulls at happy hour, but this Victorian-style pub survives the *Yellow Tie Brigade* to serve up hearty American fare, including

burgers, crabcakes, and steaks. Brunch features a *Bloody Mary* bar. ♦ American ♦ M-F 11:30AM-2AM; Sa 11:30AM-3AM; Su 10:30AM-2AM. 410 1st St SE (D St-N. Carolina Ave) Reservations recommended. Metro stop: Capitol South. 543.5005

30 Capitol Hill Hotel $$ One hundred fifty-three suites in a former apartment building on a quiet residential block just 3 blocks from the Capitol. Fully equipped kitchens, Continental breakfast, concierge service. Nonsmoking rooms. Student rate for children under 18 staying with parents. ♦ 200 C St SE (2nd-3rd Sts) Metro stop: Capitol South. 543.6000, 800/424.9165; fax 547.2608

30 Chesapeake Bagel Bakery Real bagels in Washington, hot out of the oven in a half-dozen permutations, with the requisite schmears and sandwich fillings. Carry out or eat in; good bulletin board, too. ♦ M-F 7AM-9PM; Sa 7AM-8PM; Su 7AM-5PM. 215 Pennsylvania Ave SE (2nd-3rd Sts) Metro stop: Capitol South. 546.0994. Also at: 1636 Connecticut Ave NW. 328.7985; 4000 Wisconsin Ave NW. 966.8866

It's more expensive to deliver a baby in Washington DC than in any other city. Average cost: $4210.

TICKETS: Most area theaters sell advance tickets over the phone, charged to your credit card for a small fee. Don't forget to ask about student and senior citizen discounts if you qualify. Tickets for sellout events such as **Redskins** games are often available through ads in the *Washington Post*'s classifieds at hefty markups, as well as through the ticket brokers listed below:

Concertline Tickets Brokers for tickets for local and national events, from concerts at **Merriweather Post Pavilion** and the **Kennedy Center** to sporting events (Redskins, Capitals, Bullets) to Broadway performances. ♦ Fee. M-F 10AM-10PM; Sa-Su noon-5PM. 9102 Edmonston Court, Suite 102, Greenbelt MD. 474.2055

Orioles Baseball Store Walk-in purchase of tickets to Orioles' baseball games. (No telephone charges.) Also, great selection of baseball souvenirs and Orioles' mementoes. ♦ M-F 9AM-6PM; Sa 10AM-3PM. 914 17th St NW (Eye-K Sts) Metro stop: Farragut North. 296.2473

The Ticket Outlet Inc. Tickets for Redskins games, rock concerts, and other hard-to-book events. Prices based on popularity of the event. ♦ M-F 9AM-7PM; Sa 10AM-5PM. 105 E. Annandale Rd, Suite 208. Falls Church VA. 538.4044

TicketPlace The place to buy half-price tickets for performances at most Washington-area theaters, including the **Arena Stage**, **Kennedy Center**, and **Warner** and **National** theaters—the day of the show. Full-price tickets are available in advance and can be charged to a credit card. Performances for which half-price tickets are available are posted outside the kiosk. Cash only on half-price tickets; a small service charge is added. Tickets for Sunday performances sold on Saturdays. A project of the **Cultural Alliance of Greater Washington.** ♦ Fee. M noon-2PM; Tu-Sa 11AM-6PM. Kiosk: F St Plaza (12th-13th Sts NW) Metro stop: Metro Center. 842.5387 (TIC.KETS)

Ticket Center Tickets by phone for events at the Capital Centre and major theaters, including **Wolf Trap**. Outlets throughout the Washington metropolitan area, Richmond, and Baltimore. ♦ Fee. Daily 10AM-10PM. 432.0200

Ticket Connection Tickets to concert, theater, and sporting events, operated by the same firm that runs **Concertline Tickets.** ♦ Fee. M-F 11AM-7PM; Sa noon-5PM. 8121 Georgia Ave, Suite 101, Silver Spring MD. 587.6850

Ticket Finders Brokerage of tickets for sellout events, including Redskins games and rock concerts; prices rise according to the popularity of the event. ♦ M-F 9AM-6PM; Sa 10AM-4PM. 5502 Kenilworth Ave, Suite 305. Riverdale MD. 277.4779

Ticketron Advance-sale tickets for theaters and professional and collegiate sports events. Also at some Sears and Woodward and Lothrop stores. ♦ Fee. M-F 10AM-5:30PM. 1101 17th St NW (L St) Metro stop: Farragut North. 659.2601

Top Centre Ticket & Limousine Service Brokers for Redskins games and other sporting events, as well as concerts and theatrical performances. ♦ Fee. M-F 9AM-5PM; Sa 10AM-5PM. 1911 Pennsylvania Ave NW (19th-20th Sts) Suite M100. Metro stops: Farragut West, Foggy Bottom. 452.9040

Washington Performing Arts Society is the city's largest nonprofit arts organization, with 6000 members. It sponsors concerts at the **Kennedy Center**, **Corcoran Gallery**, and the **Lisner Auditorium**, with offerings ranging from opera (**Dame Joan Sutherland**, **Kiri Te Kanawa**), to foreign orchestras (**Moscow State Symphony**, **Israel Philharmonic**), to a guitar series, folk and piano music, dance, and a **Handel** festival. ♦ Box office M-F 10AM-6PM. 1029 Vermont Ave NW (L St) Metro stops: McPherson Sq, Farragut North. 393.3600

30 Moon Blossoms & Snow Contemporary American crafts: stained glass, ceramics, jewelry, and handwoven and hand-painted women's clothing. ♦ M-F 11AM-6PM; Sa 10AM-5PM. 225 Pennsylvania Ave SE (2nd-3rd Sts) Metro stop: Capitol South. 543.8181

31 Taverna The Greek Islands ★★$ Try the moussaka, lamb pie, stuffed grape leaves, kabobs, and other specialties, as well as one of several varieties of Greek wine. ♦ Greek ♦ M-Sa 11AM-11:30PM; Su 4-11PM. 307 Pennsylvania Ave SE (3rd-4th Sts) Metro stop: Capitol South. 547.8360

31 Toscanini ★★$$ Northern Italian specialties include veal with watercress or artichoke hearts, fettucine verde, and pizza *di mare*. All desserts are homemade. ♦ Italian ♦ M-F 11AM-midnight; Sa 5PM-midnight. 313 Pennsylvania Ave SE (3rd-4th Sts) Reservations recommended. Metro stop: Capital South. 544.2335

31 Hawk and Dove ★$$ Dark, archetypal burger-and-brew joint peopled with an intriguing mix of Hill insiders, Georgetown law students, and rugby players. ♦ American ♦ M-Th 10AM-2AM; F-Sa 10AM-3AM; Su 9:30AM-2AM. 329 Pennsylvania Ave SE (3rd-4th Sts) Metro stop: Capitol South. 543.3300

31 Tune Inn ★$ Half hick bar that looks as if it belonged in Kenosha, half preppie hangout, the *Tune* is a Washington landmark legendary for cheap beer, greasy burgers, and cantankerous help. Don't miss the stuffed deer derrières over the bathroom doors. ♦ American ♦ Daily 8AM-2AM. 331½ Pennsylvania Ave SE (3rd-4th Sts) Metro stop: Capitol South. 543.2725

32 Hill Cafe ★★$$$ Competent Japanese standards and often-inspired East-meets-West specials served in an artfully cool modern decor. ♦ Japanese/Japanese-American ♦ M-F 11:30AM-11:30PM; Sa 5-11:30PM. 332 Pennsylvania Ave SE (3rd-4th Sts) Metro stop: Capitol South. 547.8668

33 Eastern Market (1871, Adolph Cluss) Inside, greengrocers and butchers tempt you with the freshest food that money can buy, handpicking each item and wrapping it for you as if you were **Princess Di**—and at times, charging royal prices as well. Outside, farmers from Pennsylvania and Maryland sell their produce, cider, flowers, and baked goods. Saturday mornings are the wildest, as Capitol Hill residents crowd the market. Sunday mornings, the food stalls are replaced by an ad hoc flea market selling knickknacks and old furniture. ♦ Tu-Sa 6:30AM-6PM. 7th St SE (N. Carolina Ave-C St) Metro stop: Eastern Market

Depending on the day's temperature, the cast-iron dome of the Capitol will expand and contract as much as 4 inches.

Within Eastern Market:

Market Lunch ★★$ The lines snake out the door for this luncheonette's Saturday breakfasts, and with good reason. Try a weekday lunch for smaller crowds and the best-ever crabcakes on homemade bread with coleslaw and hot sauce. ♦ American ♦ Tu-Sa 7:30AM-2:30PM. 225 7th St SE (N. Carolina Ave-C St) No credit cards. 547.8444

34 Provisions ★$ Primarily a coffee/tea/specialty foods shop. Customers can order thick sandwiches of turkey breast, imported

Capitol Hill/Northeast/Southeast

cheeses, curried tuna salad, and other ingredients, and steaming cups of cappuccino for takeout or to be consumed in a quaint dining niche. ♦ American ♦ M-F 9AM-7PM; Sa 8AM-6PM; Su 10AM-4PM. 218 7th St SE (Independence Ave-C St) Metro stop: Eastern Market. 543.0694

34 Tunnlcliff's ★$ Scenes of the old Eastern Market are etched on the glass dividers that decorate this charming place. Cajun specialties, fresh fish, steaks. Outdoor dining in warmer weather. ♦ American ♦ Daily 11AM-11PM. 222 7th St SE (Independence Ave-C St) Reservations recommended. Metro stop: Eastern Market. 546.3663

34 Anilian Gallery Watercolors and oils by area artists. ♦ Th-Sa noon-6PM; Su 3PM-6PM. 232 7th St SE (Independence Ave-C St) Metro stop: Eastern Market. 544.5711

35 Lincoln Park Two of the city's finest and most moving sculptures grace this compact city park. The *Emancipation Monument*, sculpted in 1876 by **Thomas Ball**, shows a life-size **Abraham Lincoln** holding the *Emancipation Proclamation*. At Lincoln's feet, a slave is just beginning to rise, his chains finally broken. The man's face was modeled after a photo of **Archer Alexander**, the last person to be taken under the *Fugitive Slave Act*. All funds for the monument were donated by former slaves.

One of the city's happiest monuments is the sculpture of black educator/activist **Mary McLeod Bethune**. The former adviser to **Franklin Delano Roosevelt** is seen passing her legacy to 2 children: it reads in part "I leave you a thirst for education. I leave you a respect for the use of power. I leave you faith. I leave you racial dignity. I leave you a desire to live harmoniously with your fellow man." ♦ E. Capitol St NE (11th-13th Sts) Metro stop: Eastern Market

36 Machiavelli's ★$ A fun place. The margaritas and pizzas are good, the jukebox plays **Nat King Cole**, **Sinatra**, and classic rock 'n' roll, and the decor is Art Deco-ish. ♦ Italian ♦ M-Th, Su 5-11PM; F-Sa 5PM-midnight. 613 Pennsylvania Ave SE (6th-7th Sts) Metro stop: Eastern Market. 543.1930

Restaurants: Red   **Hotels**: Blue
Shops/Parks: Green   **Sights/Culture**: Black

37 Friendship Settlement (The Maples) (1795, William Lovering) Despite the fact that it has served many uses—from residence to hospital—its Federal-era character and integrity remain. Past refurbishing efforts have been executed with taste and care. ♦ 619 D St SE (6th-7th Sts) Metro stop: Eastern Market

38 Trattoria Alberto ★★$$ An honest-to-goodness trattoria, multileveled, friendly, and slightly kitschy. Good cheap wine, abundant portions of homemade pastas, and tender and diverse veal dishes. ♦ Italian ♦ M-Th 11:30AM-2:30PM, 5:30-10:30PM; F 11:30AM-11PM; Sa

Capitol Hill/Northeast/Southeast

5:30-11PM. 506 8th St SE (D-E Sts) Reservations recommended. Metro stops: Eastern Market, Potomac Avenue. 544.2007

JULIO'S
CAPITOL HILL

38 Julio's ★$ Pizzas, pastas, and a knockout all-you-can-eat weekend brunch with made-to-order Belgian waffles and omelets, all in a lively, if noisy, 2-tiered room. Dancing on Friday and Saturday nights. ♦ Italian/American ♦ M-Th 11:30AM-midnight; F-Sa 10AM-2AM; Su 10AM-midnight. 801 Pennsylvania Ave SE (8th-9th Sts) Metro stops: Eastern Market, Potomac Avenue. 546.0060. Also at: 1604 U St NW. 483.8500

38 Las Cazuelitas ★★$$ Authentic Mexican kitchen emphasizing seafood specialities such as shrimp in chile, garlic, and cilantro, with nary a burrito in sight. ♦ Mexican ♦ M-F 11:30AM-10PM; Sa 4-11PM; Su 4-10PM. 500 8th St SE (D-E Sts) Metro stops: Eastern Market, Potomac Avenue. 543.0002

39 Cool Breeze's ★$ A small, family-style chili parlor. The Texas-style (hot!) and vegetarian chilis are especially good. ♦ American ♦ Tu-F 11:30AM-10PM; Sa 5-10PM. 507 11th St SE (Pennsylvania Ave) Metro Stop: Eastern Market. 543.3184

39 Newman Gallery and Custom Framing Good stock of political cartoons and posters for incorrigible political junkies. ♦ Tu-Sa 10AM-6PM. 513 11th Sts (D-E Sts) Metro stop: Potomac Avenue. 544.7577

About 12 percent of the US population lives in the Potomac Basin area.

Capitol Hill hasn't had a new building since the 1960s. All of that will change with the completion of the **Judiciary Office Building** (scheduled completion, 1991, **Edward Larabee Barnes/John M.Y. Lee and Partners**). The 7-story trapezoidal structure will provide 600,000 square feet of office space and 2 levels of underground parking. A 5-story atrium will be planted with bamboo trees.

40 Bakery Potomac Metro A mecca for serious baked goods, from sturdy croissants and rye bread to spectacular tortes, cakes, and order-ahead party specials. ♦ Tu-Sa 6AM-6PM; Su 7AM-2PM. 1238 Pennsylvania Ave SE (12th-13th Sts) Metro stop: Potomac Avenue. 543.2960

41 Christ Church, Washington Parish (1806, Benjamin Latrobe) Quite likely the oldest church building in DC, and one of the first Gothic Revival designs in the country (although the design has been significantly altered). Many of Washington's important and famous have been members of the Episcopalian congregation. Presidents **James Madison**, **Thomas Jefferson**, and **John Quincy Adams** worshiped here. ♦ By appointment. 620 G St SE (6th-7th Sts) Metro stop: Eastern Market. 547.9300

42 Women's Community Bakery Since 1975, this nonprofit collective has been whipping up hearty muffins, honey whole wheat bread, eight-grain bread, cookies, and granola. Monday is *cookies-only day*. ♦ M-T, Th-F, Su 2PM-6PM. 736 7th St SE (G-Eye Sts) Metro stops: Eastern Market, Potomac Avenue. 546.7944

43 The Broker ★★$$$ This spacious and quiet dining room of blond wood and brick is renowned for its Sunday brunches, cheese and chocolate fondues, wonderful black currant sorbet, homemade breads and croissants, and uniformly excellent Swiss cuisine. ♦ Swiss ♦ M-Th 11:30AM-2:30PM, 5:30-10:30PM; F 11:30AM-2:30PM, 5:30-11PM; Sa 5:30-11PM. 713 8th St SE (G-Eye Sts) Jacket and tie requested. Reservations recommended. Metro stops: Eastern Market, Potomac Avenue. 546.8300

Marine Corps button design, circa 1804.

44 Marine Corps Barracks America's first Marine post is still home to the *Eighth and Eye* Marines. The **Commandant's House** (1805), with its Classical overtones and crisp bay windows, is the only original building still standing on the grounds.

The Marine Corps holds Friday evening parades outdoors in the courtyard of the Marine Barracks from mid May through early September. It's a great experience, even if you're not particularly wild about rifle drills and precision marching. If you can't get in, check out the shorter sunset version of the parade, performed Tuesday evenings at 7PM, last week of May through mid August, on the grounds of the Iwo Jima Memorial in Arlington. ♦ Drills F 8:45PM, mid May-early Sep. 8th St SE (G-Eye Sts) Reservations required 3 weeks in advance. Metro stops: Eastern Market, Potomac Avenue. Reservations 433.6060

45 Washington Navy Yard (1800, Benjamin Latrobe) Kids of all ages play and learn at the same time in this **historic precinct**, which served as the **Naval Gun Factory** during the entire 19th century. The original planning and design was by the prolific Benjamin Latrobe; although various refurbishings have eroded his influence, the main gates (1804) still show his mark. It is speculated that he also designed the **Commandant's House**. Splendid officers' mansions once lined the waterfront here. Now the functional factory and warehouse buildings draw tourists.

The **Navy Memorial Museum** gives a 200-year historical rundown of naval weapons, famous ships, and entire battle scenes. The various exhibitions have been designed for the young and energetic: gun turrets move, periscopes rise, and the ships are open to the attacks of boisterous young admirals. The authentic submarine room is not for the claustrophobic, who will prefer looking at large dioramas where heroes damn the torpedoes and go full speed ahead. Techniks will appreciate the inertial guidance systems, and the World War II uniforms by naval couturier **Captain Guy Molyneux** will delight the fashion-conscious.

The Navy offers a free summer audiovisual presentation on Navy history and lore Wednesday evenings on the **Parade Grounds**. Reservations are recommended (433.2218).

Buffs of military pomp and protocol should visit the **Marine Corps Museum** next door, which features flags and trophies as well as personal effects of big-name soldiers. Here, honor is first and action second: flags and trophies are arranged in a proud chronological display mixed with personal relics of famous mariners. ◆ Free. Navy Museum: M-F 9AM-4PM; Sa-Su 10AM-5PM, Jan-Apr, Sep-Dec; M-F 9AM-5PM; Sa-Su 10AM-5PM, May-Aug. Marine Corps Museum: M-Sa 10AM-4PM; Su noon-5PM, Jan-mid May, Sep-Dec; M-Th, Sa 10AM-4PM; F 10AM-4PM, 6-8PM; Su noon-5PM, mid May-Aug. M St SE (1st-11th Sts; entrance at 9th and M Sts) Metro stops: Eastern Market, Potomac Avenue. Navy Museum 433.4882, Marine Corps Museum 433.3534 &

46 Tracks A nightclub with a huge dance floor and irresistible deejay-spun music. The clientele is predominantly gay, and many DC gay-community events are held here, but everyone is welcome. ◆ Cover W-Su after 9PM. M-Tu 6PM-2AM; W-Th, Su 8PM-4AM; F-Sa 8PM-6AM. 1111 1st St SE (M-N Sts) 488.3320

Capitol Hill/Northeast/Southeast

47 Frederick Douglass National Historic Site (Cedar Hill) The simple white Victorian home, completed in 1854, was the abolitionist and statesman Frederick Douglass' residence from 1877 to his death in 1895. Douglass, who was born a slave on a Maryland plantation in 1817, escaped at the age of 21, and finally became an adviser to 4 presidents and an eloquent spokesman for the antislavery movement. During the Civil War, Douglass advised **President Abraham Lincoln** and supported postwar constitutional amendments that gave blacks citizenship and the right to vote. His home, much restored to its original era, holds furniture, and several gifts from Lincoln and other contemporaries, including **Harriet Beecher Stowe** and **William Lloyd Garrison**. One of the most remarkable features of Cedar Hill is the self-taught philosopher's personal library, containing over 1200 volumes.

Cedar Hill rests on a hilltop. Its large airy porch, punctuated by Doric columns, offers breathtaking vistas of the Capitol and its Downtown vicinity. The **Visitor Center** is located at the bottom of the grounds to maintain the unobstructed view from the home.

An accurate and moving picture of Douglass' work is recaptured in a short film presentation, held every hour on the hour at the Visitor Center, which also contains **Ed Dwight**'s life-size statue of Douglass. Period-costumed guides conduct tours every half hour. Group tours can be arranged by calling in advance. Limited parking provided. ◆ Free. Daily 9AM-4PM, Jan-Mar, Oct-Dec; daily 9AM-5PM, Apr-Sep. 1411 W St SE (14th-15th Sts) 426.5960/1 &

48 Anacostia Museum Founded in 1967 as a branch of the **Smithsonian Institution**, this museum celebrates black culture and history through exhibitions, educational lectures, films and concerts, and hands-on demonstrations reflecting black music, art, and dance. There is a picnic area with tables and grills. Tours for groups of 10 or more may be arranged by calling in advance. ◆ Free. Daily 10AM-5PM. 1901 Fort Pl SE (Pearson-Bruce Pls) 287.3369.

A swimming pool and a steam room for affluent railroad patrons were part of the original design for **Union Station**. They never came to fruition.

49 Congressional Cemetery "Being interred beneath these grounds adds a new terror to death" is how a US senator described the dull solemnity of the Congressional Cemetery, reserved for senators, diplomats, and prominent members of Congress. The process of filling 100 burial reservations started in 1807. Seventy years later, Capitol Hill architects **William Thornton** and **Robert Mills**, one Choctaw chief, and finally **John Philip Sousa** were among the last to find their places under **Benjamin Latrobe**'s stern predesigned gravestones; photographer **Mathew Brady** and **J.**

Edgar Hoover are also buried here. Information and memorial maps given by the gatekeeper. ♦ Daily dawn-dusk. Entrance at 1801 E St SE (17th St-Anacostia Park) Metro stop: Stadium-Armory. 543.0539

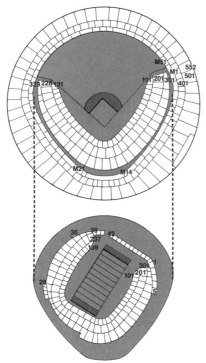

50 RFK Stadium/DC Armory Hall/Starplex
Two impressive plants, the **Robert F. Kennedy Stadium** (1962, **David Volkert & Associates**) and the historic **DC Armory Hall** (1947), comprise this huge concert, trade show, and sports complex. The 5-tiered circular amphitheater, home to the **Washington Redskins**, provides 55,000 seats to sports fans who come to watch football played on 3¹/₂ acres of natural grass.

Rock concerts and religious convocations also attract sellout crowds to the arena. During the events, 35 concession stands operate at full speed, serving delicatessen and ethnic specialties in addition to regular fast food. Intermissions rapidly fill the **Sports Lounge** with fans, who watch action replays on several monitors and a 7-foot video screen. Added to these

diversions is the **Starplex Hall of Stars**—heroes immortalized in paintings and photographs that line the walls of the lounge.

Next to the stadium is the **Armory Hall**, a huge domed structure with 2 levels, totaling over 133,000 square feet. The column-free main hall hosts everything from *Holiday on Ice* to political conventions; Starplex technicians transform the hall into such different settings as ice rinks, circus arenas, boat-show forums, and ballrooms. ♦ Box office M-F 10AM-5PM. Event information office M-F 9AM-5:30PM. 2001 E. Capitol St SE. (22nd St between C St and Independence Ave) Metro stop: Stadium-Armory. DC Armory/RFK Stadium 547.9077, Starplex ticket office 546.3337, Redskins ticket office 546.2222

Within RFK Stadium:

Farmers Market Local farmers set up camp in the RFK Stadium parking lot and sell fresh produce, cheeses, and breads. Sponsored by the DC government. ♦ Tu, Th, 7AM-dusk; Sa noon-dusk. Parking Lot 6

For more than 200 years, Washington DC's black community has been a vital force in shaping both the nation's capital and its history. The **Black National Recreation History Trail**, which opened in February 1988, was the brainchild of **Willard Andre Hunt**, a DC resident who first conceived of it while a 17-year-old Eagle Scout. In 1979, Hunt proposed the idea to the **National Park Service**, which brought together DC officials and citizens to select the first 6 sites; more may be added in the future.

The trail was dedicated in memory of **Carter G. Woodson**, a Washington historian instrumental in promoting recognition of the contributions of black Americans and in the designation of February as national *Black History Month*. One of the first blacks to receive a doctorate from Harvard University, he taught at several high schools and lived in Washington until his death in 1950. His house at 1538 9th St NW, privately owned, is a **National Historic Landmark**.

Two sites on the trail, the **Mary McLeod Bethune Council House National Historic Site** (page 99), and the **Frederick Douglass National Historic Site** (page 29), are affiliated with the National Park Service. Free maps and pamphlets describing the sites and their history are available at both places. The trail is not so much a specific route as a suggestion of places to visit. The sites and their neighborhoods illustrate aspects of black Washington from the slavery era through the New Deal.

Of the 171,300 tulips planted on federal properties in Downtown Washington each year, 103,750 are red; 27,400 are yellow; 24,200 are white tinged with red; 7200 are pink; 5950 are pure white; and 2800 are orange. The White House grounds are planted with approximately 18,000 red tulips.

James H. Billington
Librarian of Congress

My favorite place in Washington is the Jefferson Building of the Library of Congress. As a reader and researcher long before I had an office in the library, I learned to appreciate the awesome collections in the Main Reading Room, with its 160-foot-high domed ceiling. The glorious Italian Renaissance style, and the frescoes and statues all reflect the exuberance and optimism of America in 1897 as well as the skills of 50 American artists. The collections within, of nearly 90 million items in more than 450 languages, are the largest in the world; and the library's 3-building complex across from the Capitol touches every library system in the nation, and most in other countries, through its cataloging, interlibrary loan program, exhibitions, and publications, and through its use of new technology in sharing information. The pursuit of truth is the highest form of the pursuit of happiness, and there is no place on earth where more of it can be found by anyone who cares to look.

Ann W. Lewin
President, The National Learning Center

The squeals of delight when children, over a million of them to date, spot 15-foot-tall *Cootie*, a retiree of Macy's Thanksgiving Day Parade, and begin scampering up this wonderful behemoth on the Capital Children's Museum lawn.

The awe of young and old alike upon entering the Nek Chand Garden, where dozens of colorful larger-than-life fabric sculptures of India's folk life make you feel as if you have entered that exotic faraway land.

The aroma of tortillas and hot chocolate that visitors are cooking for themselves in the exhibition *Mexico*.

Everyone's surprise when Rosie, our elderly goat who lives in *Mexico*, moves or *maaas*, and they realize she is alive!

The air of suspense as visitors enter the Ice Age Cave.

The concentration on children's faces as they confront the story of the Holocaust in the *Remember the Children* exhibition.

The sight of a 3-year-old trying on real firefighters boots almost up to her armpits.

The delight of a father whose son is using 45-pound cinderblocks, pulleys, and levers to explain basic mechanical principals to his friends.

The wonder in children's eyes as they touch the puppets who are their favorite storybook characters.

The noises emanating from the *Tower of Babble:* the satellites and computers, the radio studio, the televisions, and other machines of the information age—sounds that are ushering in a future full of potential.

The intensity with which children imitate signing in *Sound and Silence*, an exhibition on deaf culture.

The excited chatter as children pull their parents to come see their favorite activities.

Daniel Boorstin
Librarian of Congress Emeritus

The Giant Bible of Mainz

Staff of the Library of Congress

Swann Collection of Political Caricatures

Hans Kraus Collection of Francis Drake Materials

Collections of bird's-eye views in the Geography and Map Division

Great Hall in the Jefferson Building

Listening to the Stradivarius in the Library of Congress

Bests

Robert W. Duemling
President and Director, National Building Museum

The museum's Great Hall—an eye-popping atrium 15 stories high and longer than a football field, surrounded by a double colonnade and containing the largest Corinthian columns in the world.

The panoply of temporary exhibitions on architecture, engineering, and building, from early American historical styles to the most avant-garde.

The intimate collection of artifacts excavated from the foundations and recalling the museum's builders 100 years ago: button shoes, bottles, coins, and rueful comments from the architect's journal.

The fountain splashing in the Great Hall, accompanied by musicians in scheduled concerts.

Troops of teenagers learning the fundamentals of design by improvising a paper envelope in which to drop a raw egg from the second-floor gallery (without having it break!).

Elliott Carroll, FAIA
Executive Assistant, Architect of the Capitol

The Cast-Iron Dome. Favorite thing: that it couldn't have been built had not cast-iron technology advanced, making it possible to bear the new, larger, cantilevered dome on Bulfinch's old masonry drum, which had supported the old copper-covered wooden dome. The old drum is 20 feet back of Walter's stage-set base of $1/2$-inch cast iron. All inspired by Leningrad's St. Isaac's Cathedral, not St. Paul's or St. Peter's, as is popularly supposed.

The Rotunda. The grandest space of all.

Old Senate Chamber.

Old Supreme Court.

Tobacco-leaf and corn-cob capitals by Latrobe, following Thomas Jefferson's direction. Survived the British fire of 1814. Tobacco blossoms are white, but these are painted red! Artistic license.

The Grotto. A lovely spring house in a glade.

The view from the West Terraces (or any window).

The Brumidi corridor and stairs. Walter and Brumidi Burial Vault, Bulfinch and Lincoln Catafalque. Designed to receive the bodies of George and Martha Washington, but family refused their removal from Mt. Vernon.

The Mall/SW

The **Mall**, the green swath that runs through the center of monumental Washington, is both the symbolic center of government and the nation's front yard.

Its bench-lined gravel paths are convenient walkways for visitors to the **Smithsonian** museums, the **National Gallery of Art**, and the **Lincoln** and **Vietnam Veterans** memorials. For residents, the Mall is a popular jogging park and playing field for after-work softball in the competitive congressional leagues. In midsummer, the Smithsonian's *Folklife Festival* turns the Mall into a small-town fair. On the Fourth of July, tens of thousands of people gather with picnics and blankets to listen to a free concert by the **National Symphony** and to watch fireworks explode behind the **Washington Monument**. And as always, the Mall serves as the point of convergence for demonstra-

The Mall

tions and protests—often-historic events ranging from the 1963 *March on Washington* (during which **Dr. Martin Luther King, Jr.**, gave his *I Have a Dream* speech from the steps of the Lincoln Memorial) to the record-breaking 1989 *March for Women's Equality and Women's Lives*.

In its earlier years, the Mall was put to more mundane uses: in the 1800s, railroad tracks ran down one side, and during World War II, a double line of wood-and-stucco temporary office buildings flanked the **Reflecting Pool** between the Washington Monument and the Lincoln Memorial.

Southwest Washington was intended to be the city's commercial center. Instead, it became a working-class residential neighborhood that deteriorated over the years. In the 1950s, the old neighborhood was effectively obliterated in the first rush of enthusiasm for massive urban renewal projects. Today, Southwest DC harbors the city's **Waterfront**, including a marina, restaurants, and a popular fish market, as well as the regional **Arena Stage** and a collection of high-rise federal office and apartment buildings.

1 White House (1792, James Hoban, Benjamin Latrobe, and many others) When **John Adams** arrived at his new home on 1 November 1800, he found a shantytown of workmen's shacks firmly rooted near the front door, and inside, the walls were not yet plastered. In fact, not one room was finished. The central staircase was still a pile of timbers on the floor, and only when fires blazed in at least 13 different fireplaces was he able to ignore the chilly dampness. That night, in a letter to his wife, **Abigail**, the nation's second president and the Executive Mansion's first tenant wrote, "I pray Heaven to bestow the best of blessings on this house and all that shall hereafter inhabit it. May none but honest and wise men ever rule under this roof."

Since that less-than-auspicious first day, 40 families have called this house *Home*. The only US president not to list 1600 Pennsylvania Avenue as his home address was **George Washington**, who served his term in Philadelphia while the capital city was being built.

It was, in fact, George Washington who personally selected the site for the *President's Mansion*, or the *President's Palace*, as it was more frequently called. When Washington staked out

the site in 1791, the city was nothing more than an unpopulated wooded flatland, with one distinguishable rise in elevation that would later be known as **Capitol Hill**. Washington declared that the Executive Mansion would be built one mile west of the hill, offering a commanding vista of the Potomac and, beyond that, Alexandria.

James Hoban, the original architect, was an Irishman, and despite many alterations the house remains as crisp, elegant, and white as fine Irish linen. The Georgian country house he designed was first altered by **Thomas Jefferson**, who had lost the original design competition to Hoban but used his clout as third president to make up for it. During the War of 1812, the British decided to take remodeling into their own hands. They gutted the interior and, for good measure, burned a sizeable portion of the exterior. Hoban was enlisted to reconstruct the building after the fire. The building's Virginia sandstone was painted white to cover fire damage—hence the moniker *White House*. Other alterations have included the front portico (1829); the wings (1902, **McKim, Mead & White**); and modern amenities including running water (1833), gas (1848), bathrooms (1878), and electricity (1890). The house has been remodeled twice: in 1902, in conjunction with the wing additions, and in the late 1940s, after it was discovered to be structurally too unsound to allow **President Harry Truman** to move in. The project took 3 years and required that the building be completely taken apart and reconstructed. It currently comprises 132 rooms.

Down through the years the mansion has witnessed one presidential wedding (**Grover Cleveland**), 5 first family weddings, 11 births, 7 presidential funerals, at least 39 redecorations—and numerous scandals. Designed to serve not only as the home but also as the office of the president, it was not uncommon for the 2 functions to get crossed. In 1902, the second floor was at last set aside for the exclusive use of the president's family, but as late as 1962 the first family's meals were still being served on the nonprivate first floor, since the second floor had no kitchen.

When **Jacqueline Kennedy**, wife of the 35th president, **John F. Kennedy**, arrived at the White House in 1961, she found the interior decor to be a mishmash of at least 34 different decorating tastes, with very few historically accurate (or original) objects left intact. Deciding that "everything in the White House must have a reason for being there," Mrs. Kennedy spearheaded an extensive restoration project aimed at bringing back to the White House the furnishings and possessions used during previous presidential administrations. Significant artifacts were scattered around the globe but were available: early in the 20th century, the descendant of a British soldier had graciously returned **James Madison**'s medicine box, pilfered during the burning of the White House in 1814. Under Mrs. Kennedy's direction, people from all over the world pitched in on

Courtesy Bureau of Engraving & Printing

the project. Thanks in large part to the efforts of Jackie Kennedy and subsequent administrations, which have continued the collection, today's White House is as much a museum of priceless Americana as it is a home and an office.

The White House tour takes you through 5 rooms on the mansion's first floor. The **East Room**, where Abigail Adams hung her laundry to dry and where **Theodore Roosevelt**'s children improved their roller-skating, is today used for receptions, press conferences, concerts, and dances. On the east wall is **Gilbert Stuart**'s famous painting of George Washington, purportedly rescued by **Dolley Madison** with no time to spare when the British invaded the city in 1814. Seven presidents who died in office, including Lincoln and Kennedy, have lain in state in this room.

Connecting doors lead from the East Room through the small reception room known as the **Green Room** into the oval-shaped **Blue Room**. Grover Cleveland used this room as a wedding chapel in 1886 when he married **Frances Folsom**. The White House Christmas tree usually stands here. Just off the Blue Room is the **Red Room**, where **Rutherford Hayes** secretly took the oath of office after the contested 1877 presidential race. The final tour stop is the **State Dining Room**. Be sure to note the inscription on the marble mantel, ordered put there by **Franklin Delano Roosevelt**—it's John Adams' White House prayer.

Each December, a candlelight tour of the White House dressed for Christmas is offered. In the spring and fall, an afternoon **Garden Tour** opens the usually off-limits White House grounds to the public. On Easter Monday, the traditional White House **Easter Egg Roll** takes place. Just show up at the Southeast Gate between 10AM and 2PM; some people arrive as early as 7AM.

No tours are offered during state visits, so call ahead. Between Memorial Day and Labor Day, visitors must assemble on the Ellipse; wait there until a National Park Service ranger escorts your group to the White House Gate. In the off-season, line up at the East Gate on E. Executive Ave no later than 10AM. (People with handicaps need not wait in line; go directly to the Northeast Gate on Pennsylvania Ave.)

The Mall

Be forewarned that especially during the summer months, the wait in line can be as long as 2 hours (you must be present to get a ticket) and the tour as short as 10 minutes. The best advice: contact your senator or congressperson far in advance of your visit (6 months is not too soon) and arrange for a VIP tour. This tour is offered earlier in the day than the regular tours (7:30-10AM) and generally lasts about 30 minutes. ♦ Free, but tickets are required between Memorial Day and Labor Day. Tickets available at booths on the Ellipse, south of the White House, at 8AM. White House: Tu-Sa 10AM-2PM, Memorial Day-Labor Day; Tu-Sa 10AM-noon, Jan-Memorial Day, Labor Day-Dec. Signed tours for the hearing-impaired available Tu-Sa 8AM; call 456.1414 to make advance arrangements. 1600 Pennsylvania Ave NW (15th-16th Sts) Metro stops: Farragut North, Farragut West, McPherson Sq. Tours and events 456.7041, National Park Service 755.7798 &

For details on White House tours, write: President's Park, 1100 Ohio Drive SW, Washington DC 20242; or call 755.7798.

You would expect many creaks and knocks in an old mansion like the **White House**, but some residents and visitors claim that there's more to the noises than the house settling on swampy Potomac riverbank soil. The White House's most famous ghost is **Abraham Lincoln**, who commonly frightened the domestic staff, as **Harry Truman** recorded in his diary. **Eleanor Roosevelt**, it has been noted, was visited by Abe's ghost on more than one occasion.

Willy Lincoln, the 11-year-old son of Abraham, died at the White House while his father was in office. His ghost was sometimes seen during the **Grant Administration** but hasn't appeared since. Visits by apparitions resembling **Dolley Madison** and **Abigail Adams** have also been reported .

The US president still remains one of the most sought-after public figures. He receives more than 20,000 letters daily.

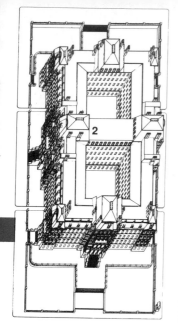

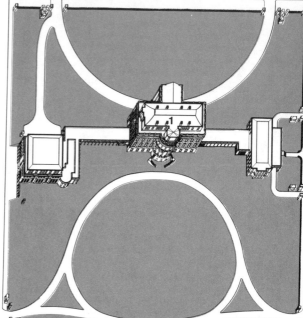

 The White House Grounds

The 18 acres known as the *President's Park* contain more than 80 varieties of trees planted over the years by almost every presidential family. The giant American Elm on the Center Oval was first a seedling from **John Quincy Adams**' home in Massachusetts. **Andrew Jackson** brought a magnolia from Tennessee as a memorial to his wife. The other magnolia near the east entrance to the White House was planted by **Warren Harding** in memory of the animals killed during WWI. More recent trees include the **Gerald Ford** family's white pine, a giant sequoia set by **Richard Nixon** in the Center Oval, and little **Amy Carter**'s tree house, built on poles and shielded by a magnificent silver Atlas cedar. Perhaps the most famous part of the park is **Ellen Wilson**'s **Rose Garden**, planted in 1913 and redesigned by **Mrs. Paul Mellon** at the request of **John F. Kennedy** in 1962. The rendition of an 18th-century garden shows osmanthus and boxwood hedges, tulips, narcissus, chrysanthemums, and heliotrope. The grounds are closed to visitors except during the White House garden tours and the annual **Easter Egg Roll**, the biggest and best-attended party the government throws—but you don't need a tuxedo. Since grass stains are almost inevitable, jeans and sneakers are just fine. All children 8 years old and under (and accompanied by an adult) are welcome. In 1989, 27,000 people frolicked on the grass while **Barbara Bush** officiated and life-size cartoon characters provided entertainment.

According to local legend, the kids of DC were big egg rollers over 100 years ago. Their favorite spot was the gently rolling slope of the Capitol lawn, which they destroyed on an annual basis. Fortunately, the wife of **President Hayes** was passing by when they were chased away in 1877. She took pity on the crying urchins and invited them to the White House. They've been coming back ever since.

Reports from **President Grover Cleveland**'s day say that children swarmed the grounds, crowding around the White House basement door asking for drinks of water. Some of the kids even invaded the East Room where Cleveland was greeting the adult public. They had heard a rumor that the president wanted to meet them, and although this was not the case, Cleveland obligingly shook many small grubby hands.

During World War II, **Franklin Delano Roosevelt** canceled the egg roll. However, accounts of the last pre-cancellation event show how popular it had become with the public. Over 53,000 people braved scorching weather to be there. Ten were treated for heat exhaustion, 4 passed out, and 78 children temporarily lost their parents.

The egg roll remained suspended for 12 years, long after the war was over. The White House social secretary under Truman defended this gross humbuggery by calling the ceremony an orgy of wasted eggs.

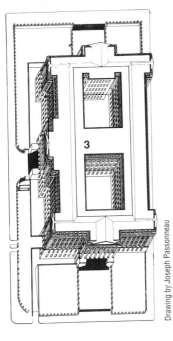

Drawing by Joseph Passonneau

2 Old Executive Office Building (1871–1888, Alfred B. Mullett) Originally designed to house the Navy and the departments of War and State, the outrageous French Second Empire building was so hated by the time of its completion that no one wanted to pay Mullett's fee. At the same time, nobody could justify the cost of demolishing the building, which has 4-foot-thick granite walls and iron door and window frames, trimming, and baseboards, all cast in an on-site foundry. The building, which is used for senior-level White House offices, is now in the midst of a felicitous renovation. Particularly notable are the stained-glass skylights over the cantilevered staircases, the **State Department Library,** with 4 cast-iron balconies and **Minton**

tile floors, and the **Indian Treaty Room**, with marble wall panels, bronze torchieres, and elaborate ironwork. The **War Department Library**, now the **White House Law Library**, features eclectic cast iron, including Moorish, Gothic, classical, and Baroque designs plated with bronze and brass. Not open to the public during the week; tours by reservation. Also, be aware that to make those reservations visitors must supply their name, birthdate, and social security number. *An RSW recommendation.*
♦ Free 1-hour tours Sa 9AM-11:40AM, every 20 minutes. 17th St and Pennsylvania Ave NW. Reservations required two months in advance. Metro stops: Farragut West, McPherson Sq. Reservations 395.5895, M-F 9AM-noon

3 Treasury Building (East wing, 1842, Robert Mills; south, west, and north wings, 1855–1869, Thomas U. Walker, consulting architects Ammi Young, Isaiah Rogers, and Alfred B. Mullett) After years of Congressional foot-dragging, **Andrew Jackson** impatiently chose this site, even though the exquisite Greek Revival building blocks L'Enfant's intended view of the Capitol from the White House. The building, which took 33 years to complete due to such mishaps as the Civil War, still houses the administrative offices of the Treasury Department and is undergoing extensive renovations to restore the interior to its former glory. In 1989, the curator's office began public tours, by reservation only, on a staggered schedule of alternate Saturdays; call for current schedule. As with the Old Executive Office Building, visitors must include their birthdate and social security number when making reservations.
♦ Alternate Sa 10, 10:20AM. Pennsylvania Ave NW and 15th St. Reservations required 2 months in advance. Metro stops: Farragut West, McPherson Sq. 343.9136

4 Ellipse The 52-acre oval-shaped yard south of the White House is best known as the site of the **National Christmas Tree**, which is lit by the president each December. Carolers and other holiday celebrants fill the area with pageantry throughout the holiday season. During the rest of the year, vendors, chess players, and strollers fill the park on sunny days. ♦ 15th-17th Sts NW (E St-Constitution Ave)

Traditionally, the event is hosted by the First Lady, and it was **Mamie Eisenhower** who decided that happy times warranted a comeback in the '50s. After more than a decade, no one knew quite what to expect. Yards of storm fencing were put up to protect flower beds and the president's putting green. Restrooms and drinking fountains were hastily erected.

When the great day arrived, the lawn was mobbed. Kids threw more eggs than they rolled, and the Eisenhower children retreated rapidly to the White House. The president, who was holding his baby granddaughter, had to be rescued from an adoring throng by Secret Service agents. Though the lawn was a matted mess of eggs, jellybeans, and marshmallows, the event was declared a huge success.

Nowadays, the government has more experience with this kind of thing, and mopping-up rarely takes more than an afternoon.

The latest change in the event came in 1981 with the Reagan administration. All participants were given wooden eggs with the White House insignia on them as a prize. In addition, the White House sends out thousands of eggs to politicians and sports and entertainment celebrities to be autographed and returned. These eggs are used in the **Easter Egg Hunt**, which takes place off to the side of the White House concurrently with the egg roll.

All rolling now takes place in 8 well-marked lanes, but real eggs and long-handled spoons are still used. Twenty-five kids at a time are allowed into the enclosure used for the egg hunt.

The White House has also begun sending out eggs to respected American artists and foreign embassies for special decoration. Actually they get 2 eggs each—one for practice. The finished results, which are often quite wonderful, are exhibited in a display case on the lawn.

Ladies First

While the Chief of State is usually the focal point of the nation's attention, several **First Ladies** have managed to capture both press headlines and the public's imagination. Whether due to a flamboyant fashion sense or a radical political stance—or even just for speaking up in public way back when—the women in the White House have left their mark on both the capital and the country.

1801—Wife of one president and mother of another, **Abigail Smith Adams** rarely stifled a political opinion, discussing current events freely with her male dinner guests. Despite her outstanding intellect, Abigail Adams remains best known for

stringing clotheslines through a vacant White House audience room.

1809—While journalists continually tried to rename her Dorothea, **Mrs. James Madison** insisted her true name was just plain *Dolley*. She furthered the Adams style of drawing room diplomacy well past her days as First Lady. Her White House successors—as well as their husbands—sought her social and political opinions until the day she died (1849). Always a style setter, Dolley's trademark was a turban highly decorated with flowers and feathers.

1845—At 41, the popular **Sarah Childress Polk** took her religion and her role as First Lady seriously, gaining great respect for what today seem conservative standards. The Polks banned dancing and serving wine or liquor at the White House—the first considered frivolous, the second somewhat sinful. On inauguration night, when the Polks arrived, the dancing was ordered stopped. Following the First Couple's 2-hour stay, the music resumed and the guests danced freely.

1877—The first First Lady with a college degree, **Lucy Webb Hayes** was an alumna of Wesleyan Female College in Cincinnati, Ohio. Mrs. Hayes brought the Easter Egg Roll to the White House grounds when DC's children were banned from the Capitol lawns. Referred to as *Lemonade Lucy*, Hayes forbade even wine to be served at the White House.

1885—The only First Lady to be married in the White House was **Frances Folsom Cleveland**. The president insisted on a small private ceremony inside, but crowds were allowed to peek through the windows.

1889—While replacing a china closet, **Mrs. Benjamin Harrison** became interested in the bits and pieces of china she found. She began a White House collection of past presidents' china. Active politically, in 1891 she was elected the first president-general of the newly formed Daughters of the American Revolution.

1909—Not a woman to hide in the president's shadow, **Helen Herron Taft** set a precedent by riding beside her husband in the inaugural procession down Pennsylvania Ave to the White House. Mrs. Taft set other precedents as well by allowing her cow, named **Mooly-Wholly**, to graze the White House lawn, and by introducing musicales at state dinners. She also suggested placing cherry trees around the Washington Tidal Basin.

1915—The second wife of President Woodrow Wilson, **Edith Bolling Galt Wilson** proved invaluable to him and to the nation during his failing health. She allowed few to bother the president during his illness, serving as a de facto president, sending news and policy from the president to his administration.

1933—Often criticized and always controversial, **Anna Eleanor Roosevelt** traveled 38,000 miles in her first year as First Lady, and kept up the pace throughout her tenure. Called The First Lady of the World, Mrs. Roosevelt spoke her mind freely in her syndicated column, "My Day," on radio broadcasts, and in special press conferences for women reporters.

1961—Setting the fashion trends for the '60s, **Jacqueline Bouvier Kennedy** was the first First Lady to appoint a personal dress designer. Women all over the world wore copies of her suit dresses and pillbox hats. Mrs. Kennedy also brought culture to the mansion—by inviting distinguished guests to perform and be honored.

1974—Known for her outspokenness on social issues, **Betty Ford** brought new candor to her office. She opened up the issues of breast cancer and chemical dependency for public discussion.

1978—The only First Lady to hold the office after a film career, **Nancy Reagan** became discontented with mere fame and decided to do something with it halfway through her husband's administration. Expressing a deep concern over the increase of drug abuse among the country's youth, Mrs. Reagan began a personal campaign to educate them about its dangers, making frequent television appearances and imploring youngsters to "Just Say No" to drugs. Mrs. Reagan's opinionated nature was one cause of friction between herself and **Raisa Gorbachev** during a visit to Russia, when she criticized her Soviet counterpart for discounting the religious content of several paintings during a tour. ("How can she ignore it?" Mrs. Reagan said. "I mean, there it is!")

1989—Known even before her arrival at the White House as the *Silver Fox*, **Barbara Bush** impressed many detractors by demonstrating a self-mocking sense of humor during her first address as First Lady. Criticized before the election for her somewhat dowdy fashion sense—fake pearls and matronly dresses—she paused during her speech to model her latest unremarkable outfit. Taking a cue from her predecessor, Mrs. Bush is setting her own agenda for personal causes: she wants to use her position as First Lady to improve the quality of education in America.

5 Constitution Gardens (1976, Skidmore, Owings & Merrill) Located between the Washington Monument and the Lincoln Memorial, where temporary Naval buildings from WWI stood until after WWII. SOM originally designed a lovely 50-acre park, but recession-era budget cuts marred the plan, and the result is considered disappointing by many. The 7¹/₂-acre lake with a landscaped island is surrounded by paths and biked trails. Over 5000 trees create their own islands of shade. *The Memorial to the 56 Signers of the Declaration of Independence* (1984, **Joseph E. Brown**) is at the east end of the gardens. ♦ 17th-23rd Sts NW (Constitution Ave) Metro stop: Foggy Bottom/GW

Within Constitution Gardens:

Vietnam Veterans Memorial (1983, Maya Ying Lin)

In 1980, Congress authorized the construction of a memorial to the veterans of the Vietnam War on this plot near the Lincoln Memorial. After a national design competition with 1421 entries, the jury unanimously chose the design of 21-year-old Yale University architecture student Maya Lin. She conceived the monument's polished black granite walls as a park within a park, a quiet place. The walls point to the Washington Monument and the Lincoln Memorial, and the 58,156 names of those killed in the war are inscribed in chronological order of the date of casualty, beginning at the vertex of the walls, at the memorial's deepest point. In a very real sense, the names become the memorial.

Lin's unconventional design raised a storm of controversy: a bronze sculpture of three soldiers by Washington sculptor **Frederick Hart**, and a flagpole, were added nearby to mollify critics. However, Lin's work has transcended the initial criticism. The memorial is one of the nation's most emotional public monuments. Veterans' groups maintain a vigil here, and visitors leave flowers, medals, letters, and other tokens of remembrance. The National Park Service is saving these offerings. Volunteers are available to help find names and make rubbings. A directory of names on Lin's memorial can be purchased by calling 889.3800. ♦ 21st St and Constitution Ave NW. 634.1568 ♿

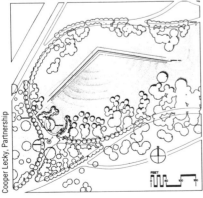

Cooper Lecky, Partnership

6 Reflecting Pool This shallow pool captures reflections of both the Washington Monument and the Lincoln Memorial on its glassy surface. The pool is 350 feet long by 180 feet wide; its depth is a uniform 3 feet. It has been the site of many celebrations and demonstrations, including the 1963 Civil Rights *March on Washington*, which climaxed with **Martin Luther King, Jr.**'s *I Have a Dream* speech given to 250,000 people crowded around, and in, the pool. (King stood on the steps of the Lincoln Memorial.) ♦ West end of Mall, between the Lincoln Memorial and the Washington Monument.

"Reader, suppose you were an idiot. And suppose you were a member of Congress. But I repeat myself." **Mark Twain**

Washington DC: The Last Colony

Strange as it may seem, the disenfranchised residents of the District of Columbia did not gain the right to vote until 1964—and that was just for president and vice president. In 1975, the privilege was amended to include the right to vote for mayor, 13 city council representatives, and a nonvoting member of Congress. Until then, the district had been run by the District Committee of the House of Representatives, controlled by Southerners: John McMillan, a crusty South Carolina Democrat, headed the committee for 25 years and ran the district like his own private fiefdom. Residents of DC, which is predominantly black, had lobbied for years for some form of self-governance, but were continually defeated in a conflict permeated with paternalism and racism.

Finally, in 1973, after the defeat of several anti-home rule congresspeople, Congress approved a compromise self-government act. It was overwhelmingly approved by DC voters in 1974 and went into effect on 2 January 1975. "We were not ready for home rule," said the Rev. Douglas E. Moore, a member of the city's first elected council, on the 10th anniversary of the act in 1985. "We were not ready. But who's ever ready for freedom?"

However, that freedom remains limited. The district now sets its own budget, but the House of Representatives retains oversight over DC's laws. In recent years, the district and Congress have quarreled over a number of issues, including management of DC's overcrowded prisons, funding for abortions for the poor, and the right of homosexual organizations to organize at Georgetown University.

District residents do not have senators or voting representatives on Capitol Hill. The city's court system is under federal control. Full statehood for DC is a perennial campaign topic, and one that promises to remain only that for the foreseeable future.

VERTEX
10'-1.56"
2'-6.71"
7'-6.85"

7 The Lincoln Memorial (1922, Henry Bacon; sculpture, Daniel Chester French) This building, so perfectly etched on Washington's landscape—not to mention the backs of the penny and the $5 bill—was built only after much debate on its shape and location. Among the early proposals were an obelisk, a pyramid, and—sponsored by car and real-estate interests—a 72-mile-long memorial parkway between Gettysburg and Washington.

The site eventually chosen was a flea-ridden, soggy swamp that had to be drained and landfilled before construction could begin in 1914. Now a better choice seems unimaginable. The classically-styled memorial anchors the east-west axis of the Mall. Lincoln gazes over the **Reflecting Pool** toward the Washington Monument and the Capitol. To the rear, a symbolic imaginary line connects him with **Robert E. Lee**'s home in **Arlington Cemetery**.

The building is essentially a Greek-style temple ("Coolly cribbed from the Parthenon," reported one critic) with a Roman-style attic or roof. The entrance is on the broad side facing the Mall rather than on one of the narrow ends, as would have been typical in antiquity.

A colonnade of 36 Doric columns rims the building; the columns are tilted inward to avoid the optical illusion of a bulging top. Above them is a frieze inscribed with the names and admission dates of the 36 states in the union at the time of Lincoln's death. (The date for Ohio is off by one year.) Higher up on the attic frieze are inscribed the names of the 48 states in the union at the time of the memorial's dedication in 1922.

Daniel Chester French's statue, often called *the Brooding Lincoln*, commands the center of the memorial. French designed the statue but only supervised the carving. It took the **Piccarilli Brothers** 4 years and 28 blocks of white Georgia marble to execute it. The 16th president leans back in a monumental throne adorned with fasces, the Roman symbol of the authority of the state. Much attention has been focused on the massive hands, which seem alive with emotion. Just before sculpting Lincoln, French had done a statue of **Albert Gallaudet**, famed teacher of the deaf. A close and perhaps imaginative examination of Lincoln's hands shows one forming the sign of the letter A and the other signing the letter L.

From heel to head the statue measures 19 feet, and if Lincoln—our tallest president—were to stand, he would tower above the crowd at a height of 28 feet.

On the north and south walls of the memorial are murals 12 feet high and 600 feet long by **Jules Guerin**. One depicts the Angel of Truth liberating a slave. The other depicts allegorical figures of Truth and Justice.

When the memorial was dedicated in 1922, one of the speakers was **Dr. Robert Moton**, the black president of Tuskegee Institute. Ironically, upon Moton's arrival, a Marine usher escorted him from the dais to the all-black section that was separated from the memorial and the rest of the audience by a roadway. Since that time the memorial has become a powerful symbol of the struggle for racial equality. In the '40s, the **Daughters of the American Revolution** refused to allow a performance by **Marian Anderson** at Constitution Hall. She sang her concert before more than 75,000 people from the steps of the memorial.

A magnificent sight at all times, the Lincoln

Memorial is most impressive at dawn and dusk. Note: **The Cave Under Lincoln**, a vast stalactite- and stalagmite-filled cavern created by excavations for the memorial, and later by water dripping from the marble steps, has been closed temporarily due to the recent discovery of asbestos in the cave. When the cleanup is completed (by 1991), visitors will be able to see the substructure of the original building—columns over 45 feet high support the 900-ton statue. ♦ 24 hours. Ranger on duty 8AM-midnight. 23rd St NW (west end of Mall) Metro Stop: Foggy Bottom. 426.6841 ♿

The Right to Assemble

Every year in DC, more than 1400 permits are issued for every type of public gathering, be it an assembly of 200,000 on the steps of the Lincoln Memorial or a solitary sign-carrying protester pacing back and forth in front of the White House. Unless someone else has already requested the same spot at the same time, permits are automatically granted.

The most sought-after sites are the Capitol and Lafayette Square, just opposite the White House. It's extremely rare that a visitor to DC does not encounter at least one type of public gathering. These expressions of the first amendment are part of what makes Washington a source of amazement for visiting foreigners, many of whom could be censured, if not imprisoned, for carrying out similar activities in their own countries.

Below are just some of the public events that have taken place in Washington over the last few decades:

1963 Martin Luther King, Jr., *I Have a Dream* speech rally (the steps of the Lincoln Memorial)—250,000

1967 March on the Pentagon (the Mall and environs)—200,000

1969 Vietnam War Moratorium (the Mall and environs)—250,000

1971 Anti-Vietnam War *Out Now* Rally (the Mall and environs)—500,000

1972 Nixon Inaugural Parade (Connecticut Ave, from the Capitol to the White House) 200,000

1976 Bicentennial Fireworks (the Washington Monument and environs)—1,000,000

1981 Martin Luther King, Jr., Birthday Celebration (the steps of the Lincoln Memorial)—200,000

1983 Redskins Super Bowl Celebration (along Pennsylvania Ave)—500,000

1988 Names Project (the AIDS quilt ceremony) (on the Ellipse and at the Lincoln Memorial)—200,000

1989 Bush Inaugural Parade (Connecticut Ave, from the Capitol to the White House)—300,000

1989 March for Women's Equality and Women's Lives (from the Washington Monument to the Capitol)—600,000

8 Potomac Parks/Hains Point These parks —**East Potomac** being the peninsula created by the Washington Channel, **West Potomac** being the area around the Tidal Basin and extending to the Lincoln Memorial—cover 700 acres at the west, Potomac River-end, of the Mall. Scattered with monuments, pools, and trees, as well as some of the city's best views, they offer excellent recreational space. You can play golf at either of 2 public golf courses, ride a bike, paddle a boat, picnic, or just enjoy the Potomac sunshine. At Hains Point, the peninsula's southern tip, you'll find cool breezes, a respite from the city's bustle, and *The Awakening*, **Seward Johnson**'s unusual 1980 aluminum sculpture that shows a figure rising out of the ground, as

if just waking up. ♦ South of Independence Ave, west of 14th St SW. Information 426.6841

9 Tidal Basin One of DC's most stunning outdoor areas, this park and breeze-swept lake is even more breathtaking when the 600 surrounding cherry trees are in bloom. An ideal place to picnic, jog, and read, with great views of the city, Jefferson Memorial, and Washington Monument. On the east side are gardens of seasonal flowers—especially brilliant in spring, when the tulips bloom—and a concession stand that sells hotdogs and burgers and rents the little blue paddleboats that skim the lake. Near East Basin Drive is the **Japanese Pagoda**, and near the **Kutz Memorial Bridge** is the **Japanese Lantern**. The basin was created in 1897 to capture water from the Potomac and empty it into the Washington Channel, possible because the river is an estuary and rises with the tide.

The best way to see the Tidal Basin blossoms is on foot. In fact, driving can be a miserable experience, with traffic backed up and drivers becoming irate. Park the car and use public transportation to reach the Mall area, then walk through the lovely, lively park, where the festive blossoms bring out vendors and street performers. Other places to see Japanese cherry trees are the **Washington Monument** grounds (3000 trees) and **East Potomac Park**, where almost 2000 pink double-blossomed trees bloom 2 weeks later than their cousins at the Tidal Basin. Take the 14th St Bridge and head south on Ohio Drive to the park. (Call Bethesda/Chevy Chase Chamber of Commerce for information on cherry blossoms in suburban Washington, 301/652.4900.) ♦ Concession daily 11AM-dusk, Apr-Nov. 15th St at Ohio Dr SW (East Potomac Park) 484.0206

10 Jefferson Memorial (1943, John Russell Pope; landscaping, Frederick Law Olmsted, Jr.; sculpture, Rudolph Evans) This monument is a fitting tribute to a man who was an accomplished architect as well as a powerful statesman.

Essentially an adaptation of the Roman Pantheon beloved by Jefferson, the memorial recalls Jefferson's own designs for his home, **Monticello**, and for the rotunda of the **University of Virginia**. The circular building is rimmed by 54 Ionic columns and is fronted, on the side facing the Mall, with a classical portico and a pediment supported by even more columns. Three other entrances bring light and fresh air into the gracefully proportioned chamber.

Like so much of the Mall, the Jefferson Memorial site was under brackish water until the commencement of an 8-year-long dredging project. The land reclaimed wasn't strong enough to support the memorial, whose every column weighs 45 tons, without a specially prepared foundation. Concrete-filled steel cylinders were driven 135 feet into the earth before reaching bedrock.

Any local postcard stand will handily prove that the Jefferson Memorial is one of the most popular attractions in a city where you can hardly take 2 steps without tripping over something monumental in either bronze or marble. But it wasn't always so. At the time of its construction, the memorial was denounced as being too sweet and feminine. The columns caused it to be called a "cage for Jefferson's statue," and its low circular shape prompted one critic to rename the memorial "Jefferson's muffin."

The interior of the coffered dome (a series of honeycomblike recesses) is of Indiana limestone. The walls are of white Georgia marble and the floors of pink-and-gray Tennessee marble.

The interior is dominated by a 19-foot-high statue of Jefferson—who stood 6 feet 2½ inches in life. He wears knee breeches, a waistcoat, and a fur-collared greatcoat given him by the Polish patriot **Thaddeus Kosciusko**.

Rudolph Evans' design was chosen over 100 other submissions. During dedication ceremonies, officiated at by **Franklin Delano Roosevelt**, the sculpture was represented by a plaster model. It couldn't be cast in bronze until several years later when the wartime ban on domestic metal use was lifted. Some parking is available near the memorial. ♦ Daily 8AM-midnight. Rotunda open and lighted through the night. 14th St and East Basin Dr SW (East Potomac Park) &

Located in East Potomac Park near the Jefferson Memorial, the **National Park Service** (NPS) is the visitor's No. 1 source for essential information. Part of the Interior Department, the Park Service offers free information and brochures on almost every aspect of Washington—and beyond.

The NPS maintains much of DC's great outdoors. It manages the **Chesapeake & Ohio Canal**, the **Petersen House,** where Lincoln died, **Dyke Marsh**, the **Old Stone House**, and the **Art Barn Gallery** in **Rock Creek Park**. Of special interest are NPS's *Bird Walks* through Rock Creek Park and *Historical Walks* through famous buildings. The NPS also cosponsors, with the **Association of Concert Bands of America**, a series of concerts at **Wolf Trap Farm Park**.

During summer months, the NPS also offers tours through the various parks and landmarks every Sunday afternoon. Other walking tours are available daily. Check the NPS monthly newsletter, *Kiosk,* or the *Washington Post's Weekend* section, or call the NPS office for each week's meeting places and tours. Main events are advertised on the Mall.

You can request information from or visit NPS at 1100 Ohio Drive SW, Washington DC 20242 (phone 485.9666). It also has staff members at the **Washington Visitor Information Center** at 1455 Pennsylvania Ave NW, 789.7000.

"Peace, commerce and honest friendship with all nations—entangling alliances with none."
        Thomas Jefferson
        First Inaugural Address

Cherry Trees

Part of the magic of **cherry blossom time** is that you never know exactly when it will arrive. Yet every spring—sometime between 20 March and 17 April—the trees bloom, lovers swoon, and traffic around the **Tidal Basin** comes to a standstill.

Blossoms or no, each year the **Cherry Blossom Festival** begins with the ceremonial lighting of the Mall's **Japanese Lantern**. For a full week, pageants, parades, concerts, and even a marathon celebrate the return of the beloved blossoms. Festival planners have settled on the first week of April, and nature usually obliges. About 2 weeks before the blooming, the meteorologists at National Capital Park Service make their predictions.

The history of the trees is almost as colorful as their blossoms. Responding to a hint from **Mrs. William Howard Taft**, the Japanese sent over a shipment of saplings in 1909. They were hardly uncrated before the Department of Agriculture declared them infested and had them destroyed. Apologies were tendered and accepted, and in 1912, 3000 more trees arrived in Washington. The hundreds planted around the Tidal Basin have become the most popular. The majority are *Akebeno* trees, with delicate white blossoms; scattered among them are *Yoshino* trees, whose petals are pale pink.

The public was so taken with the trees that in the 1940s, when it was announced some would have to be moved to make way for the Jefferson Memorial, nature lovers chained themselves to tree trunks, while the more militant occupied holes left by already uprooted trees. Later, after the Japanese bombing of **Pearl Harbor**, some of the trees were vandalized. In 1965, the US sent cuttings to Tokyo so the Japanese could replenish native stocks that had been weakened by war and pollution.

When the **steam-operated elevator** first opened in the **Washington Monument** in the late 1800s, it was considered so unsafe that only men were allowed to ride in it. The more delicate women had to climb the 898 steps to the summit. Today there is an electric elevator and the trip takes only 70 seconds.

11 Washington Monument (1848–1885, Robert Mills) The Washington Monument's presence, both simple and grand, is felt over the entire city. At 555 feet 5 1/8 inches, it is the tallest structure in DC and was the tallest in the world when it first opened to the public in 1886.

The *Monument Committee*, which launched a nationwide competition to select a landmark for the capital, favored Robert Mills' marble tower over L'Enfant's equestrian statue of Washington that was to stand on the current site of the Jefferson Pier. The original winning design had a richly decorated obelisk (stone tower) rising like a giant

The Mall

birthday candle from behind a circular Greek-style temple that would have held the tombs of Revolutionary War heroes. In front, there was to be a massive marble statue of Washington driving a *quadriga*—a Roman chariot pulled by 4 horses. Lack of money and public support for these frills have left us with this simple gleaming tower—the most recognizable symbol of Washington the City as well as of Washington the Man.

Funds for the monument initially came from private groups that solicited $1 apiece from citizens across the nation. Construction of the tower proceeded smoothly for 7 years— until a single block of marble for the building was donated by **Pope Pius IX**. This infuriated the antipapist *Know-Nothing Party*, which stole the *Pope's stone* and sabotaged attempts to raise funds for the monument. Then the Civil War intervened, and the project was abandoned for almost 20 years. In 1876 after the war and the *US Centennial Exposition*—public interest was renewed and the project was turned over to the **Army Corps of Engineers**. They strengthened the foundation (although it still sinks 1/4 inch every 30 years) and redesigned the monument, much improving the proportions of the original design. A slight change of color in the stone marks the point at which construction resumed. Four years later, the pyramidion was finally capped with a 9-inch tip made of solid aluminum (an exotic material at the time) and wired with 144 platinum lightning conductors. The $1 million tab was picked up by the government. Today, you can take a 70-second elevator ride up and down. The view from the top is magnificent. Or, if you like to walk, on weekends the **National Park Service** conducts *walking-down-step tours*, during which you'll see 188 carved memorial stones that were donated in the 19th century by various private citizens, societies, states, and nations. On Saturday or Sunday, call 426.6840 to see if a tour is being offered that day. ♦ Free. Daily 9AM-5PM, Jan-Mar, Sep-Dec; daily 8AM-midnight, 1st Su in Apr-Labor Day. Mall, south of White House. Metro stop: Smithsonian &

The Mall

Obelisks—tall, slender, 4-sided monoliths that taper to a point or pyramid—were first used by the Egyptians. Pairs of the graceful geometric figures were used to adorn the doorways of temples. They were most often carved of red granite and honored **Ra**, the Egyptian sun god. Traditionally, obelisks were designed so that their height was 10 times the width of their flat bottom. The stone column was usually set upon a circular base.

Several Egyptian obelisks have survived the ages, including those at the **Great Temple at Karnak** in Thebes. During the period of European colonialism, several of these Egyptian treasures were moved to Europe and the US. The obelisk at Paris' **Place de**

left to right: Stele of Hammurabi, Egypt; Obelisk at Axum, Egypt; Obelisk in India; Cleopatra's Needle, London; Stele at Axum, Egypt; Obelisk in Rome

la Concorde once stood at Luxor. Twin obelisks, each known as **Cleopatra's Needle**, have been separated: one now stands at London's Embankment, the other in New York City's Central Park.

Of course, the **Washington Monument** is obelisk-shaped and follows the Egyptian formula for an obelisk's height. But the fact that it isn't a single, solid stone—a monolith—keeps it from being a true obelisk.

The Washington Monument

600'

Design by Robert Mills, chosen in the 1836 competition.

Actual Construction

555' 5 1/8"

1884

410'

1883

340'

1882

250'

1881

176'

156'

1878 to 1880

1848 to 1858

12 Sylvan Theater This outdoor theater with a huge lawn regularly presents—weather permitting—delightful musicals, Shakespearean festivals, and military bands. Thousands of people flock to the small stage during hot summer nights and claim the best picnic spots in front of the stage by spreading picnic blankets or setting up their own lawn chairs. Daily concerts are held during the summer. Call for program information. ♦ Free. 15th St SW at Jefferson Dr SW. Metro stop: Smithsonian. 426.6841

13 Department of Agriculture (1930, Ranking, Kellogg & Crane) The first building erected by the **McMillan Commission**, which was charged at the turn of the century with resurrecting L'Enfant's plan for a gracious, ceremonial capital city. ♦ 14th St and Independence Ave SW (Jefferson Dr-C St) Metro stop: Smithsonian

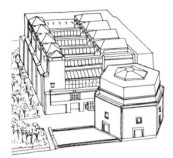

14 United States Holocaust Memorial Museum (Scheduled completion, 1990, James Ingo Freed/I.M. Pei & Partners) This building will honor the 6 million Jews and millions of others who died in the World War II *Holocaust*, in a midblock site between the red-brick Victorian-style **Auditors' Building** and the Greek Revival **Bureau of Engraving and Printing**. The privately funded museum will include a 6000-square-foot atrium, **Hall of Witness**, exhibition space over 3 floors, and a hexagonal **Hall of Remembrance**, designed for spiritual reflection. ♦ Raoul Wallenberg Place (Independence Ave-D St SW) Metro stop: Farragut North. 822.6464

15 Bureau of Engraving and Printing Once every fiscal year the Federal Reserve puts in an order at the Bureau of Engraving and Printing. The order is for paper money—so much of it, in fact, that the presses must roll 24 hours a day all year to print it. In 1987, 6,595,000 notes were printed at a face value of $77,105,600. To put this all into perspective, if you were to have that much money in $1 bills and spend it at the reasonable rate of a $1 per second, it would take you a little over 7 years to go broke.

The bureau prints more than money: 40 billion postage stamps, treasury notes, military certificates, and invitations to the White House are turned out every year. In the past it's printed food stamps, and during the oil embargo of 1973, it had an order—never fulfilled—to print coupons for gas rationing.

Watching crisp sheets of money roll off the presses is great fun for kids and provides much

fuel for fantasies for adults. The bureau offers a free 20-minute tour. Enter through the main lobby, where some of the bureau's products, including stamp sheets 4 times the size of those found at your local post office as well as part of a press plate, and some first-rate examples of counterfeiters' nefarious art are displayed.

Continue to the gallery, which is one story above the production floor and offers an excellent view of large sheets of money being printed, checked, overprinted with the treasury seal, cut, stacked, and bundled for shipment. A recorded explanation of the sights plays over a PA system as you move along.

The tour ends in the **Visitors Center**, where presidential portraits and commemorative coins

are on display and for sale. There are also additional exhibitions about the engraving process and the activities of the bureau. If you like, you can buy small bags of shredded money. ♦ Free. Tours M-F 9AM-2PM. 14th and C Sts SW. Metro stop: Smithsonian. 447.9709, 447.9916

While coins are minted in several cities, all the paper currency in the country is made in Washington at the **Bureau of Engraving and Printing**. (You may have noticed the names of other cities on the Federal Reserve Seal: these are Federal Reserve Bank branches to which the money is shipped for distribution.) The bureau is authorized to make 1-, 2-, 5-, 10-, 20-, 50-, 100-, 500-, 1000-, and 5000-dollar bills, but in 1969 they stopped making anything over $100 because of lack of use. Some of the higher denomination bills may still be in the hands of collectors, but when they turn up at a bank they are pulled from circulation and destroyed.

About $20 billion worth of currency is printed each year, largely to replace bills that have worn out. The most common bill made is the $1 bill. Production of this bill alone takes up more than half the bureau's time, which is why it was so eager to reissue the $2 bill in 1976. Unfortunately, the new bill—along with the **Susan B. Anthony** dollar coin—was a resounding flop with the public and is no longer printed.

The value of the dollar you earn may be declining, but the quality of the paper it's printed on keeps improving. The stock (manufactured by a private firm under government contract) is 25 percent linen and 75 percent cotton. The longer fibers of this pulp give the paper exceptional strength. The paper is also shot through with minuscule fibers of blue and red silk to help thwart counterfeiters. In fact, making a similar paper is against federal law. The average life span of a 1-dollar bill is 18 months—up almost 10 months since 1960. It costs 2.5 cents to make a note of any denomination. That's 25 bucks per 1000 bills.

Money is still printed—as very few things are today—by an intaglio process. The design is cut deep into a *plate* and then, under great pressure, embossed on the paper. The process begins when a master engraver gouges out the

45

design on a soft metal plate. After the plate has been cut and approved, it is casehardened by being dipped into a cyanide bath heated to 1800 degrees. The plate is then taken to a transfer table, where a small cylindrical steel roller is passed over it until the impression has been transferred. The master plate is returned to a vault and the new plate, called the *roller die*, is casehardened. The roller die is put on a step-and-repeat machine. The design, now raised, is pressed under great pressure onto a flat sheet of metal that will become the *press plate*. Once the design has been fixed on the plate and checked under a magnifying glass for mistakes, the process is repeated until the press plate holds the image of 32 bills. The new plate must

be cleaned, trimmed, chrome-plated, and curved to fit on the press before it's ready to print money. If you were allowed to look at a master plate, you would see how much the minute amount of distortion that results from curving the image is accounted for in the original design.

In fact, it's very rare that a new master plate must be engraved. The last time was in 1976, when the 2-dollar bill was reissued with design changes.

After the now-cylindrical press plate has been inked and scraped—so that ink remains only in the indentations—80 tons of pressure is used to force the paper against it. The back of each bill is first printed with green ink (hence the nickname *greenbacks*). Twenty-four hours later the front is printed with black ink.

The average press plate is good for 300,000 sheets of bills. A good pressman will look at the fine line that borders all money; if he notices any deterioration, the plate is pulled. It's stripped and replated, emerging strong enough for another 300,000 sheets. Old press plates are cut up and melted down. Contrary to what you may

have seen in the movies, no counterfeiter has ever managed to steal one.

The printed sheets are moved to COPE machinery—which does nothing to help you cope with the rising cost of money. It stands for *Currency Overprinting and Processing Equipment*. This gismo uses a different type of ink and the offset printing process to print the Treasury seal, serial numbers, signatures, and the Federal Reserve seal on the bills. (They once put sizing—like laundry starch—on the bills at this stage to make them crisp, but changes in the paper have made this unnecessary.)

In the final stage before shipping to appropriate Federal Reserve banks, the COPE machinery cuts and stacks the bills in 100-note packages. These are assembled in 40-unit groups called *bricks*.

Later, banks around the country funnel money back to Federal Reserve banks, where automatic counting machines sort the money and pull out worn bills, shred them, and replace them with new ones.

Paper money design has changed very little since 1928, when the size of the notes was reduced. In 1935 the Great Seal, front and back, was added to the 1-dollar bill, and in 1960 the words *In God We Trust* were put on the backs of all notes.

During World War II, special money was printed that was easily differentiated from regular currency and could be declared void if it fell into enemy hands. American troops in North Africa and Sicily had bills whose Treasury seal was printed in yellow. Another issue was printed for Hawaii and combat areas in the Pacific. The Treasury seal and serial numbers were printed in brown, and the word *Hawaii* was overprinted on the face of the bill.

The old 2-dollar bill was discontinued in 1963. When it was reissued in 1976, the picture of Monticello on the back was replaced with a reproduction of a painting by **John Trumbull** of

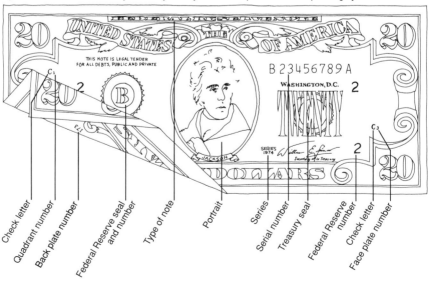

the signing of the *Declaration of Independence*. There wasn't room to reproduce the whole thing, so 6 of the signers were left out, greatly upsetting several state historical societies.

Before the Civil War, roughly one-third of all circulating paper money was bogus. Of course, having 1600 separate state banks each designing and issuing its own notes only made the counterfeiter's life easier. The government responded by adopting a national currency in 1863. However, the new money was soon so widely counterfeited that the government created the Secret Service, whose special task was, and is, to fight enterprising crooks who stashed printing presses in their basements.

The fight continues, and according to the Treasury Department, supersophisticated commercial copying machines make the fight harder.

One solution under consideration is to print each denomination in a different color. Among the ideas still being considered are the addition of special threads to the paper that would be visible only under refracted light; background tinting of the bills with minute flecks of color; and optically variable printing, a method that gives a slight 3D effect and is hard to duplicate.

No change will be made until the Treasury decides to do it and new equipment is manufactured and tested. The new greenbacks, whatever their eventual color, will gradually be phased in, and outmoded currency slowly withdrawn, the same way gold and silver certificates have been phased out in the past.

DC Weather
Not good. Best times for a visit are mid April through mid May for the sensational spring flowers and mid September through mid October for fall foliage; these are also the most temperate months. Summer is hot and humid, winter cool and damp. Every other year, there is a light snowfall, which can close the city down. Tourists wear whatever they please; business travelers are expected to dress conservatively no matter how uncomfortable that may be, and the classier bars and restaurants demand the same.

	High	Low	Mean
Jan	42.6	27.4	35.0
Feb	44.4	28.0	36.2
Mar	53.0	35.0	44.0
Apr	64.2	44.2	54.2
May	74.9	54.5	64.7
June	82.8	63.4	73.1
July	86.8	68.0	77.4
Aug	84.4	66.1	75.3
Sep	78.4	59.6	69.0
Oct	67.5	48.0	57.8
Nov	55.1	37.9	46.5
Dec	44.8	29.8	37.3

Rainfall is evenly distributed throughout the year.

SMITHSONIAN INSTITUTION

Washington, D.C. 20560
U.S.A.

16 The Smithsonian Institution Building
(1855, James Renwick) Popularly known as the *Castle* because of its marvelous spires, towers,

The Mall

turrets, and crenelated parapets, this was the Smithsonian's first building. Built of red Seneca sandstone and widely recognized as one of the finest Gothic Revival buildings in America, its occupants include the Smithsonian's administrative offices as well as the headquarters of the **Woodrow Wilson International Center for Scholars**. Also within is the **Crypt Room**, tomb of the Smithsonian's benefactor, **James Smithson**. In July of 1989, the mother building reopened after extensive renovations. ♦ Free. Daily 10AM-5:30PM. 1000 Jefferson Dr SW (10th St) Metro stop: Smithsonian. 357.2700

Washington's most often quoted cliché is probably "You could spend a week just seeing the **Smithsonian Institution**." More than 27 million people take up that challenge each year. The Smithsonian's collection, which attracts more visitors than any other tourist center in the nation, is in fact so big that only a tiny portion of its inventory can be displayed at a given time, despite its 14 museums (including 6 DC galleries) and zoo.

Yet the Smithsonian is in no way limited to exhibitions encased in buildings. It is both a seeker and a source of education, a patron of scientific expeditions, and a publisher of over 300 books and monographs each year. Its 6 research centers focus on everything from the history of art to the life cycles of fish.

When **Thaddeus Lowe** convinced **Abraham Lincoln** to use hot air balloons to observe Civil War military movements and conflicts, the Smithsonian was there. When **John Wesley Powell** led his party of wooden rafts through the raging white waters of the Grand Canyon in 1869, it was under the sponsorship of the Smithsonian. Each time a satellite circles the globe, it owes a part of its history to the Smithsonian and a young experimenter named **Robert Goddard**, who found an encouraging sponsor and publisher in the Smithsonian when no one else would listen. Goddard is today recognized as the father of modern rocketry and of the US space program. Whatever the field, if the acquisition and propagation of knowledge is involved, so, too, is the Smithsonian Institution.

The criteria for the institution's work were established in 1826 in one of history's most unusual wills. **James Smithson**, a highly regarded British scientist, decreed that if the nephew who was his only heir died childless, the Smithson fortune would go to the United States of America "to found at Washington, under the name of the Smithsonian Institution, an establishment for the increase and diffusion of knowledge among men." The irony of the bequest was that Smithson had never even visited the US!

Stigmatized through life as the bastard son of a duke and a descendant of **King Henry VII**, Smithson had fought back by excelling as a scientist. Sadly, despite his many professional

accomplishments, including the isolation of zinc carbonate (smithsonite), Smithson never broke free from 19th-century Britain's prejudice against illegitimacy. "The best blood of England flows in my veins," the scientist wrote, "but this avails me not."

Smithson's nephew died childless in 1835; 2 years later, to Washington's amazement, the US capital learned that it was heir to more than a half-million dollars, a vast sum in that day. Congress appointed **Joseph Henry**, America's most distinguished scientist in the mid-1800s, to act as the Smithsonian's first secretary. Henry's principles still govern the institution: "The great object is to facilitate...the promotion of science,...to foster original research, and to enlarge the bounds of human thought."

By Joseph Henry's decree, no branch of knowledge should be excluded from the Smithsonian's attention. Today, its channels for disseminating knowledge are almost as varied as its treasures, and include a television show and the award-winning magazines *Smithsonian* and *Air & Space/Smithsonian*. For fun facts about current astronomical events, call **Dial-a-Phenomenon** at 357.2000. To check up on museum events, call **Dial-a-Museum** at 357.2020.

Parking in and around the Mall is extremely limited; use public transportation. ◆ Metro stops: Smithsonian, L'Enfant Plaza, Federal Triangle, Archives. For Smithsonian information, call 357.2700

Infinity, a gleaming strip of stainless steel stretched into a lyrical loop that turns in on itself, was sculpted by **Jose de Rivera** in 1967. It is the first piece of abstract art commissioned by the government. The sculpture, located at Madison Drive NW at The National Museum of American History, makes a full revolution on its base every 6 minutes.

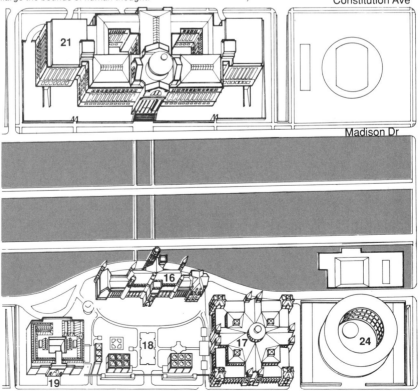

Drawing by Joseph Passonneau

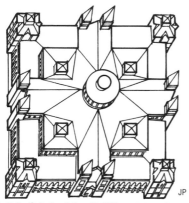

JP

17 Arts & Industries Building (1881, Cluss & Schulze) Restored in 1976, this building houses one of the most extensive collections of American Victoriana in existence. Many of the items, collectively called *1876: A Centennial Exhibition,* are the same items displayed in the *Philadelphia Centennial Exposition* of that year: horse-drawn carriages, machinery, pistols, silverware, furniture, and unusual *objets d'art,* all celebrating the exciting brassy glory that typified America during the 19th century. Even the building, built as a partner to the administration building next door, is a Victorian fantasy: an elaborate polychrome/brick affair with giant industrial trusses and meandering iron balconies. The museum shop includes replicas of Victorian picture frames, paper-doll cutouts, and jewelry.

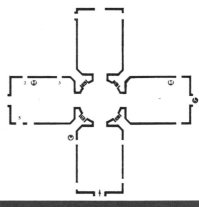

The **Discovery Theater**, Tuesday through Saturday, offers a series of changing programs, ranging from puppet shows to mimes to dance troupes. ♦ Museum: free. Daily 10AM-5:30PM. Tours M-Sa 10:15AM. Discovery Theater: admission. Shows: Tu-F 10, 11:30AM; Sa 1, 3PM. 900 Jefferson Dr SW (9th St) Metro stop: Smithsonian. 357.2700, tours 357.3030, theater tickets and reservations 357.1500 ♿

Recipients of the **Smithson Medal,** established in 1965 in memory of the Smithsonian Institution's founder, have included **Queen Elizabeth II** (1976) and **Pope John Paul II** (1979).

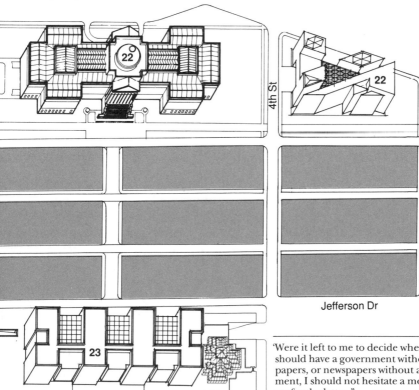

4th St

3rd St

Jefferson Dr

'Were it left to me to decide whether we should have a government without newspapers, or newspapers without a government, I should not hesitate a moment to prefer the latter." **Thomas Jefferson** *Writings, VI*

18 The Quadrangle (1987, Shepley, Bulfinch, Richardson and Abbott) Pressed by a need for more exhibition and office space, the **Smithsonian Institution** slipped its newest museums beneath a garden that lies between the **Arts & Industries Building** and the **Freer Gallery of Art**, directly south of the *Castle*. Nearly 96 percent of the 3-story complex is underground,

Shepley Bulfinch Richardson and Abbott

The Mall

beneath the 4.2-acre **Enid A. Haupt Garden**. The domed roofs of the **National Museum of African Art** pavilion recall the arch motif of the Freer, while the pyramidal silhouette of the **Arthur M. Sackler Gallery** pavilion echoes the roof lines of the Arts & Industries Building.
♦ Independence Ave SW (south of the *Castle*) Metro Stop: Smithsonian.

18 Enid A. Haupt Garden (1987, Jean Paul Carlhian) The garden (conceived by Smithsonian Institution Director Emeritus **S. Dillon Ripley**) frames the Sackler Gallery and the National Museum of African Art, and is named after **Enid Annenberg Haupt** of New York, who contributed $3 million toward its construction. The central Victorian parterre is a retreat from the museum bustle, with 40 antique wrought-iron park benches and beds of bright flowers that form patterns designed after the sunken garden at Philadelphia's 1876 *Centennial Exposition*. The main entrance, in front of the parterre, is known as the *Renwick Gate*, after *Castle* architect **James Renwick**, who sketched a carriage gate in 1849 that was never built. The gate's 4 stone pillars are made from the same red Seneca sandstone that was used to build the Smithsonian Institution building.

Two minigardens, one on either side of the parterre, reflect the mandate of the museums below. The **Moongate Garden** near the Sackler Gallery features two 9-foot-tall pink granite moongates, one on either side of a pool paved with half-round pieces of granite and shaded by two weeping cherry trees. The **Fountain Garden** near the African Art museum is designed as a haven on hot, sunny days, with a waterfall and thornless hawthorns. ♦ Free. Daily 7AM-5:45PM, Jan-Memorial Day, Oct-Dec; daily 7AM-8PM, Memorial Day-Sep. Independence Ave at 10th St SW (south of the *Castle*) Metro stop: Smithsonian

---

If all the **Smithsonian treasures** were lined up in one long exhibition and you spent just one second looking at each item, it would take you more than 2½ years of 24-hour-a-day nonstop touring to see them all—and by then the Smithsonian would have acquired an additional 2½ million items.

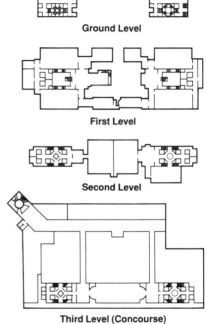

Ground Level

First Level

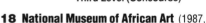

Second Level

Third Level (Concourse)

18 National Museum of African Art (1987, Jean Paul Carlhian) This is the only museum in the US dedicated to the exhibition and study of the traditional arts of sub-Saharan Africa. Founded by **Warren Robbins** in 1964 as a private institution in a series of connected row houses on Capitol Hill (one of which belonged to **Frederick Douglass**), the museum became a branch of the Smithsonian in 1979. The collection demonstrates how the continent's 900 distinct cultures interweave art with daily life in ways quite different from European and American art. Religious forms find expression not only in masks and figures created for ceremonial purposes but in the objects of everyday existence. Thus, the museum's collection includes splendid sculptures, textiles, building elements, and household items. Most are made from organic materials, such as wood, that do not last long; the bulk of the works in the collection were created in the late 19th and 20th centuries. The first level includes a gallery of 100 of the collection's highlights, many of which have never been displayed before, as well as an exhibition of metal sculpture from Benin. The second level includes a gallery for temporary exhibitions, and the museum's learning center. ◆ Free. Museum: daily 10AM-5:30PM. Walk-in tours: M, Th-F 10:30AM; Tu-W 10:30AM, 1PM; Sa-Su 11AM, 1, 3PM. Library: by appointment. Closed 25 December. 950 Independence Ave SW (9th St) Metro stop: Smithsonian. 357.4600 &

18 Arthur M. Sackler Gallery (1987, Jean Paul Carlhian) The museum's 3 floors of below-ground galleries give the Smithsonian its first real opportunity to showcase its extensive collection of Eastern art. The foundation of the collection is 1000 masterworks donated by **Dr. Arthur M. Sackler**, a New York medical researcher who also donated $4 million toward the construction of the museum. Included are Chinese bronzes from the **Shang** (1523–1028 BC) through **Han** (206 BC–AD 220) dynasties, 475 Chinese jades, from 3000 BC into the 20th century, and 156 Near Eastern works in silver, gold, bronze, and lesser minerals. The first level holds 15 masterpiece Persian and Indian paintings, Chinese **Ming** dynasty furniture, and an exhibition of Chinese interpretations of animal motifs highlighted by a zodiac display, as well as the museum shop. The second level includes a display of 493 Chinese bronzes and neolithic jades, some dating from the fourth millennium BC. The second-level library houses 35,000 volumes, half in Chinese or Japanese, and more than 200 periodicals. ◆ Free. Galleries daily 10AM-5:30PM. Walk-in tours M-F noon. Library M-F 10AM-5PM. 1050 Independence Ave SW (12th St) Metro stop: Smithsonian. 357.2700

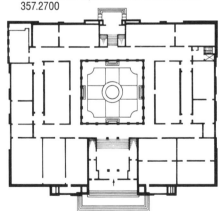

19 Freer Gallery of Art (1923, Charles Platt) This is an eclectic collection of Oriental art, as well as of late 19th- and early 20th-century American art showing a Far Eastern influence. The eclectic collection is a reflection of the passions of **Charles Lang Freer**, a wealthy Detroit businessman who began collecting Eastern art on the advice of his close friend, painter **James McNeill Whistler**. The museum's flamboyant *Peacock Room*, painted by Whistler, is a highlight of the collection. The Freer is closed for renovation through 1990 or 1991. Many of its activities will be continued by the Sackler Gallery. Call for information on the Freer's status. ◆ Jefferson Dr at 12th St SW. Metro stop: Smithsonian. 357.2700 &

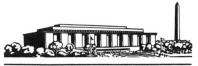

NATIONAL MUSEUM *of* AMERICAN HISTORY

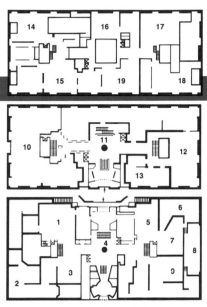

First Floor
1 Atom Smashers
2 Medical Sciences
3 Mathematics
4 Foucault Pendulum
5 Farm Machinery
6 American Maritime Enterprise
7 Vehicle Hall
8 Railroads
9 Electricity

Second Floor
10 A Nation of Nations
11 Star-Spangled Banner
12 We the People
13 First Ladies' Gowns

Third Floor
14 Ceramics
15 Printing and Graphic Arts
16 Money and Medals
17 Armed Forces History
18 Ordnance
19 Photography

20 The National Museum of American History (1964, McKim, Mead & White; completed by Steinmann, Cain & White) embodies the nation's scientific, technological, and cultural heritage. It is filled with all the things Americans love too much to throw away, even though we're not sure why we accumulated a few of them in the first place.

The museum collection began in 1858, when the US Patent Office transferred its overcrowded cabinet of curiosities to the Smithsonian. Then, in 1876, came a windfall of exhibitions from the *Philadelphia Centennial Exposition*. What you see today is an excellent cross section of America's scientific, political, cultural, and technological histories.

Behind the pink Tennessee marble exterior, the box-like building stores such highlights as the **Country Store Post Office** from Headsville WV, circa 1861 (you can still post your mail here, and it will go out with a special Smithsonian

Station postmark); farm machinery from a time when farming was strictly a family business; a **Conestoga** wagon; a 1913 **Ford Model T** (manufacturer's suggested retail price: $325); one of **Thomas Edison**'s first phonographs; the first typewriter (1829); a 1790 chemistry lab that includes equipment used by **Joseph Priestly**; **George Washington**'s false teeth; and a 280-ton steam locomotive. And that's just the first floor.

On the second floor, among many other things, you'll see the **Foucault Pendulum**, which demonstrates the earth's rotation; the original **Star-Spangled Banner**, the one **Francis Scott Key** saw *by the dawn's early light* over Fort McHenry in 1814; original home interiors dating from the

The Mall

1600s to the 1900s, and ranging from a colonial Virginia parlor to a California rancher's kitchen; campaign paraphernalia; a pocket compass used by **Lewis and Clark**; and the table and chairs used when **Robert E. Lee** surrendered at Appomatox Court House. In the museum's newest permanent exhibition, **Ceremonial Court**— a re-creation of **Cross Hall**, the grand front corridor of the White House—is a selection of inaugural gowns worn by First Ladies. Only those worn by **Jacqueline Kennedy** through **Nancy Reagan** are on view within Ceremonial Court. The rest of the dresses are undergoing renovation; the complete collection will be on display by 1991.

The relocated and expanded **Museum Shop** features current titles published by the Smithsonian presses as well as handicrafts and items—from needlepoint and pottery to jewelry and children's folk toys—that authentically relate to the exhibitions. The shop's false entrance leads browsers to a bridge that overlooks the expanded basement location. ♦ Free. Daily 10AM-5:30PM. Cafeteria: daily 10AM-5PM, Jan-June 15, Sep-Dec; daily 9:30AM-7:30PM, June 16-Labor Day. Constitution Ave at 14th St NW. Metro stop: Federal Triangle. 357.2700

21 National Museum of Natural History/ National Museum of Man (1911, Hornblower & Marshall) A treasure chest of natural sciences. Here you will see the models, live and mounted specimens, dioramas, recreations, prototypes, and artifacts used to study man's evolution, human cultures, dinosaurs, fossils, amphibians, reptiles, birds, sea organisms, mammals, insects, plants, rocks, minerals, and meteorites—in short, the entire planet Earth!

There's really too much here to digest in one visit, but some of the highlights are **Uncle Beazley**, the life-size model of a Triceratops dinosaur that greets you at the Mall entrance; a 13-foot-tall African bush elephant (you can't miss him; he's the largest known specimen of the largest land animal of modern times); a 3.1-billion-year-old fossil of a South African fig tree; dinosaur skeletons; an audiovisual show describing Ice Age glaciation's effects on the earth's surface; a freeze-dried Ice Age bison recently discovered by Alaskan gold miners;

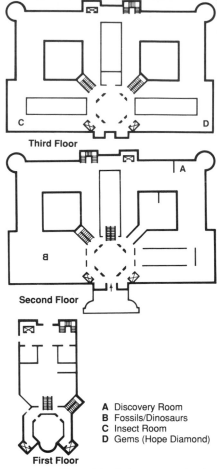

Third Floor

Second Floor

A Discovery Room
B Fossils/Dinosaurs
C Insect Room
D Gems (Hope Diamond)

First Floor

and one of Easter Island's famous stone heads. And that's only the beginning!

There is also a life-size model of a 92-foot whale; a living coral reef community housed in a king-size aquarium complete with waves; and in the mind-boggling **Hall of Gems**, more than 1000 precious and semi-precious stones, the star of which is the legendary and infamous **Hope Diamond**, a 45.5-carat dazzler with a curse to match its beauty.

Another must-see is the **Insect Zoo**, which features thousands of live insects. Volunteers display awesome creatures, such as the 3-inch-long hissing cockroach. Even after an exhaustive, and exhausting, tour, the vast majority of the museum's 118 million objects remain unseen, stored in behind-the-scenes areas that also include laboratories for the museum's scientists.

Children will especially enjoy the **Discovery Room** on the first floor, near the North American mammal exhibition. Here, hundreds of natural history specimens, from elephant tusks to crocodile heads to herb seeds, can be touched, smelled, and in some cases, even tasted. Free lectures or films are offered every Friday at noon. Receivers for a self-guided audio tour of the exhibitions are available in the second floor rotunda (charge). Cafeteria and excellent museum shop. ♦ Free passes for Discovery Room at door. Daily 10AM-5PM, Jan-June 15, Sep-Dec; daily 9:30AM-7:30PM, June 16-Labor Day. Highlight tours daily 10:30AM-1:30PM. Museum located at Constitution Ave at 10th St NW. Mall entrance: Madison Dr NW (9th-12th Sts) Metro stop: Smithsonian. 357.2700, reservations for groups of 6 or more children 357.2747

22 The National Gallery of Art

One of the world's most exceptional collections of European and American painting, sculpture, and graphic art from the Middle Ages to the present. Touring the National Gallery of Art's 2 buildings is an experience of sheer serendipity, as you discover original masterpieces you've seen reproduced countless times. In the gallery's **West Building** (1941, **John Russell Pope**), you'll find pre-20th century art by **Titian, Raphael, Rembrandt, El Greco, Rubens, Van Eyck, Fragonard, Renoir, Monet, Whistler, Gainsborough,** and **Cézanne**. The *Ginevra de' Benci* by **Leonardo da Vinci** is the Italian master's only painting outside Europe. The grand spaces inside the simple Neoclassical exterior (a Pope characteristic) serve as stage settings for the art; the Pantheon-like rotunda, complete with an oculus and marble trim from quarries in the US and abroad, is particularly majestic.

Across the **National Gallery Plaza**, connected by an underground concourse, is the **East Building** (1978, **I.M. Pei & Partners**), where visitors will find more than a sampling of 20th-century art, including **Alexander Calder**'s last major mobile, *Untitled*, and **Joan Miró**'s dramatic tapestry *Woman*. **Henry Moore**'s ever-changing sculpture, *Knife Edge Mirror Two Piece*, is stationed outside at the entrance portico. The East Building also showcases temporary exhibitions throughout the year.

One of the best modern buildings in the city, its twin triangles fit together to fill the oddly shaped site, leaving only a narrow greenbelt around the perimeter. The old quarry in Tennessee that provided the stone for the West Building's exterior was reopened for this project; Pei carefully designed the new gallery to blend with the mathematical harmonies of the older one—height, color, even the size of the marble blocks reflect the example of the West Building. Inside, the gallery spaces are strong and dramatic, and the roofline is a wonderland of space frames and towers.

Sunday lectures, given in the East Building auditorium at 4PM, feature art historians discussing their own research or part of the

collection. Sunday evening concerts, performed by the **National Gallery Orchestra** or guest artists, are free and begin at 7PM (seating begins at 6PM) in the **East Garden Court** of the West Building (no concerts in July, August, or September). *Tour of the Week* takes an in-depth look at one type of painting or special exhibition; check at the **Information Desk** to see if the tour begins in the East or West Building. *Collection Highlights* is a 15-minute lecture on a particular work. Foreign language tours (in up to 12 languages) are offered the first Tuesday of each month. Art documentaries and an adventurous program

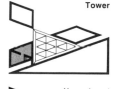

Tower

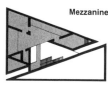

Upper Level

A North Italian
    Renaissance
B 17/18C Italian
C Central Italian
    Renaissance
D Spanish
E Flemish/German
F Dutch
G British
H American
I 19C French
J Rotunda
K 17/18C French
L Sculpture/Decorative
M Prints/Drawings
N Central Gallery
O Garden Cafe
P Bookshop
Q Cafe/Buffet
R 4th St Plaza
S Terrace Cafe

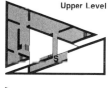

Mezzanine

Main Floor

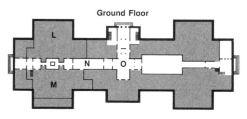

Ground Floor

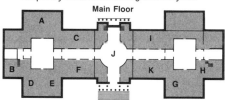

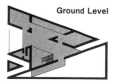

Ground Level

Concourse

R

Concourse Level

"You will find no justification in any of the language of the Constitution for delay in the reforms which the mass of the American people demand now."
Franklin Delano Roosevelt

of feature films are screened, free, in the 300-seat theater, just inside the Constitution Ave entrance of the West Building.

For inexpensive postcards or poster reproductions of works by artists from **Leonardo** to **Picasso**, the **National Gallery Bookstores** are incomparable. An excellent collection of art books is available at both the shop in the West Building and the newer one near the **Cascade Cafe** in the East Building. ◆ Free. Gallery: M-Sa 10AM-5PM; Su noon-9PM. Introductory tours meet at main floor entrance. West Bldg: M-Sa 3PM; Su 5:30PM. East Bldg: M-Sa 11:30AM; Su 12:30PM. Tour of the Week Tu-Su 1PM. Collection Highlights: Tu-Sa noon; Su 2PM. West Building: 6th St NW (Constitution-Madi-

The Mall

son Drs) East Building: 4th St NW (Constitution-Madison Drs) Metro stops: Archives, Smithsonian. 737.4215, foreign language tours and tours for 15 or more 842.6246 &

Smithsonian Outreach

The **Smithsonian's Traveling Exhibition Service (SITES)**, located in the Quadrangle, is one of that institution's least visible, most valuable services. Every year it circulates over a hundred exhibitions, ranging from wine labels and shopping bags to the treasures of Hollywood and ancient Syria, to museums across the US and abroad. For information on current offerings, call 357.3168.

A major resource for Washington residents is the **Smithsonian Resident Associate** program of lectures, educational courses, and tours. And everyone, no matter where he or she lives, can become a national member of the Smithsonian, receive its magazine, and enjoy eating in the Gothic splendor of the Castle's Commons. Membership information 357.3030.

Jacqueline Kennedy, on her first night in the White House: "I felt like a moth hanging on a windowpane."

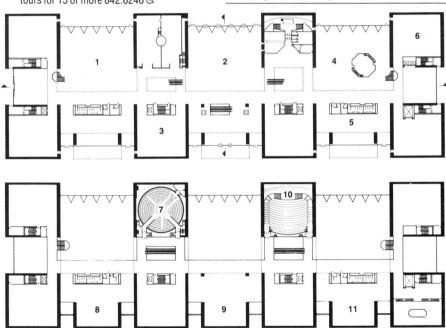

First Floor
1 Air Transportation
2 Milestones of Flight
3 Early Flight
4 Space Hall
5 Satellites
6 Rocketry and
  Space Flight

Second Floor
7 Spacearium
8 Balloons and Airships
9 Pioneers of Flight
10 Theater
11 Apollo to the Moon

Enola Gay, the plane that dropped the first atomic bomb on Hiroshima, can be seen at the Smithsonian's airplane repair shop in Suitland MD.

The portrait of **George Washington** in the East Room of the White House is one of several painted by **Gilbert Stuart**. If you look closely, you'll notice that one of the books near Washington is entitled *Constitution and Laws of the United Sates.* It seems Stuart had trouble spelling.

23 The National Air and Space Museum
(1976, Hellmuth, Obata & Kassabaum) One of the world's most popular museums, and with good reason. Here in 23 exhibition areas are reminders of the finest hours of aviation and space flight: the **Wright Brothers'** 1903 *Flyer*, **Goddard**'s early rockets; **Lindbergh**'s *Spirit of St. Louis*; **Amelia Earhart**'s *Vega*, which she used for a record-setting transatlantic solo flight; **Chuck Yeager**'s *Bell X-1*; the *Mercury Friendship 7*; the *Apollo 11* command module *Columbia*; the 1986 *Voyager*, a flying fuel tank piloted by **Dick Rutan** and **Jeana Yeager**; which flew around the world nonstop in just hours short of 9 days; and, as a fanciful tribute, the original model of the *USS Enterprise* from *Star Trek*. And that's just the beginning. You can also touch a moon rock, see simulated

landings on an aircraft carrier deck, and walk through *Skylab*.

One of the highlights of the museum is the **Langley Theater**'s *IMAX*® film projection system, with a 5-story-high screen. *To Fly*, a 30-minute film voted the *Best Film of the 1970s* by the **Independent Film Producers of America**, is so realistic your stomach may churn. The movie alternates with four others: *Living Planet*, an aerial tour over five continents; *Flyers*, the story of a young pilot and his mentor; *The Dream Is Alive*, about the space shuttle; and *On the Wind*, which compares man-made and natural flight. Showings are continuous. Tickets are available on the day of performance, and often sell out during the busy tourist season. The museum's striking glass-and-steel restaurant (1988, Hellmuth, Obata & Kassabaum) is the largest public eatery in the district. It includes the 800-seat **Flight Line** cafeteria on the main floor, serving burgers, homemade pizza, foot-long hot dogs, and salads. The mezzanine-level restaurant, the 180-seat **Wright Place**, serves seasonal specialties running from ceviche to crabcakes and Cobb salad, as well as sandwiches. There are 3 museum shops and a full-service bar. ◆ Free. Museum: daily 10AM-5PM, Jan-June 15, Sep-Dec; daily 9:30AM-7:30PM, June 16-Labor Day. Tours daily 10:15AM and 1PM, departing from the tour desk in Gallery 100. Flight Line daily 10AM-5PM. Wright Place daily 11AM-3PM. Independence Ave at 6th St SW. Metro stop: L'Enfant Plaza. 357.2700 &

It's hard to say, exactly, what the US government owns. No one in the federal government keeps an up-to-date tally of its holdings, and of those assets that are known—or acknowledged—many are vastly underestimated. Bearing this in mind, here is an abbreviated list of items that the government—and that means you—owns outright.

- Over 10,000 nuclear warheads
- 14 elephant skeletons
- The Grand Canyon
- Nearly 1000 guard geese (it costs only $25 per year to maintain a guard goose, as opposed to $50,000 for a trained guard dog and its handler)
- 56 limousines
- 4 million butterflies and moths
- Approximately 50,000 comic books
- Thousands upon thousands of pages reporting UFO sightings between 1947 and 1969
- The Hope Diamond (estimated worth: $16.5 million)
- 3 Beluga whales
- 727 million acres of land (including 80 million acres of national parks)
- John Dillinger's straw hat (he was wearing it when FBI agents gunned him down in Chicago in 1934)

Lincoln's secretary of the treasury, **Salmon P. Chase**, decided that the first US legal tender banknotes should be green.

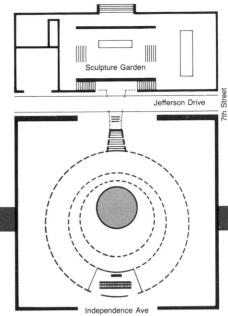

Sculpture Garden

Jefferson Drive

7th Street

Independence Ave

24 Hirshhorn Museum and Sculpture Garden

(1974, Gordon Bunshaft/Skidmore, Owings & Merrill) For the modern art enthusiast, this is the stuff of which dreams are made. The museum is, in fact, the dream child of American immigrant and self-made millionaire **Joseph Hirshhorn**. The industrialist spent over 40 years indulging his love of art and championing the cause of many yet-to-be-discovered American artists at a time when most Americans still looked to Europe for artistic legitimacy.

At its premiere, the Hirshhorn collection consisted of over 6000 items, including some 2000 pieces of sculpture, and was estimated to be worth at least $50 million. Under the Smithsonian's guidance, the collection has continued to grow and now boasts works by such sculptors as **Auguste Rodin**, **Constantin Brancusi**, **David Smith**, **Alexander Calder**, and **Henry Moore**. The museum's 19th- and 20th-century painters include such notables as **Winslow Homer**, **Thomas Eakins**, **Jean Dubuffet**, **Josef Albers**, **Georgia O'Keeffe**, **Andy Warhol**, **Anselm Kiefer**, **Kenneth Noland**, and **Jackson Pollock**, to name just a few. The Hirshhorn also mounts several major loan exhibitions each year, concentrating on a particular artist, medium, style, or theme.

The controversial doughnut-shaped building (all the circular forms look concentric, but they're actually very slightly off-center) was designed to maximize wall space while minimizing sun damage to the art. Hence, there are no exterior windows, but the third-floor balcony offers a breathtaking view.

Be sure to spend at least a few moments in the sunken garden adjacent to the museum: the terraces, reflecting pool, and works by master sculptors make it one of the city's most evocative settings. One of the most rewarding stops in the sculpture garden is Rodin's *Burghers of Calais*. This haunting piece dramatizes the moment when the town fathers of Calais, France, gave themselves up to British invaders so that their town might be saved. The 6 proud, anguished men wear nooses around their necks as they prepare to hand over the keys to the city. Thursday and Friday evenings the Hirshhorn sponsors independently produced film shorts that represent the best work of local, national, and international filmmakers (free, held from September to June). Special tour arrangements can be made by calling at least 2 weeks in advance. No baby strollers are allowed in the galleries—exchange them for infant backpacks loaned at the checkroom. Stop by the museum shop. ◆ Daily 10AM-5:30PM. Free walk-in guided tours: M-Sa 10:30AM, noon, 1:30PM;

The Mall

Su 12:30, 1:30, 2:30 and 3:30PM. Outdoor cafeteria hours vary seasonally; call for schedule. Independence Ave at 7th St SW. Metro stop: L'Enfant Plaza. 357.2700; special tours, film and lecture schedule 357.3235

25 U.S. Botanic Gardens (1902, Bennett, Parsons & Frost) The 19th-century greenhouse style, epitomized by Syon and Kew Gardens in England, lives on in this tropical mall retreat. This cast-iron-and-glass Victorian novelty houses ferns, succulents, cacti, orchids, palms, cycads, and other botanical collections. It also provides plants to Congressional offices. Group tours available; call for information. ◆ Free. Daily 9AM-5PM; June-August 9AM-9PM. 1st St SW (Independence-Maryland Aves) Metro Stop: Federal Center. 225.8333 &

26 Bartholdi Fountain (1878, Frederic Bartholdi) This 1500-pound cast-iron extravaganza was a prize-winner at the 1876 *Centennial Exposition*. Three colossal women hold up the main basin, which is rimmed with fanciful electric lamps. One of the first public displays of electric illumination, the fountain was a big hit with turn-of-the-century audiences. Bartholdi also gave us the *Statue of Liberty*. ◆ Independence Ave SW (1st St-Canal Ave) Metro Stop: Federal Center.

27 Hubert H. Humphrey Building (Department of Health & Human Services) (1976, Marcel Breuer) A vigorous and energetic design, often compared favorably to Breuer's nearby **HUD** building. The carbon monoxide funnels for I-395 (which runs under Capitol Hill) are incorporated into the structure, so the building sometimes appears to smoke. ◆ Independence Ave SW (2nd-3rd Sts) Metro Stop: Federal Center.

The **Old Executive Office Building** next to the White House still bears traces of **General Douglas MacArthur**. To lighten the facade of the colossal structure, MacArthur placed stone planters with flowers and shrubs in parallel rows from the north steps down to Pennsylvania Avenue. Although this former State, War, and Navy Department building has a new name, the planters stand as a memorial to the great general.

Restaurants: Red	**Hotels**: Blue
Shops/Parks: Green	**Sights/Culture**: Black

28 Voice of America This government-run radio station broadcasts news, culture, and information about the US through more than 112 overseas and North American transmitters. VOA announcers perform in 44 languages: you may hear broadcasts in Bengali, Slovak, Urdu, or Albanian, depending on the time of day. Tours explain the role of the VOA and its parent organization, the US Information Agency. ◆ Free. 45-minute tours M-F, except holidays, 8:40, 9:40, 10:40AM, 1:40, 2:40PM. 330 Independence Ave SW (entrance on C St, 3rd-4th Sts) Reservations required; groups limited to 25. Metro stop: Federal Center SW. 485.6231

29 Vie De France Café ★$ Domestic concept of French—fast and furious. Emphasis on baked goods and buttery croissants in the self-service section; the café has a variety of sandwiches, omelets, and pseudo-Gallic specials. Perfect for breakfast or a quick lunch. ◆ French ◆ Self-service and bakery: M-F 7:30AM-7PM; Sa 9AM-4PM. Café M-F 11:30AM-9PM. 600 Maryland Ave SW (7th St)

30 Market Inn ★$$ Settle into the noisy music-filled dining room, or opt for a darker, quieter booth in the bar. Then choose from a huge selection of fresh seafood, homemade soups, and other entrees. ◆ Seafood ◆ M-F 11AM-1AM; Sa 10:30AM-1AM; Su 10:30AM-midnight. 200 E St SW (2nd St) Reservations recommended. Metro stop: Federal Center SW. 554.2100

30 Potomac Butter & Egg Co. Inc This food warehouse, open to the public, is the place to go to stock up for parties. Items include bulk cheeses at discount prices, eggs, wines and liquor, bulk spices, crackers, frozen foods, and miscellany. ◆ M-F 6AM-2:30PM; Sa 8:30AM-2PM. 220 E St SW (2nd St) Metro stop: Federal Center SW. 554.9200

31 Department of Transportation (Nassif Building) Edward Durell Stone's insistent vertical lines and thin slab roof, rendered this time in Carrara marble. The building was privately built and is leased to the Federal Government. ◆ 400 7th St SW (D St) Metro Stop: Federal Center

32 Department of Housing and Urban Development (1983, Marcel Breuer) The grid pattern in the beige concrete exterior walls is relentless, despite the open ground floor. The unique double-Y layout (also used in Breuer's design for the NATO building in Paris) improves circulation within the building and helps minimize the alienation of endless miles of office corridors. ◆ 451 7th St SW (D St) Metro Stop: Federal Center

33 Loews L'Enfant Plaza Hotel $$$ This 4-star hostelry with spacious contemporary rooms and suites is popular with both sightseers and convention-goers. **Club 480** offers VIP service, including express check-in and -out, concierge service, a meeting parlor—and even fresh fruit, cheeses, and Godiva chocolates waiting in your suite. Special convention/business accommodations include meeting and banquet rooms, catering, and audiovisual services. There is a state-of-the-art health club and a rooftop swimming pool. Ask about weekender specials. The **Apple of Eve** restaurant and the **Greenhouse** café offer in-hotel refreshment. One flight below the hotel lobby is the **L'Enfant Plaza** shopping promenade—more than 50 shops (from **Hallmark Cards** to **Fannie Mae Candies**) and services (including cleaners, beauticians, post office, bank, and a copy center). Deli snack and café foods are also available. Children under 14 stay free. ♦ Deluxe ♦ 480 L'Enfant Plaza SW. Metro stop: L'Enfant Plaza. 484.1000; fax 646.4456 ♿

33 L'Enfant Plaza (1966, I.M. Pei) Acres of red granite were to be the soil of a garden of urban delights watered by a splashing fountain; so far, nothing's grown. The surrounding office buildings are badly placed, and all the shopping action is below plaza level. One of the few highlights is the US Postal Service's **Philatelic Sales Center**, located on the ground floor of its West Building. Another is the yellow glow of the plaza's trademark globe lamps. ♦ Frontage Rd-D St SW (L'Enfant Promenade) Metro Stop: L'Enfant Plaza

34 The Fish Market turns its share of noses on hot summer days, but locals swear by it for freshly caught and reasonably priced bounty trucked in from the Chesapeake Bay and the lower Potomac and Delaware rivers. Fish peddlers by the dozens set up shop along the Potomac's edge, some off the back of their boats, selling bushels of blue crabs, rockfish, oysters, shrimp, almost anything edible that swims in the region's waters. ♦ Maine Ave SW near 14th St Bridge. Metro stop: L'Enfant Plaza

35 Le Rivage ★★$$$ A bright spot on the all-too-pedestrian waterfront dining scene, specializing in fresh seafood served in an innovative French format: fresh trout stuffed with smoked salmon mousse and double breast of chicken stuffed with crabmeat are two creative dishes. Prix fixe pretheater menu 5:30-6:30PM. ♦ French ♦ M-Th 11:30AM-2:30PM, 5:30-11PM, F 11:30AM-2:30PM, 5:30-11:30PM; Sa 5:30-11:30PM; Su 5-9PM. 1000 Water St SW. Reservations recommended. Metro stop: L'Enfant Plaza. 488.8111

36 Hogate's ★ $$ The traditional seafood menu is unspectacular, but Hogate's waterview bar is popular with the upscale professional set after work; a deejay provides music. Raw bar Monday through Saturday evenings. ♦ Seafood ♦ M-Sa 11AM-midnight; Su 10:30AM-10PM. 900 Maine Ave SW (9th St). Reservations recommended. Metro stop: L'Enfant Plaza. 484.6300

37 El Torito ★ $$ All-you-can-eat taco happy hour draws in the after-work crowd from the EPA and other nearby government agencies. The lunch and dinner menus feature standard versions of Tex-Mex favorites. ♦ Tex-Mex ♦ M-Th, Su 11AM-10PM; F-Sa 11AM-11PM. 700 Water St SW (7th-9th Sts) Reservations recommended. Metro stop: L'Enfant Plaza. 554.5302

37 700 Water Street ★★$$$ The casual setting features 4 fireplaces and waterfront seating. Black Angus beef (a special breed with leaner meat) is used for the steaks and prime ribs, and more than 15 fish dishes are offered daily. Desserts are homemade. ♦ American ♦ M-F 11:30AM-2:30PM, 5-11PM; Sa 4-11PM; Su 10AM-2:30PM, 5-10PM. 700 Water St SW (7th-9th Sts) Reservations recommended. Metro stop: L'Enfant Plaza. 554.7320

38 Channel Inn $$ This is DC's only waterside hotel, in the midst of the Washington Channel

strip of restaurants. All rooms have balconies. The **Pier 7** restaurant specializes in seafood, including Maryland crab dishes. Live entertainment in the **Engine Room** lounge. Outdoor swimming pool. Children under 12 stay free. ♦ 650 Water St SW (6th-7thSts). Metro stop: L'Enfant Plaza. 554.2400, 800/368.5668

Unseen DC

Jeanne Fogle, a fourth-generation Washingtonian, knows her Capital City. After all, her great-grandfather, **George F.W. Streiby**, painted some of the frescoes in the Capitol. She specializes in tours of offbeat Washington—the oldest known Otis elevator, perhaps (Litwin Furniture, 637 Indiana Ave NW), or the site of **Alexander Graham Bell**'s first telephone call (the Franklin School, 13th and K Sts NW). Her list of intriguing capital sights includes:

Largest Roman columns in the world, Old Pension Building, 4th and F Sts NW.

Oldest house on Capitol Hill (1680), and the only site of opposition to the British raid in 1814, Sewall-Belmont House, 114 Constitution Ave NE.

Only district statue of a Confederate general, Brig. Gen. Albert Pike, 3rd and D Sts NW.

First outdoor use of electric lights, Bartholdi Fountain (1876), 1st St and Independence Ave NW

Largest Chinese archway in the world, Friendship Arch (1986), 7th and H Sts NW in Chinatown.

Boy Scout Memorial (1964), a scout with 2 huge classical figures, American Manhood and American Womanhood, the Ellipse, 15th St and Constitution Ave NW.

FDR Memorial, a block of marble "no bigger than his desk," just as he wished, outside the National Archives, 9th St and Pennsylvania Ave NW.

Fogle conducts small-group walking tours of offbeat Washington as part of the *Smithsonian Resident Associate Program* and by appointment. For further information, call **A Tour de Force**. 703/525.2948

38 The Gangplank ★$$ The best waterfront restaurant for sunset-watching over the marina features American seafood fare on a floating barge. ♦ Seafood ♦ M-Th, Su 11:30AM-10PM; F-Sa 11:30AM-11PM. 600 Water St SW (6th-7thSts) Reservations recommended. Metro stop: L'Enfant Plaza. 554.5000

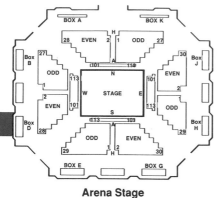

Arena Stage

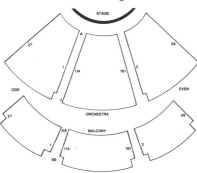

Kreeger Theater

39 Arena Stage and Kreeger Theater (1961 and 1970, Harry Weese) From its first production in 1950 in a former burlesque house, **Arena Stage** has grown into one of the nation's best regional theaters. Cofounder and producing director **Zelda Fichandler** has brought plays such as *The Great White Hope*, *The Gospel at Colonus*, and *Tartuffe* to the Arena. The Arena is a theater in the round, while the Kreeger is a proscenium stage. The **Old Vat Room** is a cabaret-style theater that features **Stephen Wade**, who has been charming audiences since 1983 with his tall tales and self-mocking songs. Saturday morning tours of theaters and offices are available. ♦ Seats: 800, 500, 180. Box office: M, Su noon-7PM; Tu-Sa 10AM-7PM. 6th and Maine Sts SW. 554.9066, box offices 488.3300

40 The Spirit of Washington As rivers go, the Potomac is not an extensively traveled one, but it is still possible to sightsee its quaint shoreline by taking a summertime cruise. The *Spirit of Washington*, a 145-foot cruiser that holds up to 450, travels past Alexandria, Fort Washington, Fort McNair, and Washington National Airport. All cruises feature live entertainment. ♦ Pier 4 (6th and Water Sts SW) 554.8000, departures and ticket rates 554.1542

41 Thomas Law House (1796, William Lovering) A classic 3-story Federal-style house, now used as a community center. ♦ 1252 6th St SW (N St)

42 Wheat Row (1790, William Lovering; restored 1966) Located in the shadow of the successful Harbor Square urban renewal project, Wheat Row is considered one of the best examples of the Federal style within DC. ♦ 1313-1321 4th St SW (N-O Sts)

43 Titanic Memorial (1931, Gertrude Vanderbilt Whitney) Sculpted in memory of the men who gave up their places in the lifeboats when the historic ocean liner sank. A granite figure stands with arms outstretched in the shape of a cross. The sculptor's own brother went down in 1915 when the *Lusitania* was sunk by the Kaiser's Navy. ♦ Washington Channel Park, 4th and P Sts SW

44 Fort Lesley J. McNair Over the years, the name and function of this strategic military post have changed. In 1791, it was planned by L'Enfant as the main fortification point of the capital. As the **Washington Arsenal**, the fort was a major distribution center for government hand weapons and cannon in the early 1800s. Immediately after the 1814 *Battle of Bladensburg*, the British invaded the fort, only to lose 40 of their own men when a supply of gunpowder accidentally exploded. Discouraged, the British left the ruined fort. The arsenal continued to store and also produce weapons. By the time of the Civil War, the fort contained more than 800 cannon, 50,000 rifles, and hundreds of gun carriages. One more explosion was needed before the government deemed the arsenal unsafe: in 1864, an ignited rocket in a row of fireworks killed or maimed over 100 women who were making rifle cartridges in the laboratory. The fort served as a warehouse and a small hospital until the **Army War College** (1908, **McKim, Mead & White**) was built on the mile-long peninsula. Later fused with the **Industrial College of the Armed Forces**, the college is still housed in its original, disciplined Beaux-Arts structure under the name of the **National Defense University**. The Inter-American Defense College and the headquarters of the US Army Military District of Washington are right next door; the Romanesque barracks and more sumptuous officers quarters add a graceful note to the military primness. Although the buildings are not open to the public, a few outside cannons and old soldiers quarters have been preserved, making the beautiful grounds well worth a visit. ♦ Grounds open daily dawn to dusk. Must present ID at gate. 4th and P Sts SW. 475.1782

45 The East Side Warehouse-turned-music-club, with live rock and New Wave bands upstairs, dancing to recorded music downstairs. ♦ W-Th 9PM-2AM; F-Sa 11PM-5AM; Su hours vary. 1824 Half St SW (T St) 488.1205

"Associate yourself with men of good quality if you esteem your own reputation; for 'tis better to be alone than in bad company."

George Washington
Rules of Civility

Pick up a starfish and watch the Beluga whales eat lunch at the **National Aquarium in Baltimore** (page 167).

Grind corn with the miller and George, the stuffed goose at **Pierce Mill** (page 137), a working 19th-century flour mill in **Rock Creek Park**.

Make friends with a computer, learn Morse code, and drive a "bus" in a museum created just for kids, the **Capital Children's Museum** (page 22).

Pet the animals at **Oxon Hill Farm** (page 148), a working replica of a turn-of-the-century farm, and at **Claude Moore Colonial Farm** (page 188), an 18th-century farm with a 1-room log cabin.

Listen as authors read their stories out loud at the **Cheshire Cat Bookstore** (page 136) and the **Noyes Children's Library** (page 145).

Ride the antique carousel in front of the **Arts & Industries Building** (page 49).

Climb on *The Awakening*, a giant-size sculpture of a giant clawing his way out of the earth, at **Hains Point** in **East Potomac Park** (page 41).

DC for Kids

Paddle a canoe or ride in a canal boat on the **C&O Canal** (page 123).

Watch a live theatrical performance especially for kids at the **Discovery Theater, Arts & Industries Building** (page 49).

Hike through the wilds of **Rock Creek Park** with a trained naturalist (page 137).

Try on a set of real antlers and other animal accouterments at the **National Zoo**'s **Zoolab** (page 139).

Touch creepy-crawly things from the world of nature at the **Discovery Room** and the **Insect Zoo**, both at the **Museum of Natural History** (page 52).

Roger G. Kennedy

Director, Smithsonian's National Museum of
American History

There is a great satisfaction in seeing people respond to the variety and range of artifacts in a museum. Several exhibitions here come to mind as standouts. Visitors react in delight to the panorama of objects in *A Material World*, like the ultramodern and high-tech *Swamp Rat* dragster, the 1912 Liberty Brush automobile, and a simple yet elegant American Beauty iron.

Field to Factory presents the point of view of black Americans who experienced the move from the South to the promise of a better life in the North shortly after the turn of this century. In one sense, it is an exhibi-

Bests

tion about families, and therefore it attracts visits from families.

The same thing can be said about our bicentennial exhibition relating the experiences of Japanese-Americans who were interned during World War II. With many of our visitors, you can almost sense the kinds of memories and feelings that are provoked by the anti-Japanese propaganda of the times, the recreated internment barracks, and the armed guards overlooking the camp.

Although the Foucault Pendulum's location has been changed to the second floor, it has not lost its place as one of the most fascinating exhibitions to both the young and the not-so-young visitors.

There is nothing, perhaps, any more moving than the display encasing the flag that inspired Francis Scott Key to write *The Star-Spangled Banner*. Visitors are riveted to attention at the roll of the drumbeat signaling the unveiling of the flag as the national anthem is played.

The elegance and individuality of the First Ladies, as represented by the gowns on display in a period room setting. Each conveys a style that evokes a time and era in our political history.

The hum and rhythm of the Howe Pinmaking machine, one of the pieces of 19th-century machinery in the *Engines of Change* exhibition, which conveys to visitors—through sight and sound—a strong sense of this country's industrial revolution period.

Listening to live performances of songs composed by some of this country's greatest composers of jazz and popular music in the museum's Palm Court with its turn-of-the-century interior. Historically, such places were designed for relaxation. This airy gathering spot is enhanced by a Horn and Hardart Automat from about 1902 and by the interior of Stohlman's Confectionery Shop from when it was located in Georgetown.

The diversity of the people explored in the exhibition *After the Revolution: Everyday Life in America 1700–1800*. Many were farmers, some were merchants, a few were rich, and many were poor. Together they were the first generation of people in this country, and the way they lived is captured in various ways.

The **first book published** by the Smithsonian Institution Press in 1848 was *Ancient Monuments of the Mississippi Valley*, by **E.G. Squires** and **E.H. Davis**.

Lois Craig

Associate Dean, School of Architecture and Planning,
Massachusetts Institute of Technology

I lived in that city for some 25 years, so in a way I know too much. At first the obvious buildings came to mind, the foreground city of official Washington with its high steps, gray colonnades, and long vistas. There is, of course, another Washington of residences, of lavish greenery, and of a fair share of urban problems, design and otherwise. And there is the city that Henry James called, "the city of Conversation." This last city can be put together in the mind's eye only over time and in many places, private and public.

Finally I decided that the advantage of long domicile is the possibility of sharing with visitors a knowledge of mostly accessible but hidden places, places behind or beyond the postcard views. So I selected mostly *inside* places:

Elizabethan Theater of the Folger Shakespeare Library

Whistler's Peacock Room at the Freer Gallery

Main Reading Room at the Library of Congress

Old house of the Phillips Collection and its drawing room for a Sunday afternoon concert

Great Hall of the Old Pension Building [now the National Building Museum]

Members Dining Room at the Smithsonian Castle (worth finding a member for the star-studded ceiling)

Exhibition Hall of the Arts and Industries Building

Model Room of the National Portrait Gallery

Lincoln Room of the National Museum of American Art

Second floor of the Renwick Gallery

Interdepartmental auditorium of the Arena Stage for a performance

Rooftop lounge of the Washington Hotel in the summer for a special view of the monumental city

Metro subway stations, especially one with a long descent—e.g. at Dupont Circle

National Cathedral for Christmas Eve service or Sunday vespers

Interiors of Old State War & Navy Building (Old Executive Office Building) and of the Department of Justice

Dumbarton Oaks Pre-Columbian Museum

The last entry is part of my favorite place-full-of-places, where I often walk, to read, to look, to meet friends, to watch children. Between 30th and 32nd at R Streets NW, one finds Oak Hill Cemetery with its old gatehouse and Renwick Chapel; Montrose Park with its rolling English landscape; Lovers Lane, which leads to Dumbarton Oaks Park, a walking park particularly beautiful in the spring when the narcissus are in bloom; Dumbarton Oaks House and Gardens, particularly notable for its formal gardens but also for its Byzantine and Pre-Columbian art collection, the latter housed in the contemporary jewel box of the Pre-Columbian Museum, located in a wooded corner of the grounds. The foregoing complex is bordered by 2 special Washington places—by Georgetown with its residential streets and courtyard gardens that recall the Southern city; and by Rock Creek Park, which winds through Northwest Washington and yields its own special spots for picnicking and hiking as well as the National Zoo with its collection of fanciful animal houses.

Walter J. Boyne

Former Director, National Air and Space Museum

The look of senior citizens as they touch a rock brought back from the surface of the moon—it seems to mean more to them than it does to a schoolchild, to whom the idea of space travel is commonplace.

The juxtaposition of the Wright Flyer of 1903, the very first airplane in the world, just 30 feet in distance and 66 years in time from the Apollo 11 spacecraft *Columbia*, in which Armstrong, Aldrin, and Collins went to and from the moon.

The sense of understanding that people seem to have in looking at Lindbergh's *Spirit of St. Louis*; there is awe at the bravery of his 33-hour flight across the Atlantic from New York to Paris, as well as a sense that, unlike the spacecraft, the *Spirit* would be an achievable thing to master.

The care with which the handicapped are attended to. There are ramps, wheelchairs, elevator service to all floors, accessible restrooms and water fountains, material for the sight- or hearing-impaired, plus a very courteous guard force and docent staff who enjoy being of assistance.

Walking through *Skylab*, the Orbital Workshop that was really America's first space station, its gold-covered exterior reflecting the crowds waiting to pass through.

Looking across an upper gallery, through the *Gossamer Condor*, the first successful manned aircraft, which is covered in transparent Mylar, past the *Pioneer 10*, the first man-made object to leave the solar system, to the orange and white *Bell X-1* in which Chuck Yeager demonstrated the right stuff in breaking the sound barrier.

Looking upward at the suspended aircraft through the glass-bubbled roof; the movement outside of the clouds imparts an illusion of movement even to the fully equipped *Douglas DC-3*, which, like all the other aircraft, sways gently in the breeze.

Strolling through the jet-age gallery, past lethal-looking jet fighters, into the theater where a section from Sid Caesar and Imogene Coca's *Your Show of Shows* depicts Sid "busting the sound barrier."

Listening to the dads explain to the kids how they flew this or that aircraft "during the big war."

Bending down to look through the sighting holes in the exhibition on Stonehenge.

Walking along the galleries and hearing the polyglot mixture of comments; seeing that children and adults from all over the world react with the same sense of humanity to the triumphs of modern technology.

Delving into the backgrounds of the various artifacts and realizing that they all proceed from the same central source of human invention and that they are all expressions of human dreams.

Going up to the library on the third floor to do research in one of the greatest collections of aviation documentary material in the world.

Taking the short ride out to Silver Hill, the Paul E. Garber Facility where Cellini-like artisans restore 70-year-old aircraft that are little more than *basket cases* to perfection.

Marion Barry, Jr.

Mayor, Washington DC

Our great sports teams: Redskins, Bullets, Capitals, Firebirds, and Hoyas

The Washington Convention Center in the middle of Downtown, which opened on budget and on schedule.

Our new Downtown, particularly the new developments of Pennsylvania Avenue.

The fifth of Washington that is all park.

The many flavors of Washington, particularly seafood and barbecue.

The diversity of our people: a multiethnic, multiracial, multinational hometown.

Bests

Our New Year's Eve celebration at the Old Post Office on Pennsylvania Avenue—an evening of free entertainment and hometown spirit.

The cleanest, most efficient Metro system in the country.

Our Potomac Riverfest celebrating the cleanness and beauty of a great and lovely river.

Our many historical and livable neighborhoods, all just minutes away from the heart of the nation.

J. Carter Brown

Director, National Gallery of Art

Duccio	*Nativity* *The Calling of the Apostles Peter and Andrew*
Fra Angelico	*The Adoration of the Magi* (with Fra Filippo Lippi)
Leonardo da Vinci	*Ginevra de' Benci*
Raphael	*The Alba Madonna*
Bellini	*The Feast of the Gods*
Giorgione	*The Adoration of the Shepherds*
Titian	*Venus with a Mirror*
van Eyck	*The Annunciation*
El Greco	*Laocoön*
Rembrandt	*The Mill* *Self-Portrait*
Vermeer	*The Girl with a Red Hat*
Fragonard	*A Young Girl Reading*
David	*Napoleon in His Study*
Turner	*Keelmen Heaving in Coals by Moonlight*
Stuart	*The Skater (William Grant)*
Cole	*The Voyage of Life*
Whistler	*The White Girl*
Manet	*Gare Saint-Lazare*
Monet	*The Artist's Garden at Vetheuil*
Renoir	*A Girl with a Watering Can*
Gauguin	*Self-Portrait*
Degas	*Four Dancers*

Foggy Bottom
West End

Decatur

Q

P

O

N

Georgetown/
Upper NW

Adams-Morgan/
Dupont Circle

M Dupont
Circle

Massachusetts Av

Connecticut Ave

Rhode Island Av

25

22 23 24

21

20

New Hampshire Ave

26

M

19

25th

24th

23rd

22nd

L

M Farragut
North

18

27

K

Downtown

7th

28

15

32

I

M Far
We

16

M Foggy
Bottom

30 31 33

H

Pennsylvania Ave

14

17

29

H

13

34

G

12

21st

F

20th

19th

18th

35 36

37

17th

2

1

E

E 3

D

5

11

C

4 7 6

10 9

Virginia Ave

8

Constitution Ave

The Mall

Potomac River

Arlington Memorial Bridge

Independence Ave

Tidal Basin

Downtown Washington's southwestern corner, composed of **Foggy Bottom** and the **West End**, has a little of everything: the offices and shops of Pennsylvania Avenue NW; the **State Department** and the **Department of the Interior**; the ceremonial expanse of Constitution Avenue, with the **Federal Reserve** and other imposing public structures; the bustle surrounding the **Kennedy Center** and the **Watergate** complex; the student hubbub at **George Washington University**; and the slick new hotels and restaurants of the formerly somnolent West End.

Foggy Bottom refers not to the keen insights of State Department diplomats but to the swampy precincts that once festered where the northern boundary of the Mall now lies—much of that area is landfill. Its higher ground was at one time one of the city's oldest residential neighborhoods. **Dolley Madison** once lived here in the **Octagon House**. Almost all the other Colonial-era houses are gone now, replaced by modern office buildings. Yet the area is graced by a number of elegant public buildings, including the Neoclassical **Corcoran Gallery of Art** on 17th St NW, and the nearby **Organization of American States** and **Constitution Hall**.

The Federal Reserve and the **National Academy of Sciences** add pomp to Constitution Ave, which was known as lowly *B Street* until 1931. The State Department's otherwise bland building hides a treasure-trove in its **Diplomatic Reception** rooms, appointed with exquisite examples of 18th- and early 19th-century American art and furniture.

By the 1950s, the neighborhood west of 21st Street NW had become one of the city's worst slums and was one of the first on the list for the bold experiment of urban renewal. The drab concrete apartment buildings here testify to the mixed success of the effort. Along the river, the old **Heurich Brewery** was razed, and the Kennedy Center and the Watergate complex rose in its stead.

North of **Washington Circle**, the residential West End, wedged in between New Hampshire Ave NW and Rock Creek Park, has become newly chic, with a half-dozen elegant hotels and attendant restaurants—an outpost of Georgetown, just across the park.

1 Corcoran Gallery of Art (1897, Ernest Flagg; Clark Wing, 1927, Charles Platt) This collection of American artworks is one of the oldest in the country and is an excellent survey of native talent. Early portraiture, primitives, the Hudson River School, American Impressionism, Abstract Expressionism, the Ashcan School, Pop, and Minimalism—all are represented. In addition, 2 substantial bequests have given the Corcoran a small but impressive collection of European masters, including works by **Degas**, **Rubens**, **Rembrandt**, **Renoir**, and **Millet**.

It's easy to forget that the Corcoran is a privately funded museum, not part of the Smithsonian empire. That independence has given it freedom to present some remarkable shows, including works by performance artists and contemporary local artists, many of whom have studied or taught at the **Corcoran Art School**. Banker and art collector **William Wilson Corcoran**'s collection formed the nucleus of today's museum; one of his favorite works, **Hiram Powers**' sculpture *The Greek Slave*, is here. Corcoran commissioned architect **James Renwick** to create a suitable home for his paintings and sculptures, but the collection quickly outgrew that building (today called the **Renwick Gallery**, just north on 17th St NW). Today's Corcoran is essentially Beaux-Arts, but American-influenced, with cleaner lines and massing. It was **Frank Lloyd Wright**'s favorite building in Washington.

West End/Foggy Bottom

The Corcoran Art School was founded along with the gallery, and Corcoran advised students to copy the works in his collection. Student and faculty exhibitions are usually very good. Often in conjunction with exhibitions, the gallery sponsors slide lectures and talks by artists and art historians in the **Frances & Armand Hammer Auditorium**. The *Musical Evening Series* presents chamber music. (One highlight is the **Tokyo String Quartet** playing on the Corcoran's prized **Amati** violins.) The **Gallery Shop** sells books, posters, reprints, and gifts. ◆ Free; admission for selected exhibitions. Tu-W, F-Su 10AM-4:30PM; Th 10AM-9PM. Free half-hour tour of highlights of permanent collection Tu-W, F-Su 12:30PM; Th 12:30 and 7PM; call for further information. 17th St and New York Ave NW. Metro stop: Farragut West. 638.3211 ⓑ

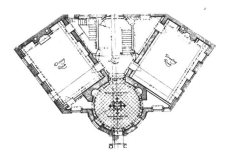

2 Octagon Museum (1798, William Thornton) Originally built as a townhouse for **Colonel John Tayloe**, the Octagon has been the center of many official and private activities. It was spared the British fire that took the White House, and served as **James** and **Dolley Madison**'s home during the fall and winter of 1814–15. It was here that Madison signed the *Treaty of Ghent*, establishing final peace with Great Britain. For several years the building changed hands and deteriorated. It was saved in 1899, when the **American Institute of Architects** took formal possession. Designed by the first architect of the Capitol, William Thornton, the Federal-style Octagon (really a hexagon!) is a successful solution to the site problem posed by radiating streets.

Because Thornton used the best building materials available, the fine restoration currently in evidence was possible. Original Chippendale and Federal-period furniture was placed in the light, high-ceilinged rooms; the cornices of the original English Coade stone mantels were replaced with exact reproductions; and the rescued circular rent table was again placed in Madison's study, believed to be the location of the treaty's signing. In 1949, the AIA moved its headquarters to a new, adjoining building. The allegedly haunted Octagon is now a registered **National Historic Landmark** owned by the AIA Foundation. Tours, including special tours for hearing-impaired persons, available on request. ◆ Admission. Tu-F 10AM-

West End/Foggy Bottom

4PM; Sa-Su noon-4PM. 1799 New York Ave NW (18th St) Metro stop: Farragut West. 638.3105

2 American Institute of Architects Bookstore Just behind the Octagon Museum and across the street from the Corcoran Gallery, this bookstore has all kinds of books relating to architecture: history, construction, design, and graphics, as well as children's books, T-shirts, and mugs. ◆ M-F 8:30AM-5PM. 1735 New York Ave NW (17th-18th Sts) Metro stop: Farragut West. 626.7474

3 Rawlins Garden Don't overlook this dainty park, where seasonal blossoms scent the air and the **National Park Service** provides entertainment—jazz concerts, puppetry, poetry—during warm weather. Two shallow pools offer excellent goldfish-watching on lazy spring days when the tulip-tree magnolia and water lily blooms are fresh. The park was named after **Grant**'s chief of staff and, later, secretary of war. ◆ E St NW (18th-20th Sts) Metro stop: Farragut West

4 The Department of the Interior Museum is as multifaceted as the department itself, encompassing exhibitions that outline the history of the **National Park Service**, wildlife preservation, land management, reclamation, geological survey, and Indian affairs. Indian crafts and artifacts, and old documents such as original land grants and surveys, are on display. ◆ Free. M-F 8:30AM-5PM. Entrance at 18th and C Sts NW. Metro stops: Foggy Bottom, Farragut West. 343.2743

Within the Department of the Interior Museum:

Geological Survey of the US Government Maps and publications. ◆ M-F 8AM-4PM. Entrance at E St NW (18th-19th Sts) Room 2650. 343.8073

Indian Craft Shop Excellent source for jewelry, baskets, blankets, and other handicrafts, all made by Native Americans. ◆ M-F 8:30AM-4:30PM. Entrance at 18th and C Sts NW. 343.4056. Also at: 1050 Wisconsin Ave NW. 342.3918

5 National Red Cross Headquarters Clara Barton organized the US branch of this international service organization in 1881. The centerpiece of its 3-building headquarters is the marble palace (1917, **Trowbridge & Livingston**), which commemorates the women who ministered to Civil War wounded. Historical exhibitions fill the lobbies of all 3 floors: included are a century of Red Cross uniforms and a fascinating collection of recruitment and public service posters. A trio of stained-glass **Tiffany** windows lights the second-floor lobby, and sculptures by such artists as **Hiram Powers** and **Felix de Weldon** decorate the buildings and grounds. To the south of the building, a small garden memorializes Red Cross workers killed in action. From this complex, over 3000 Red Cross chapters are coordinated to offer vital community services ranging from disaster relief and blood banks to children's swimming lessons. ◆ M-F 9AM-4PM. 430 17th St NW (D-E Sts) Metro stop: Farragut West. 737.8300

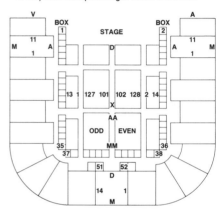

6 DAR Museum/Continental Hall (1910, Edward Pearce Casey) Members of the Daughters of the American Revolution trace their lineages back to the original colonies' fight for independence. The 4-story Memorial Continental Hall—an elaborate Beaux-Arts affair marked by a vast porte-cochere supported by enormous Ionic columns—echoes that same period. Nearly 34 rooms commemorate Colonial America and newer states, including the **Tennessee Room**, with White House furnishings from the Monroe presidency; the **Oklahoma Room**, a crude prairie farm kitchen; and the steamboat parlor in the **Missouri Room**. Children and adults will marvel at the antique toys and dolls in the **New Hampshire Attic**. Children are encouraged to play with hands-on replicas. An excellent collection of Revolutionary War-era artifacts includes silver by **Paul Revere**. Also at Continental Hall is one of the nation's finest genealogical archives (modest charge). Tours offered on a walk-in basis. ◆ Free. Museum: M-F 8:30AM-4PM; Su 1-5PM. Tours: M-F 10AM-2:45PM; Su 1:30-5PM. 1776 D St NW (17th-18th Sts) Metro stop: Farragut West. 628.1776

Washington has more historic places than any other city in the country: 158. In comparison, New York City has 111.

7 Constitution Hall (1930, John Russell Pope) Pope was a master of simple Roman forms, and this building, with its clear circulation patterns and acoustics that **Toscanini** found remarkable, is among his best. It reigned for many years as the city's major concert venue. Now supplanted in popularity by the Kennedy Center, it still attracts noted performers. ♦ Seats 4000. 18th and D Sts NW. Metro stop: Farragut West. 638.2661

8 Organization of American States (1910, Albert Kelsey and Paul Cret) Formerly called the **Pan American Union**, this coalition of the US and 26 Latin American and Caribbean nations was formed in 1948. Its headquarters is one of the capital's most striking Beaux-Arts buildings, rendered in white Georgian marble and black Andean granite. Inside are the **Hall of Heroes and Flags** (as it sounds, a collection of busts and banners) and the **Hall of the Americas**, a grand room with barrel-vaulted ceilings, columns, 3 **Tiffany** chandeliers, and parquet surfaces, that hosts OAS diplomatic soirees and recitals by artists from the member nations. At the building's center are the **Aztec Gardens**, filled with exotic plants such as guavas, banana trees, coffee trees, date plants, breadfruit plants, rubber trees, and cocoa trees. The **Peace Tree**, planted by **President Taft** in 1910, is fig and rubber grafted together, symbolic of the cultural roots of the American continents. The OAS is the oldest political organization with which the US has been associated, and it hosts lectures and symposia on improved trade and relations. Note the statue of **Queen Isabella I** outside the building's entry, a gift from Spain in 1966. Isabella rarely gets the credit she deserves—for financing **Columbus'** serendipitous expedition. Half-hour tours available. ♦ Free. M-F 9AM-5:30PM. Main entrance: 17th St at Constitution Ave NW. Metro stop: Farragut West. 458.3000

At the Organization of American States:

Museum of Modern Art of Latin America A statue of the Aztec god of flowers, *Xochipilli*, overlooks a blue-tiled fountain by **Gertrude Vanderbilt Whitney**. Beyond is this small but excellent collection, the only one of its kind in the world. Off the **Tropical Patio**, a small gift shop is filled with vibrantly colored Latin American arts and crafts. ♦ Tu-Sa 10AM-5PM. 201 18th St NW (C St-Constitution Ave) Metro stop: Farragut West. 458.6016

9 Federal Reserve (1937, Paul Cret) The increasingly ephemeral value of a dollar is set here by the *Fed*, a quasi-public institution charged with controlling the national cash flow, setting interest rates, and regulating the pace of the economy.

The Fed's board generally meets on Wednesdays at 10AM; the meetings are sometimes open to the public. Call 452.2478 for information and the agenda of topics to be discussed. The 45-minute guided tour includes architectural highlights of the Art Deco structure, as well as a 20-minute film, *The Fed: Our Central Bank*, which explains the raison d'être for this vital yet little-understood institution. If you're overwhelmed by the weighty matters at the Fed, slip into the **Federal Reserve Board Gallery**, which features art exhibitions encompassing 19th- and 20th-century painting, sculp-

ture, and works on paper. ♦ Free. Gallery Tu-F 11:30AM-2PM. Guided tours Th 2:30PM; group tours by appointment (recommended for high school age and up). Tours start at the C St guardstation. 20th-21st Sts NW (C St-Constitution Ave) Metro stop: Foggy Bottom. 452.3000, tour information 452.3149

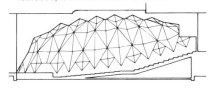

10 National Academy of Sciences (1924, Bertram G. Goodhue) Chartered under **President Lincoln** to provide an honorary society for scientists and an advisory panel for the government. As scientific knowledge exploded in the 20th century, a larger group. the **National Research Council**, was needed. Today the NRC, working in conjunction with the **Academy of Sciences, the Academy of Engineering**, and the **Institute of Medicine**, mobilizes thousands of scientists who work gratis on study committees when the government needs scientific information. Rather than doing field work, these groups evaluate and synthesize all available and often contradictory information in a given field. In the past, the NRC has reported on acid rain, toxic shock syndrome, the effects of diet on cancer, and ways in which the Secret Service might spot potential assassins.

The academy building was designed by Goodhue in a delightfully understated Greek style. The grounds are pleasant, and of particular interest is the *Einstein Memorial* (1979, **Robert Berks**) in the SW corner. (Children love to climb on the famed physicist's larger-than-life lap, demonstrating the sweetness of Berks' balloon-headed sculpture.) The building is open to the public, yet seldom visited. Be sure to note the 6 window panels: they're 2 stories high and tell the story of scientific progress from the Greeks to the moderns. The **Great**

Hall is also worth a peek. It's an ornate cruciform chamber with a 55-foot-high central dome. In the hall a **Foucault Pendulum** illustrates the earth spinning on its axis. The pendulum, however, is often taken down for receptions, so if you must see this phenomenon, visit the Smithsonian Museum of American History, where a pendulum swings perpetually.

The academy auditorium (1970, **Wallace K. Harrison/Harrison & Abramowitz**; acoustical design, **Dr. Cyril Harris**) is one of the most acoustically perfect spaces in the city. The chamber walls are a huge curving shell covered with large diamond-shaped facets joined at the edges. Call the *Art-in-the-Academy Program* at 334.2436 for information on free concerts. If you have a chance to attend one, it shouldn't be missed. Fine art, photography, weaving, and scientific exhibitions occur on a regular

West End/Foggy Bottom

basis. ♦ Free. M-F 8:30AM-5PM. 2101 Constitution Ave NW (21st-22nd Sts) Metro stop: Foggy Bottom. 334.2000

11 State Department Founded in 1789, this was the first Cabinet department created. The biggest draw for non-diplomats is the 8th floor **Diplomatic Reception** rooms, which have been decorated with an outstanding collection of 18th- and 19th-century American art and furniture, much of it historically as well as esthetically significant—**Thomas Jefferson**'s mahogany desk, at which he drafted the Declaration of Independence, is here. Once in the rooms, it's hard to believe you're in an unprepossessing modern office building, but the splendid view of the Mall reminds you that you're in Washington. Tours fill quickly in the peak season. ♦ Guided tours M-F 9:30, 10:30AM, 3PM. 2201 C St NW (21st-23rd Sts) Reservations required. Metro stop: Foggy Bottom. 647.3241

12 Kennedy Center for the Performing Arts (1971, Edward Durell Stone; acoustical design, Dr. Cyril Harris) When the Kennedy Center opened, Washington became a true focal point for the liveliest of national and international arts. Regrettably, Stone's initial curvilinear design (1959) was rejected as being too expensive, and this stripped classical box ("which the Watergate came in," according to local wits) is a depressing addition to the Potomac waterfront. The interior decor evokes an upscale mortuary; the president for whom it is named deserved better. The rooftop terrace offers spectacular views, but be warned, this is on the direct flight path of National Airport, and the planes come in at rooftop level every minute of the day.

The slain president is memorialized in a 7-foot bronze bust (by sculptor **Robert Berks**) in the **Grand Foyer**. The interior space of the foyer is 6 stories high, with more floor area than 2 football fields, and is furnished with gifts from nations around the world.

The **Hall of States**, a gallery containing the flags of each US state, and the **Hall of Nations**, displaying flags of every nation recognized by the US, help separate the theaters spatially and acoustically, and provide good circulation from the building entrances on the east side to the theater doors on the west. Check with specific theaters for events, showtimes, and ticket prices. Infrasound headsets are available for hearing-impaired persons. (A driver's license or major credit card is held as collateral; check at the usher's desk 1 hour before curtain time.) ♦ Free. Center daily 10AM-11PM. Walk-in tours daily 10AM-1PM; meet in the Hall of States. New Hampshire Ave and Rock Creek Parkway. Tour reservations required for groups of 20 or more. Metro stop: Foggy Bottom. 254.3600, tour services 254.3774, usher's desk 254.3624 ♿

Within the Kennedy Center:

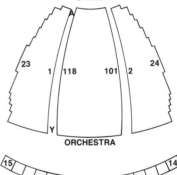

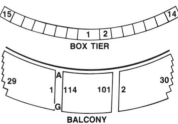

Eisenhower Theater Paneled with East Indian laurel. Small-scale musicals, dramas, dance programs. ♦ Seats 1200. Box office: M-Sa 10AM-9PM; Su, holidays noon-9PM. 254.3670

American Film Institute Theater (1973, Hardy Holzman Pfeiffer) Steeply raked seats, shoehorned into the backstage area of the Eisenhower, this place is a belated recognition of the importance of film to American culture. It was designed at a fraction of the cost of the other theaters; car hoods mounted on cinder block walls help diffuse the sound. Programs range from the earliest movies ever made (shown with live musical accompaniment at the proper speed) to the latest hit from Outer Mongolia, by way of *Casablanca* and *Gone with the Wind*. ♦ Seats 200. Information and film schedule 785.4600

"There seems reason to anticipate that in time our capital will come to be as well known as a centre of literature and art, as it is now recognized as the centre of statesmanship, law and science."

I. Edward Clarke, 1899

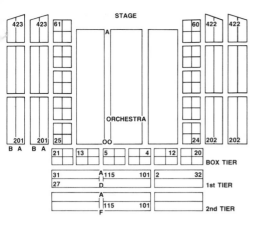

Concert Hall The gold-white theater, illuminated by Norwegian chandeliers, presents symphonies, choral groups, dance, and other musical performances. Excellent acoustics. ◆ Seats 2750. Box office: M-Sa 10AM-9PM; Su, holidays noon-9PM. 254.3776

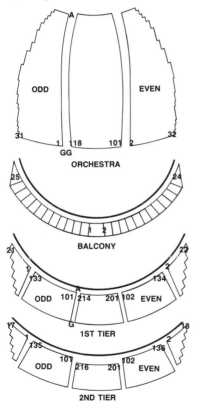

Opera House Three tiers face a golden Japanese silk stage curtain. Plays, dance programs, operas, and music programs. ◆ Seats 2300. Box office: M-Sa 10AM-9PM; Su, holidays noon-9PM. 254.3770

The statue of **Alexander Hamilton** at the south entrance of the Treasury Building proudly proclaims: "He smote the rock of the national resources and abundant streams of revenue gushed forth."

West End/Foggy Bottom

Terrace Theater This small theater hosts chamber music, poetry readings, and some dramatic productions. ◆ Seats 500. Box office: M-Sa 10AM-9PM; Su, holidays noon-9PM. 254.9895

Roof Terrace ★$$$ American regional cuisine, such as Maryland crabcakes and Cajun blackened fish, in an opulent atmosphere. ◆ American ◆ Daily 11:30AM-3PM, 5:30PM-half hour after last curtain. Reservations required. 833.8870

Curtain Call Café ★$$ Casual meals and scenery offered in a café setting. The walls are lined with photos of Kennedy Center performers. ◆ American ◆ Tu-Sa 5-8PM. 833.8870

Encore Cafeteria ★$ Serve yourself in this medium-priced crowded restaurant, which offers a great view of the Potomac and outdoor dining in the summer. ◆ American ◆ Daily 11AM-8PM. 833.8870

The Hors D'Oeuvrerie ★★$ This lavish lounge, although often crowded, strives for a sedate atmosphere with its mirrored walls and plush red furnishings. Go for a drink and special hot and cold hors d'oeuvres like wild mushroom and chicken strudels and fresh spinach baked with Gruyere. ◆ French ◆ Daily 5PM-half hour after final curtain. (Sometimes closed on M, Su; call for schedule.) 833.8870

Although the **Zero Milestone** on the Ellipse's northern tip is the legal center of the District of Columbia, the actual center is also the center of the OAS building.

In 1846, when **Charles Dickens** visited Washington, he made the following remark: "It is sometimes called the city of magnificent distances, but it might with greater propriety be termed the city of magnificent intentions." He wasn't discussing politics, but architecture, and he went on to describe the city as a place with "spacious avenues that begin in nothing and lead nowhere; streets, miles long, that want houses, roads and inhabitants; and public buildings that need only a public to be complete."

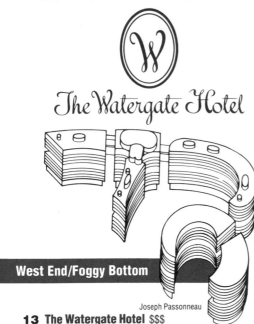

The Watergate Hotel

Joseph Passonneau

13 The Watergate Hotel $$$
Not to be confused with the other elements of this waterfront complex: the apartments, with their sweeping curves and toothy balustrades, and the outwardly unremarkable office building, across from Howard Johnson's, in which a bungled burglary of the Democratic Party's National Headquarters led to **Richard Nixon**'s resignation. The location is perfect if you plan to visit the Kennedy Center, Georgetown, the White House, or the State Department. Spacious luxury suites blend classic European and Oriental styles with contemporary decor. Pluses include a shopping mall, a health club, concierge and babysitting services, 4 fine restaurants, and 3 lounges. The **Terrace Restaurant** serves breakfast and lunch; the **Wintergarden** serves French cuisine for lunch, dinner, and supper. The **Saddle Bar** lounge is renowned for its extensive collection of one-of-a-kind saddle blankets, and the **Potomac Lounge** is tops for tea, cocktails, and piano music. Most rooms have balconies and a view of the Potomac. Children under 14 stay free.
♦ Deluxe ♦ 2650 Virginia Ave NW. Metro stop: Foggy Bottom. 965.2300, 800/424.2736; fax 337.7915⟨⟩

Within the Watergate Complex:

Les Champs One of Washington's more prestigious shopping arcades. The 30 boutiques of Les Champs also round the exterior of the Watergate **600 Office Building** and carry high-priced, high-fashion furs, crystal, antiques, imports, jewelry, and probably the city's highest concentration of designer fashions. Among the shops are **Colette of the Watergate** for Italian and California designer sportswear and prêt-à-porter; **Saint Laurent Rive Gauche**; **Saks-Jandel** for top-dollar designer fashions; **Gucci I** and **Gucci II** for renowned men's and women's clothing, accessories, and leather goods. ♦ Mall hours M-Sa 10AM-6PM. New Hampshire and Virginia Aves NW (near the Kennedy Center) 338.0700

Jean-Louis at the Watergate ★★★$$$$
This tiny bastion of nouvelle cuisine is often mentioned as one of the most expensive—and one of the finest—restaurants in America. (Restaurateur **George Lang** was involved in its original design.) Jean-Louis' service, wine list, and imaginative cooking assure a top-flight dining experience. Menus offer a wide range of choices divided into 4 pricings. Cold first courses include terrines of foie gras, truffles, and wild mushrooms. Next come warm seafood salads and other fishy creations, then meat and chicken, frequently prepared with exotic fruits and spices. While the pastries used to be among the best in the country, it will take some time to see how the new pastry chef measures up. Pretheater menu 5:30-6:30PM. ♦ French ♦ M-Sa 5:30-10PM, Jan-July, Sep-Dec. 2650 Virginia Ave NW (New Hampshire Ave) Jacket and tie requested. Reservations required. 298.4488

Watergate Pastry On the lower level of the Watergate apartment complex, a mall provides residents one-stop shopping and services, including valet, barber shop, a Safeway supermarket, optician, and florist. This bakery is noted for its oven-baked delicacies, including a variety of mousse cakes, French pastries, and memorable wedding and birthday cakes with unusual fillings. There are also 25 flavors of homemade chocolate, including rum, almond, honey, and orange. ♦ M-F 8AM-7PM; Sa 9AM-7PM; Su 10AM-5PM. 2534 Virginia Ave NW (New Hampshire Ave) 342.1777

14 Howard Johnson's Motor Lodge $ A great bargain in a ritzy neighborhood. The hotel's spacious rooms are functionally furnished (all have refrigerators), and some have a balcony overlooking the Potomac. Dining in **Bob's Big Boy**. Free underground parking and an outdoor pool for summertime swimming. Ask for the room the Watergate burglars used. ♦ 2601 Virginia Ave NW. Metro stop: Foggy Bottom. 965.2700; 800/654.2000

15 River Inn $$ A small all-suite hotel perfect for longer stays. Within walking distance of the Kennedy Center, Georgetown, and the State Department. Children under 12 stay free. ♦ 924 25th St NW (Eye-K Sts) Metro stop: Foggy Bottom. 337.7600, 800/424.2741

Within the River Inn:

Foggy Bottom Cafe ★★$$ Small and attractively appointed, this trendy spot serves eclectic fare like sesame noodles, triple eggs Benedict, and steak tartare. The perfect spot for pre- or post-Kennedy Center dining.
♦ American ♦ M-F 7-10:30AM, 11:30AM-2PM, 5:30-11:30PM; Sa 8AM-2PM, 5:30-11:30PM; Su 8AM-2PM, 5:30-10:30PM. Reservations recommended. 338.8707

16 The Inn at Foggy Bottom $$ One of the best buys in the neighborhood and a good place to bring families. The hotel restaurant (**Gloria's**) is enjoyed by starwatchers as well as by stars and government officials. Children under 12 stay free. ♦ 824 New Hampshire Ave NW (H-Eye Sts) Metro stop: Foggy Bottom. 337.6620

17 Guest Quarters Hotel $$ Each of the 101 suites features a traditional-style living room, dining area, spacious bedroom, large closets, and a fully equipped kitchen. Standard amenities include room service (no restaurant on the premises), secretarial and telex services, self-service guest laundry, audiovisual equipment, and temporary memberships to nearby health clubs. The Guest Quarters also offers grocery delivery service, a bestseller lending library, babysitters, and dog-walking (pets 25 pounds or less are allowed at a nominal fee—put your pooch on a diet). Children under 12 stay free. ◆ 801 New Hampshire Ave NW (H-Eye Sts) Metro stop: Foggy Bottom. 785.2000, 800/424.2900; fax 785.9485. Also at: 2500 Pennsylvania Ave NW. 333.8060, 800/424.2900

18 Wyndham Bristol Hotel $$$ European ambiance in a 239-room hotel convenient to Georgetown and the Kennedy Center. (Many Kennedy Center performers stay here.) Amenities include the **Bristol Grill**, the **Bristol Bar**, in-house movies, parking, and valet service. Children under 17 stay free. ◆ 2430 Pennsylvania Ave NW (24th-25th Sts) Metro stop: Foggy Bottom. 955.6400, 800/822.2430; fax 955.5765 &

19 Two Vikings ★★★$$$ The café seating out front adds to the charm of this classy French restaurant. Among the winning dishes: Two Vikings Papillote (baked seafood with a heady curry sauce), sea scallops, and shrimp flambé. ◆ French ◆ M-Sa 11:30AM-2:30PM, 5-11PM; Su noon-11PM. 2513 Pennsylvania Ave (25th St) Reservations recommended on weekends. Metro stop: Foggy Bottom. 822.0862

19 One Step Down Hot jazz sounds emanate from this dark and smoky little hangout. The lineup of local musicians attracts fans of all ages. Late-night shows on Fridays and Saturdays; all-day jam sessions on Sundays. On Tuesdays and Wednesdays a jazz jukebox substitutes, playing everything from vintage Dixieland to fusion. Limited menu offers sandwiches, pizzas, and the like. ◆ Cover. M-Th, Su 10AM-2AM; F-Sa 10AM-3AM. Shows: M, Th 9; F-Sa 10, 11:30, 1. 2517 Pennsylvania Ave NW (25th-26th Sts) Metro stops: Foggy Bottom, Dupont Circle. 228.2828

19 Marshall's ★$$ Traditional Northern Italian fare, like linguini with seafood, and roast chicken surrounded by artichoke hearts, peas, and capers—and during the summer, mango-lime mousse pie. ◆ Italian ◆ Daily 11:30AM-midnight. 2525 Pennsylvania Ave (25th-26th Sts) Metro stop: Foggy Bottom. 659.6886

Canova Lions. Two lions—one asleep, the other watchful—grace the entrance to the **Corcoran Gallery.** They are bronze copies of marble originals sculpted by **Antonio Canova** in 1792 to commemorate **Pope Clement XIII.**

20 The Grand Hotel $$$ (1984, Skidmore, Owings & Merrill; interior design, Charles Pfister) Old World-style elegance in a modern setting: all-marble bathrooms with extra-deep tubs, in-room minibars, 24-hour concierge and room services, fitness center, 2 restaurants (**Mayfair Restaurant**, **Promenade**), and the **Rose and Crown Pub**. Children under 15 stay free. ◆ 2350 M St NW (23rd-24th Sts) Metro stop: Foggy Bottom. 429.0100, 800/848.0016; fax 429.9759 &

21 The Westin Hotel $$$ (1988, Vlastimil Koubek) Just across the M Street Bridge, this sparkling 9-story building houses 405 rooms (each with minibar), 2 restaurants (try the **Collonade**), a salon, and one of DC's state-of-the-art health clubs: a pool, squash and racquetball courts, aerobic classes, and fitness evaluations are among its features. Hotel

West End/Foggy Bottom

amenities include 24-hour room and concierge services, and on-site parking. Note the luxurious bar, lounge, and restaurant contained within glazed arches that face onto an interior garden. Civilized, airy retreat for a light lunch or drinks. Children under 18 stay free. ◆ 2401 M St NW (24th-25th Sts) Metro stop: Foggy Bottom. 429.2400, 800/228.3000; fax 457.5010 &

21 1250 24th Street (1988, Don Hisaga) Light, elegant office building, designed within existing walls; leaven in the dough of neighboring developments. There's a recessed bow front, fully glazed behind a white grid; inside, walkways lead around a sparkling, leafy atrium. ◆ M-N Sts NW Metro Stop: Foggy Bottom

22 Park Hyatt $$$ (1986, Skidmore, Owings & Merrill) This spacious hotel is the addition to the new hotel nexus at 24th and M Sts. Accommodations for the handicapped, a health club, 24-hour room and concierge services, and parking. The Park Hyatt's restaurant, **Melrose**, serves American cuisine. Children under 12 stay free. ◆ 1201 24th St NW (M-N Sts) Metro stop: Foggy Bottom. 789.1234, 800/922.7275; fax 457.8823 &

23 Bread and Chocolate Tearoom ★★$ Quiches and other egg dishes, soups, flaky croissants, and rich cakes and pastries. Take-out, too. ◆ Café/bakery ◆ M-Th 7AM-6PM; F-Sa 7AM-11PM; Su 8AM-7PM. 2301 M St NW (entrance on 23rd St) Metro stop: Foggy Bottom. 833.8360

24 City Cafe ★★$$ Nora Pouillon's latest venture (her original restaurant, **Nora**, is near Dupont Circle), this jazzy Postmodern joint with tiny triangular tables can feel cramped, but it's always fun, with new angles on the usual free-range roast chicken and minipizzas. ◆ American ◆ M-Th noon-10:30PM; F noon-11:30PM; Sa 6-11:30PM. 2213 M St NW (22nd-23rd Sts) Reservations recommended. Metro stop: Foggy Bottom. No credit cards. 797.4860

| **Restaurants**: Red | **Hotels**: Blue |
| **Shops/Parks**: Green | **Sights/Culture**: Black |

25 Embassy Suites Hotel $$ All 318 suites look out over a soaring interior courtyard that contains a garden and a duck pond. Service is foremost here: complimentary breakfast and happy hour, concierge service, room service 11AM-midnight, and an exercise room are among the hotel's amenities. Children under 12 stay free. ◆ 1250 22nd St NW (N St) Metro stops: Foggy Bottom, Dupont Circle. 857.3388, 800/362.2779; fax 293.3173 ♿

Within the Embassy Suites Hotel:

Vivande ★★$$ The sky-blue ceiling reflects this café's sunny approach to Northern Italian food, with inventive pastas, pizzas, fish, and artful desserts. ◆ Italian ◆ Daily 11AM-11PM. Reservations recommended. 223.0747

26 Ramada Renaissance Hotel $$$ Located in Washington's fashionable West End, this 350-room (16 suites) convention hotel is ideal

West End/Foggy Bottom

for executive meetings, with its 8 conference rooms and audiovisual center. Rooms have work desks—an example of the Renaissance's attention to the business traveler. Ask about the **Renaissance Club**, which includes complimentary breakfast, afternoon tea and cocktails, and concierge service. Foreign currency exchange service, government and corporate rates available. Three restaurants, multilingual staff, babysitting, health club facilities, and indoor valet parking. Children under 12 stay free. ◆ 1143 New Hampshire Ave NW (22nd St) Metro stop: Foggy Bottom. 775.0800, 800/642.4616, fax 331.9491 ♿

Nearly all of the riverfront property in the district is owned by the government.

27 West End Cafe ★★$$ Two spacious dining rooms, one decorated with **Yousuf Karsh** celebrity portraits, the other outfitted with a bar and grand piano, make this a great place for romantic dinners or quiet luncheons. The food—entrees like steak bearnaise, chicken breast with apples in cream sauce, or lighter fare like eggs Benedict and various salads—is moderately priced and carefully prepared. ◆ American ◆ M-Th 7-10AM, 11:30AM-2:30PM, 6-11:30PM; F 7-10AM, 11:30AM-2:30PM, 6PM-midnight; Sa 8-10:30AM, 11:30AM-3PM, 6PM-midnight; Su 8-10:30AM, 11:30AM-3PM, 6-10PM. 1 Washington Circle NW (New Hampshire Ave) Reservations recommended. Metro stop: Foggy Bottom. 293.5390

28 Le Gaulois ★★$$$ First-rate country French fare at bargain prices ensures that this cluttered 2-story dining room is always filled to capacity. The pot-au-feu is a perennial winner, but it's hard to go wrong with anything. ◆ French ◆ M-Th 11:30AM-2:30PM, 5:30-11PM; F 11:30AM-2:30PM, 5:30PM-midnight; Sa 5:30PM-midnight. 2133 Pennsylvania Ave NW (21st-22nd Sts) Reservations recommended. Metro stop: Foggy Bottom. 466.3232. Also at: 1106 King St, Alexandria. 739.9494

29 George Washington University The first president of the United States had hoped to establish a national university, and so left his stock in the **Potowmack Canal Co.** (the precursor of the **Chesapeake & Ohio Canal**) as an endowment. But Congress could not agree on the federal government's role in such an institution, and the endowment was forfeited. Madison also pursued the issue, but with the same results.

Finally, in 1821, the Baptist Church raised funds to create the nonsectarian **Columbian College**; less than 100 years later this became George Washington U, the country's first national university.

GWU is the city's second largest landholder (after the federal government, of course), and therein lies its true prestige. Its present site is its third, and when the school settled here in 1912 it wisely engulfed many of the neighborhood's fine old homes, converting them into offices and dormitories. Now 20 full blocks of central DC are GWU-owned, making it a one-institution urban renewal force. ♦ 19th-24th Sts NW (Pennsylvania-New Hampshire Aves) Metro stop: Foggy Bottom. 994.4949

30 Lisner Auditorium of George Washington University
Built as a classic modern structure in the 1940s, Lisner Auditorium not only is the home of the **Washington Ballet**, but also houses the **Dimock Gallery** in the lower lounges. Exhibitions of local, faculty, and student artists change monthly. A permanent artwork to be seen at the auditorium is **Augustus Tack**'s abstract mural, painted on the stage fire curtain. Most performances are by various independent production companies such as **Theatreworks USA**, but occasionally the university presents concerts and other artistic events. The box office opens 1 hour before performances to offer last-minute tickets. Check local newspapers for listings of performances. ♦ Seats 1500. 21st and H Sts NW. Metro stop: Foggy Bottom. 994.6800

31 2000 Pennsylvania Avenue
(1983, Hellmuth, Obata, Kassabaum) The renovation of the **Lion's Row** townhouses gained kudos for retaining the brick townhouse facade. There is a mini-mall within the building ♦ 20th-21st Sts. Metro stops: Farragut West, Foggy Bottom

Within 2000 Pennsylvania Avenue:

E.E. Wolensky's Bar and Grill ★$$ The ever lively bar and moderate prices make this courtyard café popular with office workers and students alike. Burgers, salads, and homey café fare. ♦ American ♦ Restaurant: M, Su 11:30AM-11PM; Tu-Sa 11:30AM-midnight. Pub: M-Th, Su 11:30AM-2AM; F-Sa 11:30AM-3AM. 463.0050

Tower Records Salvation for tapeheads, audiophiles, VCR addicts, and others seeking a late-night media fix, no matter what night of the year. ♦ Daily 9AM-midnight. 331.2400

Devon Bar and Grill ★$$ Grilled seafood is the draw in the upstairs dining room; a lively bar scene and light meals downstairs. ♦ American ♦ Daily 11:30AM-10PM. 833.5660

Restaurants: Red   **Hotels**: Blue
Shops/Parks: Green   **Sights/Culture**: Black

32 Primi Piatti
★★$$$ Trendy, high-style Italian, a modest cousin of **Galileo** (page 109). Simple, delicious dishes with an emphasis on pastas and antipasti as the name suggests. But the tables are set too close together, the service can be ragged, and the din from the omnipresent crowd of young professionals is deafening. ♦ Italian ♦ M-Th 11:30AM-2:30PM, 5:30-10:30PM; F 11:30AM-2:30PM, 5:30-11:30PM; Sa 5:30-11:30PM. 2013 Eye St NW (20th-21st Sts) Reservations recommended. Metro stops: Farragut West, Foggy Bottom. 223.3600

33 Dominique's
★★$$$ Snazzy, fun, oftentimes outrageous. The seemingly endless menu lists everything from alligator

to rattlesnake, the champagne flows freely, and the desserts are named after famous patrons (chocolate truffles for **Elizabeth Taylor**). Hoopla notwithstanding, the simpler dishes are the best: crab soup, lamb stew, duck, quail, or the fresh fish of the day. End with a crunchy almond amaretto soufflé ♦ M-Th 11:30AM-2:30PM, 5:30PM-midnight; F 11:30AM-2:30PM, 5:30PM-1AM; Sa 5:30PM-1AM. 1900 Pennsylvania Ave NW (19th St) Jacket and tie requested. Reservations recommended. Metro stop: Foggy Bottom. 452.1126

34 International Monetary Fund Visitors Center
Headquarters for the multilateral development bank includes exhibitions of art from its collection, as well as traveling shows of works by prominent artists, crafts of Third World countries, an ongoing film series by the **International Cine Club**, and cultural events. Reading room and bookstore. ♦ M-F 9:30AM-6PM; tours by appointment. 700 19th St NW (G-H Sts) Metro Stop: Farragut West. 623.6869

35 Maison Blanche
★★$$$$ Within crawling distance of the White House, this luxuriously appointed dining room was a favorite with movers and shakers in the Reagan administration. Chef **Pierre Chambrin** specializes in French classics like calf's liver, veal stew, and bouillabaisse. The prix fixe pretheater menu is a bargain. ♦ French ♦ M-F 11:45AM-10PM; Sa 6-10PM. 1725 F St NW (17th-18th Sts). Jacket and tie requested. Reservations recommended. Metro stop: Farragut West. 842.0070

36 Crown Books
One of 40 DC outlets of this discount chain. ♦ M-F 9AM-7PM; Sa 10AM-6PM. 1710 G St NW (17th-18th Sts) Metro stop: Farragut West. 789.2277

37 Winder Building
(1848, William H. Winderin) This was the city's first high-rise office building (5 stories). It was also the first to use structural cast iron and central heating. It is now used as offices for the executive branch. ♦ 604 17th St NW (F-G Sts) Metro stop: Farragut West

Art Buchwald

Syndicated Columnist

My house in Washington. It tripled in value when Reagan became president.

The Smithsonian Air and Space Museum

The John F. Kennedy Center

RFK Stadium—when the Redskins are winning

The Corcoran Gallery of Art

The Phillips Collection

The War Room in the White House

The Four Seasons and Madison hotels

The C&O Canal

Rock Creek Park on Sunday

The Maison Blanche restaurant

Dumbarton Oaks

Bests

Robert McNulty

President, Partners for Livable Places

A leisurely walk or jog along the C&O Canal—any time of the year. Stop and watch the US Whitewater Kayak Team practice at Lock #6.

The quiet refuge of the Bishop's Garden at the National Cathedral.

Drinks and conversation around a winter fire at the Hotel Tabard Inn.

Midnight on the steps of the Jefferson Memorial.

Lunch in the Moveable Feast at Hillwood at the former Marjorie Merriweather Post estate (now the Hillwood Museum).

The urban archaeology project of Alexandria VA—a wonderful window on the past that can be seen at the Torpedo Factory in Old Town Alexandria.

A short drive down Old Chain Bridge Road between Loughboro Rd and MacArthur Blvd in Washington DC. This is a 19th-century rural country lane in the heart of the nation's capital. Stop and explore the Civil War site at Battery Kimball Park.

A meal anyplace in Adams-Morgan, but especially El Tamarindo Restaurant for El Salvadoran food.

The view, taking off or landing, from the north at Washington's National Airport—one of America's most meaningful vistas.

Milo C. Beach

Acting Director, Arthur M. Sackler Gallery and Freer Gallery of Art

Watching museum visitors stop to really look at an intricately designed, richly colored 17th-century Indian painting on display in the Sackler Gallery.

Joining parents and tiny children as they listen to Asian folktales enacted among the art on view in the Sackler Gallery.

Being a part of the extraordinary interaction that takes place between audience and performer during the Sackler Gallery concerts of Asian music.

Bates Lowry

Former Director, National Building Museum

The National Building Museum. The great frieze of soldiers, sailors, and wounded warriors that has been encircling the building for over 100 years. Its design was due to the architect of the building, General Montgomery C. Meigs, who dictated its subject and encouraged the sculptor, Caspar Buberi, to study the photographic evidence produced by Muybridge about how horses moved, but to take at the same time the Parthenon frieze as a model for artistic expression. The meaning of the frieze as described by Meigs makes it a very moving national monument. He wished it to be a memorial to *all* men who believed so deeply in an ideal that they would willingly give their lives to defend it. Spoken at a time so shortly after the divisive Civil War, these words make the frieze a symbol of the bonds that had to be refashioned to make our nation whole.

Once the visitor has overcome an initial experience of the vast size of the central court (316 feet by 116 feet) and begins to try to compare it with other spaces, it is well to remember that a) it is higher than the nave of Notre Dame in Paris, b) the columns are higher than those at Baalbek, usually thought of as the tallest columns in the world, c) the square footage exceeds that of Hagia Sophia by over 9,000 square feet, d) the Pantheon of Rome could be fit within its walls, e) a contemporary 15-story building could be erected in its central court. All of these statistics except for the last were known and described by General Meigs.

With a lively imagination and a keen ear one should be able to hear any number of historic pieces of music that still linger in the Great Hall from the many presidential inaugural balls held here beginning in 1885 before the building was totally finished. They continue to be held here today, although Victor Herbert has long since been replaced as the bandleader.

When visiting the museum galleries, one should realize that these open flowing spaces represent the architect's goal of bringing fresh air and natural light into offices, and they make marvelous museum galleries!

In climbing the stairways, note their gentle rise and generous size. One is ascending the first stairways especially designed for the handicapped, a feature introduced by the architect because many of the employees of the Pension Bureau were maimed veterans.

The sky-blue ceiling of the Great Hall results from the architect's desire that it appear to be an open courtyard like its Italian prototypes. The surrounding arcade—another typical feature of the Renaissance palace—serves the functional purpose of being a circulation corridor within the building. The architect opted for this design to avoid the central corridor circulation pattern used in earlier government offices, which produced dark, gloomy, and fetid areas.

The richness of the colorful, decorative scheme reflects the architect's belief that bright colors set off good architecture by adorning and emphasizing it. The lavish use of bronze coloring was much admired by early users of the building, one of whom believed that there had been nothing so splendid since Solomon's Temple. In the center court, the series of plaster busts that enrich the upper cornice were intended by Meigs to achieve "a variety of forms, lights and shadows."

The Lincoln Memorial. The most perfect architectural monument anywhere! Aside from honoring the Great Emancipator, its beautiful proportions and delicate detailing create a harmonious whole of such serene, yet majestic, effect that all can see why Classical architecture was so long considered the finest model for the architect to follow.

For an amusing architectural mirage, look down 16th St from Meridian Hill toward the White House. At this point the dome of the Jefferson Memorial joins the roof of the Executive Mansion to create a more Palladian Presidential Palace.

The Federal Triangle Buildings. A first-class product of Beaux-Arts training in design and planning and the most colossal example ever to be built. Although the Federal Triangle was, unfortunately, never completed, there are many lessons for future architects to follow in the way the enormous facades are articulated by the strategic repetition of colonnades and pedimented pavilion blocks (note the echoing of these motifs in the IRS and Commerce buildings). The great sweeping hemicycles in the center of the design are particularly handsome, and if the circular plaza intended on 13th St had been completed, it would now be the architectural center and wonder of DC.

Attention should be given to all the details embellishing these buildings, particularly the decorative metal grills and lamp fixtures. Unfortunately, the interiors of only a few of these buildings can be visited (the Art Deco decoration of the Justice Building is one of DC's forbidden fruits for the architecture buff), but step into the green marbled entry hall of the Commerce Building; visit the elaborately sculpted rotundas and entry hall of the Interstate Commerce Commission Building, and enjoy the imperial splendor of the auditorium (note particularly the hanging chandeliers and richly coffered ceilings along the window walls).

The view from the south end of the White House lawn never loses its appeal. From here, the not-very-noble White House does, nevertheless, appear so, and the fact that this impression is due, in good part, to the original, sensitive landscape design worked out by Thomas Jefferson adds to the pleasure of the experience.

In Chinatown, still in the area along and off of H Street between 6th and 9th Streets, are some of the original dwellings built to house the government functionaries when they moved here in 1800 from Philadelphia. Although not in themselves remarkable buildings, they should be noted for their diminutive size because only then can one appreciate what a powerful, colossal impact must have been made in those early days by such public buildings as the Bulfinch dome of the Capitol, the great colonnade of the Treasury, and the massive, gigantic portico of the Patent Office. (Now the home of the National Portrait Gallery, one enters it at basement level, its majestic flight of steps having been cut off in 1936 to widen F Street which, ironically, has now been turned into a pedestrian mall.)

A trip to the roof terrace of the Washington Hotel brings one of the best and most comfortable public views of southwest DC, as well as glimpses of the White House and its garden over the roof of the Treasury. An especially pleasing panorama of the red tile roofs of the Federal Triangle buildings makes the overall plan of this vast complex clear.

The Vietnam Veterans Memorial—the most emotion-provoking memorial in DC. Its black granite gash into the lush green of the Mall aptly symbolizes what a terrible self-inflicted wound that conflict was for our country. A continuous stream of quiet visitors brushing their fingers over the inscribed names of lost sons, friends, or husbands is a poignant part of the monument that becomes, by that act, an enormous braille tablet allowing those unable to see the dead to make contact with them. The tributes often left there —cowboy boots, last letters, and guitars—are carefully collected at the end of each day and stored away.

The Old Executive Office Building is a must on many lists simply due to the exuberance of its design,

which appears to have been freely poured out of a cornucopia filled with pediments, columns, cornices, and other architectural delights. But the architecture buff should also ponder the lesson to be learned about *style* by taking into account the fact that the ground plan of this building is almost identical to that of the very staid Treasury Building on the other side of the White House.

The most impressive, breathtaking architectural interior anywhere in the world is to be experienced in the vast but carefully articulated space of the Great Hall of the old Pension Building (National Building Museum). The experience is made all the more striking because the closeup impression of the exterior is of a long, low structure that in no way suggests the enormous height and length of the hall within.

Finally, all who have endured the traffic fracas of DC and cursed its city planner should reflect on the incredible boldness and vision of its designer. When L'Enfant proposed his audacious scheme, he truly found only one supporter—George Washington. It was the military and political father of our country who insisted upon this plan being put into execution. He truly was a visionary figure who foresaw how great would become the union of the 13 little colonies and believed that only a capital city many times larger than any city then existing on the continent would be appropriate for that nation. That his name should have been given to the Federal City was an entirely appropriate decision. Unfortunately, a comparable honor has not yet been accorded its planner.

Gardening enthusiasts shouldn't miss the **Tulip Library**, located near the Tidal Basin between Independence Ave and Raoul Wallenberg Place (formerly 15th Street SW). Each fall the **National Park Service** plants over 10,000 tulip bulbs here. In the spring (usually the first week in April), this area nestled between the Washington Monument and the Jefferson Memorial bursts into a riot of color. After blooming, the floral beds are replanted with a massive display of annuals, making the library a colorful attraction throughout the summer and fall.

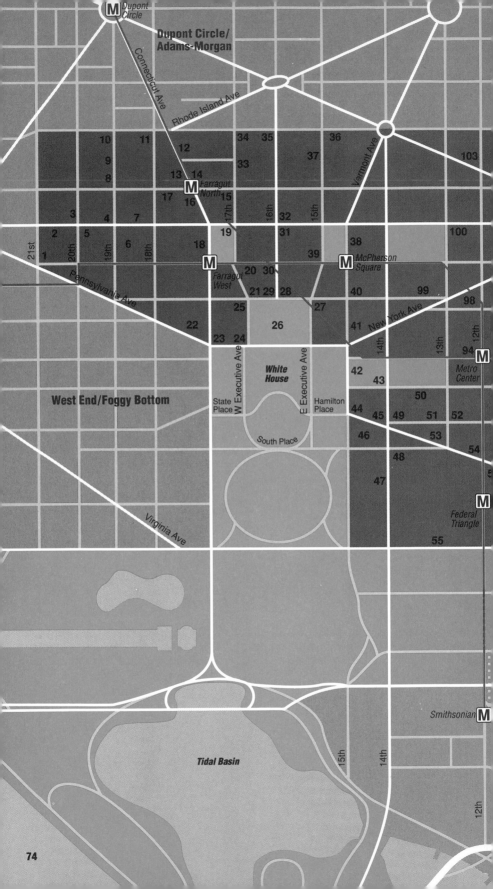

Dupont Circle/
Adams-Morgan

Dupont
Circle

Connecticut Ave

Rhode Island Ave

10   11
12

9   34   35   36
8   13 14   33
17 16
Farragut
North

15

19

32
31
39
38

McPherson
Square

103

100

2   5
1   6
21st   20th   19th   18th

18

Farragut
West

20 30
21 29 28

25
23 24   26

22

27

41

40

New York Ave

99

98

14th

13th

94

12th

Metro
Center

Pennsylvania Ave

Vermont Ave

16th

15th

17th

West End/Foggy Bottom

W Executive Ave

E Executive Ave

White
House

State
Place

Hamilton
Place

42   43

44 45 49 51 52
46

50
48
53

47

54

Federal
Triangle

55

South Place

Virginia Ave

Tidal Basin

15th   14th

Smithsonian

12th

Downtown

Logan Circle

M

L New York Ave

Pierce

77

101

78

Massachusetts Ave

New Jersey Ave

96

79

K

I

H

80

81 76

95

G Place 9th

82

10th

83

8th

84

6th

5th

Gallery
Place

3 89

90 88

92 91

G

F

4th 3rd

75

74

2nd

73

E

85

87 86

64

Judiciary
Square

M

65 66

1st

57

60 Indiana Ave

Pennsylvania Ave

59 61

C

58

M
Archives

62 63

Constitution Ave

72

No. Capitol

M Union
Station

71 Union
Station

70 69

68 69

Louisiana Ave

Delaware Ave

Capitol Hill

Madison Dr

The Mall

Jefferson Dr

The Capitol

Independence Ave

Maryland Ave

C

Virginia Ave

D

M
L'Enfant
Plaza

M
Federal
Center SW

9th

7th

6th

E 4th

Southwest Fwy

G

Ask where **Downtown** Washington lies, and you'll get a half-dozen different answers: the traditional F Street shopping area; Pennsylvania Avenue's ceremonial promenade; the dreary facades of K Street, known as *lawyers' canyon* and *Moscow West;* the tiny shops and restaurants of **Chinatown**. All of the above are correct. Downtown Washington is in the process of overcoming decades of neglect, particularly in its eastern parts, and is on its way to becoming a true city center once again. The F Street shopping corridor has been spruced up with a new **Hecht's**, and both **Garfinckel's** and **Woodward & Lothrop** have been remodeled. The historic **National Press Building**, outfitted with a new facade, anchors the **Shops at National Place**: 3 levels of boutiques and eateries. Pressure for office space has extended the Downtown renaissance as far north as Chinatown, the **Convention Center**, and the **Techworld** office development.

Pennsylvania Ave, on Downtown's southern border, serves as the ceremonial parade route for inaugurals and other events of national importance. For much of the 19th and 20th centuries, however, the avenue

Downtown

was flanked with neighborhoods of less-than-sterling character. Dentist **Henry Cogswell** built his *Temperance Fountain* there for a reason. The area where the **District Building** now stands was once so infamous that one of the Union's foremost commanders, **General Joseph Hooker**, was ordered to clean it up. The area was called *Hooker's Brigade*—its businesswomen, *hookers*.

Pennsylvania Ave now sports more respectable commerce. The imposing **Old Post Office** has been turned into a shopping and eating pavilion. The **Willard Hotel** has been triumphantly renovated, as has the **Hotel Washington** next door. The **National Theatre**, on the same site since 1835 and the place where Washingtonian **Helen Hayes** saw her first play, has received a much-needed overhaul, and once again showcases Broadway tryouts and musicals. The **National Archives** and the **J. Edgar Hoover FBI Building** stand as reminders that the avenue's business is *not* all play. But these days, *the Nation's Main Street* is looking brighter than ever.

1 Arts Club of Washington (1806, Timothy Caldwell) In 1916, the one-time residence of **James Monroe** became the permanent home of the Arts Club, a local association open to aficionados of 19th- and 20th-century art. The 55 rooms, spread over 2 floors and 2 buildings (the house next door was annexed to provide more space), present a fascinating spectrum of lesser-known artists and their work. While the exhibition upstairs is permanent, the lower level is a rotating gallery: exhibitions change every 3 weeks and feature paintings by contemporary artists. The Arts Club has received donations of period furniture to complement Caldwell's strong Georgian design. ◆ Free. Tu-F 10AM-5PM; Sa 10AM-2PM; Su 1-5PM. 2017 Eye St NW (20th-21st Sts) Metro stops: Farragut West, Farragut North. 331.7282

Restaurants: Red	**Hotels**: Blue
Shops/Parks: Green	**Sights/Culture**: Black

2 Prime Rib ★★$$$$ The portions are large, the prime ribs tops, and the atmosphere formal. Aside from the juicy 2-inch thick signature entree, this restaurant does a superb rack of lamb and crab Imperial. Soft sounds from the glass-topped grand piano create a pleasing ambiance. ◆ American ◆ M-Th 11:30-3PM, 5-11PM; F 11:30-3PM, 5-11:30PM; Sa 5-11:30PM. 2020 K St NW (20th-21st Sts) Metro stops: Farragut West, Farragut North. 466.8811

2 Florian ★$$$ A Parisian brasserie specializing in seafood, lamb, and a variety of salads. ◆ French ◆ M-F 11:30AM-2:30PM, 5-10:30PM; Sa 5-10:30PM. 2020 K St NW (20th-21st Sts) Reservations recommended. Metro stop: Farragut West, Foggy Bottom. 331.0200

2 Crown Books Bargain lovers' browserie is crammed with coffee-table books at big discounts, odd but interesting publishers' overstocks, and the latest bestsellers and popular paperbacks. Good selections of nonfiction, cookbooks, and kids' books. Everything is less than list price. ◆ M-F 9AM-8PM; Sa-Su 9AM-6PM. 2020 K St NW (20th-21st Sts) Metro stops: Farragut West, Farragut North. 659.2030

3 Takesushi ★★$$$ No tatami room or cooked dishes—just fresh, tender fish served as sushi or sashimi the Tokyo way. Small, informal, and very authentic; sample the bite-size *ikura-uzura* (salmon roe with quail egg), or try the California roll, cone-style. ◆ Japanese ◆ M-F noon-2:30PM, 5:30-10PM; Sa 5:30-10PM. 1010 20th St NW (K-L Sts) Reservations recommended. Metro stops: Farragut West, Farragut North. 466.3798

4 Tiberio ★★$$$$ Long a fixture of expense-account K Street, pretty Tiberio continues to charm regulars with its conservative Northern Italian menu. The agnolotti, veal chops, and linguini are standard favorites. Be prepared to shell out a ridiculous sum, especially for wine. ◆ Italian ◆ M-Sa 11:45AM-2:30PM, 6-11PM. 1915 K St NW (19th-20th Sts) Jacket and tie requested. Reservations required. Metro stops: Farragut West, Farragut North. 452.1915

5 Sholl's Colonial Cafeteria ★$ A cafeteria that offers hearty food at bargain prices—a favorite with tourists and office workers alike. ◆ American ◆ M-Sa 7AM-8PM. 1990 K St NW (18th-19th Sts) Metro stops: Farragut West, Farragut North. No credit cards. 296.3065

6 International Square This mini-mall includes a ground floor of fast-food eateries and a variety of stores, including **Franz Bader Books** (art) and **Sidney Kramer Books** (politics). ◆ 1911 Eye St NW (18th-19th Sts) Metro stops: Farragut West, Farragut North

7 Bombay Palace ★★$$ Part of an international chain, Bombay Palace is known for its reasonable prices and reliable food. The tandoori chicken, barbecued in a clay oven, and the *samosas* (meat- or vegetable-stuffed pastries) are among the city's best. The handsome setting has light aqua walls that display small brass sculptures. ◆ Indian ◆ M-F noon-2:30PM, 5:30-10PM; Sa-Su noon-2:30PM, 5:30-10:30PM. 1835 K St NW (18th-19th Sts) Reservations recommended. Metro stops: Farragut West, Farragut North. 331.0111

7 Jean-Pierre ★★★$$$$ Owner **Jean Michel Farrat** does an admirable job of keeping up with DC's ever-increasing number of outstanding French restaurants. Jean-Pierre's staff is solicitous and efficient, the wines are expertly chosen, the food is inventive and, for the most part, delicious. Sea scallops with tangerine sauce, venison with white rice, and a delicate Dover sole are top choices. ◆ French ◆ M-F noon-2PM, 6-10PM; Sa-Su 6-10PM. 1835 K St NW (18th-19th Sts) Jacket and tie requested. Reservations required. Metro stops: Farragut West, Farragut North. 466.2022

8 Jos. A. Bank The label of this discount men's haberdasher is found inside the jacket of many a K Street crusader. ◆ M-W, F 9AM-6PM; Th 9AM-8PM; Sa 9AM-5:30PM. 1118 19th St NW (L-M Sts) Metro stops: Farragut West, Farragut North. 466.2282

8 T.H. Mandy is the best Downtown discount store for women's sportswear, carrying designs by **Sasson**, **Kasper**, **John Meyer**, and others. Prices are cut up by up to 50 percent, the selection is good, and the service is attentive and friendly. ◆ M-W, F 9AM-7PM; Th 9AM-8PM; Sa 10AM-6PM; Su noon-5PM. 1118 19th St NW (L-M Sts) Metro stops: Farragut West, Farragut North. 659.0024

9 Luigi's ★$$ Candlelit, crowded, and casual, this is one of the most reasonable and reliable Italian restaurants in DC. The pizza is crusty, the pasta available with a variety of sauces, the house wine good and cheap. ◆ Italian ◆ M-Th 11:30AM-midnight; F-Sa 11:30AM-2AM; Su noon-midnight. 1132 19th St NW (L-M Sts) Metro stop: Farragut West. 331.7574

10 Rumors ★$$ An archetypal 19th Street *meet market*, Rumors goes ballistic on weekends and warm summer evenings ◆ American ◆ M-Th 11AM-2AM; F 11AM-3AM; Sa 5PM-3AM; Su 5PM-2AM. 1900 M St NW (19th St) Metro stop: Farragut North. 466.7378

11 Chocolate Moose Even Washingtonians laugh every month or so. Cards, jewelry, and silly gifts to tweak the soberest funny bone. ◆ M-Sa 10AM-6PM. 1800 M St NW (18th St) Metro stops: Farragut West, Farragut North. 463.0992

12 Wellington Jewels Darling, you simply must get one of the Madame's faux diamonds, set in 14-karat gold and indistinguishable from the genuine article. ◆ M-F 10AM-5PM; Sa 10AM-4:30PM. 1147 Connecticut Ave NW (L-M Sts) Metro stops: Farragut West, Farragut North. 638.3593

12 Tiny Jewel Box Estate jewelry and other little treasures in DC's most charming jewelry store. ◆ M-Sa 9:30AM-5PM. 1143 Connecticut Ave NW (L-M Sts) Metro stops: Farragut West, Farragut North. 393.2747

12 Camalier & Buckley Handbags, briefcases, and luggage of superior quality. ◆ M-W, F-Sa 9:30AM-6PM, Th 9:30AM-7PM. 1141 Connecticut Ave NW (L-M Sts) Metro stops: Farragut West, Farragut North. 783.1431. Also at: 1260 F St. 347.2400

13 Claire Dratch An exceptional fashion salon for women, featuring such designers as **Perry Ellis**, **Albert Nipon**, and **Anne Klein**. ◆ M-W, F-Sa 10AM-6PM; Th 10AM-7PM. 1224 Connecticut Ave NW (L-M Sts) Metro stops: Farragut West, Farragut North. 466.6500

14 The Mayflower Hotel $$$ (1924, Warren & Wetmore) One of the most luxurious and historic hotels in DC, the yellow-brick-and-limestone Beaux-Arts building houses a 475-foot-long lobby accented with Italian marble, brilliant chandeliers, and ornate ceilings. Ask for a renovated room with furnishings by **Henredon**. The ornate **Grand Ballroom** is one of the last in the world; its Wedgwood-like bas-reliefs, terraces, and balconies are topped by

Downtown

a 21-foot ceiling. This centrally located 654-room hotel has been serving Washington's most glittering clientele with elegance and style for the last half-century. Valet parking, 24-hour room service, concierge service, nonsmoking rooms. Some suites have wet-bars. Children under 18 stay free. ◆ Deluxe ◆ 1127 Connecticut Ave NW (L-M Sts) Metro stop: Farragut North. 347.3000, 800/HOTELS/1; fax 466.9082 ♿

Within the Mayflower Hotel:

Nicholas Restaurant ★★★$$$$ New American specialties like blackened mahimahi with ginger or orange sauce; sweetbread with pistachio and wine sauce; and a light cheesecake stuffed with fresh pears, topped with a caramel sauce, then garnished with crème anglaise. The surroundings are appropriately lush. ◆ American ◆ M-F 11:30AM-2:30PM, 6-10:30PM; Sa-Su 6-10:30PM. Jacket and tie required. Reservations required. 347.3000

14 Connecticut Connection, located at the **Farragut North Metro station**, was among the first of a new breed of lunch-crowd malls built around Downtown Metrorail stops. With a couple dozen shops and restaurants in 2 underground levels that are reminiscent of Montreal's subway shopping, it serves Washington's central business district with specialty shopping. Stores include **Crabtree and Evelyn**, an international soaps-toiletries-spices-herbs shop, and **Theodore Nye Jewelers**, for custom designs and the area's largest distributor of the **Rolex Oyster** watch. ◆ M-Sa 10AM-6PM. 1101 Connecticut Ave NW (L St) Metro stop: Farragut North. 783.1101

15 Twenty-One Federal ★★★★$$$$ This sleek outpost of the justifiably renowned Nantucket eatery concocts stylish new American fare with exotic overtones. Two winning dishes: linguini with salmon and scallops in Chinese black bean sauce; red snapper with tomato sauce, crayfish, sausage, and corn pudding. ♦ American ♦ M-Th 11:30AM-2:30PM, 6-10PM; F 11:30AM-2:30PM, 6-10:30PM; Sa 6-10:30PM. 1736 L St NW (17th St-Connecticut Ave) 5th floor. Reservations recommended. Metro stop: Farragut North. 331.9771

Downtown

Le PAVILLON

16 Le Pavillon ★★★★$$$$ A singular dining experience. Owner/chef **Yannick Cam** and his wife, **Janet**, have created a restaurant of austere beauty and constant culinary surprise. The nouvelle cuisine menu changes daily. Meals consist of many small contrasting courses—fish, meat, vegetables, seafood, superb desserts—thrilling to both the eye and the palate. Stunners include: beet ravioli with osetra caviar served in a chive butter sauce; venison with caramelized tomato flan and pepper sauce; a healthy dollop of white chocolate mousse sitting in a tulip-shaped sugar cookie topped with hazelnut praline. Be prepared to pay for such artistry. ♦ French ♦ M-F noon-2PM, 7-10PM; Sa 7-10PM. 1050 Connecticut Ave NW (K-L Sts) Jacket and tie requested. Reservations required. Metro stops: Farragut West, Farragut North. 833.3846

16 Duke Zeibert's ★★$$$$ Seems like yesterday that Duke, legendary DC restaurateur, retired from his New York-style eatery—but now he's back and eager to please. This is a new spruced-up location, and the deli staples —calf's liver, brisket, chicken- and beef-in-the-pot—are as good as ever. Dependable steak, soft-shell crab, crab cakes, lobster, and other seafood. Save room for one of the mammoth desserts. ♦ American ♦ M-Sa 11:30AM-11PM; Su 5-10PM. 1050 Connecticut Ave NW (K-L Sts) Terrace level. Dinner reservations recommended. Metro stops: Farragut West, Farragut North. 466.3730

"Fellow Citizens! God reigns, and the Government at Washington still lives!"
James A. Garfield, speech on assassination of Lincoln, April 1865.

17 Brooks Brothers Setting the tone for the lower Connecticut Ave area, where there are more lawyers per square foot than anywhere else in America. This traditional menswear store keeps a hefty stock of 3-piece blue pinstriped suits. ♦ M-W, F-Sa 9:30AM-6PM; Th 9AM-8PM. 1840 L St NW (18th St) Metro stops: Farragut West, Farragut North. 659.4650

18 Barr Building (1930, Stanley Simmons) Although English High Gothic decorations encrust the facade of this office building, they don't conceal the emerging modern structural form. Its more utilitarian neighbors are a striking contrast. Not open to the public. ♦ 910 17th St NW (Eye-K Sts) Metro stops: Farragut West, Farragut North

19 Admiral David G. Farragut (1881, Vinnie Ream Hoxie) Civil War hero and the first admiral in the US Navy, it was Farragut who said, "Damn the torpedoes, full speed ahead!" The sculpture was cast from the metal propeller of the *USS Hartford*, Farragut's flagship. ♦ Farragut Sq, 17th and K Sts NW. Metro stops: Farragut West, Farragut North

20 Map Store Maps of every area in the world, plus good guide and travel books. ♦ M-F 9AM-5:30PM; Sa 10AM-4PM. 1636 Eye St NW (16th St-Connecticut Ave) Metro stop: Farragut West. 628.2608

21 Bombay Club ★★$$$ Top choices here are the kabob platter (lamb, shrimp, and chicken served with a mint yogurt sauce), green chili chicken, and *rasmalai* (cottage cheese in sweetened milk garnished with pistachios). Live piano music nightly. ♦ Indian ♦ M-F 11:30AM-2:30PM, 5-11PM; Sa 11AM-3PM, 6-11PM; Su 11AM-3PM. 815 Connecticut Ave NW (H-Eye Sts) Jacket and tie requested. Reservations required at lunch, recommended at dinner. Metro stop: Farragut West. 659.3727

21 US Chamber of Commerce Building (1925, Cass Gilbert) Another of DC's innumerable Roman temples, this one trimmed with a wall of Ionic columns to harmonize with the nearby Treasury Building. ♦ 1615 H St NW (Connecticut Ave) Metro stop: Farragut West. 659.6000

22 Franz Bader Gallery The oldest art gallery in the city, Bader gives contemporary European art an extensive representation. American paintings and prints, including the virtuoso graphics of **Peter Milton**, are shown as well. An annual highlight is an exhibition of new Eskimo carvings and prints from Canada. ♦ Tu-Sa 10AM-6PM. 1701 Pennsylvania Ave NW (17th-18th Sts) Metro stops: Farragut West, Farragut North. 659.5515

"It is our national capital. It belongs to us, and whether it is mean or majestic, whether arrayed in glory or covered with shame, we cannot but share its character and its destiny."
Frederick Douglass

Washington has more lawyers—the highest per capita ratio in the nation.

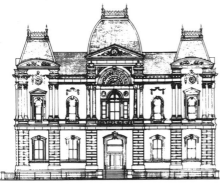

23 Renwick Gallery, National Museum of American Art (1859, James Renwick) Designed to display the private art collection of banker **William Wilson Corcoran**, who then moved his holdings to bigger digs at the Corcoran, this Second Empire mansion is now a **Smithsonian Institution** museum (acting director, **Elizabeth Broun**), emphasizing American crafts and decorative art. Past exhibitions have included Art Deco furniture, fiber art, contemporary glass, Utah beehive-motif folk art, and architecture. The opulent upstairs rooms, designed after the **Louvre** in Paris, give little hint that the building served as a Quartermaster General's post during the Civil War and as the **US Court of Claims** from 1899–1964. The gift shop features jewelry, ceramics, and weavings by contemporary artists as well as the usual books and cards. ♦ Free. Daily 10AM-5:30PM; group tours by appointment. Pennsylvania Ave and 17th St NW. Metro stops: Farragut West, Farragut North. 357.2700, 357.2531 &

24 Blair House (The Blair-Lee Houses) (1824; restoration, 1931, Waldron Faulkner; restoration, 1988, Mendel, Mesick, Cohen, White) Actually 4 townhouses used to accommodate visiting foreign dignitaries. Not open to the public. ♦ 1650 Pennsylvania Ave NW (17th St-Jackson Pl) Metro stops: Farragut West, Farragut North

25 Decatur House (1818, Benjamin Latrobe) **Commodore Stephen Decatur**, brave and reckless hero of the War of 1812, built this house, many say with proceeds from government-sanctioned privateering. Its simple exterior and formal interiors—especially the splendid second-floor ballroom—represent the best of the Late Federal style. ♦ Admission. Tu-F 10AM-2PM; Sa-Su, holidays noon-4PM; walk-in tours every 30 minutes. 748 Jackson Pl NW (H St) Metro stops: Farragut West, Farragut North. 842.0920 &

26 Lafayette Park Designed by **L'Enfant** as part of *President's Park*, this area was made public land by **Thomas Jefferson**. It was here that laborers camped and bricks were dried during White House construction. First called *Jackson Square*, it was renamed for Revolutionary War hero **Major General Marquis de Lafayette** at a reception held during his last US visit. Lafayette's statue is at the park's SE

corner. He is shown standing before the French people asking them to support the American Revolution. As a fiery 19-year-old, Lafayette traveled to America, where he became a close friend of **George Washington**. At Yorktown VA, he successfully led colonial troops against the British. *Andrew Jackson*, however, still towers at the park's center. He is shown riding a spirited horse as he reviews troops before the *Battle of New Orleans*. The first equestrian statue cast in the US, it was sculpted in 1853 by **Clark Mills**. Around its base are 4 Spanish cannon captured by Jackson at Pensacola FL. **Major General Comte de Rochambeau**, another Frenchman who distinguished himself in the US Revolutionary War, is at the park's SW corner. **Brigadier General Thaddeus Kosciusko**, Polish-born hero of Saratoga, is at the NE corner. **Baron Von Steuben**, Prussian native and leader at Valley Forge, is at the park's NW corner.

During the turbulent 1960s, the park was often the scene of demonstrations. Today, lunchtime brown-baggers and tourists outnumber the few dedicated protestors camped on the sidewalk, hoping to catch the president's eye. During summer, the **National Park Service** hosts noontime concerts. ♦ Pennsylvania Ave-H St NW (Jackson-Madison Pls, just north of the White House) Metro stops: Farragut West, Farragut North

27 Dolley Madison House (1820) Now part of the Claims Court complex, this was the house where the widowed former First Lady lived until her death in 1849. Power seekers and the social elite flocked to the area in the 1840s, so much so that the Lafayette Square house, its symbolic center, earned a reputation as the real lobby of the White House. Not open to the public. ♦ H St at Madison Pl NW. Metro stop: McPherson Sq

28 St. John's Church and Parish House (1816, Benjamin Latrobe; remodeling, 1883, James Renwick) Called the *Church of Presidents*, since *Pew 54* has been occupied (at least once) by every man to hold that office since the building was built. It was also the architect's own church: a simple Greek Cross plan that did not include the portico, extended nave, or steeple. Renwick enlarged the seating and added the Palladian windows. The nearby Parish House is a French Second Empire opus that lost no elegance in its scaled-down form. ♦ Sunday services (Episcopal): 8, 9, 11AM. 1525 H St NW (16th St) Metro stop: McPherson Sq. 347.8766

29 Hay-Adams Hotel $$$ (1927, Harry Wardman) The site of **John Hay**'s and **Henry Adams**' homes is now one of the city's most exclusive hotels, with 140 Edwardian and Georgian rooms (25 suites), many of which overlook Lafayette Square and the White House. (**Ollie North** and his pals wooed potential contributors to their private Contra

Downtown

fund in the hotel's bar and restaurants.) Amenities include full concierge service, 24-hour maid and butler service, valet parking, and 3 restaurants (including the **John Jay Room** for classic French cuisine and a fancy afternoon tea). ♦ 800 16th St NW (H St) Metro stops: Farragut West, McPherson Sq. 638.6600; fax 638.2716

30 Tuckerman House (1886, Hornblower & Marshall) An odd blending of Richardsonian Romanesque and classical influences. Its resemblance to Richardson's now-gone Hay and Adams houses, which stood nearby, has led to speculation that he may have been personally involved with this design. ♦ 1600 Eye St NW (16th St) Metro stops: Farragut West, McPherson Sq

31 Sheraton Carlton $$$$ (1926, Harry Wardman) Renovated in 1988, this elegant pied-à-terre features 200 rooms (17 suites), with butler service on every floor, as well as a restaurant and bar. If you happen to be in the **Crystal Room** at 8AM any weekday morning, chances are you'll catch sight of a DC journalist interviewing a political bigwig. These one-on-ones are known as *Sperling Breakfasts*, after *Christian Science Monitor* reporter **Godfrey Sperling**. ♦ 923 16th St NW (K St) Metro stops: Farragut West, McPherson Sq. 638.2626, 800/325.3535; fax 638.4231

Within the Sheraton Carlton:

Allegro ★★$$$ Classic Italian cuisine in a grand café setting. Lunch and dinner start with Italian bread and a fragrant pesto spread. Special dishes include *penne* with sausage and paprika sauce, and a changing roster of fresh pizzas. ♦ Italian ♦ Daily 6:30AM-2:30PM, 6-11PM. Reservations recommended. 879.6900

Restaurants: Red   **Hotels**: Blue
Shops/Parks: Green   **Sights/Culture**: Black

32 Capital Hilton $$$ Centrally located and extensively refurbished since it was called the **Statler Hilton**. It now has several serviceable restaurants, plus gift, flower, and candy shops in the lobby. Ask for a corner room for more windows and a doubly nice view. Amenities include a multilingual staff, babysitting, a health club, and concierge service. Children under 18 stay free. ♦ 16th and K Sts NW. Metro stops: Farragut West, Farragut North. 393.1000, 800/HILTONS; fax 393.7992

Within the Capital Hilton:

Trader Vic's ★★$$$ A wonderfully corny jungle setting for fresh fish and meat dishes and the *most* exotic tropical cocktails—the Mai Tai Scorpion is a lethal combination of rum, brandy, and fruit juices served in a large scorpion-shaped bowl with 4 long straws! ♦ Polynesian ♦ M-F 10AM-2PM, 5PM-midnight; Sa-Su 5PM-midnight. Reservations required. 393.1000 ext 1641

33 International Union of Operating Engineers (1957, Holabird, Root & Burgee) Still the handsomest International-style office building in Washington, the IUOE headquarters took its inspiration from New York's landmark **Lever House**. Aqua glass, stainless steel, and a variety of white, black, and green marbles form the building's elegant surfaces. ♦ 1125 17th St NW (L-M Sts) Metro stops: Farragut West, Farragut North

34 National Geographic Society/Explorers Hall (1964, Edward Durell Stone) The National Geographic Society has been funding worldwide exploration, and publishing its perennially optimistic monthly travelogue since 1888. Its format and high quality have remained virtually unchanged in all that time, although its subscriber base has grown from 1000 to 11 million.

This modern structure is the society's headquarters. The first of Stone's many Washington buildings, it may also be his best, balanced and restrained. On its ground floor it houses **Explorers Hall**, a low-key museum that can be experienced in an hour's time. Dioramas illustrate the lives of Southwest American cliff dwellers. There is an ancient Olmec stone head (**Henry**, a live macaw, resides next to it), one of the sleds **Admiral Robert Peary** used to reach the North Pole, and a piece of moon rock retrieved by *Apollo 12*. Probably the best-known object in the hall is the giant hand-painted freestanding globe that has become the symbol of the society—it's 11 feet tall and 34 feet in circumference at the equator. (A new globe was installed, the same size, in the fall of 1988—it took 3172 hours to complete.)

At the north end of Explorers Hall is the permanent exhibition **Geographica**. Slated to be completed in 1991, it is an interactive center for the study of geography. Among its many features are touch screen modules that chronicle undersea explorations and tell the stories of early science heros. At **Earth Station One**, a 72-seat amphitheater that simulates a futuristic space station, visitors ask questions of the pilot/narrator (really a computer) by pushing buttons next to their seats. The answers then appear on a large screen.

You will also find frequently changing exhibitions, most of which relate to society-funded studies. The publication desk has an excellent collection of National Geographic maps, atlases, and lavish photography books. The society's M Street building (1984, **Skidmore, Owings & Merrill**), which houses offices and the **Gilbert H. Grosvenor Auditorium**, resembles a terraced ziggurat.

Marabar, a monumental 1984 environmental sculpture by **Elyn Zimmerman**, sits on the plaza between the 17th St and M St buildings. It consists of a dozen large pieces of granite quarried in South Dakota. Some of the surfaces have been left in their natural state, while others have been sheared clean and polished to reflect a small man-made pool. ♦ Free. M-Sa 9AM-5PM; Su 10AM-5PM. 17th and M Sts NW. Metro stop: Farragut North. 857-7588, tours and groups 857.7689 &

35 **Hubbard Memorial Library** (1902, Hornblower & Marshall) A simple, massive Italianate library building with enormous Romanesque windows lighting the second story. ♦ 1146 16th St NW (M St) Metro stop: McPherson Sq

35 **Metropolitan AME Church** (1854–1881, Samuel T. Morsell) Members of the congregation once hid slaves escaping on the *Underground Railroad* behind this broad Victorian Gothic facade. The influential black congregation has been active in the civil rights struggle ever since. This is the national headquarters of the **African Methodist Episcopal Church**. Funeral services for **Frederick Douglass** were held here. Of architectural interest are the 2-foot-thick brick bearing walls on the first floor, which support the vast second-story sanctuary. ♦ Services Su 8, 11AM. 1518 M St NW (15th-16th Sts) Metro stop: Farragut North, McPherson Sq. 331.1426

36 **The Madison Hotel** $$$ The classiest of Washington's older hotels and accustomed to dealing with the many whims of visiting heads of state, the Madison even features a top-security floor, favored by the Russians. Amenities include a multilingual staff, valet parking, several restaurants and bars, non-smoking rooms, and health club access. Even if you're staying elsewhere, take a peek at the gorgeous antiques in the lobby. ♦ Deluxe ♦ 1177 15th St NW (M St) Metro stops: Farragut North, McPherson Sq. 862.1600, telex 710.822.0145; fax 785.1255 &

Within the Madison Hotel:

Le Montpelier ★★$$$$ An opulent dining room of blue and gold, adorned with magnificent china and roses, and run by a discreet and efficient staff. All of the extremely expensive traditional dishes—sautéed halibut, roast pork or lamb, apple tart—are well prepared. ♦ French/American ♦ M-F noon-2PM, 6-10PM; Sa 6-10PM; Su 11AM-3PM, 6-10PM. Jacket and tie required. Reservations recommended. 862.1712

36 **Vista International** $$$ A modern luxury hotel with 396 rooms (23 suites) around a

soaring atrium. Music in the lobby nightly, as well as in the sing-along piano bar. Amenities include a concierge floor, valet parking, and a sauna and workout room. The **Verandah Restaurant** serves light fare, while the **American Harvest Restaurant** specializes in wild game, seafood, and creatively sauced seasonal vegetables. ♦ 1400 M St NW (15th St-Vermont Ave) Metro stop: Farragut North, McPherson Sq. 429.1700, 800/VISTA-DC; fax 785.0786 &

37 **The Washington Post**, one of the nation's most influential newspapers, was started in 1877 and immediately began to founder. In 1933, **Eugene Meyer**, a Wall Street tycoon and former governor of the Federal Reserve Board, bought the paper at a bankruptcy auction. Suddenly the *Post* began gaining recognition, first under Meyer, and later under his son-in-law, **Philip Graham**, who critics say used the paper as his personal soapbox. However, the *Post* really became a national force under the leadership of editor **Ben Bradlee** and former publisher **Katharine Graham**, who took over after the death of her husband, **Philip**. Ms. Graham's son, **Donald**, became publisher in 1979.

The *Post* is in large measure responsible for a renaissance in American journalism that started with the publication of the ***Pentagon Papers*** (discussing a secret study of US involvement in Vietnam) in 1971 and reached its apogee with the relentless investigative reporting of **Watergate** and its aftermath.

Actually, the *New York Times* beat the *Post* to the *Pentagon Papers* but was stopped by a temporary restraining order instigated by the Nixon administration. The *Post* then got hold of the documents and printed excerpts before it, too, was restrained. An appeals court eventually decided that the press could reprint the documents.

Since the mid-1970s, the *Post* has experienced a seesaw of triumph and defeat. In 1975, a pressmen's strike over modernization erupted into violence. There have been libel suits and accusations of shoddy reporting: **Janet Cooke** won and then returned a Pulitzer Prize for a series of articles on a child heroin addict. The subject, it turned out, was a fictional composite, not a real person.

Yet the *Post*'s reporting of Watergate has helped restore the romance to journalism. In 1974—even before **Robert Redford** and **Dustin Hoffman** played *Post* reporters **Bob Woodward** and **Carl Bernstein** in the movie *All the President's Men*—there was a 15-percent jump in journalism school enrollment over the previous year.

Forty-five-minute tours include the newsroom, pressroom, and museum—a brief history of this Fourth Estate institution. Individuals or groups of up to 40; students must be at least 11 years old. ◆ Tours M, Th 10AM-

Downtown

3PM. 1150 15th St NW (L-M Sts) Reservations required. Metro stop: McPherson Sq. 334.7969

38 Jacques French Restaurant ★★$$$
Inventive cuisine in a softly lit dining room. Chef **Mato** offers specialties of duckling with truffles, salmon and crabmeat in beurre blanc sauce, venison in wine, and white chocolate mousse. ◆ French ◆ M-F 11:30AM-2:30PM, 5:30PM-midnight; Sa 5:30PM-midnight. 915 15th St NW (Eye-K Sts) Jacket and tie requested. Reservations required. Metro stop: McPherson Sq. 737.4445

39 McPherson Grill ★★$$$ In 1988, the creators of the justifiably successful Occidental opened this airy 1930s-style restaurant in the otherwise-bereft McPherson Square area. It's not up to its predecessor's standards, but the sauces and side dishes are fresh and inventive; desserts are superb. (The chocolate-and-walnut raspberry torte will send you heavenward.) ◆ Continental ◆ M-F 11:30AM-10PM; Sa 5:30-10PM. 950 15th St NW (Eye-K Sts) Reservations recommended. Metro stop: McPherson Sq. 638.0950

40 Southern Building (1912, Daniel Burnham) Here Burnham's typical flamboyance is restrained to a large degree: the clean lines, carefully chosen materials, and balanced proportions (designed to make the building blend gracefully with its neighbors) show great discipline. But it may have been too much for him. Look up at the florid cornice! Architect **Moshe Safdie** restored this commercial office building according to its original specifications, since Burnham settled for fewer floors than planned. ◆ 1425 H St NW (14th-15th Sts) Metro stop: McPherson Sq

When **Pierre Charles L'Enfant** died in 1825, the designer of Washington DC left an estate valued at a mere $46.

41 Prime Plus ★★★$$$$ Part of Downtown's resurgence, Prime Plus offers, appropriately, new American cuisine. The menu is short but impressive: you'll find contentment in the smoked chicken, grilled venison, or salmon in any form. The prix fixe pretheater dinner is artfully arranged and a relative bargain. The wine selection is quite good. ◆ American ◆ M-Th 11:30AM-9:30PM; F 11:30AM-10PM; Sa 5-10PM. 727 15th St NW (H St-New York Ave) Jacket and tie requested. Reservations required. Metro stop: McPherson Sq. 783.0166

41 National Savings & Trust Co. (1880, James Windrim) The remodeled National Savings building is part of the Bankers' Classic Group, which includes 3 other Roman temple structures: **American Security and Trust Co.** (1899, **York & Sawyer**) at 15th St and Pennsylvania Ave NW; **Riggs National Bank** (1898, York & Sawyer), 1503 Pennsylvania Ave NW; and the **Union Trust Building** (1906, **Wood, Donnard & Deming**), SW corner of 15th and H Sts NW. Windrim's design, which uses whimsical turrets and a strange mixture of Victorian ornamentation, is in direct juxtaposition to the other 3, which echo the Treasury Building with their massive exterior columns. The intention was to give Washington's financial area a distinct and imposing face, a fashionable concept with bankers of that era. ◆ 15th St at New York Ave NW. Metro stop: McPherson Sq

42 Old Ebbitt Grill ★★$$ Now a member of the **Clyde's** restaurant family, the Ebbitt has been transformed into an upscale eatery outfitted in lush Victorian decor, popular for after-work and after-theater dining. Worth a visit. ◆ American ◆ M-F 7:30AM-1AM; Sa 8:30AM-1AM; Su 9:30AM-1AM. 675 15th St NW (F-G Sts) Reservations recommended. Metro stop: Metro Center. 347.4800

42 Metropolitan Square (1983, Vlastimil Koubek) When the facade of the **National Metropolitan Bank** was incorporated into this office/retail complex, preservationists weren't the only ones who complained: the Secret Service said the upper floors offered a far-too-clear view of the White House. ◆ 655 15th St NW (F-G Sts) Metro stop: Metro Center.

43 Garfinckel's has been the city's most prestigious department store since 1938, and is keeping up with the competition, thanks to a multimillion-dollar face-lift completed in 1988. Designer and quality men's and women's clothing, gifts, and accessories. Take a break from shopping at the **Greenbrier Restaurant**: good salads, burgers, and pastas. ◆ M-W, F-Sa 10AM 6PM; Th 10AM-7PM. 1401 F St NW (14th-15th Sts) Metro stop: Metro Center. 628.7730

44 Hotel Washington $$ (1918, Carrère and Hastings) This refurbished Italian Renaissance 350-room hotel boasts of being Washington's oldest continuously operating hotel. Nearly every US president of the 20th century and thousands of national and international dignitaries have stayed here. In addition to the 3 restaurants (the **Sky Terrace** has a panoramic view of the White House, the Treasury, and the Mall), a complimentary afternoon tea and hors d'oeuvres are served daily to hotel guests in the lobby. A health club is in the works. Two nonsmoking floors. Children under 14 stay free. ♦ 15th St at Pennsylvania Ave NW. Metro stops: Federal Triangle, Metro Center. 638.5900; fax 638.4275 ⟁

45 Occidental ★★★★$$$$ Named after a Washington classic, the Occidental is quickly earning its own place in history with American inventions in an elegant upstairs dining room. Among chef **Jeff Buben**'s creations: grilled quail with duck liver flan, oyster stew, brochette of swordfish and tuna with 5-peppercorn shallot butter, and lemon soufflé with raspberry purée. The wine list is extensive. ♦ American ♦ M-Th 11:30AM-2PM, 5:30-10:30PM; F 11:30AM-2PM, 5:30-11:30PM; Sa 5:30-11:30PM. 1475 Pennsylvania Ave NW (14th-15th Sts) Reservations recommended. Metro stops: Federal Triangle, Metro Center. 783.1475

Downstairs from the Occidental:

The Occidental Grill ★★$$ Papered from floor to ceiling with glossies of famous Washingtonians, this lively and stylish restaurant scores with a menu that ranges from burgers to grilled swordfish to airy fried onion rings. Excellent American wines are available by the glass. ♦ American. ♦ M-Sa 11:30AM-11:30PM. Reservations recommended. 783.1475

45 Washington Visitor Information Center First stop for the 20 million people who arrive each year camera in hand. There are brochures on sightseeing, accommodations, and dining, as well as a staff eager to offer assistance. Sponsored by the **Convention and Visitors Association**. ♦ Free. M-Sa 9AM-5PM. 1455 Pennsylvania Ave NW (14th-15th Sts, inside Willard Collection shops) Metro stops: Federal Triangle, Metro Center. 789.7000

In his Pulitzer Prize-winning novel, *Advise and Consent*, **Allen Drury** wrote the following about DC: "Like a city in dreams the great white capital stretches along the placid river from Georgetown on the west to Anacostia on the east. It is a city of temporaries, a city of just-arriveds and only-visitings, built on the shifting sands of politics, filled with people just passing through."

Restaurants: Red   **Hotels**: Blue
Shops/Parks: Green   **Sights/Culture**: Black

45 Willard Inter-Continental Hotel $$$ (1901, Henry J. Hardenbergh; 1986, Vlastimil Koubek) During its various incarnations, the Willard has served as temporary home for 10 presidents-elect, including **Lincoln**, **Harding**, and **Pierce**, and as temporary White House for **Calvin Coolidge** in 1923. This imposing Beaux-Arts marble building, abandoned in the 1970s, has been renovated to its previous glory. The former front desk, now used by the concierge, is a petal-shaped wonder of marble, glass, and polished wood. Highlights include **Peacock Alley**, **Round Robin** and **Nest** bars, and the **Café Expresso** coffee shop. Twenty-four-hour room service and nonsmoking rooms. Children under 15 stay free. ♦ 1401 Pennsylvania Ave NW (14th St) Metro stops: Metro Center, Federal Triangle. 628.9100, 800/ 327.0200; fax 637.7326 ⟁

Within the Willard Inter-Continental Hotel:

Willard Room ★★$$$$ Opulent Edwardian decor and secluded banquettes set the stage

for formal dining on new-American-style fare: fresh Hawaiian prawns, roast rack of lamb, and breast of guinea hen are among the dishes offered here. ♦ American ♦ M-F 7:30-10AM, 11:30AM-2PM, 6:30-10PM; Sa 8-10AM, noon-2PM, 6:30-10PM. Jacket and tie required for dinner. Reservations required. 637.7440

46 Pershing Park This little swatch of turf offers a shimmering pool, a thicket of trees, a kiosk selling beer, wine, and goodies, and tables and chairs—a stark contrast to **Freedom Plaza** just west. Skating rink open in the winter. ♦ Kiosk daily 10AM-6PM. Pennsylvania Ave (14th-15th Sts) Metro stops: Federal Triangle, Metro Center. 737.6938

47 The National Aquarium One of Washington's oddest attractions, this dank little corner in the depths of the **Commerce Building** (1932, **York & Sawyer**), also known as the *Herbert Hoover Building*, offers a cool escape for monument-weary tourists. It is the nation's oldest aquarium, originally established under the Federal Fish Commission in 1873 and spread out over a variety of locations, including Woods Hole MA and the present grounds near the Washington Monument. (The now-centralized aquarium became a private institution in 1982.) Sixty-five tanks display over 1200 fresh- and saltwater marine specimens as well as a green sea turtle and alligators. There is also a **Touch Tank** for children to handle live critters. Slide presentations, gift shop, cafeteria. ♦ Nominal admission. Aquarium daily 9AM-5PM. Cafeteria daily 8:30AM-2PM. 14th St and Constitution Ave NW. Metro stop: Federal Triangle. 377.2825/6

Pennsylvania Avenue Walking Tour

During America's post-World War II urban exodus, many city centers became neglected, and many of the nation's best-loved main streets fell into disrepair. But now that we are rediscovering our city's vital centers, those same streets are finding new life.

Pennsylvania Avenue, the broad *Main Street of the US*, has just such a history. The 1.3-mile-long connection between the Capitol and the White House has seen the back-and-forth parades of victory, anger, and tragedy that read like mercury rising and falling on a thermometer—a measure of the nation's political temperature. Seas of women have marched here seeking the right to vote and equality under the law; blacks have marched here demanding racial equality—and the Ku Klux Klan has gathered here in an effort to deny equality. After WWII, **General Dwight Eisenhower** paraded victorious American forces down the street. Less than 20 years later, a riderless horse led **John F. Kennedy**'s funeral cortege through the capital as Washingtonians and the nation said their final farewells.

Meanwhile, the central city's shops and offices were moving to new suburban centers, and Pennsylvania Ave was left with dingy storefronts and struggling businesses.

But no longer. Today the *Avenue* is undergoing a dramatic rebirth, preserving the old and adding compatible new structures. The face-lift includes parks, shade trees, brick sidewalks, kiosks, and benches. A total of 22 blocks are included in the redevelopment. Two **Metrorail** stops—one at the **Pavilion at the Old Post Office** and another at 7th Street near **Market Square**—also make the *Avenue* convenient for visitors, including suburban shoppers who are rediscovering Downtown, government and central city workers, and visitors from around the country and the world who come to see DC's many historic attractions.

Downtown

48 District Building (1908, Cope & Stewardson) Once reviled as a monstrosity, this overblown Beaux-Arts edifice is now finding many fans. Headquarters for DC's administration.
♦ 1350 Pennsylvania Ave NW (14th St) Metro stop: Federal Triangle

49 J.W. Marriott $$$ Conveniently located between the **National Theatre**, the **National Press Building**, and the **Shops at National Place**, this 774-room convention hotel includes 4 restaurants and is the flagship of the locally-based Marriott chain. Health club for guests and in-house movies. Non-smoking rooms; children under 18 stay free.
♦ 1331 Pennsylvania Ave NW (14th St) Metro stops: Federal Triangle, Metro Center. 393.2000, 800/228.9290; fax 626.6991 &

The ghost of an actor whose stage name was **John McCollough** is said to roam the **National Theatre**. As the story goes, he and another actor were in the basement of the theater washing their clothes when they got into a fight that ended in McCollough's murder. The killer then stuffed McCollough's body between the theater's old and new foundation walls —an area now known as the *cemetery*. In 1876, an employee thought he recognized McCollough walking around onstage, but the figure disappeared when called to. The ghost has been sighted a number of times, and about 5 years ago electricians found a piece of a Springfield military musket—which is believed to have been the murder weapon.

The White House

Drawing by Carlos Diniz

In 1861, **Julia Ward Howe** attended a huge military review of Union forces in Virginia, and was so taken with the spectacle that she returned to her **Willard Hotel** room and wrote the *Battle Hymn of the Republic*. A plaque on the wall of the Pennsylvania Ave side of the hotel commemorates this historic event.

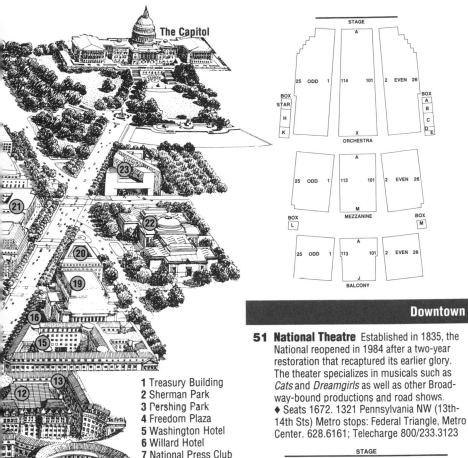

The Capitol

1 Treasury Building
2 Sherman Park
3 Pershing Park
4 Freedom Plaza
5 Washington Hotel
6 Willard Hotel
7 National Press Club
8 National Theater/
  National Place
9 J.W. Marriott
10 District Building
11 Dion Building
12 Pavilion at the Old Post Office
13 Internal Revenue Service
14 J. Edgar Hoover Building
15 Department of Justice
16 FDR Memorial
17 Navy Memorial
18 Market Square
19 National Archives
20 Federal Trade Commission
21 Canadian Embassy
22 National Gallery of Art West Building
23 National Gallery of Art East Building

Downtown

51 National Theatre Established in 1835, the National reopened in 1984 after a two-year restoration that recaptured its earlier glory. The theater specializes in musicals such as *Cats* and *Dreamgirls* as well as other Broadway-bound productions and road shows. ◆ Seats 1672. 1321 Pennsylvania NW (13th-14th Sts) Metro stops: Federal Triangle, Metro Center. 628.6161; Telecharge 800/233.3123

50 The Shops at National Place The newest of Downtown Washington's impulse malls: 125,000 square feet of retail shopping pleasures—more than 85 boutiques (from **Casual Corner** to **Joyce Selby**), fast-food shops, and restaurants (from **Roy Rogers** to **American Cafe**). The dark wood-and-brass interior opens to the lobby of the **J.W. Marriott**'s flagship hotel and extends to the **National Press Building** at the east end of the block. ◆ Stores: M-W, F-Sa 10AM-7PM; Th 10AM-8PM; Su noon-5PM. F St NW (13th-14th Sts) Metro stops: Federal Triangle, Metro Center. 783.9090 &

52 Warner Theatre Opened in 1924 as the **Darle**, a vaudeville house, the theater has also flourished as a movie house, and is now a venue for concerts. The gilded ceiling and threadbare Art Deco decor make for an atmospheric, if not elegant, evening. ◆ Seats 2000. Box office: M-F 10AM-6PM; Sa hours vary. 513 13th St NW (E-F Sts) Metro stops: Federal Triangle, Metro Center. 626.1050

L'Enfant's bill for the design of **The Federal City of Washington** totaled $95,000; after 8 years of silence, he finally accepted Congress' offer of $2500.

53 Freedom Plaza (1980, Venturi, Rauch and Scott Brown) This block-long plaza was designed as a witty re-creation of the disrupted axis between the Capitol and the White House, but was compromised when local censors eliminated its vertical elements, leaving only the inlaid map of **L'Enfant**'s city plan. The open plaza is used mainly by skateboarders and occasionally for outdoor concerts. ◆ Pennsylvania Ave NW (13th-14th Sts) Metro stop: Federal Triangle

54 Anton's 1201 Club ★★$$$ Bill Anton's sleek supper club features American cuisine and solid headliners like **Peggy Lee**. ◆ American ◆ Cover, minimum. M-F 11:30AM-2:30PM, 5PM-1AM; Sa 5PM-1AM. Shows: Tu-W 8:30; Th-Sa 8:30, 10:45. 1201 Pennsylvania Ave NW (11th-12th Sts) Metro stop: Federal Triangle. 783.1201

54 Dion Building (1984, David Childs) This huge building is a modern salute to the monolithic old office blocks that surround it. Heavy

Downtown

columns, Roman barrel vaults, and a limestone facade give it a Baroque flair, but its sheer size (12 stories, 1.2 million square feet of office space, and over 1200 windows) puts it squarely in the 20th century. Inside, over a quarter-acre of Greek and Italian tile paves the **Grand Court**, and a waterfall plunges down from the skylight 6 stories overhead. ◆ 1201 Pennsylvania Ave NW (11th-12th Sts) Metro stops: Federal Triangle, Metro Center

55 Departmental Auditorium (1935, Arthur Brown, Jr.) The unusually dynamic sculpture in the exterior pediments hints at the opulence within. Although the Neoclassical/Beaux-Arts theater style appeared in movie houses nationwide at the time, this is one of the few theaters where all the rich materials you see—gold, marble, crystal—are the real thing. The auditorium is used mainly for ceremonial events. ◆ Seats 1300. 1301 Constitution Ave NW (12th-14th Sts)

Drawing by Carlos Diniz

56 Pavilion at the Old Post Office (at the Nancy Hanks Center) (1899, W. Edbrooke; restoration, 1983, Arthur Cotton Moore) The **Evans Development Company** sponsored this first-class mix of 50 specialty shops, 5 restaurants and cafés, and 16 fast-food restaurants that serve quick cuisine (tacos, curries, crepes, and ice cream). It is the capital's most dazzling

indoor mall, built into an old and significant Romanesque Revival chateau that had been threatened by demolition. (The late **Nancy Hanks**, who headed the National Endowment for the Arts from 1969 through 1977, led the fight to save the Old Post Office. Congress rewarded her in kind.) The 315-foot clocktower is the third-tallest structure in DC. (Free tours of the tower leave from the stage level every 5 to 7 minutes.) The atrium is highlighted with Victorian brass fittings, red oak woodwork, and frosted glass; the retail and restaurant arcade is bustling, skylit, and filled with the aroma of international foods. The interior focal point is the stage, where free live entertainment—dancers, musicians, magicians—is a pleasant diversion for afternoon shoppers pausing for a fast lunch.

A feisty example of urban revitalization, the Pavilion has pumped new life into the staid and bureaucratic **Federal Triangle**. Because the Old Post Office is a federal building, retailers had to wait for the 1976 *Cooperative Use Act* to share open space with the government offices housed in the top 7 floors. But the 3 lower levels now offer a diversity of merchandise, from penny postcards at **Penn Station** to designer jewelry at **Impulse**. **Gifts at the Pavilion** offers high-ticket items by **Boda**, **Seiko**, and **Kosta**. **Kinder Haus Toys** features imported children's playthings, while **Modigliani** caters to adults with its silky lingerie and sultry perfumes. ◆ Store hours: M-Sa 10AM-8PM; Su noon-6PM. Tours: daily 10AM-5:45PM, Jan-Mar, Sep-Dec; daily 8AM-11PM, 1st Su in Apr-Labor Day. 1100 Pennsylvania Ave NW (12th St) Metro stop: Federal Triangle. 289.4224

57 J. Edgar Hoover FBI Building (1975, C.F. Murphy) The national police force keeps track of *Most Wanted* criminals and expands the science of criminology from this unpopular brutalistic beige concrete building. (Rumor has it that Hoover himself helped design it.)

Created in 1908 by **Teddy Roosevelt** to fight political corruption, the FBI began to realize its powerful potential after 1924, the year Hoover was appointed director. You'll learn more about the FBI in an introductory video presentation; then tour the high-tech laboratories and exhibitions tracing the FBI's history through the gangster years to the Cold War decade of espionage to its current science fictionlike crime-fighting techniques. The tour ends with the ever-popular firearms demonstration by a special agent. ◆ Free. Tours M-F 8:45AM-4:15PM. 10th St at Pennsylvania Ave NW; enter on E St NW (9th-10th Sts) Reservations recommended for large groups. Metro stops: Metro Center, Gallery Pl, Federal Triangle, Archives. 324.3000

Only 600 special agents are hired from 10,000 hopefuls who apply to the FBI's 59 field offices each year. The trainees, all college graduates between 23 and 35, get 16 weeks of training, including over 100 hours of firearms instructions. An agent must qualify in 8 yearly shooting tests.

IDENTIFICATION ORDER NO. 1217
March 12, 1934.

DIVISION OF INVESTIGATION
U. S. DEPARTMENT OF JUSTICE
WASHINGTON, D. C.

Fingerprint Classification

12 9 R 0
14 U 00 9

WANTED

JOHN DILLINGER, with alias,

FRANK SULLIVAN

NATIONAL MOTOR VEHICLE THEFT ACT

DESCRIPTION

Age, 31 years
Height, 5 feet 7-1/8 inches
Weight, 153 pounds
Build, medium
Hair, medium chestnut
Eyes, grey
Complexion, medium
Occupation, machinist
Marks and scars, 1/2 inch scar
back left hand; scar middle
upper lip; brown mole between
eyebrows
Mustache

Photograph taken January 25, 1934

John Dillinger

CRIMINAL RECORD

As John Dillinger, #14395, received
State Reformatory, Pendleton, Indiana,
September 16, 1924; crime, assault and
battery with intent to rob and con-
spiracy to commit a felony; sentences,
2 to 14 years and 10 to 20 years re-
spectively;
   As John Dillinger, #13225, received
State Prison, Michigan City, Indiana,
July 16, 1929; transferred from Indiana
State Reformatory; paroled under Reformatory jurisdiction, May 10, 1933;
parole revoked by Governor - considered
as delinquent parolee;
   As John Dillinger, #10587, arrested
Police Department, Dayton, Ohio, September 22, 1933; charge, fugitive;
turned over to Allen County, Ohio,
authorities;
   As John Dillinger, received County

Jail, Lima, Ohio, September 28, 1933; charge, bank robbery; escaped October 12, 1933;
   As Frank Sullivan, arrested Police Department, Tucson, Arizona, January 25, 1934; charge, fugitive; turned
over to Lake County, Indiana, authorities;
   As John Dillinger, #14487, arrested Sheriff's Office, Crown Point, Indiana, January 30, 1934; charge,
murder - bank robbery; escaped March 3, 1934.

(over)   Issued by: J. EDGAR HOOVER, DIRECTOR.

The photos of 10 fearsome faces that grace the walls of your local post office are an outgrowth of the **Public Enemy Number 1** phenomenon, largely a creation of the media in the 1930s gangster era. The FBI discovered that all the publicity was instrumental in capturing criminals, so in 1950 they created the *Ten Most Wanted List*. To make the list, a criminal must have broken a federal law and must be seen as a particular menace to the public (armed, fleeing, a history of violence, etc.), and the agency must believe that publicity will aid in his or her capture. Fugitive **Patty Hearst**, for instance, wasn't put on the list because the FBI thought her face was sufficiently well known.

When a spot opens up on the list—due to death, capture, or, in rare cases, expiration of federal warrants—it's quickly filled by one of several thousand people in the **Identification Order** (or *I.O.*) **File**. New pictures are sent out to field offices, local police stations, and media outlets across the country. The policy has proven very effective. Out of the 350 people apprehended since the 1950s, 114 were captured through the aid of citizen identification.

The FBI has fingerprints—about 185 million sets of them—and maintains that it still hasn't found 2 sets alike.

The fingerprint cards are divided into criminal and civil files. The criminal file contains the prints of anyone who has ever been arrested for a serious crime or felony (over 21 million people). The civil file contains the prints of military personnel, federal workers, and those who have passed through immigration and naturalization. The file is rounded out by another 5 million or so prints called *Personal IDs*. These are prints sent in voluntarily by citizens across the country; they have proved useful in finding amnesia victims and missing children.

The **Latent Fingerprint Analysis Unit** is the unit that examines evidence—guns, car doors, etc.—for fingerprints. These are the people you see in the movies spreading powder everywhere. The first step in identifying a set of prints is to determine into which of 3 basic categories the prints fall—loops, arches (tented or plain), or whirls. The ridges are then counted outward from a central point, narrowing the possibilities even more. At this point, the classified prints are fed into a computer, which quickly searches the master file for a matching set. The final match is always done by eye.

Under the *Freedom of Information Act* you may find out if the FBI has a file or fingerprint card for you. Request the information in a notarized letter. Send it to: Director of the FBI, J. Edgar Hoover Building, 10th St and Pennsylvania Ave NW, Washington DC 20535.

When the US government moved from Philadelphia in 1800, the entire federal staff consisted of 150 people.

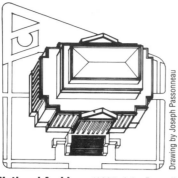

Drawing by Joseph Passonneau

58 National Archives (1935, John Russell Pope) Fifty years ago, after the documents that serve as the foundation of our government were variously lost, mistaken for worthless paper, threatened by advancing armies, or left to crumble in dark vaults, a suitable home was finally created for the *Declaration of Independence*, the *Bill of Rights*, and for the US *Constitution*.

Downtown

The National Archives serves as the nation's safe-deposit box: a 21-floor collection of treaties, laws, maps, land claims, bills of sale, sound recordings, and other important documents—enough to fill 250,000 4-drawer filing cabinets! The current archivist of the US is **Dr. Don Wilson**.

The stories and memorabilia in this collection are endless: **Richard Nixon**'s letter of resignation is kept here, as are the *Emancipation Proclamation*, the surrender documents of Japan's World War II government, and a letter from the **King of Siam** to **Abraham Lincoln** expounding the efficiency of elephant labor. There is also a copy of the *Magna Carta*.

The archives' main attractions, though, are familiar to every US schoolchild: the *Declaration of Independence, Constitution*, and *Bill of Rights*. These profoundly influential documents are on permanent display in the domed **Rotunda**, accessible via the Constitution Ave entrance. They are sealed in protective helium to guard against aging and lowered into deep vaults at night in case of emergency. **Barry Faulkner**'s massive murals depicting the forging of these papers encircle the display .

In the National Archives' **Exhibition Hall** around the Rotunda, changing exhibitions are displayed. Most are thematic, celebrating an aspect of the American people, such as the Yankee genius for invention, or a single remarkable person. Many of the exhibitions use photographs and engravings from the collection's pictorial records. The collection spans the history of photography and includes many historical pictures, such as **Matthew Brady**'s Civil War photos. Moving pictures— 140,000 reels—and miles of sound recordings, from **FDR**'s *Fireside Chats* to **Tokyo Rose**'s propaganda messages, are also on file.

The National Archives serves the public as more than a museum: access to important records and research assistance are available for genealogical searches. (One story researched here was **Alex Haley**'s *Roots*.) Immigration records, ships' logs, slave transit and ownership records, treaties with American Indian tribes, and masses of information on taxes, military service, births, and deaths help families rediscover their heritage.

The building that houses so much American minutiae has a shimmering white exterior trimmed with Corinthian columns, evidence of Pope's facility with classical forms. The Pennsylvania Ave entry is a welcome change from all the raised rusticated bases supporting other buildings in the Federal Triangle area.

Special *Behind the Scenes* tours by appointment, preferably made 2 weeks in advance. The gift shop sells document facsimiles, cards, and books. ♦ Free. Rotunda and Exhibition Hall: daily 10AM-5:30PM, Jan-Mar, Sept-Dec; daily 10AM-9PM, Apr-Labor Day. Tours M-F 10:15AM-1:15PM. Research areas: M-F 8:45AM-10PM; Sa 9AM-5PM. Constitution Ave at 8th St NW. Researchers use Pennsylvania Ave entrance. Metro stop: Archives. 523.3000, tours 523.3183, film series 523.3097, genealogical information 523.3285 ♿

59 Market Square (Slated for completion 1990, Hartman-Cox) This 2-tower office-retail-residential complex will include 210 apartments, a visitors' center, restaurants, and an open-air park. ♦ 701-801 Pennsylvania Ave NW (7th-8th Sts) Metro stop: Archives

Within Market Square:

Navy Memorial (1987, Conklin Rossant) A 100-foot-diameter circular plaza features a sculpture of the *Lone Sailor* (1987, **Stanley Bleifeld**), which stands on the largest grid map *of* the world *in* the world. Free military band concerts in the summer. ♦ 524.0830

60 Dutch Mill Deli ★$ Gigantic sandwiches and platters, okay soups. Serve yourself, cafeteria-style. Great proximity to the National Gallery and surrounding museums. ♦ American ♦ Daily 7AM-5PM. 639 Indiana Ave NW (6th-7th Sts) Metro stop: Archives. 347.3665

61 Temperance Fountain (1880) **Henry Cogswell**, an eccentric California dentist, liked to dedicate these fountains—on which his name would be prominently inscribed—to any city that would have one. He hoped the pedestrian would slake his or her thirst with cool water rather than booze. Prohibition has since been repealed, and the city long ago stopped maintaining the obsolete cooling system hidden in the fountain's base. So, while America may no longer be dry, Cogswell's fountain is. ♦ Pennsylvania Ave at 7th St NW. Metro stop: Archives

62 Mellon Fountain (1952, Sidney Waugh) An elegant fountain comprising 3 concentric bronze basins; the outermost is the largest ever cast. A 20-foot-high plume of water gushes from the center. ♦ Constitution and Pennsylvania Aves NW. Metro stop: Archives

63 Canadian Embassy (1988, Arthur Erickson) Embassy as edifice, this massive marble building includes a 175-seat theater, an art gallery, and a library, plus a 3-story rotunda set in a pool in a titanic courtyard. ♦ 501 Pennsylvania Ave NW (6th St-Marshall Pl) Metro stops: Archives, Judiciary Sq

64 Darlington Fountain (1923, Carl Jennewin) Dedicated by **Joseph Darlington**'s lawyer friends, this Art Deco sculpture of a naked nymph standing beside a fawn created quite a stir among the barristers' Baptist coreligionists. In a pointed retort, Carl Jennewin said that the lady was "direct from the hands of God instead of from the hands of a dressmaker." ♦ Judiciary Sq (5th-D Sts NW) Metro stop: Judiciary Sq

65 District of Columbia Courthouse (Old City Hall) (Original building, 1820, George Hadfield) One of the earliest Greek Revival buildings in the city. The east wing was completed in 1826, the west in 1849. ♦ 4th and D Sts NW. Metro stop: Judiciary Sq. 879.1010

66 US Tax Court (1982, Victor Lundy) This building is a showpiece of engineering. Granite and bronze-tinted glass sheath the exterior; the third-floor court chambers are each suspended from the ceiling by over 100 3-inch steel cables. The building was originally designed to span the nearby freeway, and although the plan was abandoned, the building's form still reflects the original intent. Concrete and teak lend texture to the interior surfaces. You can't just wander in—ask the guard at the entrance for permission to look around. ♦ 3rd St NW (D-E Sts) Metro stop: Judiciary Sq. 376.2724

67 Hyatt Regency Capitol Hill $$$ Not wanting to be upstaged by its ponderous Capitol Hill neighbors, the well-appointed Hyatt Regency offers both an extensive gift shop and **Atrium Park** (the lobby filled with exotic vegetation) to create its own niche in the neighborhood. There are 20 different meeting and banquet rooms, a health club and indoor pool, and a variety of restaurants and lounges in café-like settings. Indoor parking available. Some nonsmoking rooms; children under 19 stay free. ♦ 400 New Jersey Ave NW (1st-E Sts) Metro stop: Union Station. 737.1234, 800/228.9000; fax 737.5773

68 Quality Hotel Capitol Hill $$ The 341 newly decorated rooms offer one of the best values in town, including special family and weekender plans. Each spacious room features a pair of double beds and free HBO movies. There is also free indoor and outdoor parking. The **Coach and Parlor** restaurant offers traditional American food; the **Whistlestop** lounge serves cocktails and complimentary hors d'oeuvres. Tour buses leave from the hotel to historic sites. Some nonsmoking rooms; children under 17 stay free. ♦ 415 New Jersey Ave NW (D-E Sts) Metro stop: Union Station. 638.1616, 800/228.5151; fax 638.0707 &

69 La Colline ★★$$ This elegant brasserie a few blocks from Union Station offers a nice menu at bargain prices. Choose from a prix fixe menu, or go à la carte with a smoked salmon appetizer and entrees such as duck breast with cassis sauce, coq au vin, a tender veal cutlet in mushrooms and cream, or fresh fish. You should definitely investigate the dessert carts and the wine list. (Order individual glasses from a selection of featured wines changed weekly.) ♦ French ♦ M-F 7:30-10AM, 11:30AM-3PM, 6-10PM; Sa 6-10PM.

400 N. Capitol St NW (D St) Reservations recommended. Metro stop: Union Station. 737.0400

70 Bellevue Hotel $$ Tiny, efficiently run hotel just 2 blocks from Union Station has cozy rooms with Queen Anne-style furnishings and room service (from the **Packard Grille**) 7AM to midnight, and delivers the *Wall Street Journal* with breakfast. Children under 17 stay free. ♦ 15 E St NW (New Jersey Ave-N. Capitol St) Metro stop: Union Station. 638.0900, 800/337.6667; fax 638.5132

Within the Bellevue Hotel:

Tiber Creek Pub ★$$ This polished wood-paneled restaurant/lounge offers hearty steaks, burgers, and daily specials. Live jazz on weekends. ♦ American ♦ M 7AM-12:30AM; Tu 7AM-1AM; W 7AM-1:30AM; Th 7AM-2AM; F-Sa 7:30AM-2:30AM; Su 7AM-midnight. Reservations recommended. 638.0900

71 Phoenix Park Hotel $$ Remodeled as a small Continental hotel with a Dublin flair. Amenities include concierge service, and room service 6AM to midnight. Kids under 12 stay free. ♦ 520 N. Capitol St NW (F St) Metro stop: Union Station. 638.6900, 800/824.5419; fax 393.3236 &

Within the Phoenix Park Hotel:

Powerscourt ★★$$$ The part-Irish menu, discreet location, and excellent service attract politicians. ♦ Irish/American ♦ M-F 7:30-10AM, 11:30AM-2PM, 5-10PM; Sa 5-10PM. Reservations required. 737.3776

71 The Dubliner ★$ A bit o' Ireland, where pints of **Guiness** (on tap) follow shots of **Jameson** and **Paddy's**, and where each night Celtic bands encourage customer sing-alongs and plenty of blarney. ♦ Irish/American ♦ M-Sa 11AM-11PM; Su 7:30AM-11PM. 520 N. Capitol St NW (F St) Metro stop: Union Station. 737.3773

71 The Irish Times ★★$ Incogruously housed in what looks to be a former Chinese restaurant—check out the pagoda-style roof—is a boisterously Irish restaurant and bar that caters to a regular crowd of Capitol Hill staffers and embassy employees. Generous portions of stewed chili and fish 'n' chips are favorites during the busy lunch hour. The jukebox plays Irish hits nonstop, from **Molly Malone** to **U2**. ◆ Irish ◆ M-Th, Su 9:30AM-2AM; F-Sa 9:30AM-3AM. 14 F St NW (N. Capitol-1st Sts) Metro stop: Union Station. 543.5433

72 Government Printing Office & Bookstore A mecca for information freaks, the center publishes 1.4 billion volumes a year. According to the *Guiness Book of World Records*, it's the world's largest in-plant printing operation (5000 workers) and uses enough paper yearly to fill 25 miles of train cars. Main offerings include the *Congressional Record* (sent to Capitol Hill bound in Moroccan leather with marbled end papers) and the *Federal Register*, the daily trade paper for the federal government.

Downtown

Thousands of consumer-information books and booklets are published here. The all-time bestseller, *Infant Care*, has sold over 17 million copies since its first 1914 printing. The bookstore stocks over 3000 titles and offers 17,000 more in its catalog, plus **NASA** and **National Park Service** posters, how-to books, government guides, histories, and most government publications.

The main building (1901) is a massive Romanesque Revival edifice composed entirely of handmade brick. ◆ Bookstore M-F 8AM-4PM. 710 N. Capitol St NW (G-H Sts) Metro stop: Union Station. 275.2092. Also at: 1510 H St NW. 653.5075

73 Georgetown University Law Center (1971, Edward Durell Stone) Designed at the same time and by the same architect as the **Kennedy Center**, the Law Center has been widely criticized as an inhospitable mass of brick. ◆ 600 New Jersey Ave NW (F-G Sts) Metro stop: Union Station

74 Jewish Historical Society of Greater Washington (1876) Housed in a modest red brick structure that was built for *Adas Israel*, the city's oldest synagogue, the society keeps records and oral histories of the community's Jewish heritage and mounts special exhibitions of Judaica. A **National Historic Shrine**, the building itself is officially called the **Lillian and Albert Small Jewish Museum**. ◆ Free. Tu, Th, Su 11AM-3PM or by appointment. 701 3rd St NW (G St) Metro stop: Judiciary Sq. 789.0900, 301/881.0100 &

Rumor has it that **Ulysses S. Grant** coined the word *lobbyist* to describe the men who hung around the **Willard Hotel** lobby in hopes of making contact with political bigwigs.

DC ranks Number 1 (69.2%) in number of women in the workforce; 33% are in high-status jobs.

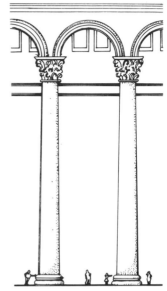

75 National Building Museum/Old Pension Building (1882, General Montgomery Meigs) For years, this low-budget Victorian version of the Palazzo Farnese in Italy was ridiculed as a white elephant. Its central court (the city's largest indoor space) and offices held 1500 clerks processing pension payments for pre-WWI veterans and their families. Over some 40 years, the clerks doled out $8 billion.

In the middle of this century the building was threatened with destruction, then happily rediscovered. In 1980 it became the home of this museum.

The NBM is dedicated to documenting and explaining the US's vital building trade, from the craft of hardhats to the art of architects. Along with exhibitions, the NBM highlights controversial building and design issues with film and video. It has put together an archives/data bank of thousands of models, drawings, blueprints, and documents.

The building's most stunning display, though, is itself. The central court is as long as a football field and approximately 16 stories high. Four tiers of balconies—some supporting ornate iron grillwork—climb its interior walls. In the center are the 8 largest Corinthian columns in the world—each one required 70,000 bricks to build and measures 76 feet high and 25 feet in diameter.

The inspired design of Army Quartermaster General Montgomery C. Meigs, who also engineered the White House dome, has offices radiating off the central court and its balconies.

There are hundreds of windows that eliminate the dark, stale hallways typical of early office buildings, while they provide natural light and ventilation without the heat of a conventional skylight.

One architect remarked that only a thunderstorm or an inaugural ball could fill the vast space. In fact, the inaugural celebrations of **Cleveland**, **Harrison**, **FDR**, **Nixon**, **Carter**, **Reagan**, and **Bush** were held here. ◆ M-F 10AM-4PM; Sa-Su noon-4PM. Walk-in tours: Tu, F 12:30PM; Sa-Su 1PM; group tours by appointment. F St NW (4th-5th Sts) Metro stop: Judiciary Sq. 272.2448 ⟨⟩

76 Comfort Inn $$ This 197-room hotel offers simple accommodations just 4 blocks from the Convention Center. Valet service, fitness room, laundromat, some rooms with jacuzzis. **Cafe Express** coffee shop. Nonsmoking rooms; children under 18 stay free. ◆ 500 H St NW (5th-6th Sts) Metro stop: Gallery Pl. 289.5959, 800/228.5150 ⟨⟩

77 A.V. Ristorante Italiano ★★$$ This simple family restaurant has been serving a rich variety of Central and Southern Italian fare for nearly half a century. Everything from pizza to lasagna to veal in all its permutations. ◆ Italian ◆ M-Th 11:30AM-11:30PM; F 11:30AM-midnight; Sa-Su 5PM-midnight. 607 New York Ave NW (6th St) Metro stop: Gallery Pl. 737.0550

77 Marrakesh ★★$$ The exotic Moroccan setting—pillows strewn on low sofas and waiters in Moroccan dress—is further enhanced by belly dancers who perform nightly. In keeping with the sensual nature of the place, diners eat with their hands (which the staff wash and dry before the meal). The 7-course prix fixe dinner lasts for several hours. If you're still conscious at the end of the evening, top off the experience with baklava and mint tea. ◆ Moroccan ◆ M-F 6-11PM; Sa seatings 6, 9PM; Su 5:30-11PM. 617 New York Ave (6th-7th Sts) Reservations required. Metro stop: Gallery Pl. No credit cards. 393.9393

78 Mt. Vernon Square (1903, Ackerman and Ross) Built as DC's **Carnegie Library**, this splendid marble Beaux-Arts building has been restored for use by the University of the District of Columbia, Mt. Vernon Campus, and awaits the renaissance of the rest of the neighborhood with the coming of Metro's Green Line. ◆ New York and Massachusetts Aves NW

79 Szechuan ★★$$ Probably your best bet for inexpensive Chinese food. Enlist your waiter's help in choosing from the vast menu of often-fiery appetizers and main courses. Excellent hot and sour soup, stir-fried vegetables, chicken with wine sauce, and garlicky jumbo shrimp. Tea brunch served on weekends. ◆ Szechuan/Hunan ◆ M-Th, Su 11AM-11PM; F-Sa 11AM-11:45PM. 615 Eye St NW (6th-7th Sts) Metro stop: Gallery Pl. 393.0130

The Algonquin Indians who lived along the lower river called it *Potowmek*—the trading place.

80 Ruby Restaurant ★$$ Dim sum (Chinese dumplings of all shapes, textures, and flavors) are this restaurant's forte; order a selection. Take your chances on an otherwise hit-or-miss menu. ◆ Cantonese/Szechuan ◆ M-Th 11AM-3AM; F-Sa 11AM-4AM. 609 H St NW (6th-7th Sts) Reservations recommended. Metro stop: Gallery Pl. 842.0060

80 Tony Cheng's Mongolian Restaurant ★★$$ Fun food: you pick the raw ingredients from the buffet, and chefs stir-fry it before your eyes on a massive Mongolian griddle. Upstairs, try **Tony Cheng's Seafood Restaurant** for fresh fish, Cantonese-style. ◆ Mongolian/Cantonese ◆ M-Th 10AM-11PM; F-Sa 10AM-midnight; Su 11AM-11PM. 619 H St NW (6th-7th Sts) Metro stop: Gallery Pl. 842.8669, 371.8669

80 Da Hua Food One-stop shopping for Oriental chefs, with fresh meat and fish, produce, and Pan-Asian staples and cookbooks. ◆ Daily 10AM-7PM. 623 H St NW (6th-7th Sts) Metro stop: Gallery Pl. 371.8888

Downtown

80 China Inn ★★$$ For over 40 years, this recently renovated bustling mainstay of DC's Chinatown has offered a seemingly endless array of satisfying Cantonese dishes: steamed chicken with Chinese sausage, roast duck, rice noodles with roast pork, spareribs in black bean sauce. Try the house specialties, especially the sea bass and other seafood dishes. ◆ Cantonese ◆ Daily 11AM-11PM. 631 H St NW (6th-7th Sts) Metro stop: Gallery Pl. 842.0909

81 Hunan Chinatown ★★$$ White tablecloths, attentive service, and well-prepared Northern Chinese favorites make this a consistent winner. ◆ Hunan ◆ M-Th, Su 11AM-11PM, F-Sa 11AM-1AM. 624 H St NW (6th-7th Sts) Metro stop: Gallery Pl. 783.5858

82 Golden Palace ★$$ The splendid red and gold dining room compensates for the sometimes uneven performance of the kitchen. Stick to dim sum or plain Cantonese standbys and you'll enjoy a pleasant meal. ◆ Cantonese ◆ M-Th, Su 11AM-10PM; F-Sa 11AM-midnight. 720 7th St NW (G-H Sts) Metro stop: Gallery Pl. 783.1225

Chinatown
This tiny neighborhood, generally located between H and K Streets NW from 6th to 9th Streets, is holding its own against the explosion of new office construction. It's a good place for an afternoon of exploring dusty little shops or for an evening of Chinese food. You can't miss the massive and ornate entrance gate! The street signs are in Chinese and English.

A plaque at 604 H St reads: "A Historical Landmark/Surratt Boarding House/ Conspirators plotted the abduction of U.S. President Abraham Lincoln/Plaque by Chi-Am Lion's Club."

Restaurants: Red	**Hotels**: Blue
Shops/Parks: Green	**Sights/Culture**: Black

83 Martin Luther King, Jr., Library (1972, Ludwig Mies van der Rohe) The main branch of the DC public library system is more than just a stack of books. Besides sponsoring a citywide arts program, the library's permanent collection of paintings, sculpture, and photographs is on display in the **Anteroom Gallery** and throughout the building. There are programs for children, poetry readings, theatrical performances, and music concerts. But back to the stacks: among the system's vast offerings are the **Washingtoniana Room**—the largest collection of DC-related information in the world (books, registers, photos, etc.) from the beginning of the 19th century—and the **Star Library**, masses of information from the old *Washington Star* newspaper. The simple black steel-and-glass box epitomizes Miesian design and was among his final works. Underground parking is available. ♦ M-Th 9AM-9PM; F-Sa 9AM-5:30PM; Su 1-5PM. 901 G St NW (9th-10th Sts) Metro stops: Gallery Pl, Metro Center. 727.1111 &

Downtown

84 National Museum of American Art and National Portrait Gallery (Old Patent Office) (1836-67, Robert Mills) When it served for 92 years as the US Patent Office, this building held an archive of American technical ingenuity. Now the arched and pillared marble hallways display American artistic talent in 2 patriotic collections.

The **Old Patent Office** building itself is a century-old replica of the Parthenon, rendered in Virginia freestone, a dignified home for the art it houses. The building's saddest role was as hospital and morgue after the battle at Antietam. **Clara Barton** and **Walt Whitman** ministered to the wounded. Today, a pair of elms enlivens the cool courtyard between the 2 great museums. Bring your own snack and picnic here, or eat at the pleasant **Patent Pending** cafeteria within the building.

The National Museum of American Art, on the building's north side, celebrates 2 centuries of native talent. A reinstallation of the entire museum, with the works more chronologically ordered, makes it easier to trace the development of native styles and movements.

This is the country's oldest art collection. The museum now owns over 33,000 pieces, including works by **Edward Hopper**, **Andrew Wyeth**, **Winslow Homer**, **Gene Davis**, and **Benjamin West**. There are selections of **Hiram Powers**' sculpture, oils by **Albert Pinkham Ryder**, and the country's largest collection of New Deal art.

The subjects preserved on canvas and in bronze lead visitors on a walk through America, past and present: the wild landscapes and frontier lifestyle depicted by **Thomas Moran** and **Albert Bierstadt**; portraits of Americans

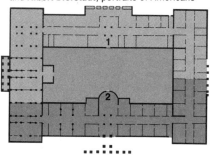

1 National Museum of American Art
2 National Portrait Gallery

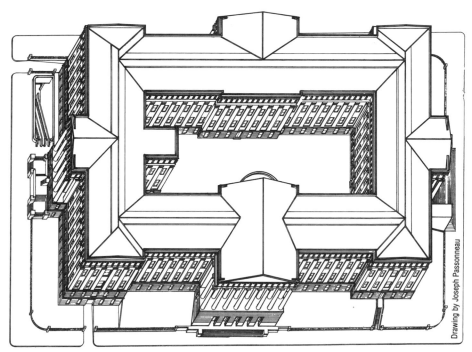

Drawing by Joseph Passonneau

both common and uncommon painted by **Cecilia Beaux** and **Charles Willson Peale**. The third-floor **Lincoln Gallery**, the site of the 1865 inaugural reception, offers the energy of the 20th century as captured in the works of **Franz Kline**, **Willem de Kooning**, **Robert Rauschenberg**, and **Helen Frankenthaler**.

The museum has a large collection of miniatures, folk art, a 45,000-volume library, and the **Archives of American Art** (open to researchers), which also serves the National Portrait Gallery.

The **Renwick Gallery** (see entry **31**) of the NMAA exhibits American crafts. The **Barney Studio House** at Sheridan Square depicts a turn-of-the-century artist's home and studio. Besides permanent and rotating exhibitions, the NMAA hosts lectures and film series. ♦ Free. Daily except Christmas Day 10AM-5:30PM. Walk-in tours: M-F noon; Sa-Su 2PM. 8th and G Sts NW. Metro stop: Gallery Pl. 357.3176, 357.2700, lecture and film information 357.3095 &

The National Portrait Gallery, on the Old Patent Office's south side, is full of old friends: images of **George Washington** that we first saw on our schoolroom walls, portraits of the explorers, military heroes and heroines, thinkers and doers in the arts and sciences, philanthropists and first families that people our history books. It's both humbling and inspiring to stand face-to-face with so much greatness.

The federal government unwittingly began this collection when it commissioned a series of presidential portraits in 1857. Now the gallery contains paintings, sculpture, etchings, photographs, and silhouettes. Works by artists such as **John Singleton Copley**, **John Singer Sargent**, **Thomas Sully**, **Augustus Saint-Gaudens**, and **Charles Willson Peale** can be found here. Call for information on special exhibitions and lectures. Walk-in tours of the collection are available weekdays 10AM to 3PM, and weekends 11AM to 2PM. ♦ Free. Daily 10AM-5:30PM. 7th-9th Sts NW (F-G Sts) Metro stop: Gallery Pl. 357.2700, lectures, films, events 357.2920 &

d.c. space

85 d.c. space ★$ In a city decidedly lacking in things avant-garde, this bar/café stands out. Narrow, noisy, and *neoned*, it's home to denizens of nearby rock 'n' roll clubs, Corcoran Art School students, and other nouveau bohemian types. Good burgers, salads, vegetarian dishes. Music or cabaret acts on some weekends. ♦ American ♦ Tu-Th 11:30AM-2AM; F 11:30AM-3AM; Sa 6PM-3AM. 443 7th St NW (E St) Metro stop: Gallery Pl. 347.1445

86 Zenith Gallery Exhibitions of contemporary fine art and neon. ♦ M-F 10AM-6PM; Sa 11AM-6PM; Su noon-4PM. 413 7th St NW (D-E Sts) Metro stops: Archives, Gallery Pl. 783.2963

86 Zygos Gallery Paintings, sculpture, and engravings by contemporary Greek artists. ♦ Tu-Sa 10:30AM-5:30PM; Su noon-5PM. 403 7th St NW (D-E Sts) Metro stops: Archives, Gallery Pl. 347.7740

87 406 Group Located in the middle of the Smithsonian art museum/gallery complex, this building is a bonus for the visitor with spare time: 2 first-rate art galleries occupy the building's 3 floors, adding richness to the 7th Street cultural corridor. ♦ 406 7th St NW (D-E Sts) Metro stops: Archives, Gallery Pl

Within the 406 Group:

B.R. Kornblatt focuses on contemporary American paintings, sculpture, and prints, often showing big-name artists like **Robert Motherwell**, **Kenneth Noland**, and **Frank Stella**. ♦ Tu-Sa 10:30AM-5:30PM. 638.7657

David Adamson Gallery, owned by a master printer, emphasizes graphics by artists such as **Kevin MacDonald** and **Michael Clark**. ♦ Tu-Sa 10:30AM-5PM. 628.0257

Downtown

87 Washington Project for the Arts, founded in 1975, supports and promotes local artists in a town often perceived as cold and cruel by anyone whose work isn't already hanging in the National Gallery. WPA has also labored to keep the struggling 7th Street NW arts corridor alive, and moved into new digs there in 1988. WPA holds shows in its 2 galleries, as well as sponsoring performance works and videos and an annual fall auction that is one of the best places to snap up work by up-and-coming artists. A yearly membership includes performance discounts, a newsletter, invitations to openings, and a discount at the **Bookworks**. ♦ Tu-F 10AM-5PM. Bookworks: M-F 11AM-6PM; Sa 11AM-5PM. 400 7th St NW (D St) Metro stops: Archives, Gallery Pl. 347.4813, information tape 347.8304 &

88 Riggs Bank (1891, James G. Hill) One of the few Chicago School buildings in a city that preferred European Beaux-Arts styles to the uncluttered boldness of the American Midwest. ♦ 9th and F Sts NW. Metro stops: Gallery Pl, Metro Center

Instigated in 1978 by **Bill Worrell**, native Washingtonian and founder of **dc space**, **District Curators** is a nonprofit organization dedicated to bringing contemporary music and interdisciplinary theater to Washington. It sponsors several dozen performances a year, as well as the Fourth of July **DC Free Jazz Festival** and the **ADD (Activities for Downtown Development)** Arts Festival, Labor Day weekend. Performers have included composer **Philip Glass**, performance artist **Laurie Anderson**, and **Sankai Juku**, a Japanese Butoh dance troupe. A yearly membership includes discounts on performances, priority seating at events, and a quarterly newsletter. Stop by weekdays between 9:30AM and 6PM at 1116 F St NW, Suite 400 (Metro stop: Metro Center), or call 783.0360.

89 Fifth Column Three-story dance hall-cum-art gallery catering to the young and black-clad with deejay music and videos. ♦ Cover. Tu-W 9PM-2AM; Th-Sa 9PM-3AM. 915 F St NW (9th-10th Sts) Metro stops: Gallery Pl, Metro Center. 393.3632

90 9:30 Club DC's pioneer live music club in the punk era now features top local and national bands, from New Wave to go-go, in a grungy storefront. ♦ Cover. M-Th, Su 8PM-2AM; F-Sa 9PM-3AM. 930 F St NW (9th-10th Sts) Metro stops: Gallery Pl, Metro Center. 393.0930

Courtesy National Park Service

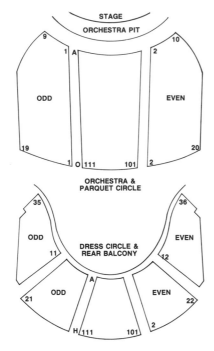

STAGE

ORCHESTRA PIT

ORCHESTRA & PARQUET CIRCLE

DRESS CIRCLE & REAR BALCONY

91 Ford's Theatre (1863, James J. Gifford; restoration, 1968, Macomber & Peter, William Haussman) **Abraham Lincoln** was shot here on 14 April 1865 during a performance of *Our American Cousin*, and the building was closed out of shame for over 100 years. The basement has a small but select museum of personal mementos of both the president and his assassin. On display are the suit of clothes in which Lincoln died and the flag that covered his casket, as well as the derringer that **John Wilkes Booth** used to commit his crime and the diary in which he recorded his resolve to

do the deed. Upstairs you can catch a glimpse of the flag-draped box where the president was sitting when Booth crept up behind him.

The theater is used for professional productions of contemporary plays and musicals such as *Hot Mikado* and *Michael Feinstein in Concert*. The **National Park Service** maintains the theater, as well as the **House Where Lincoln Died (Petersen House)** across the street. Ford's Theatre does not offer tours during matinees and rehearsals, so call ahead. All tours are self-guided. ♦ Seats 699. Free. Daily 9AM-5PM. 511 10th St NW (E-F Sts) Metro stop: Metro Center. 426.6924, box office 347.6262 ♿

Courtesy National Park Service

92 The House Where Lincoln Died (Petersen House) This house, across the street from **Ford's Theatre**, is where government leaders carried dying **President Lincoln** in 1865. The parlor where **Mary Todd Lincoln** waited through the night and the back room where the president died are furnished with period authenticity. Only the first floor is open. ♦ Free. Self-guided tours daily 9AM-5PM. 516 10th St NW (E-F Sts) Metro stop: Metro Center. 426.6830

93 Woodward & Lothrop Glittering again after an interior overhaul, the flagship store of venerable **Woodie's**, serving the city since 1880, offers a complete range of clothing for men, women, and children, as well as kitchenware, furniture, services, and 3 restaurants. ♦ M-Sa 10AM-8PM; Su 11AM-6PM. 1025 F St NW (10th-11th Sts) Metro stop: Metro Center. 347.5300

94 Hecht's Metro Center This flagship store for the local chain opened in 1985 and emphasizes midpriced men's and women's clothing as well as children's wear, kitchenware, and linens. The **Georgetown** restaurant is fine for a quick bite. ♦ M-Sa 10AM-8PM; Su 11AM-6PM. 1201 G St NW (12th-13th Sts) Metro stop: Metro Center. 628.6661

95 Grand Hyatt $$$ The 907 rooms include 60 suites (3 are *presidential* suites with private saunas). The 12-story atrium features a 7000-square-foot lagoon and 3 restaurants, including **Zephyr's** New York-style deli, **Grand Cafe** coffee shop, and **Hamilton's Chop House**. At **Impulse**, a high-tech nightclub, guests *let it all hang out*. Parking, valet, pool, and fitness center. Nonsmoking rooms; children under 17 stay free. ♦ 1000 H St NW (10th-11th Sts) Metro stop: Metro Center. 582.1234, 800/228.9000; fax 637.4781 ♿

Washington Convention and Visitors Association

WASHINGTON CONVENTION CENTER

Welton Beckett Associates Architects

96 Washington Convention Center This sparkling state-of-the-art meeting hall has come to symbolize DC's intensive urban renewal effort. Since its opening in 1983, the Convention Center has hosted over 1000 events—from car, boat, and RV (recreational vehicle) exhibitions, to antique, flower, and travel shows, political rallies, and the local high school district's graduation ceremonies. All this is estimated to have brought in over $900 million in spending by out-of-towners—proof that Downtown DC is worth the spruce-up efforts. The Convention Center provides 378,000 square feet of show and exhibition space, 40 meeting rooms, and ultramodern facilities—from audiovisual support to language translation to satellite conferencing. ◆ 900 9th St NW (H St-New York Ave) Metro stops: Gallery Pl, Metro Center. 789.1600 ♿

97 Spectrum ★★$$ Sleek neon-ceilinged room features lively variations on French and Mexican recipes: veal Française, angel hair pasta with shrimp in saffron sauce, enchiladas. ◆ Mexican/French ◆ M-F 11:30AM-3PM, 5:30-10:30PM; Sa-Su noon-3PM, 5:30-10PM. 919 11th St NW (K-L Sts) Metro stop: Metro Center. 638.7505

98 National Museum of Women in the Arts Collector **Wilhelmina Holladay** founded the museum in 1981 in order to promote women artists. In 1987, the collection and library were moved to a 1907 Renaissance Revival building formerly occupied by the **Town Theater**. Exhibitions include items from the growing collection as well as showcases of individual artists. ◆ Voluntary contribution. Tu-Sa 10AM-5PM; Su noon-5PM. Group tours by appointment. 1250 New York Ave NW (12th-13th Sts) Metro stop: Metro Center. 783.5000 ♿

99 Cafe Mozart ★★$ Classic home-cooking of Valkyrian proportions—*landjaeger* sausage, *kalbsschnitzel*, sauerbraten, and sauerkraut—served with oom-pah-pah piano music on Saturday nights. Carry-out delicatessen on the premises. ◆ German ◆ M-F 7:30AM-10PM; Sa 9AM-10PM; Su 11AM-10PM. 1331 H St NW (13th-14th Sts) Metro stop: Metro Center. 347.5732

100 Franklin School Building (1868, Adolph Cluss) The ornate brickwork, mansard roof, and Italianate window arches of this building brought new prestige to public schoolhouses and influenced their design citywide. The —children of presidents **Andrew Johnson** and **Chester Arthur** studied here, and **Alexander Graham Bell** made his first light-transmitted wireless telephone call from the building. ◆ 13th and K Sts NW. Metro stops: McPherson Sq, Metro Center

101 Henley Park Hotel $$$ Fashioned after England's fine hostelries, this refurbished apartment building seems truly royal. Catch

afternoon tea in the **Wilkes Room** off the hotel's parlor. Amenities include babysitting and a multilingual staff. Children under 16 stay free. ◆ 926 Massachusetts Ave NW (9th-10th Sts) Metro stop: Gallery Pl. 638-5200, 800/222.8474; fax 638.6740

102 The Morrison-Clark Inn $$$ In 1988, after 2 years of restoration and renovation work, the former **Soldiers, Sailors, Marines and Airmens Club** was converted into **Washington's first historic inn**. All 54 rooms are furnished with 19th-century antiques or reproductions; original red mahogany gold leaf pier mirrors and carved marble fireplaces decorate the bar and restaurant. Amenities include complimentary Continental breakfast, in-room modem hookup, and concierge service. ◆ 1015 L St NW (11th St-Massachusetts Ave) Metro stops: Gallery Pl, Metro Center. 898.1200; fax 289.8576

Within the Morrison-Clark Inn:

The Morrison-Clark Restaurant ★★★$$$ Inventive American cooking with a spiritual base in the South: ordinarily benign trout becomes "angry" when smothered with a hot pecan sauce; veal T-bone is enlivened with 5 types of seared onions. Desserts include an intoxicating pecan sandwich and the only-slightly-more-down-to-earth farmer's cheese mousse. ◆ American ◆ M-Th 11AM-3PM, 5:30-10PM; F 11AM-3PM, 5:30-10:30PM; Sa 5:30-10:30PM; Su 5:30-10PM. Reservations recommended. 898.1200

103 Church of the Ascension of St. Agnes (1875) A High Victorian Gothic composition that befits a High Church congregation known for its musical tradition. The interior includes cast-iron columns, walnut pews, a vigorous gold and silver leaf mural, and more recent abstract windows in the nave. ◆ Services Su 8, 10AM, 12:30PM. 1217 Massachusetts Ave NW (12th St) Metro stop: McPherson Sq. 347.8161

95

Duke Zeibert
Owner, Duke Zeibert's Restaurant

Laurel Race Track
Bowie Race Track
Pimlico Race Track
RFK Stadium
Capitol Centre
Kennedy Center
Georgetown
Woodmont Country Club
Joe & Mo's Restaurant
The Palm Restaurant
The YMCA on Rhode Island Avenue
Arthur Adler's Men's Stores
The Madison Hotel
The Iwo Jima Memorial
Geographical Location—near Atlantic City, New York, Philly, Baltimore

Bests

Lloyd E. Herman
Former Director, Renwick Gallery

Although the Renwick Gallery is a relatively small building as Smithsonian museums go, its namesake, architect James Renwick, understood the illusions of grandeur. He created tall doorways leading to high-ceilinged galleries, and even made the wainscot extra high to dwarf the human presence. Yet even with these tricks few visitors are prepared for the experience when they climb the grand staircase and behold the opulent room we call the Grand Salon—tasseled and draped, and hung with tiers of paintings to resemble a grand painting drawing room of the 1870s. Once the main painting gallery when the building opened as the Corcoran Gallery of Art, it is one of the most spectacular 19th-century period rooms in America. I have seen harried executives hiding out with their business papers in its quiet on a midweek midafternoon to escape phone calls or office callers. But it is at its best when the resident chamber music group fills the air with its melodies from the past. The sight and sound combine to make one almost wish to have lived before the automobile and central air conditioning! It is a mood to treasure.

Joseph Passonneau
Architect

I never met a city (particularly an old city) I didn't like, but Washington is special. The city combines some of the best principles of both French (work of L'Enfant, the McMillan Commission, etc., etc.) and English (Olmsted's Capitol grounds, Georgetown, Capitol Hill, Dupont Circle neighborhoods, the parkways) town and country planning. L'Enfant's 18th-century Baroque image was reinforced by the building height limitation, clamped on early in the 20th century. Pennsylvania Avenue, everyone's favorite street, now renewed, shows what the rest of the wide avenues can become: great outdoor rooms to rival the Paris boulevards. L'Enfant's large, squarish city blocks have spawned an unusual (for America) building type: large doughnuts with sunlit holes in the middle. Some are open to the sky. My favorite is the National Portrait Gallery (for lunch, in the courtyard, a fine delicatessen sandwich and beer or wine). The FBI Building, brutal on the outside, has a charming open courtyard with fountains, flowers, and comfortable benches. The courtyards of most new private buildings are glassed over: International Square (at the Farragut West Metro Station) has one of the finest, with a decent and inexpensive lunch in pleasant surroundings.

The old Library of Congress (all 3 buildings) has the loveliest interiors in Washington; the Jefferson Building always has an interesting, often offbeat exhibition. Among the many free Washington concert series, the library's is the most distinguished. Washington is full of mounted metal generals: by far the most evocative is *General Grant*, slouched on his horse, just west of the Capitol, flanked on both sides by stirring $^3/_4$-scale Civil War battle scenes. The city's consistently best restaurant—2 blocks north of General Grant—is La Colline (the name is suggestive). An elaborate reasonably priced menu is served in pleasant dining rooms. For lunch, try the City Cafe (fancier than the Portrait Gallery courtyard)—a little too *California*, but everything superb—the best hamburgers in town despite claims for The Sign of the Whale. For an even more elegant, still reasonably priced lunch, try the lower dining room of the Occidental.

Nature lovers will like walking/jogging along the C&O Canal, starting at Rock Creek; if driving, go out Rock Creek Parkway, north from the Canal.

Abram Lerner
Former Director, Hirshhorn Museum and Sculpture Garden

A great collection of American and European 20th-century paintings.

Probably the best sculpture collection of from 1850 on, anywhere.

The least tiring museum in the world.

The view from the ambulatories onto the fountain while lolling in comfortable chairs; these are ideal spots for quiet reading as well.

The spectacular view from the Balcony Room onto the array of great national museums on the mall; the Balcony Room's quiet, comfortable, restful atmosphere.

The outdoor Sculpture Garden, a must for art lovers and connoisseurs, with its Moores, Rodins, Smiths, etc., amid greenery-lined pathways; the garden's reflecting pool and the sound of its fountain.

The outdoor Sculpture Plaza's large abstract pieces and their backgrounds of sky and curving architecture; the dramatic roar and refreshing sight of the courtyard's fountain waters in summertime.

Diana McLellan
Syndicated Columnist

Saturday shopping at the Eastern Market. You go to Capitol Hill's bustling indoor-and-outdoor farmers market to buy the freshest fish, poultry, sausage, eggs, and vegetables. The greasy-spoon Market Lunch makes the finest crabcakes, squash-rings, and fresh lemonade in the East. Stand in line, then take them outside and gobble them at a picnic table on the sidewalk outside the huge, homely red brick building. It was designed in 1870 by Adolph Cluss.

Seeing in the New Year at the Hay-Adams Hotel. Six big Georgian windows along that skinny ballroom look smack out at the White House across the street, brilliantly illuminated and decorated for Christmas. Peter Duchin plays. There are feathered head-dresses, favors, a grand noise. Nearby is the John Hay Room—coziest year-round spot in the city for cocktails. It feels exactly like the hall of a great but cozy English or Irish country house. It costs.

Wandering in the garden at Dumbarton Oaks in spring. A place to propose marriage. It was even better when, as students in the '50s, we used to sneak in at 3AM to swim in the pool by moonlight. Nowadays, you can take your picnic next door to Montrose Park.

The Kennedy Center on a sunny day. Nothing is more beautiful than sitting at an outdoor café in the middle of all that white marble gazing down the tree-lined Potomac, drinking cold beer.

Swimming at the Washington Hilton's Racquet Club. It's mid city, outdoors, and just a few yards from the spot where John Hinckley shot Ronald Reagan. But the Gazebo there serves something divine called *Maria's Health Salad* and ridiculous fruit-and-rum drinks; the pool, next to the tennis courts, is beautiful; and the fact that the hotel guests may use it gives members—who include lots of shrinks, lawyers, lobbyists, and journalists—plenty to grumble about in the shower.

The Hirshhorn Gallery and Sculpture Garden. The art was chosen not because of artists' names but because Joe Hirshhorn liked it. The little guy had a great eye. Set aside a day.

Copenhaver's. This Washington stationer engraves everything perfectly for ambassadors and cabinet officers, and has since 1896. Your engraved calling cards or stationery are exactly *comme il faut*. Don't be frightened. The folks who run it have steered our very finest rubes along the path to Correctness.

Going to any play at the Shakespeare Theatre at the Folger. It's a precise copy of the Globe Theatre in Elizabeth I's London. The productions are often stunning, the atmosphere magical. The *Folger Consort* sings madrigals here and plunges you into the 14th century, where you wouldn't want to live, but it's nice to visit.

A 3-hour dinner at the Marrakesh Restaurant. It's in a horrible neighborhood, next to the Midas Muffler Shop. Inside, it's Ali Baba's cave—a wonderful place to go with friends and to finger-eat your food. You are treated like a guest in an upper-crust Moroccan house. Nobody mentions prices. But relax, they're tiny.

Lunch at Le Pavillon. World-class nouvelle food so beautiful it makes you want to weep. Let a waiter decide what you eat. Let somebody else pay the bill.

The Iron Gate Inn. Romantic outside in dappled sunlight beneath the grape arbor, or inside by fire-light. Middle-Eastern food.

Margot Starr Kernan, Video Producer
Michael Kernan, Journalist

New Year's Eve at the Hotel Tabard Inn. The dancing takes place upstairs in paneled rooms that look more like a London private house than a Washington hotel. A seasoned combo plays show tunes; there's champagne and funny hats for old and young.

Maya Lin's Vietnam War Memorial. They've added little flags and made it more official-looking, but nothing can detract from the power of walking down that path, reading all those names, and seeing one's own face reflected in the mirror surface of black stone.

Bests

The Washington Project for the Arts at 406 7th St NW. This bold alternative arts environment is where to go when you're feeling *Malled*. The bookstore has avant-garde video and audio tapes, limited edition artists' books, hard-to-find magazines from all over the world, and great silly postcards.

Free Saturday afternoon film programs—Godard, Wenders, Tarkovsky, Brakhage, and more—at the superb modern theater in the East Building of the National Gallery of Art. The showings usually begin at 2:30PM, but get there early if you want a seat.

Anne and Patrick Poirer's *Promenade Classique* at the TransPotomac Canal Center on the Alexandria waterfront. A marble lightning bolt, a huge carved stone eye, and columns with a pool and fountain create a witty Postmodernist archaeological find on the Virginia side of the Potomac.

Sunday Gospel Mass at St. Augustine's Roman Catholic Church. The guitar music and joyous gospel singing will warm up the chilliest winter day. You can't sit still—the beauty and the energy of this ceremony would make Scrooge jump up and shout "Hallelujah!"

In springtime, the fresh shad roe and asparagus at the Bistro Français in Georgetown. This friendly, unpretentious French restaurant has posters on the wall and a purple mimeographed list of daily specials. Nothing nouvelle here, not even the prices.

A summertime bike ride or a Sunday morning stroll along the Potomac at Haines Point—Washington's own *Grand Jette*. Multigenerational families wash their cars, listen to their stereos, fish, and picnic. Here Washington becomes a Southern small town.

A summer night tour on the Potomac—floating past the Watergate Hotel, the glittering terraces of the Kennedy Center, and the wild wooded outline of Roosevelt Island. A moon, the soft lapping of water, fireflies on the shore. Magic.

Washington's north central area, composed of the **Logan Circle** and **Howard University** neighborhoods, runs east from 16th Street to North Capitol Street, and encompasses some of the city's most historic residential and commercial neighborhoods, as well as some of its most troubled.

The broad boulevard of 16th St NW, which travels due north from the White House, is lined with imposing ranks of churches, temples, embassies, and apartment buildings, many of which are undergoing renovation. Much of the street's character is the result of the remarkable **Mrs. John Henderson**, who built herself a now-gone castle along it, directed the development of **Meridian Hill Park**, and had a number of impressive buildings put up in order to attract foreign missions. Several are still standing, including the elaborate white stone **Spanish Embassy** (1925, **George B. Totten**). In 1912, Mrs. Henderson had the street rechristened *Avenue of the Presidents*, a change that stuck for only a year. Further up 16th St, the elegant residential neighborhoods favored by the city's black professionals have been nicknamed the *Gold Coast* and the *Platinum Coast*.

While the 14th Street corridor north of M Street still bears the scars of the riots that followed the assassination of **Dr. Martin Luther King, Jr.**, completion of the **Frank D. Reeves Municipal Building** at 14th and U streets in 1986 brought hope to an area plagued by a high crime rate and drug dealers. Craft shops and experimental theaters have dug in and thrived here, and a number of public/private sector development projects are in the works, particularly in the **Shaw** neighborhood along 7th Street and in the Victorian mansions of Logan Circle. Construction has finally begun on the long-awaited **Metrorail Green Line**, which will run north beneath 9th Street NW and include stops at Shaw, U Street, Columbia Heights, and Georgia Avenue before proceeding into Prince George's County.

Howard University, which overlooks the city from a hill along Georgia Ave, has served as both beacon and anchor for the black community since its founding in 1867. **Le Droit Park**, the neighborhood just to the south, is listed on the **National Register of Historic Places** both for its Romantic Revival mansions and for its role as home to the rising black intelligentsia of the early 1900s. These are neighborhoods where the district shakes off its magisterial robes and reveals a real city in all its beauty and complexity.

Scott Circle marks the effective end of Embassy Row—note the stylized bronze kangaroo and emu holding the Australian seal in front of the country's bland modern embassy at 1601 Massachusetts Ave NW. *General Winfield Scott* (1874, **Henry Kirk Brown**) rides through the circle, and *Daniel Webster* (1900, **Gaetano Trentanove**) stands in the small triangular park just to the west. The **General Scott Apartments** at 1 Scott Circle (1942, **Robert O. Scholz**) is one of the city's last and best Art Moderne buildings, and the first to be centrally air-conditioned. ♦ 16th St and Massachusetts Ave NW. Metro stop: Farragut North

---

Restaurants: Red   **Hotels**: Blue
Shops/Parks: Green   **Sights/Culture**: Black

Radisson Park Hotel $$ An attractively remodeled hotel 5 blocks from the White House, with 189 rooms and 33 apartments. Outdoor pool, parking, meeting rooms. Children under 16 stay free. ♦ 1515 Rhode Island Ave NW (15th-16th Sts) Metro stop: Farragut North. 232.7000, 800/424.2461; fax 332.7152 &

Chardonnay ★★$$$ As the name implies, Chardonnay's claim to fame is a superb wine list showcasing American varietals at reasonable prices. The regional American cuisine has its ups and downs but shines with simple grilled dishes and irresistible homemade desserts. ♦ American ♦ M-F 6:30-10:30AM, 11:30AM-2:30PM, 5:30-10:30PM; Sa 7-10:30AM, 5:30-10:30PM; Su 11:30AM-3PM, 5:30-10:30PM. Reservations recommended. 232.7000

3 Grace Reformed Church (1903, Abner Ritcher) **Teddy Roosevelt** and his family worshipped here; he laid the cornerstone for the present building. Presidents **Eisenhower** and **Nixon** prayed here, too. ♦ 1405 15th St NW (S-T Sts) 387.3131

Thomas Circle In the center of this busy circle, *Major General George H. Thomas* (1879, **John Quincy Adams Ward**), a statue of the man known as the *Rock of Chickamauga*, surveys Downtown to the south. ♦ 14th St at Massachusetts Ave NW. Metro stop: McPherson Sq

5 National City Christian Church (1930, John Russell Pope; addition, 1952, Leon Chatelain, Jr.) The bigger-than-life scale of this Colonial-style church is heightened by its position on a small knoll. This perch, coupled with the elegant steeple, makes it one of the highest buildings in town. Presidents **James Garfield** and **Lyndon Johnson** worshipped here. ♦ Daily 9AM-4:30PM. Services (Disciples of Christ) Su 11AM. 5 Thomas Circle (14th St-Massachusetts Ave NW) Metro stop: McPherson Sq. 232.0323

6 Luther Place Memorial Church (1870, Judson York; addition, 1952, L.M. Leisenring) This Civil War-era church is a soaring neo-Gothic structure of red sandstone that provides a fitting balance to the National City Christian Church across the street. ♦ M-F 9AM-5PM. Services Su 8:30, 11AM. 1226 Vermont Ave NW (14th-N Sts) Metro stop: McPherson Sq. 667.1377

7 Bethune Museum and Archives Born in South Carolina in 1875, **Mary McLeod Bethune** was the 15th of 17 children of freed slaves. Through her work in the early days of the civil rights struggle, she became a counselor to 4 presidents. Bethune rose to prominence as a founder of **Bethune-Cookman College** in Daytona Beach FL. Under **Calvin Coolidge** and **Herbert Hoover**, she worked for the **National Child Welfare Commission**. In 1935, Bethune came to Washington as special

99

advisor on minority affairs to the Roosevelt administration and as director of the **Division of Negro Affairs** in the **National Youth Administration**. She organized black officials into the *Black Cabinet*, lobbying for a fair share in New Deal programs, and founded the **National Council of Negro Women**. This Victorian townhouse served as headquarters for the council from 1943 to 1966 and is now a center for black women's history. A **National Historic Site**. ◆ Free. M-F 10AM-4:30PM. 1318 Vermont Ave NW (13th-14th Sts) Metro stop: McPherson Sq. 332.1233

8 Logan Circle The 3- and 4-story Victorian mansions built here between 1874 and 1887 made Logan Circle one of DC's most fashionable neighborhoods. The racial makeup shifted in the 1920s and '30s, and by 1940 the city's most prominent black politicians and social leaders lived here. Decades of neglect and the neighborhood's struggle with prostitution, drug dealing, and the attendant property crime have taken their toll, but determined preservationists are in the process of restoring many of the circle's buildings. ◆ 13th St and Vermont Ave NW. Metro Stop: McPherson Sq

Logan Circle

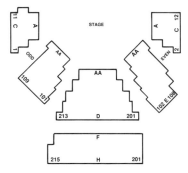

9 Studio Theatre Professional productions in an intimate theater. Five productions yearly include classic and contemporary works, often with a social bite, such as the *Slab Boys* trilogy and *Ma Rainey's Black Bottom*. ◆ Seats 200. Shows: W-Su 8PM; Su 2PM. (Some shows vary this schedule; call ahead to check.) Box office: M-F 10AM-6PM; Sa-Su noon-6PM. (Box office open until 8PM on performance nights.) 1333 P St NW (14th St) 232.7267, box office 332.3300

"In a sense we've come to our nation's capitol to cash a check. When the architects of our republic wrote the magnificent words of the Constitution and the Declaration of Independence, they were signing a promissory note to which every American was to fall heir. This note was the promise that all men, yes, black men as well as white men, would be guaranteed the unalienable rights of life, liberty, and the pursuit of happiness."
Rev. Martin Luther King, Jr.

10 Woolly Mammoth Theater The Woolly's repertory season invariably includes some of DC's most audacious productions, such as **Harry Kondoleon**'s *Christmas on Mars* and **Wallace Shawn**'s *Aunt Dan and Lemon*. ◆ Seats 130. Box office daily noon-6PM. 1401 Church St NW (P-Q Sts) Metro Stop: Dupont Circle. 393.3939

11 Temple of the Scottish Rite (1915, John Russell Pope) One of Pope's earliest contributions to *Monumental Washington*, the temple was inspired by the *Tomb of Mausolus* at Halicarnassus in Greece, one of the Seven Wonders of the World. The proportions of the building are based on numbers significant to Masonic mysticism and reflect an array of styles from Egyptian to Roman. The 2 huge sphinxes that guard the entrance to the shrine, each cut from a solid block of limestone, were sculpted in 1915 by **Alexander Weinman**. There are some stunning interior spaces to be seen here as well. This is now the **Headquarters of the Supreme Council of the Southern Jurisdiction of the Thirty-third Degree of the Ancient and Accepted Scottish Rite of Freemasonry**. ◆ 1733 16th St NW (R-S Sts)

12 Source Theatre A force in Washington's experimental theater community, the Source offers classics and new plays, as well as late-night comedies. The **Washington Theater Festival**, a 4-week showcase of new plays, runs each July. ◆ Seats 108. Box office Tu-Sa noon-6PM. 1835 14th St NW (S-T Sts) 462.1073

13 Ben's Chili Bowl ★$ Check out this hole-in-the-wall café, a long-favored hangout of Howard students, civil rights leaders, and musicians. **Bill Cosby** stops in when he comes back to town. ◆ American ◆ M-Th 11AM-11PM; F-Sa 11AM-1AM. 1213 U St NW (12th-13th Sts) No credit cards. 667.0909

15 Meridian Hill Park Also known as *Malcolm X Park*, this 12-acre park (opened in 1936) on a steeply slanted hillside is a spectacular site. A central series of cascading pools and waterfalls connects French and Italian Renaissance-style gardens. Unfortunately, not a safe place to visit alone, even during daylight hours. ◆ W. Euclid St NW (15th-16th Sts)

16 All Souls Unitarian Church (1924, Coolidge & Shattuck) **James Gibbs**' design for St. Martin-in-the-Fields (located on London's Trafalgar Square) has been much copied, but critics hail this as one of the best re-creations. In the Unitarian tradition, the simple interior is devoid of all religious icons. ◆ Tu-F 10AM-6PM; Su 9AM-3PM. Services Su 11AM. 2385 16th St NW (Harvard St) 332.5266

14 Florida Avenue Grill ★★★$ Down-home Southern cooking in an old-fashioned diner. Breakfasts include scrapple (a Philadelphia specialty), home fries, grits, and biscuits. For lunch and dinner, try the pan-fried chicken, spareribs, or ham hocks, all served with greens or cabbage, sweet potatoes, and beans or rice. The homemade corn muffins can't be beat. ◆ Southern ◆ M-Sa 6AM-9PM. 1100 Florida Ave NW (11th-12th Sts) No credit cards. 265.1586

17 Howard University Founded in 1867 by **General Oliver O. Howard**, head of the *Freedmen's Bureau* and an outspoken champion of civil rights, Howard has become one of the most prestigious predominantly black universities in the nation, with nearly 13,000 students in 18 different schools, including medicine, law, and theology, in a 150-acre campus overlooking Georgia Ave. Alumni include Supreme Court justice **Thurgood Marshall**, Atlanta mayor **Andrew Young**, and the late **Patricia Roberts Harris**, secretary of the Department of Health and Human Services. The **Founders Library** on the south side of the quadrangle contains black history exhibitions and the **Moorland-Spingarn Research Center**, the nation's largest collection of black literature. ◆ M-Th 9AM-7:30PM; F-Sa 9AM-4:30PM. 4th St-Georgia Ave NW (Harvard-U Sts) 636.7239

At Howard University:

Blackburn University Center features a continuing schedule of films and live performances open to the public, often at no charge. Private campus tours arranged by calling 2 weeks in advance. ◆ 6th St and Howard Pl NW. Campus information 636.6100

Howard University Gallery, renowned for its dedication to the arts, holds Italian Renaissance paintings from the **Kress Collections** and a permanent display of African art, as well as works by outstanding black American artists. Special exhibitions change regularly. ◆ M-F 9AM-5PM. College of Fine Arts, 2455 6th St NW (Fairmont St) 636.7047

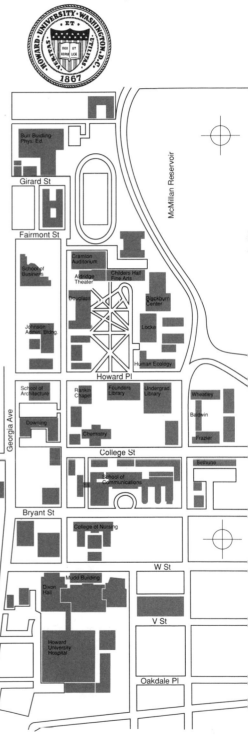

Frederick Douglass' first Washington residence was at 316 A Street NE, which in more recent years housed the Museum of African Art.

Florida Avenue is also known as *Old Boundary Road*, since it marks the outer limits **L'Enfant** had planned for the city of Washington.

18 Howard Inn $ The closest hotel to Howard University features an African motif, 150 rooms, an indoor pool, a Jacuzzi and spa, and 2 restaurants and lounges. ♦ 2225 Georgia Ave NW (Bryant-W Sts) 462.5400, 800/368.5729; fax 667.0973 ♿

19 LeDroit Park In the 1870s, architect **James McGill** designed 64 homes in the picturesque Romantic Revival style with patterned slate roofs. Fifty or so remain: see the 400-block of U Street and the 500-block of T Street. By 1920, LeDroit Park became the premier address for middle-class blacks and a center for black-owned businesses and black culture. The neighborhood is now a **historic district**. ♦ Rhode Island Ave-Elm St NW (2nd St-Florida Ave)

20 Old Soldiers' Home (1843–1852) The oldest military retirement facility in the country is a Norman fortress complete with crenelated battlements. The house was reportedly built with ransom money that **General Winfield Scott** took from Mexico City. Some of the newer buildings rival the original structure in presence. ♦ 3rd and Webster Sts NW (across from St. Paul's)

Logan Circle

The Foremost of Freedoms

Ever since newly freed slaves first emigrated here over 100 years ago, Washington's black community has striven to enjoy its constitutional freedoms. Today, with 5 weekly newspapers and a monthly business journal, blacks are still struggling to cultivate the foremost of those freedoms: the freedom of the press.

The struggle has a number of causes, some common to many young publications: lack of initial capital, little staff, competition from more established organs for both readers and talent. But the black press also faces more particular problems, not the least of which is that much of the community does not see the need for it since desegregation became law. Readership has dwindled since the height of the civil rights movement in the late 1960s, causing many papers to fold.

While it is true that the national climate has become more open to the concerns of blacks, the best place to read about black life in the US may still be in the DC hometown press. Most of these papers are distributed without charge in an effort to stress that they are community-based and rely solely on advertising to stay afloat.

Among the publications getting the word out: the *Washington Informer*, the *Metro Chronicle*, the *Washington New Observer*, the *Washington Afro-American*, the *Capital Spotlight*, and the monthly business journal *Black Networking News*. Although they may not compete with the mainstream press in terms of circulation, these papers continue to profile black citizens and events, and remain a vital part of the African-American voice.

21 Rock Creek Cemetery The city's oldest cemetery is filled with historic graves, including the **Adams Memorial**, a haunting statue of a woman (1890, **Augustus Saint-Gaudens**) erected by writer **Henry Adams** in honor of his wife, who committed suicide. Its setting was designed by **Stanford White**, and is surrounded by tall holly bushes. *Grief*, its nickname, seems apt. Other local notables interred here: **Julius Garfinckel**, **Henry Lansburg**, and **Montgomery Blair**. ♦ Daily 7:30AM-dusk. Rock Creek Church Rd NW (N. Capitol St-New Hampshire Ave) 829.0585

Within Rock Creek Cemetery:

St. Paul's Episcopal Church (1775; reconstruction, 1922, Delos H. Smith) The area's first church was built on this spot in 1775—63 years after the congregation had originally convened here! Of the original, only the brick walls remain, due to a 1921 fire. Now reconstructed, its Federal splendor includes several excellent stained-glass windows. ♦ Services Su 8, 11AM. 726.2080

22 Walter Reed Army Medical Center (1979, Stone, Marracini & Patterson) Walter Reed's hospital facilities are located within a huge 7-story square. Another building worth noting is the windowless **Armed Forces Institute of Pathology** headquarters, built in the late 1940s as a prototype of *atomic bomb-proof* buildings that were envisioned to be the future standard for Downtown Washington architecture. The development of the hydrogen bomb in the early 1950s made that vision —and this building—almost immediately obsolete. ♦ 6900 Georgia Ave NW (Fern-Aspen Sts) 576.3501

On the grounds of Walter Reed Army Medical Center:

National Museum of Health and Medicine Founded in 1862 to research medical problems of the Civil War. (Most soldiers died from diarrhea or dysentery.) Amputation was the basic treatment for wounds, hence the museum's collection of severed limbs—not a sight for the squeamish. Also on view are models of battle evacuation methods and rescue efforts. Mule-drawn litters, trains, and horse-drawn ambulances all correlate in some fashion to modern methods of evacuation, such as helicopters.

The museum concentrates on the interrelationships between exhibitions on view and the cultural, social, and historical aspects of medical care: the ways in which we view the human body, in health as well as in sickness. A multimedia exhibition addressing the medical, cultural, and historical impact of AIDS will be on display as long as the disease exists. ♦ Free. M-F 9:30AM-4:30PM; Sa-Su 11:30AM-4:30PM. Building 54. 576.2348

Otis Historical Archives has about 1,000,000 documents and an equal number of photographs and glass-plate negatives dating back to the Civil War. ♦ By appointment. Building 54. 576.2418

Views

For a glorious view of DC, especially at dusk, visit the **Iwo Jima Memorial**, just across the Potomac River in Virginia. Not only can you inspect this huge bronze statue, which commemorates the raising of the American flag over Mount Suribachi during World War II, you can also **enjoy the twinkling panorama** of the Lincoln and Jefferson memorials, the Washington Monument, and the Capitol in the distance.

In warm weather, take a break and relax at the **Sky Terrace**, the canopied rooftop of the Washington Hotel. From there you can look over the Treasury Building and the White House or **contemplate the southern view** toward the Mall and the Potomac.

If you're visiting the nation's capital on the holiday weekends of Memorial Day, the Fourth of July, or Labor Day, pack a picnic supper and head for the **west lawn of the Capitol grounds** (between the Capitol and its reflecting pool). The National Symphony Orchestra offers a free, first-class performance, so eat, drink, listen to the wonderful music, and **absorb the twilight atmosphere** while **gazing down the Mall** toward the Washington Monument and the Lincoln Memorial. (Check local newspapers for day and time of performance.)

The **Washington Monument** thrusts 555 feet skyward. It is the city's highest and most spectacular viewing station (you can **see the horizon**). This is a popular spot. Call ahead to check the wait; it can be as long as 3 hours. If *Vertigo* is your middle name, a perfectly nice view can be had from the monument's base.

As you race down 16th Street toward Downtown, **pause at the top of Meridian Hill**. The sight of the White House directly in front of you and the Washington Monument and Jefferson Memorial beyond it are sure reminders of the city's historical and political importance.

The **Clocktower** in the Old Post Office Pavilion is Washington's **3rd-highest vantage point** (315 feet). See Downtown and the monuments: the Capitol looks magnificent from here. Victorian brass fittings, red oak woodwork, and frosted glass decorate the building's lovely atrium.

Take the elevator up to the **Roof Terrace** of the Kennedy Center for a **panoramic view of the city** and especially of the Potomac. You can also **enjoy the view while dining** in the Roof Terrace restaurant.

The Potomac looks glorious from any distance. Sit on its banks in **West Potomac Park**; the best stretch is from just south of the Lincoln Memorial to Haines Point. **Daytime is best** for this particular view.

Due west of DC, across Memorial Bridge, is **Arlington House** (formerly called the Custis-Lee Mansion). From its portico on the bluff, you can **look across the Potomac** directly toward the Lincoln Memorial. Below lie the graves of President John Kennedy (marked by an eternal flame) and his brother Robert. Arlington National Cemetery, carved from the plantation Robert E. Lee's family abandoned during the Civil War, stretches throughout the hills around the mansion.

From the **Pilgrim Observation Gallery** of the Washington Cathedral, you can survey Wisconsin Avenue down into Georgetown and beyond into Virginia. Turn in the other direction and you'll see into suburban Maryland. Crowning the highest hill in the district, the cathedral's tower provides a **panoramic view** like no other in DC. (Accessible by elevator.)

To view the landscape of Old Town Alexandria, **venture to the top of the George Washington Masonic National Memorial**. Its observation deck, at over 300 feet up, furnishes a breathtaking, and sometimes windy, view of Alexandria. On a clear day you can see into DC.

A quick cab ride across the Key Bridge takes you to Rosslyn VA, where, from the **USA Today Building's Windows** restaurant, you can **gaze across the Potomac** at Downtown Washington and the monuments.

For a trip through time, stop on the grounds of **Mount Vernon** in Virginia. From here, it's easy to imagine the way the Potomac and the surrounding countryside looked in George Washington's time. (Every effort is being made to keep the scenery free of suburban sprawl.) With **nothing but trees, water, and sky to see**, it's one of the best vistas in the Washington area.

Sights and Sounds

DC Radio

The following is a list of DC's top 15 radio stations according to a 1989 **Arbitron** survey:

Format	Frequency	Station
Adult Contemporary	97.1	WASH-FM
Contemporary Hits	105.1	WAVA-FM
Classic Rock	105.9	WCXR-FM
Urban Contemporary	100.3	WDJY-FM
Beautiful Music	99.5	WGAY-FM
Classical	570/103.5	WGMS-AM/FM
Progressive	99.1	WHFS-FM
Urban Contemporary	96.3	WHUR-FM
Urban Contemporary	93.9	WKYS-FM
Light Rock	94.7	WLTT-FM
Personalities/News	630	WMAL-AM
Country	1390/98.7	WMZQ-AM/FM
Urban Contemporary	95.5	WPGC-FM
Contemporary Hits	107.3	WRQX-FM
News	1500	WTOP-AM
Album Rock	101.1	WWDC-FM
Oldies	104.1	WXTR-FM

Long before man took possession of Washington, the area was inhabited by much larger beasts—the colossal **dinosaurs**. In the 1920s, footprints and tail-draggings older than 200 million years were discovered at Oak Hill, a private residence designed by **James Hoban** and **Thomas Jefferson** for their mutual friend, **James Monroe**.

Adams-Morgan
Dupont Circle

National Zoo

Monroe

92-94

Mt. Pleasant

Irving

Hobart

Harvard

Woodley Rd

Ⓜ Woodley Park Zoo

Rock Creek and Potomac Pkwy

Adams Mill Rd

Summit Pl

Lanier Pl

Columbia Rd

Fuller 91

Euclid

67 Calvert

68

69

Biltmore

70

66 71

72

Champlain

Ontario Rd

Crescent

90

89

64

65 73 74

62

63

75 76

77

18th

20th

18th

Kalorama Rd

Rock Creek Park

Belmont Rd

Kalorama Circle

Kalorama Rd

56

California

Vernon

78

U

Wyoming

57

61

Willard

88

55

Tracy

Florida Ave

79

T

California

58

60

Swann

54

59

Bancroft

S

80

24th

23rd

53

Decatur

52

46

45

44

43

Riggs

87

47

48

42

R

51

50

49

41

39

81

Corcoran

86

31 30

33

32

34

40

38

Q

82

85 84

29

35

37

Church

P

O

28

27

26

36

2

Dupont Circle

4

Massachusetts Ave

83

Georgetown/
Upper NW

25

24

19

Connecticut Ave

Rhode Island Av

New Hampshire Ave

Logan Circle

23

21

20

18

17

N

10

9

8

7 6

5

22

16

15

13 12 11

14

Ⓜ Farragut North

26th

25th

24th

23rd

22nd

21st

20th

19th

18th

L

17th

16th

15th

West End/Foggy Bottom

17th

Pennsylvania Ave

Ⓜ Foggy Bottom GWU

If the city of Washington has a heart, it lies not on the ceremonial expanse of the Mall but somewhere amid the tree-shaded streets of **Dupont Circle**. No other DC neighborhood has undergone so many permutations over the decades, or weathered them so gracefully. Today, Dupont Circle is one of the city's most fashionable residential and commercial neighborhoods, much as it was in the late 1800s. In 1875, **Senator William M. Stewart** of Nevada built a mansion on the circle where **Riggs Bank** is now. His contemporaries mocked it as *Stewart's Folly*, but the senator was soon joined by the young capital's wealthiest citizens.

Between then and now, Dupont Circle has gone through many changes. The stock market crash of 1929 nipped millionaires' pocketbooks: many of their mansions were divided into apartments or sold for use as embassies. In the 1950s and 1960s, cheap apartments attracted the Beat Generation and their heirs, the hippies. The elegant *Dupont Fountain* became a popular staging area for antiwar demonstrations, sit-ins, and sing-alongs. In the 1970s, Dupont Circle became home to the city's gay community, which helped promote gentrification, particularly east of Connecticut Avenue. The elegantly restored townhouses and the host of restaurants and boutiques along Connecticut Ave make it the city's best pedestrian neighborhood. It is easy to spend an afternoon just exploring the ever-expanding group of art galleries on R Street NW. Although most people associate **Embassy Row** with Massachusetts Avenue west of the circle, its eastern reaches as well as the **Kalorama Circle** neighborhood north of Massachusetts Ave are crowded with chanceries—from elegant estates like Japan's to tiny suites maintained by threadbare Third World domains.

Kalorama Circle, an elegant precinct of 1920s' houses and apartment buildings, is home to notables like Supreme Court **Justice Sandra Day O'Connor**. The soaring **Taft Bridge** carries Connecticut Ave high above **Rock Creek Park**. East of Kalorama lies **Adams-Morgan**, the city's most ethnically diverse neighborhood and one of its liveliest.

Named after two neighborhood schools, Adams-Morgan is the district's bohemian quarter, with a lively ethnic mix. Its longtime black residents have been joined by DC's large Salvadoran community as well as by Ethiopians and other African immigrants. It seems as though every time there's a revolution overseas, another crop of restaurants springs up near the intersection of 18th Street and Columbia Road, the heart of Adams-Morgan. In recent years, young professionals have immigrated in droves, but they have so far failed to dilute its verve, racial diversity, and homey character. The success of Adams-Morgan's many restaurants, clubs, and shops has spawned parking problems and charges that it will soon become another Georgetown—an insult in residents' eyes. On **Adams-Morgan Day** and during the **Hispanic American Festival**—both annual events—the streets are gridlocked with local bands and stalls selling every ethnic food known to man. Will success spoil Adams-Morgan?

1 Dupont Fountain (1920, Daniel Chester French) There was once a bronze statue here of Civil War admiral **Samuel Francis Dupont**. Fortunately, the Dupont family whisked it away to Delaware, replacing it with this graceful marble fountain. Below the basin are figures representing the wind, the sea, and the stars. Dupont Circle's benches and lawn are popular for political demonstrations, chess, and just hanging out. ♦ Dupont Circle (intersection of Connecticut, New Hampshire, and Massachusetts Aves) Metro stop: Dupont Circle

2 Dupont Plaza Hotel $$$ The location of this unremarkable hotel—right on Dupont Circle—makes it a winner. Amenities include indoor parking, babysitting, valet service, 312 rooms with wetbars and refrigerators, weeknight entertainment in the lobby, and laundry and dry cleaning services. Nonsmoking rooms. Children under 12 stay free. ♦ 1500 New Hampshire Ave NW (18th-19th Sts) Metro stop: Dupont Circle. 483.6000, 800/421.6662; fax 328.3265

3 Washington Club (Patterson House) (1902, Stanford White) Another wedge-shaped building fronting Dupont Circle. This gleaming white Italian palazzo was built for the publisher of the *Washington Times Herald*. It now houses a women's club. ♦ 15 Dupont Circle

Adams-Morgan/Dupont Circle

NW (New Hampshire Ave-P St) Metro stop: Dupont Circle. 483.9200

Drawing by Edward F. Fogle

4 National Trust for Historic Preservation (McCormick Apartments) (1917, Jules Henri de Sibour) The McCormick Building was once the most opulent apartment house in DC, with one 11,000-square-foot apartment on each of its 5 floors. Notables like **Andrew Mellon** lived here. It is the best of de Sibour's many DC works (which include the nearby former **Canadian Chancery**), bringing a Parisian flair to the neighborhood. Now national headquarters for the nonprofit National Trust, which labors hard to save buildings like this. ♦ 1785 Massachusetts Ave NW (17th-18th Sts) Metro stop: Dupont Circle. 673.4000

"You and I, dear friend, have been sent into life at a time when the greatest lawgivers would have wished to live. How few of the human race have ever enjoyed an opportunity of making an election of government for themselves and their children." **John Adams**

Restaurants: Red **Hotels**: Blue
Shops/Parks: Green **Sights/Culture**: Black

5 Jefferson Hotel $$$ **Rose Narva**, doyenné of Washington hoteliers, gives this 69-room, 35-suite hotel the feel of an extremely elegant private British estate. It served as home base for a good many Reagan administration honchos. Amenities include concierge and valet services, 24-hour room service, valet parking. Children under 5 stay free. ♦ 1200 16th St NW (M St-Rhode Island Ave) Metro stop: Dupont Circle. 347.2200, 800/368.5966; fax 331.7982

Within the Jefferson Hotel:

The Hunt Club ★★$$$$ A wood-burning fireplace, Federal-period furnishings, and lots of nooks and crannies make the Hunt Club a cozy spot. Special dishes include vegetable strudel served with jicama salad and Jefferson macaroni (**Thomas Jefferson** introduced pasta to the US after his European travels). ♦ American/French ♦ Daily 6:30AM-10PM. Jacket and tie requested. Reservations recommended. 347.2200

6 Sumner School Museum and Archives (1872, Adolph Cluss) This historic red brick schoolhouse, home of the first school for black children in DC, has been renovated and now houses the archives of the DC public schools and revolving exhibitions on local history and culture. ♦ Free. M-Sa 9AM-5PM.

Adams-Morgan/Dupont Circle

1201 17th St NW (M St-Rhode Island Ave) Metro stop: Dupont Circle. 727.3419 &

7 B'nai B'rith Klutznick Museum Twenty centuries of history, with emphasis on early Jewish-American settlements, are represented by more than 500 objects, making the permanent collection one of the largest in the US. Artifacts such as thousand-year-old coins and a 16th-century Torah wrapper help to introduce visitors to Jewish history. Subjects from archaeology to modern art are covered in a series of annual exhibitions. Free films are scheduled year-round, and nationally known columnists and speakers hold lectures on a weekly basis. Next to the museum's gift shop is the **National Jewish Visitors Center**, providing hospitality services and information on Jewish sights and events in Washington. Group and multilingual tours can be arranged in advance. Library not open to the public. ♦ Voluntary contribution. M-F, Su 10AM-5PM except Jewish holidays. 1640 Rhode Island Ave NW (16th-17th Sts) Metro stop: Farragut North. 857.6583 &

8 Herb's ★★$$ Transferred from his old P Street digs, Herb still serves up zesty American food in a café setting that reflects his longtime support for the Washington arts scene. The sesame chicken salad is a winner. ♦ American ♦ Daily 7AM-midnight. 1616 Rhode Island Ave NW (16th-17th Sts) Metro stop: Dupont Circle. 333.4372

"Indeed I tremble for my country when I reflect that God is just." **Thomas Jefferson** *Notes on Virginia*

9 Iron Gate Inn ★$$ One of the prettiest garden restaurants in town, with an Old World atmosphere. Solid Middle Eastern cooking: hummus, baba ghanouj with baskets of warm pita, good stuffed grape leaves, lamb dishes, baklava. ♦ Middle Eastern ♦ Daily 11:30AM-2:30PM, 5:30-10PM. 1734 N St NW (17th-18th Sts) Dinner reservations recommended. Metro stops: Dupont Circle, Farragut North. 737.1370

10 Canterbury $$ Comfortable and elegant lodgings. Each suite has a sitting area, dressing room, and wetbar; complimentary Continental breakfast. Ask about the *Suite and Luxurious Weekend Package*. Nonsmoking rooms. Children under 11 stay free. ♦ 1733 N St NW (17th St) Metro stops: Dupont Circle, Farragut North. 393.3000, 800/424.2950; fax 785.9581

Within the Canterbury:

Chaucer's ★★$$$ Sit in the cheery basement dining room or the skylit courtyard and enjoy well-prepared specialties such as gingery red snapper or shrimp in pernod and butter. ♦ American ♦ M-F 7-9:30AM, 11:30AM-2:30PM, 5:30-10:30PM; Sa 8-10AM, 5:30-10:30PM; Su 10AM-2PM, 5:30-10:30PM. Reservations recommended. 296.0665

10 The Tabard Inn $$ A haven for Anglophiles, this friendly bed-and-breakfast has only 39 rooms. Many rooms have fireplaces, and at least one 2nd-floor room has an upright piano. Guests congregate in a large 1st-floor parlor and cocktail lounge. Most of the staff have been with the inn for many years. Breakfast is included in the room price. ♦ 1739 N St NW (17th-18th Sts) Metro stops: Dupont Circle, Farragut North. 785.1277; fax 785.6173

Within the Tabard Inn:

Tabard Inn Restaurant ★★$$ A casual, bustling dining room hung with folk art, and featuring a menu of healthy, inventive dishes: lavish salads, fresh fish with crisp vegetable garnishes, burgers covered with Stilton cheese or salsa verde, fresh pastas. Homemade desserts. Garden dining in warm weather. ♦ American ♦ M-F 7AM-10PM; Sa-Su 8AM-10PM. Reservations recommended. 833.2668

11 St. Matthew's Cathedral (1899, Heins & LaFarge) **John F. Kennedy** worshiped in this church, and his funeral Mass was said here; an inscription marks the spot of the casket. The dome, reminiscent of the Cathedral of Santa Maria del Fiore in Florence, and the simple brick geometries of the exterior give no hint of the florid interior's fine mosaic work. ♦ Daily 7AM-6PM. Services: Sa 5:30PM; Su 7, 8:30, 10, 11:30AM, 1, 5:30PM; Spanish Mass Su 6:30PM. 1725 Rhode Island Ave NW (Florida Ave-Leroy Pl) Metro stop: Dupont Circle. 347.3215

Common rules of an 18th-century tavern: No tinkereres or razor grinders taken in, all organ grinders to sleep in the washhouse. No more than 5 in a bed, and no boots worn in bed.

Restaurants: Red	**Hotels**: Blue
Shops/Parks: Green	**Sights/Culture**: Black

11 Longfellow Building (1940, William Lescaze) The first modern glass box in DC, its historical claim to fame is that it was among the very first buildings anywhere to articulate office space and service area as separate design elements. ♦ 1741 Rhode Island Ave NW (17th-18th Sts) Metro stop: Dupont Circle

11 Joe & Mo's ★★$$$$ The place for chowing down on massive steaks while rubbing elbows with the power-lunch gang. ♦ American ♦ M-F 7:30-10AM, 11:30AM-10PM; Sa 6-10PM. 1211 Connecticut Ave NW (M-N Sts) Reservations recommended. Metro stop: Dupont Circle. 659.1211

12 Le Lion d'Or ★★★★$$$$ The oldest of this city's fine French restaurants, Le Lion is known for its simple but masterful preparation of specialties like duck sausage with port, poached scallops, roast pigeon with garlic cloves, crab in remoulade, and squab with wild mushrooms. Chef **Jean-Pierre Goyenvalle** is the force behind these splendid creations. Service is impeccable, the gold-striped dining room plush. ♦ French ♦ M-F noon-2PM, 6-10PM; Sa 6-10PM. 1150 Connecticut Ave NW (entrance at 18th and M Sts) Jacket and tie required. Reservations required. Metro stop: Dupont Circle. 296.7972

12 Cantina D'Italia ★★$$$$ Although Cantina is no longer the city's most innovative Italian restaurant, its fresh pastas, risottos, hearty game, and traditional desserts still satisfy. ♦ Italian ♦ M-F noon-2PM, 6-10:30PM; Sa 6-10:30PM. 1214-A 18th St NW (M St-Jefferson Pl) Metro stops: Farragut West, Farragut North. 659.1830

12 The Roxy Cramped, yes; bad acoustics, yes; but still a great place to dance to reggae, rock, and blues bands. ♦ W-Su 8PM-2AM. 1214 18th St NW (M St-Jefferson Pl) Metro stops: Farragut West, Farragut North. 296.9292

13 Sign of the Whale ★$$ This preppied-out singles bar serves surprisingly good burgers and sandwiches—if your mind's on food. ♦ American ♦ M-Th 11:30AM-2AM; F 11:30AM-3AM; Sa 10:30AM-3AM; Su 10:30AM-1:30AM. 1825 M St NW (18th-19th Sts) Metro stop: Dupont Circle. 223.0608

On 4 July 1826, **John Adams** was dying. Not knowing that **Thomas Jefferson** was dying that same day in Virginia, he said, "Independence forever, Jefferson survives." These were his last words.

The only time the Capitol was open all night was when **John F. Kennedy** lay in state in the Rotunda.

i RICCHI

14 i Ricchi ★★★$$$ Currently one of the hottest restaurants in town, serving authentic Tuscan fare. **President Bush** and the French ambassador's chef are among its many fans. *Pappa al pomodoro* and grilled rabbit in rosemary and sage garnished with fried polenta are highpoints. Homemade Florentine almond and hazelnut cookies are served, ready for dunking, alongside *Vino Santo*. High ceilings, large columns, and golden stucco walls decorated with murals help create an enchanting space. ♦ Italian ♦ M-F 11:30AM-2:30PM, 5:30-10:30PM; Sa 5:30-10:30PM. 1220 19th St NW (M-N Sts) Reservations recommended. Metro stop: Dupont Circle. 835.0459

15 The Palm ★★$$$$ Heavy-duty lobbyists and sports figures love the clubby feel and steak-and-potatoes fare. Decor is confined to the caricatures of the famous scribbled on the wall. ♦ American ♦ M-F 11:45AM-10:30PM; Sa 6-10:30PM. 1225 19th St NW (M-N Sts) Reservations required. Metro stop: Dupont Circle. 293.9091

James Smithson's fortune, willed to the US government in 1835, amounted to $541,379.63.

Adams-Morgan/Dupont Circle

Embassy Row is a concentrated diplomatic community in the city's Northwest quadrant that houses representatives from over 130 foreign governments. Although security tends to be tight, visitors are free to look at the facades, coats-of-arms, and multicolored flags. At 2020 Massachusetts Ave NW is the **McLean Mansion**, now the Indonesian Embassy. The 1908 **Moran House** (the **Pakistani Embassy**), 2311 Massachusetts Ave, and next door, the 1909 **Fahnestock** House (formerly the **Chinese Embassy**) at 2314 Massachusetts Ave, are shining stars from the neighborhood's heyday. Notice the twin carved elephants that guard the door to the **Indian Embassy** at 2701 Massachusetts Ave NW. Many of the contents of the former **Iranian Embassy**, 3005 Massachusetts Ave NW, were auctioned to pay abandoned Iranian government debts when the shah was deposed. **Olavo Redig de Campos**, the late architect of Rio de Janeiro's Museum of Modern Art, designed the **Brazilian Embassy** (3006 Massachusetts Ave NW), a floating cube of glass that enlivens Embassy Row. The **British Embassy** is a stately English country house at 3100 Massachusetts Ave NW. Far removed from the circle is the new **Canadian Embassy** at 5th St and Pennsylvania Ave NW. Farther out is the **German Embassy**, easily the finest piece of diplomatic architecture in Washington. And the future **USSR Embassy** sits on a hilltop (1825 Phelps Pl NW), presumably to facilitate electronic eavesdropping. Metro stop: Dupont Circle.

16 Bacchus ★★$$ Excellent Middle Eastern goodies served in a charming little dining room. The baba ghanouj is perfect. ◆ Middle Eastern ◆ M-Th noon-2:30PM, 6-10PM; F noon-2:30PM, 6-10:30PM; Sa 6-10:30PM; Su 6-10PM. 1827 Jefferson Pl NW (18th-19th Sts) Reservations recommended. Metro stop: Dupont Circle. 785.0734

16 Trattu ★★$$ Tiny, modern Northern Italian trattoria; the linguine with red caviar and cream redefines the pasta genre. ◆ Italian ◆ M-F 11:30AM-2:30PM, 5:30-11PM; Sa 5:30-11PM. 1823 Jefferson Pl NW (18th-19th Sts) Reservations recommended. Metro stop: Dupont Circle. 466.4570

17 Olsson's Books and Records A top full-service general bookstore with a wide selection of pop, jazz, country, and blues LPs. DC's best bookstore. ◆ M-Sa 10AM-9PM; Su noon-6PM. 1307 19th St NW (Dupont Circle-N St) Metro stop: Dupont Circle. 785.1133. Also at: 1239 Wisconsin Ave NW. 338.9544; 12th and F Sts. 383.8990; 7647 Old Georgetown Rd, Bethesda MD. 652.3336

18 Lawson's Gourmet Great finds, from salads and breads to pastries and wines. Catering and delivery services. ◆ M-F 7:30AM-8PM; Sa 10AM-6PM. 1350 Connecticut Ave NW (19th St) Metro stop: Dupont Circle. 775.0400

Adams-Morgan/Dupont Circle

Chicago Bar and Grill and North Shore Beach Club Twin dance clubs popular with young pros and the international set. The Chicago Bar and Grill plays high-energy dance music in a modern decor, while the North Shore Beach Club sports surfboard tables, Astroturf floors, surfing posters, and rock 'n' roll. Munchies are served in both clubs. ◆ Cover Th-Sa. M-Th 5PM-2AM; F 5PM-3AM; Sa 9PM-3AM. 1330 19th St NW (Sunderland Pl-Dupont Circle) Metro stop: Dupont Circle. 463.8888

19 Euram Building (1971, Hartman-Cox) One of Washington's more imaginative contemporary buildings. Eight slick stories of brick, glass, and prestressed concrete surround an inner courtyard. ◆ 21 Dupont Circle NW (19th St-New Hampshire Ave) Metro stop: Dupont Circle

Drawing by Edward F. Fogle

20 Columbia Historical Society/Heurich Mansion (1880, J.G. Myers) Once a poor German immigrant, the wealthy 19th-century beer magnate **Christian Heurich** was one who spared no expense. His legacy to Washington, a 31-room turreted Romanesque Revival mansion, gives an accurate picture of life at the turn of the century. Many of the opulent interiors are intact, and the building houses Washington DC's local historical association, the **Columbia Historical Society**. The society maintains a wonderful collection of books, clippings, detailed journals, photos, and arti-facts focusing on the social mores of the city. ◆ Mansion: admission. W-Sa noon-4PM. Tours on a walk-in basis. Historical Society Library: free. W, F-Sa 10AM-4PM (Th noon-4PM for members only) 1307 New Hampshir Ave NW (20th-21st Sts) Metro stop: Dupont Circle. 785.2068 ♿

21 Hampshire Hotel $$ Not as lavishly deco-rated as others in the neighborhood, but this **Best Western** hotel has comfortable accom-modations and a warm and responsive staff. Suites are spacious, with stocked wetbars and sitting-room areas. Located within walking distance of Georgetown's shops and restau-rants. Nonsmoking rooms. Children under 12 stay free. ◆ 1310 New Hampshire Ave NW (20th-21st Sts) Metro stop: Dupont Circle. 296.7600, 800/368.5691; fax 293.2476

Within the Hampshire Hotel:

Lafitte ★★$$ Not everyone knows about this classy Cajun eatery, which is too bad: the barbecued shrimp induce instant bliss. ◆ Cajun ◆ M-F 7:30-10AM, 11:30AM-2:30PM, 5:30-10:30PM; Sa 6-11PM; Su 6-10PM. Reservations recommended. 296.7600

22 Embassy Square Suites Hotel $$ An air of Washington elegance is apparent in the lobby's oil portraits, fine woods, and high ceilings. Also unusual are the 250 suites: choose from 4 different decor styles. Ask for one overlooking the courtyard, or for Suite 117, the nicest in the house. Other pluses: a multilingual staff, complimentary health club, underground parking, a restaurant and night-club (**Rhapsody**), a garden courtyard with pool, and stocked kitchens and minibars. Ask about weekend specials. Nonsmoking rooms. Chil-dren under 16 stay free. ◆ 2000 N St NW (20th-21st Sts) Metro stop: Dupont Circle. 659.9000, 800/424.2999; fax 429.9546 ♿

23 Marston Luce Gallery Nineteenth-century American folk art—weather vanes, furniture, decoys, carvings, signs, paintings. A specialty is Pennsylvania majolica ware—brightly painted lead-glazed earthenware—now enjoy-ing a resurgence among collectors. ◆ M-Sa 11AM-6PM. 1314 21st St NW (N St-Newport Pl) Metro stop: Dupont Circle. 775.9460

24 Second Story Books is DC's leading used-book store. Floor-to-ceiling shelves feature old, used, rare, and out-of-print books—all at reasonable prices. Free search service and appraisals. ◆ Daily 10AM-10PM. 2000 P St NW (20th St) Metro stop: Dupont Circle. 659.8884. Also at: 4836 Avenue Rd, Bethesda MD. 656.0170

"What is government itself, but the greatest of all reflections on human nature? If men were angels, no government would be necessary." **James Madison**

24 Galileo ★★★$$$ Forget the veal marsala and go nuts over the meltingly rich risotto and other authentic Northern Italian specialities on the handwritten menu—like *bollito misto* or wild game. Homemade breadsticks and rolls accompany all the dishes. The pretty room is simple in decoration—textured white walls, a plant and a picture here and there—and the tables are arranged with privacy in mind. ♦ Italian ♦ M-Th noon-2:30PM, 5:30-10PM; F noon-2:30PM, 5:30-10:30PM; Sa 5:30-10:30PM; Su 5-8:30PM. 2014 P St NW (20th-21st Sts) Metro stop: Dupont Circle. 293.7191

24 Sala Thai ★★$ Splendidly authentic Thai food, right down to the ultrasweet iced tea, in a cool neon-lit basement room. ♦ Thai ♦ M-Th 11:30AM-2:30PM, 5-10:30PM; F 11:30AM-2:30PM, 5-11PM; Sa noon-11PM; Su 5-10:30PM. 2016 P St NW (20th-21st Sts) Metro stop: Dupont Circle. 872.1144

25 Pan Asian Noodles ★★$ The best noodles in town. Try *drunken noodles*: a plate of steamed flat noodles topped with a stir-fry of minced chicken in a spicy basil sauce. ♦ Pan-Asian ♦ M-Th 11:30AM-3PM, 5-10:30PM; F 11:30AM-3PM, 5-11PM; Sa noon-3PM, 5-11PM; Su 5-10PM. 2020 P St NW (Hopkins St) Reservations recommended. Metro stop: Dupont Circle. 872.8889

Bed-and-Breakfast

For visitors who don't feel like springing for a Downtown hotel room and who enjoy living like the locals, B&B accommodations are the answer. A growing number of Washington area residents provide a room and breakfast; many also provide tips on sightseeing, restaurants, and transportation. The following reservations services will connect you with bed-and-breakfasts in the Washington area; all 3 recommend that you call ahead to discuss what you're looking for.

The Bed and Breakfast League, Ltd.
In 1988, the Bed and Breakfast League merged with another longtime bed-and-breakfast service, Sweet Dreams and Toast, and now lists about 70 hosted homes and apartments in Washington and the suburbs, including Victorian homes in Capitol Hill and Dupont Circle. ♦ Booking fee. P.O. Box 9490, Washington DC, 20016. 202/363.7767

Bed 'n' Breakfast Ltd. Over 60 hosted private homes and apartments in the metropolitan area, from Victorian homes to modern homes. Unhosted efficiencies and one-bedrooms available. ♦ No booking fee. P.O. Box 12011, Washington DC, 20005. 202/328.3510

Inns of the Shenandoah Valley, an organization of 12 independent B&B inns, provides accommodations in several rural and historical places. Try the Belle Grae Inn, a former Victorian mansion in Staunton, or the Jordan Hollow Farm Inn, a 45-acre horse farm in Stanley. ♦ No booking fee. 11 N. Main St., Lexington VA, 24450. 703/463.2044

25 Cafe Japone ★$$ How did you manage to live without sumo-video sushi, or sushi pizza? ♦ Japanese ♦ M, Su 5PM-midnight; Tu-Th 11AM-2:30PM, 5PM-midnight; F 11AM-2:30PM, 5PM-1:30AM; Sa 5PM-1:30AM. 2032 P St NW (20th-21st Sts) Metro stop: Dupont Circle. 223.1573

26 Obelisk ★★★$$$$ Innovative Italian fare served in a stark and elegant setting. Start with grilled bread topped with herb goat cheese; move on to lasagna with venison ragout or squab with polenta and wild mushrooms; wind down with poached pears swimming in a frothy zabaglione. ♦ Italian ♦ M-Sa 6-10PM. 2029 P St NW (20th-21st Sts) Reservations recommended. Metro stop: Dupont Circle. 872.1180

27 Backstage Books, scripts, sheet music, and publications inspired by the performing arts. Also dancewear, stage makeup, and record albums. ♦ M-W, F-Sa 10AM-6PM; Th 10AM-8PM. 2101 P St NW (21st St) Metro stop: Dupont Circle. 775.1488

27 The Omni Georgetown Hotel $$ Not really Georgetown, but Dupont Circle on the verge of Rock Creek Park isn't bad. An outdoor pool, a sauna, an exercise room, and valet and concierge services are among the amenities. The **Café Beaux Arts** has a pretty Bauhaus decor

but an unremarkable American menu. Non-smoking rooms. Children under 16 stay free. ♦ 2121 P St NW (21st-22nd Sts) Metro stop: Dupont Circle. 293.3100, 800/843.6664; fax 857.0134 &

28 The Brickskeller ★★$ Beer mavens worldwide know the Brickskeller, and the Brickskeller knows what they want: more than 500 brands of beer in a basement pub conducive to quaffing. ♦ American ♦ M-Th 11:30AM-2AM; F 11:30AM-3AM; Sa 6PM-3AM; Su 6PM-2AM. 523 22nd St NW (P-Q Sts) Metro stop: Dupont Circle. 293.1885

29 Buffalo Bridge (1914, Glenn Brown/Bedford Brown) This impressive span across Rock Creek Park sports aqueductlike arches and 4 handsome buffalos sculpted by **A. Phimister Proctor**. The bridge's arches are supported underneath by Indian heads in full war bonnet, visible from Rock Creek Parkway. ♦ 23rd and Q Sts NW. Metro stop: Dupont Circle

30 Sheridan Circle A 1909 statue of **Union General Philip H. Sheridan** on his favorite horse, **Rienzi**, looks east across this peaceful formal circle. (The sculpture is by **Gutzon Borglum**, who also did Mount Rushmore.) Along the outside curb in the southeast quadrant sits a small memorial to Chilean ambassador **Orlando Letelier** and aide **Ronni Karpen Moffitt**, who were killed when a remote-controlled bomb destroyed their car here on 21 September 1976. Chilean secret police and army officials were later convicted. ♦ Massachusetts Ave at 23rd St NW. Metro stop: Dupont Circle

31 Barney Studio House Part of the Smithsonian's **National Museum of American Art**, the 1902 house built by **Alice Pike Barney** served as her home and studio. It features her work and early 20th-century artifacts. ♦ Free tours by appointment only, W-Th 11AM, 1PM; 2nd and 4th Su each month 1PM. 2306 Massachusetts Ave NW (23rd St) Metro stop: Dupont Circle. 357.3111

32 Addison/Ripley Gallery Ltd. Contemporary American painters and sculptors, including local artists **Edith Kuhnle** and **Rebecca Cross**. ♦ Tu-Sa 11AM-5PM. 9 Hillyer Ct NW (Q-R Sts) Metro stop: Dupont Circle. 328.2332

33 Cosmos Club (Townsend Mansion) (1900, Carrère and Hastings) A railway baron's wife commissioned this palace, which features one of the most ostentatious facades in the city. In 1988, this private club of achievers in the arts, politics, and science voted to admit women members. ♦ 2121 Massachusetts Ave NW (21st-22nd Sts) Metro stop: Dupont Circle

The Phillips Collection

34 The Phillips Collection (1897, Hornblower & Marshall; additions, 1920, 1923, McKim,

Mead & White; adjoining building, 1960, Wyeth & King; restoration, 1984, Arthur Cotton Moore Associates) In 1921, **Duncan** and **Marjorie Phillips** opened their 4-story brownstone home to the public, thus creating the first museum of modern art. Duncan had already established an exemplary collection, starting with American Impressionists and expanding into French Impressionists and the Post-Impressionists. Eventually, the Phillipses' holdings spanned not only European and American Modernism, but also sources of Modernism such as **Goya**, **El Greco**, and **Delacroix**.

Today, the Phillips Collection preserves the private home atmosphere while displaying its inventory to best advantage. The museum is a delight for art lovers, who can stroll through the oversize rooms or take advantage of the many couches and chairs in which to rest and ponder particular works.

Duncan Phillips tried to create exhibition units, either of an artist's whole body of work or a comparison of several artists' pieces. He sought interesting colors and unique qualities, encouraging lesser-known talents by being the first to collect their works. He insisted upon rearranging paintings to show off their best qualities—and did so even from his deathbed.

About 2500 pieces now occupy most of Phillips' original home as well as an adjoining building that was created in 1960. A 1984 restoration improved illumination and safety at the museum.

Degas, **Monet**, **Van Gogh**, **Cézanne**, and **Renoir** hold important positions throughout the museum, as do **Bonnard**, **Klee**, **Marin**, **Rothko**, **Dove**, and **O'Keeffe**. Following Phillips' wishes, the museum sponsors exhibitions, publications, and loans to other museums' special exhibitions.

The **Goh Annex**, a section that opened in spring of 1989 (**Arthur Cotton Moore Associates**), doubles the exhibition space (allowing the permanent collection to remain on view) and provides an entire floor for temporary exhibitions.

Gallery talks take place at 12:30PM the first and third Thursdays of each month. Free tours are offered at 2PM Wednesday and Saturday; group tours should be arranged one month in advance. Free Sunday afternoon concerts are given at 5PM September through May. Gift shop and tearoom on premises. ♦ Voluntary contribution. Tu-Sa 10AM-5PM; Su 2-7PM. 1600 21st St NW (Q St) Metro stop: Dupont Circle. 387.2151, tour information 387.0961

35 Anderson House/Society of the Cincinnati (1900, Little & Brown) In 1783, a group of Revolutionary War officers facing demobilization proposed this elite fraternal organization to preserve their select camaraderie. At the time, such organizations played an important part in gentlemanly civic and political advancement. Membership is limited to male descendants—usually firstborn—of those original officers, plus a few exceptions; even the French have a chapter, due to the role they played in the Revolution. The group is named for **Lucius Quinctius Cincinnatus**, a Roman leader whose life Washington's paralleled. The town of Cincinnati OH was named by a member of the society. Anderson House, where the Society of the Cincinnati is headquartered, is a **Historic House Museum** and is not to be missed. Behind the stately Palladian facade is one of the city's finest townhouses, with lavish and opulent interiors filled with artistic treasures from the US, Europe, and the Orient, including society members' portraits by famous American painters. **Gilbert Stuart**, **John Trumbull**, **Daniel Huntington**, and **Cecilia Beaux** are among the artists represented. The **Harold Leonard Stuart Memorial Library** of reference works on the American Revolution is open to the public. Walk-in self-guided tours are available, as well as guided tours for groups of 20 or more. ♦ Free. Tu-Sa 1-4PM. 2118 Massachusetts Ave NW (21st-22nd Sts) Metro stop: Dupont Circle. 785.2040 &

"The mists of the morning still hung around...[the] magnificent building when first it broke upon our view....We were struck with admiration and surprise. None of us, I believe, expected to see so imposing a structure on that side of the Atlantic. The beauty and majesty of the American capitol might defy an abler pen than mine to do it justice. It stands so finely too, high, and alone."

Frances Trollope

35 The Ritz-Carlton $$$ The Ritz's 240 rooms are decorated with American antiques and reproductions: niceties such as handcarved mahogany headboards and embroidered English chintz bedspreads are standard. Valet parking, a multilingual staff, secretarial assistance, and 24-hour room service are among the hotel's amenities. The **Fairfax Bar** offers cocktails, light lunches, and afternoon tea in a marvelously intimate series of alcoves. Nonsmoking rooms. Children under 12 stay free. ◆ Deluxe ◆ 2100 Massachusetts Ave NW (21st St) Metro stop: Dupont Circle. 293.2100, 800/241.3333; fax 293.0641 ♿

Within the Ritz-Carlton:

Jockey Club ★★★$$$$ Clubby elegance, a staff schooled in the grand old manner, and a subtle French menu. The soft-shell crabs and the sautéed John Dory with asparagus and fresh truffles are prizewinners. ◆ French ◆ Daily 6:30-11AM, noon-2:30PM, 6-10:30PM. Jacket and tie required. Reservations recommended. 659.8000

36 Blaine Mansion (1881, John Fraser) A Victorian fortress that was once the home of 3-time presidential hopeful **James Blaine**. ◆ 2000 Massachusetts Ave NW (20th St) Metro stop: Dupont Circle

37 Trocadero Asian Art Owner **Kitty Higgins** carries a wide range of Asian pieces—5th-century Chinese stone sculpture, Imperial porcelain, Ming furniture, Himalayan bronzes, and *thangka* (Buddhist meditation paintings) — as well as high-quality neolithic pottery. ◆ Tu-Sa 10:30AM-6PM. 1501 Connecticut Ave NW (19th St-Dupont Circle) Metro stop: Dupont Circle. 234.5656

37 Kramerbooks & afterwords: A café ★$ Building a café at the rear of a bookstore isn't a new idea—but the browsing bookworms, artists, and neighborhood gadflies confirm it's a good one. This Dupont Circle institution specializes in popular hardcovers and paperbacks, a little quiche, and a split of wine. Open 24 hours over the weekend. ◆ American ◆ M-Th 7:30AM-1AM; F 7:30AM-M 1AM. 1517 Connecticut Ave NW (Q St-Dupont Circle) Metro stop: Dupont Circle. 387.1400

37 Cafe Splendide ★★$ A cheery and intimate tearoom offering friendly service and large portions of Austrian food—hamburgers seasoned with green peppers and bacon, brochette of beef and pork tenderloin, homemade strudel and other pastries. One of the least pretentious eateries in the neighborhood. Good breakfasts.

◆ Austrian ◆ Daily 9AM-11:30PM. 1521 Connecticut Ave NW (Q St-Dupont Circle) Reservations recommended. Metro stop: Dupont Circle. No credit cards. 328.1503

38 Osuna One of the district's most highly regarded galleries exhibits contemporary American works and Old Masters, with occasional forays into European and Latin American realms. Its stable includes 2 of Washington's strongest artists, **Manon Cleary** and **Rebecca Davenport**. ◆ Tu-Sa 10AM-6PM. 1919 Q St NW (19th-20th Sts) Metro stop: Dupont Circle. 296.1963

39 Kathleen Ewing Gallery Specializing in 19th-century vintage and 20th-century masterwork images, this photography gallery holds monthly exhibitions and represents 30 American and European photographers. ◆ W-Sa 11AM-6PM. 1609 Connecticut Ave NW (Q-R Sts) Metro stop: Dupont Circle. 328.0955

39 Whatever Lola Wants "Rags"and jewelry for the girl who wouldn't be caught dead in a suit-and-bow blouse. ◆ M-F 11AM-7PM; Sa 11AM-6PM; Su 1-5PM. 1617 Connecticut Ave NW (Q-R Sts) Metro stop: Dupont Circle. 265.3200

40 Vincenzo ★★★$$$$ Seafood is prepared with a knowing Italian flair within Vincenzo's chic and austere interiors. Start with antipasto:

Adams-Morgan/Dupont Circle

bean and pepper salad, sardines, stuffed whole artichokes, or good ham. Then choose from pastas prepared with fragrant seafood sauces and main courses like fritto misto or grilled whole fish cooked with lemon, fresh herbs, and olive oil. Interesting wine list. ◆ Italian ◆ M-F noon-2PM, 6-10PM; Sa 6-10PM; Su 6-9PM. 1606 20th St NW (Q-R Sts) Jacket and tie requested. Reservations required. Metro stop: Dupont Circle. 667.0047

40 Cherishables Eighteenth- and 19th-century furniture and American folk art are the specialties of this shop, with particular emphasis on quilts. Weather vanes, decoys, whirligigs, and hand-carved wooden architectural collectibles are customary items as well. ◆ M-Sa 11AM-6PM. 1608 20th St NW (Q-R Sts) Metro stop: Dupont Circle. 785.4087

40 Childe Harold ★$ Local bar and DC institution; bluegrass star **Emmylou Harris** performed here in her salad days. Burgers downstairs; more formal dining upstairs. ◆ American ◆ M-Th, Su 11:30AM-2AM; F-Sa 11:30AM-3AM. 1610 20th St NW (Q-R Sts) Metro stop: Dupont Circle. 483.6702

41 Americana West Gallery One of the few places besides the Department of the Interior's Indian Craft Shop to find American West-influenced art—this by contemporary painters, sculptors, and ceramists. ◆ M-Sa 10AM-8PM; Su noon-5PM. 1630 Connecticut Ave NW (R St-Hillyer Pl) Metro stop: Dupont Circle. 265.1630

Restaurants: Red	**Hotels**: Blue
Shops/Parks: Green	**Sights/Culture**: Black

42 Fourways ★$$$ The cuisine is opulent and expensive, but fails to live up to the elegance of this beautifully restored old mansion. Banquet facilities are available; call for information. ♦ French ♦ M-F noon-2:30PM, 6-10:30PM; Sa 6-10:30PM; Su 11:30AM-3PM, 6-10:30PM. 1701 20th St NW (R St) Jacket and tie requested. Reservations recommended. Metro stop: Dupont Circle. 483.3200

43 Ginza Futons, kimonos, paper jewelry, porcelain, and other artful Japanese gismos. ♦ M-Tu, F 10AM-6:30PM; W-Th 10AM-8PM; Sa 10AM-6PM; Su noon-6PM. 1721 Connecticut Ave NW (R-S Sts) Metro stop: Dupont Circle. 331.7991

43 Larimer's Gourmet grocery and wineshop, with a bona fide butcher and weekly specials well worth going out of the way for—plus they deliver. ♦ M-F 10AM-7PM; Sa 9AM-7PM; Su 11AM-6PM. 1727 Connecticut Ave NW (R-S Sts) Metro stop: Dupont Circle. 332.3366

Suzanne's

43 Suzanne's ★★$$ Gourmet carry-out shop, and a chic and friendly little restaurant up a narrow flight of stairs. In the restaurant,

Adams-Morgan/Dupont Circle

choose from a blackboard full of specials— meats wrapped in pastry, fresh pastas, fresh salmon, selected cheeses. The desserts are great, especially the chocolate chestnut cake. ♦ American. ♦ Restaurant: M-Th 11:30AM-2:30PM, 6-10:30PM; F-Sa 11:30AM-2:30PM, 6-11PM. Bakery and take-out: M-F 10AM-8PM; Sa 10AM-7PM. 1735 Connecticut Ave NW (R-S Sts) Metro stop: Dupont Circle. 483.4633

44 The News Room In a town of diplomats, politicians, and media junkies, this shop's comprehensive collection of out-of-town and foreign newspapers and magazines is a necessity. ♦ M-Th, Su 6:30AM-10PM; F-Sa 6:30AM-midnight. 1753 Connecticut Ave NW (S St) Metro stop: Dupont Circle. 332.1489

45 Katmandu ★★$$ This enchanting restaurant is a find for the adventurous palate! The cooking of Nepal is one of the least spicy, most subtle of Asian cuisines. Meats and poultry are grilled and served with a yogurt sauce. Try the *shalgam* (turnip) curry, the fish or shrimp stew, or the pork fried in mustard oil. ♦ Nepalese/Kashmiri ♦ M-Th 11:30AM-2:30PM, 5:30-10:30PM; F 11:30AM-2:30PM, 5:30-11PM; Sa 5:30-11PM; Su 5:30-10:30PM. 1800 Connecticut Ave NW (Florida Ave-S St) Jacket and tie requested. Reservations recommended. Metro stop: Dupont Circle. 483.6470

"We know that there are chiselers. At the bottom of every case of criticism and obstruction we have found some selfish interest, some private axe to grind."
Franklin D. Roosevelt

45 Smull's A whimsical collection of clothing, jewelry, ceramics, masks, and toys, presided over by the amazing **Andi Smull**. ♦ M-F 11AM-7PM; Sa 11AM-6PM. 2031 Florida Ave NW (Connecticut Ave-S St) Metro stop: Dupont Circle. 232.8282

46 Friends Meeting of Washington (1930, Walter H. Price) This simple slate-roofed stone building eloquently embodies the Quakers' disdain for ostentation, reminiscent as it is of a country cottage. **President Herbert Hoover** and his wife worshipped here. ♦ M-F 8AM-4PM. Services W 7PM; Su 9, 10, 11AM. 2111 Florida Ave NW (S St-Decatur Pl) Metro stop: Dupont Circle

47 Uzzolo Home furnishings and clothing for trendy *urbanoids*. ♦ M-Sa 11AM-7PM; Su noon-6PM. 1718 Connecticut Ave NW (R-S Sts) Metro stop: Dupont Circle. 328.0900

47 Cafe Pettito ★$ Pizza for grownups, topped with sun-dried tomatoes and the like. A fine antipasto buffet. ♦ Pizza ♦ Daily 11:30AM-midnight. 1724 Connecticut Ave NW (R-S Sts) Metro stop: Dupont Circle. 462.8771

47 Timberlake's ★$ Archetypal burger-and-fern joint, with a crowded and noisy bar and elephantine onion rings. ♦ American ♦ M-Th 11:30AM-midnight; F 11:30AM-1AM; Sa 10:30AM-1AM; Su 10:30AM-midnight. 1726 Connecticut Ave NW (R-S Sts) Metro stop: Dupont Circle. 483.2266

48 Toast & Strawberries Exotic dresses from around the world and by California and New York designers. Jewelry and accessories from Africa, India, Latin America, Asia, and England, plus plenty of advice on putting it all together. They do alterations here—or if you don't have any clothes to alter, bring in your own fabric and they'll whip up something spectacular. ♦ M-Sa 10AM-6PM; Su 1-6PM. 2009 R St NW (20th-21st Sts) Metro stop: Dupont Circle. 234.2424

49 Gallery K European and American contemporary paintings, sculptures, and drawings as well as American folk and Indian art are shown. Washington area artists **Jody Mussoff** and **Fred Folsom** are often featured. ♦ Tu-Sa 11AM-6PM. 2010 R St NW (20th-21st St) Metro stop: Dupont Circle. 234.0339

49 Gallery Affrica Traditional arts of Africa, including masks, textiles, and beadwork. ♦ W-Sa noon-6PM. 2010 1/2 R St NW (20th-21st Sts) Metro stop: Dupont Circle. 745.7272

49 Marsha Mateyka Gallery American and European contemporary work, from **Robert Motherwell**'s prints to Washingtonian **Judy Bass**'s mixed-media works on paper. ♦ W-Sa 11AM-5PM. 2012 R St NW (20th-21st Sts) Metro stop: Dupont Circle. 328.0088

49 Baumgartner Galleries is known for its dedication to contemporary local, national and international artists, as well as to Viennese Magic Realist **Friedensreich Hundertwasser**. ♦ Tu-F 11AM-6PM; Sa 11AM-5:30PM. 2016 R St NW (20th-21st Sts) Metro stop: Dupont Circle. 232.6320

49 Art, Science & Technology Institute
Holographic art from the US and Europe, including holographic eyeglasses. Tours on a walk-in basis. Gift shop. ♦ Admission. Tu-Su 11AM-6PM. 2018 R St NW (20th-21st Sts) Metro stop: Dupont Circle. 667.6322

49 AFR Fine Art Contemporary local and international sculpture; paintings, drawings, and prints by **Gordon Bailey**, **Cy Twombly**, **Roni Horn**, and **David Lowe**, among others. ♦ W-Sa 11AM-5:30PM or by appointment. 2030 R St NW (20th-21st Sts) Metro stop: Dupont Circle. 265.6191

50 Anton Gallery **Gail Enns** and **John Figura** feature Washington artists like **Al Carter**, **Tom Nakashima**, **Mary Annella Frank**, and **Wolfgang Jasper**. ♦ Tu-Sa noon-5PM. 2108 R St NW (21st St-Florida Ave) Metro stop: Dupont Circle. 328.0828

50 Fonda Del Sol Visual Arts and Media Center A showcase for Latin American artists and Hispanic culture. ♦ Tu-Sa noon-5:30PM. 2112 R St NW (21st St-Florida Ave) Metro stop: Dupont Circle. 483.2777

50 Franklin Parrasch Galleries Contemporary works by **Thomas Hucker**, **Tage Frid**, and **Barry Yavener**. ♦ Tu-Sa 11AM-5:30PM; Su noon-4PM. 2114 R St NW (21st St-Florida Ave) Metro stop: Dupont Circle. 328.8222

51 Restaurant Nora ★★$$$ In recent years, Nora has lowered her prices to their pre-expense-account levels, while maintaining her high-quality American cuisine—homegrown herbs, organic vegetables, and additive-free meats—in a lovely country-style dining room and outdoor courtyard. ♦ American ♦ M-Th 6-10PM; F-Sa 6-10:30PM. 2132 Florida Ave NW (R St) Reservations recommended. Metro stop: Dupont Circle. No credit cards. 462.5143

51 Brody's Gallery Art for the adventurous, from **Andrea Way** and **Phyllis Bramson** to **Andrew Hudson** and **Susan Rothenberg**. ♦ Tu-Sa 11AM-5:30PM. 1706 21st St NW (R-S Sts) Metro stop: Dupont Circle. 462.4747

52 Decatur Terrace Here 22nd Street ends in a delightful staircase and fountain. ♦ 22nd St NW (Decatur Pl-S St) Metro stop: Dupont Circle

The studio of Civil War-era photographer **Mathew Brady** was located at 627 Pennsylvania Ave NW, at the corner of 7th Street. **Abraham Lincoln** visited Brady's studio on 23 February 1861 for his first official portrait as president.

53 Textile Museum (1916, John Russell Pope) In 1896, **George H. Myers** purchased an Oriental rug for his college room and began a lifelong fascination with the art of textiles. In 1925, he turned his home and its rich collection—now over 14,000 textiles and 1300 rugs—into this privately endowed showcase. The collection comes from all over the world, notably the Mediterranean and North Africa, the Near and Far East, and Central and South America. Within the museum is a 7000-book resource library on textiles.

Call the museum for information on its current special exhibition, lectures, and workshops. The gift shop, housed in what was once Myers' library, offers textiles, gifts, and publications. ♦ Voluntary contribution. Tu-Sa 10AM-5PM;

Adams-Morgan/Dupont Circle

Su 1-5PM. 2320 S St NW (23rd-24th Sts) Metro stop: Dupont Circle. 667.0441

53 Woodrow Wilson House (1915, Waddy B. Wood) This **National Historic Landmark** serves as a museum commemorating our 28th president, whose accomplishments included creation of the Federal Reserve Board and participation in the establishment of the League of Nations. Wilson's distinguished career as author of 9 books, college professor, president of Princeton University, and governor of New Jersey is covered in exhibitions and photographs. Special museum events include walking tours of the surrounding Kalorama neighborhood, Christmas open house á la 1920, and Veterans Day services. ♦ Admission. Tu-Su 10AM-4PM. 2340 S St NW (23rd-24th Sts) Metro stop: Dupont Circle. 673.5517

54 Japanese Embassy (1931, Delano & Aldrich) The original chancery building, with its iron gates and austere courtyard, manages to look both neo-Georgian and Japanese. ♦ 2520 Massachusetts Ave NW (California St)

55 Islamic Center (1955, Mario Rossi) The Islamic nations that maintain embassies in Washington collaborated on a cultural and religious center for their staffs to use, and the result is one of the most interesting sights in town. Fine craftworks by Middle Eastern artisans furnish the white marble building; the walls are inlaid with turquoise and gold. The actual mosque is a structure in the center of a courtyard, oriented toward Mecca. A minaret rises 160 feet above the complex.

Moslems from over 40 countries comprise the center's congregation, which is among the most active in the country. The center publishes informative literature and conducts lectures. A bookstore is on the premises. Call for schedule of services. Tours arranged by request. ◆ Daily 10AM-5PM. 2551 Massachusetts Ave NW (Belmont Rd) 332.8343

56 The Lindens (1754, Robert Hooper) This New England-style Georgian house is actually the oldest building in DC. But it loses that title to the **Old Stone House** in Georgetown on a technicality: it wasn't in the district until 1934, when it was disassembled and moved from its original home in Danvers MA. ◆ 2401 Kalorama Rd NW (24th St-Belmont Rd) Metro stop: Dupont Circle

57 Normandy Inn $$ Visiting French officials appreciate the charm of this 74-room hotel, with its chic tearoom and patio and Tuesday evening wine and cheese receptions. A complimentary breakfast is served under the *Weekend Package* plan. Nonsmoking rooms. Children under 12 stay free. ◆ 2118 Wyoming Ave NW (Connecticut Ave-23rd St) Metro stop: Dupont Circle. 483.1350, 800/424.3729; fax 387.8241 &

58 The Highland Hotel $$ This 140-room hotel is geared toward longer stays: some

Adams-Morgan/Dupont Circle

suites have kitchens, and all rooms have wetbars and sitting areas. Valet and babysitting services and a multilingual staff are among the Highland's amenities. Nonsmoking rooms. Children under 14 stay free. ◆ 1914 Connecticut Ave NW (California St-Leroy Pl) Metro stop: Dupont Circle. 797.2000, 800/424.2464; telex 494.1795 &

59 Cubi XI Abstract sculptor **David Smith** used steel, nickel, and chrome to powerful and startling effect. Standing 11 feet tall, the precariously balanced squares and rectangles of gleaming metal seem to hold the force of gravity temporarily at bay. ◆ Universal North Building, 1875 Connecticut Ave NW (Florida Ave-Leroy Pl) Metro stop: Dupont Circle

60 Washington Hilton and Towers $$$ Remembered primarily as the place where **John Hinckley** shot **Ronald Reagan**, this huge hotel is always filled with conventioneers. Amenities include a multilingual staff, a jogging course, and exercise rooms. The lighted tennis courts and olympic-size pool are open to health club members and hotel guests. Nonsmoking rooms. Children under 18 stay free. ◆ 1919 Connecticut Ave NW (Columbia Rd-19th St) Metro stop: Dupont Circle. 483.3000, 800/HILTONS; fax 265.8221 &

61 Middendorf Gallery Occupying a light-filled former embassy building, this handsome gallery focuses on mainstream American painting, sculpture, prints, and photography. National avant-garde trends can be studied here. The gallery also specializes in American Modernists from the first half of the century. ◆ Tu-F 11AM-

6PM; Sa 11AM-5PM. 2009 Columbia Rd NW (20th-California Sts) Metro stop: Dupont Circle. 462.2009

62 Omega ★★$ Once the only reason to eat in Adams-Morgan, this granddaddy of Cuban restaurants still serves the best black beans and rice in town in a formica-plain decor. ◆ Cuban ◆ Tu-Th, Su 11:30AM-10PM; F-Sa 11:30AM-11PM. 1858 Columbia Rd NW (Mintwood Pl-Belmont Rd) Metro stop: Dupont Circle. 462.1732

63 Kalorama Guest House $ For budget-minded travelers, this guesthouse (situated in 2 Victorian townhouses) offers comfort at a reasonable price. Amenities include complimentary Continental breakfast and evening sherry, free laundry-room use, and free local calls. Some rooms have private baths; all have brass beds, thick comforters, and late-Victorian antiques. Children under 6 not permitted. ◆ 1854 Mintwood Pl NW (Columbia Rd-19th St) Metro stop: Woodley Park/Zoo. 667.6369

64 La Plaza ★★$$ Utterly romantic candlelight and Impressionist paintings provide an unusual and delightful setting for excellent Spanish and Mexican fare. The outdoor terrace opens for warm weather dinner. Valet parking at dinner M-Sa. ◆ Mexican/Spanish ◆ Daily noon-midnight. 1847 Columbia Rd NW (Biltmore St-Mintwood Pl) Reservations recommended. Metro stop: Woodley Park/Zoo. 667.1900

65 Enriqueta's ★★$$ Real Mexican food, not Tex-Mex, in this colorful outpost of the Georgetown classic. Smooth, piquant guacamole, succulent peppers in fruit sauce, good beers. ◆ Mexican ◆ Daily 11AM-11PM. 1832 Columbia Rd NW (18th St) Metro stop: Woodley Park/Zoo. 328.0937

65 El Caribe ★★$$ Small, very noisy, and featuring distinctly Latin American decor and a strolling guitarist, this place offers the finest of Central and South American cuisines. ◆ Latin American ◆ M-Th 11:30AM-11PM; F 11:30AM-11:30PM; Sa noon-11:30PM; Su noon-11PM. 1828 Columbia Rd NW (18th St-Belmont Rd) Reservations recommended. Metro stop: Woodley Park/Zoo. 234.6969

66 Perry's ★$$ New Wave video sushi—more of an event than a culinary experience. The rooftop deck has a great view. ◆ Japanese ◆ M-Th, Su 6-11:30PM; F-Sa 6PM-12:45AM. 1811 Columbia Rd NW (Biltmore St-Mintwood Pl) Metro stop: Woodley Park/Zoo. 234.6218

67 Calvert Restaurant ★$ Proprietor **Mama Ayesha** holds court in this dark cozy bastion of Middle Eastern cuisine. Try the hummus and baba ghanouj appetizers, followed by a main course of eggplant with ground lamb and pine nuts, or a chicken dish. Round out your meal with honey baklava. ◆ Middle Eastern ◆ M-Th, Su 11:30AM-11:30PM; F-Sa 11:30AM-midnight. 1967 Calvert St NW (20th St) Reservations recommended. Metro stop: Woodley Park/Zoo. 232.5431

Restaurants: Red	**Hotels**: Blue
Shops/Parks: Green	**Sights/Culture**: Black

68 Dakota ★$$ The disco up front caters to the hip young crowd, while the **Montana Café** in the back serves light American salads, burgers, and grilled food in a casual, less frenetic atmosphere. ♦ American ♦ Tu-Th, Su 6:30-11PM; F-Sa 6:30PM-midnight. 1777 Columbia Rd NW (Euclid St-Ontario Rd) Metro stop: Woodley Park/Zoo. 265.6600

69 City Bikes Two former bicycle messengers own this impressive store, which rents as well as sells all-terrain **Miyatas, Giants,** and **Terry Precision Bicycles for Women**. Great service. ♦ M-Sa 10AM-7PM; Su noon-5PM. 2501 Champlain St NW (Columbia Rd) 265.1564

"Nothing can be more unfounded and false [than] the prevalent opinion that all men are born free and equal...[for] it rests upon the assumption of a fact which is contrary to universal observation."

John C. Calhoun

Eating The Globe

Residents of Adams-Morgon can almost track global events by the arrival of new cuisines: first Vietnamese and Cambodian, then Ethiopian, and most recently Salvadoran.

Increasingly, ethnic restaurants are springing up in neighborhoods where the adventurous diner used to be at a loss to get beyond McDonald's. Suburban Arlington, home of Little Saigon, is noted for the Vietnamese restaurants clustered along Washington Blvd. Several serve the anise-scented *pho*, Vietnam's national soup. In Adams-Morgan, Africa and Central America collide, with a good half-dozen Ethiopian restaurants that feature a soft pancakelike bread (*injera*) and richly spiced stews (*wats* and *alechas*), and another half-dozen Salvadoran restaurants that serve typical Latino fare and turnoverlike *pupusas*. Adams-Morgan also harbors a good selection of other Latin cuisines, including Mexican, Caribbean, and Spanish.

Washington's Chinatown, at 7th and H Sts NW, has profited from an infusion of restaurants that range from elegant to hole-in-the-wall, and groceries that carry ingredients for a variety of Asian cuisines. Since 1980, Thai restaurants have sprung up practically everywhere, be they expense-account restaurants on K St or minuscule mom-and-pop operations tucked into neighborhood shopping centers from Silver Spring to Annandale. Of course, there are German, Northern and Southern Italian, and Tex-Mex restaurants galore, stalwart French bistros, Argentine BBQ, and Korean *bulgogi* sandwich shops. If you don't find your fancy, don't worry—it will be here soon.

70 New Orleans Cafe ★★$$ Narrow, noisy, with the kitchen right in the center of the place. Order a spicy Creole omelet (served with home fries, homemade biscuits, and jam), crawfish balls, jambalaya, or *pain perdu* (French toast made with French bread). The house coffee is a strong chicory-laced milky brew. ♦ Cajun/Creole ♦ M-Th, Su 8:30AM-10PM; F-Sa 8:30AM-11PM. 1790 Columbia Rd NW (18th-Euclid Sts) Metro stop: Woodley Park/Zoo. 234.5111

70 Red Sea ★★$ The first of Adams-Morgan's many Ethiopian restaurants, featuring spicy meat-and-vegetable stews scooped up with spongy fermented bread called *injera*. Live music nightly. ♦ Ethiopian ♦ M-Th, Su 11:30AM-midnight; F-Sa 11:30AM-1AM. 2463 18th St NW (Columbia Rd) Metro stop: Woodley Park/Zoo. 483.5000

70 Le Cafe Riche ★$$ A weird and fun café where you're as likely to see patrons dancing on the tables as sampling the eccentric owner's culinary concoctions. ♦ French/African ♦ Daily 6PM-2AM. 2455 18th St NW (Belmont-Columbia Rds) Reservations recommended. Metro stop: Woodley Park/Zoo. 328.8118

71 Millie & Al's ★$ *The* neighborhood bar for casual conversation, a golden oldie jukebox, and good pizzas. ♦ Pizza ♦ M-Th 4PM-2AM;

Adams-Morgan/Dupont Circle

F-Sa noon-3AM; Su noon-2AM. 2440 18th St NW (Belmont-Columbia Rds) Metro stop: Woodley Park/Zoo. No credit cards. 387.8131

71 Meskerem ★★$ Sit at a woven-straw table and dine on specialties like *kitfo* (a spicy version of steak tartare) and shrimp *wat* (shrimp combined with a host of fiery spices). ♦ Ethiopian ♦ M-Th 5PM-midnight; F-Su noon-midnight. 2434 18th St NW (Belmont-Columbia Rds) Reservations required F-Su. Metro stop: Woodley Park/Zoo. 462.4100

72 La Fourchette ★★$$ A French bistro replete with floor-to-ceiling murals of French café scenes. Daily specials include bouillabaisse and other rich soups, duck, rabbit, and lobster with cream and peppercorns. ♦ French ♦ M-Th 11:30AM-10:30PM; F 11:30AM-11:30PM; Sa 4-10:30PM; Su 4-10PM. 2429 18th St NW (Belmont-Columbia Rds) Metro stop: Woodley Park/Zoo. 332.3077

73 Cities ★★$$$ An open-air sidewalk bar, a restaurant that changes cuisine and decor (Rio, Bangkok, Leningrad) every 5 months, and an upstairs disco. ♦ International ♦ M-Th 6-11:30PM; F-Sa 6PM-midnight. 2424 18th St NW (Belmont-Columbia Rds) Reservations recommended. Metro stop: Woodley Park/Zoo. 328.7194

73 Fish, Wings & Tings ★★$ Spicy rum-dashed jerk chicken and other Jamaican treats in a tropical-bright café. Carry-out if it's too crowded. ♦ Jamaican ♦ M-Th noon-10PM; F-Sa noon-11PM. 2418 18th St NW (Belmont-Columbia Rds) Metro stop: Woodley Park/Zoo. 234.0322

73 Idle Time Books Three floors of used books in a browser's paradise. ◆ Daily 11AM-9PM. 2410 18th St NW (Belmont-Columbia Rds) Metro stop: Woodley Park/Zoo. 232.4774

73 Belmont Kitchen ★★$$ It's worth suffering the trendiness for the upside-down Chicago-style pizzas and home-style desserts. A *Washington Heart Menu* that features low cholesterol meals is also available. ◆ Italian ◆ M-Th, Su 11:30AM-10PM; F-Sa 11:30AM-11PM. 2400 18th St NW (Belmont Rd) Reservations recommended. Metro stop: Woodley Park/Zoo. 667.1200

74 Homeworks Ltd. Furniture and furnishings from Art Deco to early *Honeymooners*. ◆ W-Sa 11AM-6PM; Su noon-6PM or by appointment. 2405 18th St NW (Kalorama-Columbia Rds) Metro stop: Woodley Park/Zoo. 483.1897

75 Sun Gallery Goldsmiths Jamal Mims draws on his African experience to design exquisite modern gold and silver jewelry, some with amber and precious stones. ◆ Tu-Sa 11AM-7PM. 2322 18th St NW (Belmont Rd) Metro stop: Woodley Park/Zoo. 265.9341

76 Bradshaw's ★★$$ Bradshaw's upper floors offer relatively formal dining on a variety of fresh fish, meats, and salads. Downstairs, the

Adams-Morgan/Dupont Circle

scene is entirely different. Deejays spin vintage '60s rock 'n' roll, and customers are free to hang out at the bar. Just one sour note: because of Bradshaw's proximity to area clubs, DC zoning laws prohibit dancing in the restaurant. ◆ American ◆ M-Th, Su 6PM-midnight; F-Sa 6PM-1AM. 2319 18th St (Kalorama-Belmont Rds) Dinner reservations recommended. Metro stop: Woodley Park/Zoo. 462.8330

76 Adams-Morgan Spaghetti Garden ★$ A family place serving cheap and hearty Italian fare. Outdoor rooftop dining in seasonable weather. ◆ Italian ◆ M-Th noon-midnight; F-Sa noon-1AM; Su noon-11PM. 2317 18th St NW (Kalorama-Columbia Rds) Metro stop: Woodley Park/Zoo. 265.6665

77 Kalorama Cafe ★$ Hearty vegetarian fare, with particularly good brunch food and occasional live music. ◆ American ◆ Tu-Sa 11:30AM-10PM; Su 11:30AM-3PM. 2228 18th St NW (Kalorama Rd-Wyoming Ave) Metro stop: Woodley Park/Zoo. 667.1022

78 Kilimanjaro A sophisticated, integrated nightclub with 2 big dance floors featuring top African and reggae bands; deejay dancing, too. ◆ Cover Th-Su. M-Th, Su 5PM-2AM; F-Sa 5PM-4AM. 1724 California St NW (18th St-Florida Ave) Metro stop: Dupont Circle. 328.3838

The Capital Beltway was first proposed by the National Capital Parks and Planning Commission in 1928. Congress did not approve the proposal until 1955, and construction was not completed until 1964, at a cost of nearly $190 million.

79 Le Tam Tam ★★$$ The meaty peanut-laden cuisine of West Africa served in a charming neighborhood restaurant/discothèque. Well-prepared French dishes are also available. For those who stay after the kitchen closes, international music is performed Friday and Saturday nights from 11PM to 2AM. ◆ West African ◆ M-F 11:30AM-2:30PM, 5-11PM; Sa-Su 5-11PM. 1910 18th St NW (T St-Florida Ave) Reservations recommended F-Su. Metro stop: Dupont Circle. 483.0505

80 Lauriol Plaza ★★$$ Wonderful Spanish and Latin American food in an airy, if sometimes noisy, modern café. During warmer months, eat outside on the terrace. ◆ Spanish/Latin American ◆ M-F noon-midnight; Sa-Su 11AM-midnight. 1801 18th St NW (S-Swann Sts) Reservations recommended. Metro stop: Dupont Circle. 387.0035

81 Belmont House (Eastern Star Temple) (1908, Sanson, Trumbauer) Architect **Ernest Sanson** was imported from France specifically for this project (American **Horace Trumbauer** was the project manager), and the resultant building exhudes Gallic romanticism. The shape was mandated by the wedge-shaped lot. The opulent interiors, complete with **Louis Tiffany** glass, brought the total construction cost to $1.5 million. Much of the original owner's art collection remains in the house, although it was sold (actually given—the price a paltry $100,000) to the Order of the Eastern Star in 1937. ◆ 1618 New Hampshire Ave NW (R-18th Sts) Metro stop: Dupont Circle

82 American Playwrights Theatre is a quaint and intimate theater dedicated to the production of new American plays and other contemporary works. ◆ Seats 125. Shows: Tu-Sa 8PM; Su 3, 7PM. Box office: Tu-Sa noon-8PM; Su 1-7PM. 1742 Church St NW (17th-18th Sts) Metro stop: Dupont Circle. 232.1122

83 First Baptist Church (1955, Harold E. Wagoner) The massing of this neo-Gothic church, reminiscent of **Frank Lloyd Wright's** work leads the eye upward to a steeple that isn't there. ◆ Daily 9AM-5PM. Services: Su 11AM. 1328 16th St NW (Entrance on O St) Metro stop: Dupont Circle. 387.2206

84 Foundry United Methodist Church (1904, Appleton P. Clark) Rusticated gray granite is formed into the fan vaults characteristic of High Gothic Revival; the low dome contributes to this building's renowned acoustical qualities. Its name honors Georgetown foundry owner **Henry Foxhall**, who founded the church. ◆ Services Su 9:30, 11AM. 1500 16th St NW (O-P Sts) Metro stop: Dupont Circle. 332.4010

Want to make your opinion known to the president? Call the White House directly at 202/456-7639, weekdays from 9AM to 5PM. Comments are noted, summarized, and presented to the president each day.

85 Skewers ★★$$ An exotic decor (Middle Eastern fabric hangs from the ceiling; the walls are painted in peacock blue, mint green, and red) and great kabobs at reasonable prices, all served with saffron rice or homemade pasta and a skewer of fresh vegetables crowned with almonds and raisins. Live jazz Monday through Saturday. ◆ Middle Eastern ◆ M-Th 8AM-11PM; F 8AM-1AM; Sa 11AM-1AM; Su 5-11PM. 1633 P St NW (16th-17th Sts) Reservations recommended. Metro stop: Dupont Circle. 387.7400

86 Trio Restaurant ★$ Long before 17th Street became *restaurant row*, the Trio was dishing up meat loaf, waffles, and other hearty diner stuff—a neighborhood institution. There's an outdoor terrace for warm weather dining; also a bar and carry-out pizza. ◆ American ◆ Daily 7:30AM-11:30PM. 1537 17th St NW (Q St) Metro stop: Dupont Circle. 232.6305

87 El Bodegon ★★$$ Flamenco dancers, flowing sangría, a garrulous staff, and crowded, festive dining rooms make this a particularly lively place. Good thick soups, excellent seafood paella, chicken with sausage, ham, and sliced potatoes in brown sauce, and an abundance of beef dishes. Flamenco dancing nightly. ◆ Spanish ◆ M-F 11:30AM-2:30PM, 5:30-11:30PM; Sa 5:30-11:30PM. 1637 R St NW (16th-17th Sts) Reservations recommended. Metro stop: Dupont Circle. 667.1710

88 Julio's Rooftop Pizza ★$ Respectable pizza, irresistible all-you-can-eat weekend brunches, and a nice view from the roof deck add up to a neighborhood winner. ◆ Italian ◆ M-Th, Su 10AM-midnight; F-Sa 10AM-1AM. 1604 U St NW (16th-17th Sts) Metro stop: Dupont Circle. 483.8500

88 Stetson's ★$ Enchiladas and their like, and as close as you'll get here to a real live Texas bar. A favored local hangout. ◆ Tex-Mex ◆ M-Th, Su 11:30AM-2AM; F 11:30AM-3AM; Sa 4PM-3AM. 1610 U St NW (16th-17th Sts) Metro stop: Dupont Circle. 667.6295

89 White-Meyer House (1912, John Russell Pope) The Georgian-style mansion built for **Ambassador Henry White**, an American diplomat, was annexed by Meridian House International in 1987. Together they form a block-long international campus. ◆ 1624 Crescent Pl NW (16th-17th Sts) Metro stop: Woodley Park/Zoo

89 Meridian House International (1915, John Russell Pope) A limestone-faced Louis XVI townhouse built for **Irwin Boyle Laughlin**, a former ambassador to Spain and member of the Pittsburgh steel family. The entrance hall, loggia, and dining room are particularly impressive. Since 1961, the mansion has been home to Meridian House International, a nonprofit foundation dedicated to bringing the international community together through exhibitions, concerts, and cultural events, as well as through tours and seminars for thousands of foreign visitors to the US each year. ◆ Free. M-F 1-4PM. 1630 Crescent Pl NW (16th-17th Sts) Metro stop: Woodley Park/Zoo. 667.6800

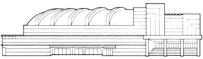

90 Citadel Motion Picture and Video Center (1947, Frank Grad & Sons; renovations, 1989, Doug Robinson/Robinson & Willis) The recent conversion of this 3-story, 121,000-square-foot building into one of the East Coast's largest sound studios is the latest in a string of remarkable reincarnations. Designed as an Art Deco-style combination roller rink and bowling alley—and built with excess profit taxes from WWII—the building has also functioned as self-storage locker space, a parking garage, and DC's first self-service gas station. In addition to a vast sound stage, there are video sets, screening rooms, a carpentry shop, administrative offices, and a public restaurant (the reborn **D.C. Diner**). **Francis Ford Coppola** shot *Gardens of Stone* here in 1986, before renovations were underway. Tours are available upon request. ◆ 1649 Kalorama Rd (16th-17th Sts) 667.0344

91 Inter-American Defense Board (1906, George Oakley Totten, Jr.) Also known as the *Pink Palace*. A Gothic version of the Ducal Palace in Venice (note the windows), but the

massing is somewhat awkward. ◆ 2600 16th St NW (Euclid-Fuller Sts) Metro stop: Woodley Park/Zoo

92 Gala Hispanic Theater Professional theater, producing contemporary Latin American works in both Spanish and English in a Mount Pleasant school. ◆ Seats 100. Shows: Tu-Sa 8PM; Su 7PM. 1625 Park Rd NW (16th-17th Sts) 234.7174

93 Fio's ★$$ Admittedly an acquired taste, this Italian café in the basement of the massive **Woodner Apartments** is a blast out of the 1950s, with its leatherette booths, menu leaning heavily to red sauce and fried calamari, bargain prices, and familial service. ◆ Italian ◆ Tu-Su 5-10PM. 3636 16th St NW (Spring Pl-Oak St) 667.3040

94 Carter Barron Amphitheatre Operated by the **National Park Service**, this open-air amphitheater features a 7-week summer festival of pop, rock, and jazz. Open June through August. ◆ Seats 4250. 16th St and Colorado Ave NW. 829-3202 (June-Aug), 426.6837 (year-round)

517 Sixth Street Southeast: The Best Little Rowhouse in Washington—or is it Miami? Behind this innocuous facade, erstwhile model **Donna Rice** joined former Colorado senator **Gary Hart** for the 1987 weekend tryst that torpedoed the then-front runner's presidential hopes. Still a private residence.

"This generation of Americans has a rendevous with Destiny."
Franklin D. Roosevelt

Georgetown
Upper NW

Brandywine

92-100

91

Albemarle

Tenleytown

M

Yuma

Van Ness

46th

44th

Nebraska Ave

89

Dalecarlia Pkwy

Tilden

Massachusetts Ave

49th

Rodman

Quebec

88

Rockwood Pkwy

85

MacArthur Blvd

Macomb

Loughboro Rd

Lowell

84

Sherrier Pl

Klingle

86

Cathedral Ave

Potomac Ave

Cathedral Pl

Arizona Ave

44th

Galena Pl

Garfield

87

49th

83

Calve

Foxhall Rd

Bento

W

W

Reservoir Rd 55

Canal Rd

MacArthur Blvd

**Northern
Virginia**

George Washington Memorial Parkway

118

Connecticut Ave

102

103

Van Ness-106
UDC
M 107

104

105

Tilden

82

Wisconsin Ave

81

80

101

109

108

Cleveland
Park

110
M 111
112
113

Klingle Rd

79
78

Macomb

Woodley

77

76

75

Garfield

Cleveland Ave

Edmunds

72

71

73

70

74

Massachusetts Ave

115   114

116   M   Woodley
Park Zoo

Calvert   118   117

119

Rock Creek and Potomac Pkwy

Connecticut Ave

Adams-Morgan/Dupont Circle

69

68

67   R

66   65

58   64

56   63

59   62

53   50

54   52   51   60   61

49

35th

M

1-48
see page 121   30th

Reservoir Rd 57

Wisconsin Ave

Francis Scott
Key Bridge

West End/Foggy Bottom

New Hampshire Ave

M   Dupont
Circle

Farragut
North

Pennsylvania Ave   M

119

The little Maryland tobacco port of **Georgetown** thought its fortune made when it was included in the land set aside for a Federal District. Business was expected to come flooding in, real-estate values to soar. What happened was quite different. Not only did Georgetowners fail to grow rich, they discovered that they had lost the right to vote for the president who was to live among them and that they no longer had a congressman. A century later, in the 1890s, they were to lose their city as well, as Washington swallowed Georgetown whole. Perhaps it was spite, or perhaps the assertion of a strong spirit of independence, but during the Civil War, when DC was the capital of the Union, Georgetown was a hotbed of secessionism.

By the early 20th century, much of Georgetown, like much of the rest of DC, had become poor and run-down. Still, it managed to nurture the talents of young **Duke Ellington**, who grew up here. The neighborhood's appeal to the well-to-do began with a massive population growth during the '40s and its discovery by members of the New Deal.

Despite changing demographics, the neighborhood has never lost its sense of separate identity. The area is officially known as **West Washington**, but everyone thinks of it still as Georgetown, and its people continue to refer to themselves as Georgetowners; some even give their address as *Georgetown DC*.

And they have kept their distance in other ways as well. They wanted nothing to do with the subway, so it doesn't stop here. They wanted nothing to do with the city's lottery, so no tickets are sold here.

Georgetown/Upper Northwest

Georgetown's independence has finally paid off—but it may be a mixed blessing. The area is home to numerous chic restaurants and boutiques and has become the shopping heart of the city to such a degree that shopping malls, such as the elegant **Georgetown Park**, are squeezed between the existing 18th- and 19th-century buildings. Of course, real-estate values finally did soar. The tiny homes originally built by Irish *navvies* (laborers on the **Chesapeake & Ohio Canal**) who wanted to be near the Jesuit fathers' **Georgetown University** now sell for $300,000 and up. Georgetown's homes, of course, were not all built by navvies. **Tudor Place**, a private home, has been in the same family for 2 centuries and has hosted such notables as **Martha Washington**, the **Marquis de Lafayette**, and **Robert E. Lee**. **Dumbarton Oaks** is now open to the public, as are its famous gardens. The **Kennedy** house, where JFK lived when he was a senator, is still a private home, but many people seek it out.

The tree-lined C&O Canal, one of the city's favorite spots for bicycling and canoeing (vehicles for both may be rented at **Fletcher's Boat House**, 3 miles upriver) or just strolling, is a failed 19th-century effort to bring island commerce to the city's ports. (Baltimore started its railroad in 1828, the same year Washington started its canal; a textbook case of the wrong technology at the wrong time.) Locals thank **Justice William O. Douglas** for the C&O's survival: in the blacktop-happy '50s, it was almost turned into a 4-lane highway.

Georgetown is also the pedestrian heart of the city. Not only are its narrow old sidewalks crowded at most hours of the day, but when Washingtonians gather together, whether to celebrate a **Redskins** triumph or to participate in the local rites of Halloween, it is to the brick sidewalks of Georgetown that they take. Washington may have swallowed Georgetown administratively, but in daily life it sometimes seems to be the other way around.

Upper Northwest, the area of Washington west of **Rock Creek Park**, remains the city's wealthiest section and one of the wealthiest residential areas in the nation. During **President Grover Cleveland**'s term, **Cleveland Park** and **Woodley Park** were summer retreats from the sweltering lowlands Downtown. Today, the elaborate Victorian houses along **Newark Street** and **Highland Place** are coveted homes for senators, lawyers, and lobbyists.

On the city's highest point, **Mount Saint Alban**, looms the **Cathedral Church of St. Peter and St. Paul** (known as the **Washington Cathedral**), whose soaring Gothic stone walls were started in 1910 and are just being completed today. To the south lies the **Naval Observatory**, a working astronomical station whose usefulness has been lessened by the encroaching lights of the city. The large house on the observatory grounds has served as the vice president's house since the **Gerald Ford** administration.

Rock Creek Park offers a habitat for birds and wild animals, and a soothing retreat and playground for its human visitors. The **National Zoo**, most famous for its two rare pandas, the only ones in the United States, also harbors a large collection of other exotic species. With such distinctive attractions to its credit, Georgetown certainly deserves recognition as a city all its own.

The Four Seasons Hotel $$$$ Luxuriously appointed, elegant and relaxed, this is a favorite resort of Hollywood stars, musicians, and other nonpolitical celebrities. Many of the 197 rooms overlook the historic C&O Canal or Rock Creek Park. Amenities include a multilingual staff, accomodations for the handicapped, 24-hour room service, complimentary weekday limo service, audiovisual communications facilities, health club access, and valet parking. The **Garden Terrace** bar, with soft flowered sofas, a piano, and a profusion of greenery overlooking Rock Creek, is one of the city's best cocktail-hour rendezvous spots; high tea is served here every afternoon, and light food all day. Children under 12 stay free. ◆ Deluxe ◆ 2800 Pennsylvania Ave NW (Rock Creek Park-29th St) 342.0444, 800/268.6282; fax 944.2076 ♿

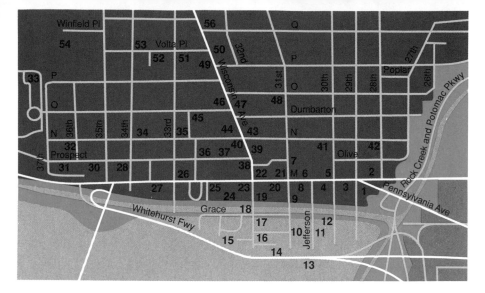

Within the Four Seasons:

Aux Beaux Champs ★★$$$$ This ultra-posh dining room features nouvelle cooking, including foie gras, caviar, lobster, and wild game, as well as lighter spa specialties. ◆ French ◆ M-F 7-11AM, noon-2:30PM, 6:30-10:30PM; Sa-Su 8AM-2:30PM, 6:30-10:30PM. Jacket and tie requested. Reservations required. 342.0810

1 Lorenzo Five floors of men's clothing direct from Italy. **Missoni**, **Ermegildo Zegna**, and **Luciano Soprani**, among others, at prices that look as if they were quoted in lire. ◆ M-Sa 10:30AM-7:30PM; Su 1-5PM. 2812 Pennsylvania Ave NW (28th-29th Sts) 965.6149

1 Bone Jour Cafe-Boutique Owner **Becky Pugh** makes certain the well-bred pooch can get every itch scratched—the letters from **Nancy Reagan** and **Barbara Bush** on behalf of their canines are proof. Specialties include personalized pet dishes and doggie tuxedos. ◆ M-Sa 10AM-6PM; grooming Tu-Sa 8:30AM-6PM. 2818 Pennsylvania Ave NW (28th-29th Sts) 333.8349

1 Basile Elegant tailored women's clothing by the Italian designer Basile, including suits, dresses, and sportswear. ◆ M-Sa 10:30AM-7:30PM. 2822 Pennsylvania Ave NW (28th-29th Sts) 337.0622

2 The Craft Shop Toys, gifts, and decorative objects from around the world, some of them produced by **Save the Children Federation** projects designed to encourage native craftspeople. ◆ M-F 11AM-7PM; Sa 11AM-6PM. 2803 M St NW (28th-29th Sts) 342.8096

2 Enriqueta's ★★$ Although Tex-Mex staples like enchiladas are delicious, Enriqueta's claim to fame is as Washington's original Mexican restaurant, featuring the varied cuisine of the country's provinces, from pork in fruit sauce to chicken mole, and prepared well enough to make you swear off tacos forever. ◆ Mexican ◆ M-Th 11:30AM-10PM; F 11:30AM-11PM;

Sa 5-11PM; Su 5-10PM. 2811 M St NW (28th-29th Sts) Reservations recommended. 338.7772

2 Biograph Theatre The Biograph remains true to repertory and revival, scheduling extensive retrospectives of foreign and domestic films, animation festivals, and showcases of local filmmakers. The snack bar, with **Cadbury** chocolate bars and theme snacks (tea and

Georgetown/Upper Northwest

pastries for the Australian films, say), more than compensates for the uncomfortable seats. ◆ 2819 M St NW (28th-29th Sts) 333.2696

3 Janis Aldridge Inc. Seventeenth- through 19th-century architectural and botanical prints (including **Beslers** and **Piranesis**) set off by exquisite French mats glow softly on the walls of this little shop. Decoupage screens and other decorations worthy of a Georgetown manse are available as well. ◆ Tu-Sa 10AM-6PM. 2900 M St NW (29th-30th Sts) 338.7710

3 The American Hand showcases works by contemporary American ceramists, silver-smiths, and jewelers, as well as elegant housewares from the **Museum of Modern Art** collection. Wedding Gift Central. ◆ M-Sa 11AM-6PM; Su 1-5PM. 2906 M St NW (29th-30th Sts) 965.3273

4 Georgetown Marbury Hotel $$$ This 164-room hotel offers guests a dozen floor plans, including a spacious duplex suite and rooms surrounding an outdoor pool. Amenities include accommodations for the handicapped, and VCRs. The hotel is conveniently located in the heart of Georgetown. Children under 16 stay free. ◆ 3000 M St NW (30th-Jefferson Sts) 726.5000, 800/368.5922; fax 337.4250

The 1989 presidential inauguration week was insured for over $30,000,000. The premium cost American Bicentennial Presidential Inaugural Inc. approximately $400,000.

5 Garrett's ★$ When you're tired of overpriced, overcute nightspots, it's time for Garrett's. The downstairs bar is a neighborhood pub, and the upstairs terrace restaurant serves basic saloon fare and diner food: burgers, nachos, meat loaf, and a prime-ribs special. ♦ American ♦ Daily 11:30AM-11:30PM. 3003 M St NW (30th-31st Sts) 333.1033

6 Loughboro-Patterson House (1806; restoration, 1964, Macomber & Peter) An authentic Federal-period restoration made more interesting by a single delicate dormer in the roofline. ♦ 3039-3041 M St NW (30th-31st Sts)

Within the Loughboro-Patterson House:

Junior League Shop of Washington is the place to experience Georgetown anthropology via Buffy and Bitsy's castoffs—monogrammed **Mark Cross** handbags, furs, worn-once designer wear—as well as good-quality secondhand clothing from not-so-famous Washingtonians. ♦ M-W, F 9:30AM-3PM; Th 9:30AM-3PM, 6:30-9PM; Sa 10AM-3:45PM; Su noon-5PM. 337.6120

6 Old Stone House (1765, Christopher Layman; kitchen, 2nd-floor dining room, and 3rd-floor bedroom, 1767, Cassandra Chew) This little cottage is believed to be the only surviving pre-Revolutionary building in DC. Layman was a Pennsylvania cabinetmaker. The building has served many owners as both home and place of business. The house is furnished in 18th-century style; its old-fashioned gardens

with fruit trees and masses of blooms are a welcome respite from the bustle of M Street. A **National Park Service historic site**. ♦ Free. House W-Su 9:30AM-5PM. Gardens W-Su 9AM-5PM. 3051 M St NW (30th-31st Sts) 426.6851

6 Fendrick Gallery Barbara Fendrick has earned a solid reputation for showing good up-and-coming artists as well as solid successes, including **Albert Paley**'s romantic modern ironwork and **Wendell Castle**'s furniture. The **Young Collector**'s gallery features relatively inexpensive works. ♦ M-F 10AM-6PM, Jan-June, Sep-Dec; Tu-Sa 10AM-6PM, July-Aug. 3059 M St NW (30th-31st Sts) 338.4544

7 Washington Post Office, Georgetown Branch (1857, Ammi Young) A timelessly simple composition of heavy plain stone walls; acclaimed as one of the best Italianate Federal buildings ever built. ♦ 1221 31st St NW (M-N Sts)

7 Booked Up This antiquarian bookstore, owned by **Larry McMurtry**, author of *Lonesome Dove* and *The Last Picture Show*, features a broad collection ranging from first editions of *The Maltese Falcon* to 15th-century incunabulae. Secluded corners invite curling up on rainy afternoons. ♦ M-F 11AM-3PM; Sa 10AM-12:30PM. 1209 31st St NW (M-N Sts) 965.3244

8 Dar es Salam ★★$$ The rooms are tiled and painted like a Moroccan fantasy, the belly-dancers twirl like Scheherazade, and the food is celebratory, authentic, and delicious. Multi-course Moroccan dinners, eaten by hand, include salads, sweet chicken and phyllo dough, couscous, and spit-roasted lamb. ♦ Moroccan ♦ M-Tu 5-11PM; W-Sa 5PM-3AM; Su 5-10PM. 3056 M St NW (30th-31st Sts) Reservations required. 342.1925

9 Paper Moon ★$$ The neon-lit Manhattan-style decor is fun when you're in the mood for noise from the young European bar crowd and want to be seen in the wide-open dining room. Good pastas served in enormous bowls, pizzas, and salads. ♦ Italian ♦ M-W, Su 5:30-11:30PM; Th-Sa 5:30PM-2AM. 1069 31st St NW (K-M Sts) Reservations recommended. 965.6666

9 Tout Va Bien ★★$$ A small, posh café serving reasonably priced nouvelle fare: duck with raspberry sauce, chicken galantine, baby salmon, fruit tarts made to order. ♦ French ♦ M-Th 11:30AM-2:30PM, 5:30-11PM; F 11:30AM-2:30PM, 5:30-11:30PM; Sa-Su 11:30AM-3PM, 5:30-11:30PM. 1063 31st St NW (K-M Sts) Reservations recommended. 965.1212

10 La Ruche ★★$$ This serene café is renowned for its fresh-fruit tarts, chocolate mousse, and luscious cakes. But don't forget the huge salads, rich slices of zucchini pie and quiche, and low-priced daily specials like mussels, chicken breast with apples, and trout amandine. Outdoor dining in warm weather. ♦ French ♦ M-F 11:30AM-midnight; Sa-Su 10AM-1AM. 1039 31st St NW (K-M Sts) 965.2684. Also at: White Flint Mall, Bethesda MD. 468.1155

10 Yes! Bookshop The nation's largest New Age book- and networking store stocks subjects from holistic medicine, nutrition, and mysticism to healing and East-West philosophy. The recordings section is great for peculiar but choice items: Eastern meditative music, natural sounds from the African jungle, medieval hymns, or Celtic tunes. See page 139 for **Yes! The Natural Gourmet**. ♦ American ♦ M-Sa 10AM-10PM; Su noon-6PM. 1035 31st St NW (K-M Sts) 338.6969

Restaurants: Red	**Hotels**: Blue
Shops/Parks: Green	**Sights/Culture**: Black

11 Chelsea's DC's large Latino community has long trooped to Chelsea's to shake to the latest salsa from live bands. The club also offers Friday performances of *Side by Side by Sondheim*, a musical revue, and Saturday performances of the satirical cabaret revue *Capitol Steps* by a bunch of congressional aides who get their revenge on stage. ♦ Cover Tu-Sa. *Side by Side* F 8PM. *Capitol Steps* Sa 8PM. Swing music Tu 7:30-10PM. Latin bands: Tu 10:30PM-2AM; F-Sa 10:30PM-5AM. Live Persian music W, Su 10PM-2AM. Box office: Tu-Sa 10AM-10PM; Su 1-10PM. 1055 Thomas Jefferson St NW (K-M Sts) 298.8222

12 Chesapeake & Ohio Canal is one of the last and best preserved of the great system of canals that helped move goods westward in the late 18th and early 19th centuries. An engineering marvel, the canal employs 74 locks and the 3100-foot **Paw Taw Tunnel** carved through the stone mountains of western Maryland. The C&O extends 184^1/$_2$ miles, from Georgetown to Cumberland MD, where the Allegheny Mountains interrupted its intended meeting with the Ohio River. **George Washington** had envisioned such a canal and invested $10,000 in the Potowmack Canal Company—those stocks were eventually left to endow **George Washington University**—and supervised much of the work on this early canal, precursor of the C&O. **John Quincy Adams** broke ground for the larger canal on 4 July 1828, and for several decades mule-drawn canal clippers carried lumber, coal, whiskey, and grain from the West at about 4 miles per hour. By the end of the 19th century, the **Baltimore & Ohio Railroad** had stolen most of the canal's customers; by 1924, the C&O was obsolete.

The best preserved portion of the C&O is a 22-mile stretch from Georgetown to Seneca MD, but you can hike or bike the old **Towpath** for the entire length of the canal. The **National Park Service** sponsors some guided hikes and maintains campsites. The timberland that nestles along the waterway and its rich wildlife make the spot perfect for such activities, as well as for rock climbing (by permit) on its rugged overhangs, canoeing, boating, and in winter, ice-skating. There are even some old gold mines, battle sites, and cabins along the route.

Catch the mule-drawn *Georgetown* at the dock, 30th and M Sts in Georgetown (there's a charge for the ride; call 472.4376 or 653.5844 for information), or the *Canal Clipper* at the famous old **Great Falls Tavern** in Potomac MD (299.2026, 299.3613).

Canoes and boats can be rented at **Fletcher's Boat House**, 4940 Canal Rd NW, just 3 miles north of Georgetown; **Jack's Boats** at 3500 K St NW; or **Swain's Lock**, on River Rd just north of Potomac MD. ♦ *Georgetown* departures: W-F 1, 3PM; Sa 10:30AM, 1, 3, 5PM; Su 10:30AM, 1, 3PM, mid Apr-mid Oct. *Canal Clipper* departures: Sa 10:30AM, 1, 3PM; Su 10:30AM, 1, 3, 5PM, mid Apr-mid Oct. C&O District Headquarters 301/739.4200, Fletcher's Boat House 244.0461, Jack's Boats 337.9642

13 Washington Harbour (1986, Arthur Cotton Moore) The cement factory that long occupied this riverfront site was an eyesore, but it never pretended to be otherwise. The Fine Arts Commission recommended a park to replace it but settled for this bombastic mixed-use development, which seems to have strayed in from a low-budget epic on the Decline and Fall of the Roman Empire. One trembles to think what a future Gibbon will write of the American Empire while contemplating the ruins of this and its neighbors, the Watergate and the Kennedy Center. Its one redeeming feature is the riverside promenade, a popular spot in fine weather. ♦ 3000 K St NW (31st St) 342.7366

At Washington Harbour:

Hisago ★★★$$$$ Handsome decor, meticulous service, and authentic Japanese cuisine make Hisago worth consideration, but its Tokyo-style prices make it a sometimes thing for all but Japanese businesspeople on expense accounts. ♦ Japanese ♦ M-F noon-11PM; Sa-Su 6-11PM. Reservations required. 944.4181

Jaimalito's ★★$$ This genial restaurant features Southwestern cooking with a Santa Fe touch—enchiladas with blue corn tortillas—and a desert-toned bar with on-tap frozen margaritas. ♦ Southwestern ♦ M-Th, Su 11:30AM-10:30PM; F-Sa 11:30AM-11:30PM. 944.4400

Georgetown/Upper Northwest

Artie's Deli & Cafe ★★$ Enormous deli sandwiches on miniloaves of homemade bread and well-seasoned salads, to either carry out for a riverside picnic or eat in the little café area. ♦ Deli ♦ M-F 10:30AM-7PM; Sa-Su 11AM-6PM. 944.4350

Tony and Joe's Seafood Place ★$$ Fish is it, but that's okay when it's as fresh and simple as Tony and Joe's and served in this casual and comfortable dining room. ♦ Seafood ♦ M-Th 11AM-11PM, F-Sa 11AM-midnight; Su 11AM-10PM. 944.4545

14 The Bayou attracts a young-to-not-so-young crowd (you must be 20 to gain admission) with nationally known performers from the jazz, fusion, and blues arenas. The casual split-level nightclub seats 500 and is concert-oriented; drinks, sandwiches and pizza are served. During intermissions, a large screen features Top-40 videos. Deejays spin post-show dance tunes until closing time. Tickets are available at the box office or at Ticketron outlets. Some shows are free. ♦ M-Th, Su 8PM-2AM; F-Sa 8PM-3AM. 3135 K St NW (31st St-Wisconsin Ave) 333.2897

"I am goddamned tired of listening to all the babble for reform....America is a hell of a success....The country don't need any legislation."

Joseph Gurney Cannon
Speaker of the House, 1903–11

15 The River Club ★★$$$$
Outfitted like an Art Deco ocean liner, this classy supper club features East-meets-West cuisine: Chinese smoked lobster and sesame-seeded salmon with papaya Thai basil sauce are just 2 possibilities. For those who like to dance while they dine, there is swing music nightly from 9 to 11PM, then the kitchen closes and things get more modern with '50s and '60s rock 'n' roll. ◆ American-Far Eastern ◆ M-Th 6-11PM; F-Sa 6PM-midnight. 3223 K St NW (Cecil Pl-Wisconsin Ave) Reservations recommended. 333.8118

16 Classic Clothing Although its prices are higher than other vintage shops, Classic goes out of its way to supply a wide selection of *retroduds*, from beaded evening dresses and men's suits and overcoats to authentic Hawaiian shirts. ◆ M-Sa 10AM-7PM; Su noon-6PM. 1015 Wisconsin Ave NW (K-M Sts) 965.2120. Also at: 3146 M St NW. 965.0505

17 Grace Episcopal Church (1866) Early Gothic Revival stone church established as a mission to the boatmen on the Chesapeake & Ohio Canal. ◆ 1041 Wisconsin Ave NW (M-South Sts)

18 Conran's British designer **Terence Conran** knew what he was doing when he created this

Georgetown/Upper Northwest

virtual department store of clean-lined reasonably priced furniture, kitchenware, and furnishings designed for first-time apartment dwellers and for those who still shop like they are. ◆ M-F 10AM-9PM; Sa 10AM-7PM; Su noon-6PM. 3227 Grace St NW (Wisconsin Ave-Potomac St, or enter through Georgetown Park) 298.8300. Also at: 10400 Old Georgetown Rd, Bethesda MD. 564.9590

19 Filomena's ★$$ A huge and noisy basement space with trendy types gobbling up okay pasta and veal, seafood, and chicken dishes. ◆ Italian ◆ M-F 11:30AM-3PM, 5-11:30PM; Sa-Su 5-11:30PM. 1063 Wisconsin Ave NW (K-M Sts) Reservations required. 338.8800

19 The Pleasure Chest Ltd. Racy lingerie, blue movies, and naughty adults-only toys for respectable folk who don't care to venture into one of the dwindling number of "dirty" bookstores Downtown. ◆ M-Tu 10AM-10PM; W-Sa 10AM-midnight; Su noon-7PM. 1063 Wisconsin Ave NW (K-M Sts) 333.8570

The **National Zoo** receives 3 million visitors a year.

The new red-brick commercial blocks (Foundry, Georgetown Park, etc.) that have restored commercial life to the Georgetown waterfront are strictly whitebread; ironically, one relic of a bolder era—the **Incinerator Building** on 31st St, foursquare with a soaring chimney—stands desolate.

19 Houston's ★$ There's a line outside the door for a reason. Houston's menu of burgers, ribs, salads, and grilled chicken with a Texas touch may not be anything remarkable, but this casual pub pulls the formula off with consistency and value. ◆ American ◆ M-W, Su 11:15AM-11PM; Th 11:15AM-midnight; F-Sa 11:15AM-1AM. 1065 Wisconsin Ave NW (K-M Sts) 338.7760

19 Blues Alley ★$$ This intimate nightspot is filled with jazz fans who come to hear big stars like **Dizzy Gillespie**, **Wynton Marsalis**, and **Nancy Wilson**. To complement the music, Blues Alley serves regional New Orleans-style dishes, medium-priced seafood, and steaks. Dinner guests are given preferential seating during the shows. It's possible to enjoy the music and the candlelit ambiance without eating, but there is a cover charge. In either case, reservations are a must. (In 1982, Washington's oldest and most prominent jazz club officially donated its name to the street it stands on.) ◆ Southern ◆ Cover. M-Th, Su 6PM-midnight; F-Sa 6PM-2AM. Shows: M-Th, Su 8, 10PM; F-Sa 8, 10PM, midnight. Box office: M-Th, Su noon-midnight; F-Sa noon-2AM. 1073 Wisconsin Ave NW (K-M Sts) Main entrance on Blues Alley. Reservations recommended. 337.4141

20 Nathan's ★★$$$ Pinstriped politicos, lobbyists, and businesspeople gravitate to the huntclubby bar with intimate booths and a quality view of the passing sidewalk crowd. Given the lively bar scene, the food is surprisingly good: handmade pasta, fresh seafood, and veal. For brunch, try the 10 different takes on eggs Benedict. ◆ American ◆ M-W 11AM-3PM, 6-11PM; Th-F 11AM-3PM, 6PM-midnight; Sa 9AM-3PM, 6PM-midnight; Su 9AM-3PM, 6-11PM. 3150 M St NW (Wisconsin Ave) Reservations recommended. 338.2000

20 Georgetown Tobacco & Pipe Stores Inc. Native Washingtonian **David Berkebile** has been keeping the city smoking since 1964— **Anwar Sadat** used to stock up on the store's special-blend pipe tobacco. ◆ M-Sa 10AM-9PM; Su noon-8PM. 3144 M St NW (31st St-Wisconsin Ave) 338.5100. Also at: Montgomery Mall, Bethesda MD. 469.6161; Tyson's Corner Mall, McLean VA. 893.3366

20 Bistro Français ★$$ Francophiles will delight in the authentic bistro fare prepared in a romantic wood- and mirror-paneled restaurant. This café has maintained its tradition of serving good food at reasonable prices. Great for after the theater. ◆ French ◆ M-Th, Su 11AM-3AM; F-Sa 11AM-4AM. 3128 M St NW (31st St-Wisconsin Ave) 338.3830

20 Mr. Smith's ★$ Fresh fruit daiquiris and the garden patio are the big advertised draws for this casual bar and restaurant, but the piano bar packs 'em into the front room. Good burgers and sandwiches. ◆ American ◆ M-Th 11:30AM-2AM; F 11:30AM-3AM; Sa 11AM-3AM; Su 11AM-2AM. 3104 M St NW (31st St-Wisconsin Ave) 333.3104

21 Urban Outfitters The source for dorm room furnishings, **Esprit** and **Gennera** casual clothing, wacky postcards, gelati, and just about every other necessity for the Georgetown University set. ◆ M-Th 10AM-10PM; F-Sa 10AM-11PM; Su noon-8PM. 3111 M St NW (31st St-Wisconsin Ave) 342.1012

22 American Cafe ★$$ This neon-bright café starred with tarragon chicken salad, sesame noodles, and other fresh, innovative salads and sandwiches when everyone else was still flipping burgers. Although often crowded and noisy, this original restaurant for the chain is still going strong. The upstairs takeout section features many of the same dishes. ◆ American ◆ M-Th 11AM-3AM; F-Sa 11AM-4AM; Su 11AM-2AM. 1211 Wisconsin Ave NW (M-N Sts) 944.9464. Also at: 227 Massachusetts Ave NE. 547.8500; 5252 Wisconsin Ave NW. 363.5400; 1331 Pennsylvania Ave NW. 626.0770

23 J Paul's ★$$ This *meetmarket* caters to the under-30 preppy crowd, while the restaurant features decent bar food like fresh seafood, pastas, burgers, chicken, and ribs. You can check out the population at the bar through the large picture windows. ◆ American ◆ M-Th 11:30AM-2AM; F-Sa 10:30AM-3AM; Su 10:30AM-2AM. 3218 M St NW (Wisconsin Ave-33rd St) 333.3450

24 Georgetown Park By any standards, this 100-million-dollar shopping complex with more than 100 stores, boutiques, and shops impresses. Billed as *the World's First Shopping Park*, it is the only such commercial venture that overlaps a national park—the historic C&O Canal that has supported Georgetown trade since 1831. Certainly, it was the first DC shopping mall to capture the imagination of well-heeled shoppers and reverse the retail traffic pattern back into West Washington. And it may be the first shopping mall anywhere to be included on group-tour itineraries.

Built in 1981 behind the preserved and reconstructed century-old facades at the heart of commercial Georgetown, the mall boasts a magnificent Victorian interior. Its 3 levels of brass-and-iron-railed mezzanine shopping encircle a grand atrium and an indoor garden that flourishes under the block-long skylight roof. All the details, from the brass-and-glass elevators to regular performances of classical music by local musicians, give Georgetown Park an aura of sophistication. The prices do,

too. This is not a bargain hunter's paradise. Sale signs are small, unobtrusive—and rare. Buzzwords like *European-tailored, chic,* and *unique* aren't exaggerations. This is snob shopping at its best.

Among the internationally flavored shops and stores is, for instance, the first East Coast branch of **Abercrombie & Fitch** since the fun, excessive sporting emporium fled New York City for Texas and California a few years back, with merchandise ranging from complete safari outfits to dwarf billiard tables. An elegant branch of **Garfinckel's** that caters mainly to women is the largest store among the mall's many small and tony boutiques, such as **Cache**, a high-fashion women's shop from Miami. Contemporary home furnishings and craftwork are featured at **Scan**. For fine toys, there's **F.A.O. Schwarz**, and the **Chesapeake Knife and Tool Co.** carries an international selection of cutlery, hunting and collectors' knives, and accessories. **Narragansett** goes for the traditional in men's and women's clothing. Visit **Godiva Chocolatier** for calories; **Waldenbooks** for paperback bestsellers and fine art, literature, and history books at big discounts; and **Uno** for one-of-a-kind handcrafted gold and silver jewelry.

The mall's 1987 addition includes **Polo Ralph Lauren** for designer's men's wear and **Victoria's Secret** for naughty and nice lingerie. Underground parking at reduced rates with

a shop validation sticker. ◆ Mall: M-F 10AM-9PM; Sa 10AM-7PM; Su noon-6PM. Individual store hours may vary. 3222 M St NW (Wisconsin Ave) Entrances on Wisconsin Ave and M St. 342.8180

25 Clyde's ★$$ This archetypal fern bar turned 25 in 1988 and has matured nicely, thank you. Innovations such as swordfish with fresh salsa have surfaced on the menu, but it's the Clyde's classics that bring people back: the quintessential cozy pub decor, good thick burgers, and brunch—still the best omelets and Bloody Marys around. ◆ American ◆ M-Th 7:30AM-2AM; F 7:30AM-3AM; Sa 9AM-3AM; Su 9AM-2AM. Omelet Room: M-F 7:30AM-2:30PM, 6PM-1AM; Sa-Su 9AM-2:30PM, 6PM-1AM. 3236 M St NW (Wisconsin Ave-33rd St) 333.0294

26 Thai Taste of Georgetown ★★$ This little brother of the popular Connecticut Ave restaurant is the Georgetown place to wallow in the delights of chicken with basil and shrimp with lemon grass. ◆ Thai ◆ M-Th, Su noon-10PM; F-Sa noon-11PM. 3287 M St NW (Potomac-33rd Sts) 965.7988

27 Zed's Ethiopian Cuisine ★★$$ Excellent *wats* and *alechas* (spicy sweet stews) and the best *injera* (a soft bread with a slightly acidic taste used in place of utensils) in DC. ◆ Ethiopian ◆ M-Th, Su 11AM-11PM; F-Sa 11AM-2AM. 3318 M St NW (33rd-34th Sts) Reservations required for 4 or more. 333.4710

27 Madurai ★★$$ Vegetarian cooking from southern India in all its complexity and inventiveness. Novices might go with the Madurai Special, a sampler that includes fried eggplant, an assortment of curries, cucumbers in yogurt, mango chutney, rice, and *poori* (puffy breads). More experienced diners should try the *dosais* (crisp rice-based pancakes) and mushroom and vegetable curries. On Sunday, Madurai offers an all-you-can-eat buffet. ◆ Indian ◆ M-Th 5:30-10PM; F-Sa 5:30-10:30PM; Su noon-4PM, 5-10PM. 3318 M St NW (33rd-34th Sts) 333.0997

27 Bill's of Beverly Hills ★★$ Eight varieties of pizza, with more than 20 toppings. Ingredients are extremely fresh (including live yeast), all sauces are homemade, and no oils are used in cooking. Low-calorie pizza? Delivery available within a 20-minute radius by bicycle. ◆ Pizza ◆ M-Th noon-midnight; F-Sa noon-3AM; Su 10AM-5PM. 3340 M St NW (33rd-34th Sts) 333.4063

28 Stoddert House (1787, Benjamin Stoddert) A large, rangy, and ornate Federal townhouse. Owner and architect Stoddert called it *Halcyon House*. Although the north facade has been completely redesigned, the south side, interiors, and garden remain as they were 2 centuries ago. Private residence. ◆ 3400 Prospect Ave NW (34th-35th Sts)

29 Quality Hill (1798, John Thomson Mason) The entire neighborhood may once have been

Georgetown/Upper Northwest

called *Quality Hill* after its many fine homes; somehow, this house inherited the nickname. Private residence. ◆ 3425 Prospect St NW (34th-35th Sts)

30 Prospect House (1788, James M. Lingan) The view (or prospect) of the Potomac commanded from this sharply detailed Federal house is the basis for the name. Private residence. ◆ 3508 Prospect St NW (35th-37th Sts)

31 3600 Prospect Street *The Exorcist* was filmed at this red brick building owned by Georgetown University. It was modified for the story, but you can see the steep steps where the title character met his fate. ◆ 36th St NW

32 1789 ★★$$$ Situated in an 18th-century house, this dining room boasts fireplaces, early American furnishings and etchings, and an extensive menu featuring dishes like chicken breast with pecans and morels, salmon with 2 caviars, and oysters in puff pastry. Intriguing but overpriced wine list. ◆ French ◆ M-Sa 6-11PM. 1226 36th St NW (Prospect St) Jacket requested. Reservations recommended. 965.1789

Interred in the **National Cathedral** are the bodies of **President Woodrow Wilson**, **Admiral George Dewey** of the Spanish-American War, **Helen Keller** and her teacher, **Anne Sullivan Macy, Mabel Boardman,** who was head of the American Red Cross, and **Cordell Hull,** the secretary of state during WWII.

32 F. Scott's ★★$$$ The music of Broadway and the Big Band era, Art Deco flourishes, and movers and shakers in politics and the arts fill this ultrachic bar and restaurant. Good pastas, grilled dishes, and salads. ◆ American ◆ M-Th 6PM-2AM; F-Sa 6PM-3AM. 1232 36th St NW (Prospect-N Sts) 342.0009

32 Georgetown University Shop was preppy before preppy was cool, and has a reputation for quality men's wear and classic sportswear for women. ◆ M-Sa 10AM-6PM. 1248 36th St NW (Prospect-N Sts) 337.8100. Also at: 45 Wisconsin Ave NW, Chevy Chase MD. 656.4004

Georgetown University

33 Georgetown University The country's oldest Roman Catholic university is a pleasant place to walk along shady cobblestoned streets. Founded by **John Carroll** in 1789, the school has always been open to "students of every religious profession," and today includes those from 91 countries.

Old North Building was the original structure, finished in 1792. The fortresslike **Healy Building** (1879, **Smithmeyer and Pelz**) is a grim German Gothic affair topped with an amazing spire. (When you're across the river in Arlington, you'll catch the best view of the school's famous spires.)

The building was named for the **Reverend Patrick Healy, SJ**, the country's first black man to earn a Ph.D. GU's highly regarded School of Medicine sponsors a 535-bed hospital. Other colleges include schools of arts and sciences, nursing, dentistry, and language, as well as the country's most applied-to law school. The university's location in the nation's capital is one reason it includes the country's first and largest foreign service program.

Campus tours can be arranged by calling the undergraduate admissions office 3 weeks in advance. ◆ 37th St NW (Reservoir Rd-Prospect St) Main entrance at 37th and O Sts. 687.0100, admissions and tours 687.3600

34 Cox's Row (1817) Often acclaimed as the finest series of Federal row houses in Georgetown. Some of the middle houses were remodeled during the Victorian era; the end houses are as built. Private residences. ◆ 3327-3339 N St NW (33rd-34th Sts)

35 Smith Row (1815, Walter & Clement Smith) Six Federal houses, side by side and identical except for the most subtle variations in color and form. Private residences. ◆ 3255-3263 N St NW (Potomac-33rd Sts)

36 Booeymonger ★$ This small café and take-out assembles huge specialty sandwiches. ♦ American ♦ Daily 8AM-midnight. 3265 Prospect St NW (Potomac St) No credit cards. 333.4810

36 Golf Par-Tee Miniature golf is strange enough, but this latest twist on what most of us think of as an outdoor sport is designed for only the most serious addicts of the game. Here players don't have to deal with the elements. All action takes place in a small room, where physical exertion consists of putting balls over a tiny computerized green toward any one of several of the world's most luxurious courses, which are projected onto a large screen at one end of the room. Call for an appointment. ♦ 3251 Prospect St NW (N St) Reservations required. 333.3537

37 Morton's of Chicago ★★$$$ A favorite of Capitol Hill regulars and other powerbrokers, this macho steakhouse makes a show of parading its raw beef, chicken, even onions, before customers in order to demonstrate quality and freshness. ♦ Steakhouse ♦ M-Sa 5:30-11PM. 3251 Prospect St NW (Potomac St-Wisconsin Ave) Jacket and tie requested. Reservations required. 342.6258

38 Key Theaters Four screens in a tiny building, but this is an independent operation, not a chain. It presents some of the best new art films, often for extended runs, and its owners care about the quality of the sound and projection. ♦ 1222 Wisconsin Ave NW (M-Prospect Sts) 333.5100

39 Olsson's Books & Records Possibly the best stocked and certainly the most popular book and record store in town. The staff is knowledgeable and will special-order books. The classical recordings section is tops. Famous authors appear now and then to autograph their latest offerings. ♦ M-Th 10AM-10:45PM; F-Sa 10AM-midnight; Su noon-7PM. 1239 Wisconsin Ave NW (M-N Sts) 338.9544. Also at: 1307 19th St NW 785.1133; 1200 F St NW. 347.3686; 106 S. Union St, Alexandria VA. 684.0007; 7647 Old Georgetown Rd, Bethesda MD. 652.3336

39 Britches of Georgetowne is the uncontested headquarters for young professionals seeking a distinctively trendy look. **Britches Great Outdoors for Women** is only 2 blocks up Wisconsin Ave (at 1357). Several locations throughout the DC metropolitan area. ♦ M-F 10AM-9PM; Sa 10AM-6PM; Su noon-6PM. 1247 Wisconsin Ave NW (M-N Sts) 338.3330. Also at: 1219 Connecticut Ave NW. 347.8994; Montgomery Mall, Bethesda MD. 365.2995; Fair Oaks Mall, Fairfax VA. 385.4788

40 Alexander Julian Shop features the designer's exciting and colorful men's clothing. ♦ M-W, F-Sa 10AM-6PM; Th 10AM-8PM; Su noon-5PM. 1242 Wisconsin Ave NW (Prospect-N Sts) 333.1988

Restaurants: Red **Hotels**: Blue
Shops/Parks: Green **Sights/Culture**: Black

40 Martin's Tavern ★★$$ The oldest tavern in Georgetown—warm, classy, and quieter than most other Irish pubs. Tiffany lamps and the gold-framed paintings give the place a clubby feeling. The conservative clientele comes for the Virginia crabcakes or the excellent lamb stew. ♦ Irish/American ♦ M, Su 8AM-midnight; Tu-Sa 8AM-1:30AM. 1264 Wisconsin Ave NW (N St) 333.7370

Drawing by Edward F. Fogle

41 John Laird Mansion (Laird/Dunlop House) (1799, William Lovering) Originally the home of tobacco merchant John Laird. **Robert Todd Lincoln**, son of the president, also once owned this Federal-period mansion. Private residence. ♦ 3014 N St NW (30th-31st Sts)

42 Decatur House (1813, John Stull Williams) After **Commodore Stephen Decatur**, the dashing naval hero of the War of 1812, was killed in a duel, his widow moved to this stately Federal-style home. Private residence. ♦ 2812 N St NW (28th-29th Sts)

Georgetown/Upper Northwest

43 Paolo's ★★$ On the site of the former **Maison des Crepes**, this hugely popular bar/restaurant is run by **Capital Management Corporation**, who have given the narrow site a sense of space and style. Brisk, friendly service; fresh, modern menu on which the pastas, salads, and fish of the day are standouts. ♦ Italian ♦ M-Th 11:30AM-midnight; F-Sa 11:30AM-3AM; Su 11AM-midnight. 1303 Wisconsin Ave NW (N-Dumbarton Sts) 333.7353

43 Susquehanna Antiques American and English antiques of the 18th and 19th centuries, including some 19th- and 20th-century paintings. ♦ M-F 10AM-6PM; Sa 10AM-7PM. 1319 Wisconsin Ave NW (N-Dumbarton Sts) 333.5843

43 Aux Fruits de Mer ★★$ An illuminated window aquarium decorates the exterior of this informal seafood establishment. Order from a large selection of fresh fish, broiled lobster stuffed with crabmeat, frog legs, slaw, and mounds of fries. ♦ Seafood ♦ M-Th, Su 11:30AM-2AM; F-Sa 11:30AM-3AM. 1329 Wisconsin Ave NW (Dumbarton St) 965.2377

The center of the dome of the old **Naval Observatory** at 23rd and E Sts (now the **Navy Medical Command**) is the location of the Washington meridian established by Congress in 1850. From that precise point, the boundaries of most plains and western states were drawn.

43 Au Pied de Cochon ★$ This bustling, affable round-the-clock bistro serves hearty French fare: omelets, crepes, quiches, pigs' feet, ratatouille. The black bean soup is great, but when available, the best buy is lobster. In nice weather, the outdoor café is perfect for meeting friends; during the colder months, it becomes an enclosed greenhouse where you can keep warm with mugs of coffee and watch the rain or snow. ♦ French ♦ 24 hrs. 1335 Wisconsin Ave NW (Dumbarton St) 333.5440

44 The Georgetown Inn $$$ This 95-room hotel, in a series of restored 18th-century buildings, features a traditional decor. Rooms have poster beds, **Martha Washington** spreads, and **Crabtree & Evelyn** toiletries. Children under 16 stay free. Free parking. ♦ 1310 Wisconsin Ave NW (N-O Sts) 333.8900, 800/424.2979; fax 337.6317

Within the Georgetown Inn:

Georgetown Bar and Grill ★$$ Gorgeously decorated with green marble and wood paneling, but the food is fairly ordinary: grilled salmon, crabcakes, pasta with pesto. ♦ American ♦ Daily 7AM-2:30PM, 5PM-midnight. 333.8900

44 Georgetown Coffee Tea and Spice A floor-to-ceiling collection of coffee equipment, kitchenware, and gourmet bulk coffees and teas. ♦ M-W 10AM-7PM; Th-Sa 10AM-8PM; Su noon-6PM. 1330 Wisconsin Ave NW (N-O Sts) 338.3801

Georgetown/Upper Northwest

44 Sarinah Satay House ★$ Delicious renditions of Indonesian cuisine in a secluded garden setting. Subtle, complex spices and festive national dishes, including rijsttafel. ♦ Indonesian ♦ Tu-Sa noon-3PM, 6-10:30PM; Su 6-10:30PM. 1338 Wisconsin Ave NW (N-O Sts) Reservations recommended F-Su. 337.2955

45 St. John's Episcopal Church, Georgetown Parish (1809, Dr. William Thornton; renovation, 1870, Starkweather & Plowman) The second-oldest Episcopal church in DC. Like Thornton's design for the Capitol, this Georgian edifice was drastically altered in later years. ♦ M-F 9AM-4:30PM. Services Su 8, 9, 11AM. 3240 O St NW (Potomac St-Wisconsin Ave) 338.1796

46 Commander Salamander Heavy emphasis on multicolored leopard designs, rhinestone sunglasses, and the latest in hairspray colors draw a clientele worth seeing. ♦ M-Tu 10AM-9PM; W-Th 10AM-10PM; F-Sa 10AM-midnight; Su noon-8PM. 1420 Wisconsin Ave NW (O-P Sts) 337.2265

47 Appalachian Spring Fine country-look American crafts: pottery, baby quilts, jewelry, and clothing. ♦ M-W, F-Sa 10AM-6PM; Th 10AM-8PM; Su 1-6PM. 1415 Wisconsin Ave NW (Dumbarton-O Sts) 337.5780. Also at: Union Station, 50 Massachusetts Ave NE. 682.0505

47 Little Caledonia A treasure-trove of furnishings for Anglophiles. Kitchenware, fabrics, furniture, lamps, and one of the best Christmas card collections going. ♦ M-Sa 10AM-5:50PM. 1419 Wisconsin Ave NW (O-P Sts) 333.4700

48 Christ Church, Georgetown (1886, Henry Laws) A scaled-down Gothic cathedral with an unusual gabled tower. Although it's too small to be really awe-inspiring, it fits neatly into the neighborhood. **Francis Scott Key** was a member of the congregation; the church was founded in 1817. ♦ Episcopal services Su 8, 9, 11AM. 31st and O Sts NW. 333.6677

49 Adams Davidson Galleries Eighteenth- and 19th-century American oils, watercolors, and drawings are the specialties of this gallery. The place to view Hudson River School landscapes from the 1850–75 period by such masters as **Thomas Cole** and **Frederic Church**. ♦ Tu-F 10AM-5PM; Sa noon-6PM. 3233 P St NW (Wisconsin Ave-33rd St) 965.3800

49 The Phoenix A quality collection of handcrafted items from Mexico: wedding dresses, contemporary silver jewelry, women's clothing, candelabras, and pottery. ♦ M-Sa 10AM-6PM; Su 1-6PM. 1514 Wisconsin Ave NW (P St-Volta Pl) 338.4404

49 Secondhand Rose Contemporary women's clothing in almost-new condition at good prices, with many designer names and cocktail dresses. The really cheap stuff's in the bathroom. ♦ M-Sa 10AM-6PM, Jan-June, Sep-Dec; Tu-Sa 10AM-6PM, July-Aug. 1516 Wisconsin Ave NW (P St-Volta Pl) 337.3072

50 Silhouette **Hugo Boss**, **Byblos**, and other au courant designer sportswear for men and women. ♦ M-W, F-Sa 10AM-7PM; Th 10AM-8PM; Su noon-6PM. 1517 Wisconsin Ave NW (P-Q Sts) 337.8334

50 Santa Fe Style Home furnishings for **Georgia O'Keeffe** wanna-bes. Rustic carved furniture, whimsical sculptured animals, flatware, and jewelry. ♦ M-Sa 10AM-6PM; Su noon-5PM. 1525 Wisconsin Ave NW (P-Q Sts) 333.3747

51 New Volta Place Gallery Handcrafted Mexican folk arts, including ceramics, handblown glass, copper, pewter, and furniture. ♦ M-Sa 10AM-5PM. 1531 33rd St NW (Volta Pl-P St) 337.7864

52 Pomander Walk (1885) Renovation in the 1950s changed this from a blighted alley to a charming set of small homes. Private residences. ♦ Volta Pl (33rd-34th Sts NW)

53 Volta Bureau (1893, Peabody & Stearns) A strange amalgam of early Greek temple and office building, and home to the **American Association for the Teaching of Speech to the Deaf**. **Alexander Graham Bell** funded the building with money he received from his invention of the telephone, and within the building is a small monument to him. ♦ 1537 35th St NW (Volta Pl)

54 Convent of the Visitation (1820–1872) The convent's 3 buildings—an 1820 Federal-style chapel, a Gothic monastery (1832–1857),

---

Restaurants: Red   **Hotels**: Blue
Shops/Parks: Green   **Sights/Culture**: Black

and an ornate Victorian school building dating from 1872—represent a merry pastiche of 19th-century tastes. ♦ 35th St NW (P St-Reservoir Rd)

55 Embassy of the Federal Republic of Germany (1964, Egon Eiermann) A lot of working space cleverly fits into a narrow, sloping site. A white steel trellis lightens the bulk of the building and makes it compatible with the residential neighorhood. A cool, sophisticated design that's vastly more imaginative than most Washington embassies. ♦ M-F 9AM-noon. 4645 Reservoir Rd NW (Foxhall Rd-Whitehaven Parkway) 298.4000

56 Audubon Naturalist Book Shop This is the city's best collection of bird and nature books and avian gifts and accessories. ♦ Tu-W, F-Sa 10AM-5PM; Th 10AM-7PM. 1621 Wisconsin Ave NW (Q St-Reservoir Rd) 337.6062. Also at: 8940 Jones Mill Rd, Chevy Chase MD. 652.3606

56 French Market A dependable standby with all the basic meats, breads, wines, and sandwiches to go. ♦ M-Tu, Th-Sa 8:30AM-6PM; W 8:30AM-1:30PM. 1632 Wisconsin Ave NW (Q St-Reservoir Rd) 338.4828

57 Mackall-Worthington House (1820, Leonard Mackall) A large Federal home that was once the focal point of the neighborhood it occupies. The incongruous mansard roof was added later. Private residence. ♦ 1686 34th St NW (Reservoir Rd-R St)

58 Tudor Place (1794, Dr. William Thornton; wings added 1805–1816) **Martha Washington**'s granddaughter, **Martha Parke Custis**, and her husband, **Thomas Peter**, were the original occupants of this house; their descendants lived here until 1983. Now open to the public as a **historic house**, with period furnishings and formal gardens. ♦ Voluntary contribution. Tours Tu-Sa 10, 11:30AM, 1, 2:30PM. Tour reservations required. 1644 31st St NW (Q-R Sts) 965.0400

Drawings by Joseph Passonneau

59 Cookes Row (1868, Starkweather & Plowman) Although Georgetown is perhaps best known for its Federal-style buildings, this group of mid-Victorian charmers offers a welcome twist on the row house theme. The 4 duplexes contain twice that many residences, each with a side yard and over 4000

square feet of space. The exterior details—bay windows, dormers, porches—give each building its own character (2 are in the French Mansard style; the other pair is vaguely Germanic). But inside, they are not nearly as individual as they look: all 4 have the same floor plan. Private residences. ♦ 3009-3029 Q St NW (30th-31st Sts)

60 Miller House (1840, Benjamin Miller) A New England clapboard house set down in the midst of the city's original neighborhood. The portico is an early hint of the Greek Revival styles that gained popularity soon after it was built. Private residence. ♦ 1524 28th St NW (P-Q Sts)

60 Reuben Daw's Fence (1860s) This fence, made of musket barrels from the 1848 Mexi-

can-American War, encloses 3 houses on P St and a pair on 28th St. ♦ 2803 P St NW (28th-29th Sts)

61 John Henry's All-cotton garments and active sportswear in every color, from shy to shocking. ♦ Tu-Sa 10AM-6PM. 2601 P St NW (26th St) 338.1414

62 Dumbarton House (1800–1810) Known until 1932 as **Bellevue**, this is a very typical early 19th-century Georgian home complete with oval rooms, ornate mantels, and breezy hallways. **Benjamin Latrobe** installed the rear bays. Now owned by the **National Society of the Colonial Dames of America**, who have maintained the Federal furnishings, which include **Hepplewhite** and **Sheraton** pieces, and fine collections of silver and china. Worth a visit. ♦ Voluntary contribution. M-Sa 9AM-12:30PM, Jan-June, Sep-Dec. 2715 Q St NW (27th-28th Sts) 337.2288

63 Evermay (1801, King and Hedges) This was considered the most elegant house in the city, even back when opulence was the norm. Now occupied by **DuPont** heirs, it has been restored to its former extravagance, and features a garden of such Southern favorites as azaleas, magnolias, and boxwood. Private residence. ♦ 1623 28th St NW (Q-R Sts)

"The whole of Government consists in the art of being honest." **Thomas Jefferson** *Works, VI, 186*

64 Beall House (1784) George Washington's great-nephew, **Colonel George Corbin Washington**, and his bride, **Elizabeth Beall**, were given this house as a wedding gift by her father. The original Georgian structure has been much altered. Private residence. ♦ 30th and R Sts NW

65 Oak Hill Cemetery Given to the city by **William Wilson Corcoran**, such notables as **John Howard Paine** (author of *Home, Sweet Home*), statesmen **Edwin M. Stanton**, **James G. Blaine**, and **Dean Acheson**, and socialite **Peggy O'Neil** are buried here. The **Gatehouse** (1839, **George la Roche**) and the simple Gothic Revival chapel (1850, **James Renwick**) are architecturally noteworthy. ♦ M-F 9AM-4:30PM. Entrance at 30th and R Sts NW. 337.2835

66 Montrose Park A small, quiet woodland park with tennis courts, playground, picnicking, walking trails. **Lovers Lane**, a cobblestone walking path, forms the western border, separating Montrose and Dumbarton Oaks parks. Tennis courts available on a first-come, first-served basis. ♦ R St NW (30th-31st Sts) 426.6827

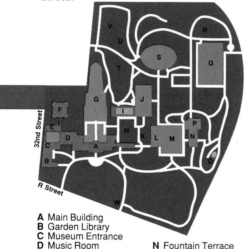

A Main Building
B Garden Library
C Museum Entrance
D Music Room
E Byzantine Collection
F Pre-Columbian Museum
G North Vista
H Green Garden
I Swimming Pool
J Pebble Garden
K Beech Terrace
L Urn Entrance
M Rose Garden
N Fountain Terrace
O Lovers Lane Pool
P Arbor Terrace
Q Cut Flower Garden
R Cherry Hill
S Ellipse
T Crabapple Hill
U Forsythia Hill
V Fairview Hill
W Garden Entrance

67 Dumbarton Oaks (House, 1800) This lovingly preserved 19th-century estate is one of the capital's very special places, famous both for the lavish mansion where groundwork for the United Nations charter was laid and for its exquisite gardens. Originally part of the Port of Georgetown land grant made by **Queen Anne** in 1702. In the 1920s, the ramshackle estate was purchased by former ambassador to Argentina **Robert Woods Bliss**, and he and his wife began creating the present museum and garden. A small pre-Columbian museum (1963, **Philip Johnson**), a grouping of 9 domed glass cylinders, houses excellent collections of works by Byzantine and pre-Columbian artisans, including jewelry and metalwork. The restored home is a collection of European art and architectural treasures. In the music room, the Blisses entertained—and were entertained by—such noted friends as pianist **Jan Paderewski** and composer **Igor Stravinsky**, who wrote his *Concerto in E Flat*, the *Dumbarton Oaks Concerto*, to commemorate the couple's 30th anniversary. **El Greco's** *The Visitation* hangs in the room.

Several libraries house books reserved for scholars, although the **Rare Books Room** is sometimes open for viewing. The estate has over 100,000 books on landscape gardening and Byzantine and pre-Columbian art. The 16 acres of gardens designed by **Beatrix Farrand** and Mrs. Bliss are a wonderland of manicured walkways and thematic culs-de-sac. One of the favorite garden spots is the **Pebble Garden Fountain**, an expanse of intricately patterned pebble mosaics that in spring and summer are flooded with a thin layer of water. A graceful Italianate fountain features a pair of putti romping on seahorses while water springs from the hands of a third. ♦ Free. Dumbarton Collections Tu-Su 2-5PM. 1703 32nd St NW (R-S Sts) 338.8278, tours (groups of 12 or more) 342.3212 ♿

Within Dumbarton Oaks:

Dumbarton Oaks Gardens is 27 acres of natural woodlands noted for its profusion of spring wildflowers. The fact that it's only accessible by foot, via **Lovers Lane** off 31st and R Sts, helps keep it unspoiled. No picnicking or pets allowed on the grounds. ♦ Jan-Mar, Nov-Dec: free. Daily 2-5PM. Apr-Oct: admission. Daily 2-6PM, weather permitting; senior citizens free W. 338.8278

68 Japan Inn ★★$$$ Sit at a communal table in the **Teppan-Yaki Room** and have your steak, chicken, or shrimp cooked on a stainless-steel grill right before your eyes. If you want a more private experience, reserve a tatami room upstairs, where you'll sit at a low table and sup on sukiyaki and *shabu shabu* prepared by a kimonoed waitress. Or have a full dinner of sashimi, sushi, or tempura. ♦ Japanese ♦ M-F noon-2PM, 6-10PM; Sa 6-10PM; Su 5:30-9:30PM. 1715 Wisconsin Ave NW (R-S Sts) Jacket and tie requested. Reservations recommended. 337.3400

69 Miller and Arney Antiques, Inc. Eighteenth- and 19th-century American and English antiques, as well as lamps, rugs, and accessories. ♦ M-Sa 9:30AM-5:30PM. 1737 Wisconsin Ave NW (S St) 338.2369

69 Peter Mack Brown Antiques This veteran antiques dealer is well-regarded for 19th-century European furniture. Pottery and porcelain are other specialties of the shop. ♦ M-Sa 11AM-6PM. 1742 Wisconsin Ave NW (S St) 338.8484

In 1884, **Belva Lockwood** became the first woman to run for US president—she captured 4149 votes.

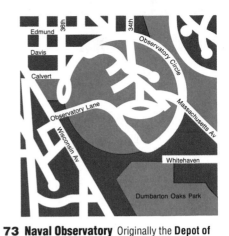

70 Sushi-Ko ★★$$ DC's first sushi bar is still one of its best. Expert chefs prepare a vast range of raw and cooked fish and seafood, as well as tempura and a few broiled dishes. ◆ Japanese ◆ Tu-F noon-2:30PM, 6-10:30PM; Sa 5-10:30PM; Su 5-10PM. 2309 Wisconsin Ave NW (Whitehaven-Calvert Sts) 333.4187

71 Le Caprice ★★★$$$ Chef **Edmond Foltzenlogel**, formerly of the French embassy, makes inventive use of fresh and seasonal ingredients in such dishes as lobster sausage, medallions of venison with wild mushrooms and green lentils, and chocolate terrine. There are also bistro basics like roast chicken with tarragon. Short, fairly priced wine list. Charming ambiance with atmospheric lighting and well-spaced tables. The prix-fixe menus are an excellent value. ◆ French ◆ M-F 11:45AM-2PM, 5:30-10PM; Sa 6:30-10:30PM; Su 6-10PM. 2348 Wisconsin Ave NW (Calvert St-Hall Pl) Reservations recommended. 337.3394

71 Germaine's ★★★$$$ A pristine dining room featuring Pan-Asian cuisine (Vietnamese, Thai, Korean, Chinese, and Indonesian). Order from a wide offering of appetizers: sate (skewered meats with peanut sauce), scallop salad, dumplings, Korean beef. Superb seafood dishes. Charming Germaine will no doubt visit you during your meal and make sure all is well. ◆ Pan-Asian ◆ M-Th noon-2:30PM, 5:30-10PM; F noon-2:30PM, 5:30-11PM; Sa 5:30-11PM; Su 5:30-10PM. 2400 Wisconsin Ave NW (Calvert St-Hall Pl) Jacket and tie requested. Reservations recommended. 965.1185

71 Austin Grill ★★$ This jaunty eatery draws a casual young crowd, but the 3 salsas on the table show it's serious about the food: fajitas, Austin enchiladas, and grilled chicken, shrimp, and porkchops. Don't miss the killer margaritas. ◆ Tex-Mex ◆ M 5:30-11PM; Tu-Th 11:30AM-11PM; F-Sa 11:30AM-midnight; Su 11:30AM-10:30PM. 2404 Wisconsin Ave NW (Calvert St-Hall Pl) 337.8080

71 The Ice Cream Shop Featuring **Bob's Famous Ice Cream**, this is the first store opened by **Bob Weiss**, the local lawyer-turned-ice-cream-maker who invented Oreo ice cream, Mystic Mint, and Mozambique—and made the world a better place to live in. ◆ Daily noon-midnight. 2416 Wisconsin Ave NW (Calvert St-Hall Pl) 965.4499

72 Savoy Suites $$ Right across the street from the new Soviet Embassy, which cannot be occupied until the bugs are removed from the US Embassy in Moscow. Some rooms have kitchens or jacuzzis. Restaurant and outdoor pool. Nonsmoking rooms. Children under 12 stay free. ◆ 2505 Wisconsin Ave NW (Calvert-Davis Sts) 337.9700; fax 337.3644 ⅙

Restaurants: Red   **Hotels**: Blue
Shops/Parks: Green   **Sights/Culture**: Black

73 Naval Observatory Originally the **Depot of Charts and Instruments**, located in Foggy Bottom and charged with keeping navigational charts. The first astronomical involvement was for the testing of ship chronometers. **Observatory Circle** was created to distance the delicate instruments from the rumblings of city traffic. Collections include atomic clocks and a 26-inch refractor telescope that was used in the 1877 discovery of the Martian moons. ◆ Valid ID required for entrance. Free 2-hour observatory tours Monday evenings, except federal holidays; gates open 7:30PM. Tour limited to first 100 visitors. Group tour reservations must be made in advance. 34th St at

Georgetown/Upper Northwest

Massachusetts Ave NW. 653.1543, tour reservations 653.1541

On the grounds of the Naval Observatory:

Vice President's House In the early 1970s, Congress decided that too much money was being spent on security measures for the homes of US vice presidents. In 1975, over the protests of the Navy, it co-opted this house, which for decades had been home to naval admirals. Despite the fact that it is located on a navy post, which makes it easy to defend, the large sunny Victorian home with acres of lawn doesn't seem like a fortress at all. Not open to the public.

74 British Embassy (1931, Sir Edward Luytens) Luytens' grandiose classicism glorified the British Raj in Delhi; here he created a country house in the style of **Sir Christopher Wren** to house HMG's representatives. Back in the '30s, they received hardship pay for enduring the rigors of Washington summers —but at least the building and its ample lawns reminded them of home. The statue of **Sir Winston Churchill** (1966, **William McVey**) outside seems to be trying to hail a cab. He hasn't had any luck in the 20-odd years he's been standing here; neither will you. ◆ 3100 Massachusetts Ave NW (Observatory Circle-Whitehaven St)

For an announcement of the Naval Observatory's **Master Clock Time**, call 900/410.8463.

75 Santa Sophia Greek Orthodox Church
(1956, Archie Protopappas) The largest Greek
Orthodox congregation in the country meets in
this magnificent Byzantine-inspired building.
The mosaic work is definitely worth seeing.
♦ M-F 10AM-3:30PM or tours by appointment.
Services Su 10AM. 36th St at Massachusetts
Ave NW. 333.4730

76 Primavera ★★★$$$$ Located within the
Alban Towers apartment building. Dine inside
or al fresco (in an enclosed inner courtyard)
on fresh pasta and seafood. The swordfish and
fried calamari are winners, as is the tiramisú.
♦ Italian ♦ M-Sa 6-11PM; Su 11:30AM-3PM, 6-
11PM. 3700 Massachusetts Ave NW (Wisconsin Ave) Reservations recommended. 342.0224

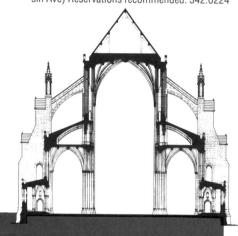

**77 Cathedral Church of St. Peter and St.
Paul** (Begun 1907, Vaughn & Bodley; scheduled completion, 1990) High on Mount Saint
Alban, the limestone towers of this Gothic
cathedral (aka **Washington Cathedral**) rise
above the treetops of the city of Washington.
For most of this century it has been growing
slowly in size and splendor. The final phase
of construction will be completed by 29
September 1990.

The work began nearly 100 years ago when,
in 1893, the Protestant Episcopal Cathedral
Foundation was created by an act of Congress,
and **Henry Yates Statterlee**, first Bishop of
Washington, began securing the land and
raising funds—a duty that would last a lifetime.
Two architects were hired, **Dr. George Bodley**
of Britain, and **Henry Vaughn**, an American.
Although they had to exchange drawings
across the Atlantic, the design—for what
would become the sixth-largest cathedral in
the world—was completed in only 13 months.
No less important was the hiring of the **George
A. Fuller Company** as chief contractors, which
it remained until 1980. Over the years the company maintained a staff of technicians able to
build with limestone in the Gothic style of the
14th century.

In 1907, **Teddy Roosevelt** officiated at ground-
breaking ceremonies for the cathedral, using
the silver trowel **George Washington** used
when laying the cornerstone of the US Capitol.

Architect **Philip Frohman** took over the project
in 1919, refining the design and supervising
every facet of construction. During 40 years of
service he never tired of the project. He could
be seen climbing the scaffolding into his 70s.

If America were to have an official national
cathedral, this would certainly be the one. No
federal money was used in its creation, but
citizens from every part of the country have
contributed funds. Over the years it has been
the site for the burial services of presidents
Wilson and **Eisenhower** and generals **Bradley**
and **MacArthur**. Services for US servicemen
killed in Vietnam were held here, as were prayer
services for the Iranian hostages and a memorial service for **Anwar Sadat**.

Although the cathedral is the seat of the Washington Episcopal Diocese, it has maintained the
ecumenical stance of its founders. It has no
standing congregation, but opens its doors to
worshippers of all denominations.

The church is built in the shape of a cross, with
twin towers (still under construction) in the
west and a **Gloria in Excelsis Tower** in the
center. Ninety-six angels, each with a different
face, pose in a frieze around the tower, which
holds a 10-bell peal and a 53-bell carillon.

As you tour the cathedral, remember that in
Gothic architecture, structure and symbol
merge into one. The design must communicate
as much as the hymnals, but often without
words, so look closely for the narratives and
references in the intricate carvings and lumi-
nous windows.

Enter the cathedral at the **North** or **South Transept**, or through the doors at the west end.
Entering from the west you will find yourself in
the **narthex** (an enclosed porch). Laid into the
mosaic floor are seals of the 50 states.

In the **nave** above the **Warren Bay** is the **Space
Window**. It commemorates the scientists and
astronauts of *Apollo XI*. An actual piece of
moon rock retrieved on that mission is embed-
ded in the glass! Further down is **Wilson Bay,**
containing the tomb of the only president
buried in the District of Columbia. Carvings
symbolize aspects of **Woodrow Wilson**'s life.
A crusader's sword on the sarcophagus symbolizes his quest for peace through the League
of Nations. Look for a thistle (his Scottish heritage) and for the seal of Princeton University
(Wilson was once its president).

A few steps toward the center of the cathedral
should place you in the **Crossing**, a magnificent
space where the transepts bisect the nave. Four
massive stone piers soar 98 feet up to meet the
vaulted ceiling. The pulpit is made of stones
from **Canterbury Cathedral**, and it was here
that **Martin Luther King, Jr.**, delivered his last
sermon before his assassination in Memphis,
Tennessee.

The charming **Children's Chapel** shouldn't
be missed. Everything is scaled down and
designed to delight the child. The windows tell
the stories of **Samuel** and **David** as boys, and
the kneelers are embroidered with all manner
of animals—pets as well as wild beasts. The

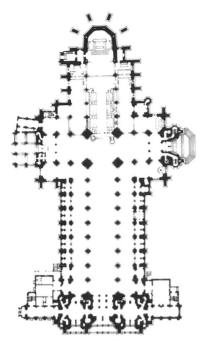

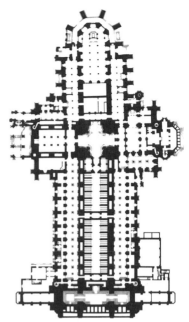

ceiling—the only fan vaulting in the cathedral
—is as delicate as a christening gown's lace.

The altar panel in the **Holy Spirit Chapel** was
painted on wood by **N.C. Wyeth**, father of
Andrew Wyeth. Golden-haloed angels sing the
praises of God on a piercing field of blue.

If you've been walking along the aisles, now
might be a good time to step more toward the
center and admire the nave. Part of the genius
of Gothic architecture was the flying buttress,
which by transferring the weight of the roof off
the walls and outside the building allowed the
walls to be opened up with stained-glass windows. As you walk down the nave, scores of
windows on either side depict biblical themes
as well as great artists who have glorified God
in their works, such as **Dante**, **Milton**, **Bach**,
and **Sir Christopher Wren**. Turn toward the
western end of the cathedral for the dazzling
West Rose Window designed by **Rowan
LeCompte**. It is a fiery wheel (25 feet 11 inches
in diameter) that burns with kaleidoscopic
color, particularly as it catches the last rays
of a setting sun.

On the lower floor, or **Crypt**, you will find 4
more chapels, burial vaults, a **gift shop/book-
store** (with excellent cathedral guides), a **visitors center**, and a **brass-rubbing center**.

Before leaving the cathedral, you might want to
go up to the **Pilgrim's Observation Gallery**,
which can be reached by an elevator in the west
end of the main level. Located in the twin towers, the 70 windows of the gallery provide a
panoramic view of Washington, Maryland, and
Virginia, as well as a bird's-eye view of some of
the cathedral's exterior carvings.

The cathedral's **Close** (grounds) is a 57-acre
plot that includes 5 schools, a preachers college, and some delightful gardens. A stroll here
can be a restful way to end the afternoon.

Leave the building from the **South Transept** or
West Doors and go to the **Herb Cottage**, where
sachets, herbs, honeys, and herb vinegars are
for sale. Outside, a small herb garden is redo-
lent with the scent of rosemary and mint.

Georgetown/Upper Northwest

Continue south to the **Bishop's Garden**. Pass
through a Norman arch and enter one of the
city's loveliest garden spaces. Actually a series
of several gardens, it includes a rose garden,
a medieval herb garden, boxwood, magnolias,
and the **Shadow House**, a small stone medieval
summer cottage that's cool in the summer and
dry in the rain—a perfect spot to relax in.

A bit further down the hill is the statue of **Lieutenant General George Washington** (1959,
Herbert Hazeltine), a heavily gilded bronze of
young Washington astride a graceful well-
muscled horse—according to rumor, the spit-
ting image of the famous racehorse **Man O' War**.
In the style of the ancient Egyptians, the horse's
eyes are made of glass.

You might also take a walk on the **Woodland
Path**, maintained by local garden clubs. It starts
at a Japanese footbridge and makes its way up a
wooded hill planted with wildflowers.

The **Cathedral Greenhouse** southeast of the
church raises rare herbs. A catalog of those on
sale is available on request.

Tours are free, take about 40 minutes, and leave
continuously from the west entrance Monday
through Saturday between 10AM and 3:15PM
and Sunday between 12:15 and 2:45PM. Or you
can take your own tour until 4:30PM (until
8:30PM from May through Labor Day).

The Summer Festival, a series of free outdoor
orchestra and choral concerts featuring international and multifaith music, is offered Wednes-

day evenings at 8PM. The carillon is played every Saturday afternoon, and organ recitals follow afternoon prayers on Sunday; call for more information. Served by most of the Massachusetts and Wisconsin Ave buses. ♦ Church: M-Sa 10AM-5PM; Su 8AM-5PM, Jan-Apr, Labor Day-Dec; M-F 10AM-9PM; Sa 10AM-5PM; Su 8AM-5PM, May-Labor Day. Services: M-F 7:30AM, noon, 4PM; Su 8, 9, 10, 11AM, 4PM. Pilgrim's Observation Gallery daily 10AM-3:30PM. Wisconsin-Massachusetts Aves NW (34th-Garfield Sts) 537.6200, recorded information 364.6616

78 University Pastry Shop Traditional shortening-laden cakes and cookies and homemade ice cream, in flavors like fresh peach and strawberry. ♦ Tu-Sa 8AM-6PM; Su 8AM-1PM. 3234 Wisconsin Ave NW (Macomb St-Woodley Rd) 966.5218

78 Zebra Room ★$ After a quarter-century, the Zebra Room still packs in families and softball teams on Tuesdays and Thursdays, when its thin-crust pizza is half price. There's an open-air patio for warm-weather dining. ♦ Pizza ♦ M-Sa 8AM-2AM; Su 9AM-midnight. 3238 Wisconsin Ave NW (Macomb St-Woodley Rd) 362.8307

79 Thai Flavor ★★$ This quiet neighborhood restaurant showcases subtly spiced Thai classics; all are garnished with carved vegetables and graciously served. When it's warm, eat in the sidewalk café. Carry-out service. ♦ Thai ♦ M-Sa 11:30AM-midnight; Su 5PM-midnight.

Georgetown/Upper Northwest

3709 Macomb St NW (Wisconsin-Idaho Aves) 966.0200

80 Rosedale (1793, Uriah Forrest) A genteel and breezy clapboard house, built as a country home before the city grew out to surround it. Private residence. ♦ 3501 Newark St NW (34th-36th Sts)

81 Winthrop Faulkner Houses (1964, Winthrop Faulkner) Three mid 20th-century houses that fit into their surroundings by using the vernacular of their older neighbors very effectively. Private residence. ♦ 3530 Ordway St NW (35th-36th Sts)

82 Friends School Administration Building (The Highlands) (1822, Charles Joseph Nourse) Built as a country home, this stone Georgian house features unorthodox but handsome square columns that were not part of the original design. Private grounds. ♦ 3825 Wisconsin Ave NW (Rodman-Quebec Sts)

83 Glover-Archbold Park When you tire of the bustle and cold monumental marble of the capital, this is the most perfect escape: a deliciously unkempt 183 acres where you'll be just another member of the wildlife that finds sanctuary here. Paths wind through the park, crossing Foundry Beach creek. A good place for bird-watching and picnicking. The 3.6-mile nature trail is smooth enough for jogging. ♦ C&O Canal Towpath-Upton St NW (39th-42nd Sts) 426.6829

84 Sutton Place Gourmet Washington is a comprehensive, one-stop food store that has prime meats (the aged filets are unmatched), freshly baked pastries and breads, produce from around the world, cheeses, wines, fresh seafood, and prepared entrees ready to take home and serve. Outrageously expensive. ♦ M-Sa 9AM-9PM; Su 9AM-8PM. 3201 New Mexico Ave NW (Klingle-Lowell Sts) 363.5800. Also at: 10323 Old Georgetown Rd, Bethesda MD. 564.3100; 600 Franklin St, Alexandria VA. 549.6611

85 Foxhall Square Mall An indoor mall with 2 dozen small shops, including **Just So** (fancy children's clothing), **New Conceptions** (designer maternity wear), and **Tree Top Toys**. ♦ 3301 New Mexico Ave NW (Macomb-Lowell Sts) 363.0027

Within Foxhall Square Mall:

Jackie Chalkey Fine Crafts has a dual personality—part fine handcraft shop, part high-fashion store—carrying signed porcelains, earthenware, metal collage jewelry, and exquisite knitwear, all priced as art. A sweater can sell for over a thousand dollars! ♦ M-Sa 10AM-5:30PM. 686.8884. Also at: 1455 Pennsylvania Ave NW. 638.3060

86 Battery Kemble Park Named after **Gouvernor Kemble**, a former president of West Point Foundry in Cold Spring NY, this green pocket is ideal for summer picnics and Frisbee tosses. In winter, it's ideal sledding territory. The jogging path connects south to the C&O Canal Towpath. A small cannon battery, part of the capital's chain of Civil War defenses, is preserved by the **National Park Service**. Cars enter via Chain Bridge Rd off MacArthur Blvd NW. ♦ C&O Canal-Foxhall Rds NW (Chain Bridge Rd-49th St) 426.6829

87 Listrani's ★$ A storefront café featuring good pizzas and pastas; free home delivery within a limited area. No liquor license. ♦ Italian ♦ M-Th, Su 11AM-10PM; F-Sa 11AM-11PM. 5100 MacArthur Boulevard NW (Dana-Edmunds Pls) 363.0619

88 The American University One of the area's leading educational and cultural forces, Methodist-affiliated AU was incorporated in 1893 by an act of Congress. Among the colleges attended by the university's 11,000 students are arts and sciences, law, n ursing, and public and international affairs. FM radio station **WAMU** broadcasts **National Public Radio**, bluegrass, and locally produced public affairs programs. **Hurst Hall**, the oldest building on the 77-acre campus, dates to 1896. The public is welcome at many of the university's activities, including movies at the **Wechsler Theater**, lectures at **Gaston Hall**, and concerts in the **New Lecture Hall**, where the **Opera Theater of Washington** makes its home. **Watkins Art Gallery** hosts undergraduate and graduate exhibitions. ♦ Guided campus tours by appointment. 4400 Massachusetts NW (Nebraska Ave) 686.2000, Wechsler Theater 483.5825, New Lecture Hall 483.5825, Watkins Art Gallery 885.6000, Gaston Hall 532.5972

89 Caspian Tea Room ★$$ An elegant Persian haunt squirreled away in a Spring Valley office building, featuring lamb stews and eggplant, as well as standards like pasta. Turkish coffee and pastries for dessert. ♦ Persian ♦ M-Sa 9AM-10PM. 4801 Massachusetts Ave NW (48th-Yuma Sts) 244.6363

90 Roche Bobois Furniture for lounge lizards and other well-heeled, tasteful types. ♦ Tu-Sa 10AM-6PM. 4200 Wisconsin Ave NW (Van Ness-Warren Sts) Metro stop: Tenleytown. 966.4490

90 Sansar An American crafts furniture gallery with a sprinkling of Asian artifacts such as Indonesian carvings. ♦ Tu,Th-Sa 10AM-6PM; W 10AM-8PM. 4200 Wisconsin Ave NW (Van Ness-Warren Sts) Metro stop: Tenleytown. 244.4448

90 Armand's Chicago Pizzeria ★★$ Armand's serves inch-thick Chicago-style pies, as well as a popular all-you-can-eat lunch. Free delivery. ♦ Pizza ♦ M-Th, Su 11:30AM-midnight; F-Sa 11:30AM-2AM. 4231 Wisconsin Ave NW (Van Ness Ave) Metro stop: Tenleytown. 686.9450. Also at: 226 Massachusetts Ave NE. 547.6600; 4400 Massachusetts Ave NW. 966.4800

91 Dancing Crab ★★★$$ Crabs, crabs, and more crabs. Grab a mallet and a pitcher of beer, and go to it. Dress in keeping with the casual atmosphere—the tablecloths are brown paper; the napkins, paper towels. Come hungry. ♦ Seafood ♦ M-Th 11AM-11PM; F-Sa 11AM-midnight; Su 10:30AM-11:30PM. 4611 Wisconsin Ave NW (Brandywine St) Reservations recommended. Metro stop: Tenleytown. 244.1882

91 Dona Flor ★$$ Brazilian specialities, including seafood cooked with coconut milk and palm oil, and feijoada, the national dish—a sturdy stew of black beans, pork, and sausage. ♦ Brazilian ♦ M-F 11:30AM-11:30PM; Sa-Su noon-11:30PM. 4615 41st St NW (Brandywine St-Wisconsin Ave) Metro stop: Tenleytown. 537.0404

92 Yosaku ★$$ Sushi, tempura, and other Japanese favorites in an airy dining room and sidewalk café. ♦ Japanese ♦ M-Th 11:30AM-2:30PM, 5:30-11PM; F 11:30AM-2:30PM, 5:30PM-midnight; Sa 5:30PM-midnight; Su 5:30-11PM. 4712 Wisconsin Ave NW (Chesapeake-Ellicott Sts) Metro stop: Tenleytown. 363.4453

93 El Tamarindo ★$ Zero atmosphere but hearty El Salvadoran-style enchiladas, tacos, and the usual variations on the theme, at rock-bottom prices. ♦ El Salvadoran ♦ M-Th, Su 11AM-1:30AM; F-Sa 11AM-2:30AM. 4910 Wisconsin Ave NW (Fessenden-Ellicott Sts) Metro stop: Tenleytown. 244.8888. Also at: 1785 Florida Ave NW. 328.3660

Teddy Roosevelt's favorite pastime in Washington was taking strenuous walks, "perhaps down Rock Creek, which was then as wild as a stream in the White Mountains."

93 Floriana Ristorante ★$ A neighborhood trattoria specializing in traditional pastas and meat dishes. ♦ Italian ♦ M-F 11:30AM-2:30PM, 5-11PM; Sa 5-11PM; Su 5-10PM. 4936 Wisconsin Ave NW (Fessenden-Ellicott Sts) Reservations required F-Sa. Metro stop: Tenleytown. 362.9009

94 Hamburger Hamlet ★$ Dressed-up burgers in a casual atmosphere, as well as omelets, nachos, and other fun foods. Crayons are provided for drawing on the paper tablecloths. When it's warm, eat in the sidewalk café. ♦ American ♦ M-Th 11:30AM-10PM; F-Sa 11:30AM-midnight; Su noon-9:30PM. 5225 Wisconsin Ave NW (Jenifer-Ingomar Sts) Metro stop: Friendship Hts. 244.2037. Also at: 3112 M St NW. 965.6970; 10400 Old Georgetown Rd, Bethesda MD. 897.5350

MAZZA
GALLERIE

95 Mazza Gallerie A high-fashion indoor mall anchored by **Neiman-Marcus**. Among the more than 50 other stores are **Raleighs** for men's and women's clothing; **The Forgotten Woman**, for fashionable large sizes; **F.A.O. Schwarz**; **Williams-Sonoma** for fine housewares; **Pierre Deux**, for country-French fabrics and furnishings; **Jane Wilner**, for exquisite linens, and **Kron Chocolatier**. Movie theaters are on the lower level, as is **McDonald's**. ♦ M F 10AM-

Georgetown/Upper Northwest

9PM; Sa 10AM-6PM; Su noon-5PM. 5300 Wisconsin Ave NW (Western Ave-Jenifer St) Metro stop: Friendship Hts. 966.6114

Within Mazza Gallerie:

Pleasant Peasant ★$$ The pretty dining room features new American fare like grilled swordfish and jumbo portions of homemade cakes, tarts, and ice cream desserts. ♦ American ♦ M-Th, Su 11:30AM-3PM, 5:30-11PM; F-Sa 11:30AM-3PM, 5:30PM-midnight. 364.2500

96 Harriet Kassman Inc. European and American designer clothing for women by **Genny**, **Byblos**, **Norma Walters**, and **Calvin Klein**. ♦ M-W, F-Sa 10AM-6PM; Th 10AM-9PM. 4400 Jenifer St NW (Western Ave-44th St) Metro stop: Friendship Hts. 363.1870. Also at: 1425 Pennsylvania Ave NW. 393.2276

97 Lord & Taylor The DC branch of the traditional New York department store carries high-quality women's and men's clothing, shoes, linens, china, and accessories. Two-hour free parking for customers. ♦ M-F 10AM-9:30PM; Sa 10AM-6PM; Su noon-5PM. 5225 Western Ave NW (Jenifer St-44th St) Metro stop: Friendship Hts. 362.9600. Also at: Fair Oaks Mall, Fairfax VA. 691.0100; White Flint Mall, Bethesda MD. 770.9000

The real **Uncle Tom's Cabin** is thought to have been part of what is now a private home on Old Georgetown Rd in Montgomery County MD.

98 Magruder's Bedlam masquerading as a supermarket. Customers claw through the narrow aisles to stock up on the fantastic bargains on the daily specials in the produce and meat departments. Parking in the rear. ♦ M-W 8AM-8PM; Th-F 8AM-9PM; Sa 7AM-8PM; Su 9AM-6PM. 5626 Connecticut Ave NW (McKinley St-Chevy Chase Circle) Metro stop: Friendship Hts. 244.7800. Also at: 6936 Braddock Rd, Annandale VA. 703/941.8864; 170 Halpine Rd, Rockville MD. 301/881.1181

99 Bread and Chocolate ★$ A tearoom featuring soups, salads, and French-influenced entrees, as well as a carry-out bakery. Good for after-movie Sacher torte binges. ♦ French-American ♦ M-Th 7AM-9PM; F-Sa 7AM-11PM; Su 8AM-7PM. 5542 Connecticut Ave NW (Morrison-McKinley Sts) 966.7413. Also at: 4200 Wisconsin Ave NW. 363.3744; 3251 Prospect St NW. 338.5722; 666 Pennsylvania Ave SE. 547.2861

99 American City Diner ★$ This re-creation of a 1950s' diner is authentic down to the Coke machine, but the food is nostalgic only if your mother specialized in hockey-puck burgers and thin milkshakes. No liquor license. ♦ American ♦ 24 hours. 5532 Connecticut Ave NW (Morrison-McKinley Sts) 244.1949

99 The Cheshire Cat Children's Bookstore Former schoolteachers are the minds behind this inviting bookstore, which in addition to books features records, maps, and coloring

Georgetown/Upper Northwest

books. A play area occupies small children while their parents browse. Authors visit in the spring and fall. ♦ M-Sa 9:30AM-5:30PM. 5512 Connecticut Ave NW (Livingston St) 244.3956

99 Swiss Cafe ★★$$ Fondue, spaetzle, and other typically tame fare from the mid Continent serves as a cover for longtime piano bar artist **Ken Foy**, who holds forth in the **Geneva Lounge**. ♦ Swiss ♦ Tu-Sa 5-11PM. 5510 Connecticut Ave NW (Livingston-Morrison Sts) 966.7600

100 Politics & Prose This full-service bookstore specializes in the books and interests of local authors, be it public policy or fiction. Great book-signing parties. ♦ M-Sa 10AM-10PM; Su 11AM-6PM. 5010 Connecticut Ave NW (Nebraska Ave-Fessenden St) 364.1919

101 Hillwood There are at least 4 good reasons to visit the estate of the late **Marjorie Merriweather Post**, cereal heiress and longtime cornerstone of DC—and American—society. The house, a 40-room Georgian mansion of red brick, dates from the 1920s, when it was a showpiece of Gatsbyan formality. It was purchased by Post in 1955, and under her direction Hillwood surpassed its earlier opulence. The heiress' staff included a chef, a butler, a footman, and a resident curator. The latter is a clue to the estate's second raison d'être: it is every bit a museum, displaying an excellent and eccentric collection of French and Imperial Russian art. Included are gilded icons and ecclesiastical vestments, fine portraiture and folk art, Fabergé eggs, gold and silver craftsmanship, and fine porcelain—including the royal service of **Catherine the Great**. (Post had traveled with one of her husbands, the first ambassador to the Soviet Union following the Revolution.) Fine French furniture and tapestries fill the house.

Outside, on the 25-acre estate, are formal Japanese and French gardens, a 1-room Russian summerhouse (dacha), and a **Rose Garden**. **Perry Wheeler** created the gardens—

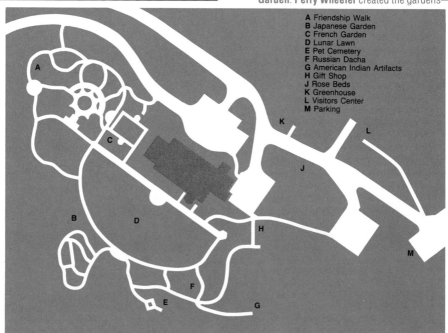

A Friendship Walk
B Japanese Garden
C French Garden
D Lunar Lawn
E Pet Cemetery
F Russian Dacha
G American Indian Artifacts
H Gift Shop
J Rose Beds
K Greenhouse
L Visitors Center
M Parking

it was he who designed that more famous Rose Garden at the White House—which exhibit over 3500 varieties of flora. Within the greenhouse alone are over 5000 kinds of orchids. Finally, to the southeast, over the treetops of Rock Creek Park, is a stunning view of the Washington Monument. A 2-hour tour is offered, featuring a film on the history of Hillwood narrated by Post's daughter, **Dina Merrill**. Reservations must be made several weeks in advance, and children under 12 are not allowed on the tour. An on-the-premises café serves light fare and a proper tea with scones. ♦ Admission. Tours M, W-Sa 9, 10:30AM, noon, 1:30PM. Café M, W-Sa 10:30AM-3PM. 4155 Linnean Ave NW (Tilden St) Metro stop: Van Ness/UDC. 686.5807&

102 Kitchen Bazaar The big fix for cooking junkies, with china, bakeware, utensils, books, gadgets, appliances, and plenty of advice. ♦ M-W, Sa 10AM-6PM; Th-F 10AM-9PM; Su noon-5PM. 4401 Connecticut Ave NW (Van Ness-Albemarle Sts) 244.1550

103 University of the District of Columbia Formed in 1976 by the merger of 3 colleges, UDC is a commuter school: more than 2/3 of its 14,000 students attend part-time. The 10-building complex at the urban Van Ness campus houses the colleges of liberal arts, engineering, and life sciences, as well as a 1000-seat auditorium, a physical activities center, outdoor tennis courts, an FM radio station (**WDCU**), and an athletic field. ♦ 4200 Connecticut Ave NW (Van Ness-Uma Sts) Metro stop: Van Ness/UDC. 282.7300

104 Kuwaiti Embassy, Cultural Division (1982, Skidmore, Owings & Merrill) This gracefully balanced cube artfully plays with the Islamic motif of rotated squares. Note how the square tinted windows are cut diagonally by steel tubes. ♦ 3500 International Dr NW (Tilden-Van Ness Sts) Metro stop: Van Ness/UDC. 364.2100

105 The Intelsat Building (1985, John Andrews International Pty. Ltd.) A silvery spaceship, improbably located on a bustling commercial strip, houses the United Nations of satellite communications. Octagonal office "pods," protected from the sun by louvers of photogray glass, and cylindrical stair towers faced in glass brick are clustered around 4 top-lit atria. John Andrews laid out the complex with the local firm of **VVKF** to create an ideal, energy-efficient working environment. Existing trees were preserved, but Intelsat makes no attempt to hide itself from public gaze. Tours available. ♦ Tours: Tu 10AM: Th 3PM. 3400 International Dr NW (Tilden-Van Ness Sts) Metro stop: Van Ness/UDC. 944.6800, tours 944.7841

106 Royal Warrant ★★$ A pianist works the vinyl-padded piano bar Thursday through Saturday nights for patrons who remember the first time martinis were fashionable. (A guitarist is featured Tuesdays and Wednesdays.) Music nightly from 9PM; food until midnight. ♦ American ♦ M-Th 11:30AM-2AM; F-Sa 11:30AM-3AM; Su noon-8PM. 4201 Connecticut Ave NW (Van Ness-Albemarle Sts) Metro stop: Van Ness/UDC. 244.3200

107 Brazilian-American Cultural Institute For the authentic Carioca spirit, or a taste of Bahia, this is the place: live music, the best new artists, films, samba and language lessons, and a tropical salad mixed by the ever-inventive **Dr. José Neistein**. ♦ M-F 8AM-9PM. 4103 Connecticut Ave NW (Upton-Van Ness Sts) Metro stop: Van Ness/UDC. 362.8334

108 Sedgwick Garden (1931, Mihran Mesrobian) Highlight of the subdued Art Deco apartment blocks along this once fashionable stretch of Connecticut Ave. Rich detailing animates the expanses of brick, and there is a splendid zigzagged porte-cochere. ♦ 3726 Connecticut Ave NW (Rodman-Sedgwick Sts) Metro stop: Cleveland Park

109 Rock Creek Park In 1890, **President Benjamin Harrison** signed Congress' million-dollar endowment of Rock Creek Park, mandating the preservation of this rugged 1700-acre stretch, once the home of the Algonquin Indians. Over the centuries it has nurtured bear,

Georgetown/Upper Northwest

elk, and even bison; early settlers tapped the creek's swift waters to power their grist- and sawmills. Later, the woodlands allowed a moment of escape for such harried leaders as **John Quincy Adams** and **Teddy Roosevelt**. The park still stubbornly maintains its sense of ruggedness as it winds for 4 miles along Rock Creek. Wildlife and wildflowers are abundant here. You can still see the occasional deer and perhaps even a fox. Nature lovers haunt the place, searching for thrushes, chickadees, and ducks. **Fort DeRussy**, a link in the capital's chain of defenses against the Confederate Army, is still in evidence. (If all this seems too idyllic, it is. Rock Creek's waters are sour with pollution, and many of the fish have died. Fishing, swimming, and wading are prohibited.)

Rock Creek Park's bike/foot path begins in West Potomac Park just below the Kennedy Center and winds along the creek and beside park roads. Sites near the route include the **Watergate** and the **National Zoo**, where the hilly terrain is an especially pleasant challenge for running enthusiasts. The path ends just north of the **Old Pierce Mill** at the city's outskirts, a 9-mile trek from the Mall. ♦ Potomac Park-Needwood Rd NW (Oregon-Colorado Aves) Park information 426.6828

Within Rock Creek Park:

Rock Creek Nature Center is the place to orient yourself to the park. This **National Park**

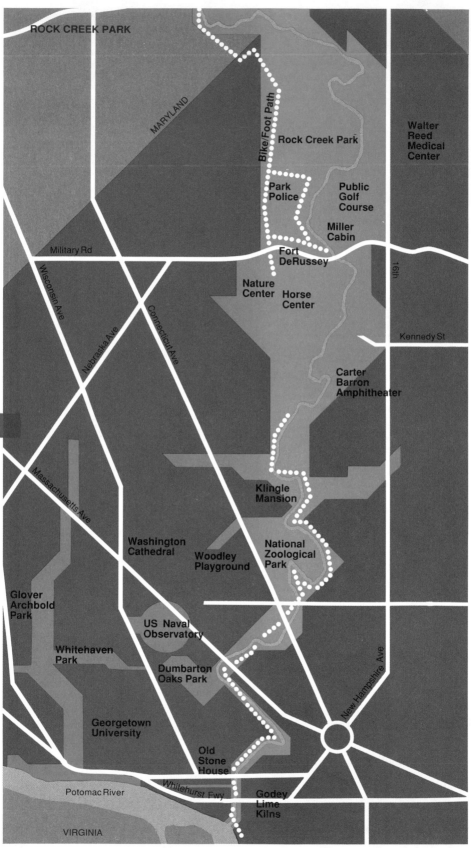

ROCK CREEK PARK

Rock Creek Park

Walter Reed Medical Center

Bike/Foot Path

MARYLAND

Park Police

Public Golf Course

Miller Cabin

Military Rd

Fort DeRussey

Nature Center

Horse Center

16th

Kennedy St

Wisconsin Ave

Nebraska Ave

Connecticut Ave

Carter Barron Amphitheater

Klingle Mansion

Massachusetts Ave

Washington Cathedral

Woodley Playground

National Zoological Park

Glover Archbold Park

US Naval Observatory

Whitehaven Park

Dumbarton Oaks Park

New Hampshire Ave

Georgetown University

Old Stone House

Potomac River

Whitehurst Fwy

Godey Lime Kilns

VIRGINIA

Service is especially great for kids, who can view wild-animal exhibitions or watch the workings of a beehive behind glass. There are nature films, planetarium shows, and guided hikes. ♦ Daily 9AM-5PM. 5200 Glover Rd NW (Oregon Ave) 426.6829

Biking The bicycle path runs from the Lincoln Memorial into Maryland, and connects via the Memorial Bridge to the Mount Vernon bike trail in Virginia. Beach Drive between Military and Broad Branch roads is closed to cars from 7AM Saturday until 7PM Sunday and on holidays.

Golf The **Rock Creek Golf Course**, an 18-hole public course with a clubhouse, can be reached from 16th and Rittenhouse Sts NW. Club and cart rental, lockers, and snack bar. ♦ Daily dawn-dusk. 882.7332

Picnicking There are 30 picnic areas scattered throughout the park for groups of up to 100. Advance reservations are required year-round. ♦ 673.7646

Playgrounds The large playing field at 16th and Kennedy Sts NW includes soccer, football, volleyball, and field hockey areas. Some can be reserved through the DC Department of Recreation. ♦ 673.7646

Riding The **Rock Creek Park Horse Center**, located near the Nature Center, offers guided trail rides. On weekends, reserve a place in advance by leaving a deposit in person. Riding lessons include special classes for the disabled. Children under 12 may not ride. ♦ Fee. Trail rides: Tu-F 3, 4:30PM; Sa noon, 1:30, 3, 4:30PM (additional ride at 6PM, Memorial Day-Labor Day); Su 1:30, 3, 4:30PM. 5100 Glover Rd. 362.0117

Tennis The **Washington Tennis Center** at 16th and Kennedy Sts NW features 17 soft-surface and 5 hard-surface courts, open April through November. Reservations must be made in person through **Guest Services Inc.** (722.5949). Six soft-surface courts off Park Rd, just east of Pierce Mill, are open May through September. Go to the courts to make reservations in person through **Washington Area Tennis Patrons** (328.3636).

110 Vace A real Italian deli, with fantastic fresh pastas and sauces, takeout pizzas, cheeses, and salamis. All you need is the wine. ♦ M-W, Sa 9AM-8PM; Th-F 9AM-9PM. 3504 Connecticut Ave NW (Ordway-Porter Sts) Metro stop: Cleveland Park. 363.1999

110 Ivy's Place ★$ Indonesian and Thai specialties like stuffed squid, shrimp with broccoli, and wonton soup. A good place for a bite after a movie at the nearby Cineplex Odeon and Uptown Theater. ♦ Indonesian/Thai ♦ M-Sa 11:30AM-midnight; Su 3:30PM-midnight. 3520 Connecticut Ave NW (Porter St) Metro stop: Cleveland Park. 363.7802

111 Club Soda Dancing to rock 'n' roll oldies, with live music Wednesday through Saturday, deejays the other nights of the week. ♦ Cover F-Sa. M-Th, Su 4PM-2AM; F-Sa noon-3AM. 3433 Connecticut Ave NW (Macomb-Ordway Sts) Metro stop: Cleveland Park. 244.3189

111 Yes! The Natural Gourmet The Georgetown stalwart has moved to Upper Northwest, but still offers bulk grains and spices, fresh milk and yogurt, and organic toiletries. Yes, this is related to **Yes! Bookshop**, page122. ♦ M-F 9AM-9PM; Sa 9AM-7PM. 3425 Connecticut Ave NW (Macomb-Ordway Sts) Metro stop: Cleveland Park. 363.1559

111 Roma Raw Bar ★$ Raw mollusks and simple seafood dishes in a tiny wood-paneled bar. Watch the tropical fish or the football games on TV. ♦ Seafood ♦ Daily 5PM-midnight. 3419 Connecticut Ave NW (Macomb-Ordway Sts) Metro stop: Cleveland Park. 363.6611

112 Cineplex Odeon and Uptown Theater One of the last places in town to see a big movie on a big screen. ♦ 3426 Connecticut Ave NW (Ordway St) Metro stop: Cleveland Park. 966.5400. Also at: 4000 Wisconsin Ave. 244.0880

112 Ireland's Four Provinces ★$ The Gaelic music, from local and bona fide Irish musicians, is the big draw, but don't overlook the Harp on tap, corned beef and cabbage, and other authentic touches in this cavernous club. There's a sidewalk café for warm-weather dining. ♦ Irish ♦ M-Th, Su 5PM-2AM; F-Sa 5PM-3AM. 3412 Connecticut Ave NW (Newark-Ordway Sts) Metro stop: Cleveland Park. 244.0860

Georgetown/Upper Northwest

113 Gallagher's Pub ★$ A friendly neighborhood pub with burgers, Irish stew, Guinness, and local bands playing folk, bluegrass, and Irish music Wednesday through Saturday. Open mike Sunday and Monday. ♦ Irish/American ♦ M-Th 4PM-2AM; F 4PM-3AM; Sa noon-3AM; Su noon-2AM. 3319 Connecticut Ave NW (Macomb-Ordway Sts) Metro stop: Cleveland Park. 686.9189

114 The National Zoological Park, also called the **National Zoo**, sprawls over 163 acres, allowing plenty of room for its 4000 animals.

Established in 1889 under the direction of the **Smithsonian Institution**, the zoo moved from the Washington Mall to Rock Creek Valley when **Samuel Pierpont Langley**, the Smithsonian's third secretary, persuaded Congress to provide funds to establish a site to protect the American bison from extinction.

When you enter the zoo, follow **Olmsted Walk**, the main pedestrian pathway. Along the walk you'll find the new **Gibbon Exhibit**, the **Great Ape House**, and new invertebrate exhibitions. A circular walkway overlooks 3 large outdoor yards for a close-up view of the great cats. The area features full-maned Atlas lions and rare blue-eyed white tigers, plus leopards and cheetahs. All of the zoo's tigers are descendants of **Mohini**, a white tiger brought from India in 1960.

At least one dozen species call the **Monkey House** home, including the Celebes crested

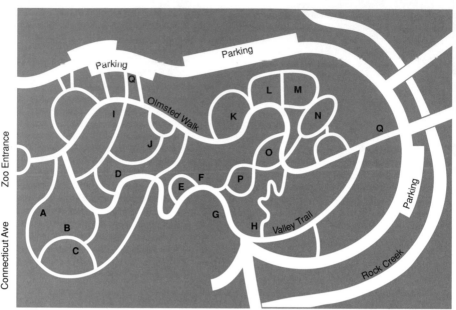

A Hoofed Animals	**J** Elephants & Giraffes
B Great Flight Cage	**K** Great Ape House
C Bird House	**L** Reptile House
D Birds	**M** Monkey House
E Beavers & Otters	**N** Lion-Tiger Hill
F Wolves	**O** Monkey Island
G Seals & Sea Lions	**P** Bears
H Pumas & Jaguars	**Q** Information & Baby
I Pandas & Panda Cafe	Strollers

Georgetown/Upper Northwest

macaques, and the endangered lion-tailed macaques from India.

In the **Reptile House**, a compound heating system warms some of the collection's 91 species of amphibians and reptiles, from the smallest snakes to the venomous king cobras, giant pythons, and anacondas.

Designed in 1931 by **Albert Harris**, the building is an Italian-Romanesque-style structure. Its stone corbels are carved with intricate reptilian heads and its columns rest on carved stone turtles.

Outside the Reptile House, 550-pound Aldabra tortoises wander in the summer months. Crocodiles bathe in crocodile pools—indoors in winter, outdoors in summer. Also watch for the giant Komodo dragon lizards and alligators.

The **Great Ape House** gives you and the apes a perfect look at one another. Four-hundred-pound lowland gorillas watch visitors from indoors and out. The building, specially designed for apes, features sculptured steel-frame trees.

All of the Great Ape House orangutans were born in zoos. Their housing is carefully constructed, as orangutans like to unbolt and take things apart.

The **Small Mammal House**'s exotic creatures include meercats; golden lion tamarins, small blond monkeylike creatures; the foxlike fennecs; and tiny elephant shrews.

The **Elephant House** guides you to elephants, hippos, rhinoceroses, and giraffes. Favorites include the versatile-trunked Asiatic elephant and the African elephant with its large ears.

By far the most popular exhibition is the 2 giant pandas, **Ling-Ling** (*Cute Little Girl*) and **Hsing-Hsing** (*Bright Star*), a gift from the People's Republic of China in 1972. Repeated attempts to breed the pair have been disappointing: 4 tiny cubs were either stillborn or died within a few days of birth. The pandas spend most of their time in separate enclosures, waking only occasionally to gnaw on bamboo. Even asleep, they're cute.

The recently installed **Invertebrate Exhibit**, behind the reptile building, includes octopuses, giant crabs, cuttlefish, spiders, and microscopic organisms.

At the upper west end of the zoo roam kangaroos, antelopes, zebras, and deer. The **Bird House** has over 1000 birds comprising 155 species, from the seldom seen kiwi to the endangered Bali mynah. Special features include the **Indoor Flight Room** and the outdoor **Great Flight Exhibit**.

Along the **Valley Trail** are otters, gray seals, sea lions, beavers, and timber wolves. Nearby is **Smoky Bear II**, the model for firefighters' Smokey the Bear. His legend began in 1950, when a small badly burned black bear club was rescued and brought to the zoo.

Zoo centers treat visitors to zoology lessons at **Zoolab** in the **Education Building**, **Herplab** in the **Reptile Building**, and **Birdlab** in the **Bird House**. The zoo offers free films, lectures, slide shows, and wildlife films in the Education Building auditorium.

The zoo also runs a 3100-acre preserve near Front Royal VA for the study of endangered species.

Parking accessible from Connecticut Ave NW and Beach Drive in Rock Creek Park. Lots fill by

10AM on busy days, and parking on nearby side streets is limited.

The zoo is also accessible from the bike path in Rock Creek Park. No bicycle riding allowed within the zoo. Gifts are available at the **Panda Gift Shop**, the **Mane Gift Shop**, the **Bookstore/Gallery**, and the **Seal Shop**. ♦ Grounds: daily 8AM-6PM, Jan-Apr, Sep 16-Dec; daily 8AM-8PM, May-Sept 15. Buildings: daily 9AM-4:30PM, Jan-Apr, Sep 16-Dec; daily 9AM-6PM, May-Sept 15. Main entrance at 3000 block of Connecticut Ave NW (Cathedral Ave) Metro stop: Woodley Park/Zoo. 673.4800 &

115 Mrs. Simpson's ★★★$$$ A jewel box of a dining room, wittily decorated in honor of the **Duchess of Windsor** and featuring a frequently changing menu of new American dishes, including renditions of grilled chicken and shrimp, and a lemon mousse to die for. ♦ American ♦ M-Sa 5:30-10PM; Su 10:30AM-2:30PM, 5:30-10PM. 2915 Connecticut Ave NW (Cathedral Ave-National Zoo) Reservations recommended. Metro stop: Woodley Park/Zoo. 332.8300

116 Sheraton Washington Hotel $$$ Almost a city in itself, this vast hotel (1505 rooms) is usually filled with intown businesspeople taking advantage of the exhibition, meeting, banquet, and ball rooms. Escapes from the workaday world include a game room, a huge outdoor swimming pool (open May through September), beauty and barber shops, and lounges. Culinary pleasures range from the pies, cookies, and European-style pastries at **Wolfgang's Pastry Shop** to American-style dining at **Americus**. Amenities include multilingual concierge service, nonsmoking rooms, exercise facilities, a post office, and a gift shop/newsstand. Children under 18 stay free. ♦ 2660 Woodley Rd NW (Connecticut Ave-29th St) Metro stop: Woodley Park/Zoo. 328.2000; 800/325.3535; fax 234.0015

117 Tandoor ★★$$ Juicy grilled lamb and chicken and other refined Indian dishes in a dramatic setting. ♦ Indian ♦ M-F 11AM-10:30PM; Sa 5:30-10:30PM; Su 5:30-10PM. 2623 Connecticut Ave NW (Calvert-Garfield Sts) Reservations recommended. Metro stop: Woodley Park/Zoo. 483.1115

117 Captain Day's ★★$ This reasonable little seafood restaurant has left its Downtown alley and come uptown. Fresh lobster, crabcakes, and fritto misto as well as seafood pasta dishes. ♦ Seafood ♦ M-F 11:30AM-3:30PM, 5-11PM; Sa-Su 5-11PM. 2619 Connecticut Ave NW (Calvert-Garfield Sts) Metro stop: Woodley Park/Zoo. 234.8445

117 Khyber Pass ★$ An unpretentious introduction to Afghan food, including ravioli-like *aushak* (a dish made of noodles, green onions, yogurt, and meat sauce), lemony chicken kabobs, and flatbread. ♦ Afghan ♦ M-Su 5:30-11PM. 2309 Calvert St NW (Connecticut Ave-Woodley Pl) Metro stop: Woodley Park/Zoo. 234.4632

| **Restaurants**: Red | **Hotels**: Blue |
| **Shops/Parks**: Green | **Sights/Culture**: Black |

118 Thai Taste ★★$$ An intricate menu, an attentive, extremely helpful staff, and a revamped Art Deco interior. Try duckling with mixed vegetables, fish cakes, or charcoal-grilled marinated fish. ♦ Thai ♦ M-Th 11:30AM-10:30PM; F-Sa 11:30AM-11PM; Su 5-10:30PM. 2606 Connecticut Ave NW (Calvert-Garfield Sts) Metro stop: Woodley Park/Zoo. 387.8876

118 New Heights ★★$$$ Nouvelle American cuisine in the food-as-art school—braided fish, for example. Unusual combinations like foie gras crowned with lentils and spinach can be sensational or, occasionally, disastrous. The room overlooking Rock Creek, with its American crafts furniture, is a knockout. ♦ American ♦ M-Th 11:30AM-3PM, 5:30-10:30PM; F 11:30AM-3PM, 5:30-11:30PM; Sa 5:30-10:30PM; Su 11AM-3PM, 5:30-10:30PM. 2317 Calvert St NW (Connecticut Ave-24th St) Reservations recommended. Metro stop: Woodley Park/Zoo. 234.4410

119 Omni Shoreham Hotel $$$ (1929, Harry Bralove) A luxurious hotel overlooking the beautiful woods of Rock Creek Park. The historic Shoreham has hosted many presidential inaugurations. **President Truman** held his private poker games in room D-406. The hotel's ambiance has attracted such luminaries as **Clark Gable**, **Rudy Vallee**, **Marilyn Monroe**, and **Gary Cooper**. The **New Leaf** restaurant serves French and American cui-

Georgetown/Upper Northwest

sines. The **Marquee Lounge** offers Big Band sounds in an Art Deco setting. Try the elegant Sunday brunch featuring champagne and piano music in the **Garden Court**. Amenities include nonsmoking rooms, limousine and babysitting services, tennis courts, and an outdoor pool. Tennis and Swim Club memberships are available to residents. Children under 18 stay free. ♦ Deluxe ♦ 2500 Calvert St NW (Connecticut Ave-28th St) Metro stop: Woodley Park/Zoo. 234.0700, 800/THE OMNI; fax 234.0700 ext 3117 &

"Government, even in its best state, is but a necessary evil; in its worst state, an intolerable one."

Thomas Paine
Common Sense

"The ladies from Georgetown and in the 'city' have many of them visited me. Yesterday I returned fifteen visits—but such a place as Georgetown! I felt all that Mrs. Cranch described when she was a resident there. It is the very dirtyest Hole I ever saw for a place of any trade or respectability of inhabitants. It is only one mile from me, but a quagmire after every rain. Here we are obliged to send daily for marketing. The Capitol is near two miles from us. As to roads, we shall make them by the frequent passing before winter! But I am determined to be satisfied and content, to say nothing of inconvenience, etc."

Abigail Adams
Letter to her sister, 21 November 1800

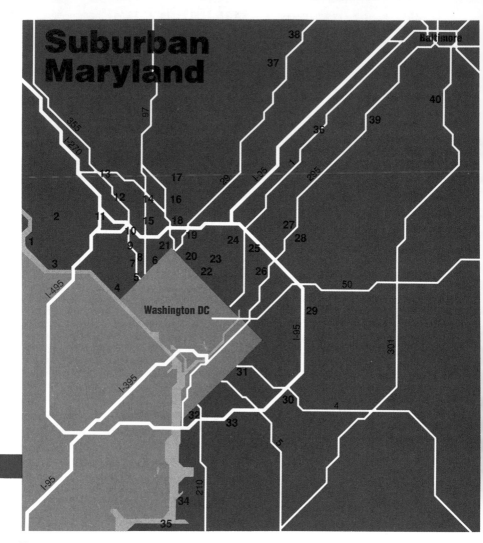

Montgomery County

In the last decade, Montgomery County has experienced an unprecedented surge in population and development. Downtown **Bethesda**, once a quaint local shopping district, has become a business destination in its own right. With the coming of Metrorail, up-county areas like **Gaithersburg** have been transformed from farmland to neighborhoods, and the **I-270** corridor has emerged as a high-technology center. Ethnically diverse **Silver Spring**, long neglected, is the next to undergo transformation—the extent of redevelopment remains a hot political topic. Still, there are little pockets of Montgomery County that retain something of its quiet past: **Glen Echo Park**, perhaps, or sleepy downtown **Rockville**. *Area code 301 unless otherwise indicated.*

1 C&O Canal National Historic Park offers scenic overviews of the **Great Falls of the Potomac**, as well as access to the 184-mile-long canal—great for walks and bicycling. Within the **Great Falls Tavern** (food and drinks are *not* served) is a tiny museum with photographs and artifacts of 19th-century life. Rides on the mule-drawn *Canal Clipper* (fee) are offered April through October. The **Billy Goat Trail**, along clifftops overlooking scenic **Mather Gorge**, is not for the timid. Operated by the **National Park Service**. ♦ Free. Daily dawn-dusk. 11710 MacArthur Blvd (Falls Rd) Potomac. 299.3613

2 Normandie Farm ★★$$ Traditional country-French cooking in a romantic, almost-rural setting. Normandie Farm is known for its popovers; other specialties include veal Oscar and poached salmon. ♦ French ♦ Tu-Th 11:30AM-2:30PM, 6-10PM, F-Sa 11:30AM-2:30PM, 6-11PM; Su 11AM-2PM, 5-9PM. 10710 Falls Rd (River Rd-Kentsdale Dr) Potomac. Reservations recommended. 983.8838

3 Old Angler's Inn ★$$$ The food never measures up to the decor, but it has far and away the most romantic fireplace in town. One of the specialties is tuna marinated in honey and peppercorns, then sautéed and served rare with a peppercorn butter sauce. There is an outdoor terrace for warm-weather dining. ♦ French/American ♦ Tu-Su noon-2:30PM, 6-10:30PM. 10801 MacArthur Blvd (Brickyard-Falls Rds) Potomac. Reservations required. 365.2425

4 Glen Echo Park Built in 1891 as the base of the *Chautauqua Movement*, Glen Echo is better known for its 70-year career as an amusement park. It's been a **National Park Service site** since 1971 and houses artists studios, classroom space, and a wonderful ballroom. ♦ Daily 10AM-5PM. 7300 MacArthur Blvd (Goldsboro Rd) Glen Echo. 492.6282

Within Glen Echo Park:

Clara Barton National Historic Site The last residence of the founder of the **American Red Cross**. In 1897, 86-year-old Clara Barton moved to the **Glen Echo House**, originally built as a warehouse for Red Cross supplies. After removing some of the 72 concealed closets, deep enough to store wheelchairs, the indefatigable Clara expanded the house to 36 rooms. Her personal effects and furniture remain as they were during the heroine's last years. Guided tours upon request. ♦ Free. Daily 10AM-5PM; last tour leaves 4:30PM. Closed federal holidays. 5801 Oxford Rd (MacArthur Blvd) 492.6245

5 Tila's ★★$$ Elegant Southwestern restaurant, an offshoot of Washingtonian **Clive Du Val**'s establishment in Houston, which presents innovative variations on traditional ingredients. Standouts include the black bean soup, roast pork with fresh bananas, fajitas, and grilled marinated chicken. ♦ Southwestern ♦ Daily 11:30AM-10PM. 2 Wisconsin Circle NW (Western Ave) Chevy Chase. Reservations recommended. 652.8452

6 Audubon Naturalist Society (1828, John Russell Pope) Located on 40 acres of wildlife sanctuary, the society makes its home in a Georgian mansion designed by the architect of the **Jefferson Memorial**. A $3/4$-mile nature trail leads around the estate, which is known as **Woodend**. Self-guided tours Monday through Saturday; on Sunday at 1PM, from mid April to mid May, a guided tour is offered. The bookshop is open daily. ♦ Free. Grounds daily dawn-dusk. Bookshop: M-W, F 10AM-5PM; Th 10AM-7PM; Sa 9AM-3PM; Su noon-5PM. 8940 Jones Mill Rd (Jones Bridge Rd-Woodhollows Dr) Chevy Chase. 652.9188

Bethesda

7 China Coral ★★$ This bustling restaurant specializes in seafood. Try China Coral Bird's Nest (lobster, king crab, shrimp, and scallops sautéed with fresh vegetables). Excellent dim sum. ♦ Chinese ♦ M-Th 11:30AM-10:30PM; F-Sa 11:30AM-11:30PM; Su 11:30AM-10PM. 6900 Wisconsin Ave (Bradley Blvd-Leland St) Reservations recommended F-Su. 656.1203

Restaurants: Red	**Hotels**: Blue
Shops/Parks: Green	**Sights/Culture**: Black

7 Bethesda Crab House ★★$$ Fresh, perfectly cooked crabs in a setting that focuses on the business at hand: the tables are covered with newspapers, and utensils consist of a wooden mallet and a small knife. If you don't want to go the all-you-can-eat route, feel free to order up to a dozen—jumbo or extra large. Be sure to call ahead—the crab supply can be limited—and arrive on time. ♦ Seafood ♦ M-Sa 9AM-midnight; Su 11AM-midnight. 4958 Bethesda Ave (Arlington Rd-Clarendon Dr) No credit cards. 652.9754

8 Johnny's ★★$$$ Supersleek restaurant shines with new American fare like sharp goat cheese-basil ravioli. Homemade pasta and creative entrees like boneless salmon wrapped in risotto and served in a puff pastry with coriander butter. ♦ American ♦ M-Th 11:30AM-3PM, 5:30-10:30PM; F-Sa 11:30AM-3PM, 5:30-11PM; Su 11AM-3PM, 5:30-10:30PM. 7200 Wisconsin Ave (Bethesda Ave) Reservations recommended. 654.8822

8 Lowen's Great selection of toys, art supplies, and children's books. An extra treat—the in-store ice-cream parlor! ♦ M-W, F-Sa 9:30AM-6PM; Th 9:30AM-9PM; Su noon-5PM. 7201 Wisconsin Ave (Willow Ln-Bethesda Ave) 652.1289

9 Windows of the East ★★$$ Well-prepared Vietnamese cuisine with French influences, in an elegant room. ♦ Vietnamese ♦ M-Th 11:30AM-2:30PM, 5:30-10PM; F 11:30AM-2:30PM, 5:30-10:30PM; Sa 5:30-10:30PM; Su 5:30-10PM. 4747 Elm St (Woodmont-Wisconsin Aves) Reservations recommended. 654.6444

9 China Gourmet of Bethesda ★★$$ A favorite among Bethesda's Sinophiles, who come to feast on exotics like lemon duck or crystal shrimp, Hong Kong-style. ♦ Chinese ♦ M-Th, Su 10:30AM-10:30PM; F-Sa 10:30AM-11:30PM. 4711 Montgomery Ln (Wisconsin Ave-Arlington Rd) 657.4665

9 Hyatt Regency Bethesda $$ A large hotel (380 rooms) with an indoor pool, workout area, and 2 restaurants, the **Plaza Cafe** and **Breton's Bar & Grille**. Membership in the **Regency Club** offers special amenities: call for details. Nonsmoking rooms. Children under 18 stay free. ♦ 1 Bethesda Metro Center (Wisconsin Ave-Old Georgetown Rd) 657.1234, 800/233.1243; fax 657.6453

9 Bethesda Cinema 'n' Drafthouse ★$ Second-run movies are shown on the movie screen, accompanied by beer and wine, pizzas, nachos, and deli-style foods in a living-room setting. Must be 21 or with parent to enter. ♦ Pizza/deli ♦ Daily 6PM-midnight. Showtimes vary; box office opens $1/2$ hour before showtime. 7719 Wisconsin Ave (Middleton Ln-Cheltenham Dr) 656.3337

Maryland—named for the Virgin—was settled by the **Calvert** family, English Catholics seeking a religious haven.

9 Tastee Diner ★$ The genuine wood-paneled and chromed article. Be prepared to wait for seating. ♦ American ♦ 24 hours. 7731 Woodmont Ave (Cheltenham Dr) No credit cards. 652.3970

9 Foong Lin ★★★$$ The place for a traditional Hong Kong tea lunch. The dim sum are fresh and tender—some to sample: grilled turnip cakes, stuffed ducks' feet, spareribs with black bean sauce. The regular menu offers Cantonese, Szechuan, and Peking specialties like Five Flavored Shrimp, stuffed scallops with black-bean sauce, and lemon chicken. ♦ Chinese ♦ M-Th 11AM-10PM; F-Sa 11AM-11PM; Su noon-10AM. 7710 Norfolk Ave (Fairmont-Woodmont Aves) 656.3427

9 Rio Grande Cafe ★★$$ Bustling Tex-Mex joint serving some of the best fajitas and margaritas to hit the East Coast. ♦ Tex-Mex ♦ M-Th 11:30AM-10:30PM; F 11:30AM-11:30PM; Sa noon-11:30PM; Su noon-10:30PM. 4919 Fairmont Ave (Old Georgetown Rd-Norfolk Ave) 656.2981

9 La Miche/L'Hippocampe ★★$$$ A people-watcher's paradise. The café-style menu goes beyond simple *croque-monsieur*, with surprises like poached oysters topped with caviar or mussels in cream and almonds. Piano music is offered Thursday through

Suburban Maryland

Saturday evenings. ♦ French ♦ La Miche: M-F 11:30AM-2:30PM, 6-10PM; Sa 6-10PM. L'Hippocampe: M-F 4:30-11PM; Sa 6-11PM. 7905 Norfolk Ave (St. Elmo-Cordell Aves) 986.0707

9 Le Marmiton ★★★$$$ Everything on the extensive Provençal menu, which is printed daily, is beautifully rendered—from the country pâté with green peppercorns to the veal topped with shiitake and oyster mushrooms, to the delicate pastries and the strong, rich coffees. ♦ French ♦ M-F 11:30AM-2:30PM, 6-10PM; Sa 6-10:30PM. 4931 Cordell Ave (Old Georgetown Rd-Norfolk Ave) Reservations recommended. 986.5188

9 Travel Books Unlimited An exhaustive collection of guidebooks, novels, and essays for the traveler, armchair or otherwise. ♦ Tu-Sa 10AM-9PM; Su noon-5PM. 4931 Cordell Ave (Old Georgetown Rd-Norfolk Ave) 951.8533

10 National Institutes of Health Professionals affiliated with the medical sciences and interested public are welcomed to the **Visitors Center**, where tours of the clinical center (by appointment) include films and slideshows. The **National Library of Medicine**, adjacent to the Visitors Center, is the world's largest research library in a single professional field. ♦ NIH: M-Th 7:45AM-10PM; F 7:45AM-6PM; Sa 8:30AM-6PM; Su 1-5PM. NLM: M-Th 8:30AM-9PM; F-Sa 8:30AM-5PM, Jan-Memorial Day, Labor Day-Dec; M-Th 8:30AM-9PM; F-Sa 8:30AM-5PM, Memorial Day-Labor Day. Library tour M-F 1PM. Meet in lobby of Lister Hill Center. Tours by appointment M-F 8AM-4PM. 8600 Rockville Pike (Old Georgetown Rd-Cedar Ln) NIH 496.1156, Visitors Center 496.1776, NLM 496.6308

10 Marriott Bethesda Hotel $ A step up from the usual suburban accommodations, this 405-room hotel features a large outdoor swimming pool, an indoor lap pool, lighted tennis courts, and an exercise room. Three restaurants—Polynesian, Northern Italian, and family-style American—provide a variety of cuisines and prices. For an extra treat, ask about the *Executive Kings* room, an upgraded minisuite. Nonsmoking rooms. Children under 17 stay free. ♦ 5151 Pooks Hill Rd (Rockville Pike-the Beltway) 897.9400, 800/228.9290; fax 897.0192 ♿

11 Cabin John Regional Park Over 500 acres of park grounds run by Montgomery County. Ice-skating, outdoor tennis courts (on a first-come-first-served basis), miniature train rides, summer concerts. ♦ Grounds daily dawn-dusk. Ice skating: fee. Daily dawn-dusk, Jan-Mar, Oct-Dec. Train rides: fee. M-F 10AM-4PM; Sa-Su 10AM-6PM, Apr-Sep. 7400 Tuckerman Ln (Democracy Blvd-Westlake Dr) 299.4555

12 White Flint Even the mannequins at this 3-tiered fashion mall have high cheekbones and that perfectly manicured look. **I. Magnin**, **Bloomingdale's**, and **Lord & Taylor** are the big-leaguers anchoring more than 120 smaller shops and fashion boutiques in an interior of rosewood and copper terrazzo floors. Additional stores at White Flint include **Black, Starr and Frost**, the oldest high-fashion jewelry outfit in the country; **Andre Bellini**, men's and women's imported clothing; and **St. Laurent Rive Gauche**, prêt-à-porter with a haute couture look. ♦ Mall: M-Sa 10AM-9:30PM; Su noon-6PM. 11301 Rockville Pike (Nicholson Ln) 468.5777

Rockville

12 Kum San Oak ★★$$ Koreans frequent this restaurant for a taste of home, Westerners for a chance to sample delicacies like grilled sliced beef, minced-pork-and-vegetable pancakes, and dumplings in a rich broth. Order several of the side dishes—ask your waiter for suggestions. ♦ Korean ♦ M-Th 11AM-10:30PM; F-Su 11AM-11PM. 4870 Boiling Brook Parkway (Nicholson Ln) 770.7791

Restaurants: Red	**Hotels**: Blue
Shops/Parks: Green	**Sights/Culture**: Black

12 G Street Fabrics No longer on G Street, but still the most amazing fabric store you'll ever find, with designer textiles, a full bridal facility, and sewing classes. ♦ M-F 10AM-9PM; Sa 10AM-6PM; Su noon-5PM. 11854 Rockville Pike (Montrose Rd) 231.8998

12 Yesterday & Today A record shop where the current and the obscure share equal billing. Specializes in LPs and 45s. ♦ M-F 10AM-9PM; Sa 10AM-7PM; Su noon-6PM. 1327-J Rockville Pike (within Sunshine Square Shopping Center) 279.7007

13 Beall-Dawson House (1815) **Upton Beall** entertained **General Lafayette** here. Owned by the **Montgomery County Historical Society**. House features furnishings dating from 1815 through the Victorian era. Also on the grounds are the small medical museum and office of **Dr. Stonestreet**, with medical implements from 1852–1903, and a gift shop. Tours on a walk-in basis. ♦ Fee. Tu-Sa noon-4PM; 1st Su of the month 2-5PM. 103 W Montgomery Ave (S. Adams St) 762.1492

13 St. Mary's Church (1817) Hard to believe, but novelist **F. Scott Fitzgerald** and his wife, **Zelda**, are buried in the Roman Catholic church's cemetery. (Zelda was born in Rockville.) ♦ Daily dawn-dusk. Services M-F 7, 9AM; Sa 9AM, 6:30PM; Su 7:45, 9, 10:30AM, 12:25PM. 520 Viers Mill Rd (Rockville Pike) 424.5550

13 Vietnam Taste ★$$ Straightforward presentation of spring rolls, *bo cuon* (beef tenderloin rolls), and other classics, at modest prices. ♦ Vietnamese ♦ M-F 11:30AM-10:30PM; Sa-Su 10:30AM-10:30PM. 2007 Viers Mill Rd (Twin Brook Rd) 279.8870

14 Antique Row More than 40 shops, some in malls and others in small buildings nearby, make up this collection of styles, periods, and prices. Items range from Art Deco and railroad memorabilia to stained glass, folk art, and vintage clothing. ♦ Howard Ave-Connecticut Aves. Kensington

15 Temple of Latter-Day Saints (1974, Wilcox, Markham, Beecher & Fetzer; landscape design, Irwin Nelson) This massive traffic-stopper stands on a 57-acre hill in Maryland's countryside. The 15-million-dollar building is 248 feet long and 136 feet wide and has a height equivalent to a 16-story commercial building. Its foundation is built on solid rock to withstand any tests of the elements; the building itself is sheathed in 173,000 square feet of Alabama white marble, enough to cover 3^1/2 football fields. Even the windows are made of marble, ^{5}/8 of an inch thick and translucent, giving the interiors an otherworldly quality. The fortress is topped with 6 gold-plated steel spires, the highest of which supports a gold-leaf statue of the angel **Moroni**. The temple interior—open to members only—has a multitude of rooms on its 9 levels, reserved for important occasions like weddings and baptisms. A formal 30-minute tour guided by volunteers passes through the **Visitors Center**, where photographs, sculptures, and a religious theater with lifelike mannequins tell the story of Mormonism. Three theaters show films on this and other temples throughout the world. ♦ Tours daily 10AM-9PM. 9900 Stoneybrook Dr (Capital View Ave) Kensington. 587.0144

15 Noyes Children's Library A Montgomery County library built just for preschoolers, with more than 10,000 volumes and story-reading programs. ♦ Tu, Th, Sa 9AM-5PM. Carroll and Montgomery Aves. Kensington. 949.3780

16 Brookside Gardens This 50-acre section of **Wheaton Regional Park** includes a conservatory with tropical plants and a large formal garden. Have a question about horticulture? The people at Brookside Gardens are here to help. Call 949.8227 between 9:30AM and noon, Tuesday through Thursday.♦ Grounds daily 9AM-sundown. Conservatory daily 9AM-5PM. 1500 Glenallen Ave (Randolph-Kemp Mill Rds) Wheaton. 949.8230

Silver Spring

17 National Capital Trolley Museum, built as a replica of an old terminal, offers a look at trolley memorabilia from Austria, Germany, and Washington DC. A real trolley will take you on a 1^1/2 -mile ride through the neighboring countryside. Gift shop. ♦ Fee. Sa-Su noon-5PM, Jan-June, Sep-14 Dec; W, Sa-Su noon-4PM, July-Aug. 1313 Bonifant Rd (Layhill-Notley Rds) Northwest Branch Regional Park. 384.6088

18 Round House Theater Provocative productions of contemporary plays, plus an ongoing chamber music series. The 5-play season runs from September to June. ♦ Seats 218. Shows:

Suburban Maryland

F-Sa 8PM; Su 2PM. Box office Tu-Sa 11AM-5PM and 1 hour before performances. 12210 Bushey Dr (Viers Mill-Randolph Rds) 468.4234

18 Old St. John the Evangelist Church and Cemetery (Our Lady Queen of Poland) (1790) Jesuit churchman **John Carroll** founded his private Evangelist Mission chapel on this site in 1774, and served here until his appointment as official head of the newly legislated US Roman Catholic Church 10 years later. The small frame building is an exact reproduction of the original structure, with all fixtures and sacred vessels intact. In essence, the church stands as a memorial to Maryland's influential Carroll family. The church also serves the area's Polish community, to whom it is known as Our Lady Queen of Poland. ♦ Services Su 10AM, Polish Mass 11:30AM. Church by appointment. Cemetery dawn-dusk. 9700 Rosensteel Ave (Forest Glen Ave) 681.7663

Harriet Tubman was born a slave in 1820 in **Bucktown**. A wildly successful slave-runner, she guided more than 300 slaves from the Eastern Shore to freedom in Canada. In 10 years she made 19 trips and not one slave was caught.

The first guidebook to Washington was published in 1812.

19 Quality Hotel $ Two hundred rooms recently remodeled in well-appointed style. There is an American restaurant, as well as a Northern Italian dining room named **Mamma Regina's**. The health club—indoor pool, sauna, and exercise room—is open to hotel patrons and guests. Special weekend rates. Children under 18 stay free. ♦ 8727 Colesville Rd (Spring St) 589.5200, 800/228.5151; fax 588-1841 &

19 Han II ★★$$ Great Korean barbecue—which diners cook at the table on small recessed grills or portable gas grills—dumplings, and *yook hwe* (Korean steak tartare). The quality of the food is confirmed by the largely Korean clientele. ♦ Korean ♦ Daily 11AM-10:30PM. 8511 Fenton St (Colesville Rd-Ellsworth Dr) 585.8600

19 China ★★$$ Although this small family-run restaurant specializes in elaborate banquets (a minimum of 4 guests; call at least 1 day in advance), don't hesitate to wander in for pan-fried dumplings, Hong Kong pork, and Szechuan beef. ♦ Chinese ♦ Tu-F 11:30AM-2:30PM, 5-9:30PM; Sa 5-9:30PM; Su 4-9PM. 8411 Georgia Ave (Bonifant-Wayne Aves) Reservations required F-Sa. No credit cards. 585.2275

20 Crisfield ★★★$$$ Outstanding regional specialties like Chincoteague oysters, Maryland crabs (every way but steamed), and fresh clams are offered on a menu that has been the same for the past 50 years. ♦ Seafood ♦ Tu-Th 11AM-10PM; F-Sa 11AM-11PM; Su noon-9:30PM. 8012 Georgia Ave (East-West High-

Suburban Maryland

way-Blair Mill Rd) No credit cards. 589.1306. Also at: 8606 Colesville Rd. 588.1572.

20 Sakura Palace ★★$$ Great sushi bar in the dining area, flanked by tatami rooms for larger parties going completely Japanese. Fried, steamed, boiled, and broiled complete dinners, including salt-broiled salmon, *tonkatsu* (deep fried pork cutlet), tiny clams, and Pacific oysters in season. ♦ Japanese ♦ Tu-F 11:30AM-2:30PM, 5:30-10PM; Sa-Su 5-10PM. 7926 Georgia Ave (King St-Eastern Ave) Reservations recommended. 587.7070

21 Parkway Deli and Restaurant ★★$ Regularly voted the best deli in the Washington area, the Parkway offers *big* bowls of matzo ball soup, kosher sandwiches, chopped chicken liver, dried herring and whitefish, and, of course, lox and bagels. Eat in or carry out. ♦ Deli ♦ M-Th, Su 7AM-9:30PM; F-Sa 7AM-10PM. 8317 Grubb Rd (Washington Ave-East-West Highway) No credit cards. 587.1427

Takoma Park

22 Andean Trading Hand-woven, natural-fiber clothing from Third World countries. ♦ Daily 11AM-7PM. 7030 Carroll Ave (Laurel-Tulip Aves) 270.6064

Takoma Park, Maryland, nicknamed the *City of Azaleas*, is also a nuclear-free zone.

22 House of Musical Traditions sells, rents, and repairs musical instruments, from kazoos and tambourines to concertinas, fiddles, drums, guitars, and banjos. It also stocks an extensive line of records, tapes, and CDs in a wide variety of musical styles, including a special section of Washington DC artists. Lessons are also available. ♦ M, Sa noon-5PM; Tu-Th, Su noon-7PM; F noon-9PM. 7040 Carroll Ave (Laurel-Tulip Aves) 270.9090

22 Takoma Kids Owner **Andrea Stevenson** makes a line of clothes called **Sarah's Closet** from materials in paisleys, stripes, and small floral prints; Takoma also carries standard children's dresses and overalls, books and toys, and maternity wear. ♦ Infant-children's size 8. M-F 11AM-6:30PM; Sa 10AM-5PM; Su 10AM-2PM. 7040 Carroll Ave (Laurel-Tulip Aves) 853.3237

23 Braxton's Bonsai Artistry An impressive selection of indoor and outdoor bonsai. Owner **Philip Braxton** also imports *penjing*, miniature potted trees accompanied by landscapes composed of tiny pagodas, rocks, and human, animal, and bird figurines. ♦ M, W-Sa 9AM-7PM. 1109 Sligo Creek Parkway (New Hampshire Ave) 270.5512

Prince George's County

Maryland's second-largest county is already the most populous jurisdiction in the Washington area, with nearly 700,000 residents, but the frenetic growth blighting its rolling hills promises to make short work of that statistic. Prince George's claims some historic firsts: **Captain John Smith** set foot here in 1608; the first American airport was built in **College Park** in 1908—**Wilbur** and **Orville Wright** were teachers here. **NASA**'s **Goddard Space Flight Center** in Greenbelt continues the pioneering tradition.

23 Ledo ★$ Among the many options, bacon-cheese pizza on a thin flaky crust is the ticket at this longstanding Prince George's hangout. ♦ Italian ♦ M-Th, Su 8AM-11:30PM; F-Sa 8AM-12:30AM. 2420 University Blvd East (Riggs-Adelphi Rds) Hyattsville. 422.8622

23 Publick Playhouse for the Performing Arts A performing arts center sponsoring dance, chamber music, and theatrical series. ♦ Seats 462. Shows: F-Sa 8PM; Su 2PM. Box office M-F 9AM-4PM and 1 hour before performances. 5445 Landover Rd (Annapolis Rd) Hyattsville. 277.1710

Care to take in a game of polo? There are free matches every Sunday afternoon on the field at the Lincoln Memorial. In June and from September through October, matches start at 3PM; they begin at 2PM in May and at 4PM in July and August. Call 485.9666 for information.

24 University of Maryland The main campus of this coeducational state-supported facility has over 38,000 students and 2000 faculty members; physics, mathematics, and computer science are the departments that have earned Maryland U a place among the country's top 10 public universities. ♦ Guided tours given by admissions office by appointment only, M-F 11AM, 1, 3PM. Baltimore Ave (Adelphi Rd-Campus Dr) College Park. Main campus 454.3311

25 Recreational Equipment Inc. (REI) A mecca for backpackers, climbers, and other woodsy types, this cooperative gives a substantial year-end rebate on purchases. ♦ M-F 10AM-9PM; Sa 10AM-6PM; Su noon-5PM. 9801 Rhode Island Ave (Baltimore Ave-Greenbelt Rd) College Park. 982.9681

26 Greenbelt National Park Only 12 miles from Downtown Washington, this green pine-forest is a haven for deer, red fox, and gray squirrel; the streams are filled with small fish, and the air is fragrant with the scent of flowers. Twelve well-marked walking trails, camping facilities, and picnic areas dot the 1100 acres. ♦ Park daily dawn-dusk. Administrative offices M-F 8AM-4:30PM. 6565 Greenbelt Rd (Kenilworth-Good Luck Rds) Greenbelt. 344.3948

27 Agricultural Research Center Seven thousand five hundred acres of land inhabited by cattle, pigs, and poultry, under research by the USDA. The center is devoted to solving such problems as environmental protection and global food supply. ♦ Free. M-F 8AM-4:30PM; tours by appointment. Powder Mill Rd (Good Luck Rd-Edmonston Ave) Beltsville. 344.2483

28 Goddard Space Flight Center (NASA) NASA's museum, directly on its research facility, offers a solar telescope for sunspot viewing and several dismantled rockets and other space objects, plus exhibitions ranging from outer space satellite transmissions to everyday TV weather maps. Film clips of NASA's adventures in space are screened nonstop; you can also watch outtakes from the pressure-cooker drama at ground control before a rocket takeoff or landing. Model rocket launches are held on the 1st and 3rd Sundays of each month at 1PM. ♦ Free. W-Su 10AM-4PM. Guided tours W-F 2:30PM; group tours by appointment. Soil Conservation Rd (Baltimore-Washington Parkway-Greenbelt Rd) Greenbelt. 286.8981 ♿

Prince George's County (established 1696) was named after the prince consort to Queen Anne of England, Prince George of Denmark.

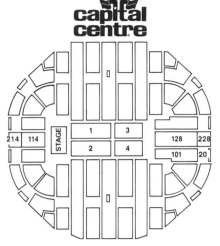

29 Capital Centre One of America's foremost showcase auditoriums, the vast arena has played host to some of the most popular contemporary events in the country. The steady procession of sports events includes the **World Professional Ice Skating Championship**, hockey (**Capitals**), all-star basketball tournaments (**Bullets**, **Georgetown Hoyas**), professional wrestling, and closed-circuit boxing. Other sellout events have included **Elvis Presley**, the **Rolling Stones**, and **Bob Dylan**, in monumental concerts. In 1988, **Michael Jackson** played to a capacity crowd 4 nights running.

Suburban Maryland

There are 12 concession stands and 2 full-service restaurants on the premises: the elegant French/American **Capital Club**, with reservations necessary 2 weeks in advance; and the **Showcase Pub & Eatery**, a deli/restaurant and bar that seats on a first-come-first-served basis. A more original feature: the **Parents Quiet Room**, a soundproof area where adults can wait in peace for their children who are screaming their heads off at the rock concert upstairs. ♦ Seats 20,000. Box office daily 10AM-5:30PM or until start of event. 1 Harry Truman Dr (Landover Rd-the Beltway) Landover. 24-hour information 350.3400

29 Wild World is an amusement park filled with the customary rides, shows, concessions, and attractions guaranteed to drive youngsters wild and parents crazy. Assorted waterslides, an innovative children's pool, and **Wild Wave**, the world's largest wave pool, provide big splashes of fun. There are 4 different shows, and special events each weekend. Open some weekends in the off-season: call for information. ♦ Admission. Daily 10AM-10PM, 16 June-Labor Day. 13710 Central Ave (Rte 301) Largo. 249.1500

30 Andrews Air Force Base This strategic military base is used for presidential comings and goings; unfortunately, it is closed to the public. ♦ Allentown Rd (Pennsylvania-Branch Aves) Camp Springs

31 Paul E. Garber Facility The **National Air & Space Museum**'s preservation and restoration facility exhibits 92 wondrous aircraft, together with models, kites, and astronautical artifacts. Many of the antique foreign planes are war prizes, collected by the USAF at the end of WWII. More recent aviation achievements are equally represented: the **Bell** *Model 30*, the first 2-bladed helicopter, and the 1960 **Able-Baker** nose cone from the *Jupiter* craft that carried 2 monkeys into space. Plan ahead: tours require reservations 2 weeks in advance. ♦ Free. Tours M-F 10AM; Sa-Su 10AM, 1PM. Old Silver Hill Rd at Branch Ave. Suitland. Reservations required. 202/357.1300

32 Oxon Hill Farm City folks can try out the lifestyle of country bumpkins on this working farm, where home-woven charms abound. The cows are milked and the fields plowed, and all the farm animals provide plenty of diversions for incredulous asphalt-raised children. Family activities include summer hayrides and special events, such as **Draft Horse Day** and **Dairy Day**. A forest, an orchard, and a

vegetable garden complete the rustic picture. Administered by the **National Park Service**. ♦ Free. Daily 8:30AM-5PM. 6411 Oxon Hill Rd (Indian Head Highway-the Beltway) Oxon Hill. 839.1177

33 Rosecroft Raceway Fall and winter night harness racing with a view from the terrace dining room restaurant. ♦ Mid Jan-May, Oct-Dec. Post times: W-Sa 7:30PM; Su 6:30PM. Restaurant: W-Sa 6-11PM; Su 5-10PM. 6336 Rosecroft Dr (Bock-Brinkley Rds) Fort Washington. Reservations 567.4045, information 567.4000

34 Fort Washington (1824, Lt. Col. Walker K. Armistead) The fort that now occupies this site is the successor to the original **Fort Warburton**, destroyed by British fires in 1814. The present structure was manned as a river defense post, at times with the strength of nearly 350 men. High brick and stone walls enclose the 3-acre fort; the entrance has a drawbridge suspended over a dry moat, preventing attacks from the enemy. The ramparts, the casement positions, and the water battery (designed by **L'Enfant**) 60 feet below the main fort could deliver lethal bombardments from 3 levels. Volunteer guides in period costume give musket demonstrations during peak season. Several trails lead to picnic areas in the 300-acre historical park surround-

ing the fort. Tours on request. ♦ Admission. Daily 9AM-5PM. Visitors Center daily 10AM-4:30PM. Tours M-F by request; Su noon, 1, 2, 3, 4PM. Fort Washington Rd. (Livingston Rd) Fort Washington. 763.4601

35 National Colonial Farm A working re-creation of an 18th-century tobacco plantation, offering a fascinating glimpse into Colonial life in southern Maryland. Managed by the **National Park Service**. ♦ Admission; children under 12 free. Tu-Sa 10AM-5PM. 3400 Bryan Point Rd (Piscataway Park) Accokeek. 283.2115

36 Savage Mill (1842) First built to manufacture cotton duck for sail canvas, the factory complex ceased operation after World War II. It has been rehabilitated as a 12-building crafts center, with studios, shops, and cafés. ♦ M-Sa 10AM-5:30PM; Su 11AM-5:30PM. 8600 Foundry Street (Howard St-Gorman Rd) Savage. 498.5751

Columbia

37 Merriweather Post Pavilion Outdoor amphitheater in a 50-acre park hosts major rock and pop concerts in the summer. Lawn or pavilion seating; tickets sold through major DC outlets. ♦ Reserved seats: 5000. 10475 S. Entrance Rd. 730.2424, recorded performance information 982.1800

37 Holiday Inn Columbia $ Free in-room movies, meeting rooms, an outdoor pool, and a restaurant and bar are among the amenities. Nonsmoking rooms. Children under 12 stay free. ♦ 7900 Washington Blvd (Rte 1) 799.7500, 800/HOLIDAY; fax 799.1824 ♿

37 Columbia Hilton $$ A comfortable hotel with an indoor pool and sauna, meeting rooms, 2 restaurants, and a bar. Children under 13 stay free. ♦ 5485 Twin Knolls Rd (Thunderhill Rd) 997.1060 ♿

37 The Columbia Inn $$ The hotel is a member of the nearby **Columbia Association**, a state-of-the-art athletic facility with full health-club services and tennis courts. Free transportation is provided for guests. The hotel itself offers concierge service, meeting rooms, and a restaurant and bar. Children under 12 stay free. ♦ 10207 Wincopin Circle (Rte 29) 730.3900, 800/638.2817; fax 730.1290

37 King's Contrivance ★$$ A historical country-estate setting for veal Provençal and other classic dishes. ♦ French ♦ M-Th 11:30AM-2:30PM, 5:30-9PM; F 11:30AM-2:30PM, 5:30-9:30PM; Sa 5:30-9:30PM; Su 4-9PM. 10150 Shaker Dr (Rte 32) Reservations required. 995.0500

The state motto of Maryland is *Fatti Maschii, Parole Femine* (Manly Deeds, Womanly Words).

Ellicott City

38 Crab Shanty ★$$ Classic Maryland seafood, from steamed crabs to more formal grilled dishes. ♦ Seafood ♦ M-Th 11:30AM-2:30PM, 5-10PM; F 11:30AM-2:30PM, 5-11PM; Sa 5-11PM; Su 2-9PM. 3410 Plumtree Dr (Rte 40W) 465.9660

39 Blob's Park ★$ Beer, sauerbraten, and live polka music draw families to this cavernous beer garden. ♦ German ♦ F-Sa 7PM-1AM; Su 2-10PM. 8024 Blob's Park Rd (Jessup Rd) Jessup. 799.0155

BAGGAGE CLAIM/LOWER LEVEL
TICKETING/UPPER LEVEL

PIER C
PIER D
PIER B
PIER E
PIER A

ARRIVALS/LOWER ROADWAY
DEPARTURES/UPPER ROADWAY

40 Baltimore-Washington International Airport is located 10 miles south of Baltimore and 32 miles north of Washington, a 45- to 60-minute drive. BWI used to be called *Friendship International* (and still is by some old-timers), but its new name, along with a major reconstruction job, reflects its growing importance in the region. The airport serves over 110 cities in the nation and the world and handles 60 percent of all regional cargo.

The main terminal is a 2-level building with access roadways on each level. Ten monumental red-tiled pillars support an airy *space-frame roof* of glass and steel. Natural light filters into the terminal, while the roof, which hangs over the pillars, effectively shelters arriving and departing passengers from the elements. The bilevel design effectively separates arriving and departing passengers. You can walk directly from individual airline entrances to a ticket counter no more than 50 feet away. From there, all 40 departure gates are easily accessible. There are 5 departure piers, 3 of which are the long finger-pier type. Loading bridges connect directly with the planes.

Arriving passengers go directly to the lower level, where they find 2 baggage-claim areas, customs, car rentals, and ground transportation. Airport services include the usual complement of bars, restaurants, and a duty-free shop. Twenty-four-hour assistance in different languages is available. The **Bank of Maryland** has a branch in the airport, and in **Pier A** there is a 24-hour snack bar. ♦ General nonflight airport information, 859.7111, 202/261.1000

When driving to the airport from DC, take Hwy I-495 (the Beltway) to the Spellman Parkway or to the Baltimore-Washington Parkway to Rte 46, which is the airport access road. Taxi service is available to Baltimore and Washington. A dispatcher is always on duty. ♦ Airport taxi 859.1100

Limo/van service is available from **Airport Connection**, which operates 46-passenger motorcoaches as well as vans that stop at Greenbelt (for passengers traveling to Prince George's and Montgomery counties) and at 1517 K St NW in Downtown DC (next to the Capital Hilton). ♦ Buses leave at quarter past each hour: M-F, Su 4:15AM-12:30AM; Sa 5:15, 6:15, 8:15, 9:15, 11:15AM, 12:15, 2:15, 3:15, 5:15, 6:15, 8:15, 9:15PM. Ground Transportation Desk, lower level of BWI. 859.3000

Maryland Limousine offers door-to-door service throughout the Washington and Baltimore metropolitan areas. Accepts all major credit cards. ♦ Daily 5AM-midnight. Pier C, lower level of BWI. 850.4100

Washington Flyer offers door-to-door van and bus service throughout Montgomery and Prince George's counties; also travels to terminal at 1517 K St NW in Downtown DC. ♦ Daily at quarter past the hour 5:15AM-midnight. Ground Transportation Desk, lower level of BWI. No credit cards. 202/685.1400

Amtrak's **BWI Rail Station** is 2 miles from the airport. Trains pass through on their way to Northeast Corridor cities like Washington, Philadelphia, New York, and Boston. The airport runs a free shuttle bus to and from every train. ♦ 800/872.7245

In 1982, a couple from Maryland's Eastern Shore sighted and videotaped a 30-foot-long dragonlike creature at Chesapeake Bay's Love Point. The humpbacked aquatic monster was instantly named **Chessie**, after its illustrious relative in Loch Ness, Scotland.

Suburban Maryland

In 1963, Maryland senator **J. Glenn Beall** protested—on the floor of the Senate—that "no Marylander would recognize" the so-called Maryland crabcakes served in the Senate dining room. In response to his outburst, Maryland First Lady **Avalynne Tawes** sent Beall her recipe for the Real Thing, which he promptly had reprinted in the *Congressional Record*:

Avalynne Tawes' Maryland Crabcakes
1 pound crab claw meat
dash of Tobasco sauce
2 medium eggs, beaten
1 tablespoon parsley, chopped
2 tablespoons mayonnaise
1 cup crushed saltine crackers
   (about 10)
$^1/_4$ teaspoon salt
$^1/_8$ teaspoon pepper
cooking oil for frying

Combine all ingredients except crackers and cooking oil, and mix lightly together. Form mixture into desired size of cake or croquette. Do not pack firmly, but allow mixture to be light and spongy. Bread the crabcakes with cracker crumbs. Do not use prepared cracker crumbs. Fry in pan with approximately 1 inch of oil until golden brown, turning once. Drain on absorbent paper and serve hot. Serves 4 people.

Dr. LaSalle D. Leffall, Jr.

Chief Surgeon, Howard University Hospital

University Pastry Shop, where the homemade ice cream, especially the peach, brings back memories of every happy day of your childhood.

The quaint Francis Scott Key Bookshop in Georgetown, for the best personal and thoughtful service while locating any special book requested. The Pyramid Bookstore just off the Howard University campus provides equally fine service.

In order to satisfy my conservative taste in clothes, an annual trek to Brooks Brothers for fittings, but only under duress.

A morning at Howard University's Moorland-Spingarn Research Center (a leading repository of black Americans), ending at the Howard Inn for lunch and stimulating conversation.

The Jockey Club in the Ritz Carlton Hotel, 21 Federal, or Le Pavillon, for the food as well as the ambiance.

My favorite neighborhood restaurants: Mrs. Simpson's, Germaine's, and La Ferme (Chevy Chase), where the food and coziness are of equal rank.

The view from the roof of the Washington Hotel, vying with those from the terraces of the State Department and the Kennedy Center as one of the best in the city.

Tennis at the Arlington Y or at St. Alban's Tennis Club, followed by a pleasant stroll on the Washington Cathedral grounds, with a "forbidden" peek in the Bishop's Garden.

A visit to the Frederick Douglass Memorial Home and

Bests

Visitors Center, and before departure enjoying the beautiful panoramic view of the metropolitan area.

An early morning commute through Rock Creek Park with its seasonal foliage.

Listening to modern jazz at Blues Alley in Georgetown, particularly when Miles Davis or my friend Nat Adderley is appearing.

A walk in my neighborhood, Forest Hills, with its magnificent huge trees and rolling hills–an urban pastoral tranquility.

For a special treat, spending time on a cold snowy day at the National Gallery of Art, the Museum of African Art, the Corcoran, or the Anacostia Neighborhood Museum—all stimulating and engrossing.

Alan Fern

Director, National Portrait Gallery

National Portrait Gallery Building. A wonderfully dignified series of spaces, with a courtyard that is an oasis in Downtown Washington.

Mary Cassatt, by Degas. One of the most subtle and tantalizing portraits in the Portrait Gallery. Here is a major French painting in a collection devoted to portrayals of noted Americans.

Benjamin Franklin, by Duplessis. Here, the elderly statesman is shown in his plain suit without a wig, as he appeared before the elegant French. Commissioned by an intimate acquaintance in Paris, this portrait remained in her family until recently. Franklin's expression—at once sharply observant and on the point of a witty remark—never ceases to intrigue.

The Mezzanine and Great Hall of the National Portrait Gallery. After a fire in 1877, the third floor of the Greek Revival Patent Office Building was reconstructed in highly colored, high-Victorian style. Above the magnificent Great Hall is told the story of the War Between the States and Reconstruction—a suitable installation for the space in which President and Mrs. Lincoln had received their guests at Lincoln's second inaugural ball. In the Civil War collection are many exceptional portraits, including daguerreotypes, paintings, and prints of all the major participants.

NPG Permanent Collection. I like to show my guests the many surprises: red-headed Marianne Moore and her mother, painted by Marguerite Zorach when they all were young; Se-Qou-Yah holding the Indian alphabet he devised; 19th-century black actor Ira Aldrich in costume as Othello; Jo Davidson's brilliant sculptured portraits of his contemporaries.

Robert Jenkins

Former Director, National Aquarium in Baltimore

The thematic design of the building.

The rain forest on the roof.

The ecosystem of the exhibition, showing the animal as it looks in the wild.

The Flashlight Fish that produces its own light.

Poison Arrow Frogs in vivid rainbow colors, particularly the powder-blue ones.

The multipurpose use of the building—purely educational or as a place to have fun.

The Giant Tarpon swimming in the Coral Reef tank.

The Porkfish, who earns his keep by picking parasites off his neighbors.

A tankful of the Lionfish, frilly but venomous critters who kill with the spine.

The people who come: it makes the job worthwhile.

George Stevens, Jr.

Filmmaker, Founder of the American Film Institute

Nora's Restaurant. Quiet, with an ever-inventive menu and homegrown vegetables.

i Ricchi. Fine Florentine food. Space between tables means you can hear yourself think.

The Westin Fitness Center. Excellent swimming pool offsets fine Florentine food.

Par T Golf in Georgetown. On a wintry day, play Pebble Beach indoors.

Cineplex Odeon, Wisconsin Ave. Big screens and good sound, in contrast to the dreadful minitheaters in Georgetown.

Corn A Plenty. Superb popcorn by the bag or to send away as gifts.

Cavalier Motors, Arlington. A service manager named Al Marshall may give auto repair a good name.

William Donald Schaefer
Governor of Maryland

One of the most important things to keep in mind if you live in Washington, or visit here, is that you are virtually surrounded by the great state of Maryland. That's important to know if you want really good steamed crabs or want to see a major-league baseball game, go sailing on the world's greatest bay, or spend a day at the beach.

Maryland is a great place to visit and to live. I've lived in Maryland for more than 65 years, most of them right in Baltimore. Baltimore is one of the most interesting and diverse cities in the world. There's always something going on. Besides baseball on a summer evening, there's the Inner Harbor with its restaurants, its shops, and its view of the water. There's the National Aquarium and the new Fishmarket entertainment center, as well as Maryland's Science Center, a terrific hands-on experience for children and adults.

Baltimore is a *market town*...for years and years farmers and watermen have brought fresh produce and seafood to our markets. When you visit Baltimore, be sure to stop for lunch at the world-famous Lexington Market downtown. You'll get a real introduction to the wide variety of people and foods of Maryland.

Annapolis is another special place in Maryland. Just 30 minutes from Washington, Annapolis is a walker's and a water-lover's delight. You can stroll through the grounds of the U.S. Naval Academy, wander through historic houses and museums, or sit on the City Dock to watch the fishermen come and go with their catches. There is water on every side, so it's no surprise that Annapolis is the sailing capital of the United States.

I have a hard time picking out one or two places to talk about in Maryland. There's so much to see and do in every part of the state. Of course, there's Ocean City in the summer—one of the best beaches on the East Coast. And in the fall, a trip to Western Maryland to see the foliage...and maybe a stop at Antietam, the historic Civil War battlefield just north of Washington in Frederick County.

We call Maryland "America in miniature." You'll find the best of everything in Maryland.

John Naisbitt
Author, *Megatrends*

The C&O Canal. Starts at the Four Seasons Hotel in Georgetown and winds almost 200 miles along the Potomac River to Cumberland MD. The 8- to 11-foot-wide towpath is one of the great places to run in the world, partly because much of it overlooks the more beautiful bends in the Potomac. Also ideal for bicycling and just plain walking. Nicely populated on weekends.

Trocadero Asian Art. Located in a beautiful triangular glassed-in building on Dupont Circle. Talk with Kitty for an education in Oriental art. Modest prices for impressive pieces.

Tea at the Four Seasons Hotel. The perfect break from Georgetown shopping; formal afternoon tea in a lush setting.

East Wing of the National Gallery of Art. This I.M. Pei building is a piece of sculpture in itself, with a tremendous Calder mobile as its centerpiece. Revolving exhibitions are beautifully staged, and the permanent David Smith room is a religious experience in a sacred space.

The News Room. Best range and selection of out-of-town newspapers, city magazines, and special-interest magazines in town. Ice cream, quiche, or cappuccino are available while you browse.

Dumbarton Oaks. Owned by trustees of Harvard University, this beautiful museum houses a fabulous pre-Columbian collection and is surrounded by a variety of gardens that are breathtaking all year round. Picnic afterwards in adjacent Montrose Park.

Yes! Bookstore. The East Coast's best bookstore for New Age religion, philosophy, and self-development. A bookstore with an intensely spiritual atmosphere and a far-reaching inventory.

The Phillips Collection. A private, eclectic collection of primarily American and French artists, Impressionists (including Renoir's *The Luncheon of the Boating Party*), Post-Impressionists, and Modernists. Favorites are Edward Hopper, Arthur Dove, Paul Klee, de Stijl. Exhibited in what was the Phillips home, this 1890s' house has been renovated and offers a lovely, intimate way to enjoy art.

Kramer Books and Afterwards Cafe. Washington's No. 1 bookstore. Singles scene; that's where I met my wife. Good luck!

The Jefferson Memorial at night. This tribute to America's architect and greatest citizen must be seen and experienced at night. It is located at the Tidal Basin; take a cab and have it wait.

Bests

Michael Webb
Architecture Critic

What I've missed most since moving to Los Angeles: dogwoods and cherries in bloom during the all-too-brief spring.

Fireflies in the garden on a still summer's night.

Crispness of fall in Georgetown and along Skyline Drive.

Welcoming the world's best filmmakers to the AFI Theater in the Kennedy Center.

Old Pension Building, Union Station, and the Willard Hotel: heroic survivors, gloriously restored, that far outshine the new.

Insider gossip on politics around the dinner table.

National Gallery of Art's sybaritic study center.

Spicy steamed crabs at the Eastern Shore.

Early morning on the Mall: a standing stage set awaiting the players.

The Kennedy grave sites in Arlington National Cemetery: heartbreaking reminders of a nation's loss.

Chesapeake Bay

The tentacles of this great waterway saw the birth of America. Here we struggled to survive and prosper, here we nurtured all that is unique about us. But *our* survival has long since been assured. Now the question is, can the Chesapeake survive us?

The history. Important chapters of our history have been written on the shores of fertile Chesapeake Bay and her tributaries, from the founding of Jamestown—the first permanent English settlement in America—to the ending of the Revolutionary War at Yorktown, to the testing of WWII naval landing boats in the 1940s. The waters that run into the Chesapeake pass by the steel-producing country of Pennsylvania, the farmland of Virginia, the corridors of power in Washington DC, and the ports of Baltimore, Annapolis, and Newport News.

But even before a single colonist set foot in the region, it was bustling with activity. The *Delmarva Peninsula*, as it is commonly known, was alternately covered with jungle and choked with ice. Muskrat and fox now live on land where saber-toothed tigers and mastodons once roamed. There may have been Indians in the region 10,000 years ago, and scientific dating techniques have shown that by 5550 years ago the Indians were enjoying the same breeds of oysters that we enjoy today. The Indians would leave the shells in large piles known as *midden heaps*. The biggest and oldest heap was found near the Potomac; it was 20 feet deep and covered 30 acres.

Some who came from across the ocean to settle the land were adventurers looking for a quick profit far from royal interference. Others, like those led by the **Calvert** clan, came in search of religious freedom. In 1632, the Calverts were granted 12 million acres—all of Maryland and half of Pennsylvania—where they would have plenty of room to practice tolerance.

Chesapeake Bay

These ideals—free trade and freedom of belief—faced many challenges in the New World, but they ultimately forged themselves into the American character.

The geology. Maryland on a map looks eaten away, as though something voracious had chomped through the state and divided it into 2 parts. The jagged bite is the Chesapeake Bay.

The bay is a drowned river. When the glaciers melted 18,000 years ago, the sea rose to fill the valley of the Susquehanna River. The river had flowed south from western New York 400 miles away, its valley and the valleys of all the rivers joining it became Chesapeake Bay. The 48 rivers and 102 branches and tributaries are navigable for 1750 miles. Maryland's 24 rivers give her more river frontage than any other state.

The Chesapeake Bay is both a bay and an estuary, a place where fresh water mingles with salty tidal water. It is 195 miles long and varies from 22 miles wide at the Potomac River to 4 miles wide at Annapolis. Its surface area is 4316 square miles (one-third the size of Maryland itself) and it drains a total land area of 64,170 square miles. At any moment the bay contains about 18 trillion gallons of water; about 45 billion gallons flow in and out of it each day.

The land around the bay is sinking at about one foot per 100 years. Each year the bay swallows about 326 acres from the shore. Whole islands have divided or disappeared. In 1850, **Sharp's Island** covered 600 acres; by 1944 only 6 acres of marsh was left. Now even that is gone, leaving a solitary lighthouse. Further south, **James Island** has lost 150 acres in this century alone.

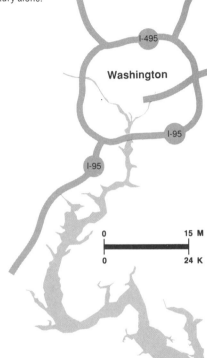

Dredging to maintain a navigable channel has been necessary since the early 1800s because erosion or sedimentation is constantly filling it in. Towns that were once ports are now landlocked or claim only a trickle of water. (**Easton**, though, was saved by mud in 1812 when a British invasion ran aground in the Tred Avon River.) The shipping channel through the bay is 161 miles long and 42 feet deep, but the bay's average depth is less than 28 feet. Here and there are deep stagnant pools formed millions of years ago. One pool near **Bloody Point** is 174 feet deep.

The weather. Nature's tumults have always marked Chesapeake Bay. Every generation seems to have its great storm. The most recent was Hurricane Agnes in 1972, one of the worst natural disasters in American history. The tremendous quantities of rainwater that the storm shed into the bay lowered its salinity and devastated the shellfish industry. The bay is still recovering.

But severe weather is now much less common. Winters especially seem milder, and ice has become less of a hazard—or convenience. At times in the past it was possible to walk or ride all the way down (1856) or across (1780) the iced-over bay—but not within the last 50 years.

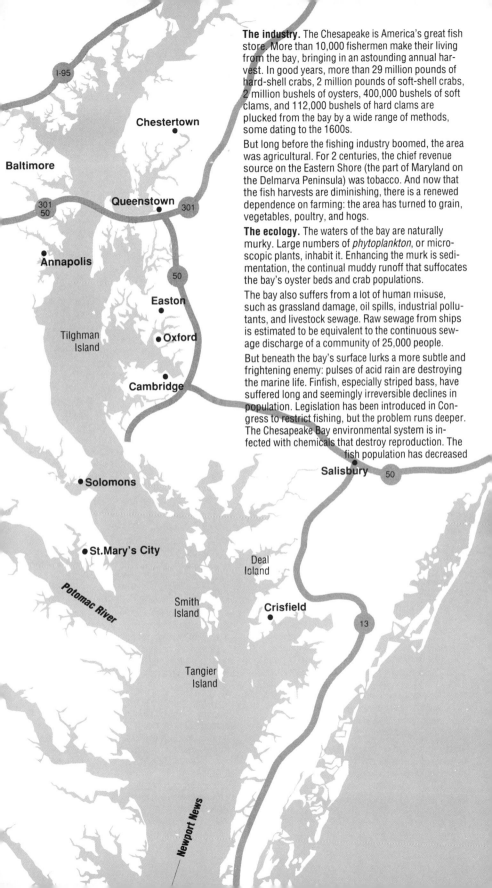

The industry. The Chesapeake is America's great fish store. More than 10,000 fishermen make their living from the bay, bringing in an astounding annual harvest. In good years, more than 29 million pounds of hard-shell crabs, 2 million pounds of soft-shell crabs, 2 million bushels of oysters, 400,000 bushels of soft clams, and 112,000 bushels of hard clams are plucked from the bay by a wide range of methods, some dating to the 1600s.

But long before the fishing industry boomed, the area was agricultural. For 2 centuries, the chief revenue source on the Eastern Shore (the part of Maryland on the Delmarva Peninsula) was tobacco. And now that the fish harvests are diminishing, there is a renewed dependence on farming: the area has turned to grain, vegetables, poultry, and hogs.

The ecology. The waters of the bay are naturally murky. Large numbers of *phytoplankton*, or microscopic plants, inhabit it. Enhancing the murk is sedimentation, the continual muddy runoff that suffocates the bay's oyster beds and crab populations.

The bay also suffers from a lot of human misuse, such as grassland damage, oil spills, industrial pollutants, and livestock sewage. Raw sewage from ships is estimated to be equivalent to the continuous sewage discharge of a community of 25,000 people.

But beneath the bay's surface lurks a more subtle and frightening enemy: pulses of acid rain are destroying the marine life. Finfish, especially striped bass, have suffered long and seemingly irreversible declines in population. Legislation has been introduced in Congress to restrict fishing, but the problem runs deeper. The Chesapeake Bay environmental system is infected with chemicals that destroy reproduction. The fish population has decreased drastically (up to 90 percent less shad and bass for example), and the numbers will go even lower. The *good* news is that a 10-year bay cleanup plan was signed in May 1989. Highlights of the plan, which will cost several billion dollars: preserve forest buffers and wetlands from development; aim for a 40-percent reduction of oxygen-choking nutrients and toxic chemical discharges; carry out a July 1989 plan to preserve oysters, American shad, and blue crabs.

Despite these real and scary flaws, despite all the economic realities and ecological hazards, the bay area seems remarkably resistant to change. Even without the vast forest, which became ships and shelters, it looks old-country and feels down-home. The wide open flatlands still have tremendous natural dignity and permanence. Minimal renewal, few theaters, and fewer bookstores (and almost no patrolling police cars) express its torpor—and its calm isolation. *Area code 301 unless otherwise indicated.*

Chestertown itself is a terrifically rich, thoroughly satisfying town experience where walking is a pleasure. The wide main street runs between large, comfortable trees away from the Chester River, site of this town's own Tea Party rebellion in 1774. Lined with elegant homes and harmonious commercial buildings of all sizes and styles, the whole area has been designated a **National Historic Landmark**. Above Chestertown, the upper Chesapeake Bay gets skinny and branches west and north into Pennsylvania (the Susquehanna River) and east into the Chesapeake-Delaware Canal and Delaware Bay.

1 Water Street. One architectural show-stopper after another lines the street overlooking the Chester River. The variety of Georgian, Federal, and Victorian-embellished structures is enough to satiate any appetite. A *Candlelight Walking Tour* of historic homes (fee) is conducted once a year: September's third Saturday, 6 to 10PM. Call 778.3499 for information.

Chesapeake Bay

1 White Swan Tavern $$ This bed-and-breakfast inn occupies structures as old as 1733 and is restored to a turn. Each of the 6 rooms has a double and a single bed and a private bath. Continental breakfast included. ◆ 231 High St (Maple Ave) No credit cards. 778.2300

1 Chester River Once one of the busiest shipping lanes (to Chestertown) on the Chesapeake, it has some of the oldest farm plantations and the best goose hunting on the bay. In the late 1800s, illegal oyster dredgers started the infamous **Oyster Wars** here. The wars lasted 30 years and killed 50 men, including policemen from the Maryland Oyster Navy, which was commissioned in 1868.

Queenstown, a pleasant old town, lies within the site of the *Great Thumb Grant* of 1654. **Lord Baltimore** gave his supporter **Henry Coursey** all the land his thumb could cover on a map. It turned out that Henry had a 1600-acre thumb.

A drive of 90 minutes (except on summer weekends) takes you due east from the Capitol over the **Chesapeake Bay Bridge**, down Route 50 to Easton, and out a bit west to the tip of St. Michael's Peninsula. You pass through all that is characteristic of the Eastern Shore. The immense sky presses the landscape flat and diminishes large, isolated farmhouses to dots in the distance. Glimpses of the bay itself beyond the fields stretch to eternity—the world really seems flat after all.

The Chesapeake Bay Bridge isn't 1 bridge, it's 2. Built in 1952 and 1973, they are among the largest continuous overwater steel structures in the world. Stolid engineering determination probably made the style and structure of the 2 spans completely different, but anyway, after 350 years of boat crossings, a leap from shore to shore can now be made in minutes.

Drawing by Mary Anne McLean

Wye Mills consists of, obviously, a mill (which ground grain for Washington's troops during the Revolution and is still operating) and 1 terrific tree. The **Wye Oak** stands 104 feet high, is 160 feet wide and 32 feet around the trunk, and is well over 400 years old. All by itself it was made the **Wye Oak State Park**, the only 1-tree state forest in the country.

The **Annual Jousting Tournament** has been held in Cordova, near Wye Mills, every August since 1868 (for information call 822.6915). The medieval sport took hold in Maryland around 1840 and was proclaimed the state's official sport in 1962. Maryland is the only state to have an official sport.

Easton itself was once the capital of the Eastern Shore. Still a trading, banking, and cultural center, the slow infusion of wealthy riverfront property-owners has brought chic to town. Old spruced-up and new Colonial buildings grace the streets surrounding the 1711 **Talbot County Courthouse** (on Washington St, weekdays 8:30AM to 4:30PM). To the south is the **Third Haven Quaker Meeting House**, considered America's oldest religious frame building. Lord Baltimore attended, and **William Penn** preached on its broad lawns. When you hear people speaking about the Eastern Shore, they are probably referring to places like **St. Michael's**, **Oxford**, and the **Tred Avon River**, all within a rocket's red glare of Washington and Baltimore.

The crooked neck road out of Easton (Maryland has incredibly fine road conditions) takes you to **St. Michael's**, home of the shipbuilders to the bay. The British attacked the town at night in 1813. The town blacked itself out (a warfare first), hung lanterns in nearby trees, and the British shot at the lights instead. Ah, where would our history be without the British? The town is now undergoing low-watt restoration, but behind the ferns and quaint signs is still an honest, working village. The old Baltimore clipper and log-canoe shipyards are gone, but the fishing docks are operating and can be closely inspected.

3 Tidewater Inn $ (1949) Not so old and quite large (119 rooms, 7 conference rooms), the Tidewater still somehow pays a cunning allegiance to the old Colonial publick-house look. Restaurant and outdoor swimming pool. ♦ Restaurant daily 7AM-10PM. Dover and Harrison Sts. Restaurant reservations recommended. 822.1300

3 Chesapeake Bay Maritime Museum displays all 28 principal types of bay boats, watermen's tools, and the screwpile lighthouse from **Hooper Strait**. ♦ Fee. Sa-Su 10AM-4PM, Jan-Feb; daily 10AM-4PM, Mar-Memorial Day, Labor Day-Dec; daily 10AM-5PM, Memorial Day-Labor Day. Tours by appointment. Navy Point. 745.2916

The bay's marine life is tremendously varied. There are normal (gray) or pink or green oysters, clams, blue crabs, and 238 recorded varieties of finfish. Some are biggies, like 100-plus-pound drumfish and, in Colonial times, sturgeon 12 feet long. There are hogchokers (the American sole), toadfish (ugly but tasty), bull sharks and brown sharks (some more than 8 feet), eels, seals, porpoises, and stinging jellyfish, a species 500 million years old. Whales used to breed in the bay during the Miocene Age, and some still drop in. Marine Turtles (diamondback terrapins) were enormous and innumerable in the 1700s, in fact so plentiful and cheap that slaves were given little else until laws were passed limiting their turtle meals to one a week.

Oysters were abundant beyond the colonists' dreams. They first tasted them in 1607, when they surprised Indians in the middle of an oyster roast. In 1610, oysters were found 13 inches long—one-oyster dinners.

An oyster pumps about 50 gallons of water a day, extracting oxygen, proteins, carbohydrates, fats, salts, and minerals–a natural final-stage sewage treatment plant. If healthy, the bay could provide 2.3 million bushels of oysters a year; in its present condition it gives up less than a million. They are caught by a variety of methods: tonging, dredging, and diving. Oysters take 30 months to grow to market size, a time that controlled breeding can halve. But their enemies are many. Manmade pollutants like acid rain, oil spills, and indiscriminate sewage-dumping have been devastating, but so has the bay's natural pollutant, ever-encroaching sediment.

Crabs shed their shells 18 to 20 times in their 2-year (female) to 3-year (male) life spans. They have been found as big as 14 inches across; fishermen say they are biggest and tastiest when the moon is full. In 1915, 50.5 million pounds were harvested; today the annual yield is about 33 million, two-thirds of the national total. Around fishing docks you will see wood-lattice shedder floats in which crabs are kept until they drop their hard shells. While soft, they are packed in seaweed and ice and shipped live to market.

The migrating habits of these creatures are fascinating. When a bunch were let loose up near the Chesapeake-Delaware Canal the speedy creatures scrambled east and west at a rate of 4 miles a day. Some crawled 97 miles in 27 days. Because they would shed any kind of tag along with their shells, they are now branded with laser beams.

3 The Patriot of St. Michael's Excursion boat offers 90-minute trips up the Miles River to see ospreys nesting, historic houses, and watermen at work at Navy Point. ♦ Daily 11AM, 1, 3PM, May-Oct. Departure Chesapeake Bay Maritime Museum. Navy Point. 745.3100

3 The Inn at Perry Cabin $$ Six bedrooms and 4 dining rooms within a wedding cake house topped with cupolas. Seasonal flocks of geese visit the tremendous grounds. The great emancipator **Frederick Douglass** lived here—in the slave quarters. ♦ Restaurant: M-Th 11:30AM-4PM, 5-10PM; F-Sa 11:30AM-4PM, 5-11PM; Su 10AM-2PM. Reservations recommended F-Sa. 308 Watkins Ln (Rte 33) 745.5178

3 The Crab Claw ★★$$ An Eastern Shore tradition, with casual indoor/outdoor service of steamed crabs and other Eastern Shore delicacies. Come hungry, grab a mallet and a roll of paper towels, and go to it. (The placemat describes how.) The *Annapolitan* excursion boat from Annapolis docks here daily during the summer.♦ Seafood ♦ M 11AM-4PM; Tu-Sa 11AM-10PM. Navy Point. No credit cards. 745.2900

4 Harrison's Country Inn $ The locals will tell you Harrison's has the bay's best seafood. Direct and simple fare (try *Angels on Horseback*), served with bustle. And they'll put you up in an honest little room that your Uncle Murray would like. Fishing packages April through October. ♦ Restaurant daily 7AM-9PM. Tilghman Island. Reservations recommended for inn. 886.2123

Oxford existed long before Baltimore but it seems to have fallen asleep. During the mid 1700s, this small village was Maryland's largest port, with a heavy

fishing and tobacco trade. Now an exquisite quiet prevails—so much the better for cozy-town lovers.

5 Robert Morris Inn $$ (1710) The most notable inn on the Eastern Shore still has a grand air, despite 275 years of continual enlargement. Robert Morris built it in a manner befitting the town's leading citizen. (He was later killed by wadding from a ship's guns fired in his honor, the only man known to be killed by his own salute.) His son, **Robert Morris, Jr.**, risked all his savings on the new concept of a United States and helped finance the Revolution. Their house is now an inn with a decent restaurant. **James Michener** rated its crabcakes 9.2 (out of 10) because they bulged out the sides, but alas, they don't bulge anymore. A separate **Lodge on the River** has quieter, larger rooms with screened-in porches and a view of the river. ♦ Restaurant: M-Sa 8-11AM, noon-3PM, 6-9PM; Su 8-11AM, noon-8PM. 314 N. Morris St (Tred Avon River) 226.5111

Animal life around the bay, beyond the usual, included wolves menacing the villages in the 1600s. Talbot County paid a bounty of 100 pounds of tobacco for each wolf's head.

5 Masthead Club ★★$$ A dark horse (maybe a bit too dark) but a must. The place looks so-so, but everything is prepared and delivered with elegance and flair. The menu changes weekly, but chances are good that it will feature fresh red snapper, grilled shrimp and andouille sausage, or crabcakes, with a choice of Derby or chocolate chip cookie pie for dessert. The dining room closes early, but will stay open late "if the bar crowd warrants it." ♦ American ♦ M-Th 11:30AM-2:30PM, 6-9PM; F-Sa 11:30AM-2:30PM, 6-10PM; Su 11AM-3PM, 6-9PM. 101 Mill St (Tilghman St) Reservations recommended. 226.5303

On the **Western Shore**, south of **Prince Frederick**, is **Calvert Cliffs**, where you can explore the bay's prehistoric life. Bird teeth (yes, teeth), shark teeth, crocodile jaws, and whale skulls reveal the creatures that flew over and swam in the ancient Calvert Sea 10 to 12 million years ago. The cliffs were discovered in 1608 by **Captain John Smith**; they stretch 30 miles long and 120 feet high.

Solomons on the **Patuxent River** is a pleasant old town that is rapidly becoming a pleasure-boat mecca on a par with Annapolis. The town is also known for its fishing, crabbing, and deepwater harbor—the deepest on the East Coast—an ideal site for the **Chesapeake Biological Laboratory** (part of the University of Maryland), which researches area marine life and water quality.

6 Calvert Marine Museum includes exhibitions on slave ships, naval battles, marine biology, boat building, and the waterman's trade. (A waterman is a person licensed to take any legal catch of fish and shellfish on Chesapeake Bay.)Take a walk through the 1887 **Drum Point Lighthouse** (fee). ♦ Museum: free. M-F 10AM-4:30PM; Sa-Su noon-4:30PM, Jan-Apr, Oct-Dec. M-Sa 10AM-5PM; Su noon-5PM, May-Sep. Solomon's Island Rd (Lore St) 326.2042

Cambridge is across the **Choptank River** on the Eastern Shore's Route 50. After seeing the town (which you must), you have 3 choices. Due west on Route 343 is continuous Eastern Shore landscape, on and on through handsome land, tiny towns, and past an odd little windmill built in 1850. Southwest from Cambridge on Route 16 is **Taylors Island**, with more of the same scenery but no windmill. But branch off 16 onto 335 at **Church Creek** (settled in the 1670s) and you will enter **Blackwater National Wildlife Refuge**, and marsh heaven. The road ends on **Hooper Island** (actually 3 bridge-connected islands), where you find yourself surrounded by the almost disturbing beauty of the tidal wetlands. The islands stretch to the bay on all sides, broken by little inlets, coated with spiky, silky grass. In the evening, the low light enhances the muted color tones and the wind brings a pulse to the land.

Cambridge sits on land bought from the **Choptank Indians** for 42 cloaks. The main drag (**Race Street**), reminiscent of an Edward Hopper painting, branches off into supremely mixed Colonial-Georgian-Victorian neighborhoods (around **High Street**) punctuated by some weird architecture of uncertain origin. You could say it works, but you'd have to be tolerant. The encroaching highway interchanges herald major redevelopment. This little city holds the annual **National Outdoor Show**, featuring such particular attractions as a beauty pageant, a log-sawing contest, and muskrat- and raccoon-skinning championships (last weekend in February, 397.3517), and a series of **Powerboat Regatta Classics** with corn roasts and crab feasts, June through September (476.5113).

7 Old Trinity Church Six miles west of Cambridge is the oldest active church in the United States. Built around 1675, it suffered some Gothic modernizing but was restored 30 years ago. As was common, its cemetery surrounds it. ♦ M, W-Su 9AM-5PM, Mar-Dec. Rte 16 near Church Creek. 228.2940

8 Blackwater National Wildlife Refuge

 Eighty thousand Canada geese and 30,000 ducks call this place home in the fall. Also hiding here are 4 endangered species: the bald eagle, Delmarva fox squirrel, peregrine falcon, and the red-cockaded woodpecker. There is a 5-mile **Wildlife Drive**, observation tower, and a number of foot trails. Lots of nature. ♦ Trails dawn-dusk. Visitors Center: M-F 8AM-4PM Sa-Su 9AM-5PM, Jan-Memorial Day, Labor Day-Dec; M-F 8AM-4PM, Memorial Day-Labor Day. Key Wallace Dr (Rte 335 near Church Creek Park) 228.2677

Salisbury is distractingly urban compared to the rest of the shore—and may disturb your countryside tune. If so, you will be grateful for Route 50's detour around the city—the most damaging visual aspects of this route are a few fast-food joints and a Sheraton Inn.

On the other hand, Salisbury does spell relief. Founded by **Colonel Isaac Handy** (who called it *Handy's Landing* more than 250 years ago), it was leveled twice by fire. It has shown great vitality in its revivals, spurts of development, and activities. A **Wildfowl Carving Exhibition** is held here on the first weekend of October (admission; write 655 Salisbury Blvd, Salisbury MD 21801, or call 742.4988). Salisbury also hosts park band concerts, art exhibitions, Civil War reenactments, rodeos, auto shows, and boat shows as well. There is a nice little zoo with wild ponies from Assateague Island. ♦ Contact Wicomico County Convention and Visitors Bureau. Civic Center. Glen Avenue. Salisbury MD 21801. 548.4914, 24-hour information 749.TOUR

As you continue south into **Somerset County**, the blue-collar Eastern Shore emerges. Fishing and farming are the orders of life. The land continues flat, if possible flatter, always blending into the plane of the bay. Absolutely effortless bicycle country.

Restaurants: Red	**Hotels**: Blue
Shops/Parks: Green	**Sights/Culture**: Black

Princess Anne, the county seat since 1744, is venerable and dignified, with magnificent sycamores lining the streets. The **Manokin River** once made Princess Anne a busy port, but the river is no longer navigable—in fact it no longer *is* at all. The town now raises chickens. Some structures date back to 1705, but most of the architecture is Federal and Victorian. Many buildings can be toured during **Olde Princess Anne Days**, which take place the second weekend in October (for information call Somerset County Tourism at 651.2968 or 800/521.9189).

9 Washington Hotel $ (1744) It sits in the middle of town offering unpretentious accommodations and most definitely unpretentious meals. ♦ Restaurant and coffee shop M-Sa 6AM-9PM. Somerset Ave (Prince William St) 651.2525

9 Teackle Mansion, an elegant 5-part brick house built in 1801, is a bit Late Georgian and a bit Tudor. It figures prominently in an antebellum novel (*The Entailed Hat* by **George Alfred Townsend**) about the Eastern Shore's most notorious slave-kidnapper and smuggler, **Lucretia Patty Cannon**. There is a candlelight walking tour in December. ♦ Admission. Su 2-4PM. (During Olde Princess Anne Days: Sa 11AM-5PM; Su noon-5PM.) Mansion St (Prince William St) 651.1705

Deal Island is one of the last refuges for the sailing **skipjack**. Hop down from Princess Anne on Route 353, past the church cemeteries lined with cement sarcophagi, to **Wenona**. Here the boats can be seen close at hand.

Skipjacks are the bay's most famous throwbacks. The state limits the use of power in collecting deepwater oysters, so these boats continue to do what similar boats have done for 300 years. There were once 150 skipjacks at Deal Island. But as the oysters diminished, so have the boats: they now number around a dozen. Flat-bottomed and sloop-rigged, from 30 to 60 feet long, always white with a hefty raked mast and coarse work sails, they are arresting sights. They use iron-pronged, jawlike dredges to scrape oysters off the bottom. Look just beneath the bowsprit for the trailboard carvings of the boat's name embellished with gold leaf and bright colors.

Crisfield is a factory town. Somber but honest, it looks like the hardworking town it is. In season, the vacationers somehow mix well with the workers. Find the shell-shedding tanks behind the packing houses and watch nature's process of turning hard-shell crabs into soft-shell crabs.

Crab picking and crab races are held during the **National Hard Crab Derby and Fair** in September, a 3-day affair with fireworks, bands, and carnivals. (For information call 968.2682.)

10 The Captain's Galley ★$ This restaurant suits the town—straight-up meals on kitchen table settings. Sort of a seaside truck stop with quite good oyster stews. ♦ Seafood ♦ M-Th 8AM-9PM; F-Sa 8AM-11PM; Su 8AM-10PM. Main St (Rte 413) 968.1636

In the famous painting *Washington Crossing the Delaware*, a young **James Monroe** is seen behind **Washington** holding the flag.

10 Aunt Em's ★$ Looks awful, an all-American highway food stop. For some reason it makes an extra effort on clam chowder. ♦ American ♦ M-Th, Su 6AM-10PM; F-Sa 6AM-11PM. Richardson Ave (Standard Ave) No credit cards. 968.0353

11 Smith Island and **Tangier Island** These two islands off Crisfield have retained the rustic charm of the waning days of Chesapeake watermen. Residents of the islands have been so isolated, many still speak with an Elizabethan lilt; **Captain John Smith** was the first white visitor, in 1607. Both are ideal for walking, bicycling, or sampling the hearty Chesapeake fare prepared by local women, including *she-crab* soup, crabcakes, and stuffed ham.

The 65-foot *Captain Tyler II* cruises from Crisfield to Smith Island daily during the summer. ♦ Daily departure 12:30PM, returns 5:15PM, Memorial Day-Oct. Somers Cove Marina. Capt. Alan Tyler 425.2771

The 90-foot *Steven Thomas* cruises to Tangier Island daily from Memorial day through October. ♦ Daily departure 12:30PM, returns 5PM. City Dock at Main Street Tangier Island Cruises 968.2338

Below Crisfield, as you enter Virginia, the Eastern Shore thins to a scraggly finger pointing at **Cape Henry** and **Newport News**. The flat terrain approaches the desolate. The huge forests of the 1600s were long ago turned into boats and villages, leaving the land open and agricultural by default. Violent gales could carry ships deep ashore into the diminishing woods.

Accomac, the county seat, has more restored Colonial buildings than any other town of its size. ♦ Accomac Chamber of Commerce 804/787.2460

Onancock (*Foggy Place* to the Algonquin Indians) is a pearly little town with a museum operated by the

Virginia Historical Society. ♦ Museum: fee. Tu-Sa 10AM-4PM, Mar-Dec. Kerr Place (Market St) 804/787.8012

In 1665, in **Pungoteague**, 7 miles south, 3 men performed *Ye Beare and Ye Club*, the first play staged in the New World. As it was illegal, they were charged with *acting a play*. Despite the costumes and script shown in evidence they were declared innocent.

The peninsula of the Eastern Shore ends 45 miles below Accomac. Hopping the mouth of the bay is the **Chesapeake Bay Bridge and Tunnel**. It is 17.6 miles long including 2 mile-long tunnels beneath the ship channels, 1 high bridge, and four 8-acre islands. "One of the seven wonders of the modern world," it takes 23 minutes to cross (fee) and has a restaurant and fishing pier on the way.

If you continue your tour north up the Western Shore back to Washington, then Williamsburg, Jamestown, and Fredericksburg will be just minutes off your path.

Captain John Smith crosshatched the Lower Chesapeake with his sailing treks. He fished ("that abundance of fish, lying so thicke with their heads above the water as for want of nets we attempted to catch them with a frying pan"), he mapped, he named (**Tangier Island** after his enemies the Tangier pirates, and **Stingray Point** after eating one that bit him), and he shot (or claimed he shot) 148 ducks with 3 shots.

Pirates appeared in the Chesapeake as soon as there was anything to steal. They were first recorded in 1610, only 3 years after Jamestown was colonized. In 1685, **Roger Makeele** and his crew of 13 men and 4 women crime-waved the bay; in 1717, **Blackbeard** blockaded the mouth of the bay at **Cape Henry** and demanded tribute for passage.

Piracy begat privateering. The difference between the two was that the government encouraged and honored privateersmen, while it hanged pirates. Privateers formed a very effective navy during the Revolutionary War, and in the War of 1812 their fleet of 126 ships captured 556 British ships. They certainly weren't wanting for style: one **Captain Thomas Boyle** announced to London that he was blockading the entire coast of Britain and Ireland with his 1 schooner and 16 guns.

The boats have always mirrored the bay's activity. Before the quick schooners of the privateers, log canoes with sails were fashioned from Indian dugouts; they evolved into larger versions called *brogans* and *bugeyes*. There were *shallops*, *deals*, *wherries*, *bateaux*, and *scows* (all utility, fishing, or church boats), *sloops*, *clippers*, *skipjacks*, and *rams* for increasingly serious pirating, fishing, and trade. The most famous of these was the *Baltimore Clipper*, built like a souped-up schooner in the late 1700s. It was long, low, extremely raked, and very fast—popular among pirates and slavers. Around 1860, in came decent laws and out went the clippers—they just couldn't carry enough honest cargo.

Steamboat lines crisscrossed the Chesapeake from 1787 (when **James Rumsey** ran one up the Potomac) to 1959, when the last 2 sidewheeling steamers were used to break the bay's ice. Some steamers could be quite long (200 feet), but they were always

Chesapeake Bay

slender—the Chesapeake-Delaware Canal restricted their width to no more than 24 feet, the width of the locks. In the late 1800s, the steamers were the last word in classy travel. They served cheap, extraordinary meals with their own silverware (which still turns up in local antique shops) in genteel, paneled salons and cabins.

But a steamer's career could be mixed. The *Chauncey M. Depew* was built in 1913 for the Maine Central Railroad, was used as a day cruiser on the Hudson River, then became a troop carrier in World War II, went back to the bay and then to Bermuda as a cruiser and back to the bay again to be scuttled; then it was raised and turned into a dock-locked restaurant. The bay steamboat *President Warfield* became the *Exodus* in 1947. Although her capacity was only 300, she safely carried 4554 Jews from France to Palestine in one monumentally dangerous trip. She later caught fire, sank in Haifa Harbor, and was sold for scrap.

The naming of the bay's towns has been variously historical, logical, and exotic. **Hadlock** was called *TB* for 130 years because **Thomas Bell**, a man with an exaggerated sense of property, burned his initials into shingles and plastered them on the town's trees. Elsewhere, there are towns called **Gratitude** (after a steamboat), **Bivalve** and **Shelltown** (origins obvious),

and **Accident** (origin uncertain). **Two Johns Landing** on the Choptank River came from an 1880 vaudeville team of two 300-pound men who lived there—both named John. **Plaindealing Creek** was named by the Indians after the honesty of the Quakers they traded with—evidently they found incidents of honesty so rare they felt they should be commemorated.

Drum Point Lighthouse, Solomons

Drawing by Mary Anne McLean

Lighthouses were first used here in 1791. By 1910, more than 100 had been built. But these and the few lightships used were not satisfactory. They were either too far from the danger they marked or too low. So, the *screwpile* method of on-water construction was developed. Pilings were corkscrewed down into the soft, mucky bay bottom until they formed a stable base, and stone riprap was added to protect the pilings. Neat little hexagonal cottage-lighthouses were built on top, poised on girders above the water like fantasy houses on spider legs. The 110-year-old **Thomas Point Light** near Annapolis was automated in 1986. The other 2 are retired, one to the Maritime Museum in St. Michael's, the other to the Calvert Marine Museum in Solomons. Today, all other operating lights are automated affairs except for the **Cove Point Lighthouse** north of the **Patuxent River**. Two Coast Guardsmen and their families run it—the last family light station on the bay.

Text by Peter Bradford

A Dozen More Maryland Crab Houses:

Captain John's Crab House and Marina, Inc. Rte 254, Cobb Island. 259.2315

Fin & Claw 104 Smallwood Village Shopping Center, St. Charles. 645.2529

Fisherman's Inn Rte 18, Grasonville. 827.8807

Dave Harper's Hemingways Pier 1 Marina, Stevensville. 643.2196

Harrison's Chesapeake House Rte 33, Tilghman Island. 886.2121

Hayman's Crab House 3105 Solomon's Island Rd, Edgewater. 956.2023

Red Roost Restaurant Clara Rd, Whitehaven. 546.5443

Robertson's Crab House Pope's Creek Rd, Newburg. 934.9236

Rod-n-Reel Rte 261 and Mears, Chesapeake Beach. 257.2735

Schaefer's Crab House 208 Bank St, Chesapeake City. 885.2200

Shymansky's Rte 254, Cobb Island. 259.2881

Bish Thompson's Seafood Restaurant 7935 Wisconsin Ave, Bethesda. 656.2200

January Presidential inauguration, every 4 years, steps of the Capitol, followed by a parade down Pennsylvania Ave to the White House; Opening of Congress; Robert E. Lee birthday celebration, Stratford Hall Plantation, Stratford VA; Stonewall Jackson birthday celebration, Lexington VA; Annapolis Heritage Antique Show, Edgewater MD; Chesapeake Bay Boat Show, Convention Center, DC; Martin Luther King, Jr., birthday celebrations throughout DC

February Abraham Lincoln birthday celebrations throughout DC; George Washington birthday celebrations, Washington's Birthplace, near Oak Grove VA, and Mount Vernon; Chinese New Year's Parade, Chinatown, DC; Casonova Point-to-Point Races, Warrenton VA

March Annual Fine Arts Festival, Fredericksburg VA; Baltimore Antique Bottle Show and Sale, Timonium MD; Winter Wine Preview Weekend, Charlottesville VA; St. Patrick's Day parades, DC, Baltimore MD, and Annapolis MD; Maryland Days Weekend, St. Mary's City MD; Civil War Relic Show, Fredericksburg VA

April Cherry Blossom Festival, DC; Historic Garden Week, Charlottesville and Albemarle VA; Rappahannock River Run and Walk, Old Town Fredericksburg VA; Annual Dogwood Festival, Charlottesville VA; Easter Egg Roll, White House, DC; Champagne and Candlelight Tour of Ash Lawn-Highland, Charlottesville VA; Prince George's Dressage and Maryland Horse Fair, Upper Marlboro MD; Wreath Laying Ceremony commemorating birthday of Thomas Jefferson, Monticello, Charlottesville VA; William Shakespeare birthday festivities, Folger Shakespeare Library, DC; Spring Garden Tour, White House; Gross National Parade, from the White House to Georgetown; Annual Old Town Tour of Homes and Gardens, Alexandria VA; Annual Foxfield Horse Races, Charlottesville VA; Annual Festival of 18th-Century Life, Sully Plantation, Chantilly VA

May Memorial Day ceremonies, Arlington National Cemetery and Vietnam Veterans Memorial; National Symphony concert, west lawn of Capitol; Annual Shenandoah Apple Blossom Festival, Winchester VA; George Mason Day, Gunston Hall, Lorton VA; Flower Mart, Baltimore MD; Baltimore African Violet Show, Towson MD; Preakness celebration, Pimlico Race Course, Baltimore MD; Commissioning Week, US Naval Academy, Annapolis MD; Chesapeake Bay Bridge Walk, Sandy Point MD; Queen Henrietta Maria's Festival of Roses and May Flowers, William Paca Garden, Annapolis MD

June Annual Ash Lawn-Highland Summer Opera Festival, Charlottesville MD; Potomac Riverfest, DC; Dupont-Kalorama Museum Walk Day, DC; Festival of American Folklife, Smithsonian Institution, DC; Showcase of Nations Ethnic Festivals, Baltimore MD; Chesapeake Bay Bridge Swim Race, Annapolis MD; Virginia Wineries Festival, Front Royal VA; Blackwater Wildlife and Water Celebration, Cambridge MD; Tilghman Island Seafood Festival, Tilghman Island MD; Marine Corps Sunset Parade, Iwo Jima Memorial, Arlington VA; National Flag Day celebration, Fort McHenry, Baltimore MD

July Independence Day celebrations throughout DC; Annual Colonial Crafts Festival, Washington's Birthplace, VA; Hispanic-American Cultural Festival, DC; Annual Virginia Scottish Games and Gathering of the Clans, Alexandria VA; Solomons Island Regatta, Annapolis MD; Annual Naturalization Ceremony, Monticello, Charlottesville VA; Blue Bayou Music Festival, Marlboro MD; J. Millard Tawes Crab and Clam Bake, Crisfield MD

August Tavern Days, Gadsby's Tavern, Alexandria VA; 1812 Overture, Washington Monument grounds, DC; Annual Wine Festival, Middleburg VA; Annual Antique Auto Show, Fredericksburg VA; Governor's Cup Yacht Race, Annapolis MD; Queen Anne Joust, Queen Anne MD; Capital Classic Horseshow, Marlboro MD; Maryland Renaissance Festival, Annapolis MD

September International Children's Festival, Wolf Trap Farm Park, Vienna VA; National Hard Crab Derby and Fair, Crisfield MD; Skipjack Races and Festival, Deal Island MD; Waterman's Boat Docking Contest, Salisbury MD; Trolley Car Extravaganza, National Capital Trolley Museum, Wheaton MD; Annual Draft Horse and Mule Day, Leesburg MD; Annual Gunston Hall Car Show, Lorton VA; Foxfield Steeplechase Races, Charlottesville VA; Labor Day Concert by National Symphony Orchestra, west lawn of Capitol, DC; Opening of Redskins football season

October Reenactment of formal visit of the Marquis de Lafayette, Boyhood Home of Robert E. Lee, Alexandria VA; United States Sailboat and Powerboat Show, Annapolis MD; Foxfield Steeplechase Races, Charlottesville VA; Monticello Wine Festival, Charlottesville VA; Opening of Supreme Court, DC; Chesapeake Appreciation Days Festival, Annapolis MD; Halloween Insomniac Tour, Baltimore MD

November Marine Corps Marathon, Iwo Jima Memorial, Arlington VA; Veteran's Day celebration, Arlington National Cemetery and Vietnam Veterans Memorial; Maryland Handel Festival, University of Maryland, College Park MD; Oyster Day, St. Michaels MD; Thanksgiving Day parades, DC and Baltimore MD; Annual Crafts Festival and Exhibit, Fredericksburg VA

December Pageant of Peace and Lighting of National Christmas Tree, Ellipse, DC; Candlelight tour of the White House, DC; Annual Scottish Christmas Walk, Alexandria VA; Drum Point Lighthouse Open House, Solomons MD; Christmas Parade of Yachts, Annapolis MD; New Year's Extravaganza, Inner Harbor, Baltimore MD; New Year's Eve Celebration, Old Post Office Pavilion, DC; Annual First Night, Charlottesville VA

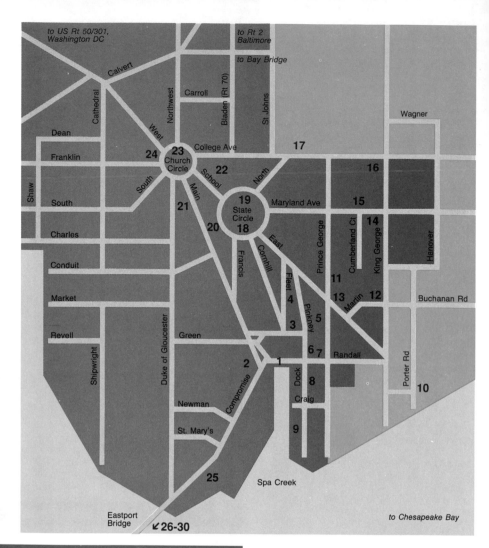

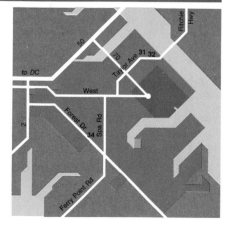

In 1770, **Reverend Jonathan Boucher** described Annapolis as "the genteelest town in North America....I hardly know a town in England as desirable to live in."

Annapolis, just 30 miles east of DC on the Chesapeake Bay, has been the capital of Maryland since early Colonial days. First settled by Puritans in 1649, Annapolis took its present name 50 years later from **Princess Anne**, crowned Queen of England soon thereafter. The city began to thrive in the 1740s as colonists grew increasingly independent of British rule. The many handsome 18th-century buildings still standing today—many built prior to the Revolution—attest to the city's important role as a port and commercial center for Maryland colony. (After years of struggle to ensure the safety of this country's greatest collection of 18th-century buildings, an enforceable historic-district zoning law was finally passed in 1969.) From November 1783 through August 1784, Annapolis served as the US capital—**George Washington** resigned as commander-in-chief of the Continental Army here and the *Treaty of Paris* was ratified, officially ending the American Revolution.

When it was established in 1845, the **United States Naval Academy** became the center of attention in Annapolis. The academy brings its own rich history, in addition to flocks of white-hatted midshipmen, or *middies*, as they are commonly known.

The maritime atmosphere in Annapolis has also attracted flocks of sailing enthusiasts, many of world-class caliber, turning the city into an East Coast sailing mecca. The in-the-water sailboat show in October is the largest in the nation. The water has also beckoned many well-to-do professionals from Baltimore and Washington in search of respite from their hectic city lives. *Area code 301 unless otherwise indicated.*

1 City Dock The old dock marks the historic city center where the tobacco ships loaded their cargoes. Today it is a popular hangout, particularly in midsummer, when boaters cruise the narrow channel, checking out the action. ♦ Main and Randall Sts

At City Dock:

Visitor Information Center is a good source of facts about the city and surrounding areas, tours, and various buildings. For further information, contact the **Tourism Council of Annapolis and Anne Arundel Counties** (280.0445) or the **Greater Annapolis Area Chamber of Commerce** (268.7676), both at 6 Dock St, Annapolis MD 21401. ♦ Daily 10AM-6PM, Memorial Day-Oct. (Days and hours vary during off-season: call for schedule.) 268.8687

Market House at City Dock The first Market House at this location was built in 1788, the next in 1858. A renovated version opened in 1972. Shops feature vegetables, bakery goods, and, of course, fish. ♦ Daily 10 AM-9PM. Market Sq. 267.0363

2 Victualling Warehouse Maritime Museum (1810) The *Maritime Annapolis 1751–1791* exhibition is housed within this building. Other displays focus on trade and commerce. Commissary stores stood here during the Revolution. ♦ Fee. Daily 11AM-4:30PM. 77 Main St (Green-Compromise Sts) 268.5576

3 Riordan's ★★$$ This saloon and 2nd-floor dining room is well-known for its reliable seafood —especially crabcakes—and prime ribs. ♦ American ♦ M-Sa 11AM-1AM; Su 10AM-midnight. 26 Market Space (Cornhill St) 263.5449

4 The Barracks Furnishings here represent the living conditions of Revolutionary War soldiers awaiting sea passage to battle sites. ♦ Fee. Sa-Su 11AM-4:30PM, mid Apr-mid Oct. 43 Pinkney St (East St-Market Sq) 268.5576

Upon seeing Chesapeake Bay, one of the very first Maryland colonists exclaimed that "this baye is the most delightful water I ever saw between 2 sweet landes...." And about the *Patowmeck*: "This is the sweetest and greatest river I have seene, so that the Thames is but a little finger of it."

Restaurants: Red	Hotels: Blue
Shops/Parks: Green	Sights/Culture: Black

5 Shiplap House and Garden (1713, Edward Smith) The **Historic Annapolis** group purchased and restored the building in 1958. First a private home, then a tavern, Shiplap House now houses archaeological finds from digs throughout Annapolis. Gift shop. ♦ Free. Daily 11AM-4PM. 18 Pinkney St (East-Randall Sts) 267.8149

6 Tobacco Prise Warehouse Tobacco-processing tools and equipment are on exhibit in this restored warehouse. ♦ Fee; tickets at Victualling Warehouse, 77 Main St. Sa-Su 11AM-4:30PM, mid Apr-mid Oct. 4 Pinkney St (Market Sq) 268.5576

7 Harbour House Restaurant ★$$ Modern version of beamed-ceiling tavern. Seafood, prime ribs, and bouillabaisse are specialties. A fine view of the port. ♦ American ♦ Daily 11:30AM-2:30PM, 5-10PM. 87 Prince George St (Randall St) 268.0771

8 Harbor Square Treat yourself to some wonderful chocolates before dashing off to the haberdashery among the square's half-dozen specialty shops. ♦ Dock St (Randall-Prince George Sts)

9 United States Naval Academy Established in 1845, its buildings include the **Chapel** and French Renaissance-style **Bancroft Hall**. The chapel houses the tomb of

John Paul Jones, who is often called the *Father of the US Navy*. Naval officers are memorialized in the chapel's stained-glass windows. Just outside the chapel entrance lie anchors from the *New York*, a cruiser used to blockade Cuba in 1898.

The **Visitor Information Center** at Ricketts Hall is open daily 9AM to 4PM. The **Gift Shop** is open daily 10AM to 4PM. ♦ Fee. Walking tours: M-Sa 10AM-3PM on the hour, Su 11AM-3PM, Mar-May, Labor Day weekend-Thanksgiving weekend; M-Sa 9:30AM-4PM every half hour, Su 11AM-4PM, June-Labor Day weekend. Group tours by reservation only. Visitor Gate, King George St (Maryland Ave) 267.6100, Naval Academy Guide Service 267.3363 or 263.6933

Within the United States Naval Academy:

Preble Hall features 30,000 nautical relics, from ships models to uniforms to oil paintings and engravings. ♦ M-Sa 9AM-5PM; Su 11AM-5PM. 267.2108

10 Governor William Paca House (1765, William Paca) A signer of the Declaration of Independence and 3-time governor of Maryland built this 5-part mansion. The restored and refurbished building is now used as a conference center for the US State Dept. ♦ Fee. M (federal holidays only); Tu-Sa 10AM-4PM; Su noon-4PM. 186 Prince George St (East St-Maryland Ave) 263-5553

11 William Paca Gardens Restored Colonial garden with sculptured terraces, waterways, a canal, and a Chinese Chippendale bridge. Among the plants are wildflowers, myrtle, and roses. ♦ Fee. M-Sa 10AM-4:30PM; Su noon-4:30PM, Jan-Apr, Nov-Dec; M-Sa 10AM-4PM; Su noon-5PM, May-Oct. 1 Martin St (King George St) 267.6656, 299.0601

12 Brice House (1774, James Brice) This Georgian mansion, restored and repainted in its original colors, is one of the largest homes in Annapolis. Note the triple pediment windows above the main entrance and the huge chimneys. A registered **National Historic Landmark**. ♦ Admission. Group tours by appointment only. 42 East St (Prince George-King George Sts) 267.8149

13 Hammond-Harwood House William Buckland's 18th-century Georgian mansion features egg-and-dart moldings and Ionic columns at the front door. Rose festoons frame the fan above the front window. ♦ Fee. Tu-Sa 10AM-4PM, Su 1-4PM, Jan-Mar, Nov-Dec; Tu-Sa 10AM-5PM, Su 2-5PM, Apr-Oct. 19 Maryland Ave (King George St) 269.1714

14 Chase-Lloyd House Samuel Chase, later a signer of the Declaration of Independence, sold this unfinished house to **Edward Lloyd** in 1771. It is now a ladies retirement home. ♦ Fee. 1st-floor rooms Tu-Sa 2-4PM. 22 Maryland Ave (Prince George-King George Sts) 263.2723

Annapolis

15 Ogle Hall First occupied by Royal Governor **Samuel Ogle** in 1739, this hall was purchased by the Naval Academy in 1949 to serve as a graduate guest home. Not open to the public. ♦ 247 King George St (College St-Maryland Ave)

16 St. John's College Opened in 1696, the college was one of the first US public schools. During the Civil War, it served as a Northern parole and hospital center. **McDowell Hall**, built in 1742 as a residence for Governor **Thomas Bladen**, became known as *Bladen's Folly* for its grandiose style. The **Liberty Tree**, on the campus' northern side, is a tulip poplar over 400 years old. ♦ Bladen-King George Sts (College-Taylor Aves)

In 1876, the **Annapolis Convention** brought together commercial interests from the various states. Dissatisfaction with the *Articles of Confederation* expressed there led to the **Federal Constitutional Convention** in Philadelphia the next year.

17 Old Treasury Building Built in 1735 to store Bills of Credit, this brick building with arched ceilings serves as the tour office of **Historic Annapolis Inc.**, which conducts 1½-hour walking tours of Annapolis' historic district. The company also arranges group tours of historic homes ordinarily closed to the public. ♦ Fee. M-F 9AM-4:30PM. Tours M-F 1:30PM. State House Grounds at State Circle. 267.8149

18 Maryland State House Built between 1772 and 1779, this is the oldest US state capitol in continuous legislative use. Congress met in the Old Senate Chamber from late 1783 to mid 1784, when Annapolis was serving as the US capital. Senate and House chambers currently occupy a newer 1902 section.

The structure's dome is the largest wooden dome in the US. Officials climb 149 steps twice daily to raise and lower the state flag. Guided tours of 1st-floor public rooms, with slide orientation program. ♦ Free. Daily 10AM-5PM. Walk-in tours daily at 11AM, 2, 4PM. Group tours by reservation. State Circle (School St-Maryland Ave) 974.3400

19 MFA Gallery on the Circle The Maryland Federation of Art operates this gallery of ever-changing art exhibitions. ♦ Free. Tu-F 11AM-5PM; Sa 10AM-5PM; Su noon-5PM. 18 State Circle (School-Francis Sts) 268.4566

20 Maryland Inn $$ (1776) Once billed as a *house of entertainment*, this cozy 43-room inn around the corner from the State House has offered food, lodgings, and good cheer since 1782. The **Treaty of Paris Restaurant** specializes in Chesapeake Bay seafood and French dishes; the **King of France Tavern**, first used in 1784 and restored in the mid 1970s, features national and regional jazz acts. Children under 18 stay free. ◆ 16 Church Circle (Duke of Gloucester-Main Sts) 202/261.2206, 269.0990, 800/847.8882 (800/638.8902 in MD); fax 268.3813 &

21 Governor's Mansion (1866) This Victorian-style house owned by the Naval Academy was converted to a Georgian-style structure in the 1930s and is now used as the residence of the governor of Maryland. The 1st-floor rooms have been recently renovated with antique furnishings, vintage Oriental rugs, and 6 Waterford crystal chandeliers. ◆ Group tours Tu-Th 10AM-2PM by appointment only. School St (State-Church Circles) 974.3531

22 St. Anne's Church The first church on this site was constructed in the 1600s; the present structure, the third church built on this site, dates back to 1858. ◆ Daily 9AM-4PM. Services (Episcopal) Su 7:30, 10, 11:15AM. Church Circle. 267.9333

23 Banneker-Douglass Museum of Afro-American Life and Culture A historical and cultural overview of the lives of black residents of Maryland. Films, lectures, and art classes. ◆ Free. Tu-F 10AM-3PM; Sa noon-4PM. 84 Franklin St (Shipwright-South Sts) 974.2894

24 Annapolis Hilton Inn $$ Located in the historic district. The **Penthouse Wardroom Restaurant**, **Skipper's Pub**, and **Afterdeck Bar** are all here for your refreshment. Some rooms have balconies overlooking the harbor. The outdoor patio is a great place to watch the boats cruising City Dock. Special packages available. Children under 12 stay free. ◆ 80 Compromise St (St. Mary's St) 268.7555, 800/HILTONS; fax 263.8999

25 Fawcett Boat Supplies Inc. Ultimate boat chandlers, with hardware, charts, clothing, gifts, and books for the Topsider crowd. ◆ M-F 8:30AM-5:30PM, Sa 11AM-4PM, Jan-Memorial Day, Labor Day-Dec; M-Th, Sa 8:30AM-5:30PM, F 8:30AM-7:30PM, Su 11AM-4PM, Memorial Day-Labor Day. 110 Compromise St (St. Mary's-Duke of Gloucester Sts) 267.8681

26 International Sailing Products The motherlode for the area's hard-core windsurfers: boards, wetsuits and drysuits, sailing gear, and safety equipment. Lessons and rentals are available. ◆ M-Sa 10AM-6PM; Su noon-5PM. 318 6th St (Spa Creek Drawbridge) 269.6160

27 Carrol's Creek Cafe ★$$ Light renditions of fresh seafood, with a Cajun touch. Overlooks Spa Creek. ◆ Seafood ◆ Daily 11:30AM-4PM, 5-10PM. 410 Severn Ave (4th-5th Sts) 263.8102

28 Marmaduke's Pub ★★$ A casual burger-and-seafood joint favored by sailboat maniacs; the race videos are the clue. ◆ American ◆ Daily 11:30AM-11PM. 301 Severn Ave (3rd-4th Sts) 269.5420

Three men from Annapolis signed the Declaration of Independence: **William Paca**, **Samuel Chase**, and **Charles Carroll**.

29 C. Plath, North American Division Traditional brass compasses and other exquisitely crafted marine accessories; you don't need to own a boat to appreciate them. ◆ M-F 9PM-5PM. 222 Severn Ave (2nd-3rd Sts) 263.6700

30 Chart House ★★$$ California-style seafood, steaks, and salad bar. Overlooks the harbor. ◆ American ◆ M-Th 5-10PM; F-Sa 5-11PM; Su 11AM-2PM, 5-10PM. 300 2nd St (Severn Ave) 268.7166

31 Helen Avalynne Tawes Garden Named after one of Maryland's former First Ladies, this 6-acre botanical garden is in fact several gardens, each a well-cultivated representation of Maryland nature. Designed to exemplify the objectives of the **Department of Natural Resources** (preservation, development, wise use, and enjoyment), the garden is an environmentalist's delight, an excellent blend of conservation and landscape architecture. There are picnic areas, a visitors center, a cafeteria, and a gift shop staffed by volunteers; the latter 3 are closed state holidays. ◆ Free. Garden daily dawn-dusk. Visitors center M-F 8AM-5PM. Cafeteria M-F 7:30AM-3PM. Gift shop M-F 11AM-3PM. Tours by appointment. 580 Taylor Ave (Roscoe Rowe Blvd) 974.3717

32 Northwoods ★★$$ Pastas, grilled meats, and fresh fish. The coho salmon is especially good when topped with pine nuts, capers, or hearts of palm. For dessert, made-to-order zabaglione. Extensive wine list. ◆ Italian ◆ M-F 11:30AM-3PM, 6-10PM; Sa 6-10PM; Su 5-9PM. 609 Melvin Ave (Ridgely Ave) 268.2609

33 Cantler's Riverside Inn ★★★$ Ultimate crabhouse, with indoor dining at long tables or outdoor dining overlooking Mill Creek. ◆ Seafood ◆ M-Th, Su 10AM-11PM; F-Sa 10AM-midnight. 458 Forest Beach Rd (Rte 50E) 757.1311

34 Holiday Inn $ Conveniently close to the historic district; equipped with HBO and meeting and banquet facilities. Children under 19 stay free. ◆ 210 Holiday Court (Forest Dr) 224.3150, 800/HOLIDAY; fax 224.3413 &

35 London Town Publik House and Gardens This restored Colonial inn overlooks the South River. The only building remaining from an 18th-century town. Eight acres of gardens as well. ◆ Admission. Tu-Sa 10AM-4PM; Su noon-4PM, Mar-Dec. 839 London Town Rd (Rte 2-Mayo Rd) Edgewater. 956.4900

In 1611, **Lord De-La-Ware** stated the following: "This is a goodly River called Patomack, upon the borders whereof there are growne the goodliest Trees for Masts, that may be found elsewhere in the World: Hempe better than English, growing wilde in aboundance: Mines of Antimonie and Leade."

About 70 percent of Maryland's settlers arrived as indentured servants.

163

Rich in character, a fascinating place to explore, **Baltimore** is much earthier and more varied than Washington. Highlights include the sights and smells of the harbor, a lively ethnic mix, some of America's finest 19th-century streets, great seafood, and a world-class collection of **Matisse** paintings.

Founded in 1729, Baltimore has always been a water city, harboring every kind of sailing, steaming, and diesel craft. At times the immense fishing fleets, or later the coffee, pineapple, and coal fleets, made Baltimore look like a city of ships. Shipbuilding flourished during the Revolutionary War and the 1800s; the great Baltimore clippers maintained a lucrative overseas trade even in times of conflict.

In 1827, businessmen feared that the new Erie Canal would threaten their profitable trans-Allegheny traffic,

Baltimore

as goods and settlers moved westward from the East Coast cities and ports. In response, the **Baltimore & Ohio Railroad**, the first public railroad in North America, was established. The successful run of **Peter Cooper**'s *Tom Thumb* train in 1830 introduced steam locomotives to the B&O. A replica of it still stands in the **B&O Railroad Museum**.

Like so many of America's older cities, Baltimore began to deteriorate in the 1950s and by the '60s was a prime target for urban renewal. Dismayed and alarmed by the city's disintegration, a group of businesspeople formed the **Greater Baltimore Committee** and drew up plans for revitalization. With the city government's help—particularly that of **Mayor William Schaefer** in the '70s—these plans have become reality.

The results? A sparkling inner harbor, spruced-up homes, and a recharged downtown. The first makeover gave us **Charles Center**, a 15-building office and apartment complex that covers 33 acres of downtown Baltimore.

The **Inner Harbor** was transformed by the success of **Rouse Company**'s **Harborplace**. The 18-million-dollar project attracts huge crowds with its 2 glass pavilions topped with green aluminum roofs. The 2 marketplaces meet at a right angle, and from everywhere inside offer a view of the water and its ships.

Other projects for the harbor have included the 30-story **World Trade Center** and the **Maryland Science Center**. The **National Aquarium** brings visitors face-to-face with fish and sea mammals—as close as possible without getting wet. The amazing concrete-and-glass structure juts out over **Pier 3**.

To further rehabilitate the city, innovative homesteading programs have allowed homebuyers to purchase abandoned houses for $1; when repaired, these formerly dilapidated row houses become valuable properties. *Area code 301 unless otherwise indicated.*

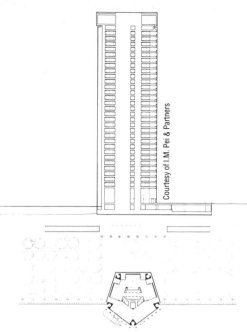

Courtesy of I.M. Pei & Partners

1 World Trade Center (1977, I.M. Pei & Partners) The world's tallest pentagonal high-rise reflects Pei's fondness for strong geometries and is perhaps the most recognizable feature of Baltimore's new downtown skyline. There's a great observation deck on the 27th floor called the *Top of the World*: you'll see the entire city, as well as creative displays of the port, its attractions, and its people. Buttons, levers, and viewers will especially delight kids and first-time visitors. ♦ Fee. Sa-Su 10AM-5PM, Jan-May, Oct-Dec; M-F 10 AM-5PM, Sa 10AM-7PM, Su noon-6PM, Jun-Sep. 401 E. Pratt St (Commerce St) 837.4515

2 Harborplace (1980, Benjamin Thompson & Associates) Acclaimed as the nucleus of the **Inner Harbor** renewal effort, the 2 glass-enclosed pavilions seem to float on the edge of Baltimore's inner harbor. Put together with great attention to color and detail, Harborplace offers 142,000 square feet of shops, taverns, and restaurants. ♦ M-Sa 10AM-10PM; Su noon-8PM. 200 E. Pratt St (Light St) 332.4191

At Harborplace:

The Gallery at Harborplace (1987, Zeidler Roberts Partnership) A 1.7 million-square-foot, 28-story development linked to Harborplace by a skyway. The **Stouffer Hotel at Harborplace** ($$) contains 622 guest rooms, 18 meeting rooms, and 2 huge ballrooms (547.1200). The **Legg Mason Office Tower** is home to 20 businesses. Four levels of retail space hold approximately 75 shops, restaurants, and food stalls.

Phillips at Harborplace ★★$$ Great ocean-view patio seating, music daily at the piano bar, and live Dixieland jazz on Sundays. An assortment of some of the freshest crabs, mussels, and clams in the city. ♦ Seafood ♦ M-Th, Su 11AM-10:30PM; F-Sa 11AM-11PM. Light St Pavilion. 685.6600

Vivande ★★$$ Northern Italian specialties with a touch of California—good pizza and pasta—and a spectacular view of the water. ♦ Italian ♦ M-Th 11:30AM-9:30PM, F-Sa 11:30AM-10:30PM; Su 10:30AM-9PM, Jan-Jun, mid Oct-Dec. M-Th, Su 9AM-3:30PM, 5:30-10PM, F-Sa 9AM-4:30PM, 5:30-11PM, 1 Jul-mid Oct; Pratt St Pavilion. Reservations recommended F-Su. 837.1131

Bamboo House ★★$ For some of Baltimore's best Chinese food, try this Szechuan haven. ♦ Chinese ♦ M-Th 11:30AM-10:30PM; F 11:30AM-11:30PM; Sa noon-11:30PM; Su noon-10:30PM. Pratt St Pavilion. 625.1191

3 Hyatt Regency Baltimore $$$ Walkways connect this immense glass-paneled hotel with the Baltimore Convention Center and Harborplace. The 487 rooms have access to 2 restaurants, 3 tennis courts, a health club, and a large rooftop swimming pool. The upgraded **Regency Club** features toiletries, unlimited concierge assistance, and complimentary Continental breakfast, hors d'oeuvres, and cocktails. Children under 18 stay free. ♦ 300 Light St (Conway-Pratt Sts) 528.1234, 800/228.9000; fax 685.3362

4 Maryland Science Center & Planetarium (1976, Edward Durell Stone) This octagonal structure of soft pink brick contains 5 permanent exhibitions about Baltimore, the Chesapeake Bay, and related scientific information. The center is the home of the **Maryland Academy of Sciences**, founded in 1797. Traveling exhibitions focus on the latest in Earth and Space achievements. The **Davis Planetarium** re-creates a stellar voyage with 350 simultaneous projectors, and the **Boyd Theatre** screens films and live experiments.

Not to be missed. ♦ Fee. M-F 10AM-5PM; Sa 10AM-6PM; Su noon-6PM. 601 Light St (Key Highway) 685.5225

5 Federal Hill Park You'll get the best panoramic view of the harbor from this hill, occupied by the North during the Civil War. An area of 18th-century homes just below the park, the **Otterbein Homesteading Project**, has been restored by modern urban homesteaders who each bought their homes for a dollar. ♦ Daily 7AM-midnight. Battery St and Key Hwy

6 Baltimore Museum of Industry Once an oyster cannery, now a museum tracking the industrial history of Baltimore. Permanent exhibitions include a 1910 garment loft, a 19th-century print shop, and a 1906 steam tugboat. ♦ Admission. Tu-F, Su noon-5PM; Sa 10AM-5PM. 1415 Key Hwy (Ford Ave) 727.4808

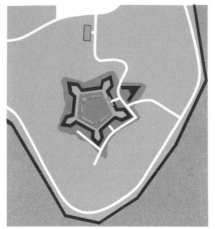

7 Fort McHenry (1794–1805, John Jacob Ulrich Rivardi) The 20-foot-thick brick walls of this star-shaped fort overlooking the harbor protected the compound from the British attack on 13 September 1814; the next morning, when he saw that the US flag was still flying, **Francis Scott Key** wrote a poem called *Star-Spangled Banner*. Later the poem was put to music, and in 1931 became the national anthem.

The **Visitors Center** offers films and exhibitions on the fort and the national anthem. ♦ Fee. Daily 9AM-5PM, Jan-May, Sep-Dec; daily 9AM-8PM, Jun-Aug. E. Fort Ave. 962.4290

8 Fell's Point One of the first great maritime communities and still a working waterfront. Settled in the early 1700s by the Fell brothers from Lancaster, England, Fell's Point preserves a flavor of its early history. Many of the buildings are 18th- and early 19th-century originals;

the streets are paved with Belgian block and have names that reflect the English ancestry of the first settlers: **Bank**, **Bond**, **Fleet**, **Lancaster**, **Shakespeare**, **Thames**, **Wolfe**. Fell's Point was the first district in Maryland to be added to the **National Registry of Historic Places**. It can be reached on a trolley car for only a quarter. Call for walking tour hours. ♦ Fee. 1 mile east of Inner Harbor. 764.8067

At Fell's Point:

Market Square A public square from the time of the Fell brothers. Local ethnic festivals are held here during the summer. ♦ Broadway and Thames St

Vagabond Players, Inc. Opened in 1916, the Vagabond claims to be the oldest continuously operating little theater in the country. ♦ Seats 102. 806 S. Broadway (Shakespeare-Thames Sts) 563.9135

China Sea Marine Trading Company The proprietor, a long time seaman himself, and his parrots (they have free run of the space) sell an eclectic mix of international merchandise, mostly from ships that have called at the Baltimore port. Maybe the oddest item: a preserved human skull in a glass case. This could qualify as a museum. Watch out for Jack, a 52-year-old parrot who will fly 2 doors down to the **Cat's Eye** for a drink. ♦ Call for hours. 1724 Thames St (Broadway-Ann St) 276.8220

The Admiral Fell Inn $$ Once a sailors lodging house, then a vinegar factory. Forty rooms with antique furnishings, including canopy beds with white lace covers. Go up to the roof and view Fell's Point in contrast to the surrounding modern landscape. Breakfast included. Weekend and other special packages. ♦ 888 S. Broadway (Shakespeare-Thames Sts) 522.7377, 800/292.4667; fax 522.4667

Bertha's Dining Room ★★$$ Its bumper stickers ordering you to Eat Bertha's Mussels give good advice. High tea reservations required 1 day in advance. ♦ Seafood ♦ M-Th, Su 11:30AM-11PM; F-Sa 11:30AM-midnight. High tea M-Sa 3-4:30PM. 734 S. Broadway (Lancaster-Aliceanna Sts) 327.5795

Robert Long House (1765, Robert Long) The oldest house in the city. Built in the Quaker style with a pent roof and a shed dormer. Tours by appointment. ♦ Fee. 812 S. Anna St (Thames St) 675.6750

Haussner's ★★$$ Heads of state are literally fixtures at this incredible restaurant, hoarding a big collection of Greco-Roman busts and antique paintings in the dining room. Enjoy a feast of sauerbraten, rabbit with spaetzle, or seafood. ♦ German/American ♦ Tu-Th 11AM-10PM; F-Sa 11AM-11PM. 3242 Eastern Ave (Clinton St) 327.8365

Unicorn Studios Vintage stained glass, gold-leafed and expertly framed. ♦ Tu-F 10AM-6PM; Sa 10AM-5PM. 626 S. Broadway (Fleet-Aliceanna Sts) 675.5412

9 Pier 6 Vaguely reminiscent of the opera house in Sydney, Australia, this addition to the Inner Harbor is the largest structure of its kind in America. The open music pavilion seats 3100 listeners both inside and outside its canvas-domed steel structure. Pop, jazz, and classical music are featured throughout the summer season. ♦ Box office M-F noon-6PM. Performance days M-F noon-8PM. 727 E Pratt St (Pier 6) 625.4230, Telecharge 625.1400

10 Submarine USS Torsk This submarine sank the last Japanese combatant ships of World War II. After that feat the *Torsk* was fortified with a snorkel-equipped *GUPPY* machine and used as a training vessel. It holds the all-time world record for having made 11,884 dives. The self-guided tour includes the *Lightship Chesapeake*, a floating lighthouse. ♦ Fee. Daily 9:30AM-4:30PM. Pier 3 at the Inner Harbor. 396.3854

For Baltimore events, call 301/837.INFO.

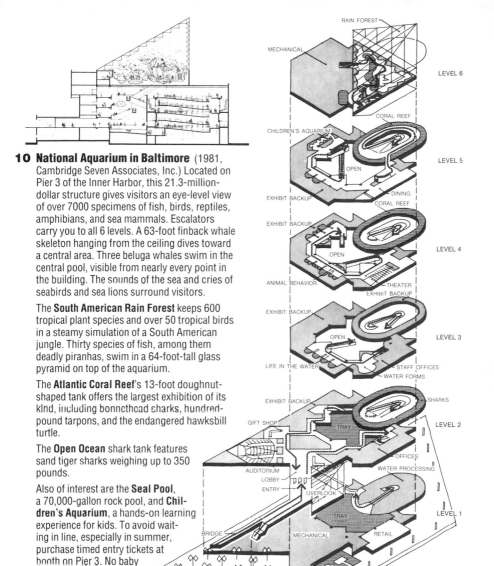

Labels on the diagram: RAIN FOREST, MECHANICAL, LEVEL 6, CORAL REEF, CHILDREN'S AQUARIUM, LEVEL 5, OPEN, DINING, EXHIBIT BACKUP, CORAL REEF, EXHIBIT BACKUP, LEVEL 4, OPEN, ANIMAL BEHAVIOR, THEATER, EXHIBIT BACKUP, EXHIBIT BACKUP, LEVEL 3, OPEN, LIFE IN THE WATER, STAFF OFFICES, WATER FORMS, EXHIBIT BACKUP, SHARKS, GIFT SHOP, TRAY, LEVEL 2, OFFICES, AUDITORIUM, WATER PROCESSING, LOBBY, ENTRY, OVERLOOK, TRAY, LEVEL 1, BRIDGE, MECHANICAL, RETAIL, SEALS, WIND SCULPTURES, RETAIL, PLAZA, **Baltimore**

10 National Aquarium in Baltimore (1981, Cambridge Seven Associates, Inc.) Located on Pier 3 of the Inner Harbor, this 21.3-million-dollar structure gives visitors an eye-level view of over 7000 specimens of fish, birds, reptiles, amphibians, and sea mammals. Escalators carry you to all 6 levels. A 63-foot finback whale skeleton hanging from the ceiling dives toward a central area. Three beluga whales swim in the central pool, visible from nearly every point in the building. The sounds of the sea and cries of seabirds and sea lions surround visitors.

The **South American Rain Forest** keeps 600 tropical plant species and over 50 tropical birds in a steamy simulation of a South American jungle. Thirty species of fish, among them deadly piranhas, swim in a 64-foot-tall glass pyramid on top of the aquarium.

The **Atlantic Coral Reef**'s 13-foot doughnut-shaped tank offers the largest exhibition of its kind, including bonnethead sharks, hundred-pound tarpons, and the endangered hawksbill turtle.

The **Open Ocean** shark tank features sand tiger sharks weighing up to 350 pounds.

Also of interest are the **Seal Pool**, a 70,000-gallon rock pool, and **Children's Aquarium**, a hands-on learning experience for kids. To avoid waiting in line, especially in summer, purchase timed entry tickets at booth on Pier 3. No baby strollers allowed inside.

School and group tours can be arranged with lots of advance notice. ◆ Fee. M-Th, Sa-Su 10AM-5PM, F 10AM-8PM, Jan-14 May, 16 Sep-Dec; M-Th 9AM-5PM, F-Su 9AM-8PM, 15 May-15 Sep. 501 E. Pratt St (Gay Sts) 576.3810

Courtesy Cambridge Seven Associates, Inc.

11 Old Otterbein United Methodist Church (1786) Built by German immigrants nearly 2 centuries ago, the Georgian building is now the oldest church in Baltimore. In the 1960s, it served as one of the anchors for the city's urban renewal plan. The interior is rather plain, except for the original stained-glass windows. Tours by appointment. ◆ Free. Sa 10AM-4PM, Apr-Oct. Conway and Sharp Sts. 685.4703

12 P.J. Cricketts ★$ Choose between the upstairs dining room and the casual atmosphere of the downstairs pub. Baby back ribs are the big push here, served with taco salad or nachos, or with fresh crabcakes as surf 'n' turf. ◆ American ◆ M-Th 11AM-2PM, 5-10PM; F 11AM-2PM, 5PM-midnight; Sa 5PM-midnight; Su 4-10PM. 206 W. Pratt St (Howard-Sharp Sts) Reservations recommended. 244.8900

F. Scott Fitzgerald once said of Baltimore, where he lived from 1933 to 1935, "I belong here, where everything is civilized and gay and rotted and polite."

Restaurants: Red **Hotels**: Blue **Shops/Parks**: Green **Sights/Culture**: Black

13 Baltimore Arena The huge hall with its jagged roofline was Baltimore's main auditorium before the Convention Center was built. On this site in 1774 the Continental Congress voted to give **George Washington** full military control. The famous *Sunday Morning Fire* began here in the cellar of the Hurst Company building. Check local listings for sports and entertainment events. ◆ Seats 10,000. Daily 10AM-5PM. 201 W. Baltimore St (Hopkins Plaza) Tape of events 347.2000; tickets 342.2010.

14 Davidge Hall (1812, Robert Carey Long, Sr.) Home to a medical teaching facility ever since it was built in 1812. Styled after a Roman temple. ◆ 522 W. Lombard St (Green-Paca Sts) 328.7454

15 Edgar Allan Poe's Grave The master of scary suspense certainly picked his lot: Westminster Church, next to the graveyard, is built directly on catacombs, where coffins filled with bones lie wide open. Tours to Poe's and the other grisly graves are held every first and third Friday evening and Saturday morning. ◆ Fee. Tours F 6:30PM, Sa 10AM, Apr-Nov. Reservations required. Fayette and Greene Sts. 328.7228

16 Lexington Market Originally an open-air market, the Lexington is the oldest of its kind in the country. Named for the Battle at Lexington, the land was donated in 1782 by **General John Eager Howard**. By the 1800s, wagons and farmers were arriving from all over the state to hawk their wares on Saturdays. A massive fire in 1949 destroyed the market, which was rebuilt in 1952 and still attracts thousands with its meats, fresh seafoods, and home-baked goods. ◆ M-Sa 8:30AM-6PM. 400 W. Lexington St (Paca-Eutaw Sts) 685.6169

17 Marconi's ★★★$$$ Baltimore's bastion of classic Italian cooking. The sweetbreads Bordelaise are as famous as the lightly fried soft-shell crabs. Save room for a cannoli. ◆ Italian ◆ Tu-Sa noon-3:30PM, 5-8PM. 106 W. Saratoga St (Cathedral St-Park Ave) Jacket required. 727.9522

Baltimore

18 Old St. Paul's Episcopal Church (1856, Richard Upjohn) Stained-glass works and mosaics by **Louis Comfort Tiffany** and the **Tiffany Studios**. Additional glass by **Maitland Armstrong** and **John LaFarge**. A **Masonic Temple**, the third built here after fire burned down the building twice, in 1890 and 1908, is adjacent to St. Paul's. ◆ N. Charles and Saratoga Sts. 685.5537

19 Omni International Hotel $$$ With 704 rooms, this is one of the state's largest hotels. The American-style bistro and café (**Jacqueline**) offers cabaret entertainment on the weekend. Amenities include concierge service and access to a health club across the street. Special weekend and promotional packages. Children under 17 stay free. ◆ 101 W. Fayette St (N. Charles St-Park Ave) 752.1100, 800/THE.OMNI; fax 752.0832

20 B&O Railroad Museum (1850; roundhouse, 1884) Standing on the site of the nation's first passenger and freight railway station, the museum displays early locomotives. Under the airy windowed roof of the roundhouse and in the station building are such treasures as a steam-powered replica of **Peter Cooper**'s early *Tom Thumb* train. Also on display are an 1836 **Grasshopper** locomotive built here at the Mount Clare shops, a red caboose from 1907, and a **Forty & Eight** boxcar.

The museum also features train memorabilia like hand-blown whiskey flasks and a collection of station clocks and railroad watches. ◆ Admission. W-Su 10AM-4PM. 901 W. Pratt St (Poppleton St) 237.2387

21 Charles Center An overhead walkway connects the 33 acres of apartments, shops, and commercial buildings of this major development begun in 1956. Although the focus of Baltimore has shifted to the Inner Harbor, Charles Center still remains a vital area. **Hopkins Plaza**, the second open square in the center, is the forum for weekend festivals and concerts: check local papers for listings. ◆ 36 S. Charles St (Baltimore St)

At Charles Center:

Morris A. Mechanic Theatre (1968, John M. Johansen) A testing ground for Broadway productions. The multifaceted concrete building is Brutalist in inspiration. ◆ Seats 1600. Box office: M-Sa 10AM-6PM (performance days 10AM-8:30PM); Su noon-3:30PM on performance days. Baltimore and Charles Sts (Hopkins Plaza) 625.4230; Telecharge 800/638.2444

22 The Peale Museum Artist **Rembrandt Peale** first built this as his own **Baltimore Museum and Gallery of Fine Arts** in 1814. In 1930, after serving temporarily as Baltimore's City Hall (1830–1875), the Peale went back to its original function as America's oldest museum building, with permanent exhibitions of Baltimore's row houses and works by the artistic Peale family. ◆ Admission. Tu-Sa 10AM-5PM; Su noon-5PM; free Sa 10AM-1PM. 225 Holliday St (Saratoga St) 396.1149

Check out the harbor for the *Pride of Baltimore II*, an authentic reproduction of an 18th-century clipper ship. The *Pride II* was launched in 1988 to replace the previous *Pride*, which sank during a storm on an ocean crossing. The *Pride II* sails to international ports to promote the city.

Restaurants: Red	**Hotels**: Blue
Shops/Parks: Green	**Sights/Culture**: Black

23 Baltimore City Hall (1875, George A. Frederick; restoration, 1974, Myers, D'Aleo & Patton) A Victorian wonder with local white marble, mansard roofs, and a cast- and wrought-iron dome designed by **Wendell Bollman**. The building's fine ironwork has been renovated and restored. Note the 110-foot rotunda and galleries of artwork depicting Baltimore's history. ♦ Free. Tours M-F 10AM or by appointment. 100 N. Holliday St (Fayette-Lexington Sts) 396.3100

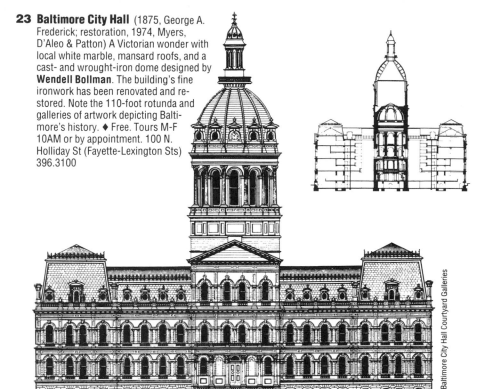

Courtesy Baltimore City Hall Courtyard Galleries

24 Visitors Information Center Maps, information, hotel bookings, and tour reservations. Call ahead for details of the City Fair, held each September, and the city's many ethnic festivals. ♦ Daily 10AM-6PM. 34 Market Pl (enter on Frederick St) 3rd fl. 727.5847

25 Custom House Walk up the front steps to the big *Call Room*, where you can gaze up at the 30- by 68-foot canvas on the ceiling that shows sailing vessels, from ancient Egyptian papyrus boats to the Baltimore clipper. ♦ Free M-F 8AM-5PM. 40 S. Gay St (Lombard St) 962.2666

26 Holocaust Memorial A pair of giant monoliths, each 75 feet long and 18 feet high, symbolizes the nightmare of Nazi Europe. Names of all World War II concentration camps in Europe are inscribed in the twin stones; the 6 rows of trees surrounding the memorial are dedicated to the 6 million Jews who perished. ♦ Lombard and Gay Sts

Connolly's ★★$ A comfortable walk from the harbor, this unpretentious neighborhood-style crab house serves seafood basics at modest prices. ♦ Seafood ♦ M-Th 10:30AM-10:30PM; F-Sa 10:30AM-11PM; Su 11:30AM-9:30PM. 701 E. Pratt St (Market St) 837.6400

In the wake of Maryland's 1856 statewide elections, violent gangs like the *Plug Uglies* and the *Blood Tubs* controlled the streets.

Baltimore City Life Museums (396.4545) is an umbrella organization that includes the following 4 museums and houses:

28 Center for Urban Archeology Displays of ceramics and glassware from 18th- and 19th-century homes, with archaeologists at work in the laboratory. ♦ Fee. T-Sa 10AM-4PM, Su noon-4PM, Jan-Mar, Nov-Dec; T-Sa 10AM-5PM, Su noon-5PM, Apr-Oct; free Sa 10AM-1PM. 800 E. Lombard St (Front St) 396.3156

28 Carroll Mansion The last home of Declaration of Independence signer **Charles Carroll**. A fine variety of Empire-style furnishings and a spiral staircase still decorate this 1812 townhouse, which is considered one of early Baltimore's finest residences. Across the street is Old Brewer's Park, where in 1983 an 18th-century brewery was excavated. (Plans to show exhibitions there are underway.) ♦ Fee. Tu-Sa 10AM-4PM, Su noon-4PM, Jan-Apr, Nov-Dec; Tu-Sa 10AM-5PM, May-Oct; free Sa 10AM-1PM. 800 E. Lombard St (Front St) 396.3523

28 Courtyard Exhibition Center Charts Baltimore's growth since the 1930s through photographs, building models, and memorabilia. ♦ Fee. Tu-Sa 10AM-5PM; Su noon-4PM; free Sa 10AM-1PM. 800 E. Lombard St (Front St) 396.9910

28 1840 House Housed in a reconstructed row house, the museum transports visitors back to Baltimore in the 1840s with reproductions of toys, furniture, and other objects from the 19th century. Since these articles are reproductions they can be handled by visitors. ♦ Admission. Tu-Sa 10AM-5PM; Su noon-5PM; free Sa 10AM-1PM. 800 E. Lombard St (Front St) 396.3279

29 Shot Tower Over 1,100,000 handmade bricks were used to build this 246-foot high landmark, where gunshot was made between 1828 and 1892. A slide show inside the tower explains the process of dropping molten lead through a sieve from the top of the tower into a barrel of cold water below. ♦ Free. Daily 8:30AM-4:30PM. 801 Fayette St (Front St) 396.2911

30 Chiapparelli's ★★$ Southern Italian cooking at its most copious and robust. Great lobster. ♦ Italian ♦ M-Th, Su noon-11PM; F noon-1AM; Sa noon-2AM. 237 S. High St (Fawn St) 837.0309

30 Capriccio ★★$$ Just a couple of blocks east of Harborplace. Northern Italian specialties in a cozy, romantic setting. ♦ Italian ♦ M-F 11:30AM-2PM, 5-11PM; Sa 5PM-midnight; Su noon-11PM. 846 Fawn St (High-Albemarle Sts) Reservations recommended. 685-2710

31 Obrycki's Crab House ★★★$ Casual atmosphere, simple decor, beer, and succulent crabs in a family-run restaurant. Baltimore's most famous crab house. ♦ Seafood ♦ M-F 11:30AM-11PM, Sa 4-11PM, Su 4-9:30PM Apr-Dec. 1727 E. Pratt St (Broadway) 732.6399

32 Great Blacks in Wax Museum More than 100 wax figures representing prominent black

Baltimore

Americans, including Olympic star **Jesse Owens** and civil rights activist **Rosa Parks**. The removal of Ms. Parks from a Montgomery, Alabama bus is captured in wax. ♦ Admission. Tu-Sa 9AM-6PM; Su noon-6PM. 1601 E. North Ave (Broadway) 563.3404

33 Bo Brooks ★★★$ Hammer your way through the best crabs in the city. Locals stand in line to feast on the little critters in all varieties: backfin, stuffed, fried, steamed, or combined with the freshest oysters, mussels, and clams available. No crabs served at lunch. ♦ Seafood ♦ M-Th 11:30AM-3:15PM, 5-10PM; F 11:30AM-3:15PM, 5-11:15PM; Sa 5-11:15PM; Su 3:30-9:30PM. 5415 Belair Rd (Frankfort Ave) 488.8144

The **Baltimore & Ohio Railroad** line was finished on Christmas Eve in 1852.

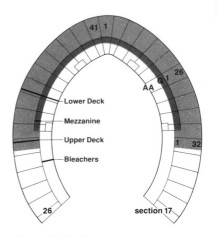

34 Memorial Stadium Home base to the **Baltimore Orioles** since its completion in 1954, the stadium seats up to 60,000 *O's* fans. The city has a new downtown stadium in the works, but fans are justifiably loyal to this classic ballpark. Concession stands with light snacks are open during game time. ♦ Box office: M-Sa 9AM-6PM, when Orioles are out of town; open 2 hours before game time when Orioles play in Baltimore; M-F 9AM-5PM in off-season. Gates open 1¹/₂ hours before game time. (Tickets also available through the Orioles Baseball Store in DC, 914 17th St NW; 202/296.2473.) 33rd and Ellerslie Ave. 338.1300

35 Prime Rib ★★$$ Sister restaurant to DC's famous beef house. Prime ribs, steaks, and other classics. ♦ American ♦ M-Sa 5PM-midnight; Su 5-11PM. 1101 N. Calvert St (Chase St) 539.1804

36 Center Stage Maryland's state theater mounts distinguished productions ranging from *Hamlet* to **Sam Shepard**'s *Fool for Love*. ♦ Seats 541. Box office M-F 9AM-5PM. 700 N. Calvert St (Monument-Madison Sts) 332.0033

37 Brown's Arcade This Neoclassical arcade—columns, arches, moldings, and all—was reconstructed and bought for the city by **Governor William Brown** after Baltimore's *Sunday Morning Fire* in 1904. Since the '70s, the ornate building has been associated with charity ventures: part of the profit from its shops and restaurants goes to support housing for the poor. ♦ 324 N. Charles St (Pleasant St)

Within Brown's Arcade:

McGinn's Irish Pub & Restaurant ★$ Try the lamb stew, corned beef and cabbage, and the stout on tap. Live music on the weekend. ♦ Irish/American ♦ Daily 11AM-2AM. 539.7504

Shogun ★★$$ Sushi bar and tatami room for pre-**Mechanic Theatre** dinners. ♦ Japanese ♦ Tu-Th 11:30AM-2:30PM, 5-10PM; F 11:30AM-2:30PM, 5-11PM; Sa 5-11PM; Su 4-10PM. Reservations required for the tatami room. 962.1130

38 Eubie Blake Cultural Center A community arts center dedicated to the life and music of Baltimore-born jazz artist **Eubie Blake**. ◆ M-F 10AM-6PM. 409 N. Charles St (Franklin-Mulberry Sts) 396.1300

39 Enoch Pratt Free Library The city's principal library also maintains prints of old Baltimore, war posters, and special collections on native sons **H.L. Mencken** and **Edgar Allan Poe**. ◆ M-Th 10AM-9PM; F-Sa 9AM-5PM. 400 Cathedral St (Franklin-Mulberry Sts) 396.5430

40 Tio Pepe ★★★$$ Perhaps Baltimore's best restaurant. A large stuccoed cave serves incomparable pheasant *Alcantara* in grape sauce, sole with banana hollandaise, and exquisite seafood paella. Say *Ole!* if you manage to get reservations after only 2 weeks of trying. ◆ Spanish ◆ M-Th 11:30AM-2:30PM, 5-10:30PM; F 11:30AM-2:30PM, 5-11:30PM; Sa 5-11:30PM; Su 4-10:30PM. 10 E. Franklin St (N. Charles St) Jacket and tie required. Reservations required. 539.4675

Drawing by Betty L. Heiges

41 Mt. Vernon Once a forest known as *Howard's Woods*, this cruciform park began with the **Washington Monument** (1815–1829, **Robert Mills**), the first monument to honor **George Washington**. The statue on top of the 178-foot marble Doric column depicts Washington as he resigns from his position as general of the Continental Army. The **Mount Vernon Methodist Church** (1872, **Thomas Dixon** and **Charles Carson**) northwest of the monument is a Charles Addams' Gothic pile in green serpen-

tine stone. **Leakin Hall** on E. Mount Vernon Place opened in 1927 as the Preparatory Department of the Peabody Institute. ◆ E. Mount Vernon Pl (Charles-Monument Sts)

At Mt. Vernon Square:

Peabody Institute (1878, Edmund G. Lind) Founded by **George Peabody** in 1856, the institute was originally conceived as a library, music academy, and art gallery. Over the years the academy has become internationally renowned, with about 450 students rigorously reelected. It is now part of **Johns Hopkins University**. Note the gates outside of **North Hall**, bronze copies of the Ghiberti gates at the Baptistery in Florence. The academy offers public concerts throughout the year. Call for information and tickets. The **Peabody Library** at 11 E. Mount Vernon Place should not be missed. Over 250,000 volumes are arranged on 6 levels of stacks, all connected by a central wall that rises 61 feet to the ceiling. ◆ Box office W-F 1-4PM and prior to concerts. 1 E. Mt Vernon Pl. 659.8100

42 Walters Art Gallery (1909, Delano and Aldrich) Engineer **William Walters** bequeathed his collection of 19th-century paintings, Chinese porcelains, and other treasures to Baltimore in 1931. With it came the fine Palladian-style building, designed after a Renaissance palazzo in Genoa. Among the gallery's treasures are artifacts from the Ancient Near East, Egyptian tomb paintings, papyrus scrolls, and Roman sculptures. The museum store sells reproductions of museum works. ◆ Admission. Tu-Su 11AM-5PM; free W. Gallery lectures W 12:30PM, Su 2PM. 600 N. Charles St (Center St) 547.9000

43 Brass Elephant ★★$$ The Northern Italian cuisine of this exquisitely restored 1860s' townhouse runs from veal Val Dostano with truffles to fish prepared many different ways. ◆ Italian ◆ M-Th 11:30AM-2PM, 5:30-9:30PM, F 11:30AM-2PM, 5:30-11PM; Sa 5:30-10:30PM; Su 5-9PM. 924 N. Charles St (Read-Eager Sts) 547.8480

Baltimore

43 Great American Melting Pot ★$ Art Deco-inspired nightspot for Baltimore's bohemians. The menu lists anything from a decent beef Wellington to fair tacos and salads. ◆ International ◆ M-Th, Su 11:30AM-2AM; F-Sa 11:30AM-3AM. 904 N. Charles St (Read St) 837.9797

43 Meredith Contemporary Art A collection of platters, vases, and baskets by **Kaette**, a leading American ceramist. A small selection of good lithos and framed posters. ◆ Tu-F 10AM-4PM. 805 N. Charles St (Read St) 837.3575

Little Italy. Portuguese-born **Saint Anthony** protects this historical part of the city, spared from a 1904 fire that raged through most of downtown. The neighborhood families proclaim 13 June *St. Anthony's Day*. Streets are closed for processions and celebrations. ◆ Presidents-Pratt Sts.

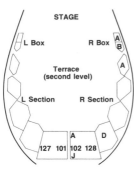
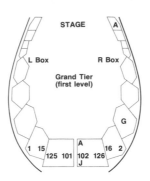
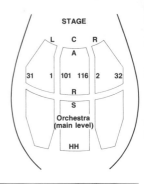

44 Joseph Meyerhoff Symphony Hall (1982, architect Pietro Belluschi; acoustics, Bolt, Beranek and Newman) The dream of **Baltimore Symphony Orchestra**'s maestro, **Sergiu Comissiona**, and its president, **Joseph Meyerhoff**, the hall presents the symphony in all its splendor. The interior surfaces are curved for perfect acoustics: 420 tons of plaster coat the double-thick walls to protect the chamber from external noise. The building's round shape gives an unobstructed view of the stage. Its grand staircases and glass-and-brick touches further treat the eye. ♦ Seats 2467. 1212 Cathedral St (Preston St) 783.8000

45 Danny's ★$$$ A traditional, somewhat pretentious establishment. The Dover sole is good, the wine list even better. ♦ French/American ♦ M-F 11:30AM-3PM, 5PM-midnight; Sa 5:00PM-midnight. 1201 N. Charles St (Biddle St) Jacket required. Reservations recommended. 539.1393

46 Belvedere $ Built on the site of an old mansion, the Belvedere is one of the most beautiful hotels in the Chesapeake Bay area. The marbled lobby with its sparkling chandeliers leads to 12 more floors of richly decorated rooms and the **Ballroom**, famous for its panoramic view of Baltimore. Amenities include a health club, an indoor swimming pool, 2 racquetball courts, a beauty salon, and a florist. **The Owl Bar** is known for its *yards of beer*

(beer served in tall, thin glasses, literally a yard high) and the owl motifs in its stained-glass windows. Children under 14 stay free. ♦ 1 E. Chase St (N. Charles St) 332.1000
Within the Belvedere:

John Eager Howard Room ★★$$
Crabcakes, Scotch salmon sautéed with tomatoes, mushrooms, and hearts of palm, and veal Française are among the dishes served in this large, sunny dining room. ♦ American ♦ M-F 7-10AM, 11:30AM-2:30PM, 5:30-10:30PM; Sa 7-10AM, 5:30-11PM; Su 10AM-12:30PM. Jacket required. Reservations recommended. 332.1000

Building the **C&O Canal** was serious business. Any slaves or hired whites who ran away from duty were sentenced to have their heads and eyebrows shaved immediately.

47 Antique Row Collectors from all over the East Coast prowl the 60-odd antique shops along the 700- and 800-blocks of Howard Street. One complex, **Antique Treasury**, houses 20 dealers (M-Sa 10AM-5PM, 728.6363). ♦ Howard St (Monument St-Martin Luther King, Jr., Blvd)

48 Inscribulus Books Old and out-of-print books. Occasionally a real rarity shows up among the children's books, art books with tipped-in prints, and first-edition mystery novels. ♦ M-Sa 10AM-5PM. 857 N. Howard St (Read-Madison Sts) 383.8845

49 Mother Seton House At the request of **Bishop John Carroll** of Baltimore, **Saint Elizabeth Seton** founded a girls school here in 1808. In 1975, she became the first American-born person to be canonized in the Roman Catholic Church. ♦ 600 N. Paca St (Franklin St-Druid Hill Ave) 523.3443

50 Babe Ruth's Birthplace and Orioles Museum The legendary baseball player is immortalized through pictures, paintings, and over 1000 pieces of professional memorabilia, including the oldest baseball in Maryland (circa 1870), the bat Babe Ruth used when he hit 60 home runs in 1927, and the Orioles' 1983 World Championship trophy. The home is decorated in late 19th-century furnishings. ♦ Fee. Daily 10AM-4PM, Jan-Mar, Nov-Dec; daily 10AM-5PM, Apr-Oct. 216 Emory St (Pratt St) 727.1539

51 Mount Clare Mansion (1760, Charles Carroll) Baltimore's oldest plantation home. Late 18th-century furniture and memorabilia of the Carroll family. ♦ Fee. Tu-F 10AM-4:30PM; Sa-Su noon-4:30PM. Carroll Park. 396.4265

52 H.L. Mencken House This stately 19th-century row house housed the *Sage of Baltimore* for more than 68 years. The home of the acerbic newspaperman has been restored with his original furniture, including his treasured Tonk baby grand piano. A brief filmstrip presents highlights of his career. Part of the **Baltimore City Life Museums**. It faces **Union Square**, a model of urbanity, which was recently restored and is a neighborhood gem. ♦ Admission. W-Su 10AM-5PM. 1524 Hollins St (Union Square) 396.7997

Restaurants: Red   **Hotels**: Blue
Shops/Parks: Green   **Sights/Culture**: Black

53 Edgar Allan Poe House Poe moved here in 1832, when he was 23 years old, and wrote *MS Found in a Bottle*, the first story to bring him recognition. The house, which belonged to his aunt **Maria Clemm**, was almost razed in a slum-clearance project; it is now a museum. ♦ Fee. Call for hours. 203 N. Amity St (approximately 7 blocks west of Lexington Market) 396.7932

54 Lillie Carroll Jackson Museum The home of the civil rights leader who founded the Baltimore branch of the **National Association for the Advancement of Colored People** and served as its president for 35 years. Exhibitions chronicle her life and the civil rights struggle. ♦ Admission. Call for hours. 1320 Eutaw Pl (Lafayette St) 523.1208

55 The Pump Room ★$ A convenient place to stop for crabs after the ball game, on your way back to DC. ♦ Seafood ♦ F-Su 6-10PM, Jan-Mar, Sep-Dec; Tu-Su 6-10PM, Apr-Aug. 133 W. North Ave (Howard St) Reservations required. 727.0369

55 Baltimore Streetcar Museum Founded in 1966, the museum features rides in authentic Baltimore streetcars from the 1890s through the 1940s. The 1¼-mile round trip runs from the North Avenue loop to the 28th Street loop by way of Falls Road. Back at the **Visitors Center**, streetcar history is recalled through photographs, displays, and a slide show. If asked, a museum volunteer will conduct tours through the **Car House**, which contains about a dozen streetcars. Tours weekdays by appointment, Jan-May, Nov-Dec. ♦ Free. Sa-Su noon-5PM, June-Oct. 1901 Falls Rd (Lafayette Ave) 547.0264

56 Lovely Lane United Methodist Church (1884, Stanford White) Considered to be the mother church of American Methodism. Lovely Lane houses one of the nation's finest museums on Methodist history. The church is Romanesque in style with Etruscan detailing. On the **National Registry of Historic Places**. ♦ Tours given, call for hours. 2200 St. Paul St (22nd St) 889.1512

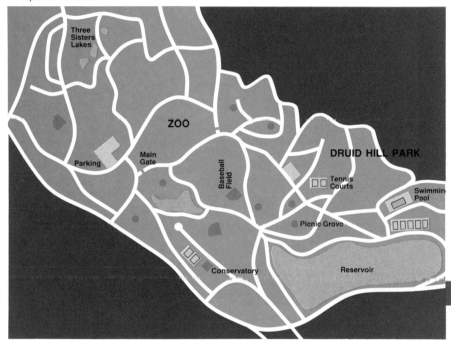

57 Druid Hill Park/Baltimore Zoo What used to be a private estate in the 1800s is now Baltimore's largest public recreational area. Tennis courts and playgrounds are scattered throughout the 650-odd acres; the Victorian picnic shelters built in 1859 are still in use; and the Olympic-size pool is open during warm weather.

The **Conservatory**, a late 19th-century domed greenhouse, features 3 massive seasonal floral displays. A tropical collection of African violets, succulent cacti, and over 500 varieties of orchids is located in a smaller greenhouse next door.

Over 1200 species of crawling, walking, and swimming animals live within Baltimore Zoo's 150 acres. The lions and giraffes are housed in an open-air exhibition; there is a hippo house and an area for rare breeds of antelope, as well as a 3-acre house and exercise area for 4 African elephants, including the affable **Dolly**. The **Children's Zoo**, an area with rabbits, sheep, and baby animals, features pony rides, a minitrain, and a carousel (fee). Feeding the animals is strictly prohibited, but you can watch the black-footed penguins get their fill daily at 3PM; the Kodiak bears eat at 2PM. Ophidiophiles should stop by the **Reptile House** outside the zoo fence on Greenspring Ave. ♦ Fee. M-F 10AM-4:30PM; Sa-Su 10AM-5:30PM. Conservatory daily 10AM-4PM. Druid Park Lake Dr exit, off I-83. 366.5466, group tours 467.4387

58 Baltimore Museum of Art (1929, John Russell Pope; numerous expansions) In the early 1900s, when Baltimore decided that it greatly lacked a serious art museum, a commission quickly decided upon Wyman Park as the site and selected J.R. Pope—the man responsible for much of monumental Washington—to design it.

Sights not to miss inside this massive Grecian temple include the 3 floors of the **American Wing**, representing life in the 18th and 19th centuries; the **Wurtzburger Sculpture Garden**, with works by **Calder**, **Moore**, and **Rodin**; the **Old Masters Collection** of European paintings; **African** and **Oceanic Art**; and the **Cone Collection** of works from 1840–1940, including the world's largest collection of **Matisse** paintings. (*The Pink Nude*, *The Blue Nude*, and *The Purple Nude* are here.) The museum shop is open during museum hours. Works by regional and international artists, available for sale or rent to museum members (396.6351). Library open to the public (396.6317). Group tours available upon request (396.6320). ♦ Admission. Tu-W, F 10AM-4PM; Th 10AM-9PM; free Th and for those under 21. Cafe: Tu-W 11AM-10PM; Th-Sa 11AM-11PM; Su 11AM-9PM (235.3930). Art Museum Dr at Charles St. 396.7101

59 Johns Hopkins University Founded in 1876 by Johns Hopkins, a prominent Baltimore merchant, this prestigious university was originally dedicated to graduate study and research. Today there are about 2800 undergrads, and its graduate schools continue to prosper, with 1000 students. This 126-acre Homewood campus houses the schools of arts and sciences, engineering, and continuing studies and is the centerpiece of the university. The medical school and hospital are in East Baltimore and the **School of Advanced International Studies** is located in DC. **Homewood Field** is home base for the thriving lacrosse program. ♦ 34th and Charles Sts. Lacrosse game information 338.7490, tour information 338.8171

Baltimore

60 Homewood **Charles Carroll** built this Federal mansion in 1801 as a wedding present for his son, **Charles**. The house, a **National Historic Landmark**, has been restored with period furnishings. ♦ Fee. M-F by appointment. 3400 N. Charles St (39th St) 338.5589

61 Pimlico Race Course Home of the famed mid-May **Preakness** race, the second horse-racing spectacular of the **Triple Crown**. Watch the daily thoroughbred racing from the aprons, or reserve window seating in the restaurant. Post time 1PM. ♦ M-Sa 11AM-5:30PM, mid Mar-first week of June. Park Heights and Belvedere Aves. 542.9400

62 Cylburn Arboretum Built by wealthy Baltimore businessman **Jesse Tyson** between 1863 and 1883, this estate sprawls over 176 acres in the heart of Baltimore.

The **Arboretum**, run by the Bureau of Parks, contains Japanese maples, native Maryland oaks, and rare trees (rubber, dove, magnolia, boxwood). The many nature trails show off Maryland's flowering plant life in its natural state. Also of interest: the **Horticultural Library**, **Children's Nature Museum**, **Fessenden Herbarium**, and the **Bird Museum**. ♦ Free. M-F 8AM-4PM. Grounds daily 6AM-9PM. 4915 Greenspring Ave (south of Northern Parkway) 396.0180

63 Villa Pace The Italianate mansion was the last home of the great American soprano **Rosa Ponselle**. The mansion is named after her debut aria. Privately owned and closed to the public. ♦ 1526 Greenspring Valley Rd

64 Hampton National Historic Site This late-Georgian mansion, built by the prominent **Ridgely** family, is one of the largest constructed in the post-Revolutionary period. Its extensive formal gardens are particularly impressive. Administered by the **National Park Service**. Gift shop and tearoom; tours available upon request. ♦ Free. Daily 9AM-5PM. Hampton Lane, Towson. 823.7054

65 Elkton, Maryland, is the closest county seat south of New York, New Jersey, and Pennsylvania. As such, the town flourished by marrying couples unwilling to wait the time other states required for marriage licenses. Cab-drivers would meet incoming trains and—for a high fee—take couples first to the courthouse for a license, then to a parson for the wedding. Signs advertised *Marrying Parson* up and down Main Street. Business came to a halt in 1938, however, when Maryland passed a 48-hour waiting period for licenses.

Baltimore is the USA's official capital of lacrosse—the **Lacrosse Foundation** and **Lacrosse Hall of Fame** are both located here. Home-team heroes, the Johns Hopkins University lacrosse team, have captured several national titles. And it's a favorite game of the city's youth, who start learning how to play as soon as they can hold a stick.

Lacrosse as we know it was derived from a form of sacred mock combat—called *baggataway play*—played in the 1400s by teams of 100 to 1000 Native Americans. In the early 1800s, French settlers in Canada adapted the game and called it *Lacroix*, because the stick resembled a bishop's crozier.

Lacrosse is a cousin of soccer, sharing that game's fast pace and back-and-forth field action. Two teams of players—10 for men, 12 for women—play on a field 60 by 110 yards; goals are at each end, with 80 yards between them. A player uses a stick, or crosse, with a basketlike net on one end to catch and throw the ball down the field for a goal.

If you're visiting Baltimore during spring or summer, take time to learn why lacrosse is a local passion. You can catch games on most pleasant evenings at local colleges or city parks. For more information, write the Lacrosse Foundation, Newton H. White Athletic Center, Homewood, Baltimore MD 21218, or call 235.6882.

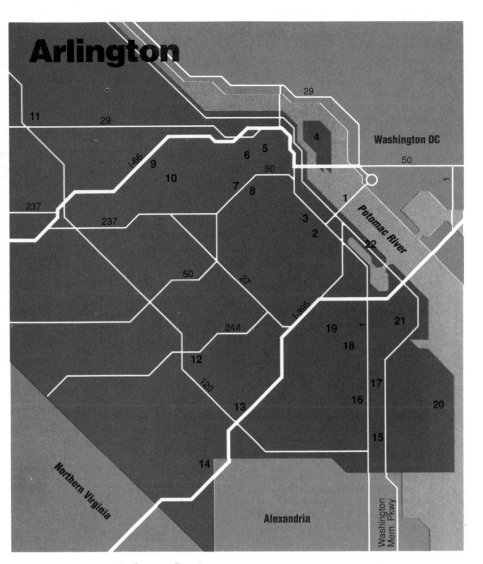

Arlington

11 29 29

I-66 9
10

237

237 50

50 27

344 I-395

12

120

13

14

Northern Virginia

4

Washington DC

5
6
50
7 8

50 1

Potomac River

3
2
22

19 21
18

17
16 20

15

Alexandria

Washington Mem. Pkwy

Arlington, directly across the Potomac River from Downtown Washington, was originally part of the District of Columbia. In 1847, on what some call one of Washington's saddest days, the 25.7-square-mile parcel was ceded back to Virginia; the federal government couldn't imagine having a need for all that extra space. Today, Arlington is a booming suburban community containing many federal offices and monuments, including **Arlington National Cemetery**, the **Pentagon**, the **Iwo Jima Memorial**, **Arlington House**, and the **Netherlands Carillon**. **Washington National Airport** stands on a landfill just south of the **Pentagon**. This small county also contains the concrete high-rise office and hotel complexes of **Rosslyn** and **Crystal City**, which, unlike DC, have no restrictions on building height. **Clarendon**, **Fairlington**, and **Shirlington** are thriving bedroom communities, and the **Wilson Boulevard** area is home to a lively immigrant community—*Little Saigon* bustles with Vietnamese shops and restaurants. Development around the Metro stops at **Ballston** and **Virginia Square** is transforming the faces of these formerly sleepy communities with new shops, restaurants, and hotels.

Area code 703 unless otherwise indicated.

1 Arlington Memorial Bridge (1926–1932, McKim, Mead & White) Although a bridge had been planned at this location for years, it took

a massive traffic jam on Armistice Day 1921 to get this one built. A long, low series of arches spans the Potomac with MM&W's usual Beaux-Arts flair. ♦ From Lincoln Memorial to Arlington National Cemetery

2 Arlington National Cemetery Lying across the Virginia hills just over the Arlington Memorial Bridge is this serene testament to the US's military sacrifices: 612 acres of rolling hills dotted with simple headstones as far as the eye can see. Arlington National Cemetery is reserved for officers and enlistees of the US military and government employees and their families. In 1868, **General John Logan** set 30 May aside to decorate Civil War

175

graves, holding the first service at the Arlington House portico. This was the beginning of Memorial Day.

Authorities believe that space at the cemetery will run out about the year 2020 and have set strict requirements for interment. The 213,000-plus buried here represent the Revolutionary War, War of 1812, Civil War, Spanish-American War, World Wars I and II, and the conflicts in Korea and Vietnam. Stop at the Visitors Center (1989, **Frances D. Lethbridge** and **Patricia Schiffelbein)** near the parking lot. This imposing modern building was designed with a giant skydome. It houses the main information offices for the cemetery, a bookstore, and the **Tourmobile** station. The only vehicles allowed on the cemetery grounds, Tourmobiles offer guided tours of the various monuments and points of interest. (202/554.5100) ♦ Entrance at Arlington Memorial Bridge. 202/692.0931

Within Arlington National Cemetery:

The **Tomb of the Unknowns** (formerly **Tomb of the Unknown Soldier**) remains the focus of sentiment and ceremony at the cemetery. Cut from a single block of white marble, it is decorated by sculpted wreaths and a 3-figure symbol of *Victory Through Valor Attaining Peace.* The inscription on the back panel reads, "Here Rests in Honored Glory an American Soldier Known But to God." Entombed in the monument are the remains of 4 US servicemen, one each from World Wars I and II, and the Korean and Vietnam conflicts.

At all times, a soldier from the *Old Guard* of the Third US Infantry protects the tomb and periodically performs the impressive *Changing of the Guard.* This routine of heel-clicking, rifle maneuvers, and salutes takes place every half-hour during summer, every hour in winter, and every 2 hours at night. The guard moves 21

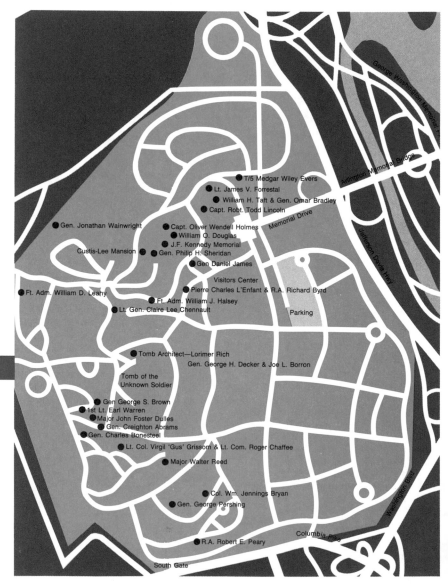

steps, stops for 21 seconds, then retraces his route. (The **Iran Memorial**, marking the aborted rescue mission of American hostages in 1980, and the **Astronaut Memorial**, created in memory of the Challenger crew, are located near the Tomb of the Unknowns.)

Arlington House, the **Robert E. Lee Memorial** (1820, George Hadfield) The story of Arlington House is really the story of 2 great Virginia families—the **Washingtons** and the **Lees**— and their struggle to hold onto this 1100-acre estate, which overlooks the Potomac River and is now Arlington National Cemetery.

John Custis, **Martha Washington**'s son, purchased the land in 1778. In 1802, his son, artist **George Washington Parke Custis** (adopted by George and Martha), started building the Greek-Revival mansion and, in turn, passed it along to his daughter **Mary Anna Randolph Custis**, who married **Lieutenant Robert E. Lee** in 1831. The mansion took its more common name, the **Custis-Lee House**, from this famous marriage.

The house is preserved as a memorial to Confederate General Lee, a man highly regarded by both sides in the Civil War. Lee wrote of this house: "My affections and attachments are more strongly planted here than at any other place in the world."

When the Union Army crossed the Potomac during the Civil War, it overran the mansion and forced the Lee family out. Then in 1864 the federal government seized the land for unpaid taxes that had been questionably imposed. Finally, in 1883, the Supreme Court ruled to return the house to Lee's son, **George Washington Custis Lee**. He sold it back to the government for $150,000, to be used as a national monument. Congress approved restoration for the ransacked house in 1925.

Extensive research and curatorial zeal have refurnished Arlington House as it was when it was the home of the Robert E. Lee family. Much of the furniture, artwork, and housewares are the actual pieces used by the Lees; others are careful reproductions. Large portions of the double parlor set have survived and now furnish the **White Parlor**; **Nellie Custis**' music case is also here. The bedchamber in which Lee resigned from the US Army in 1861 is much as it was then. Copies of many of the paintings that once hung here, among them, an 1830 Italian *Madonna* by **William George Williams**, decorate the house. Original artworks include George Washington Parke Custis' *Battle of Monmouth*, intended for the Capitol but now hanging in the **Morning Room**, and the 1831 portrait of Mary Anna Randolph Custis by **August Herview**, painted shortly before her wedding to Lee. Both floors of the house are open, and the glimpse into the lifestyle of pre-Civil War Southern gentility is a must for DC visitors. Tours are self-guided. Tourmobiles will take you on a guided tour of the various monuments and points of interest. ♦ Free. Daily 9:30AM-5PM, Jan-Mar, Oct-Dec; 9:30AM-6PM, Apr-Sep. 557.0613

Mast of the Battleship Maine The mast—its tower still in place—was raised in 1912 from the ship, which sank in 1898 in Havana Harbor. It is set in a granite base inscribed with the names of the 229 men who died in the mysterious explosion that preceded the Spanish-American War.

Arlington Memorial Amphitheater (1920, Carrère and Hastings) A memorial to the Army, Navy, and Marine Corps. Finished in white Vermont marble, it is reminiscent of Greek and Roman theaters. ♦ Seats 5,500.

The Tomb of Pierre Charles L'Enfant, the designer of DC's city grid, lies on a hillside overlooking Washington, just in front of Arlington House. His original plan (page 208) is carved on the tomb.

John F. Kennedy's grave is marked by an eternal flame and slate headstone. The simple marble terrace yields a panoramic view of the city; one low wall reminds visitors of Kennedy's power with words, showing an inscription from his inaugural address. Nearby in a grassy plot is **Robert F. Kennedy**'s grave. An adjacent granite wall and fountain memorialize the words of the late attorney general and senator.

Confederate Memorial (1914, Moses Ezekiel) Erected by the United Daughters of the Confederacy, Ezekiel's Baroque bronze monument honors the soldiers of the short-lived Confederate States of America. A female figure in the center stands for the *South in Peace*, while a frieze on the base portrays the South's women sending their men to fight. **President Woodrow Wilson** dedicated the statue.

3 United States Marine Corps War Memorial (1954, Felix W. Weldon) More popularly known as the **Iwo Jima Memorial**, this is Weldon's re-creation of **Joe Rosenthal**'s Pulitzer Prize-winning photograph. Five marines and a sailor raise the American flag on Mt. Suribachi, Iwo Jima. The 78-foot-high, 100-ton sculpture represents the World War II battle site where more than 5000 marines died. ♦ Arlington Boulevard and Meade Street, north of Arlington National Cemetery. 285.2598

On the Marine Memorial Grounds:

Sunset Parade takes place Tuesday at 7:30PM, May through August, and features the *Marine Silent Drill Team* and *Drum and Bugle Corps*. ♦ 202/433-2258. Reservations accepted, 202/433.6060

Netherlands Carillon This gift from the Netherlands has 49 stationary bells with a 4-octave range of notes. The smallest bell weighs 37.5 pounds, the largest, 12,654 pounds. ♦ Concerts Sa 10AM, Apr-May, Sep; Sa 6:30PM, Jun-Aug.

Although **Arlington National Cemetery** was used as a burial ground for Union soldiers, the first man buried there was a Confederate prisoner of war who had died in a local hospital.

4 Theodore Roosevelt Island and

Memorial In the Potomac River, between the Roosevelt and Key bridges, lie these gentle marshlands honoring the 26th president. The island's 88 acres allow red-tailed hawks, red and gray foxes, and marsh wrens to roam freely, along with groundhogs, muskrats, great owls, and wood ducks. Old sycamore, oak, hickory, and dogwood trees shade the $2^1/_2$ miles of nature trails on the island. **Paul Manship**'s 17-foot bronze memorial statue of Roosevelt stands in front of four 21-foot granite tablets, each inscribed with his thoughts on nature and The State. During summer months, surrounding fountains spurt 21-foot plumes.

The parking lot and the pedestrian bridge to the island are accessible from the northbound lanes of the George Washington Parkway (the Virginia side of the Potomac). The island can also be reached by canoe from **Thompson's Boat House** in DC (202/333.4861). Nature walks are available. ♦ Free. Daily 8AM-dusk. 285.2598

5 Windows ★★★$$$$ A 2-level dining room with lacquered walls, masses of flowers, and a gorgeous view of the Potomac. One of the first East Coast restaurants to feature the light, bright new California cuisine and designer pizzas. Chef **Pasquale Ingenito** continues to offer some of the most

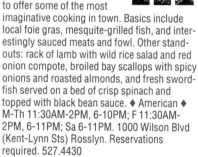

imaginative cooking in town. Basics include local foie gras, mesquite-grilled fish, and interestingly sauced meats and fowl. Other standouts: rack of lamb with wild rice salad and red onion compote, broiled bay scallops with spicy onions and roasted almonds, and fresh swordfish served on a bed of crisp spinach and topped with black bean sauce. ♦ American ♦ M-Th 11:30AM-2PM, 6-10PM; F 11:30AM-2PM, 6-11PM; Sa 6-11PM. 1000 Wilson Blvd (Kent-Lynn Sts) Rosslyn. Reservations required. 527.4430

5 Tom Sarris' Orleans House ★$ New Orleans comes to Virginia, and at bargain-basement prices. Huge portions of seafood, grilled meats, and, yes, prime ribs are served

to crowds who have waited for up to a half-hour to get inside, then happily wait again for a chance at the salad bar. Come hungry. ♦ Southern ♦ M-F 11AM-11PM; Sa 4-11PM; Su 4-10PM. 1213 Wilson Blvd (N. Moore-Lynn Sts) Rosslyn. 524.2929

5 Hyatt Arlington $$ Not as flashy as some other Hyatts, but close to both the Iwo Jima Memorial and Arlington National Cemetery. Georgetown is a quick walk across the Key Bridge. Amenities include babysitting, in-house movies, and free parking. Children under 18 stay free. ♦ 1325 Wilson Blvd (Nash St-Ft Myer Dr) 525-1234, 800/233.1234; fax 875.3393

5 Best Western Rosslyn Westpark $$ Located at Key Bridge, this modern hotel is a short drive from DC and close to major interstate highways. There is a rooftop restaurant, a health club and indoor swimming pool, and same-day valet service. (A room on one of the top floors will assure you a breathtaking view.) Children under 18 stay free. ♦ 1900 N. Fort Myer Dr (Key Blvd-Lee Hwy) Rosslyn. 527.4814, 800/368.3408; fax 522.7480 ⑁

5 Key Bridge Marriott $$ Amenities include a pool, exercise facilities, and a restaurant with a spectacular panorama of DC. Children under 18 stay free. ♦ 1401 Lee Hwy (N. Ft. Myer Dr) Rosslyn. 524.6400, 800/228-9290; fax 524.8964

5 Red Hot, and Blue ★★$ GOP chairman **Lee Atwater** (an entirely unbiased investor) raves about the hickory-smoked pork ribs and chicken, and the *pulled pig* sandwich—all served with beans and slaw or potato salad. Sit back and listen to the political gossip, or just tune in to the jukebox. ♦ Southern ♦ M-F 11AM-10PM; Sa noon-10PM; Su 3-10PM. 1600 Wilson Blvd (N. Pierce St) Rosslyn. 276.7427

5 The Cambodian Restaurant ★$ Subtle Southeast Asian cuisine, including meals cooked at the table. ♦ Cambodian ♦ M-Sa 11AM-10:30PM; Su 4-9PM. 1727 Wilson Blvd (Queens-Rhodes Sts) Reservations suggested. 522.3832

6 Jacques' Cafe ★$$ French/Italian cooking at bargain prices, live jazz Tuesday through Sunday, and a cheerful staff. ♦ French/Italian ♦ Tu-Th, Su 5-10PM; F-Sa 5-11PM. 3012 Wilson Blvd (Highland-Garfield Sts) Reservations recommended for 4 or more. 528.8500

6 My An ★$ Great spring rolls and other spicy/sweet Vietnamese dishes in a bustling café. ♦ Vietnamese ♦ Daily 9AM-10PM. 3101 Wilson Blvd (Highland St) Reservations required for 4 or more. No credit cards. 276.7110 ⑁

6 Nam Viet ★★$ A fancier version of My An, which is right across the parking lot. ♦ Vietnamese ♦ Daily 10AM-11PM. 1127 N. Hudson St (Wilson Blvd) 522.7110

6 Queen Bee ★★$ Consistently good Vietnamese and Chinese cuisine, including variations on *pho*, the fragrant Vietnamese soup/stew. ♦ Vietnamese ♦ Daily 11:30AM-10PM. 3181 Wilson Blvd (Washington Blvd) 527.3444

7 Whitey's ★$ Unreconstructed pub features "broasted" chicken and burgers, and live music from folk to jazz. ♦ American ♦ M-Th 9AM-1AM; F 9AM-2AM; Sa 8:30AM-2AM; Su 8:30AM-1AM. 2761 N. Washington Blvd (Pershing Dr) 525.9825

8 Fort Myer Neat brick barracks house troops, chiefs of staff, a clinic, and a firehouse. Its **Parade Ground** nearby has held demonstrations of aviation history's bests, including the Wright Brothers' first public display of their plane in 1909. ♦ Us Hwy 50 (Fort Myer exit) 202/696.3510

9 Holiday Inn Arlington at Ballston $$ Main features here are the large meeting rooms, complete with state-of-the-art video equipment, and an outdoor pool. On-the-premises restaurant and a nearby jogging trail. Free shuttle to local restaurants, shopping, and the Metro. Children under 18 stay free. ♦ 4610 N. Fairfax Dr (Glebe Rd) 243.9800, 800/HOLIDAY; fax 527.2677

9 Ballston Commons Enclosed mall with 120 stores including **Hecht's** and **JC Penney** department stores, **Limited Express**, **Lane Bryant**, and a court with 14 different food stalls. ♦ M-Sa 10AM-9:30PM; Su noon-5PM. 4238 Wilson Blvd (Glebe Rd) 243.8088

9 The Coffee Bean Over 100 coffees (hazelnut, coconut, Seville orange), a large selection of bulk teas and coffeepots, and tremor-inducing chocolate-covered espresso beans. ♦ M-Sa 10AM-9:30PM; Su 11:30AM-5:30PM. 4238 Wilson Blvd (Glebe Rd) 522.1650

10 Pines of Italy ★★$ Neighborhood Italian at its best: good fried zucchini, fried artichoke hearts, al dente pastas. If you're on a budget, ask for prices of the specials before ordering—they can be relatively high. ♦ Italian ♦ M, Su 11AM-10PM; Tu-Th 11AM-11PM; F-Sa 11AM-11:30PM. 237 Glebe Rd (Pershing Dr) 524.4969

11 Tachibana ★★★$$ Perfect sushi at a reasonable price. Try the lunchtime platter. ♦ Japanese ♦ M-F 11:30 AM-2PM; Sa 5-10PM. 4050 Lee Hwy (Quincy St) Reservations required. 558.1122

12 Matuba ★★$ Excellent sushi, tempura (try the soft-shell crab version), and teriyaki. Ask the staff about the sushi and kushiyaki bars. ♦ Japanese ♦ Tu-Th 11:30AM-2PM, 5:30-10PM; F 11:30AM-2PM, 5:30-10:30PM; Sa 5:30-10:30PM; Su 5:30-10PM. 2915 Columbia Pike (Garfield St-Walter Reed Dr) Reservations recommended. 521.2811

12 Arlington Cinema 'n' Drafthouse ★$ A big old movie theater that serves beer, wine, pizzas, and snacks while showing second-run movies. Comfy sofas and chairs. ♦ American ♦ M-Th, Su doors open 7PM, movies 7:30, 9:45PM; F-Sa doors open 6:45PM, movies 7:30, 9:45PM, midnight. 2903 Columbia Pike (Walter Reed Dr) No credit cards. 486.2345

12 Bob & Edith's Diner ★$ Bona fide chromed diner is the place for eggs and hash browns at 3AM. ♦ American ♦ 24 hours. 2310 Columbia Pike (Wayne-Barton Sts) No credit cards. 920.6103 &

13 Econo Lounge $ A medium-size hotel with an outdoor pool, meeting rooms, and restaurant. Children under 6 stay free. ♦ 2485 S. Glebe Rd (I-395, exit 7) 979.4100, 800/446.6900

14 The Village at Shirlington features upscale stores like **Kuppenheimer's** (men's clothes), **Bellini** (baby furniture), and **Metropolis Bike**. Restaurants include **Charlie Chang's, Bistro, Bistro,** and **Carlyle Grand Cafe**. Free parking. ♦ M-F 10AM-9PM; Sa 10AM-6PM; Su noon-5PM. I-395 at S. 28th St. 379.0007

15 Hyatt Regency Crystal City $$$ Big shiny hostelry offers all you'd expect from a Hyatt, plus the convenience of this location near National Airport. Amenities include health club with pool, in-room safes, and special weekend packages. Dine in one of the hotel's 2 restaurants. Meeting facilities. ♦ 2799 Jefferson Davis Hwy (S. Clark St) 418.1234, 800/228.9000; fax 418.1233 &

15 Embassy Suites Hotel $$ This all-suite hotel features meeting and health facilities. Complimentary breakfast. Children under 12 stay free. ♦ 1300 Jefferson Davis Hwy (15th St) 979.9799

16 Bangkok Gourmet ★★$$ A tiny dining room that serves fiery hot dishes like sliced steak with green curry and an eye-watering version of *pad thai* noodles. ♦ Thai ♦ M 5:30-10PM; Tu-F 11AM-3PM, 5:30-10PM; Sa-Su 5-10PM. 523 S. 23rd St (Eads St) Reservations recommended. 521.1305

17 Crystal City Underground Beneath an area of some 40 high-rise glass-and-concrete buildings that rise out of the flatlands near National Airport is this gem of a small mall of 120 shops and services with winding cobblestone walkways and twisting alleys that charm shoppers from one boutique to the next. The **Crystal Dinery** features international fast-food kiosks; stores include **The Complement** for luggage and handbags, **Cuff's Men's Shop**, **Casual Corner,** and a post office. ♦ M-W, F 10AM-7PM; Th 10AM-8PM; Sa-Su 10AM-6PM. Crystal Dr (15th-18th Sts) 892.4680

17 Marriott Crystal City Hotel $$ Connected to Crystal City Underground and just 5 minutes from National Airport (round-the-clock limousine service). One restaurant and a lounge. ♦ 1999 Jefferson Davis Hwy (Rte 1) 521.5500, 800/228.9290; fax 685.0191 &

17 Marriott Crystal Gateway $$$ Crystal City's newest hotel is also connected to Crystal City Underground and just 10 minutes from National Airport. Amenities include indoor and outdoor pools, a health club, concierge service, and 3 restaurants. The 16th and 17th floors offer the nicest rooms. ♦ 1700 Jefferson Davis Hwy (15-18th Sts) 920.3230, 800/228.4290; fax 979.6332

Arlington

18 Arlington County Visitors Center offers information on hotels, restaurants, and sights in DC and all of Virginia. ♦ Daily 9AM-5PM. 735 S. 18th St (Hayes St) 521.0772

19 Woo Lae Oak ★★$ You can't go wrong with an appetizer platter (a large one serves 4 or more), dumpling and noodle dishes, or hot pots of vegetables in spicy sauce. ♦ Korean ♦ Daily 11:30AM-10:30PM. 1500 S. Joyce St (15th St) Reservations recommended. 521.3706

During the Civil War, **Walt Whitman, Clara Barton,** and **Louisa May Alcott** all tended wounded soldiers in DC.

Restaurants: Red	**Hotels**: Blue
Shops/Parks: Green	**Sights/Culture**: Black

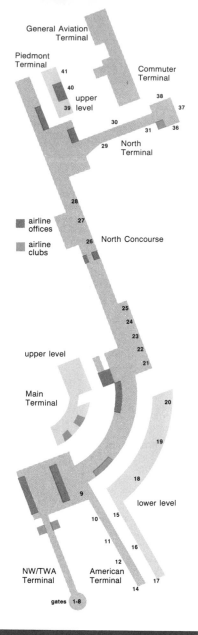

General Aviation Terminal

Piedmont Terminal

41

40

upper
39 level

Commuter Terminal

38

37

30

31   36

29   North
      Terminal

28

airline
offices   27

airline
clubs   26   North Concourse

25

24

23

22

21

upper level

Main
Terminal   20

19

18

9

lower level

10   15

11   16

12

NW/TWA   American
Terminal   Terminal   17

14

gates   1-8

Arlington

19 Washington National Airport, handling domestic and commuter flights, is the most convenient airport to Downtown Washington, just 3¹/₂ miles or a 15-minute cab ride away. However, the convenience of the location is tempered by the cramped, antiquated terminals, inadequate parking, and awkward traffic flow, particularly during peak travel times. A long-term renovation program was launched in 1989, further disrupting operations. Have patience.

Driving: To get to the airport, take the 14th St Bridge or Memorial Bridge to I-395, which connects with the George Washington Memorial Parkway. Look for the airport exit off the parkway. Parking is expensive.

Metrorail rapid rail service is without a doubt the cheapest way to or from the airport. Both the yellow and blue lines stop at the station, which is just across from the Main Terminal. A free shuttle bus runs every 5 to 8 minutes between the terminals and the station. Metrorail allows you to transfer to any point served in the system, including Union Station.

Metrobus also serves the airport, though less frequently than Metrorail. ♦ Bus stop in front of the Main Terminal

Limo service is provided by Washington Flyer, which serves 72 points in Washington, Maryland, and Virginia, including Dulles and Baltimore-Washington International. Service from 5AM to midnight (5AM to 10PM to and from Dulles). Vans leave every half hour, less often after 10PM. Downtown stops at several hotels. There is a ticketing and information booth inside the Main Terminal adjacent to the United Airlines counter and another in the NW/TWA Terminal. ♦ 24-hour information 685.1400, general nonflight airport information 8:30AM-5PM, 685-8000, parking and shuttle bus information 684.6441

20 The Pentagon The world's largest office building, the Pentagon has 3 times the floor space of the Empire State Building. The 5-sided structure—headquarters of the **Department of Defense**—covers 29 acres, with a 5-acre courtyard at its center. Built during World War II, the structure took only 16 months to complete. There are 17.5 miles of corridors, yet no office is more than 7 minutes from any other.

During the hour-long guided tours (first-come-first-served; bring photo ID), which leave from the concourse, the guide walks backward the entire time. Call ahead to arrange handicapped tours. ♦ Tours every half hour M-F 9:30AM-3:30PM (Rte 1–I-395) 202/695.1776

21 Navy and Marine Memorial (1930, Ernesto Begni dei Piatti) This is a simple, graceful representation of 7 seagulls in flight. ♦ Off the George Washington Memorial Pkwy (Arlington Memorial Bridge-14th St Bridge)

21 Lyndon Baines Johnson Memorial Grove At the south end of **Lady Bird Johnson Park** stretches 15 acres of pines, flowering dogwoods, and daffodils planted to commemorate the 36th president and his First Lady. The memorial site, marked by a large Texas pink granite monolith, is surrounded by stones inscribed with quotations by Johnson. ♦ Daily dawn to dusk. George Washington Pkwy (Arlington Memorial Bridge-14th St Bridge)

Alexandria

35-37
Pendleton
25
Oronoco
Princess
Quay
Queen
24
26
12
27
Cameron
23
13
9
22
Pitt
Fairfax
16
King (Rt 7)
11
8
2
1
21
30-34
19
17
15
10
7
3
20
14
5
4
18
Prince
Duke
Wolfe
6
Wilkes
Gibbon
to
Mount Vernon
Franklin

Henry (Rt 1 S)
Patrick (Rt 1 N)
Alfred
Columbus
Washington
St Asaph
Royal
Lee
Union
Potomac River

The handsome red-brick city of **Alexandria** (established 1749) was a principal Colonial port as well as a vital social and political center. Scotsman **John Alexander** purchased the land in 1669. **George Washington** was a native of Alexandria, as were Revolutionary War general **Henry *Light Horse Harry* Lee** and his son, Confederate general **Robert E. Lee**. Most of the city's extraordinarily rich history lies right before your eyes, in the dozens of historic buildings scattered around downtown, some of which are open to the public. **Old Town Alexandria**, the merchant district for the old seaport, has become a lively shopping and entertainment district. As in Georgetown, the main drag, **King Street**, is chaotic, but the side streets retain their dignity. Prince and Queen, east of Washington Street, have unusually handsome ensembles of early 19th-century row houses, and a riverfront park offers a retreat from the bustle of commerce. Alexandria is both a bedroom community for Washington and a place with its own distinctive identity as the unofficial capitol of Northern Virginia. *Area code 703 unless otherwise indicated.*

During the Civil War, Washington was the capital of the Union. The Confederacy was established in Montgomery AL, but moved its capital to Richmond VA soon after.

Torpedo Factory
ART CENTER

1 Torpedo Factory Works by more than 200 photographers, jewelers, sculptors, painters, and textile designers are on display in this WWII factory, formerly the major producer of naval torpedoes and parts. Although everything is for sale, the artists are more interested in explaining than hawking their works. ♦ Daily 10AM-5PM. 105 N. Union St (King-Cameron Sts) 838.4565 &

Alexandria

Within the Torpedo Factory:

Alexandria Archeology Since 1973, this organization has conducted explorations throughout Alexandria, unearthing objects from 3000 BC to the 20th century. ♦ Tu-Th 10AM-3PM; F-Sa 10AM-5PM. 3rd floor. 838.4399

1 The Fish Market ★$ A bustling chowder and seafood house within hailing distance of the waterfront. ♦ Seafood ♦ Daily 11:15AM-midnight. 105 King St (Union St) 836.5676 &

2 The Small Mall includes **Ampersand Books and Records** (549.0840) and **Serendipity** (683.3555), with American craftworks by craftspeople from across the nation. ♦ 118 King St (Union-Lee Sts)

181

3 Union Street Public House ★$$ Popular pub features microbrewery beers, plus the usual burgers and sandwiches. ♦ American ♦ Daily 11:30AM-10:30PM. 121 S. Union St (King St) 548.1785

4 Captains Row (early 1800s) The cobblestone walk from the waterfront up Prince Street is known as Captains Row because of its charming homes built by old sea captains. The rooflines, proportions, materials, and trim of these townhouses vary wildly, perhaps reflecting the independent spirits of the owners. ♦ 100-block of Prince St (Fairfax St)

5 Gentry Row The houses on this mid 18th-century block form a collage of characteristic Georgian themes. All residences are private, except the Greek Revival-style Athenaeum (below). ♦ 200-block of Prince St (Fairfax-Lee Sts)

5 Athenaeum Originally the *Bank of Old Dominion* (1851), it was purchased a century later by the **Northern Virginia Fine Arts Association** for use as an art museum and cultural activities center. Guest curators prepare original exhibitions of contemporary art and performances. The museum also hosts lectures, readings, workshops, and films. A fine example of Greek Revival architecture. ♦ Voluntary contribution. Tu-Sa 10AM-4PM; Su 1-4PM. 201 Prince St (Lee St) 548.0035 ♿

6 Old Presbyterian Meeting House The Scottish Presbyterians of Alexandria built this somber Georgian church in 1774. **George Washington**'s funeral services, canceled at Christ Church due to stormy weather, were held here. A weathered tombstone in the cemetery honors the **Unknown Soldier of the American Revolution.** ♦ M-F 8:30AM-4:30PM. Services Su 8:30, 11AM. 321 S. Fairfax St (Duke-Wolfe Sts) 549.6670

7 Why Not? Children's clothes (**OshKosh**, **Absorba**, **Imp**, **Mexx**), books, toys, and stuffed animals. ♦ Girls: infants-size 14. Boys: infants-size 7. M-W, Sa 10AM-5:30PM; Th-F 10AM-9PM; Su noon-5PM. 200 King St (Lee St) 548.4420

8 219 Basin Street Lounge ★$$$ Bourbon Street comes to Alexandria, with barbecued

shrimp and other Creole concoctions. Upstairs, traditional jazz. ♦ Southern ♦ Cover. M-Th 11:30AM-10PM; F-Sa 11:30AM-11PM; Su 10AM-10PM. 219 King St (Fairfax-Lee Sts) Jacket and tie required. Reservations recommended. 549.1141

"I think this is the most extraordinary collection of talent, of human knowledge, that has ever been gathered together at the White House, with the possible exception of when Thomas Jefferson dined alone."

John F. Kennedy
White House dinner honoring Nobel Prize winners, April 1962

8 Ramsay House/Alexandria Tourist Council (1724) After selecting the area in 1749, Alexandria's founder, **William Ramsay**, shipped his house down the Potomac and hauled it in one piece to its proper lot. The oldest house in Alexandria still contains many of Ramsay's personal belongings, purchased during his career as a merchant trader. Several rooms of the house have been rebuilt to accommodate the Alexandria Tourist Council, which provides free maps, hotel and group tour reservations, and lists of shops and restaurants in the area. ♦ Daily 9AM-5PM. 221 King St (Fairfax St) 838.4200

9 Antique Guild Antique and estate jewelry, sterling hollowware and bronzes. ♦ M-Sa 11AM-5PM. 113 N. Fairfax St (King-Cameron Sts) 836.1048

9 Carlyle House (1753, John Carlyle) Designed to resemble a Scottish manor house, this great mid-Georgian home was one of the first built in Alexandria. A number of the Carlyle family's personal effects and household items now on exhibit were found when archaeologists uncovered 5 privy shafts and trash chutes during the restoration. This is where **General Edward Braddock** and 5 Colonial governors planned the funding and strategy of the initial campaigns of the French and Indian War. Guided tours every half hour. ♦ Nominal admission. Tu-Sa 10AM-5PM; Su noon-5PM. 121 N. Fairfax St (King-Cameron Sts) 549.2997

10 Bamiyan ★★$$ Elegant service and the subtle cuisine of Afghanistan, including kabobs and *aushak* (lamb-stuffed ravioli). ♦ Afghan ♦ M-F 11:30AM-2:30PM, 5-11PM; Sa-Su 5-11PM. 300 King St (Fairfax St) Dinner reservations recommended F-Sa. 548.9006

11 Market Square/City Hall The **Townhouse Courthouse and Market** (established 1749) is the oldest continuously operating market in the US. The U-shaped Victorian building with a central courtyard was erected after an 1871 fire. In 1962, the courtyard was filled in by an addition to the building. But the farmers market goes on, set up in arcades on the south plaza of City Hall each Saturday from 5:30 to 9:30AM. Salt-cured meats, produce, homemade baked goods, flowers, and handmade crafts are sold. Underground parking garage. ♦ 300-block of King St (Royal-Fairfax Sts)

During the Civil War, Washington was the capital of the Union. The Confederacy was established in Montgomery AL, but moved its capital to Richmond VA soon after. **Jefferson Davis**, president of the Confederacy, was both US Secretary of War and a US senator from Mississippi before secession.

Restaurants: Red   **Hotels**: Blue
Shops/Parks: Green   **Sights/Culture**: Black

12 Gossypia Mexican wedding dresses and unusual women's clothing and jewelry from South America and Asia. ♦ M-Sa 10AM-6PM; Su noon-5PM. 325 Cameron St (Royal St) 836-6969 ⊛

12 Frankie Welch The best in American fashions for women, including Frankie's acclaimed scarfs and fabrics. ♦ M-Sa 10AM-6PM; Su noon-5PM. 305 Cameron St (Fairfax-Royal Sts) 549.0104

13 Gadsby's Tavern Museum (1770) In December of 1799, the proprietor, John Gadsby, offered tribute to his friend **George Washington** by hosting a gala ball in his honor. Unfortunately, it was the last time Washington would visit the tavern. He died shortly thereafter, just before his birthday. For many years, the tavern has celebrated his birthday with a traditional *Night Ball*. The inn has been completely restored, to the point of including period china and silverware, although the original ballroom interior is now in the Metropolitan Museum of Art's American Wing. What you see here is a reproduction. ♦ Nominal admission. Tu-Sa 10AM-5PM; Su 1-5PM. 134 N. Royal St (King-Cameron Sts) 838.4242

13 Gadsby's Tavern ★$$ (1792) The almost 200-year-old restaurant serves game specials, prime ribs, trifle, and a rich pecan pie. ♦ American ♦ M-Sa 11:30AM-3PM, 5:30-10PM; Su 11AM-3PM; 5:30-10PM. 138 N. Royal St (King-Cameron Sts) 548.1288

14 Not New Shop Quality silver, china, furniture, clothing, and jewelry have been sold here for over 40 years. There is also a large selection of modern cookbooks. ♦ M-Sa 10AM-4:30PM. 116 S. Royal St (King-Prince Sts) No credit cards. 549.0649

15 Holiday Inn of Old Town $$ You wouldn't know there was a modern hotel behind these Colonial brick walls. Among the amenities: a large indoor pool, a restaurant offering a great champagne brunch on Sundays, and shuttle service to National Airport every 30 minutes or upon request. The family dog and children under 18 stay free. ♦ 480 King St (Royal-Pitt Sts) 549.6080, 800/368.5047; fax 549.7777

The **National Museum of Health and Medicine** possesses the bullets that assassinated presidents **Lincoln** and **Garfield**, and it has the largest microscope collection in the world. It was also the site where the computer punch card was developed for the 1890 census.

16 Silverman Galleries, Inc. One of the area's largest collections of 18th- through 20th-century jewelry—diamonds are a specialty. Also, 18th- and 19th-century American and European furniture, silver, porcelain, and various decorative arts and furnishings. ♦ Tu-Sa 11AM-5PM; Su hours vary. 110 N. Saint Asaph St (King-Cameron Sts) 836.5363

16 Henry Africa ★★$$$ Seafood and interesting variations on traditional favorites are served in the Art Nouveau dining room. New management and talented young **Chef Bernard** have brought the place out of a slump. Music and hors d'oeuvres daily from 5 to 7PM; a jazz ensemble plays Tuesday through Sunday from 9PM to 1AM. ♦ French ♦ Tu-F 11:30AM-2:30PM, 6:30-10:30PM; Sa 11:30AM-2:30PM, 6:30-11PM. 607 King St (Saint Asaph St) 549.4010

17 Terrazza ★★$$$ Expensive, stylish Northern Italian branch of **Tiberio**. Standouts include agnolotti topped with alfredo sauce, light, fragrant cannellonis, and a heady raspberry cheesecake. Good wine list. ♦ Italian ♦ M-F 11:30AM-2:30PM, 6-10:30PM; Sa 6-11PM. 710 King St (George Washington Pkwy) Jacket required. Reservations recommended. 683.6900

17 Geranio ★$$ A comfortable, rustic trattoria for classic Northern Italian dishes. ♦ Italian ♦ M-F 11:30AM-2:30PM, 6-10:30PM; Sa 6-10:30PM. 722 King St (Washington Columbus Sts) Reservations recommended. 548.0088 ⊛

17 Scotland Yard ★★$$ Venison, quail, finnan haddie, and Scotch, of course, in a wood-paneled, clubby dining room. ♦ Scottish ♦ 728 King St (Washington-Columbus Sts) Reservations recommended. 683.1742 ⊛

18 Lyceum (1858; restoration, 1974, Carrol Curtice) Considered the historical headquarters of the city, the 2-story Grecian-style Lyceum presents Alexandria's history in etchings, daguerreotypes, photographs, video presentations, and color slides. The **Fashion Promenade** features costumed historians portraying Colonial celebrities in amusing vignettes. ♦ Free. Daily 10AM-5PM. 201 S. Washington St (Prince St) 838.4994 ⊛

19 Taverna Cretekou ★★$$ Picturesque little restaurant with a vine-covered courtyard in back. The grilled lamb, perfectly trimmed and seasoned with a lemon-herb mixture, is recommended. Authentically rowdy on Saturday nights. ♦ Greek ♦ Tu-F 11:30AM-2:30PM, 5-10:30PM; Sa noon-4PM, 5-11PM; Su 11AM-3PM, 5-9:30PM. 818 King St (Alfred-Columbus Sts) Reservations recommended. 548.8688

Key Bridge, connecting Georgetown with Rosslyn VA, was named for **Francis Scott Key**, author of the *Star-Spangled Banner*. His residence at 3512 M Street NW was dismantled in 1935 to make way for the Whitehurst Freeway.

20 Morrison House $$ Most of the 45 rooms and suites in this Colonial-style mansion have fourposter beds, brass chandeliers, and sconces. Tea is served every afternoon in the parlor. Amenities include a multilingual staff, valet service, indoor valet parking, and babysitting. ♦ 116 S. Alfred St (King-Prince Sts) 838.8000, 800/367.0800; fax 684.6283 ᭣

Within Morrison House:

Le Chardon d'Or ★★★$$$ Not as well known as big-name DC French restaurants, but an exquisite, and expensive, nouvelle cuisine restaurant with impeccable service. Specials include breast of chicken in a madeira sauce, veal kidney with red wine sauce and breast of roasted chicken in a light chive butter sauce. A la carte and prix-fixe menus daily. ♦ French ♦ Tu-Th 6-9:30PM; F-Sa 6-10PM. Jacket required. Reservations required. 838.8008 ᭣

21 East Wind ★★★$$ Vietnamese cuisine as an art form. *Bo dun* (marinated strips of beef broiled on skewers and topped with chopped peanuts and onion) makes a good starter, as do the sweet and sour soups. Delicately seasoned main courses include steamed fish in ginger sauce, and chicken, shrimp, or beef sautéed with vegetables. Stylish service in elegant surroundings. ♦ Vietnamese ♦ M-Th 11:30AM-2:30PM, 6-10PM; F 11:30AM-2:30PM, 6-10:30PM; Sa 6-10:30PM; Su 6-10PM. 809 King St (Columbus-Alfred Sts) Reservations recommended. 836.1515 ᭣

Alexandria

22 Bittersweet Imaginative soups, pâtés, salads, and hot entrees. ♦ Takeout ♦ M-Sa 11AM-3PM. 103 N. Alfred St (King St) 549.2708

23 Christ Church (1767–1773; tower, 1818, James Wren) **George Washington** paid $20 for his pew as a vestryman in this English country-style church. Much of the building, both inside and out, is original. Incumbent presidents are invited to attend services on

Radio Smithsonian, the institution's half-hour weekly magazine show, is heard on 55 public broadcasting stations in 29 states.

Restaurants: Red **Hotels**: Blue
Shops/Parks: Green **Sights/Culture**: Black

the Sunday closest to Washington's birthday. **Winston Churchill, Franklin Delano Roosevelt**, and **Robert E. Lee** attended services here. Plaques on pews mark where Washington and Lee each sat. ♦ M-Sa 9AM-5PM; Su during services and 2-5PM. Services: M-F 5:15PM; Su 9, 11:15AM. 118 N. Washington St (Cameron St) 549.1450

24 Lloyd House and Library (1798, John Wise) A distinguished example of late-Georgian architecture. After a succession of owners, Lloyd House was saved from demolition by Alexandria's preservationists. The interior has been restored for use by the **Alexandria Library**, which holds a large collection of books and documents on Virginia history. ♦ M-Sa 9AM-5PM. 220 N. Washington St (Queen St) 838.4577

25 Boyhood Home of Robert E. Lee (1795) The Lee family settled in the area before the War of 1812, and Robert E. Lee lived in this house until his West Point enrollment in 1825. Beautifully furnished with antiques and family artifacts, the brick house is a showcase of the early Federal period. ♦ Admission. M-Sa 10AM-4PM, Su noon-4PM Feb-Dec 14. 607 Oronoco St (Washington-Saint Asaph Sts) 548.8454

25 Lee-Fendall House A Greek Revival mansion built by **Philip Lee**'s grandson in 1785. Here **Henry** *Light Horse Harry* **Lee** authored a farewell address to **George Washington**; the children's room contains antique toys from many Lee generations. The Lee family lived in this house from 1785 until 1902. Tours on a walk-in basis. ♦ Nominal admission. Tu-Sa 10AM-4PM; Su noon-4PM. 614 Oronoco St (Washington-Saint Asaph Sts) 548.1789

26 Bilbo Baggins ★★$$ Wine bar and gourmet restaurant. Picnic lunches available. ♦ American ♦ M-Sa 11:30AM-2:30PM, 5:30-10:30PM; Su 11AM-2:30PM, 4:30-9:30PM. 208 Queen St (Fairfax-Lee Sts) Reservations recommended. 683.0300

27 La Bergerie ★★$$$ Robust Basque specialties like seafood stew and the classic refinement of *filet de poisson* are served in this handsome old house. ♦ French ♦ M-Sa 11:30AM-2:30PM, 6-10:30PM. 218 N. Lee St (Cameron-Queen Sts) Reservations required. 683.1007 ᭣

27 Ecco Cafe ★$$ A trendy Italian café, where the accent is on fresh pastas and inventive pizzas—how about fresh spinach with mozzarella, Parmesan, and goat cheese? The crowd is predictably young and upscale. ♦ Italian ♦ M-Th 11AM-midnight; F-Sa 11AM-2AM; Su 10:30AM-midnight. 220 N. Lee St (Queen-Cameron Sts) Reservations required. 684.0321

28 Artworks Animation Gallery Original cels for sale from **Disney Studios**, **Friz Freleng**, **Hanna-Barbera**, and **Jay Ward**. ♦ M-F 10AM-6PM. 831 S. Washington St (Jefferson-Green Sts) 836.5070 &

29 David Donnelly Mission Oak furniture and a selection of Art Deco pieces, mirrors, and '50s' neon. ♦ M-F 11AM-7PM; Sa 10AM-7PM; Su 11AM-5PM. 1314 King St (West-Payne Sts) 549.4672

30 Hard Times Cafe ★$ Chili heaven, Cincinnati- or vegetarian Texas-style. Portions are gigantic. ♦ American ♦ M-Sa 11AM-11PM; Su 4-10PM. 1404 King St (West St) 683.5340 &

31 George Washington Masonic National Memorial (1932, Harvey Wiley Corbett) This 333-foot tower, a speculative reconstruction of the Pharaoh's lighthouse in Egyptian Alexandria, contains Washington memorabilia, murals, and stained-glass depictions of his life, as well as much information on Freemasonry (Washington became charter master of the Alexandria Masonic Lodge in 1788). Forty- to 50-minute tours begin approximately every half hour, depending on the crowd. ♦ Free. Daily 9AM-5PM. King St at Callahan Dr. 683.2007

32 New Thieves Market Seventeen antique stores under one roof. Collectibles include furniture and Oriental rugs, paintings, china, and silver. ♦ M-F 10AM-5PM; Sa 10AM-6PM; Su noon-5PM. 8101 Richmond Hwy (Rte 235) 360.4200

Within New Thieves Market:

Scarlet Fox One of the largest shops in the market, containing a hodgepodge of new and antique furniture (mostly French), Venetian glass chandeliers, Georgian silver, and a selection of 19th- and 20th-century paintings. ♦ 780.3699

33 Guest Quarters $$$ Home away from home. Each of the 225 suites has a living room, dining room, bedroom, and fully equipped kitchen (the hotel will even deliver your groceries). There *is* a restaurant, **Political Club Cafe**, if you want a vacation from the stove. Complimentary Continental breakfast. Children under 18 stay free. ♦ 100 S. Reynolds St (Duke St) 370.9600, 800/424.2900; fax 370.0467 &

34 Fort Ward Museum and Park The fifth-largest Civil War fortification protecting Washington has been reconstructed with the help of photographs by **Mathew Brady**. Located in a 40-acre park with picnic facilities and an outdoor amphitheater. Soldiers in Civil War garb act out historic battles during summer weekends. ♦ Free. Tu-Sa 9AM-5PM; Su noon-5PM. 4301 W. Braddock Rd (N. Howard St) 838.4848

The **National Museum of Health and Medicine** possesses the bullets that assassinated presidents **Lincoln** and **Garfield**, and it has the world's largest microscope collection. It is also the site where the computer punch card was developed for the 1890 census.

35 The Executive Club $$ Suites only in this pretty Georgian-style building. There's a health club (universal weights, treadmill, bicycles), an outdoor pool, and complimentary Continental breakfast Monday through Friday. Non-smoking rooms. Free shuttle service to the airports and Old Town. ♦ 610 Bashford Ln (N. Washington St) 739.2582, 800/535.2582

36 Washington Sailing Marina Rentals and lessons in sailing and windsurfing; bicycle rentals for the Mount Vernon bicycle path. **Spinnaker & Spoke** sells boating and biking equipment. Snack bar. ♦ George Washington Memorial Pkwy, 2 miles south of National Airport. 548.9027

At the Washington Sailing Marina:

Potowmack Landing ★$$ A splendid view of the river and DC from this restaurant and nautical-theme bar. Just passable new American fare. ♦ American ♦ Daily 11:30AM-2:30PM, 5:30-10PM. 548.0001

37 Birchmere This threadbare bar is a mecca for Washington's bluegrass community. **Seldom Scene**, one of the nation's best bluegrass bands, plays every Thursday night. ♦ Tu-Sa 7PM-1AM. 3901 Mt. Vernon Ave (Bruce St) 549-5919 &

The **Alexandria Canal** connected the city to the C & O Canal over an aqueduct across the Potomac into Georgetown. Operations, interrupted by the Civil War, continued from 1843 to 1886. The **Tide Lock**, excavated in 1978, is now the site of the **Alexandria Waterfront Museum**.

"Take the worst parts of City Road and Pentonville, or the straggling outskirts of Paris, where the houses are smallest, preserving all their oddities, but especially the small shops and dwellings, occupied in Pentonville (but not in Washington) by furniture-brokers, keepers of poor eating houses, and fanciers of birds. Burn the whole down, build it up again in wood and plaster; widen it a little, throw in part of St. John's Wood; put green blinds outside all the private

Alexandria

houses, with a red curtain and a white one in every window; plough up all the roads; plant a great deal of coarse turf in every place where it ought not to be; erect three handsome buildings in stone and marble anywhere, but the more entirely out of everybody's way the better; call one the Post Office, one the Patent Office, and one the Treasury; make it scorching hot in the morning, and freezing cold in the afternoon, with an occasional tornado of wind and dust; leave a brick-field without the bricks, in all central places where a street may naturally be expected; and that's Washington."

Charles Dickens
American Notes

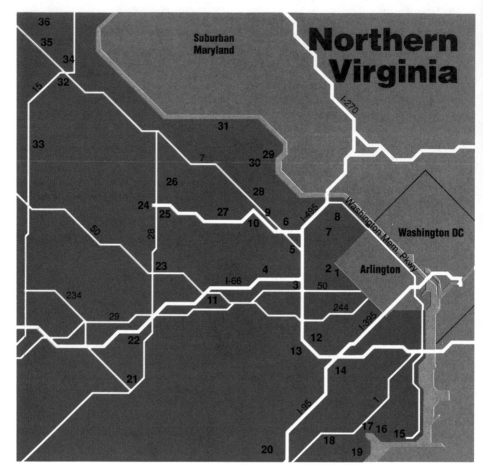

Much of the DC area's wealth is concentrated within the rapidly growing **Northern Virginia** suburbs. The region's prosperity is readily evident in **Dale City**'s **Potomac Mills Mall** and the enormous **Tysons Corner** complex of malls, as well as in the paralyzing traffic during rush hour. Behind all the hustle and newness, however, lies the *Old Dominion*—in gracious Colonial mansions like **Oatlands**, in the Civil War battlefields such as **Manassas**, and in the rolling green **Hunt Country** to the west. Rural Virginia, just an hour's drive from Downtown Washington, remains remarkably similar to the pastoral ideal so admired by **Thomas Jefferson**. *Area code 703 unless otherwise indicated.*

Northern Virginia

Falls Church

1 Falls Church (1792) The original wooden church was erected in 1732 near a road leading to the Potomac waterfalls. Sixty years later, a new structure was completed on the same site. Part of the church serves as a museum: weapons, medical instruments, and curios from the Civil War are exhibited. ♦ M-F 9AM-5:30PM. Services (Episcopal) Su 7:30, 8:45, 10:30AM, noon. 115 E. Fairfax St (Lee Hwy-Broad St) 532.7600

Restaurants: Red	**Hotels**: Blue
Shops/Parks: Green	**Sights/Culture**: Black

1 Paradise East ★$ Once you've mastered basic chopstick skills, don't hesitate to order the various raw meat or seafood combinations—dip them in your own bubbling saucepan on the table and enjoy. Forks are available upon request. ♦ Korean/Chinese/Japanese ♦ M-Sa 11AM-11PM; Su noon-11PM. 7151 Lee Hwy (Annandale Rd) 534.2552

1 Bangkok-Vientiane ★★$ Laotian and Thai dishes like deep-fried pork-filled spring rolls and seafood soup with bean thread. Excellent daily specials. Laotian rice tends to be more glutinous than Thai, and the spices less fiery hot. ♦ Laotian/Thai ♦ M-Th, Su 11AM-10PM; F-Sa 11AM-11PM. 926A W. Broad St (West St) Reservations recommended. 534.0095

1 Panjshir ★$ Top-notch *aushak* (a raviolilike creation stuffed with scallions and topped with meat sauce, yogurt, and mint), kabobs, and a wide selection of Afghan vegetarian dishes. ♦ Afghan ♦ M-Sa 11AM-2PM, 5-11PM; Su 5-11PM. 924 W. Broad St (West St) Reservations recommended. 536.4566. Also at: 224 W. Maple Ave, Vienna VA. 281.4183

1 Fortune ★★$$ Dim sum is served from rolling tea carts during the week as well as on weekends—thus allowing customers to order by sight rather than from memory. The regular menu offers beautifully prepared seafood, meat, and noodle dishes. On Saturday and Sunday afternoons, Fortune is packed with Chinese families. ♦ Chinese ♦ M-Th, Su 11AM-10:30PM; F-Sa 11AM-midnight. 5900 Leesburg Pike (Arlington Blvd) 998.8888

1 **Peking Gourmet Inn** ★★★$$ **President Bush**'s favorite Chinese restaurant is equipped with a bulletproof window (for his protection and yours), and for him they deliver. Three generations of the **Tsui** family provide dedicated service and a consistently high standard of classic dishes. The Peking duck is unusually crisp and fat-free; other specials include pork with garlic sprouts, Szechuan beef, and Jou-Yen shrimp. Handsome decor, surprisingly inexpensive, and worth a wait on the weekends. ♦ Chinese ♦ M-F, Su 11AM-10:30PM; F-Sa 11AM-midnight. 6029 Leesburg Pike (Glen Carolyn Rd) Reservations required. 671.8088

2 **National Memorial Park** A vast cemetery, noted for its gardens and sculptured fountains. The *Fountain of Faith*, the centerpiece of the grounds, was created by Swedish sculptor **Carl Milles**. Thirty-seven graceful bronze figures seem to hover in a spray of water; each face a portrait of one of the sculptor's deceased friends. The fountain represents the joy that may await us after death. ♦ Daily 8AM-dusk. 7400 Lee Hwy (Hollywood Rd-West St) 560.4400

3 **Skyline Chili** ★$ Chili, Cincinnati-style. Order it any one of 5 ways, ranging from a "bowl of plain," which is simply a bowl of sauce, to the "five-way," a plate crowded with spaghetti, beans, chili, onions, and plenty of grated Cheddar cheese—instructions on how to get the most from every bite (this involves a maneuver called the "forklift") are provided. ♦ American ♦ M-Th 10:30AM-10PM; F-Sa 10:30AM-11PM; Su noon-8PM. 8102 Arlington Blvd (Yorktown Square Shopping Center-Gallows Rd) No credit cards. 698.5669. Also at: 50 Massachusetts Ave NE (in Union Station) 202/842.4454

Vienna

1 **Nizam's** ★★$$ From suburbia to Istanbul: Middle Eastern delicacies in a romantic setting. ♦ Middle Eastern ♦ Tu-Th 11AM-3PM, 5-10PM; F 11AM-3PM, 5-11PM; Sa 5-11PM; Su 4-10PM. 523 Maple Ave (Rte 243) Reservations recommended. 938.8948

5 **Tysons Corner Marriott Hotel** $$$ Adjacent to the shopping center, this recently renovated hotel matches the surrounding area—pleasant suburbia with a touch of class. Aside from the regular amenities—free HBO, valet service, and restaurant—the 2nd floor sports a health club, complete with indoor swimming pool, whirlpool, sauna, and exercise room with locker facilities. Children under 19 stay free. ♦ 8028 Leesburg Pike (Chain Bridge Rd) 734.3200, 800/228.9290; fax 442.9301 ♿

5 **Clyde's** ★$$ Art Deco outpost is classier than the Georgetown original, with the same reliable burgers and omelets, plus seafood. ♦ American ♦ M-Tu, Su 11AM-midnight; W-Sa 11AM-2AM. 8332 Leesburg Pike (Old Chain Bridge Rd) 734.1901

5 **Embassy Suites Hotel at Tysons Corner** $$ A stone's throw from Tysons Corner Center, this large and glitzy hotel has an indoor swimming pool, sauna, Jacuzzi, in-house movies, and accommodations for the handicapped. Children under 16 stay free. ♦ 8517 Leesburg Pike (Dulles Access Rd) 883.0707, 800/EM-BASSY; fax 883.0694 ♿

Within the Embassy Suites Hotel:

Carnegie Deli ★$ Improbably located in the hotel's lobby, this branch of the Manhattan institution serves up the same colossal corned beef sandwiches and authentic matzo ball soup. Brighter and much less noisy than the original. ♦ Deli ♦ M-Th, Su 11AM-10PM; F-Sa 11AM-midnight. 790.5001

5 **Fedora Cafe** ★$$ Attractively trendy pub with pizzas, pastas, and grilled seafood; the bar is *Singles Central*. ♦ American ♦ M-Th 11:30AM-3PM, 5-10:30PM; F 11:30AM-3PM, 5-11:30PM; Sa noon-3PM, 5-11:30PM; Su 10:30AM-2:30PM, 4:30-9:30PM. 8521 Leesburg Pike (Dulles Access Rd) Reservations recommended. 556.0100

5 **Potomac Vegetable Farms** is one of the few remaining plots in an area that is being overtaken by shopping malls, offices, and housing developments. Established in the early 1960s by the **Newcomb** family, the 28-acre farm grows vegetables (snap peas, mustard greens, Chinese cabbage, basil, lettuces, tomatoes, Japanese eggplant), fruit (raspberries, blackberries, blueberries, strawberries), a variety of grains, and flowers—all without chemical pesticides. Organic methods, including natural fertilizers, cover cropping, and predator insects (ladybugs, praying mantises, lacewings), enrich the soil and help keep pests at bay. ♦ Daily 9AM-6PM Jul-Oct. Rte 7 (Beulah Rd) 759.3844

Courtesy Wolf Trap Foundation

6 **Wolf Trap Farm Park** Situated on 117 acres of woodlands, this concert/arts facility has brought the best of the arts to outdoor Virginia.

Northern Virginia

The **Wolf Trap Foundation** chooses the performers, which have ranged from **Metropolitan Opera** singers and folk singers to the **Alvin Ailey Dance Theatre** and a variety of comedians. The concert hall, **Filene Center** (1971, **MacFadyen & Knowles**), comprises a stage, a lofty scene tower, and a soaring, open-sided wooden canopy that shelters 3500 wooden seats built into a natural slope. Higher up is unprotected lawn seating for 3000 more. The romantic setting is matched by fine acoustics. Devastated by fire in 1982, the hall has since been rebuilt to its original design. Tours of the center and the park are available from the **Visitor Services Office**. ♦ Tickets required for performances. Filene Center box office: daily noon-6PM; performance days noon-9PM, Jun-Sep. 1624 Trap Rd (Leesburg Pike-Dulles Access Rd) 255.1860, box office 255.1900; Ticket Center 202/432.0200, 800/448.9009

7 Tysons Corner Center After a face-lift, the original Tysons mall now offers almost 200 stores aimed at a middle-income clientele. Major department stores are **Garfinckel's**, **Bloomingdale's**, **Woodward & Lothrop**, and **Nordstrom**, a Seattle-based department store. Among its proven retail ingredients are **Britches** and **Britches Great Outdoors** for stylish young professional and sports clothing. **Balley, Banks and Biddle** for fine jewelry, crystal, china, silver, and porcelains. ♦ M-Sa 10AM-9:30PM; Su noon-5PM. 9160 Chain Bridge Rd (Leesburg Pike) McLean. 893.9400

7 Galleria at Tysons II Opened in 1988, this megamall will eventually have 143 stores (there are now 105). **Macy's**, **Saks Fifth Avenue**, and **Neiman-Marcus** are here already. ♦ M-Sa 10AM-9:30PM; Su 11AM-6PM. 2001 International Dr (Chain Bridge Rd-Leesburg Pike) McLean. 827.7700

8 Giant Gourmet A supermarket that excels in selection and quality, carrying freshly baked (in-house) breads and pastries, more than 500 wines and 60 imported beers, and exotic meats like camel and pheasant. ♦ M-Th 10AM-8PM; F-Sa 9AM-9PM; Su 9AM-7PM. 1445 Chain Bridge Rd (Old Dominion Dr) McLean. 448.0800

8 La Mirabelle ★★$$ Elegance without pretense reigns at this classic French establishment, serving specialties *à la Escoffier* in a country-style atmosphere. ♦ French ♦ M-F 11:30AM-2PM, 5-9PM; Sa 5-9PM; Su hours vary: call for schedule. 6645 Old Dominion Dr (McLean Square Shopping Center) McLean. Reservations required. 893.8484

8 Kazan ★★$$ The tented ceiling and tuxedoed captains are in tune with the tab, slightly higher than at your usual ethnic hangout. The cuisine is a superior representation of what the Middle East has to offer, from Greek moussaka to Turkish *borek* (pastry filled with cheese, spinach, or meat). ♦ Middle Eastern ♦ M-Th 11AM-3PM, 5-10PM; F 11AM-3PM, 5-11PM; Sa 5-

11PM. 6813 Redmond Dr (Chain Bridge Rd-Old Dominion Dr) McLean. Reservations required. 734.1960

9 Claude Moore Colonial Farm at Turkey Run Amazing look at an authentic pre-Revolutionary War farm, where a costumed family (acting courtesy of staff members) performs household chores and heavy farm work with the help of original tools and utensils. ♦ Fee. W-Su 10AM-4:30PM. Closed on rainy days. 6310 Old Georgetown Pike (Dolley Madison Blvd) McLean. 442.7557

10 Meadowlark Gardens Regional Park In the shadow of Tysons' high-tech towers, a 75-acre oasis of woods and gardens, including lily ponds and an herb garden. ♦ Daily 10AM-8PM. 1624 Beulah Rd (Dulles Access Rd) Tysons Corner. 255.3631

11 George Mason University A branch of the University of Virginia until 1972, the university enrolls nearly 20,000 students. George Mason's major thrusts are toward the humanities, business, and public policy. The **Sports Recreation Complex**, commonly known as the *Field House*, boasts 69,000 square feet of basketball, tennis, and volleyball courts, a 200-meter indoor track, and archery and fencing facilities. Sporting events and concerts take place at the **Patriot Center**. Tickets sold through **Ticket Center** outlets. ♦ Patriot Center box office M-Sa 10AM-5:30PM. 4400 University Dr (Rte 123) Fairfax. 323.2000, info tape 323.2675; Ticket Center 202/432.0200, 800/448.9009

12 Duck Chang's ★$ Prime duck is the specialty of this modest neighborhood place. ♦ Chinese ♦ M-Sa 11AM-11PM; Su noon-10PM. 4427 John Marr Dr (Little River Trnpk) Annandale. 941.9400

12 Fritzbe's ★$ Suburban chic, where the residents of Annandale and occasional Beltway farers feast on meats from the grill. The Sunday brunch is impressive. ♦ American ♦ M-Th 11:30AM-1AM; F-Sa 11:30AM-2AM; Su 10:30AM-1AM. 7052 Columbia Pike (Little River Trnpk) Annandale. 354.4560

13 The Accotink Creek meanders through 479 acres of a landscaped park area (**Lake Accotink Park**), ending in a pretty lake. A historical hiking trail follows the **Old Alexandria Railroad**, whose tracks once ran through the park. Canoes, paddleboats, and rowboats can be rented at the marina facility, which also operates a mini-golf course and a seasonal snackbar. ♦ Park dawn-dusk. Marina facility 8AM-dusk, Mar-Nov. 5660 Heming Ave (Braddock-Old Keene Mill Rds) Springfield. 569.3464 &

14 The Talbots Save and look soigné at this outlet store for the popular purveyor of the town-and-country look. ♦ M-F 9:30AM-8PM; Sa 10AM-6PM; Su noon-5PM. 6815 Old Springfield Plaza (Backlick Rd-Commerce St) Springfield. 644.5115

14 Gloria Jean's Coffee Bean Over 50 varieties of coffee, from Columbian Supremo to Hawaiian Kona, teas, and all the paraphernalia to brew them. ♦ M-Sa 10AM-9:30PM; Su noon-5PM. Springfield Mall (Franconia Rd-the Beltway) 971.3280

The legend of George Washington's cherry tree originated in Fredericksburg. The story seems to have first appeared in a biography of Washington by **Parson Mason Locke Weems**.

If you don't have time to pack a picnic lunch for a day at Wolf Trap, you can order one ahead of time by calling 202/448.0800.

15 Mount Vernon (1754–1787, George Washington) The contemporary presidential home is characterized by privacy and security. Sliding iron gates, video cameras, and guard posts protect the White House, the presidential beach, and riding trail. No such security was needed in the early days of the Republic. What presidential homes then held in common were wheat and tobacco fields, mills, smokehouses, and stables. In a time of broad personal mastery, a gifted leader was often able to administer a nation, lead troops in battle, design a building, and run a profitable farm. George Washington exemplified this spirit, and his estate at Mount Vernon is its testimony. He lived here from 1754 until his death in 1799. The original building was built by his brother, **Augustine**.

In its prime, Mount Vernon comprised 8000 acres divided into 5 working farms. It was self sufficient in almost every way. There were orchards, a gristmill, and facilities for making textiles and leather goods.

"No estate in United America is more pleasantly situated than this house," Washington wrote, but during the years he was Mount Vernon's proprietor he was allowed little time there. First there was the French and Indian War, then the Revolutionary War, which kept Washington away for 8 years. When he returned, he was determined to be a successful planter. He experimented with crop rotation and compared notes with like-minded growers. His harvests were good, and he even won a "premium for raising the largest jackass" from the Agricultural Society of South Carolina. But only 4 years later, he went to Philadelphia as a delegate to the Constitutional Convention and then served 2 terms as president. Finally, in 1797, he returned home, where he lived contentedly until his death—2 years later.

The current estate, a more manageable 500 acres, is probably the best preserved 18th-century plantation in the country, and in the summer as many as 10,000 people a day come to enjoy it. The best strategy is to arrive early and tour the mansion before visiting the outbuildings and grounds.

The inside of the white Georgian mansion has been lovingly restored. All wallpaper, drapery, and upholstery are exact replicas, and the original colors have been repainted on the walls. (The Colonial palette was much bolder than you'd expect.) Note the Palladian window

in the **Banquet Hall**, and in the **Little Parlor**, the harpsichord Washington imported for his adopted daughter, **Nellie**. One of the upstairs bedrooms holds a trunk Washington carried with him during the Revolutionary War, as well as the bed in which he died. (Washington was 6 feet 2 inches and had the extra-long bed made to order.)

Ten of the outbuildings are open, including the spinning room and open-hearth kitchen house. (In days when fires were common and virtually unstoppable, the kitchen was often set apart from the main house.) You can visit the stable, where a rare 18th-century coach is on display, and a small museum with exhibitions of Washingtoniana, Colonial silver, and china. In the reconstructed greenhouse/slave quarters there is a fascinating exhibition about archaeology at Mount Vernon. (Digs are taking place on the premises now.)

On either side of the gracious bowling green are period gardens with flowers, vegetables, and boxwood hedges. Note the partially submerged walls called *ha has* that separate tended lawns and gardens from pasture. It's a pleasant walk down to the family vaults where George and Martha are buried. Plan to spend between 90 minutes and 2 hours touring the grounds; guided tours are available inside the mansion. Gift shop. ◆ Fee. Daily 9AM-4PM, Jan-Feb, Nov-Dec; daily 9AM-5PM, Mar-Oct. Tourmobile tours Jun-Sep. Southern end of George Washington Pkwy (8 miles south of Alexandria, 16 miles south of DC) 780.2000 ♿

16 George Washington Grist Mill Historical State Park (1774; restoration, 1932) The original foundations remain at this restored mill. George Washington owned the mill for almost 30 years. After his death, it began to fall into disrepair and by 1850 was in shambles. During the Depression, the **Civilian Conservation Corps** and local craftspeople and historians worked to restore it, rebuilding the walls and foundation in time for the bicentennial of Washington's birth. The contents of the mill (machinery, conveyor bolts, and their like, authentic to 1770), originally at Front Royal, were made by millwright **Oliver Evans** of Philadelphia, who made the machinery for this mill when it was in operation. ◆ Fee. Daily 9AM-4:45PM, Memorial Day-Labor Day. 5514 Mt. Vernon Memorial Hwy (just south of US 1) 780.3383

Northern Virginia

W&OD Railroad Regional Park A 45-mile abandoned railroad right-of-way (for the Washington & Old Dominion Railroad) is now a bicycle, horseback riding, and jogging path that runs from Alexandria through Arlington County, Falls Church, and Fairfax County to Purcellville in Loudoun County. Some day it will extend to the Blue Ridge Mountains. The park is open daily dawn to dusk; its trail office is located at 1860 Reston Ave, Reston (437.1910).

17 Woodlawn Plantation (1805, Dr. William Thornton) Estate bequeathed by George Washington to his adopted daughter, **Nellie Parke Custis**, and his nephew, **Lawrence Lewis**. The Georgian mansion is architecturally more coherent and impressive than Mt.Vernon, and its rooms and restored formal gardens are well worth seeing. There is a gift shop as well. Managed by the **National Trust for Historic Preservation**. ◆ Admission. Daily 9:30AM-4:30PM; guided tours every half hour. 9000 Richmond Hwy (US 1 and Rte 235, 14 miles south of DC) 780.4000

At Woodlawn Plantation:

The Frank Lloyd Wright House (Pope-Leighey House) (1940, Frank Lloyd Wright) Originally located in Falls Church VA, the house was rescued from destruction in 1964, when it was moved to Woodlawn Plantation and donated to the National Trust. Built of cypress, brick, and glass, the house contains features that were uncommon when it was built: heated concrete slab floors, a flat roof, windows designed as an integral part of the wall. A rare example of what Wright called *Usonian* architecture—well-designed housing for moderate-income families. Managed by the **National Trust for Historic Preservation**. Tours on a walk-in basis. ◆ Admission. Daily 9:30AM-4:30PM

18 Pohick Church (1774, James Wren and William West) **George Washington** and **George Mason** were on the select building committee that influenced the design of this country church. The simple block of brick is set off with handsome quoins and pediments of Aquila Creek stone cut from Washington's own quarries. ◆ Services (Episcopal) Su 8, 9:15, 11AM, Jan-Memorial Day, Labor Day-Dec; Su 8, 10AM, Memorial Day-Labor Day. 9301 Richmond Hwy (US 1, south of Alexandria) Lorton. 339.6572

19 Gunston Hall (1759) was the home of **George Mason**, a Virginia farmer, the author of the *Virginia Declaration of Rights 1776*, and a framer of the *Bill of Rights*. The Georgian-style home overlooks the Potomac River. Furnishings are 18th-century English and American. **William Buckland** was the joiner-turned-architect who designed the sumptuous Palladian drawing room, and Chinese Chippendale dining room, as well as the 2 distinctive

Northern Virginia

porches. Equally glorious are the boxhedge gardens behind the house. ◆ Fee. Daily 9:30AM-5PM. Tours every half hour. Guided tours of house; self-guided tours of outbuildings, gardens, and rest of plantation. 10709 Gunston Rd (Rte 1) Lorton. 550.9220

19 Pohick Bay Regional Park A water-oriented park with 300 campsites, an 18-hole golf course, miniature golf, Frisbee golf, sailboat and paddleboat rentals, a swimming pool, and nature trails. ◆ Entrance fee for out-of-area visitors. Daily dawn-dusk. 10651 Gunston Road (25 miles south of DC) Lorton. 339.6104

20 Potomac Mills Mall The world's largest off-price and outlet mall holds almost 200 stores, including **Ikea**, a Swedish furniture store; **Cohoes**, for men's and women's clothing; and **Waccamaw Pottery**. Take a break from shopping, at one of the mall's 10 movie theaters. ◆ M-Sa 10AM-9:30PM; Su 11AM-6PM. 2700 Potomac Mills Circle, Prince William. 643.1770, group tours 643.1605

20 Marine Corps Air-Ground Museum Great moments in Marine Corps history, 1900–1945, displayed in uniforms, weapons, artillery, and aircraft. ◆ Free. Tu-Su 10AM-5PM, Apr-Nov. Quantico Marine Base, I95 and Quantico Triangle. 640.2606

Manassas Although the town didn't exist when the famous battle took place, it boasts a pretty Victorian-era downtown with a courthouse (1892) and bank building (1896); hard to believe it's in the midst of booming suburbia.

21 Carmello's Ristorante Italiano ★$$ Homey Italian café shines with the traditionals: ravioli, minestrone, and veal dishes. ◆ Italian ◆ M-F 11:30AM-2:30PM, 5-10PM; Sa 5-10PM. 9108 Center St (Battle St) Reservations recommended. 368.5522

21 Manassas City Museum Civil War and railroad memorabilia, and maps for walking, driving, and architectural tours of downtown and surrounding area. Gift shop. ◆ Free. Tu-Su, federal holidays 10AM-5PM. 9406 Main St (Church St) 368.1873

21 Laws Antiques Complex Thirty antique shops and some 75 flea market stands flank the **H.L. Sonny Laws** auction house. The auctions include 3-day catalog affairs, first-weekend-of-the-month estate sales, and weekly Friday night disposals of household goods. One-stop shopping for antiques has been going on here for more than 20 years. ◆ Shops M, Th-Su 10:30AM-5PM. Auction house daily 9AM-5PM. 7209 Centreville Road (Rte 128) 631.0590

22 Bull Run Regional Park Several thousand acres with 150 campsites, a swimming pool, miniature golf, picnic areas, and nature trails. Semiannual dog shows and a yearly country jamboree. ◆ Daily dawn-dusk, mid Mar-Nov. 17700 Bull Run Dr (Rte 66-Rte 28) 631.0550

23 Sully Plantation (1794, Richard Bland Lee) **Richard Bland Lee**, uncle of **Robert E. Lee** and Northern Virginia's first representative to Congress, built this house, which is furnished with Federal-period antiques. Tours include the smokehouse and stone dairy. ◆ Fee. Sa-Su 11AM-4PM, Jan-Feb; M, W-Su 11AM-5PM, Mar-Dec. 3601 Sully Rd (off State Rte 28, near Dulles Airport) Chantilly. 437.1794

The **key to the Bastille** is one of the most unusual historical objects on view at **Mount Vernon**. It was sent to George Washington by Lafayette, who ordered the destruction of the prison during the French Revolution.

Restaurants: Red	**Hotels**: Blue
Shops/Parks: Green	**Sights/Culture**: Black

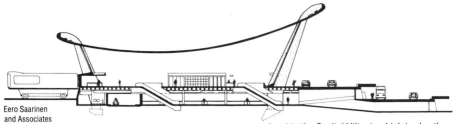

Eero Saarinen
and Associates

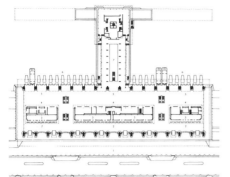

24 Washington Dulles International Airport

(1962, Eero Saarinen) Saarinen's expressive design for the main terminal epitomizes the joy of flight: this was the first airport designed for the jet age, and its airy main terminal is still spectacular. Saarinen's other bright idea, the mobile lounges designed to carry passengers to airplanes, has been overtaken by the surge in traffic. Now, most airlines use the lounges to carry passengers to midfield terminals, where they board through conventional gates. But it beats walking down a mile-long finger.

International arrivals, customs, baggage claim, ground transportation, a duty-free shop, and 24-hour car rentals are on the ground floor. You will also find information and foreign language assistance services, a post office, a bank, and an American Express disbursing machine.

There is no public transportation to Dulles. You must either drive, take a cab, or use the limousine service. ♦ Information hotline 471.4242

Driving: A 13.5-mile limited access highway runs east from the airport. It connects with Rte 123 (which is Old Chain Bridge Rd), I-495 (the Beltway), and Hwy I-66. Highway I-66 will take you over the Theodore Roosevelt Bridge and into Downtown DC in about 30 to 35 minutes.

Taxis: There is a dispatcher on duty 24 hours a day. As you approach, the dispatcher will give you a brochure, in 5 languages, with estimated rates to points in DC, Maryland, and Virginia. The cabs are metered. ♦ Fee. 471.5555

Limos: **Washington Flyer** runs bus and limo service to Washington, Maryland, and Virginia, also Baltimore-Washington Airport and Washington National Airport. Service runs frequently between 5AM and midnight, and the fare is reasonable. Hotels served in DC are the Shoreham, Sheraton Park, Capital Hilton, Mayflower, and the Washington Hilton. All routes terminate at the airport bus terminal, 1517 K St NW

(next to the Capital Hilton), which is also the major pickup point for trips to the airport. There are 2 ticketing and information booths at the top of the ramps leading to the ground transportation loading and pickup area. ♦ Fee. Departures (Dulles to DC): M-F 4:45AM-9:45PM every 30 minutes; Sa-Su 4:45AM-midnight every hour. (Trips may be available by request in off-hours. Inquire at east wing, lower level) 24-hour information 685.1400

25 Washington Dulles Airport Marriott $$

Closest hotel to the airport. Indoor/outdoor pool, Jacuzzi, weight rooms, outdoor tennis courts. Special weekend rate; children under 18 stay free. ♦ 333 W Service Rd (Dulles Access Rd) Chantilly. 471.9500, 800/228.9290; fax 661.6785 &

26 Holiday Inn Dulles Airport $$ Convenient

airport location. Indoor pool, sauna, lounge, restaurant. Children under 18 stay free. ♦ 1000 Sully Rd (Dulles Access Rd) Sterling. 471.7411, 800/HOLIDAY; fax 471.7411 ext 515

Reston

27 Reston (Begun 1962) One of the nation's few

remarkable *new towns*, Reston was envisioned by **Robert E. Simon** in the mid 1950s. (Simon's initials form the basis of the city's name.) It is a completely planned city, covering 11 1/2 square miles, and when it is completed in the 1990s, over 65,000 people will live around the 5 lakes that dominate the city plan.

Forty percent of all the land in Reston is open and/or public space. Homes are arranged in small neighborhood clusters, which are distributed evenly throughout the city; recreational amenities include golf courses, pools, ballparks, tennis courts, bridle paths, and a **Nature Center**. Yet this picture of suburban serenity has been very successful in attracting high-tech industries, and the presence of companies like **GTE**, **AT&T**, **Sperry**, and the **US Geological**

Northern Virginia

Survey has guaranteed at least one job per household in the city.

Reston's development is supervised by **Mobil Land Development Corporation**, which coordinates the design and construction of homes (ranging from small apartments to townhouses to minimansions, of varied quality and styles), schools, business complexes, and shopping centers—all with a splendid sensitivity to the surrounding woods and meadows. The landscaping far outshines the architecture away from the central core. ♦ 5 miles east of Dulles Airport. Fairfax County. 620.4730

27 Reston Art Gallery Cooperative art gallery with exhibitions of local artists' work and educational programs for adults and children. Also presents workshops, demonstrations, and poetry readings. ◆ Tu-Sa 11AM-5PM; Su noon-5PM. 11400 Washington Plaza W, Lake Anne Plaza (Baron Cameron Ave) 481.8156

27 Academy of Model Aeronautics Museum Historical exhibitions of model airplanes, ranging from a foot-long rubberband-powered plane to a 5-yard-long remote-controlled model powered by a lawnmower engine. ◆ Free. M-F 9AM-5PM; Sa 10AM-3PM. Group tours by reservation. 1810 Samuel Morse Dr (Sunset Hills Rd) 435.0750

Great Falls

28 Colvin Run Mill Historic Site This 19th-century gristmill still grinds grain. Woodcarving demonstrations take place on the first Sunday of each month from May to August. ◆ Fee. Sa-Su 11AM-5PM, Jan-Feb; M, W-Su 11AM-5PM, Mar-Dec. 10017 Colvin Run Rd (off Leesburg Pike) 759.2771

29 Great Falls Park The best view of the imposing 76-foot falls of the Potomac is from the Virginia side; during full spring flood the volume of water surpasses that of Niagara Falls: 480,000 cubic feet per second. The Observation Deck is a great place to watch kayakers play at the base of the falls.

The forest and swamps that follow along the Potomac's banks include spectacular displays of wildflowers in their seasonal blooms. The park is a migration stop for many birds, and bird watchers claim that this is one of the East Coast's best areas—even bald eagles have been spotted. The natural pools along the river attract deer, foxes, muskrats, beavers, opossums, and rabbits. An excellent system of hiking trails leads you through the woods and along the river. Picnic areas are located throughout the park (no open fires, please). The **Visitors Center** offers rotating exhibitions about nature, conservation, and safety; the helpful staff answers questions and will direct visitors to the season's special vistas.

In the late 1700s, **George Washington** came here to oversee the building of the **Potowmac Canal**, a bypass of the falls and other unnavigable parts of the river. Locks 1 through 5 and part of the canal are still visible, and the

Northern Virginia

National Park Service, which maintains the area, is working constantly to prevent further deterioration. Ruins of the canal are located southeast of the **Visitors Center**. Also visible are a chimney, a spring house, and other remnants of **Matildaville**, the city founded by **Henry** *Light Horse Harry* **Lee** in honor of his first wife.

Note: This is a beautiful yet extremely dangerous section of the river: currents are swift and the rock faces sheer. Everyone is urged to stay off the rocks near the river and out of the water near the falls. Drownings occur several times

yearly when the swift current pulls careless climbers and waders into the torrent. Parents: Watch your children! Experienced rock climbers with proper equipment can register at the Visitors Center.

Picnicking available. Take Rte 193 Exit 13 from the Beltway; park entrance is 6 miles west; Visitors Center is 1/4 mile past the entrance on the right. ◆ Fee. Daily dawn-dusk. Visitors Center daily 9AM-5:30PM. 9200 Old Dominion Dr (Georgetown Pike) 759.2915

30 L'Auberge Chez Francois ★★★$$$ Fresh country cooking in a magical sylvan setting. Chef and owner **François Haeringer** turns out such delicacies as Alsatian-style sauerkraut, salmon soufflé, and brazed sweetbreads. Book well ahead. ◆ French ◆ Tu-Sa 5:30-9:15PM; Su 1-7:30PM. 332 Springvale Rd. Reservations required. 759.3800

31 Algonkian Regional Park A 511-acre park overlooking the Potomac, with an 18-hole golf course, 12 vacation cottages, miniature golf, a swimming pool, boat launching ramp, and picnic areas. ◆ Free. Daily dawn-dusk. 1600 Potomac View Rd. Sterling. 450.4655

Leesburg

Jordan's ★★★$$$ Top regional American fare served in a Postmodern setting: grilled salmon with tarragon and beurre blanc and grilled loin of lamb served with a garlic and rosemary sauce are just 2 choices. ◆ American ◆ Tu-Sa 6-9PM. 107 Loudoun St SW (Liberty-Wirth Sts) Reservations recommended. 777.1471

32 Loudoun Museum and Information Center Historical information and maps for walking tours. ◆ M-Sa 10AM-5PM; Su 1-5PM. 16 Loudoun St SW (King St) 777.7427

33 Oatlands Georgian mansion built in 1803, now maintained as a museum to the **Carter** and **Eustis** families. Managed by the **National Trust for Historic Preservation**. Gift shop. ◆ Fee. M-Sa 10AM-5PM; Su 1-5PM, mid Mar-mid Dec. Tours every half hour. Rte 15 (3 miles south of Leesburg) 777.3174

34 Morven Park (1781) Greek Revival plantation house features rooms decorated in a wide range of styles, a carriage museum (with 125 antique buggies), and 2 nature trails. ◆ Fee. Sa 10AM-5PM, Su 1-5PM, May, Sep-Oct; Tu-Sa 10AM-5PM, Su 1-5PM, Jun-Aug. Rte 7 (just north of Leesburg) 777.2414

35 American Work Horse Museum features thousands of horse-equipment pieces, including harnesses and blacksmith and veterinary equipment. Tours on walk-in basis. ◆ Free. W 9AM-5PM and by appointment. Rte 662 at Paeonian Springs. 338.6290

36 Waterford Founded by Quakers in 1733, and possibly the only town in Virginia that recruited Union soldiers, the entire town is now a **National Historic Site**. Homes open one weekend each October for the **Waterford Homes Tour and Crafts Fair**. ◆ Main St (2nd-Bond Sts) 882.3018

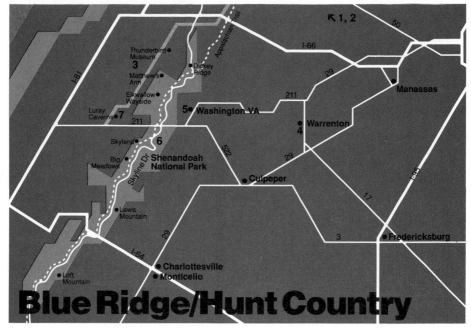

Blue Ridge/Hunt Country

Long before this nation was a nation, the gentry of the Old Dominion was living a civilized life in the rolling green countryside of the Virginia Piedmont.

Today fox hunting and point-to-point steeplechase races are still an integral part of the scene, although today's gentry is likely to be corporate bigwigs in search of an escape to a more pastoral time or Washingtonians in search of bed-and-breakfasts and antique shops. **Leesburg** and **Middleburg** retain much of their Colonial charm, and the region's smaller towns, including **Culpeper** and **"Little" Washington**, also contain much to reward history buffs and weekend Sybarites alike. *Area code 703 unless otherwise indicated.*

Middleburg

The heart of Virginia's hunt country is home to wealthy horse breeders, Fortune 500 executives, and reclusive celebrities.

1 Piedmont Vineyards & Winery An antebellum mansion surrounded by vineyards. A former dairy barn now houses the winery and tasting room. Wines: Chardonnay, Sémillon Seyval Blanc, Hunt County White, Little River White. Gift shop. ◆ Winery M-F 9AM-5PM; Sa-Su 10AM-5PM. Tours M-F 9AM-4PM; Sa-Su 10AM-4PM. Rte 626 (3 miles east of Middleburg) 687.5528

1 Meredyth Vineyards One of the state's oldest and largest wineries, making such wines as Villard Blanc, Seyval Blanc, Riesling, Chardonnay, and Cabernet Sauvignon. ◆ Winery daily 10AM-5PM. Tours daily 10AM-4PM. 2.5 miles south of Middleburg (off Rte 628) Reservations required for groups. 687.6277

Virginia was the 10th of the original 13 states to ratify the Constitution.

The first Germans arrived at Antietam Creek in 1726. Following an old Iroquois trail, they settled at Blue Ridge, past the Shenandoah Valley.

1 Red Fox Inn $$ All of the 18th-century-style rooms in this 3-house complex have 4-poster beds (some with canopies) and color televisions. Cotton bathrobes and fresh flowers provide a touch of home. The **Red Fox Tavern** turns out an impressive roster of wild game dishes. ◆ 2 E. Washington St (Marshall St) Middleburg. 687.6301, 800/223.1728; fax 687.3338

2 Oasis Vineyard One of Virginia's largest vineyards, with an annual champagne brunch and hot-air balloon rides during **Springfest** (held on the first Saturday in May). Wines: Chardonnay, Sauvignon Blanc, Gewürztraminer, Cabernet Sauvignon, and Champagne. ◆ Winery daily 10AM-4PM. Tours daily 10AM-3:45PM. Rte 635 (Rte 522-Rte 688) Hume. 635.7627

Shenandoah Valley, called the *Breadbasket of the Confederacy*, served as the chief supply site for **Robert E. Lee**'s army during much of the Civil War, and was a crucial battlefield for both North and South. In 1960, the **Virginia Civil War Commission** placed the *Circle Tour* markers at major battle sites throughout the valley, including:

Cedar Creek: Here, Confederate soldiers tried for the last time to win over the valley. Visit **Belle Meade Mansion**, where **James and Dolley Madison** honeymooned; **Front Royal**, where Jackson's men captured 750 Federal

soldiers; the **Soldier's Circle Monument**; and **the Battle of Front Royal Monument**.

Thoroughfare Gap: Where Confederate troops scored a victorious 1862 battle.

Strasburg: This village, which divides the valley in half, was used by both sides as a sentry outpost.

Waynesboro: The last battle for the North's control of Virginia took place here.

Edinburg: Headquarters for the Southern Cavalry briefly in 1862, it was burned by the North in 1864.

New Market: A Civil War museum rests on an 1864 battlefield where the South overtook Union lines.

Harrisonburg: Jackson often met with his troops here in 1862.

Cross Keys: The 1862 Northern attack failed here.

Port Republic: The South won a battle here following Cross Keys, but suffered heavy casualties.

Bath County: Entrenchments remain at Millboro Springs.

Lexington: Site of the **Virginia Military Institute** and the home of **Stonewall Jackson**. Historic Lexington Visitors Center, 463.3777.

Winchester: Changing hands 72 times during the war, Winchester saw more fighting than any other area west of Richmond. Visit the **Stonewall Jackson Home**, his headquarters in a Gothic-style house that now displays Jackson memorabilia; the Confederate Monument; **General Philip Sheridan**'s headquarters; and Stonewall Cemetery.

3 Gaspard's ★★★$$$ Inspired by the Inn at Little Washington, chef **Will Greenwood** has given Virginia standards a fresh spin. Chesapeake oysters are baked with watercress or served in a stew with shiitake mushrooms. Breast of pheasant with apple-cornbread stuffing is accompanied by peppered game sausage and applejack sauce. Seating in the bar area or in the more formal dining room. ♦ American ♦ Bar M-Sa 5PM-2AM. Dining room M-Sa 6-9:30PM. 200 N. Braddock St (Piccadilly St) Jacket required in the dining room. Reservations recommended. 662.5350

Warrenton: Beyond the fast-food shops of Route 29 lies this charming antebellum town, founded in 1810 by **Richard Henry Lee**, a US senator, a member of the Continental Congress, and a signer of the Declaration of Independence.

4 Fauquier County Historical Museum Located in Warrenton's **Old Jail** (1808). Displays of local history and maps for walking tours of downtown. ♦ Voluntary contribution. W-Sa 11AM-4PM. Tours by appointment. Court House Circle (Ashby St) 347.5525

Washington

Not only were there 8 other national capitals before Washington DC, there was even another town called

Blue Ridge/Hunt Country

Washington, and as the 220-or-so residents of that Virginia hamlet like to tell you, **George Washington** had much more to do with it than with his namesake to the northwest.

As a 17-year-old surveyor, George Washington and his 2 assistants laid out the town plan that is pretty much the same today: 2 main streets bisected by 5 shorter cross streets. This was done 43 years before DC became the capital. And if by chance you should have any

doubts about the town's authenticity, visit the stone monument, where a plaque proudly proclaims: "The town of Washington Virginia, the First Washington of All, Surveyed and Plotted by George Washington."

Washington VA is typical of all that is good about small Northern Virginia towns. Moreover, it has scrupulously avoided the developers and their cousins the gift-shop owners, who seem to be taking over the rest of the state. It's in sight of the foothills that knock up against the Blue Ridge mountains and nestled between farms, peach orchards, and apple orchards, where many owners will let you pick your own and pay by the bushel. Many of the farms have remained in the same family for over 200 years. In the village are several antique stores, art galleries, cabinetmaking studios, and a charming 1833 courthouse where justice is still handed down. An 1800s' tavern has been converted into a free museum with rooms re-creating an 18th-century kitchen and a 1-room schoolhouse.

5 The Rush River Company Craftspeople's co-operative featuring work by 20 artists as well as books and materials. ♦ Th-F 10AM-4PM; Sa-Su 10AM-6PM. Gay St (Middle-Jett Sts) 675.3410

5 Kramer and Eiland Woodworking Peter **Kramer** creates one-of-a-kind pieces that are influenced by 18th-century American, Shaker, and French Canadian designs. Kramer also does architectural woodworking. ♦ M-F 8AM-5PM. Showroom daily 8AM-5PM. Gay and Jett Sts. 675.3882

THE INN AT LITTLE WASHINGTON

5 The Inn At Little Washington ★★★★$$$$ Chef **Patrick O'Connell** combines the finest local ingredients with exotic fare to create dishes of great subtlety and originality. As a result, this superb restaurant is booked months in advance. Locally grown corn is transformed into a soup, a flan, or breadsticks; local ham is paired with fruit or local foie gras and black-eyed peas; veal is served à la Normande with apples and Calvados. Tiny whole vegetables accompany tender slices of lamb. The home-baked desserts are not to be missed. The main dining room is wood-paneled and romantically rose-lit; the garden court is a lovely place for after-dinner drinks. Extensive prix-fixe menus. If you want to spend the night, the 10 rooms range from 2 deluxe 2-story suites to queen-size rooms with a bath and shower. All rooms are double occupancy. Continental breakfast included. ♦ American ♦ M, W-F 6-9:30PM; Sa seatings at 5, 6, 8:30, 9, 9:30PM; Su 4-9PM. Middle and Main Sts. Reservations required. 675.3800; fax 675.3100

6 Shenandoah National Park Overlooking the Shenandoah River along 80 miles of Blue Ridge Mountains. In the autumn, the park shows off its fiery colors on oak, hickory, and hemlock trees. Spring and summer come to life with a rainbow of wildflowers and blossoming trees carpeting the park's 190,000 woody acres. The 105-mile-long **Skyline Drive** winds through the park near the crest of the Blue Ridge Mountains, through **Rockfish Gap**, to converge with the **Blue Ridge Parkway**.

Encircled by the Blue Ridge Mountains on the east and the Alleghenies to the west, the Shenandoah Valley runs deep with native and early American history. Its Indian name means *Daughter of the Stars*, perhaps alluding to the Indian belief that the valley was once a lake around which the stars sang every thousand years. The valley's half-billion years of development glow in its primitive volcanic rock, as old as any in existence. For a few million years, the area was smoothed by winds, uplifted and worn down again. The river's *wind gaps*, where it diverted other channels into its own waters, still lie in the Blue Ridge, now far above the river's floor. So splendid were nature's ways here that **George Washington**, a major landowner, insisted each of his tenants plant 4 acres of apple trees, as the peaceful orchards in the valley now attest.

The Shenandoah National Park, established in 1936 and dedicated by **Franklin Delano Roosevelt**, marks what was, during frontier days, the major route west.

Several companies offer canoe trips along the Shenandoah River. The park is open year-round, except in extreme bad weather. ♦ Fee. 999.2266, recorded information 999.2299

Skyline Drive's numbered mileposts guide visitors to historic and scenic features, including:

Dickey Ridge Visitor Center Picnic sites and Ranger Information. ♦ Daily 9AM-5PM, Apr-Oct. Milepost 4.6. Campground reservations 800/456 CAMP

Mathews Arm Camping and picnic areas. ♦ Milepost 22.2

Elkwallow Wayside Rest stop and trout fishing. ♦ Milepost 24.1

Skyland Lodge Horseback riding, self-guided tours, hiking, lodgings. ♦ Milepost 41.7. 999.2221

Byrd Visitor Center Museum, ranger programs, information. ♦ Daily 9AM-5PM, Mar-Dec. Milepost 51

Big Meadows, Wayside and Lodge Rest stop, store, stables, fishing. ♦ Mid May through Oct. ♦ Milepost 51.3. Lodge 999.2221, reservations 743.5108

Lewis Mountain Camping, picnicking, hiking, lodgings. ♦ Milepost 57.5

Loft Mountain Picnic area, restaurant, camping, hiking, self-guided tours. ♦ Milepost 79.5

7 Luray Caverns Near Skyline Drive, Luray Caverns boasts shiny stone columns and cavern walls that reflect every color imaginable. Discovered in 1878, the caverns have fascinated millions of visitors.

The **Great Stalacpipe Organ** fills the cavern's *Cathedral Room* with symphonic tunes made from playing the stalactites that hang from the cave's ceiling. The nation's only stalacpipe organ can be played either from the console or with automatic controls. ♦ Admission. Open daily 9AM, closing hours vary with the season; call for schedule. Off US 211. 743.6551

Plantation Tour

Stratford Hall Plantation (1730) Perhaps the greatest manor house in the area, unique in plan and handsomely refurbished. It was the boyhood home of **Robert E. Lee** (page 207). ♦ Admission. Daily 9AM-5PM; tours every half hour. State Rte 214, east of Fredericksburg. 804/493.8038

Morven Park (1781) Greek Revival plantation house features rooms furnished in a wide spectrum of historical styles (page 192). ♦ Fee. Hours vary with season: call for schedule. Old Waterford Rd (2 miles north of Leesburg) 777.2414

Hampton National Historic Site (ca. 1780) Over 2 dozen buildings depict life in the heyday of the plantation system. Impressive Late Georgian main house; 45-minute tours start every hour on the hour. ♦ Free. Daily 9AM-4PM. 535 Hampton Ln (Delaney Valley Rd) 301/962.0688

Sully Plantation (1794) Recently restored complex was the home of **Richard Bland Lee**, uncle of **Robert E.** (page 190). ♦ Fee. M, W-F 11AM-5PM, Sa-Su 11AM-4PM, Jan-Feb; M, W-Su 11AM-5PM, Mar-Dec. 3601 Sully Rd (off State Rte 28) Chantilly. 437.1794

Oatlands (early 1800s) Well-preserved Greek Revival mansion is now a major equestrian center. Tours given on a walk-in basis. Operated by the **National Trust for Historic Preservation** (page 192). ♦ Fee. M-Sa 10AM-5PM, Su 1-5PM, mid Mar-Dec. 6 miles south of Leesburg on State Rte 15. 777.3174

Sotterley Mansion (1713) Working plantation. A highlight is the intricately carved woodwork throughout the farmhouse. ♦ Fee. Daily 11AM-4PM, June-Sep. Walk-in tours. Off Rte 235, south of Waldorf, Hollywood MD. 301/373.2280

Blue Ridge/Hunt Country

As you cruise around Virginia, look for the blue **Virginia Byways** signs showing a cardinal and dogwood blossoms. These signs mark alternate, less traveled roads that may lead to a special attraction or just wind through scenic farmland, a river valley, or the Blue Ridge foothills.

Restaurants: Red   **Hotels**: Blue
Shops/Parks: Green   **Sights/Culture**: Black

Charlottesville

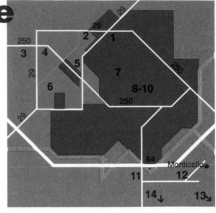

Charlottesville, one of the nicer places in the United States to live in and visit, is nestled on the eastern slope of the Blue Ridge Mountains, in the area of Virginia known as **Piedmont**, 120 miles southwest of Washington.

This quiet town of 40,000 is the home of the **University of Virginia** and, more importantly, of the university's founder, **Thomas Jefferson**. The country's third president was a gentleman-farmer, writer, architect, educator, lawyer, gadgeteer, sometime politician, and a dabbler in the arts and sciences—in short, America's favorite frontier Renaissance man. Charlottesville is *Mr. Jefferson's Country*—a lovely place of mild winters and long beautiful springs and autumns. Here one finds rolling fenced fields, white porticoes, red brick houses, flowering trees, and boxwood gardens surrounded by vistas of pale blue mountains; it is as close as one comes to an American *Arcadia*. This physical amenity, together with the area's *sense of history* and its heritage of attractive old buildings, has drawn a wide variety of retired diplomats, businesspeople, and teachers, as well as a fair assortment of rich people seeking expansive second homes. The University of Virginia adds to this special atmosphere, so that for most, save die-hard urbanists and the poor, there is a sense of *privilege*—historical, social, educational, and environmental—about being able to live here...much like a year-round resort.

Like the mythical towns of our country's collective memory, Charlottesville seems the sort of place where it is possible to live the ideal American life and *get away from it all*. It is a setting for children, dogs, and family outings, for discussions about horticulture and horses as well as about basketball and books. Significantly, it is also a place where *history* is given more than lip service. **Madison, Monroe, Mason, Washington, Henry, Lee, Jackson, George Rogers Clark**, and especially Jefferson, seem a part of one's life here. His great buildings, the **Rotunda** and the **Lawn** and **Monticello**, are not just historic landmarks but potent cultural icons—symbols, if you will, of a core of beliefs, styles, and images not yet dead. A sense of a *living past* is present here to a much greater extent than is usually found in American communities. In this sense, Charlottesville, considered a liberal frontier by tidewater Virginians in Colonial times, is close to certain European settings in both feeling and sense of place, and somewhat removed from current America.

Among the most revered artifacts of this particular cultural framework are old buildings. Architecture in Virginia colony was the central art form and is everywhere, something an educated gentleman knew about, as well as practiced, an emblem of refinement and worth. (Probably a quarter of the books on prominent display today in a bookshop in this part of Virginia deal

Charlottesville

with either Virginia history or historic buildings.) This love of old buildings and gardens extends also to furniture, china, draperies, silverware, flowers, trees—all things that adorned a Virginian's home. In such a setting, historic preservation has traditionally held a central place, so that old buildings, not new

ones, are the center of attention and emulation, even today.

The University of Virginia stands literally and symbolically at the center of the region. Founded and designed by Jefferson in 1819 (when he was 70 years old!), the original complex of buildings, what Jefferson called his *academical village*, is generally conceded to be the most significant contribution to American architecture since the founding of the Republic. By any standard it is an architectural masterpiece, the first example of the Greco-Roman Revival in the US and the model for campuses and countless civic buildings all over the country. Today, Jefferson's complex is internationally recognized as a pilgrimage for all serious students of architecture; an "ideal city of gardens and buildings, the clearest built statement of the ideas of the American Enlightenment," which, like its Oxford and Cambridge counterparts, is as vibrant and alive today as when it was conceived.

On a nearby hill, like a custodian of value, stands **Monticello**, Jefferson's villa and the citadel of his beliefs, another of our culture's seminal buildings. Here, American pragmatism and invention are melded with Palladio and French Revolutionary architecture in an extraordinarily inventive if idiosyncratic way. Monticello is both quirky and sublime, a *little mountain* of American classicism erected in the wilderness. One can sense here, better perhaps than anywhere else, Jefferson's many-sided personality: his values, priorities, and obsessions. For the architecture buff there are 2 other houses near Charlottesville from the hand of our only architect/president, **Edgemont** and **Barboursville**, the latter a Piranesi-esque ruin now surrounded by a thriving Italian-owned vineyard and what are probably the largest tree boxes in North America.

To the west lies the **Skyline Drive**, a great tourist route that is breathtaking in spring and autumn, and the **Shenandoah Valley**, a place still seemingly removed from the 20th century and not unlike parts of the Austrian Tyrol.

The 2-hour drive from Washington to Charlottesville via Route 29 can be broken at pretty **Warrenton**.The return can be made on Rte 20, through **Orange**, the **Battle of the Wilderness National Park**, and historic **Fredericksburg**, the site of another epic Civil War battle. Two exceptional houses—George Mason's **Gunston Hall** (page 190), with the first Palladian interior in the New World and a wonderful garden, and **Stratford** (page 207), the extraordinarily powerful Lee plantation on the Potomac (my favorite American house), are within an easy drive off of Route 495 and should be seen.

For those seeking the luxurious resort, there are the 2 famous mountain spas, **The Homestead** at Hot Springs VA, and **The Greenbrier** at White Sulphur Springs in West Virginia, just over the border. Both are superbly run and equipped, and come as close as anything in America to the great spa/resorts of Europe.

All in all, Piedmont, Mr. Jefferson's country, offers an ideal escape from the growing contemporary squalor of metropolitan Washington, an alternative environment in which buildings and nature still exist in harmoniuous balance.

Mr. Jefferson's Country
Jaquelin Robertson
Cooper, Robertson & Partners

Area code 804 unless otherwise indicated.

1 English Inn of Charlottesville $ Despite the name, a relatively new hotel. Sixty-seven rooms (21 suites with wet bars), 3 conference rooms, an indoor pool, sauna, whirlpool, and weightroom. The lounge and restaurant serve standard hotel fare. Country breakfast complimentary for hotel guests. Children under 12 stay free. ♦ 2000 Morton Dr (south of 250 bypass, Rte 29N) 971.9900

2 Oakencroft Vineyard & Winery Home of award-winning **Seyval Blanc**, **Chardonnay**, and **Cabernet Sauvignon**. ♦ Tours and tastings: M-F 9AM-4PM; Sa-Su 11AM-5PM, Apr-Dec. Barracks Rd (3$\frac{1}{2}$ miles west of Rte 29) 295.8175

3 Boars Head Inn $$ Probably the best known hostelry in this area. One hundred seventy-five rooms and suites built around an old gristmill and set in rolling lake country. Ask for a suite with a fireplace and lake view. Swimming, indoor and outdoor tennis, racquetball, fitness center, sauna, fishing, and biking all available. Impeccable old-fashioned service. Twelve conference rooms and a ballroom available for groups. Children under 18 stay free. ♦ Rte 250W (Ednam Forest, 2 miles from Charlottesville) 296.2181

Within the Boars Head Inn:

The Old Mill Room ★$$ The Mill Room is a large wood-beamed dining room with Colonial-costumed waiters and waitresses. Pleasant setting, particularly the glassed-in **Garden Room**. Filling but average American/ French food—although the beef Wellington is worthy of a special mention. ♦ American/ French ♦ M-F 7-10:30AM, noon-2PM, 6-9PM; Sa-Su 7:30-10:30AM, noon-2PM, 6-9PM. Jacket required at dinner. Reservations required (specify if Garden Room) ♦ 296.2181

Collections were taken up among the soldiers of **Robert E. Lee**'s army to relieve starvation and suffering among the people surviving the Battle of Fredericksburg in 1862. One Georgia regiment raised $500; **General Stonewall Jackson** personally gave $100, his headquarters $800; and **A.P. Hill**'s division donated $10,000.

3 Duner's Restaurant ★$$ Casual, with daily specials ranging from French to Indian to Thai, with an emphasis on seafood. ♦ International ♦ M-Sa 11AM-10PM; Su 10AM-3PM, 5PM-10PM. Rte 250W (in Ivy) 293.8352

4 Ivy Inn ★★$$ Dine in one of the 6 rooms of this renovated 1830s' house furnished *à la* Williamsburg. Specials are Virginia mountain trout, veal, and a seafood kettle of steamed shellfish and drawn butter. Bread and desserts are homemade. Relax and take your time: the owner believes 3 hours for a dinner among friends is reasonable. The restaurant's schedule is just as flexible (open occasionally on Sundays and for lunch), so call ahead. ♦ American ♦ M-F 11:30AM-2:30PM, 5:30-9PM; Sa 5:30-9PM; Su 11AM-3PM. 2244 Old Ivy Rd (Rte 250) 977.1222

5 Best Western Cavalier Inn $ A 5- to10-minute drive from the University of Virginia; 118 rooms with TV and air conditioning, a pool, and a restaurant that serves sandwiches and salads. Clean, generic. Children under 18. stay free. ♦ University and Emmett Sts. 296.8111

6 University of Virginia (1825, Thomas Jefferson) When Jefferson's *academical village* opened, there were 68 students and 8 professors. Now it's a small city with over 17,000 students and 1900 faculty members. It's the town's biggest single employer, and it dominates the social scene. Charlottesville is full of students who decided not to leave. They joke that you can't get a job as a waiter around here without a Ph.D. or at the very least a master's degree. There's a strong preppy contingent at UVA, with the attendant fraternities, beer parties, and sun dresses. But equally strong is the tradition of liberal academic excellence with nationally acclaimed graduate programs.

UVA was the project of Jefferson's old age, and he lovingly planned every aspect of it from the fundraising to the design of the buildings to the selection of the faculty, curriculum, and library books. His school was to be run by the teachers and have affiliation with no church or religion. All courses would be electives. Students of all ages would mix and live in a village setting among their teachers. There was no American precedent for what Jefferson created—the prototype of a modern university.

At the University of Virginia:

The Lawn The terraced lawn was the center of the old campus. It's flanked on both sides by low rows of student rooms broken up at intervals by 2-story pavilions, the whole fronted by a colonnade. Students lived in the

rooms, while faculty lived in the upstairs pavilions and taught downstairs. Students still live in the 54 lawn rooms, which have fireplaces but no bathrooms—students have to walk *outside* and down a pathway to reach the toilets and to shower. Nevertheless, residency

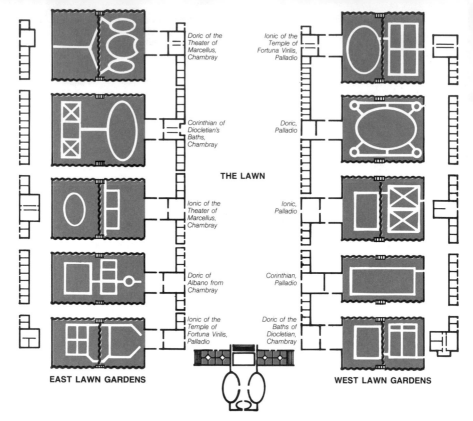

Doric of the Theater of Marcellus, Chambray

Corinthian of Diocletian's Baths, Chambray

Ionic of the Theater of Marcellus, Chambray

Doric of Albano from Chambray

Ionic of the Temple of Fortuna Virilis, Palladio

Ionic of the Temple of Fortuna Virilis, Palladio

Doric, Palladio

Ionic, Palladio

Corinthian, Palladio

Doric of the Baths of Diocletian, Chambray

THE LAWN

EAST LAWN GARDENS

WEST LAWN GARDENS

is considered a great honor and is attained by a highly competitive and political process.

A natural didactician, Jefferson decorated each pavilion with an order from a different Roman temple. He meant to expose all students, particularly those who might never travel abroad, to a classical notion of good taste.

Behind the pavilions are gardens enclosed by characteristic Jeffersonian **Serpentine Walls**. Although only one brick thick, their curved design gives them great strength. Behind the East and West Gardens are rows of additional student housing called **The Ranges**. These rows are broken up by 6 *hotels*. Now administrative offices, they were once dining halls. A different language was to be spoken at table in each one. ♦ West end of Main St. Tour information, see **Rotunda**

Bayly Art Museum An intimate museum whose eclectic collection offers the afternoon browser a taste of everything: *Art in the Age of Jefferson*; *Contemporary American Realists*, featuring such artists as **Alfred Leslie**, **William Bailey**, and **Jack Beal**; an Oriental collection; and pre-Columbian, ancient Mediterra-

Charlottesville

nean, and Chinese ceramics. Frequent traveling exhibitions. ♦ Free. Tu-Su 1-5PM. Rugby Rd (half a block from the Lawn) 924.3592

Rambunctious UVA students were once fond of riding on horseback past the Rotunda and shooting out the clock.

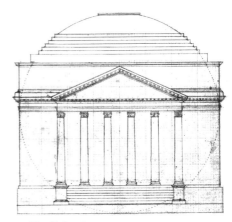

The Rotunda Considered Jefferson's *most perfect* building, it housed the library and was the focal point of the campus. Its plan, basically a sphere inscribed within a cylinder, is derived from the Pantheon; its dome is exactly half the size of the original in Rome. Jefferson's interior design called for 3 floors; the first 2 contained graceful oval rooms, the third, a dome that would house books and, he hoped, a planetarium with gilded models of the stars on the ceiling.

In 1895, the interior was destroyed by fire. Reigning architectural monarch **Stanford White** was called in to remodel, which he did, completely discarding Jefferson's plan. He removed the oval rooms and an entire floor, while adding clunky Victorian columns and a gallery. Fortunately, the original rotunda was one of the best documented buildings in America. Between 1973 and 1976, White's work was gutted and the building was restored. Upon entering the dome room you can see bookcases behind the pillars, but these vanish as you move toward the center. Allegedly, Jefferson envisioned student dances in the room and didn't want the young scholars to be reminded of their work while having fun. ♦ Guided tours 10, 11AM, 2, 3, 4PM, Jan-Nov; call for Dec schedule. 924.7969, 924.1019

Poe Room Room 13 in **The Ranges**—but of course! Furnished with the most common style of period furniture, probably what **Edgar Allan Poe** would have had as a student. Poe stayed at UVA for only 10 months (1825). He ran up big gambling debts, which he couldn't pay, and was asked to leave.

7 Blue Ridge Brewing ★★$$ Brewpub featuring 2 lagers, an ale, and stout brewed on the premises, as well as grilled Caribbean chicken and seafood, burgers, and minipizzas. Bar open until 2AM. ♦ Caribbean/American ♦ Daily 11:30AM-2PM, 5-10PM. 709 W. Main St (9th St) 977.0017

8 The Mall Seven blocks of Main Street that have been paved with brick and reserved for walkers. There are fountains, flowers, and renovated turn-of-the-century buildings housing boutiques, antiques, gift and specialty shops, restaurants, and outdoor cafés. Check out **Williams Corner Bookstore** (977.4858). *Tuesday Evening Performance Series*, a program of free outdoor concerts, is held at Central Place from June through August on Tuesday nights at 8PM. ♦ 2nd-6th Sts (E. Main-W. Main Sts)

Jefferson's design for the University of Virginia was practical as well as pretty. Decentralized modern dormitories and teaching pavilions meant that in case of a fire or epidemic the whole university needn't shut down.

Take part in a Charlottesville tradition. Put together a tailgate picnic and head for the **University of Virginia Polo Center**, Fridays and Sundays, June through October (I-64 to 5th St exit, Rte 631 south for 3¹/₂ miles, 804/979.0293).

Guesthouse Bed and Breakfast Inc. A service that specializes in dispensing Southern hospitality and romantic country weekends. The more than 50 homes and one dozen suites and cottages (many are on Charlottesville's annual garden tour, page 201) range from cozy guest rooms with a bath down the hall to suites in restored 19th-century homes to cottages on rolling country horse farms. All come with breakfast. Very private accommodations are available. On the other hand, enjoying your host's hospitality and knowledge of the area can be half the fun, so the service tries harder than most to match guests with appropriate homes. Expect to spend some time on the phone. ♦ 979.7264, 979.8327

8 Eastern Standard ★★$$ A bit of New York chic. Light, airy 1920s' decor. Fresh flowers abound, and Ella Fitzgerald and Billie Holiday croon in the background. Funky mismatched china, but excellent and eclectic food. Try Oriental chicken curry or oysters in caviar sauce. The best English trifle in town. ♦ American ♦ Daily 6PM-2AM. 102 Old Preston Ave (west end of the Mall) Reservations recommended. 295.8668

8 Le Snail ★★$$ The Viennese chef prepares excellent French food in a charming renovated old house. Try the fresh fish, beef Wellington, or baby rack of lamb. Four-course prix fixe dinner available from Monday to Thursday. ♦ French ♦ M-Sa 6-10PM. 320 W. Main St (5th St) 295.4456

8 Blue Moon Diner ★$ Classic stainless-steel diner interior. Small but fun. Good burgers, omelets, blueberry muffins, and pancakes at modest prices. Packed for brunch. The best R&B jukebox in town. ♦ American ♦ M-F 7AM-7PM; Sa-Su 8AM-4PM. 512 W. Main St (6th St) 293.3408

8 The Virginian ★$ Old wooden booths, blackboard menus, and a boisterous crowd at the bar. Food is dependable: burgers, stir-fry, international specials. Brunch could be eggs Benedict, Florentine, or Chesapeake—or French toast with fried apples on the side. ♦ American ♦ M-F 9AM-2AM; Sa-Su 10AM-2AM. 1521 W. Main St (6th St) 293.2606

8 C&O ★★★$$$ Inside a ramshackle warehouse is one of Charlottesville's best restaurants. Dine on classic French dishes like stuffed quail and beef filet with a fresh morel glaze. In the downstairs bistro, the atmosphere and fare are more casual, as are the prices. Call for a schedule of musical performances in the club (also named the C&O). ♦ French ♦ Restaurant M-Sa seatings at 6:30 and 9:30PM. Bistro: M-F 11:30AM-3PM, 5:30-10PM; Sa-Su 5:30-10PM. 515 E. Water St (east end of the Mall) Jacket and tie required for restaurant. Reservations required for restaurant. 971.7044

9 Jefferson-Madison Regional Library The **Charlottesville-Albemarle Historical Collection**, run jointly by the library and the Albemarle County Historical Society, features a library specializing in local history and genealogical research, with files on more than 1200 Old Dominion families. ♦ Main Library: M-W 9AM-9PM; Th-Sa 9AM-5PM. Historical Collection: M-F 10AM-4PM; Sa 10AM-noon. 201 E. Market St (2nd St) 296.7294

9 Fellini's ★$$ Northern Italy in the Old Dominion. Homemade pastas, breads, and some really intense chocolate desserts. The

menu changes monthly, but the steaks and home-grown veal are always good choices, as are the vegetarian specialties. ♦ Italian ♦ Daily 6-10PM. 200 E. Market St (2nd St) 295.8003

Restaurants: Red	**Hotels**: Blue
Shops/Parks: Green	**Sights/Culture**: Black

9 Lee Monument (1924) General **Robert E. Lee** sits in **Lee Park** astride his horse, **Traveller**, hat in hand. Designed by **Henry Schrady**, who did the Grant Memorial in DC. Completed after Schrady's death by **Leo Lentelli**. ♦ E. Jefferson St (1st-2nd Sts)

9 McGuffey Art Center This 1916 schoolhouse has been converted into a complex of studios for 40 artists, including painters, sculptors, photographers, jewelers, calligraphers, dancers, and a flute maker. ♦ Free. Tu-Su 10AM-5PM. 201 2nd St NW (E. Jefferson St) 295.7973

10 Albemarle County Courthouse/Court Square (1803; additions, 1859 and 1867) The old courthouse is the centerpiece of the downtown historic district. It was the political and business hub of old Charlottesville, and a passerby in the early 1800s might very well have seen **Jefferson**, **Madison**, and **Monroe** chatting together on the green. It was also the shared church of the town's 4 faiths. Jefferson wrote: "In our village...there is a good degree of religion with a small spice of fanaticism. We have 4 sects, but without either church or meeting house. The courthouse is the common temple, one Sunday of each month. Here Episcopalian, Presbyterian, Methodist and Baptist meet together...[and] listen with attention and devotion to each other's preachers, and all mix in a society of perfect harmony." The courthouse is open only when court is in session; call ahead. ♦ 501 E. Jefferson St (Court Sq-Park St) 296.6920

10 Jackson Monument (1921, Charles Keck) Old **Stonewall Jackson** is full of fire and brimstone despite the bronzing. He rides **Little Sorrel**. ♦ E. Jefferson and N 4th St (NE corner of Jackson Park, next to courthouse)

10 Court Square Tavern ★$ Shepherd's pie, hearty sandwiches, and other tavern-style fare favored by UVA students; the beer list runs to 100 imports. ♦ American ♦ M-Sa 11:30AM-midnight; Su 7PM-midnight. 500 Court Sq (5th-E. Jefferson Sts) 296.6111

10 Albemarle County Historical Society Inside is a small museum with local artwork, photographs and some old weapons and tools. The society is staffed by volunteers; if there are enough personnel they will show you around. ♦ M-F 8AM-noon. 220 Court Sq (6th-E. Jefferson Sts) 296.1492

Charlottesville

11 Thomas Jefferson Visitors Bureau The place to stop for brochures and information on the area, as well as for the permanent exhibition *Thomas Jefferson at Monticello*, which displays memorabilia and artifacts. *President's Passes*, which grant discounted entrance to Monticello and other local attractions, are available, as is a hotel and restaurant reservation service. ♦ Bureau M-F 9AM-5:30PM. Visitors Center daily 9AM-5PM. Rte 20S at Interchange 24. 293.6789

12 Michie Tavern Rumored to be the boyhood home of **Patrick** ("Give me liberty or give me death!") **Henry**. It was later sold to Mr. Michie (pronounced *mickey*), who, realizing he was on the busiest stagecoach route in town, expanded and opened a tavern, which thrived until the turn of the century.

When Monticello opened to the public in 1924, the tavern owners saw a golden opportunity. They moved the tavern stone by stone to its present location half a mile from Jefferson's home. Although it was only a 17-mile trip, it took 3 years to complete reconstruction. The tavern is now a museum with a fine collection of pre-Revolutionary War furnishings. In the **Gentleman's Parlor**, note the old-time equivalent of a taproom, where waiting coachmen could be served. There is also a ladies parlor, ballroom, dining room, and furnished bedroom. Many of the outbuildings have been re-created and are open, including a kitchen house, smokehouse (still in use), privy, and a dairy. The **Meadow Run Grist Mill**, built in 1797 and still sporting a turning waterwheel, houses a **Virginia Wine Museum** selling the state's growing variety of vintages. Next to the gristmill is the **General Store,** where Virginia handcrafted items are for sale. Michie Tavern provides an enlightening view of how the common man lived. Guided tours available. ♦ Admission. Daily 9AM-4:20PM. Rte 53 (2^1/2 miles SE of Charlottesville) 977.1234

Within Michie Tavern:

The Ordinary ★$ A Colonial buffet lunch in converted slave quarters. Southern-fried chicken, black-eyed peas, homemade cornbread—nothing fancy, but satisfying. There may be a 5-10 minute wait. ♦ American ♦ Daily 11:30AM-3PM, Jan-Mar, Nov-Dec; daily 11:15AM-3:30PM, Apr-Oct. 977.1234

13 Ash Lawn-Highland This was the home of **James Monroe** from 1799 to 1826, but Monroe wasn't around much to enjoy the place. (He called the estate *Highland*, later owners dubbed it *Ash Lawn*.) Monroe served as senator, governor, and minister to France, England, and Spain. Then he served 2 terms as president.

It was **Thomas Jefferson**, Monroe's law teacher for many years and his mentor for many more, who suggested that Monroe move to Albemarle County close to Monticello. Ever planning and improving, Jefferson was eager to create a "society to our taste" in the neighborhood. While Monroe was in France, Jefferson personally selected the site for his friend's house and sent over his own gardeners to seed the orchards.

The large yellow house is simple on the outside but beautifully appointed on the inside—a dichotomy that prompted Monroe to refer to his home as his *cabin-castle*. Sadly, Monroe was broke after 40 years of working for the government—a nice contrast to the ethics of some of today's officeholders—and had to sell the home upon completing his term as president.

Visitors can tour 5 rooms of the main house, the basement, warming kitchen, and 2 rooms of a Victorian-era addition. The furniture is all antique, much of it Monroe's own either from Ash Lawn or from the Monroe tenancy in the White House.

 Stroll through the pastures, woods, and boxwood gardens, where you may very likely meet up with a cow or one of the 10 peacocks that live on the plantation. The peacock was popular in Colonial times as a game bird and—because of its singularly loud and ugly voice—as a watch bird.

There have been some archaeological digs at the old icehouse and servants quarters that have turned up coins and pottery. If one is going on during your visit, you are welcome to watch.

A summer festival from mid June through mid August includes performances of 18th-century operas in the estate's garden. Saturday mornings, children's programs of dance and puppet shows are presented. In early July there is an excellent **Colonial Crafts Weekend**. Picnic facilities and guided tours. ♦ Admission. Daily 10AM-5PM, Jan-Mar, Nov-Dec; daily 9AM-6PM, Apr-Oct. 2¹/₂ miles from Monticello. Take Rte 53 to county Rte 795S. 293.9539

Scottsville is a lovely 20-mile drive south from Charlottesville on Route 20. This sleepy town, chockablock with Federal, Republic, and antebellum buildings, was once the county seat. River traffic kept it busy as early settlers pushed west, but its heyday came in the middle 1800s when it was the center of business on the **James River Kanawha Canal**. During the Civil War, Sheridan, Custer, and 10,000 Union troops came in and blew up all the locks. Even now it is not uncommon for residents working in their gardens to turn up a Civil War cannonball.

James River Runners Rent a canoe or a big fat inner tube for the afternoon. The service takes people upriver and lets them float or paddle down. The **James River** and its tributary, the **Rockfish**, offer Class 1 and 2 white water—fun but not too hard for a novice. The crystal-clear water is a favorite hangout for smallmouth bass, and it is not uncommon to see deer, wild turkey, mink, and beaver on the banks. Great for bird-watching. Rafts are also available and are recommended for young children and the elderly. If braving the rapids isn't your idea of fun, the **Hatton Ferry** (the last pole-drawn ferry in the state and one of only 2 remaining in the entire country) offers free rides across the James River. ♦ Fee. Daily 11:30AM-3PM. Rte 20 to Scottsville, Rte 76 south, left on Rte 625 to the river. Reservations required for rafting. 286.2338

Tourism brought $6,900,000,000 to Virginia in 1987.

Schulyer and all the area around Scottsville is **Walton Country**. Author **Earl Hamner, Jr.**, grew up in Schulyer. If there aren't too many Toyotas and Nissans around, it can look like **John Boy** might come loping around the corner at any moment. Take Rte 6 out of Scottsville, turn left onto Rte 800, and continue 2 miles to Schulyer.

14 Prospect Hill ★★$$ Romantic country inn and delightful, quirky restaurant in a restored manor house. Guests are greeted at the door with wine and invited to sit by the fire or stroll in the gardens. A bell summons all to dinner. There is no menu; the evening's 4-course dinner is always a surprise but is always good and usually French. Host leads all in short grace before the meal.

The inn ($$$) has 3 rooms in the main house, 7 restored plantation dependencies, and 1 converted slave cabin. Four of these are suites with fireplaces and 4 have Jacuzzis. Furnishings range from elegant to rustic-cozy. Country breakfast and dinner included. ♦ French ♦ Restaurant (one seating nightly): M-Th 7PM; F-Sa 8PM; Su 6PM. 14 miles east of Charlottesville, on Rte 250 near Zion crossroads. Reservations required. 703/967.0844

14 Foxfield Races Spring and fall running of nationally known steeplechase events. ♦ Foxfield Race Course, Garth Rd. 293.8169, 293.9501

14 Montdomaine Cellars One of the biggest of the area's burgeoning wineries, with more than 50 acres of vines. Wines: Villard Blanc, Skyline White, Skyline Red, La Abra Peach, Skyline Rose. ♦ Tours and tastings daily 10AM-5PM. Rte 720 south of Charlottesville. 971.8947

Historic Garden Week. This unique chance to glimpse gracious Virginia living takes place in April, timed to coincide with the colorful explosion of spring foliage. Expertly maintained gardens, some in restored 18th- and 19th-century estates, are open to the public. Special events include candlelight tours of the lawn at UVA and Ash Lawn. The selected private homes and gardens change each year, and there is an admission charge. Call the **Visitors Center** (239.2484) or **Chamber of Commerce** (295.3141) for information, brochures, and reservations.

Charlottesville's downtown is compact and encompassable, so don't be afraid to explore both sides of the street. Often what looks like a residential stretch is broken up with isolated but delightful shops and restaurants.

The Corner, centered at University Ave and Elliwood St, is the student shopping strip; expect to find a mix of casual dining

Charlottesville

spots, bookstores, and boutiques. For soup, salad, and sandwich fare, check out the patio at **Martha's Café**. **Eljo's** is the preppy clothing store of choice, and **Mincer's Pipe Shop** is a Corner institution: tobacconist, bookstore, and purveyor of university paraphernalia.

Thomas Jefferson left testimony to his public self in history books, but to glimpse the private man, one must look to **Monticello**, his home.

No other structure so fully embodies the character of its owner. It is graceful, learned, spacious, generous, ingenious, and quirky—and it is totally Jefferson. He picked the site, he designed the plan and its endless modifications. He supervised every aspect of the construction, planted the gardens, picked the furniture, and designed the draperies. The timber came from his woods; even the bricks and the nails were produced on his own land.

Thought to be the best American architect of his day, Jefferson was self-taught. Rejecting the prevailing Georgian style, he was drawn to the harmony and mathematical perfection he saw in classical Roman buildings. Monticello is decorated with the classic orders drawn directly from the books of **Palladio**, the great Renaissance scholar and architect. (One of Jefferson's beloved architecture primers is preserved in the Library of Congress, and not surprisingly, it shows signs of hard use.)

He began work on Monticello, *little mountain* in Italian, in 1769, when he was 26 years old. Three years later, when he moved into his house on a snowy night with his new bride, only one small building, the **Honeymoon Cottage**, had a roof on it. If he wasn't away on public duty, he was modifying the plans. Construction continued for the next 40 years, long after his wife had died.

When Jefferson returned from France in 1789, the house was almost complete. But he had been smitten by the domed pavilions he saw abroad and the Parisian townhouses with their emphasis on privacy and comfort. "Architecture is my delight," he said, "and putting up and pulling down one of my favorite amusements." Still, it took a very bold man to tear

Monticello

down half a house and begin again. He added a dome, a new front, 13 rooms. The new second-story bedrooms had floor-level windows tied together by a single frame with the ground floor windows. This creates the illusion that the house has one story and is much smaller than it is.

Jefferson was an inveterate entertainer who even in straitened circumstances might order 150 bottles of his favorite wine. That side of him is seen in 18-foot-high light-filled public rooms where lavish dinners, weddings, and spirited musicales were held.

But Monticello was also the home to which Jefferson came for quiet contemplation, so his own suite, seldom visited by friends or family, provided great privacy. In it is his alcove bed and his study where he read and wrote thousands of letters. The bedroom leads to a library and the glassed-in plaza where Jefferson nursed his seedlings. Monticello also reveals Jefferson the gadgeteer, the lover of mechanical ingenuity. There is a clock that tells the day as well as week. In his study is a writing table with a revolving top and the polygraph that makes a copy of a letter as the original is being written. While Jefferson didn't invent the machine, he did modify it. He owned several and was so fond of the innovation, he even lent his name to an advertisement. There are dumbwaiters hidden in the dining room mantelpiece, and under the parlor doors is a hidden chain-and-sprocket mechanism that allows both doors to swing open when only one is pushed.

The house is practical as well as pleasing. There is brick nogging (insulation) between floor and ceiling, and there are double doors to preserve heat. The natural incline of the hilltop is used to hide the service dependencies half underground. These extensions contained servants quarters, stables, kitchen, and smokehouse. Connected to the cellar by an all-weather passageway, the roofs of these wings become broad terraces that connect to the main floor of the house.

There has been much work on the grounds of the estate in recent years. Jefferson kept extensive notes on the over 250 varieties of vegetables and herbs he planted in terraced beds, organized according to whether the plant was used for root, leaf, or fruit. These are being replanted with the help of his notes. Excavation also continues on *mulberry row*, the industrial strip of the estate, where 19 buildings once stood, including stables, a nailery, and a carpentry shop. Work reviving his groves, vineyards, and berry squares goes on as well.

After almost 40 years of public service, Jefferson finally retired to Monticello. Although toward the end he was beset by debts and an army of uninvited guests, it's easy to see why he might have said, "All my wishes end where I hope my days will end—at Monticello."

A shuttle bus runs continuously between the parking lot and the house. If you'd rather walk (a leisurely 10 to 15 minutes), take the **Woodland Trail**, which goes past the family cemetery. Guided tours last 25 to 30 minutes and begin every 5 minutes. Allow 2 hours for house, dependencies, garden, and grounds. ♦ Admission. Daily 9AM-4:30PM, Jan-Feb, Nov-Dec; daily 8AM-5PM, Mar-Oct. Guided tours of gardens mid April to mid Oct: call for schedule. Little Mountain Luncheonette daily 10:30AM-3:30PM. Rtes 20 and I-64, exit 24A (2 miles SE of Charlottesville) 804/295-8181, 804/295-2657 &

Jefferson

The Albemarle County in which Jefferson grew up was the western frontier of the nation. That expansive mindset helped set the tone of this ever-exploring and restless personality.

As a young man he mastered Greek, Latin, French, Anglo-Saxon, the natural sciences, and mathematics. He was a good violinist, an excellent horseman, and a decent dancer. It's said that he may have been one of the last men to have embraced all the learning of his age—he was certainly one of the few men, then or now, to make practical use of calculus.

He went on to study law and had a successful practice, earning $3000 one year, and within 2 years increasing his caseload from 154 to 405. Yet Jefferson, not a forceful public speaker, disliked a trade whose task it was to "question everything, yield nothing, and talk by the hour." Wishing more to reform the law than profit by it, he quit the profession in 1774 and, at a most volatile moment, entered the political fray.

He was a man of tremendous energy, who even into his seventies rode 3 hours a day and wrote for 4 or 5 more. When a friend once asked him to prescribe a course of study for self-improvement, Jefferson recommended readings in science, ethics, and religion—all before eating breakfast! With such vitality, even the leanest summary of his career would sound extraordinary.

Deeply resentful of British rule, Jefferson made a name for himself in the Virginia House of Burgesses, going on to represent his state in the Continental Congress. While living in rented rooms in Philadelphia and attending meetings all day, he managed to write the Declaration of Independence in just over 2 weeks. He was 33 years old.

He became governor of Virginia and later minister to France. In Europe he took notes on architecture, farming, new inventions, anything he thought would be useful in America. He went so far as to smuggle protected grain seeds out of Europe. He was a tinkerer, believing everything could be improved, from the design of a plow—he held a patent on an improved moldboard—to the laws that govern human conduct. He worked doggedly in Virginia to guarantee religious freedom and reform the laws of inheritance.

Although Jefferson disliked cities and missed Monticello every day he was away from it, he served as secretary of state under **Washington**, vice president under **Adams**, and finally, for 2 terms as president.

He was radical as a theorist, but could be pragmatic in action. He believed that government had a strictly limited authority, yet as president, he stretched that authority to the utmost in engineering the *Louisiana Purchase*, perhaps the most important single event in US history. Characteristically, Jefferson dispatched **Lewis and Clark** posthaste to explore the area and send back samples of everything—from berries to the bones of extinct animals.

He was 6 feet 2 inches tall, with broad, angular features, a freckled complexion, a strong but loose build, and rather unkempt reddish hair. Just as his rough looks contrasted with the subtle and supple mind within, so was much of his personal conduct contradictory. At the White House he employed 14 servants and a French chef, yet he occasionally did his own shopping. Even though he made efforts to curb slavery through legal means, he owned at least 150 slaves himself, freeing only a few in his will.

Jefferson was a savvy and astute politician who often lobbied through others while keeping clear of the fray, yet he was singularly untalented when it came to his own finances. His constant rebuilding of Monticello and lavish political entertaining at his own expense kept him forever in debt. When he left the presidency, he was forced to sell his 7000-volume personal library to the government (for $23,950) to meet his obligations. (Whereupon he immediately resumed collecting books.) In describing his own views and those of his Federalist adversaries, who supported a strong central government, Jefferson wrote, "One feared the ignorance of the people, the other, the selfishness of the rulers without them." Here may lie the key to his philosophy, which was more than a cold cribbing from **Locke** or **Montesquieu** or a simple states-rights-versus-federal-rights polemic. Jefferson had an unbridled belief in the good judgment of man and his perfectibility. He believed men could choose for themselves which church to attend and which government to obey. He believed education allowed men to actively participate in their fate. Above all, he believed in freedom, as his own words make clear: "I have sworn upon the altar of God eternal hostility against every form of tyranny over the minds of men."

Jefferson

In his autobiography, **Thomas Jefferson** wrote of Williamsburg Va, "I have heard more good sense, more rational and philosophical conversations, than in all my life besides."

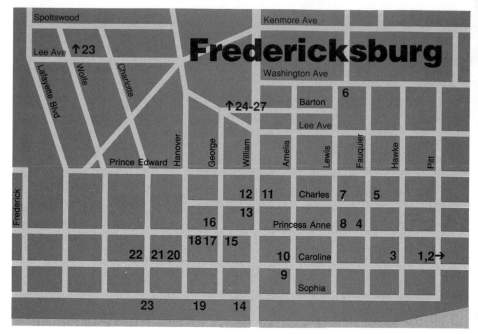

Fredericksburg sits like a giant dollhouse on the south shore of the **Rappahannock River**. The frontier port town was barely 10 years old when sandstone miner **Augustine Washington** moved his family to **Ferry Farm** on the north side of the Rappahannock in 1738. The farm became **George Washington**'s boyhood home, where he lived until appointment as the land surveyor of Culpeper County.

During the American Revolution, Fredericksburg became a center for heavy arms manufacturing. Unscathed by this war, the Southern town continued its prosperous existence until 1860, when the peace was abruptly shattered by the Civil War, during which Fredericksburg suffered massive losses and tremendous physical destruction. Although the battles permanently scarred many of the surrounding areas, several of **Old Town**'s Colonial homes were mended or rebuilt. Today, hundreds of 18th- and 19th-century buildings are still in use in the historic blocks along the river. *Area code 703 unless otherwise indicated.*

1 Belmont American artist **Gari Melchers** spent his last 16 years in the splendor of this 27-acre estate filled with European antiques and paintings by **Brueghel**, **Morisot**, and **Puvis de Chavannes**. Melchers' private studio, now converted into a gallery, exhibits more than 50 of his impressionistic works, including a version of *The Last Supper*. The artist's tools as well as medals and honorary certificates are also on view. ♦ Fee. M-Sa 10AM-4PM, Su 1-4PM, Jan-Mar, Oct-Dec; M-Sa 10AM-5PM, Su

Fredericksburg

1-5PM, Apr-Sep. 224 Washington St (off State Rte 17) Falmouth. 373.3634

2 Fredericksburg Colonial Inn $ Thirty-four rooms and 6 suites furnished in antiques from 1850 make this old-fashioned inn a faithful rendition of a pre-Civil War hostelry. Special touches include canopy or 4-poster beds and Colonial marble-top washstands; the *Stonewall Jackson Room*, also called the *Honeymoon Suite*, features a canopy bed and a pretty love settee in the sitting room. Amenities include private baths, refrigerators, radios, and color TVs. Continental breakfast available. Children under 12 stay free. ♦ 1707 Princess Anne St (Herndon-Ford Sts) 371.5666 &

3 Rising Sun Tavern (1761, Charles Washington) The revolutionary leaders of Virginia often plotted anti-British activities at this gathering place, owned by **George Washington**'s brother, **Charles**. The remarkable collection of original fixtures is put to use in the **Tap Room**, where spiced tea is served by a costumed tavern maid. ♦ Fee. Daily 10AM-4PM, Jan-Feb, Nov-Dec; daily 9AM-5PM, Mar-Oct. 1304 Caroline St (Fauquier-Hawk Sts) 371.1494

4 Smythe's Cottage Restaurant ★★$ A tavern specializing in dishes from the Colonial era: roast pork, stuffed quail, chicken potpie, cornbread. Outdoor dining in the summer. ♦ American ♦ M, W-Th, Su 11AM-9PM; F-S 11AM-10PM. 303 Fauquier St (Charles-Princess Anne Sts) Reservations recommended. 373.1645

5 St. James' House **George Washington** bought the site from his brother-in-law, **Fielding Lewis**, in 1761. A few years later, he sold it to his mother's attorney, who built the tiny gambrel-roofed house. The garden and interior have been restored with priceless European antiques to reflect handsome 18th-century living. The house is open only 2 weeks out of the year. ♦ Fee. By appointment last week of Apr, 1st week of Oct. 1300 Charles St (Fauquier-Hawk Sts) 373.1776

Restaurants: Red   **Hotels:** Blue
Shops/Parks: Green   **Sights/Culture:** Black

6 Kenmore (1752) The home of **George Washington**'s sister, **Betty Lewis**, is perhaps the most beautiful mid-Georgian mansion in Fredericksburg—some of its rooms are considered to be among the country's most elegant. Richly ornamented plaster ceilings (some say that Washington helped direct their design) complement the mahogany furniture; the carved stone portico overlooking the boxwood garden is grander than any other in town. Tea and gingerbread served in the Colonial kitchen. There is a museum on the premises with a diorama of Fredericksburg and the role of the Lewis family in it; also exhibited are silver and furniture used by the family. Gift shop. ♦ Fee. House and museum daily 9AM-4PM, Jan-Feb, Dec; daily 9AM-5PM, Mar-Nov. Tours daily every half hour. Gift shop daily 10AM-4PM, Jan-Feb; daily 9AM-5PM, Mar-Dec. 1201 Washington Ave (Fauquier-Lewis Sts) 373.3381

7 Mary Washington House Another quaint piece of Washington family real estate. Mary selected the house, and her son **George** bought it for her in 1772. Here, Mary spent her last 17 years among her favorite possessions from the Ferry Farm home. The old sundial was placed in the English garden, and the "best dressing glass" was also brought along—an 18th-century Chippendale mirror. ♦ Fee. Daily 9AM-4PM, Jan-Mar, Nov-Dec; daily 9AM-5PM, Apr-Oct. 1200 Charles St (Lewis-Fauquier Sts) 373.1569

8 Kenmore Inn $ Beautiful antebellum bed-and-breakfast inn. Each of the individually decorated rooms has a private bath. Lunch and dinner served daily in the restaurant. Continental breakfast included. ♦ 1200 Princess Anne St (Lewis-Fauquier Sts) 371.7622

9 Anrapo Antique Importers and Traditional Home Furnishings Quality American and European antique (mostly English) reproductions from the 17th through 19th centuries. Regular shipments of turn-of-the-century European furniture. Oriental rugs. ♦ M-F 10AM-5PM; Sa 10AM-6PM; Su noon-6PM. 1027 Caroline St (Amelia-William Sts) 371.7176

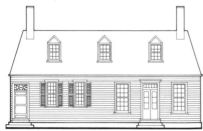

10 Hugh Mercer Apothecary Shop The Scottish doctor-turned-general (he died at the Battle of Princeton) treated Colonial ailments with snakeroot and crab claws from this 200-year-old drugstore. His office, where he sometimes performed surgery, is also part of the house. Silver pills in apothecary jars painted from the inside are among the more palatable antidotes displayed. ♦ Fee. Daily 10AM-4PM, Jan-Feb, Dec; daily 9AM-5PM, Mar-Nov. 1020 Caroline St (Amelia-William Sts) 373.3362

11 Ristorante Renato ★★$$ Homemade pasta, excellent seafood, and veal specialties. Live entertainment in the lounge on Friday and Saturday evenings. ♦ Italian ♦ M-F 11:30AM-2PM, 4:30-10PM; Sa-Su 4:30-10PM. 422 William St (Prince Edward St) Old Town Fredericksburg. Reservations required F-Sa. 371.8228

11 Slave Auction Block Pre-Civil War remnant from the dark ages of America. ♦ William and Charles Sts

12 James Monroe Museum and Memorial Library Monroe's first law office, now a showcase of his Louis XVI furnishings. The most intriguing piece is the desk where the *Monroe Doctrine* was signed. Other items of interest include Mrs. Monroe's gems and her lavish wardrobe. Thousands of books and manuscripts in the library tell us everything we want to know about Monroe and his era. ♦ Fee. Daily 9AM-5PM. 908 Charles St (George-William Sts) 899.4559

13 La Petite Auberge ★★★$$ The city's one and only French restaurant. Ample portions of country specials served in a gardenlike setting. The focus is on fresh local fish, wonderful homemade sorbets. Robust reds on the wine list. The menu changes daily. ♦ French ♦ M-F 11:30AM-2:30PM, 5:30-10PM; Sa 5:30-10PM. 311 William St (Charles-Princess Anne Sts) Reservations required. 371.2727

14 Old Stone Warehouse (Pre-1760, renovated 1975) Four stories of Civil War relics are housed in this Colonial tobacco warehouse. The underground area, once used for loading cargo aboard ships, is now a basement dig for wild boar tusks, fragments of pottery, and the like. The present ground level is really the 2nd story: Sophia Street was raised early in this century and the 1st floor was buried in the effort. For information on archaeological digs on this site, call the **Fredericksburg Area Chapter of the Archaeological Society of Virginia**, 373.1674. ♦ Free. Su 1-4PM. 923 Sophia St (William-George Sts) Fredericksburg Visitor Center 373.1776

15 St. George's Episcopal Church (1849) The stained-glass windows (including 3 signed by **Louis Comfort Tiffany**) in this 19th-century Gothic church were dedicated to **Mary Washington** by the Daughters of the American Revolution. Several friends and relatives of the Washington clan are buried in the cemetery: **Martha Washington**'s father (**John Dandridge**), **Betty Washington**'s husband (**Fielding Lewis**), and **John Paul Jones**' brother (**William**). ♦ Free. Daily 7AM-5PM. Services Su 11AM. 905 Princess Anne St (George St) 373.4133

Fredericksburg

Colonel Fielding Lewis, Kenmore's illustrious owner, has been seen puttering around in Revolution-wear just like his 250-year-old self. He favors dim corridors and his study, where he checks out the dusty ledgers for ghastly financial errors.

16 Presbyterian Church (1833) A target for Civil War bombardments in 1862, the Greek Revival structure still has cannonballs stuck in its pillars and scars in the belfry walls. The original bell was melted into cannon, and pews were torn loose to make coffins, as **Clara Barton** nursed the Yankee soldiers who lay dying inside. ◆ Free. Daily 9AM-3PM. Services Su 11AM. 810 Princess Anne St (Hanover-George Sts) 373.7057

17 Court House (1852, James Renwick) A Gothic Revival replacement of an 18th-century structure. Although the 1-room interior has been divided into offices, the original walnut ceilings, supported by hand-carved bridgework, still grace the courtroom. **Mary Washington**'s will and old city documents can be found in the Clerk's Office below. The bell tower has one of the 3 bells cast by **Paul Revere** remaining in the US. ◆ M-F 8AM-4:30PM. 815 Princess Anne St (Hanover-George Sts) 372.1066

17 The Masonic Lodge of George Washington One of the oldest lodges in America. This is where **George Washington** was initiated as a Mason in 1752; the Bible and minute book used to record this event are displayed together with his portrait. ◆ Fee. M-Sa 9AM-4:30PM; Su 11AM-4PM. 803 Princess Anne St (George-Hanover Sts) 373.5885

18 The Silversmith House (ca. 1785, James Brown) Saved from demolition by local historians, this 18th-century home is now the headquarters of the **Fredericksburg Center for the Creative Arts**. The main attractions are monthly exhibitions by living artists and craftspeople and a film series program. Call for schedule of events. ◆ Voluntary contribution. Tu-Su noon-4PM. 813 Sophia St (George-Hanover Sts) 373.5646

19 Windsor Tea Room ★$ Breakfast, lunch, and English teas with finger sandwiches and scones. ◆ English ◆ M-F 8AM-5PM; Sa-Su noon-5PM. 724 Caroline St (Charlotte-Hanover Sts) No credit cards. 899.7750

19 Fredericksburg Visitor Center A pit stop for the Fredericksburg explorer, this center offers block admission tickets, maps, and hotel and restaurant information. Twelve-minute orientation film shown upon request. ◆ Daily 9AM-5PM, Jan-mid June, Sep-Dec; daily 9AM-7PM, mid June-Labor Day. 706 Caroline St (Charlotte-Hanover Sts) 373.1776

20 Chimneys Tavern ★★$$ (1772, John Glassell) Duck, game pie, and beef Wellington are the specialties of this fine Colonial-style restaurant. The Georgian-style house, named for its massive brick chimneys at each end, was

the childhood home of **Nell Arthur**, the wife of **Chester Arthur**, the 21st US president. Inside, the original mantels and wainscoting add to the authenticity. ◆ American ◆ Tu-Su 11:30AM-3PM, 5:30-9:30PM. 623 Caroline St (Charlotte St) Reservations recommended. 371.9229

21 Copper Shop A father-and-son team hammer out 6 patented versions of the *Fredericksburg Lamp*, chandelier and tabletop size. The city gives them to visiting dignitaries—now you can have one, too. ◆ M-Sa 9:30AM-5PM; Su noon-5PM. 701 Sophia St (Charlotte St) 371.4455

22 Cardinal Pewter Classic wine goblets, plates, and bowls produced in the backyard of a home. Cottage industry at its best. ◆ M-Sa 10AM-5PM. 309 Princess Elizabeth St (Charles-Princess Anne Sts) 371.0585

23 Fredericksburg National Cemetery Three-quarters of the 15,243 Federal soldiers buried here are listed as unknown. The monuments and plaques throughout the somber grounds commemorate various Union divisions and military units. Operated by the **National Park Service**. ◆ Daily dawn-dusk. Visitor Center: daily 9AM-5PM, Jan-May, Sep-Dec; daily 8:30AM-6:30PM, June-Labor Day. Marye's Heights (Sunken Rd at Lafayette Blvd) 373.6122

24 P.K.'s Restaurant and Lounge ★$$ Small-town romantic atmosphere with Victorian accents. Baked stuffed shrimp and succulent ribs are favorite entrees, finished off with homemade chocolate-walnut pie à la mode. ◆ American ◆ M-Sa 11:30AM-2:30PM, 5-10PM; Su 11:30AM-8PM. Westwood Shopping Center, Rte 3 and I-95. 371.3344

25 Sheraton-Fredericksburg Resort and Conference Center $$ Four hundred landscaped acres with 3 tennis courts, an 18-hole golf course, fishing grounds, a large swimming pool, and a conference center. Additional amenities include cable TV and 3 restaurants. Children under 18 stay free. ◆ Rte 3 and I-95. 786.8321, reservations 800/325.3535; fax 786.3957 ⑂

26 George Washington Birthplace National Monument (Wakefield) George really slept here, and like a baby—he was born on this verdant farm in 1732. It all started in the winter of 1665, when **John Washington**, George's great-grandfather, was sailing upriver in a ship carrying Virginia tobacco to England. The ship sank. While it was being refitted, John was taken in by the charms of the countryside and a local planter's daughter. He married her, and their grandson **Augustine** (George's father) built the plantation at **Popes Creek** called **Wakefield**. Here, George was born and lived as a child and later for several years as a teenager.

Although the original estate burned down on Christmas Day 1779, the **National Park Service** has done a fine job re-creating the plantation as it might have been, and today it maintains Wakefield as a demonstration Colonial farm. Costumed employees give demonstrations in spinning, weaving, and, if staffing permits, blacksmithing, carpentry, and ox-driving.

The Park Service has faithfully rebuilt **Memorial House**, the plantation home, as well as the kitchen and spinning houses. Using 18th-century methods for the most part, the farm grows wheat, flax, corn, and tobacco—crops this plantation once produced. Vegetable and herb gardens are planted with period accuracy. Even many of the animals at Wakefield—red Devon cattle, English game hens, razorback hogs—were common on 18th-century farms.

A hiking trail leads visitors through a cedar grove to the banks of Popes Creek, where George Washington often went hunting. Picnic areas are set up on the property. Introductory film at the Visitors Center. A granite obelisk marks the entrance. Group tours available.
♦ Fee. Daily 9AM-5PM. Guided tours on the half-hour. Visitors Center: daily 9AM-5PM, Jan-May, Sep-Dec; M-F 9AM-5PM; Sa-Su 9AM-6:30PM, June-Aug. Located 38 miles east of Fredericksburg. Take Rte 3 to Rte 204. Continue for 2 miles. From DC take the Beltway to Rte 5, go south to Rte 301 to VA Rte 3, then to Rte 204. 804/224.1732

27 Stratford Hall Plantation (1730) This magnificent estate was the birthplace of **Robert E. Lee**; it was built by his great-grandfather, **Thomas Lee**. The mill was rebuilt on its original platform just before World War II and is in operation every Saturday at 1:30 and 3PM and on the 2nd and 4th Mondays of May through October. Whole wheat flour and cornmeal from the mill are sold in the gift shop. Lunch is served in a log cabin dining room, April through October. ♦ Fee. Daily 9AM-5PM. Tours every half hour. State Rte 214, Stratford Hall. From Fredericksburg, Rte 3 east to Rte 214; from DC, take Beltway to Rte 5, south to Rte 301, then Rte 3 east to Rte 214. 804/493.8038 &

Civil War Sites

As Civil War hostilities broke into open fighting, each side's capital city became a major target for the enemy. Washington DC served as the capital of the Union; Richmond VA, just over 50 miles away, was the capital of the Confederacy. Thus, the early campaigns of the war centered in the area between and around these 2 cities.

Fredericksburg & Spotsylvania National Military Park, Virginia.

A 5644-acre park commemorates the 100,000 soldiers who fell at the battles of **Fredericksburg**, **Spotsylvania**, **Chancellorsville**, and the **Wilderness**. The **Stonewall Jackson Shrine** is here as well. Driving and hiking tours are available in each of the park's 7 areas. Costumed park employees and narrative markers explain troop movements and the historic significance of each battle. ♦ Free. Daily 9AM-5PM Jan-15 June, Oct-Dec; daily 8:30AM-6:30PM 16 June-Sep. Visitors Centers: 1013 Lafayette Blvd, Fredericksburg; Rte 3, Chancellorsville. Rte 95 south to Fredericksburg; follow the signs. 703/373.4461 &

Shenandoah National Park, Virginia.

Important to the Southern army for its agricultural riches, sympathetic inhabitants, and strategic location, the valley served as a Confederate stronghold for the early part of the war. But Union troops attacked relentlessly, and dozens of battles shattered the farmland's serenity. (See page 195 for more information on the park and battlesites.) ♦ Fee. 24 hr. Rte 211 (east of Luray Va) 703/999.2243

Manassas National Battlefield Park, Virginia. Also known as **Bull Run**. Two of the war's bloodiest battles were fought on this small section of streams, woodlands, and hills. At the first major battle of the Civil War, picnickers from nearby Washington DC daytripped out to watch the military encounter; neither spectators nor soldiers expected the horror and panic that ensued. Troops clashed here again 1 year later when **General Robert E. Lee** sent **Stonewall Jackson** to protect Richmond-to-Shenandoah lines. Visitor Center (off Rte 234) has an audiovisual program explaining the military and historic aspects of both battles. ♦ Fee. Daily 8:30AM-5PM, Jan-mid June, Oct-Dec; daily 8:30AM-6PM, mid June-Sep. Take I-66 to VA Rte 34. 703/754.7107

Harpers Ferry National Historical Park, West Virginia. Site of **John Brown**'s infamous raid on a Federal arsenal; he had hoped to raise a private army to murder Southern sympathizers. The unsuccessful attack ended in the hanging of Brown and several of his men. The Harpers Ferry Visitor Center has a film on the historic town and the Civil War activity here. The 1500-acre park has special programs during the summer. ♦ Fee per car. Daily 8AM-5PM, Jan-mid June, Oct-Dec; daily 8AM-6PM, mid June-Sep. Take Rte 70 north to Frederick MD, then Rte 340. 304/535.6371 ext 6329

Antietam National Battlefield, Maryland. Also known as **Sharpsburg**. Here the Union Army successfully halted Lee's drive north toward Pennsylvania. In the bloodiest day of the war, 23,000 men were left dead or wounded. Now 810 acres are set aside to commemorate the battle. The tribute includes a film presentation. ♦ Fee. Daily 8:30AM-5PM, Jan-mid May, Oct-Dec; daily 8:30AM-6PM, mid May-Sep. Take Rte 270 to Frederick MD, Rte 70W towards Hagerstown, Rte 34 to Sharpsburg. 301/432.5124

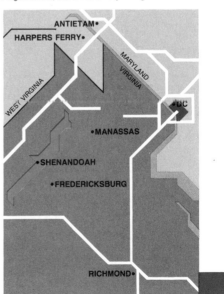

During the Civil War, Fredericksburg became a major battleground—the town changed hands 7 times.

By 1893, Fredericksburg was a prospering town for 1797 white citizens, 1124 slaves, and 287 free blacks.

L'Enfant's Plan

On 29 March 1791, **Pierre L'Enfant**'s letter to **George Washington** described, leading from Georgetown to a bridge on the Anacostia, "a large and direct avenue...planted with double rows of trees,...a street laid out on a dimension proportioned to the greatness which...the Capital of a powerful Empire ought to manifest." That street is Pennsylvania Avenue, 160 feet wide per L'Enfant's instructions, and finally, almost 200 years later, planted with double and triple rows of trees.

In his *Observations Explanatory of the Plan*, L'Enfant said, "The positions of the different Grand Edifices, and for the several Grand Squares...were first determined on the most advantageous ground, commanding the most extensive prospects," and in a memorandum to Washington he described **Jenkins Hill**, the location of the Federal House (the Capitol building), as standing "really as a pedestal waiting for a superstructure....(No other location) could bear comparison with this."

Because "avenues of direct communication (were) to connect the separate and most distant Objects with the Principal (Objects),..." the street laid out on a dimension proportioned to the greatness of a powerful Empire connected the Capitol and the President's House. Pennsylvania Avenue is bent a bit at the White House because, according to Washington's notes, the President's House was moved westward to take advantage of high ground and the view down the Potomac.

L'Enfant had surveyor **Andrew Ellicott** draw "a true Meridian line by celestial observation, which passes through the Area intended for the Congress House; this line he crossed by another due East and West." The true meridian is North/South Capitol Street and the line due east and west is the center line of the **Mall** and East Capitol Street. The east/west line and the north/south line through the President's House (16th Street) intersected at "the equestrian figure of George Washington, a monument voted on in 1783 by the late Continental Congress. These lines were accurately measured, and made the bases on which the whole plan was executed."

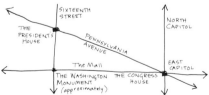

From this arrangement of "a large and direct avenue, Grand Edifices, several Grand Squares, true Meridian, and due East and West line," the rest of the plan followed in logical sequence. Eighth Street, halfway between the President's House and the Congress House was also an important locus of buildings and monuments. It is the center line of 3 of "the Squares...proposed to be divided among the several States;..." it was the location, opposite the Presi-

dent's House, of the **National Church**. Its intersection with Pennsylvania Avenue was adorned with "a grand fountain, intended with a constant spout of Water;"

and its intersection with the banks of the Potomac was the location of the *Naval Itinerary Column*, which was certainly intended as the American prime meridian, this being half a century before Greenwich was adopted worldwide as *the* prime meridian.

Twenty-third Street is Eighth Street's twin on the opposite side of the President's House, and 13th and 19th streets are the subharmonics to the basic rhythm set up by North/South Capitol, 8th, and 23rd streets. (One must go to the site to see why the subharmonic between 8th and North Capitol is missing: it would have been located in the depression now occupied by the North/South Freeway Connector, and all of these *monumental avenues* were to be located on "advantageous ground, commanding the most extensive prospects." In its place, and out of sync, are **John Marshall Place** and **Judiciary Square**, on high ground with a commanding prospect of the Mall.)

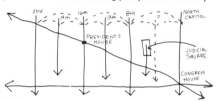

All of the 18th-century Baroque city plans proposed arrays of avenues radiating from the principal places. But except for Karlsruhe, Germany, Washington is the only city in which these plans were fully realized. New York Avenue is the twin of Pennsylvania Avenue: both radiate from the President's House. Maryland Avenue is the twin of Pennsylvania but radiates from the Congress House. Connecticut Avenue, Vermont Avenue, and F Street complete the star around President's House; New Jersey Avenue and Delaware Avenue complete the star about the Congress House.

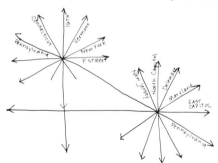

Massachusetts Avenue connects Dupont Circle (high ground at the intersection of Connecticut Avenue and 19th Street) and Mount Vernon Square (the intersection of New York Avenue and 8th Street); east of North Capitol, Massachusetts bends south to intersect East Capitol in **Lincoln Square** at the Itinerary Column (exactly one mile east of the Congress House, from which all land distances were to be measured). New Hampshire Avenue connects Dupont Circle and Washington Circle (high ground at the intersection of Pennsylvania Avenue and 23rd Street). K Street connects Washington Circle and Mount Vernon Square. And so on.

Overlaid on, and *in addition to*, this network of avenues is a grid of conventional streets, each 90 feet wide.

The logic of the plan has many consequences, a few of which are the following:

* Over 50 percent of Washington is in public rights of way; this is more street space than exists in any other major city in the world.

* Central Washington is a city designed for pedestrians, 2-legged and 4-legged. Every pedestrian-size precinct is focused on a public square, and every major street is regularly interrupted by public open spaces about a 5-minute walk apart. The city is, or should be, a pedestrian's dream, but it is a modern traffic planner's nightmare.

* The angled avenues and irregular grids create a multitude of oddly shaped blocks and intersections; these provide a variety of dilemmas for private architects and public urban designers. L'Enfant had begun to tackle that problem in ways that could have produced lovely results, but he was done in before he could finish the job.

* The topographic, ceremonial, and geometric logic of the plan is easily accessible. It reflected a capacious 18th-century enlightened view of the world, with the private life and the public life in a fine equilibrium. That original crystalline structure has been largely obscured. This is too bad, and it need not continue to be the case.

L'Enfant's city covered an area roughly the size of Paris in 1800. It took over a century for that space to be filled with buildings. In the meantime, Washington was the subject of cheap shots by visitors, particularly Europeans and particularly Englishmen. "The City of Magnificent Distances," "the great Serbonian Bog," "with shrines unbuilt and heroes yet unborn." And so on. Dickens described it this way: "Take the worst parts of (London),...[and] the straggling outskirts of Paris;...make it scorching hot in the morning, and freezing cold in the afternoon, with an occasional tornado of wind and dust,...and that's Washington. Such as it is, it is likely to remain."

Despite its 160-foot breadth and L'Enfant's proposal that it be lined with shopping arcades, East Capitol Street never became a retail street. The pull of Georgetown and the White House was too strong, and Washington early developed along the axis between the 2 Grand Edifices. But

at the time of the Civil War, most of the L'Enfant city was still unoccupied. Buildings were strung out toward Georgetown a couple of blocks on either side of Pennsylvania Avenue, and along 7th Street north to about N Street. In the Southwest, the area about 3 blocks south of the Mall was built up, and there was a settlement north of the Navy yard in Southeast Washington. Northeast Washington was still open country. What is now P Street was the northern edge of Georgetown.

Washington was, and remains, a company town. In the 19th century it was for Congressmen a temporary home. During the summer most returned to their families in other cities. Pennsylvania Avenue was bordered with hotels, rooming houses, and other houses; F Street and 7th Street were the retail streets. The city was seen by many people as a temporary place in another way: until the end of the century there were frequent movements to relocate the seat of government west of the Appalachian Mountains or, later, west of the Mississippi.

But the seeds of the modern metropolis were germinating. The **Henry Ford**s and the **Otis**es would have more effect on the shape of the modern city than would architects and city planners, and the **Boss Shepherd**s* and the **Thomas Crapper**s would have more effect on the health of populations than all of medical science before the development of antibiotics. The private automobile would permit cities to spread out over extraordinary distance at very low densities, the high-speed elevator would permit concentrations of activity in certain locations at densities previously undreamed of, and modern sanitation would help insure that there would be people to inhabit the suburbs and the skyscrapers.

And Washington would, uniquely, be shaped by changing roles for national governments, and by America's changing position in the world of nations.

***In 1848, Andrew Jackson Downing**, a landscape architect, laid out the White House grounds and the Mall as English landscape gardens, and in the 1880s the elder **Frederick Law Olmsted** designed the Capitol grounds, which remain today one of the great urban design accomplishments. But **Alexander Robey** (*Boss*) **Shepherd**, briefly head of the Department of Public Works in the early 1870s, had more effect on the city than either Downing or Olmsted. In 2 years he regraded the streets, added pavement and curbs, rebuilt bridges, built water and sewer mains, planted trees, added streetlights. The dusty village took on some of the character of a modern city. Shepherd also bankrupted the city. Like L'Enfant before them, both Downing and Shepherd were fired before they could finish their work.

From a speech by
Joseph Passonneau

Courtesy Library of Congress

L'Enfant's Plan

Timeline

Prior to the Europeans' settlement in the Potomac River area during the mid-1600s, the only known human inhabitants are the Piscataway Indians.

1749 **Settlers establish Alexandria**, the area's first town.

1765 **James Smithson**, founder of the Smithsonian Institution, is born in France.

1790 **Thomas Jefferson** successfully leads a campaign in Congress to place the nation's permanent capital in a southern state. In exchange, the southern states agree to accept a tax overcharge.

1791 At Congress' request, President **George Washington** chooses the exact site for the capital city. With city designer **Pierre Charles L'Enfant**'s help, each of the major federal buildings is given a location. Virginia and Maryland deed the necessary land to the federal government.

1792 Architect **James Hoban** wins $500 and a city lot for his winning entry in the competition to design the President's House.

18 September 1793 George Washington lays the cornerstone for the **Capitol** building.

1800 President **John Adams** and his wife, **Abigail**, move into the not-yet-finished President's House. At Adams' insistence, Congress moves from its temporary Philadelphia headquarters to its new permanent home on Capitol Hill. Approximately 5000 non-Indians have settled in the area.

1 November 1800 First joint session of **Congress** is called to order on the Hill.

1801 **Thomas Jefferson**'s presidential inauguration marks the first one held in the new federal capital.

1802 Congress sets up a **local government** consisting of a mayor and a council to help govern the city. Washington residents gain the right to elect the city council.

1814 During the **War of 1812**, British soldiers invade the city, burning many of the just-built federal buildings, including the Capitol and the President's House. With only moments to spare, First Lady **Dolley Madison** rescues many of the Executive Mansion's treasures, including **Gilbert Stuart**'s portrait of Washington, before fleeing by carriage.

1816 James Hoban is brought back to restore the President's House in time for **James Monroe** to take-up residence in 1817.

1819 Most of the damage done by the British in 1814 has been repaired. Congress moves back into the Capitol.

1820 Washingtonians win the right to elect their own mayor but still have no say in congressional or presidential elections. **Maria Hester Monroe** weds **Sam Gouverneur** in the Executive Mansion's first wedding ceremony. The **Chesapeake & Ohio Canal** opens, linking the capital with Cumberland MD. More than 500 boats regularly use the canal, creating the city's earliest freeway system.

1821 **George Washington University** is founded.
4 July 1826 **Thomas Jefferson** and **John Adams** die.

1829 **Daniel Webster** and **Henry Clay** appoint the first congressional page.

1833 Fire destroys the **Treasury.** The restored building spreads across Pennsylvania Avenue, interrupting the view between the President's House and the Capitol.

1835 The United States inherits **James Smithson**'s fortune. Congress does not decide for 8 years whether the US will accept the bequest.

1846 Virginia regains the land deeded to the nation for the capital city when the city's growth fails to meet earlier expectations. Population is approximately 50,000. Congress decides to accept James Smithson's half-million-dollar fortune and establishes the **Smithsonian Institution**. Architect **James Renwick, Jr.**, begins building the red brick castle that will house the institution.

1848 Funded by private donations, construction begins on the marble obelisk that will memorialize **George Washington**.

1850 A South Carolina congressman reads a prophetic warning to his Northern colleagues on Capitol Hill: "Let the (Southern) states we represent agree to separate and part in peace. If you are unwilling we should part in peace, tell us so, and we shall know what to do, when you reduce the question to submission or resistance."

1853 **Clark Miller**'s equestrian bronze of **Andrew Jackson** finds a home in Lafayette Square. A second fire (the first was set by the British in 1814) virtually destroys the **Library of Congress**.

1855 **Washington Monument** funds run out, and the construction stops at 55 feet.

1857 The Smithsonian begins using balloons to collect weather data. The *Washington Evening Star* reports this information daily.

1860 On the 128th anniversary of George Washington's birthday, **Clark Miller**'s statue of the first president is unveiled in Washington Circle. South Carolina leads the secession of southern states.

1861–1865 Just as the government grows in time of war, so the capital city grows. The population soars from 60,000 to 120,000, thanks in part to the thousands of freed blacks who move to Washington in search of a new life and federal protection. An enormous housing shortage develops.

1861 The fall of **Fort Sumter** and the ensuing **Civil War** turn Washington into an army camp. Soldiers are quartered in the East Room of the Executive Mansion, and the Capitol Rotunda becomes a field hospital. At night Washingtonians can see rebel campfires across the Potomac. Smithsonian Secretary **Joseph Henry** successfully encourages Lincoln to support hot-air balloon pioneer **Thaddeus Lowe**'s idea of using balloons to observe military operations.

5 February 1862 The press criticizes President **Lincoln** and his wife, **Mary**, for having thrown a gala reception at the Executive Mansion while war bitterly divides the nation. The press fails to mention that both of the Lincolns had protested against the party and that upstairs the 2 younger Lincoln sons were gravely ill. Five days later, 11-year-old **Willie Lincoln** dies.

1 January 1863 Lincoln signs the *Emancipation Proclamation* in his Cabinet room (later this room is turned into the Lincoln Bedroom).

1863 Thomas Crawford's *Statue of Freedom* is lifted to the top of the Capitol dome, climaxing a decade of building on the Capitol.

1864 Arlington National Cemetery is established.

1865 The 13th Amendment abolishes slavery.

14 April 1865 Lincoln is fatally shot while attending a performance of *Our American Cousin* at Ford's Theatre.

1867 Howard University is founded.

1868 President Andrew Johnson is impeached by the House, but acquitted in the Senate by one vote.

1871 Congress sets up a territorial government for the District of Columbia, headed by a president-appointed governor. A building for the State, War, and Navy departments is authorized.

1874 Congress revamps the local government again, putting 3 commissioners appointed by the president in charge. DC residents lose the right to vote for mayor and city council representatives.

1877 Lucy Hayes sponsors the first Easter-egg-rolling contest. Black spokesman Frederick Douglass creates a stir when he moves into a whites-only section of Anacostia (Cedar Hill) and becomes a District of Columbia US Marshal.

1881 A second Smithsonian building (later called the Arts and Industries Building) opens in time for James Garfield's presidential inauguration.

2 July 1881 President Garfield is assassinated in Washington's railroad terminal. Chester Arthur succeeds Garfield and begins redecorating the presidential residence with Victorian decor.

1884 The Washington Monument is finally completed. Unfortunately, after construction was shut down for lack of funds, the original quarry ran out of marble, so the color of the top 500 feet of the monument does not quite match the lower 55 feet.

1886 Forty-nine-year-old President Grover Cleveland marries 21-year-old Frances Folsom in the Blue Room, making Cleveland the first and only president to be married in the Executive Mansion.

1887 L'Enfant's original manuscript of the Plan of the City of Washington is rediscovered. Study shows that its guidelines have been ignored.

1890 City acquires Rock Creek Park, where the National Zoo will be built.

1897 The Library of Congress building is completed. (An annex is added in 1939.)

14 September 1901 President William McKinley dies from a gunshot wound inflicted 8 days earlier. Theodore Roosevelt becomes president and officially adopts *White House* as the name for the presidential residence.

1902 Steel magnate Andrew Carnegie endows the Carnegie Institute.

1904 Smithsonian Institution board member Alexander Graham Bell brings James Smithson's remains to DC from Italy.

1907 Construction begins on Washington Cathedral atop Mount St. Alban. (President Wilson is later buried here.)

1909 Belatedly acknowledging the hard work of the city's original architect, Pierre Charles L'Enfant, DC moves his remains to a grave site on the Custis-Lee estate overlooking the Potomac. The presidential Oval Office is built.

1910 President William Taft appoints the first Commission of Fine Arts and assigns it the task of supervising all subsequent city development.

1912 The mayor of Tokyo presents First Lady Helen Taft with a gift of Japanese cherry trees, which she plants in the recently drained Tidal Basin.

1914 World War I begins in Europe. Alley-dwelling is prohibited in the city after September 1918, but this proves unenforceable due to the housing shortage brought on by World War I.

1916 Four years before American women are given the right to vote in national elections, Montana elects 36-year-old Jeannette Rankin to Congress.

1917 The US officially enters World War I, and war once again brings a boost in population for the nation's capital. By 1918 the city's population has topped 450,000, the automobile has nudged out the horse and buggy, and the Mall has been turned into a parking lot.

1919 President Woodrow Wilson wins the Nobel Peace Prize for attempting a just settlement of World War I and advocating the League of Nations.

1922 Dedication of the Lincoln Memorial causes many Washingtonians to show a newfound respect for the Commission of Fine Arts. The commission had chosen Henry Bacon as the monument's architect and Daniel Chester French as the creator of what will become one of the most recognizable and best loved sculptures in the world.

1923 Freer Gallery of Art opens.

1924 The Washington Senators win the World Series against the New York Giants, 4 games to 3.

1930–1940 New government jobs created to ease the burden of the Depression cause a third population boom. By the time the US enters World War II, the city boasts 665,000 residents.

1932 Arkansas' Hattie Wyatt Caraway wins a Senate seat—the first woman to enter the Senate by election, not appointment.

1937 The Washington Redskins win the National Football League championship game 28-21 against the Chicago Bears.

1939 In a year that produced *Gone with the Wind*, *The Wizard of Oz*, and *Stagecoach*, the capital city premieres *Mr. Smith Goes to Washington*, starring Jimmy Stewart. Sensing an unfavorable reception, the film's director, Frank Capra, sneaks out during the screening.

1940 The Washington Redskins lose the National Football League championship game 73-0 to the Chicago Bears.

1941 On behalf of the American people, President Franklin Roosevelt accepts the National Gallery of Art, a gift from the estate of A.W. Mellon. After the Japanese bombing of Pearl Harbor, FDR makes his *Day That Will Live in Infamy* speech from the White House. The US enters World War II.

1942 The Washington Redskins win the National Football League championship against the Chicago Bears 14-6.

1945 FDR dies; Harry Truman becomes president. The war finally ends, but the world has entered the age of nuclear weapons.

1948–1952 President **Truman** and his family live in Blair House while the White House undergoes a major renovation.

1950–1952 US becomes involved in the **Korean conflict**.

1950 Population peaks at 800,000, then drops, as people migrate to the suburbs.

1954 In response to a Supreme Court decision (**Brown v. Board of Education of Topeka**), Washington becomes the first major city to integrate its schools.

1959 Francis Cardinal Spellman dedicates the **National Shrine of the Immaculate Conception**.

1960 National Museum of American History moves into its current home.

1961 The Constitution's **23rd Amendment** gives Washington DC residents the right to vote for president and vice president. **Arena Stage**, a theater-in-the-round built by private subscriptions, opens near the riverfront.

1961–1963 Jacqueline Kennedy's restoration of the White House furnishings becomes a media event, climaxed by her nationally televised tour of the Executive Mansion's refurbished first floor.

28 August 1963 In the shadow of the Lincoln Memorial, an interracial crowd of 250,000 demonstrators gathers peaceably to demand equal justice for all citizens under the law. **Martin Luther King, Jr.**, one year away from a Nobel Peace Prize, delivers his impassioned *I Have a Dream* speech, emphasizing his faith that one day all men will be brothers.

22 November 1963 President **John Kennedy** is killed in Dallas, Texas. **Lyndon Johnson** moves into the White House and in 1964 establishes the Commission for the Preservation of the White House. The commission facilitates donations to the White House and ensures that the Executive Mansion will be maintained in museum-quality condition.

1964 Washingtonians vote in their first presidential election.

1965 Construction begins on the **John F. Kennedy Center for the Performing Arts** (opens in 1971).

1966 Ground is broken for the **Hirshhorn Museum and Sculpture Garden** (opens in 1974).

1968 Following the assassination of **Martin Luther King, Jr.**, the *April Riots* plague Washington DC, resulting in 7 people being killed, 1166 injured, and 7370 arrested. Over 15,000 troops are required to quell the rioting. **Ford's Theater** reopens.

1972 Campaign workers for Republican president **Richard Nixon** break into the Democratic political headquarters at the **Watergate** apartment/office complex. The subsequent scandal leads to Nixon's 1974 resignation. The **National Zoo** receives 2 **giant pandas** from the People's Republic of China.

1973 Secretary of State **Henry Kissinger** wins the Nobel Peace Prize for his work in negotiating the Vietnam War cease-fire agreement.

1975 Washingtonians vote in their first mayoral and city council elections in over 100 years. **Walter E. Washington** becomes mayor.

1976 *All the President's Men*, based on 2 *Washington Post* reporters' investigation of the Watergate break-in, wins the Academy Award for best picture. The world's most popular museum, the **National Air and Space Museum**, opens in time for the Bicentennial Celebration. The Smithsonian sponsors an exhibition dramatizing Revolutionary War times.

1978 The **East Building of the National Gallery of Art** opens.

1981 John Hinckley, Jr., shoots President **Ronald Reagan** outside the Washington Hilton. Press Secretary **James Brady** and a police officer are also wounded.

1982 Vietnam Veterans Memorial is dedicated in Constitution Gardens.

1983 The **Washington Redskins** win Superbowl XVII. The event draws the largest TV audience ever for a live broadcast.

1984 Ronald Reagan is reelected president by a landslide, carrying 49 states; at 73 years old, he becomes the oldest man ever elected president.

1986 National Security Council aide Colonel **Oliver North** admits secretly selling arms to Iran in order to evade a Congressional ban and finance the Contras fighting the Nicaraguan government.

1987 The **Arthur M. Sackler Gallery** and the **National Museum of African Art**, 2 new Smithsonian Institution museums, open; so does the private **National Museum for Women in the Arts**, the world's first major museum for women artists.

1988 The **Washington Redskins** win the **Superbowl**, with **Doug Williams** becoming the first black quarterback to lead his team to the national championship. The **Baltimore Orioles** establish the longest losing streak (21 games) in the history of major-league baseball.

1989 The Smithsonian Institution **Museum of American History** opens the permanent exhibition *Ceremonial Court*, a re-creation of **Cross Hall**, the grand front corridor of the **White House**.

4 May 1989 Oliver North is convicted of 3 out of 12 counts: obstructing Congress, destroying documents, and receiving an illegal gratuity.

During his career as a congressman and senator, **John F. Kennedy** lived in 5 different houses. All but one were in Georgetown:

1528 31st St NW. This typically narrow Georgetown rowhouse was JFK's home when he was a bachelor freshman senator.

1400 34th St NW. As the senator began to gain clout, he found it necessary to entertain lavishly and moved into this 4-story corner house. His sister, **Eunice**, usually served as hostess.

3271 P St NW. This is where Jack Kennedy brought his new bride, **Jacqueline**.

3307 N St NW. This was the last home the Kennedys occupied before moving to 1600 Pennsylvania Ave.

(For a while, the Kennedys also lived at **Hickory Hill**, off Chain Bridge Rd near McLean VA.)

Index

Blue Ribbon Dining

Bests